MANAGEMENT TODAY

Managing Work
in Organizations

MANAGEMENT TODAY

**Managing Work
in Organizations**

THOMAS J. ATCHISON
San Diego State University

WINSTON W. HILL
California State University, Chico

HARCOURT BRACE JOVANOVICH, INC.
New York   San Diego   Chicago   San Francisco   Atlanta

To our wives, Elizabeth Pierce Atchison and Elizabeth Olson Hill, for their help, support, and understanding; and to our children, Michael, Marie, Stephen, and Patrick Atchison, and Marguerite and Nora Hill, for their patience.

ISBN: 0-15-554780-1

Library of Congress Catalog Card Number: 78-57251

Printed in the United States of America

CREDITS AND ACKNOWLEDGMENTS: The Design Quarter, p. 41, 72; Reprinted by permission of NEA, p. 75; The Design Quarter, p. 78, 101, 113, 156; Courtesy of Lufthansa Airlines, p. 159; The Design Quarter, p. 189; Copyright © 1975. Reprinted by permission of Saturday Review and Henry Martin, p. 195; The Design Quarter, p. 211, 259; William Hoest, p. 279; The Design Quarter, p. 285, 302; John Norment, p. 304; The Design Quarter, p. 336; Special permission for reproduction is granted by the author, Jay Hall, Ph.D., and publisher, Teleometrics International. All rights reserved, pp. 362-363; The Design Quarter, p. 374, 410, 427; Robert Tannenbaum and Warren H. Schmidt, "How to Choose a Leadership Pattern," Harvard Business Review, March–April 1958, page 96, Copyright © 1958 by the President and Fellows of Harvard College, all rights reserved, p. 465; The Managerial Grid Figure from The Managerial Grid, by Robert R. Blake and Janet Srygley Mouton. Houston: Gulf Publishing Company, Copyright © 1964, page 10. Reproduced by permission. See also The New Managerial Grid, Houston: Gulf, 1978, p. 11, p. 466; The Design Quarter, p. 468, 486; Sidney Harris/Sierra Club Bulletin, p. 502; The Design Quarter, p. 517, 551.

Technical Art by Evanell Towne; Chapter Opening Art by The Design Quarter.

Preface

Purpose of the Book

Management Today: Managing Work in Organizations is designed to introduce students to the nature and problems of organizational management. The book will be useful for basic courses in management, and, since we have assumed that those who study the text will be majoring in any of a variety of academic disciplines, no specialized knowledge is prerequisite.

Focus of the Book

Integration of a Wealth of Knowledge Around Work

Management Today unifies and focuses the rapidly developing body of knowledge about management around the *work* organizations do. For several decades, practitioners and researchers have studied and written about management and organization, often arguing noisily about the best approach. Out of this debate has developed a diversity of ideas and methods that sometimes seem at odds with one another. When we focus on work, however, the lines that at first appear to divide the different approaches begin to disappear.

Because work is a dynamic phenomenon, involving the *decisions* people make, the *activities* in which they engage, and the *interactions* that take place among them, our approach can be considered a *systems–contingency orientation*. But this book also incorporates management principles, organization theory, behavioral knowledge, and quantitative techniques as they relate to the effective and efficient accomplishment of work. Although the content is eclectic in its inclusiveness, we have tried to avoid merely stacking new sets of ideas on old ones.

Format of the Book

Five Parts
(1) Introduction
(2) Organization Design
(3) Factors That Affect Design
(4) Internal Managerial Activities
(5) External Managerial Activities

The book is divided into five parts. The first part serves to introduce the topics that will be developed in the chapters to come. The second part concentrates on how work is organized to produce a structure, which is the arena of the manager; and the third part focuses on factors that restrict freedom of choice in organizing: the constraints posed by human behavior, by technology, and by environmental forces. The fourth part examines those activities that managers carry out primarily inside the organization; and the fifth part deals with how managers perform their jobs to preserve and protect the organization and keep it relevant in a turbulent environment.

Special Features of the Book

This book combines several concepts of management and presents them in special ways that we believe will be relevant and helpful. Specifically, the chapters on Goals, Job Design, Technology, Environment, Decision Making, and Influence are comprehensive in their coverage and unusual in their organization.

Organizational Goals

After the two introductory chapters that constitute Part 1, we begin the discussion of Work and Organization Design in Part 2. Chapter 3 reviews the multiple and changing nature of organizational *goals,* then discusses how managers establish and work within those goals. A clear concept of organizational mission, we believe, is a prerequisite to all other discussions of organizational design and managerial activity. Chapter 4 continues the discussion of organizing by focusing on the division of goals into operational task objectives and the assignment of such work.

Job Design

Chapter 5 on Job Design elaborates alternative ways to combine tasks into people-sized jobs. Chapter 6 on Departmentation explains how jobs are grouped into departments, and Chapter 7 discusses structural coordination. Emphasized throughout is the idea that goals direct the work to be done and that the arrangement of groups of tasks, jobs, and departments creates the organization. That is, the form the organization takes results from the way work is assigned.

Contingencies

The next part treats other factors that affect the design of organizations: human, technological, and environmental variables. Chapters 8, 9, and 10 deal with humans—both as individuals and as members of groups. Chapter 11 on Technology discusses the human and mechanical techniques that affect how work is done in the performance core and in the managerial hierarchy. It also explores the effects of various technologies on people and on organization design. Chapter 12 stresses the many environments that affect organizations, the increasing environmental turbulence and change, and the effects these forces have on work and on organizational structure.

Managerial Activities

The last two parts of the book consider the managerial activities of direction and adaptation and include chapters on Decision Making, Communication, Influence, Leadership, Planning, Control, and Change. All these chapters incorporate both traditional and developing areas about managerial work. Because managers and scholars are becoming increasingly aware of the dynamics of power, politics, compliance, and conflict in organizations, we devote an entire chapter to these topics under the general heading of Influence.

The location of the Planning chapter near the end of the book may appear a bit strange to some, but we have chosen this location for two reasons. Planning is a vital kind of decison making, so we believe it should come after the chapters on decision making. In addition, planning is a major activity by which managers accommodate their organizations to changing circumstances. We believe, therefore, that it should be united with other concepts of adaptation. Of course, the part of the planning process that has to do with goal determination (Chapter 3) precedes the discussions of organizing (Chapters 4, 5, 6, and 7).

Models and Methods

Throughout the book we present ideas about management and organization in the form of *models* and *methods*. We use the term *model* to refer to a representation of reality that helps describe, predict, or control reality, and that also helps to prescribe or plan future activities. For example, the models of human behavior that we describe in Chapter 8 help to explain why people in organizations act as they do. *Methods,* which represent ways to accomplish some specific purpose, often follow from models. The personnel methods described in Chapter 9, such as incentive systems, develop from behavioral models. In Chapter 10, additional models of human behavior are presented, this time concentrating on human groups.

Sometimes it is hard to distinguish the model from the method, so the material on combining work units in Chapter 6 incorporates both the models of organizing and the methods of doing so.

Models and methods in management are neither very precise nor very linear. People who like orderly situations may be frustrated by their study of management: The field is complex because managerial ac interactions, and decisions are complicated processes. But though frustrating, management is also a challenging opportunity. Managers in our society are paid a great deal for using their judgment; their decisions are complex and have far-reaching consequences. We feel that our approach can be helpful to managers by presenting models and methods in ways that indicate the advantages and costs of certain approaches to decision making. In choosing to discuss the work of managers in terms of the complex forces acting on them, we have necessarily had to make this book comprehensive and somewhat complex. For decades our students have been complaining that "Effective management is just good common sense," but the record of organizational failures belies their argument. This book should allay their suspicions.

Use of the Book

Although we believe the order of topics in this book is both fresh and logical, those who prefer other designs will find that each chapter is a complete and coherent unit that can be used in a variety of different sequences. For example, those who prefer the planning–organizing–directing–controlling order might try the following sequence: Introduction (Chapters 1, 2); Planning (Chapters 3, 13, 14, 18); Organizing (Chapters 4, 5, 6, 7, 11, 12); Directing (Chapters 8, 9, 10, 15, 16, 17); Controlling (Chapters 19, 20).

Those who stress organizational behavior in the first management course might like to try a sequence such as this: Introduction (Chapters 1,

2); Individual Behavior (Chapters 8, 13, 14); Group Behavior (Chapter 10) and Interpersonal Relationships (Chapters 15, 16, 17, 20); Organization Design (Chapters 3, 4, 5, 6, 7, 11, 12); Personnel Methods (Chapter 9); and Organizational Adaptation (Chapters 18, 19).

At the end of each chapter, readers will find thought-provoking questions for discussion and involvement activities intended to give students practical experience in wrestling with managerial problems. We have found that students are more likely to feel committed to solving problem situations when they develop them from their own experiences. Thus the involvement activities and cases often require readers to draw on their own resources to solve the questions posed.

Instructor's Manual   The Instructor's Manual that accompanies the text contains still other experiential learning opportunities. In addition, it includes alternative class formats, learning objectives, lecture outlines, brief answers to the discussion questions, test items, and discussions of some representative media presentations.

Acknowledgments

Although the *form* of the book represents a move away from some of the traditional approaches to management theory, the *content* is not intended to be entirely original. On the contrary, it represents a compilation of the work of others. To them we are indebted, and to them we give full credit for the strengths of this work. But because the book also reflects the experience and study of the authors, we assume full responsibility for its limitations.

In addition to the contributions others have made, which have helped us formulate our models of management, we owe a more direct debt to those who have helped us complete the book. Dwight Taylor of the University of California, Terence Sharp, and Bob Clark each read an early or a later draft of the complete manuscript and made helpful suggestions from the point of view of undergraduate business students. Mary Lippitt of the University of Minnesota, and Bernard Alpert, of San Francisco State University, reviewed a previous draft of this book and made many helpful recommendations. Also we owe a debt of gratitude to Gary Burke, Barbara Rose, and Karen Bierstedt of Harcout Brace Jovanovich, Inc., who have been very helpful and supportive editors. But our greatest debt is owed to Betty Atchison and Bettie Hill, who were our major supporters, typists, critics, and prodders. They made us get it done.

THOMAS J. ATCHISON
WINSTON W. HILL

Contents

Four: Managerial Activities of Directing   329

Five: Managerial Activities of Adaptation   481

1

Basic
Concepts

During the past fifty years practicing managers and management theorists have developed a vast array of ideas and theories in their attempt to better understand how organizations are managed. But, as in any new and changing area of study, there is a continuing debate between the proponents of opposing points of view. Not long ago, for example, a major argument existed between those who believe that organizations can and should be managed according to a set of rational principles (the proponents of administrative management) and those who believe that organizations should be viewed as social systems and managed as such (the human relations theorists). Recently, these two opposing camps have joined ranks and a third, broader theory, has been worked out. That old theories die out and are replaced by new ones and that broader theories often emerge from once-conflicting viewpoints are generally accepted facts in all fields of inquiry.

With these facts in mind, the authors of this text have attempted to present as many of the old, current, and emerging theories of management as are relevant and to integrate them with a unifying framework. No claim is made that any one theory is better or worse than another, for each has its own contribution to make to the overall body of collected knowledge.

Chapter 1 develops a framework for the study of management, organizations, and, the unifying theme of this book, work. The framework consists of written and visual models of these three systems and presents them as consistent with one another and as containing certain common elements.

Chapter 2 provides a background for the study of management and organizations by detailing the major theoretical constructs that have created the field as it exists today.

1

Models of Management, Organizations, and Work

The term **management** refers to a common set of activities that are designed to promote and direct purposeful work. Thus to some degree everyone is a manager, if only of his or her own actions. It is when people get together in a formal relationship, such as that of an organization, that management becomes a major and separate field of activity. To begin to study management in this latter context, one must set a framework and develop models in order to understand what management is about. The purpose of this chapter, then, is to present models of management, organizations, and work, which will set the framework for the chapters that follow.

This morning, millions of people all over the country got up and went to work. And almost nine out of ten of these people went to work in an organization—large or small. A variety of volunteer organizations awaited the services and talents of thousands of others not in the regular work force. Even children participate in organizations—school, Little League, scouting, summer camp, and so on. Senior citizens often belong to organizations, too, such as recreational centers, retirement villages, lecture groups, and many others. Organizations are a pervasive aspect of our society. There are few people in the United States who are not, at one time or another in their lives, a part of an organization.

The goals, structures, and activities of these innumerable organizations must be thought out, implemented, and coordinated. This is the activity of managing. More and more, as organizations increase in number and in scope, managing has become an important and complex component of modern society. This book is about managerial work—what managers do and why they do it.

Whatever Happened to "Rugged Individualism"?

"Our society is an organizational society. We are born in organizations, educated by organizations, and most of us spend much of our lives working for organizations. We spend much of our leisure time paying, playing, and praying in organizations. Most of us will die in an organization, and when the time comes for burial, the largest organization of all—the state—must grant official permission."

Amatai Etzioni. *Modern Organizations*
(Englewood Cliffs. N.J.: Prentice-Hall, 1964). p. 1.

Managerial Work

In response to the increasing need for people to direct the work of others, each year many employees in organizations are promoted into the managerial ranks. Schools of management and administration exist in nearly all colleges and universities and in private institutions as well. These schools provide a steady flow of trained people to fill managerial positions. Management is an attractive occupation. It offers challenging work and provides opportunities for growth. It is often prestigious and well paid. But managing is not for everyone. Managerial activities are characterized by an unrelenting pace, brevity, variety, and fragmentation (1). To some, these characteristics are challenging and exciting; to others they are frustrating and unsatisfying.

The Field of Management

Management, like any other field of study, can be viewed from many different perspectives. So to help the reader gain a clear and comprehensive overview of the subject, this book will focus on three specific aspects of managing. These are: the arena, or context, in which managing occurs; the target, or object, that is being managed; and the whole range of activities that together define managerial work.

Where Does Managing Occur? Whenever people deliberately influence their own actions or the actions of others, they are managing. By this definition, everyone spends a good deal of time managing and has experienced both the satisfactions and traumas that accompany this endeavor. To some extent, then, much of the material that follows will be familiar. But for the purposes of this book management will be considered as including only those activities that take place within the context of an organization.

Management, as a specific set of organizational activities that constitute an occupation, occurs when a number of people have joined together to accomplish some task or goal—that is, when there is an organization. All organizations require managing, and the larger and more complex the organization, the more managing it requires.

Managers are the decision makers. They perform the same service for the organization that the brain does for the body. They initiate and process information and then issue directions for carrying out what needs to be done. This role obviously requires a thorough understanding of organizations. (Part 2 of this book deals with how organizations work.)

Managers are not involved solely with the organization, however. They must continually deal with individuals, groups, and other organizations. For this reason, it is part of the managerial task to integrate the pressures from the outside environment with the pressures and activities occurring within the organization. (Part 3 of this book addresses itself to the external environment in terms of its impact upon, and the major resources coming into, the organization.)

What Is Managed? The different types of organizations in our society are numerous. And although each is unique, they all share certain common characteristics. A focus on the unique characteristics of different organizations has produced programs in business management, public administration, educational administration, health care administration, and so on. Similarly, the separate departments within organizations also are distinctive yet the same in certain respects. For this reason, we find courses in sales management, financial management, production management, personnel management, and so on, all in the same school. Looking at the diversity of organizations and departments to be managed, some critics have gone so far as to claim that there is no such thing as management per se. According to these commentators, the word *management* must be preceded by an adjective, such as *marketing* or *engineering*.

Other theorists take an opposite position. They maintain that the similarities among organizations and departments so far exceed the differences that management can be considered a universal activity that is independent of the function being managed. A compromise is offered by Katz (2). He suggests that technical skill in the area for which the manager is responsible varies with organizational purpose, but that the other two skills required of managers, human and conceptual, are common to all managerial work irrespective of the kind of work being managed.

The position taken in this book is that the activities of managers will differ according to the combination of three primary factors—the particular task that is managed, the resources that are available, and the environment in which the task occurs. But what each of these factors has in common—and the focus of all managers—is the work of the organization. And for this reason, work is the unifying theme of this book.

What Does a Manager Do? This question might be rephrased to read: If managers do not actually perform the same work as the people they manage, what do they do? One approach to answering this question would be to look in the dictionary at the verb "manage." As usual, any dictionary gives a series of meanings. A common thread running through these is that managing is concerned with guiding, directing, and controlling behavior, especially the behavior of other people and things. Further, the definitions also give some indications of how managing should be carried out. Tactics with such positive connotations as "training" and "treating with care" are included with such negative tactics as "keeping one submissive," "manipulating," "adulterating," and "contriving." Managing, then, has both positive and negative aspects.

In the early part of this century, French industrialist Henri Fayol isolated the functions of planning, organizing, commanding, coordinating, and controlling as constituting managerial activity (3). Today this list is somewhat changed and contains the functions of planning, organizing, staffing, directing, and controlling. These activities form a sequence of related events starting with goal-setting, which is the planning stage (or the determination of where the organization is to go), followed by the structuring and staffing stages (which are necessary to attain goals), and finally, the directing and controlling stages, which ensure the continuation of purposeful, goal-oriented activity.

A more recent delineation of managerial activities is provided by Mintzberg (4). As a result of studying a number of executives at work, Mintzberg categorized the observations he made into groups of specific behaviors. These behaviors, or roles, are arranged into three distinct areas: interpersonal roles, informational roles, and decisional roles (see Figure 1-1). The first area, termed **interpersonal roles,** comprises activities that deal with the development of interpersonal relationships by the manager; they are linked directly to the manager's authority and status. Two of these roles, those of figurehead and liaison, involve the manager in contacts outside the organization. As a **figurehead,** the manager represents the organization or department in external contacts ranging from trivial to extremely important; as a **liaison,** the manager must maintain a large network of interpersonal contacts outside the organization. The third role in this category, that of **leader,** is internally oriented. It enables the manager to direct and motivate the people in the organization or department for whom he or she is responsible.

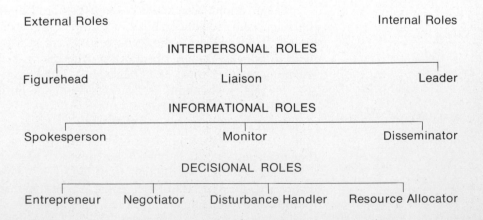

External Roles   Internal Roles

INTERPERSONAL ROLES

Figurehead   Liaison   Leader

INFORMATIONAL ROLES

Spokesperson   Monitor   Disseminator

DECISIONAL ROLES

FIGURE 1–1
The manager's roles.   Entrepreneur   Negotiator   Disturbance Handler   Resource Allocator

The second category contains **informational roles,** which enable the manager to receive and transmit information. Since the manager is, in a sense, the "nerve center" of the organization, the first of the roles in this category is that of **monitor.** As a monitor, the manager absorbs information from inside and outside the organization for processing in the directing and decision-making functions. This role is both internally and externally directed. The second role, that of **disseminator,** is internally oriented. Here, the manager passes on information to the proper places within the organization. The role of **spokesperson** is externally oriented. It allows the manager to transmit information about the organization outward to the environment.

The third category of behaviors contains **decisional roles.** Mintzberg felt that these roles are the most crucial of all managerial activities. Managerial decisions range along a continuum from innovative to reactive. The most innovative of the decision roles is that of **entrepreneur.** In this role the manager initiates and designs changes within the organization. These are not imposed changes but rather are opportunities for improvement that are observed by the manager. A second decision role is that of **disturbance handler.** Here the manager reacts to changes in the environment or in the organization. He or she deals with these changes in whatever manner is considered best for the organization. **Resource allocator** is the third role in the decision category. This role is clearly internally oriented. Once a decision has been made regarding a particular course of action, the manager must allocate, or assign, whatever resources are necessary to implement the plan. The final decision role, that of **negotiator,** is externally oriented and is somewhat different from the others. The negotiator role stems directly from the figurehead, spokesperson, and resource allocator roles. As negotiator, the manager participates in arbitrating disputes, usually those involving such important matters as management-labor relations.

A View of Managerial Work

One of the most common definitions of managing is "getting things done through other people." Although this definition does highlight the distinction between managing and doing, it does not present a useful description of managerial activities. What, for instance, are the "things" that get done? In fact, these "things" are the sum total of the organization's work. Or, more accurately, they are the myriad tasks that constitute the work of the organization. Thus, it would be more accurate to state that managing is "getting organizational work done through other people."

Now, what about the word *people*? In any organization people are an important resource; in fact, the most important resource. But people are not the only resource the manager uses to "get organizational work done." The manager has a whole range of available resources, making *resources* a better word than *people*. So, our definition now may read, "getting organizational work done through the use of available resources."

Finally, let's look at the words *getting done*. These words emphasize the influencing aspect of managing, which is unquestionably an important activity, but they do not represent the whole range of role categories discussed above. As we have learned, getting organizational work done requires the manager to deal with the environment as well as the organization itself. So a further expansion of the definition would result in the following: "Within a given environment, managing consists of (1) planning goals (the work to be done); (2) implementing the goals by obtaining, organizing, and allocating resources; and (3) leading the organization to ensure the completion of work through the roles of communicator, influencer, and controller." Now we have a definition that more adequately describes the full range of managerial work.

A Model of Managerial Work

Based on the foregoing definition of managerial work, Figure 1-2 depicts a model of the manager's many roles within the organization. The manager is shown as a "person in the middle" with two faces, one looking inward toward the organization, the other looking outward into the environment. The manager must react to and integrate the demands made from both directions.

The Outward Face of the Manager. The outward-looking face of the manager focuses on the environment. This means that in the context of directing the work of the organization (in implementing its goals), the manager must be aware of external activity. He or she must react to environmental changes and also seek new areas of opportunity.

In order to accomplish its goals, the organization must have resources. Recognizing and acquiring useful resources is another aspect of the outward face of the manager. In carrying out this function, he or she engages in the sequential activities of planning, controlling, and changing. Finally, the outward-looking face must protect the organization from the environment. The manager performs this service either by changing or

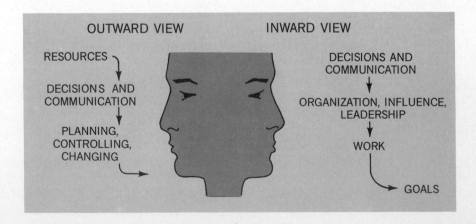

FIGURE 1-2
The two faces of the manager.

influencing the environment or by personally absorbing the demands made on the organization by the environment.

The Inward Face of the Manager. The inward-looking face of the manager is concerned primarily with leadership activities. Having decided what work is to be done, how it will be accomplished, and what resources need to be employed, the manager must then cause the organization to function. The first step here is to arrange its various parts into goal-oriented task groups. Once the organizing is accomplished, the manager must activate the groups through the use of influence. The managerial work contained in these duties generally occurs on an immediate, everyday basis and consumes the greatest portion of the manager's time.

The Managerial Arena—The Organization

Everyone knows what an organization is. Most people probably use the word with some regularity in normal conversation. But have you ever tried to define an organization? A university, for instance, is an organization. How would you describe such an organization to someone who was new to this culture? You could show him the buildings. But are these buildings *the* university? In the daytime, with people bustling about them, it seems so, but at night the buildings are only the shell of the organization. We look at the people streaming across campus and think that to call that meandering disorder an organization would be a contradiction in terms. What, then, is the organization?

The problem of accurately describing something we take for granted is a common one. Those things that are ordinary in life are often the ones we examine the least. What is needed is a systematic observation.

For the purposes of observation, our sample organization will be contained within a single building. The building itself will be observed from

the outside; it will be compared with other buildings housing organizations, and the roof will be taken off to observe what goes on inside. These internal and external views of the organization parallel the two faces of the manager described earlier.

**An External View
of the Organization**

Aside from the physical aspects of the building itself, the most obvious external characteristic of an organization is the movement that takes place into and out of the building. A variety of things constantly enter and leave, such as people, physical objects (materials), money, and information. From the organization's viewpoint, what goes in may be classified as **resources,** and what goes out may be classified as **products** or **services.** Thus, we can formulate our first observation:

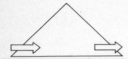

> *Observation 1.* Organizations have **inputs** and **outputs.** The inputs are resources and the outputs are products or services.

A somewhat closer look at the inputs and outputs results in two more observations. First, the inputs and outputs are of a wide variety and can be further subcategorized, and second, the outputs are different from the inputs. From this latter observation we can assume that something happens inside the building that transforms or utilizes the inputs to produce the outputs. This utilization process may be called the **work** of the organization.

> *Observation 2.* Organizations take in resources (inputs) and transform (work) them into products or services (outputs).

Resource Inputs—People. The people who are associated with an organization can be thought of as belonging to one of two major groups. The first group arrives in the morning and leaves in the evening all at approximately the same time. Activities start inside the building after the people arrive and stop as soon as they leave. It is a reasonable inference that this group constitutes the **work force** of the organization (employees).

> *Observation 3.* People are the activating resource of the organization.

The second group of people have a less permanent association with the organization. They come and go during the course of the day and typically stay only a short period of time. They have one common characteristic—they bring something into the building or take something out, or both. What appears to be taking place is some form of exchange. If we were to divide this category of people into subgroups, according to what they bring in and take out, we would see that one subgroup brings in materials and information and takes away money. These people are called **suppliers.** A second group brings in money and takes away materials and information. These are **customers.** A third and more diverse group of people are those who exchange information for information. There is no special label for this group—it consists of a wide variety of people from the general population.

Observation 4. Organizations engage in exchange relationships to obtain resources and to dispose of outputs.

Even the regular employees of the organization are engaged in exchange transactions. In exchange for their time and utilization of their skills, the organization pays them a salary. Collectively, this group takes a large sum of money out of the building.

Resource Inputs—Money. The inflow and outflow of money is easily observable and of considerable importance in terms of measuring the organization's ratio of inputs to outputs. Money leaves the building for the purpose of obtaining the resources that come into the building. By the same token, money is obtained from others in exchange for the organization's products. Thus, in several ways, money acts as a measure of value.

The input-output flow of money reflects the value, or health, of the organization in two ways. First, the amount coming in must be at least equal to the amount going out over a long period of time. A reserve of money allows the organization to remain flexible. Without such flexibility, an organization might not be able to survive difficult times. Second, money must flow in and out at a fairly constant rate. When the input of money slows down, the ability to acquire other resources is affected. In turn, a lack of resources limits the amount of output, which accelerates the downward spiral.

Observation 5. Organizations must maintain both a steady flow of resources and a positive balance of inputs over outputs.

Resource Inputs—Materials. In our sample organization (again for purposes of simplicity), the output is viewed as material in nature. Remember, however, that our hypothetical material product can be replaced by any conceivable product or service.

Two categories of materials can be observed going into the building. The first group is composed of those that come in at predictable intervals and that can be directly related to the outputs. In some form or other, the material inputs in this category can be seen as a part of the outputs that ensue later. Continued observation of inputs over a long time period would even allow one to predict the type and composition of outputs and specify a date in the future when they would appear.

The second group of material inputs is not observable as a part of the output and appears only at sporadic intervals, not on predictable schedules. These inputs are **capital equipment,** and they are directly related to a build-up of monetary reserves. A surplus of funds is often used to purchase this type of input.

The advent of capital equipment is always associated with change in other inputs and in outputs. These changes can occur in almost any area of the organization. For example, a new computer can affect human resources in that it may reduce personnel, require some employees to learn new skills, or increase personnel (specialist computer operators). Other new capital equipment may cause changes in the composition and timing of other materials, or in the ratio of monetary input to output — usually in a favorable manner. New capital equipment may also change the material output by increasing the volume or type of product.

Resource Inputs — Information. The most difficult resource input to "see" is information. It comes into the organization through the interaction of people inside and outside the building. Physically, information flows into the organization by direct personal contact, over the telephone, and through the mail.

Generally, information coming into the organization concerns events in the external environment. On an immediate level, this information includes data on all the other resource inputs, on the reactions to outputs, and about employees, customers, suppliers, and other aspects of the industry that are relevant to the organization. Other information flowing into the building is about broader aspects of the world outside. It includes such news as trends in the general economy, events in other industries, new government regulations, and current trends in society and in the local community.

Environmental information has varying degrees of impact upon the organization. Some information (such as passage of a new law) acts as an imperative; it causes the organization to make changes, which are reflected in its inputs, outputs, or both. Other information has a less direct effect. For instance, information about a new trend in fashion may initiate minor adaptations in a clothing manufacturer's output, which are not visible for several months. Before change is instituted, however, this type of information must be coupled with other supportive pieces of information from several different sources.

A special category of information has to do with better ways of producing desired outputs with given inputs. This information is directly concerned with the work that goes on inside the building. The result of combining material and information inputs is called the **technology** of the organization. It is this combination of materials with knowledge of how to best utilize resources that has been responsible for the rapid changes in industry that have taken place during the last fifty years.

Product or Service Outputs. Material leaving the building is of two types. The first, and the major one, includes all the goods or services that the organization intentionally produces — those things for which people (customers) seek out the organization. It is by these outputs that the organization is identified in the outside world. The other material output is waste, which has the characteristics opposite those of products. Waste is unintended and unusable. People do not come seeking it; in fact, the organization pays people to get rid of it. And it does not fit the needs of other organizations. Waste is created when the intentional output does not totally absorb the input. Occasionally, waste may be useful to someone outside the organization, such as sludge that is used as fertilizer for farming. But more often, classes of outputs are created that not only are unintended but that cause problems for the organization and for others.

Any one output, then, can be intended or unintended as well as useful or nonuseful. The degree to which management can design ways to minimize the number of unintended outputs is a measure of organizational **efficiency.** Also the degree to which the public views the outputs of the organization as useful instead of nonuseful or harmful is a measure of organizational **effectiveness.**

> *Observation 6.*   Outputs may be either intended or unintended from the viewpoint of the organization, and useful, nonuseful, or harmful from the viewpoint of people in the environment.

Information Outputs. Information leaving the building is also of two types, that which has to do with events and activities going on in the building and that which deals with reactions to information coming into the building. Information about what is happening inside the building tends to be more informal than formal. Sometimes other organizations, such as governmental bodies, directly request (or demand) information. At other times, information about the organization is requested from associations representing the industry of which the organization is a part. But most of the information leaving the building results from direct contact between employees and other people in the outside world. This release of information often results in conflicting or inconsistent views of the organization.

Another form of information output is the intentional release of data that are meant to influence people and groups in the world outside. This typically takes the form of advertising or public relations. Occasionally, information is released in the form of media announcements in which the organization makes public its position on certain issues that are of concern to the people—such as political endorsements, environmental-protection stances, and so on.

> *Observation 7.*   Organizations respond to the environment by either changing their internal operations (work) or by influencing the environment.

Comparing Organizations

If one were to make comparative observations of a large number of organizations, one would see that inputs and outputs vary considerably in both volume and kind. In addition, the material outputs of all the organizations observed would still represent only a fraction of the types of outputs generated throughout the world (or even throughout the country). These dramatic differences between organizations spotlight a very important aspect of organizations—that of purpose. Any one organization produces a specified and limited range of outputs. Thus, it needs to exchange resources with other organizations to continue to meet its own purposes. For this reason, organizations are related to, or interdependent on, one another.

> *Observation 8.* Organizations are purposeful and related. They exchange resources with other organizations to produce a particular and limited output.

Another interesting comparison observation is that of organizations with similar material outputs. The inputs, particularly people and materials, of these organizations would necessarily be similar also. But the volume of input and output need not be similar at all. Consider the difference, for example, between a national chain of large supermarkets and the family-owned neighborhood grocery store. The inputs and outputs are quite similar in type and composition, and the employees perform similar functions, but volume differs considerably. A variation of this observation is that similar organizations, with the same volume of inputs, produce different amounts of outputs. This leads us to:

> *Observation 9.* To produce particular outputs, certain resources are needed, but organizations differ as to how well they utilize resources.

A comparison of information inputs and outputs is also illuminating. Organizations vary considerably in the volume of their information input and output. Some organizations deal almost exclusively with information that is directly related to their outputs and, to a lesser degree, their inputs. Other organizations take in information from a wide range of sources about a great many events in the world. To some degree this variance reflects the amount of information surrounding and relevant to the organization. For example, a small-business organization in the Midwest receives and generates much less information than does a large import-export organization in New York City. The former simply does not have need of, or access to, the huge volume of information that the latter does.

> *Observation 10.* Organizations vary in the extent to which they are open to information from the environment. In part, this difference is related to the amount of information directed toward, and generated by, the organization.

An Internal View of the Organization

Although we have made a number of useful observations about the organization by viewing it from the outside, our picture, or definition, is incomplete. We still need to know what goes on inside the building that changes the resources into outputs.

The first impression of the inside of the organization is that there are too many stimuli to sort out. Motion and activity seem to be everywhere. And certainly it does not look like the neat, tidy picture shown by the organization chart hanging on the wall. There are machines and desks scattered around, and a maze of partitioned-off areas. Materials, obviously in various stages of change, are stacked around; people are moving about or standing seemingly at random; telephones are ringing constantly; and paper work is piled high on most of the desks. How is sense to be made of all this?

By separating the resources into categories, some order can be made out of the chaos. As a start, a close examination of the work flow will reduce much of the confusion. Then, an analysis of the information flow and of the specific activities in which people engage will result in a fairly ordered and complete picture of the organization.

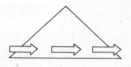

Work Flow. The most apparent observation of how work flows through the building is that it passes through a series of places (**work stations**) where materials, people, and machines come together. These work stations are themselves like miniature organizations. The materials are worked on (changed) as a result of the actions of the people and machines. This change process creates a particular output. The output in turn provides part of the material to be worked on at the next station, and so on, until the final product is ready. Each subunit (or work station), then, exists within two separate but connected environments—that of the larger organization and that of the world outside.

> *Observation 11.*   Subunits of organizations are themselves organizations, and they may be observed as separate entities.

Materials flow through the building, people move in limited directions, and machines are stationary. Machines are permanently placed at work stations, have a comparatively narrow range of activities they perform on specific materials, and are able to repeat the procedure endlessly without change. People are a little more mobile but still revolve around a particular work station most of the time. However, the operations they perform on the materials usually are more varied than those performed by machines. People adapt to variations in the materials that pass through the stations. Certainly the people do not follow the materials from one end of the building to the other. Figure 1-3 illustrates the way people, machines, and materials interact to accomplish the organization's work.

> *Observation 12.*   Resources come together at various places within the organization to form work stations. The operations performed at these stations represent the work flow of the organization.

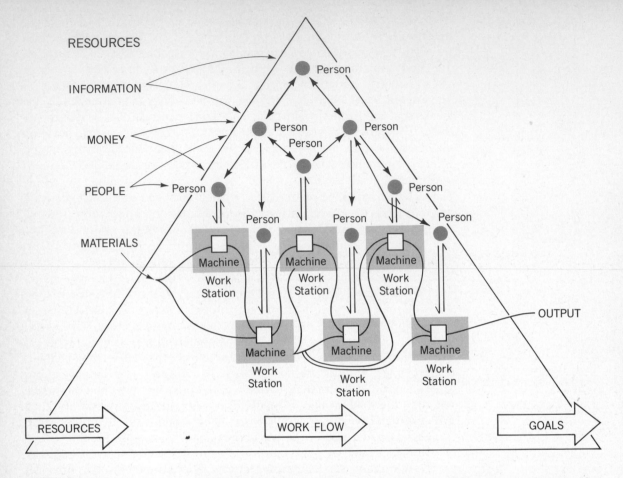

FIGURE 1–3
A model of the organization.

Information Flow. Whereas materials are the primary resource for some groups of people in the organization, information is the primary resource for other groups. Information flows through the organization in quite a different manner from the flow of materials. Only a select number of people receive information, which they then process and disperse throughout the organization for further treatment, as shown at the top of Figure 1-3.

When information arrives at the work stations, the people staffing the stations transform the data from guidelines into explicit action plans. Information also flows upward from the work stations to those who receive external information. These people may process the information from the work stations and send it out into the environment in the form of marketing, sales, or promotional material.

Information also flows along much the same paths as do materials and people. It is constantly being recombined and reinterpreted at each work station, which results in significant alteration of the information as it moves through and around the organization. The majority of the information moving around these paths deals with the internal operations of the organization. In contrast, the information that is passed down through the organizational hierarchy deals primarily with information pertinent to the external environment.

Activities of People. The first thing one notices in observing the activities of people in the organization is that not everyone is doing the same thing. People perform specialized tasks that are often similar, yet often widely diverse.

In addition to performing the tasks prescribed by the work stations of which they are a part, people are involved in many other activities within the organization. Some of these activities are directly related to the work; others are not. But a majority of these activities typically involve **interactions** with other people.

> *Observation 13.* Work that people perform in organizations is specialized, and it is both similar to and different from everyone else's work.

Interactions simply are contacts that people have with other people. They imply initiation and response; they can happen between two people or between groups of people; and they can last anywhere from a minute or two to an indefinite period of time.

Careful observation of human interactions over time allows one to delineate three broad groups of people by the way they interact. The first group consists of people who are associated with the actual flow of material and with the machines. These people are mostly responders to interactions initiated by other people. Compared to the other two groups, this group has fewer interactions, and the percentage of time the members spend in interactions is moderate. Because this group is involved most directly with changing the inputs into outputs, their energies are concentrated in that direction. Further, when these people do interact, their interactions are of short duration and take place with a limited number of people. This group is made up of the nonmanagerial employees of the organization.

The second group of people have a somewhat different pattern of interaction. They both initiate and respond; however, the length of their interactions also tends to be short. These people are the managers of the organization, and they can be further divided into three subcategories—first-line supervisors, middle managers, and top managers.

First-line supervisors initiate activity for a specified group of employees and respond to middle and top managers. Middle managers initiate activity for first-line supervisors and indirectly for the employees. They also have extensive interactions with other middle managers and with top managers. The top managers initiate activities for middle managers and, through them, for employees. They also interact, both by initiation and response, with people outside the organization. In fact, top managers spend as much, if not more, time with people outside the organization as they do with those inside. It is apparent from these observations that within the organizational hierarchy, the top-level groups initiate action for members of lower-level groups. This hierarchy of initiations and responses represents the organization's **chain of command.** When the hierarchy is charted, the organization design resembles a pyramid.

> *Observation 14.* Organizational positions form a pyramid with a few positions at the top and many at the bottom. The pyramid represents a chain of command down to the individual work stations.

The third group, composed of staff members, has a complicated interaction pattern. The members of this group have extensive contacts throughout the organization. They both initiate and respond, and their interactions are typically of longer duration than the other two groups. Much time is spent in long association with others, usually in the form of committee meetings. By observing the various interactions of these people, one can see that the subject matter of their interactions encompasses a very narrow sphere. They are experts in a variety of functions necessary to the operation of the organization, and their interactions normally pertain strictly to their areas of expertise.

Informal Interactions. The interactions we have discussed thus far have all centered around work-related associations, or interactions for the purpose of accomplishing assigned tasks. These are referred to as **formal interactions.** But another category of interactions may also be observed. **Informal interactions** occur usually within the same group rather than across groups, and they are not related to specific work activities. In this sense they may be said to be extra-organizational. These interactions do take place among definite groups of people, but ones that are not well linked together or hierarchical in nature.

> *Observation 15.* People in organizations engage also in interactions that are not associated with their work. These are called informal interactions.

An Overview of the Organization

Our mythical organization now looks something like the one depicted in Figure 1-3. This organization has a specialized, intentional output, a product it makes and exchanges with other organizations in the environment. Resources (people, money, materials, and information) must balance favorably against the outputs in order that the organization remain solvent. And the output must be seen as useful to at least some factions within the environment. Further, organizations must adapt to changes in the environment either by changing internally or by somehow changing the environment.

To produce a particular product, the organization must combine its resources with relevant technology. Such a combination constitutes the work of the organization. Resources are allocated to particular work stations where machines and people work together to recombine the resources into finished products or services. Part of this work involves complicated patterns of interactions, including decision-making activities.

Mediating between the environment and the work stations and directing and coordinating the work activities are the responsibilities of the managers. The different levels of managerial positions form the hierarchy of the organization. It is through this hierarchy that the chain of command operates, whereby policies and directives filter down from top-level managers to the various work groups.

Work

"You can't eat for eight hours a day nor drink for eight hours a day nor make love for eight hours a day—all you can do for eight hours is work. Which is the reason why man makes himself and everybody else so miserable and unhappy."
—WILLIAM FAULKNER

What is work? If you were to ask ten different people, you would undoubtedly get ten different responses. Some might equate it with play. This attempt seems reasonable enough, but how would you differentiate between the meanings of the two words? When you are "working" on your car, are you working or playing? The weekend golfer and the pro both do the same thing when they "play" golf. Which one is working? If you enjoy what you are doing is it always play? If you dislike the activity is it always work? Can you dislike activities that you call play, or enjoy activities you call work?

So far in this chapter, work has been seen as the object of managing; something that organizations do and that is performed within the context of the organization. Since we have already defined work as the transformation of resources into desired outputs, perhaps work can best be thought of as a miniature organization, one in which the complexities of its parts have been reduced to the most basic units—one person performing one set of activities. And, like organizations, work can best be understood by examining it both from an external and an internal point of view.

To remain consistent with the rest of the chapter, the following sections will also look at work in terms of the resource inputs, the activities of work, and the outputs, as illustrated in Figure 1-4.

An External View of Work

We have described how each work station within an organization is established to contribute to the overall goals and products of the organization. Work, then, does not happen at random. It is carefully designed and prescribed in ways that best meet the needs of the organization. And those who are hired to perform work tasks are those whose skills most closely coincide with the demands of the technology.

The output of work itself parallels the output of the organization—it is both intended and unintended, useful and nonuseful. Whether output is intended or unintended depends on the person doing the work. The output

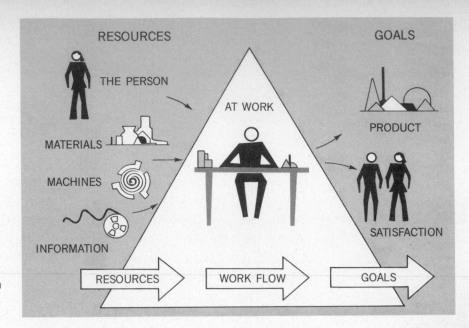

FIGURE 1–4
A representation of work. The person at work is represented as is the organization within the organizational pyramid.

"The gods hate mankind and out of spite condemn men to toil."
—HOMER

is intended if the person views it as contributing to either organizational or personal goals. Whether work output is useful or nonuseful depends on the manager's point of view, that is, whether he or she sees it as contributing to organizational goals. Conflict arises when the views of employees and managers differ as to intention and usefulness. Because the work of any one person is evaluated in terms of its contribution to organizational goals, there must be coordination of the work itself as well as of the general functions of the work stations. Maximum satisfaction (on the part of the organization and the individual) is attained when the employee and the manager collaborate on the coordination and design of work.

Work requires the same resources as does the organization; however, in work, the monetary resources are often received through indirect channels. The most obvious resource, of course, is the person doing the work. Employees possess certain sets of skills that enable them to perform given tasks. They also have their own needs and perceptions that determine the extent to which they are willing to do the work. Clearly, the happiest circumstance is one in which the work not only requires the individual's skills but also satisfies his or her personal goals.

Material and informational resources are made available by the organization. Most work requires material resources of equipment and supplies. And the kind of equipment available to a great extent determines the type of skills and extent of effort required from the employee. For example, an order-processing department that keeps its accounts on a computer requires different skills from its personnel than one that processes all orders manually.

The information available to employees determines the extent to which they are aware of how their work fits into the overall mission of the organization. Employees who are given little information generally are less highly motivated than employees who have a clear notion of how their work fits into the general scheme of things.

An Internal View of Work

What exactly do people do when they work? From the discussion of organizations in the previous section, three factors can be identified: people engage in specific activities, they interact with others, and they make decisions.

Activities. Every type of work consists of a specified set of activities. Secretaries, for example, may do filing, take dictation, type, answer phones, and perform hundreds of other discrete tasks. Gas station attendants not only put gas in your car, they also wash the windows, check the water in the radiator and battery, put air in the tires, and make mechanical repairs. Thus, secretaries have a whole range of skills that are unique to one kind of work, and gas station attendants have a set of skills that are unique to another. Certain of these skills, such as keeping accounts, may overlap, but for the most part, the activities of each job are highly specialized.

One way to distinguish different types of work, of course, is to simply look at the different physical and observational skills employed. But there are other forms of classification. One is **variety.** Does the task require many different activities, such as the two examples above, or endless repitition of the same activity, such as that performed by an assembly-line worker? Another way to classify activities is by **complexity.** Does the task require an ability to sequence the activities? Repetitious activities are limited in variety; sequential ones must be programed into a correct series; and more complex patterns require a concurrent juggling of a number of activities.

". . . if you cannot work with love but only with distaste, it is better that you should leave your work and sit at the gate of the temple and take alms from those who work with joy."
— GIBRAN

Interactions. In the performance of work, people must interact with other people and with machines. People can be both master and victim of these interactions. Employees who engage in simple sets of activities (those in which machines do most of the work) tend to be controlled by the machine. Employees whose activities are complex, and for whom machines are peripheral to the work, are in control of the machines. These differences appear to be reflected in two aspects of the activity-person relationship. First, different amounts of concentration are required. Simple sets of tasks take only a little concentration — surface attention rather than deep concentration (key punching and sweeping floors are two examples). The most complex tasks require high degrees of concentration plus commitment. People who stay with the task and remain long after others have left for the day typically are involved in highly complex tasks. Second, this simple-to-complex dimension is also reflected in people's attitudes

"No man can practice virtue who is living the life of a mechanic or laborer."
— ARISTOTLE

toward their work. People who perform routine, repetitious tasks often have a negative view of work. Complex sets of tasks, however, usually evoke a strong desire on the part of those who perform them to get to the activity and to stay with it over extended periods of time. These people often have very positive attitudes about work.

Although many types of work take place in isolation from other activities and people, more often work is performed in a group or as part of a sequence of activities. People in groups do not necessarily all perform the same sets of activities, although there are some who do. Most typically, each person in the group performs one part of the total set of activities designed to make a particular change in the material or information. Such interdependence creates a need for a good deal of interaction between people in order to accomplish the work.

Decisions. Clearly, people cannot do any kind of work they desire in the organization. On the other hand, no design or coordination of work by managers is so complete and thorough that the person does not have at least some discretion over how his or her work will be carried out. In one series of studies, known as the Glacier project, Jaques claimed that work could be defined as "the exercise of discretion with prescribed limits in order to reach a goal or objective" (5). Jaques further states that it is the discretionary aspect of work that gives the person the feeling of responsibility and the opportunity to use his or her unique abilities.

"Blessed is he who has found his work; let him ask no other blessedness."
— CARLYLE

Chapter Review

Understanding management requires a knowledge of the arena within which managing takes place (the organization), the work to be done and the nature of the resources that are used, and the activities that are common to managing. These topical areas are covered in each of the five parts of this book. The major ideas and terms that have been developed in this chapter include:

1. **Management** — planning goals (the work to be done); implementing the goals by obtaining, organizing, and allocating resources; and leading the organization to ensure completion of work through the roles of communicator, influencer, and controller.

2. **Inward** and **outward faces of the manager** — all managers are "persons in the middle." They must respond to pressures from both inside and outside the organization.

3. **Organization** — an assemblage of resources, particularly human ones, that are arranged and sequenced through technology to achieve an intended output.

4. **Inputs** — the resources that organizations gather in order to create outputs. These include people, money, technology, and information.

5. **Outputs**—the results of organizational operations that are intended to be useful to some group. A side effect is the production of unintended outputs, called waste.

6. **Work**—combining resources through the activities, interactions, and decisions of people to accomplish an organizational purpose.

Discussion Questions

1. Define *management.* Is a student a manager by this definition? Is a professor? Explain your answers.

2. Why is it important for a manager to understand organizations?

3. What does a manager do that is different from what other people in an organization do?

4. Define the term *organization.*

5. What resources or inputs do organizations need? How are they put to use?

6. What constitutes the outputs of an organization?

7. What do organizations look like on the inside?

8. How is an organizational hierarchy formed? What is the difference between hierarchy and work flow?

9. What is work?

10. How does the organization affect the work people do?

Involvement Activities

1. One way to find out firsthand what managers do is to talk with someone who is a manager. If you are employed, interview your boss. If not, talk with a friend or acquaintance who is a manager. Use the following questions as a guideline, but be sure to make up several of your own.

a. How do you spend your time?

b. What specific activities do you perform that your employees do not?

c. What are the most significant aspects of your job?

2. Describe the university or college that you are attending (or the organization for which you work) in terms of the following characteristics:

a. The resource inputs and their source.

b. The intended and unintended outputs.

c. The work flow.

d. The managerial hierarchy.

3. Are students performing work? Are professors? How would you describe studying and teaching in terms of activities, interactions, and decisions?

2

Past and Present Ideas About Managing

The purpose of this chapter is to briefly review the major theoretical and conceptual trends that have led to the current understanding of the field of management. The chapter begins with a historical review of the roots of management theory and goes on to explore the theory of organization, organization design, the factors that impinge on organization design, organizations as systems, and the role of managers in organizations.

If for centuries people ran organizations without the help of a systematic set of ideas about managing, why do we need these ideas now? And if we do need them, why did we wait this long to develop them? The answer to both these questions is that new ideas about human activities develop when traditional ways of handling problems no longer work. In this chapter we will show how major ideas about managing grew out of the need of organizations to solve problems that never before existed.

Historical Background of Management Thought

Until recently, few people thought about how work was organized and managed. Armies fought, governments rose and fell, merchants traded, and religious institutions flourished, all without benefit of an orderly scheme for understanding and improving the organizational techniques they employed. After all, in a world with limited means of transportation and poor communication, change occurred slowly, and tradition and custom determined how things were done and who did them. The children of monarchs ruled; the children of shoemakers made shoes. Everyone's role was more or less determined by birthright, and few moved out of the social class into which they were born.

However, by the end of the eighteenth century in Western Europe, the foundations had been laid for such rapid changes in the nature of work roles that customary ways of doing things were no longer satisfactory. Trading companies, chartered and protected by national rulers who were anxious to build their treasuries, brought the riches of the New World, Africa, and Asia to Europe. Soon, the increasing wealth in European nations led to a growing demand for manufactured goods. In turn, rapid market expansion led to marked improvements in the manufacture of glass and textiles, the smelting of iron, and the mining of coal. In particular, James Watt's improvements on the steam engine, which previously had been used mainly to pump water from coal mines, made large-scale, steam-powered production not only possible but inevitable.

Until this time, most products were made by skilled craftspeople serving local markets. They owned all their own tools and equipment, purchased the raw materials, and did all the work necessary to turn out a finished product for a specific customer. But because few of them had the money to buy the modern new equipment, and because their handmade products could not compete in price with machine-made goods, craftspeople gave way to those who could purchase tools, equipment, raw materials, and the work of others. These people who brought together all the means of production were called **capitalists.** At first, capitalists farmed out their work, to be done in the workers' cottages; it soon became more efficient, however, to put the equipment under one roof and hire workers to come to the plant. The factory system was thus born (1).

The Mercantile System

Mercantilism refers to a friendly, two-way — or reciprocal — relationship between the rulers and the merchants of a nation. Historically, the primary source of a nation's funds was taxes, and when recurrent wars drained national treasuries, taxes alone could not make up the deficit. Thus, merchants were called upon to replenish the national wealth by maintaining a "favorable" balance of trade — which meant exporting more products than were imported. The trouble was that all the competing nations in Europe tried to maintain a favorable balance of trade, an obvious impossibility. The answer to this dilemma was (1) to try to develop a colonial empire in the non-European world so that the home country would be virtually self-supporting, and (2) to set such high import duties on goods from competing nations that domestic or colonial goods would inevitably be cheaper. Colonies were to supply raw materials rather than manufactured goods, and they were to be taxed to further support the adventures of the mother nation.

According to plan, many European governments indeed became richer under the mercantilist doctrines. And so did the traders, the bankers, and the manufacturers. In fact, many businesses soon became large-scale monopolies. Cooperative legislatures and rulers provided armies and navies to reduce the hazards of international trade, and they subsidized other industries of all types.

The Free Enterprise System

But in 1776, in his book called *An Inquiry into the Nature and Causes of the Wealth of Nations,* the Scottish economist Adam Smith lashed out

Adam Smith (1723-1790)

Adam Smith was born in Scotland in 1723. After attending public schools and completing six years of college, he wrote a book on ethics and became a well-known author. Smith taught in schools and colleges for eighteen years but gave up his post at the age of forty-one to become a private teacher for a duke. In this capacity, Smith traveled widely throughout France with his pupil and talked with many French intellectual leaders of the day. Based on what he had learned in his travels, he spent the next ten years writing *Wealth of Nations*, which was to become the single most influential factor in ushering in the Industrial Revolution.

Smith, in fact, originated the field of economics as a separate area of thought, and revolutionized the thinking of political and business leaders throughout the Western world. To this day, Adam Smith's ideas remain a dominant force in economic thought in industrialized nations everywhere. A capsule summary of these ideas follows:

• Wealth will increase only if the value of output rises faster than the cost of inputs; that is, only as work becomes more productive.

• Increased productivity results from the division of a total task into smaller, specialized units of work. Each worker can turn out more by being a specialist, doing a limited piece of work increasingly well.

• If goods so produced are allowed to be freely exchanged in open markets, resources will flow to those nations (or firms or individuals) that can use them more efficiently than they can use other resources.

• People are motivated primarily by economic gain. They will willingly perform bits of a whole job because wealth will increase; and as the national income rises, so will the individual's wages.

Source: Adam Smith, *An Inquiry Into the Nature and Causes of the Wealth of Nations, Part One* (New York: P. F. Collier and Son, 1901), pp. 43 ff.

against the abuses of monopoly and mercantilism (2). Smith argued that wealth in a nation is not the gold collected as a result of maintaining a favorable balance of trade but rather is the result of productivity. He argued further that productivity is not enhanced by protective tariffs but rather by specialization, division of work, and free trade. Smith claimed that trade is not aided but is hampered by either governmental help or interference. The invisible hand of free market demand will channel resources to those individuals, firms, and nations that can use them most efficiently. This doctrine of **laissez-faire capitalism** (that governments should not intervene in the affairs of business and industry) swept away mercantilism and ushered in the Industrial Revolution.

The time was right for a new doctrine. Politically, the revolt of exploited colonists was imminent. Economically, the accumulation of capital could supply the expensive equipment needed for large-scale manufacturing. And scientifically, the newly born steam engine could be used to power ships and locomotives. For the first time in history, railroads made inexpensive overland transportation possible, and with the cost of transportation dramatically reduced and free trade encouraged, the modern industrial era began. The philosophy that dominated this era may be summarized by the following statement: *Productivity is a result of specialization, division of labor, and exchange.*

Organizing Work

A hundred years after Adam Smith first proposed his revolutionary economic theories, the world was vastly altered. Manufacturing had moved from workers' cottages to factories, which were rapidly increasing in size. Merchandising firms had grown and were disposing of the products of specialized manufacturers through elaborate marketing systems. Nations were knit together by complex transportation networks. Banks, which handled expanding market transactions, occupied an increasingly important position in the economies of the industrial world. And capital accumulated in the hands of manufacturers, merchants, shipping magnates, and bankers. This aggregation of wealth in the hands of relatively few people accelerated the rate of economic growth by making it possible for those with capital to invest in expensive new equipment, which, in turn, further increased their wealth. Traditional approaches to running organizations clearly were no longer sufficient. Indeed, no one really knew how to manage large, complex, and interdependent organizations. The stage was thus set for the first management theorists—the industrial engineers. Under the banner labeled **scientific management,** this new wave of theorists was led by Frederick W. Taylor.

Scientific Management

Frederick W. Taylor (1856–1915) and his successors showed how rational approaches to the design of work could increase efficiency through the implementation of specialization and division of labor (3). Growing up during the years in which industrial America came of age, Taylor was appalled at what he considered to be the waste of human and material resources permitted in the organizations he observed. He set for himself the task of applying the rational methods of science to the operations of workers, managers, and machines in industry. Taylor, who is considered the "father of scientific management," was the first efficiency expert, analyzing the motions people went through in doing their jobs. His contributions have provided a permanent place for the industrial engineer in modern society.

In his book *The Principles of Scientific Management,* first published in 1911, Taylor affirmed that the main goal of his life and work was to find and institute methods of increasing the national efficiency by discovering ways to reduce the waste of human effort. He believed that because inefficiency was the result of slipshod managerial methods, it was the obligation of management to improve the productive system by finding the "one best way" to perform tasks and then to recruit, train, and organize people for efficient work and cooperation. Taylor contended that if workers were trained to perform their tasks in the most rapid and efficient way possible, they would turn out the highest quality work permitted by their natural abilities—provided they were adequately rewarded for their performance. Rewards were to be in the form of pay, determined by examining the task, designating the most efficient methods, and establishing a standard amount of time it took to perform the task. Additional rewards (or

Frederick Taylor:
The Man with a Passion for Improving Things

Taylor's contributions to modern technology are astonishing. From his early boyhood he invented ways to improve things—in sports and around his home, as well as in industry.

SPORTS

• Fashioned a brake for his sled from a rake, which worked better than digging his feet in the snow to stop, as other boys did.

• Invented the overhand pitch while still in high school and revolutionized the game of baseball.

• Invented a spoon-handled tennis racket.

• Invented a two-handed putter. When the device was ruled out by the golfing association, he proceeded to make other improvements in the game of golf.

HOME

• Figured out a way to move entire rows of overgrown hedges without damaging the roots.

• Experimented with different mixtures of grass to develop better golfing greens.

INDUSTRY

• Developed machinery for cutting metals at high speed, thus revolutionizing the machine-tool industry.

• Developed a system of cost accounting.

• Developed the first scientific personnel-selection system, trying to fit applicants to job demands; suggested personnel administration as a separate management function.

• Developed a unique theory of business organization based on management specialists (functional foremen).

• Systematized the loading of pig iron; increased the output to 47 tons a day from the usual 19½. The secret—frequent rest pauses.

• Conducted some shoveling experiments and discovered that different kinds of shovels should be used for materials of varying weights. The result was that companies began buying the new shovels rather than having workers bring their own, and the workers felt deprived of their mark of individualism.

Frederick Taylor: Efficiency Expert

The year was 1880, the place was the Midvale Steel Company in Bethlehem, Pennsylvania. Taylor's improvements represented the first major attempt to apply the scientific method to work in industry. He found that workers could produce more when their tasks were divested of all unnecessary motions, when they were trained to do their jobs in the new way, when higher standards for output were set, and when a pay system was established that ensured that they were rewarded both for production and for additional output. Taylor quickly moved up the executive ladder at Midvale, applying his methods of scientific study to a variety of different kinds of work and extending his analysis to machines and equipment.[*]

Taylor eventually carried his ideas to the Bethlehem Steel Company. One of his famous studies there was an analysis of pig-iron handling. Taylor found the right person for the pig-iron job in one man he called "Schmidt." Of this prototype pig-iron handler, Taylor says:

> Now one of the very first requirements for a man who is fit to handle pig-iron as a regular occupation is that he be so stupid and so phlegmatic that he more resembles an ox in his mental make-up than any other type.[‡]

He was so completely sold on this bit of advice that he kept repeating it in his lectures and writings, which may help explain why some people took such a dim view of Taylorism!

Where Taylor was allowed to try his methods of rationalizing work, he regularly achieved increased efficiency. His successes were felt in an incredible number and diversity of endeavors—from shoveling to the cutting of metals.

[*] Frederick W. Taylor, "The Principles of Scientific Management" in *Scientific Management* (New York: Harper & Row, 1947).
[‡] Page 59.

bonuses) were to be offered as an incentive for workers to perform the tasks especially quickly. If the methods and rates were figured scientifically, workers could decide for themselves how much they wanted to earn. But there was always the implication that the more they earned, the more productivity would increase, and management as well as workers would benefit from the higher output. Thus the interests of management and workers became indentical. Both factions were economically motivated to maximize their incomes, which could be done if systematic methods were applied to the study of tasks. Managements that failed to develop their methods and their workers to the highest state of excellence were fulfilling neither their objectives nor their responsibilities.

Taylor maintained that for every form of labor known there is a science. Through careful study of the motions performed by a worker, it is possible, said Taylor, to eliminate unnecessary movements and to redesign the job, and the tools if need be, so that any qualified person could do the work efficiently. After an analysis of the motions of a task had been made, any capable worker could be taught to do the job as it had been designed. When the worker had become skilled, he or she would be timed and a standard set. Although Taylor's work was alleged to be against the best interests of workers and their unions, he contended to the end that he worked only for the humanitarian goal of reducing waste in order to maximize the incomes of both workers and managers.

The Results of Scientific Management

Taylor and such associates as Harry L. Gantt and Lillian and Frank Gilbreth applied the methods of scientific management throughout the industrial and commercial world. (Taylor also tried to systematize the work of various army and navy installations, which resulted in wild protests of indignation from employees at the Watertown Arsenal and a subsequent congressional investigation.) Owing to the efforts of these people, organizations became more efficient, national productivity increased greatly, and firms enjoyed both larger markets and higher profits. The rationalization of work by breaking down tasks into their component motions and combining like elements led to the development of machines designed to perform many of the most routinized functions. Taylor's ideas thus led to the increased mechanization of factories and further acceleration of the Industrial Revolution.

Eli Whitney's earlier invention of interchangeable parts (which meant that products could be manufactured through the use of standard elements instead of individually crafted units) combined with Taylor's standardization of work, led Henry Ford to combine both ideas and refine the revolutionary system of assembly-line mass production. The assembly-line system of production contributed to immense increases in productivity and resulted in the lower production costs and global mass markets we know today.

Taylor attacked the problem of managing large enterprises by analyzing the work, the worker, and the shop environment. Frank and Lillian Gilbreth carried the scientific study of motions one step further by making moving pictures of a worker and isolating every motion (4). They tagged each elementary motion with the name "therblig"—Gilbreth nearly spelled backward. Once the individual tasks were broken down into discrete motions, industrial engineers were able to substantiate the idea that the division of work led to efficiency. The Gilbreths confirmed the observation that *specialized and divided work can be made more efficient through careful study and analysis.*

Lillian Moller Gilbreth (1878–1972)

The work of Taylor was continued and extended by a number of his associates and disciples. Many are notable, but few did more to improve the efficiency of work than Lillian Moller Gilbreth and her husband, Frank Bunker Gilbreth.

Lillian Moller was born in Oakland, California, on May 24, 1878, the daughter of a German-born sugar refiner. Taught in the German tradition that a woman's responsibilities included only children, kitchen, and church, she fulfilled that role by bearing and raising twelve children; but she also maintained a full-time professional career as a psychologist, teacher, lecturer, and management consultant.

Lillian graduated Phi Beta Kappa from the University of California in 1900 with a degree in English and went on to earn her master's degree in the same field. In 1904 she interrupted work on her doctorate to marry Frank Gilbreth and changed her specialization to psychology in order to complement her husband's work in the construction industry. She completed her doctor's thesis, but the University of California would not award the degree because she had not completed the required year of study on campus. Frank, however, secured a publisher, and her thesis became the book *The Psychology of Management* (1914), which was one of the earliest considerations of the relationship between scientific management and people in industry. Gilbreth was finally awarded a Ph.D. by the University of California in 1915 in applied management after an approved year of study at Brown University.

"Lillian's training in psychology supplemented Frank's work on fatigue, motion study, the impact of the work environment on the worker, and the scientific management movement in general."[*] She wrote or collaborated on a number of books and articles, took over as president of the management consulting firm Gilbreth, Inc. after her husband died in 1924, was a professor of management at Purdue University from 1935 to 1948, and lectured throughout the world until the age of 90, when she decided to retire.

Gilbreth was acclaimed nationally and internationally, receiving twenty-two honorary degrees, three gold medals from various associations of managers and consultants, and many other accolades. The life of the Gilbreth family was popularized in books by two of her children, Ernestine Gilbreth Carey and Frank B. Gilbreth, Jr., in their biographical novels, *Cheaper by the Dozen, Belles on Their Toes,* and *Time Out for Happiness.*

Either individually or in collaboration with her husband, Lillian Gilbreth:

• Extended motion study by using moving pictures to point out wasteful and unproductive movements;

• Concentrated on finding the "one best way" to do work in hundreds of different organizations.

• Analyzed work from the viewpoint of the worker, thus laying the foundations for the study of management as a social science; and

• Instituted one of the first management-development and training programs.

[*] Daniel A. Wren, "In Memoriam: Lillian Moller Gilbreth, 1878–1972," *The Academy of Management Journal,* Vol. 15, No. 1 (March 1972), pp. 7–8. Other material in this sketch is derived from the above reference and from Carl Heyel, ed., *The Encyclopedia of Management,* 2nd ed. (New York: Van Nostrand Reinhold Co., 1973), pp. 284–285.

Administrative Management

Taylor and other industrial engineers concentrated on improving the efficiency of work at the "worker" level. With the application of science to specialized and divided work, productivity increased, the real income of industrialized nations grew, and a rise in the demand for goods followed. Accelerated demand led managers to expand their organizations so that by the end of World War I (1918), there were more large-scale organizations in the world than had ever before existed. These new organizations with their specialized production methods required not only more managers but managers who could understand how to operate complex organizations effectively. Because traditional rules of thumb were no longer appropriate for dealing with the problems of such diversified establishments, a number of successful executives, administrators, and consultants set out to define some of the principles that had helped them gain success. It was their hope that these principles might be adapted for general use by managers of mass-production organizations.

The ideas that these practitioners came up with are known as the **principles of administrative management.** These principles examined the organization of work from the point of view of senior executives rather than of the hourly worker. Some of the principal exponents of the administrative management of large organizations included Henri Fayol, General Director of the Comambault coal-mining company in France from 1888 to 1918; James D. Mooney and Alan C. Reiley, executives for General Motors in the 1920s and 1930s; Lyndall Urwick, a British management consultant; Luther Gulick, a public administrator and professor; Oliver Sheldon, a British consultant; and Henry S. Dennison of the Dennison Manufacturing Company of Massachusetts. Max Weber, a well-known German sociologist, also developed very similar ideas (5).

Coordination of Work. Organizations exist because collaboration is more efficient than individual effort. When work is divided among specialists within organizations, however, the output of each specialized work station somehow must be meshed with the output of all other work stations. In other words, individual operations need to be coordinated into a smooth and efficient whole. Thus, someone must supervise all the work of one particular operation, or all the work in one designated area. Then, to make sure that the combined work of each operation or department meshes properly with other operations or departments, the supervisors must be coordinated by other managers. Their work, in turn, is coordinated by their superiors. This kind of coordination continues all the way to the top, where the chief executive officer is charged with the final responsibility for coordinating all the work of the organization. This type of organization leads to the following observation: *The coordination of specialized tasks requires an administrative organization.*

Organizations as Hierarchies. A chart of the various offices within an organization would resemble a pyramid, with a chief executive officer at the top and the various echelons of managers and workers below. When viewed this way, organizations can be thought of as **hierarchies,** in which the work of a few (or of tens, hundreds, or thousands) is ultimately controlled by a small group of senior administrators.

The senior administrators, in turn, are controlled by outside forces in the form of cultural norms and values, societal laws and regulations, prevailing economic conditions, and public pressure and interest groups. But on a more immediate level, organizations are controlled by their owners or by owners' representatives.

When an owner or owners of an organization cannot be personally involved in the day-to-day decision-making processes, a governing board may be selected to act on their behalf. These boards appoint chief executives, set general objectives, and outline policies to guide administrative behavior. Thus the power and means of control of an organization are collected and concentrated in the hands of a few people at the top. A further observation, then, is that: *The administrative organization is hierarchical in form with those toward the top controlling those below.* (See Figure 2-1.)

Authority, Responsibility, and Accountability. When people believe that the power held by those at the top of an organization is legitimate, that power is called **authority,** an acknowledged right to command with the expectation of compliance. The managerial hierarchy of an organization can use authority to get work done. Although most authority is clustered at the top of an organization, lesser degrees of authority are delegated downward through the hierarchy so that each manager or supervisor has enough control over his or her assigned area to make certain that work is performed satisfactorily. An important requirement of

FIGURE 2–1
An organizational hierarachy.

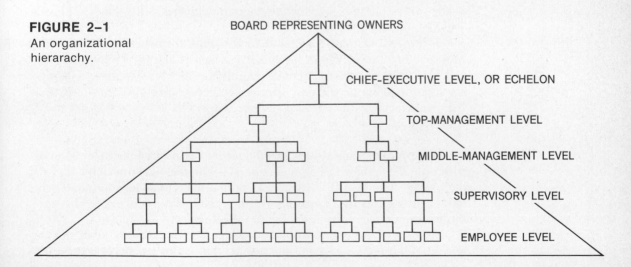

proper delegation is that the authority delegated to any position in the hierarchy be equal to the **responsibility,** or performance obligation, involved in carrying out the job. In this way each person is assured of sufficient resources necessary to fulfill the job obligation and can be held **accountable** for the adequate performance of the task. However, the person performing the work is not the only one held accountable. Persons at all levels in the hierarchy who have been involved in delegation are also held accountable for the results.

Centralization and Decentralization. A further aspect of authority covered by the administrative management theorists deals with the extent to which authority is delegated within the organization. The organizer may choose to centralize authority in the hands of a few people at the top of the hierarchy or to decentralize authority by delegating it extensively throughout the organization. The advantages and costs of centralization must be weighed against decentralization, and a plan should be selected that is most appropriate for the enterprise at the time.

Centralized authority can provide a single, coherent set of standards for the entire operation that enables easy transfer of people from one segment to another; it also adds an element of predictability and uniformity to performance. Because authority is the major coordinating power in an organization, it could be argued that the greater the need for coordination the more authority should be centralized. The organizer who wants to achieve a maximum degree of stability, control, and coordination will therefore centralize power in a top management group and provide these managers with only a few subordinates (a narrow **span of control**). In this way, managers can carefully superintend their employees' work. The fewer people each executive supervises, the narrower the span of control, the greater the number of levels required in the hierarchy, and the steeper will be the organizational pyramid. This kind of organization maximizes control and facilitates sending messages downward to the workers; however, it creates corresponding problems.

If the goal of the organizer is to stimulate local autonomy, develop well-rounded executives in the lower reaches of the hierarchy, improve upward communications, or make operations quickly adaptable to changing conditions, he or she may choose to decentralize authority, create a "flat" hierarchy with few levels between top and bottom, and opt for a wide span of control.

Harmony of Objectives. In all decisions regarding the delegation of authority, the manager as organizer must keep in mind the principle developed by the administrative management theorists called **harmony of objectives,** which states that every part of the organization and every phase of its operation must be consistent with the interests of the enterprise. Thus, the interests of the organization as a whole take precedence over the interests of the individuals and the groups that make up the operation. In

The Mystery of the Dimming Lights

The manager of a factory in which workers assemble telephone parts has applied scientific management principles to the work, divided the tasks into discrete elements, eliminated waste motions, and hired qualified workers. But still he feels the work is not as efficient as it should be. One day he notices that the quality of illumination varies throughout the plant, and he wonders whether worker efficiency could depend on the quality and quantity of light.

To check this idea, he sets up an experiment: first he increases the illumination and then he decreases it. Result: efficiency fluctuates randomly with changes in the lighting. So he tries a second experiment. Using a test group for which he changes the lighting, and a control group, for which he leaves the light alone, he finds that output increases in *both* groups even though he has altered the lighting in only one.

So the manager tries a third test, again using both a test group and a control group. He increases the illumination for the test group and leaves unchanged the lighting for the control group. Again efficiency increases in both groups. On the fourth test, he cuts back the light in the test group until it's as dim as moonlight, and to his enormous surprise, *efficiency goes up.*

What's going on?

(Can you guess what caused these results before reading on?)

building the organization, a manager must structure relationships in such a way that private interests and individual idiosyncrasies are either kept subordinate to the requirements of the organization or made harmonious with them.

The administrative management theorists have presented a view of the organization as a rationally ordered mechanism whose goal is to produce products or provide services in the most efficient manner possible. And as long as the work organization remained a design on paper, this machine-view seemed quite logical. But when this logic of efficiency and order was implemented in the design of large-scale organizations, other difficulties surfaced.

Organization Design

The best-run organizations do not owe their success simply to the careful use of organizational principles. Rather, they are the result of combining sound coordination of divided work with attentiveness to the myriad other variables that affect an enterprise, some of which may have little to do with the work itself. For example, in addition to efficiency and order, three major factors that must be considered in organization design are the **people** who do the work, the **technology** they work with, and the **environment** they work within.

How Human Behavior Influences Organization Design: A Case Study

By the middle of the 1920s the Industrial Revolution, which had begun in the United States in the early years of the nineteenth century and had picked up momentum during and after the Civil War, had dramatically changed the character of American life, work, and industry. The emphasis on organizational efficiency through task specialization and division of labor meant that workers' jobs required less skill. Unskilled laborers, who moved to the cities in droves, were eager for a chance to work and thus threatened the job security of those who were already employed. Further, new and expensive machinery required substantial outlays of cash, and most workers no longer could afford to own their own tools. They lost status, confidence, and self-reliance as they were increasingly made dependent on the large factories that employed them.

Existing theories proved inadequate for dealing successfully with workers in this new climate, and managers sought on a trial-and-error basis some solution to the motivational problems of the day. In one approach, management turned for help to industrial psychologists, such as Lillian Gilbreth, or to sociologists, such as Elton Mayo. The reasoning of these applied behavioral scientists during the 1920s was that worker restiveness might well be the result of physiological fatigue. Thus, if the pace of work along with other environmental conditions were changed, employees would be less tired and more content. As a result, restlessness would decrease and productivity would rise.

Such was the thinking that, in 1924, led the management of the Hawthorne Works of the Western Electric Company near Chicago, Illinois, to begin a series of investigations that would have far-reaching effects on future ideas about management. The Hawthorne Studies, as these investigations came to be known, began as an attempt to discover how the quality of illumination affected efficiency. During the course of the study (which lasted until 1927) it became clear that although some changes in efficiency were noted, the degree of light was not the determinative element. Still determined to make general improvements in the rate of productivity, management sought means to continue studies that would unearth the real factors responsible for the noted increases in efficiency.

They recruited a research staff from the Industrial Research Department of the Graduate School of Business at Harvard University. Under the leadership of industrial sociologist Elton Mayo, the team included a number of people destined to add important contributions to management theory (6).

In an earlier (1923) research effort, Mayo had investigated labor turnover in a textile mill near Philadelphia. He found that allowing people to take rest pauses during their working hours resulted in higher productivity and lower rates of turnover. His explanation of this result was that work breaks reduced boredom and fatigue, thereby stimulating employees to increase their output. The Hawthorne Studies further affected Mayo's thinking about the variables affecting human productivity. The data he generated pointed to interpersonal relations rather than to physiology as a motivating factor. *It was not lighting or other working conditions that affected productivity but the fact that the employees in the test group had been specially selected for observation, and that those in the control group, where the illumination did not change, knew they were part of an important experiment.*

To Mayo, the Hawthorne Studies invalidated what he called the "rabble hypothesis," which was that society consists of hordes of unorganized individuals who act solely to secure their own self-interest and who think logically and rationally to maximize their calculated goals. Mayo believed that, contrary to then-current opinion, people are not rational in solely economic terms, seeking exclusively to maximize income relative to effort (Taylor's view). They are not necessarily competitive by nature, seeking only to outwit everyone else. And they are certainly not machines. Mayo found that workers respond with something less than delighted enthusiasm when efficiency experts rationalize their work and industrial psychologists strive to create for them a "perfect" physical environment, a sterile, well-lighted and ventilated factory for the production of goods. The Hawthorne Studies showed workers to be people, not unwholesome rabble or faceless automatons. And like all people, they are partly logical and rational, and partly creatures of sentiment and feeling. At work, they develop elaborate social mechanisms for their protection and for their maintenance as members of miniature social systems within the larger social system known as the Company.

A major conclusion drawn from the Hawthorne Studies was that people at work are diversely motivated members of complex social systems. Workers could no longer be considered simply pieces of equipment to be moved around like desks according to the logic of efficiency, without penalty to the organization. People at work were found to be movitated not only by their desire for wages but by a host of other factors as well. It was found, for instance, that an important role in behavior is played by the personal history of individuals, including their life outside the plant, their values, their education, their goals, and their experiences. These personal factors in turn influence their attitudes and sentiments, which are also affected by the social situation they create at work. Behavior, then, is seen to be the result of the combined influences of past experience, first-hand awareness of what is going on, aspirations for the future, and the informal groups of which workers are likely to be a part.

Results from the Hawthorne Studies were slow in making an impact on the logic of efficiency, which was so well entrenched in industry. Early findings were published in 1933 in Mayo's book *The Human Problems of an Industrial Civilization,* and later in occasional articles (7). In 1938, T. North Whitehead published *The Industrial Worker,* in which he reviewed the Hawthorne findings (8); in 1939, Fritz Roethlisberger, a member of the Harvard research team, and William J. Dickson of the Western Electric Company issued *Management and the Worker,* a thorough review of the research and its results (9). Still, the studies had little

The Hawthorne Studies, 1927–1932
Western Electric Company, Chicago, Illinois

I. *The Relay-Assembly Test-Room Experiments.* The first study, lasting from 1927 to 1932, took place in the Relay-Assembly Test Room. It was found that the workers, who were placed in a room especially designed for the experiment, regularly increased their rate of output, irrespective of changes in such conditions as the number and length of rest pauses and wage incentive systems. Because they felt especially chosen for this important experience, the employees' attitudes toward the company and toward their work so changed that they gave management what they thought was wanted: higher productivity.

II. *The Interview Experiments.* These results (which led to the introduction of rest pauses all over the plant, and which may have instituted the great American coffee break custom) encouraged the research team to undertake a further examination of the attitudes of employees. They decided to select and train interviewers who would listen with understanding and empathy to any employee who wanted to talk. Complaints would be assembled and used for supervisory training, but the names of employees would be kept strictly confidential. The interviewer was trained to listen with understanding, to make only noncommittal remarks, and not to structure or direct the conversation in any way.

The Industrial Research Department of the company conducted the interviewing, the analysis of interviews, and the supervisory training. The interviewing program led to desirable changes in supervisory behavior because the supervisor now had an insight into worker feelings. It led also to the assembling of the intimate thoughts, sentiments, and reflections of the worker, and gave the employees a lift as the result of being recognized and of having participated in training their supervisors. Repeatedly, employees remarked on the benefits of

being able to express their feelings and emotions freely to a neutral and patient listener who was not an authority, who gave no advice, and who presented no argument.

III. *The Bank-Wiring-Room Experiments.* The researchers, because of their findings that the social environment in which people work influences productivity and that sentiments are "facts" to those who hold them (and influence their behavior), decided next to turn their attention to an analysis of the social organization of workers in the Bank Wiring Room, a study that lasted from November 1931 to May 1932. The purposes of the Bank-Wiring-Room experiments were to obtain more exact information about the social organization of workers than had been provided by the interviews and to develop a method of direct observation in place of interviewing as a means of gathering data.

On the basis of patient observations of the workers in the Bank Wiring Room during the six months of the study, the research team discovered that a complex "informal" organization existed that was at least as important as the formal organization.

The employees developed an elaborate set of informal rules of behavior, or social norms, which in many instances were diametrically opposed to the assumptions of scientific management and the best-intentioned studies of industrial engineers: that is, they established a social system to protect their group from internal indiscretions and from outside interference; they evolved their own means of social control; they imposed social ostracism for severe breaches of the norms; and they restricted output to confound the logic of technological efficiency. The conclusions of the investigation indicated that the worker is not primarily motivated by economic gain, and that work behavior is neither exclusively logical nor completely rational in an economic sense.

F. Roethlisberger and W. J. Dickson, *Management and the Worker* (New York: Wiley, 1939).

immediate impact; undoubtedly the time was not right for industrial social reform. Workers in the Depression era of the 1930s were grateful to have jobs at all, and during World War II, managers and workers alike concentrated all their energies on productivity for the war effort.

After the war, however, managerial concern with worker motivation again became critically important. Eagerly seeking ways of understanding worker behavior, managers sought out teachers and consultants to gain insight into human problems. At last the Hawthorne findings were relevant to organizational needs. During the 1950s, the demand for human relations training was so strong that it came to be a major social movement. And by the 1960s most managers were well aware that unpredictable human elements put a constraint on the logic of efficiency and the orderly grouping of organizational parts.

Now some began to wonder whether there were still other, unaccounted for, variables that would affect organization design. Can any institution be designed like any other so long as efficiency, order, and human needs are attended to? The answer came back No, and the reason was that different organizations employ different forms of technology. To find out how technology affects organization design, managers turned to the universities for help.

Technology and Organization Design

The term **technology** refers to all the knowledge, skill, tools, machines, materials, and conditions required to perform work—this includes human abilities as well as machine capacity. The relationship between technology and organization design has yet to be studied extensively, but the research that has been done indicates very clearly that technology has a definite effect on the design of an organization. In fact, Charles Perrow indicates that technology may well be the defining characteristic of an organization in that its structure is dependent on its technology (10). Perrow suggests that in planning an organization design, one might first examine the work to be done and then determine the most appropriate structure in which to do it.

The Effects of Differentiation of Work. In a job shop, one person's function might be to make a saw. The worker would move from machine to machine as necessary to complete the job. In a saw-making factory, on the other hand, one department might cut the sheet metal, another the handles, another the teeth, and another would assemble the final product. Specialized units would also oil, pack, and store the product. It seems logical that different kinds of organization designs would be necessary to coordinate the work of these two very different kinds of systems. Yet both make saws. The more the work is divided among specialists or the more it is differentiated from other work, the greater the need to coordinate or integrate to make certain that the very specialized work of one segment of the system meshes well with that of the other segments. Thus, the number of hierarchical levels might be determined by the extent of differentiation rather than by managerial choice.

The Effects of Mechanization. The greater the degree of differentiation, the more likely it is that machines can be designed to do the work, and this mechanization will have an effect on the organization design. Clearly, a fully automated production system would require a vastly different organization from one in which the work is performed by people who work machines. Yet both production systems would require a different organization from one that was hardly mechanized at all. For example, petroleum refining requires only a few people, most of whom are technicians who watch and maintain the mechanized process. Because controls are built into the equipment, the administrative organization need not be large. On the other hand, the assembly line requires both people and machines. Because the work of the operators is highly specialized and each step of the process must dovetail perfectly with succeeding steps, an integrating organization, perhaps one with several managerial levels, is necessary. Where the work is not very mechanized, as in a social welfare agency, human skills are more likely to direct the choice of organization design than are the requirements of any machinery that may be utilized.

The Effects of the Degree of Difficulty of Work and Extent of Routinization. Closely allied technological variables that affect organizations are the degree of routinization of the work and the level of difficulty of the routines. Further research is necessary to determine exactly how routinization affects an organization, but it seems logical that nonroutine and very difficult work requires a **specialist organization.** This involves a simple structure with a specialist in charge. On the other hand, highly programed and simple tasks require more controls and coordination, which means having a **bureaucratic organization** with many hierarchical levels.

The Effects of Varying Skill Requirements. If the skills, or expertise, required of the people who do the work are mimimal, there may be several organizational levels that deal with supervising, controlling, and coordinating people. If the skills required for the job are highly technical, the employees will likely require less supervision and the organization's structure may be less complex. In both cases, however, the kind of supervisory system that is instituted might depend in part on the ready availability of workers—an outside, or environmental, variable.

The Effects of the Interrelationship Between People and Technology. Earlier we noted how the technological variables interact with and affect one another and so must be taken into account when designing an organization structure. A corollary to this requirement is that to the extent the technological system involves people, the organization design must also reflect the relationship between those people and the technology they employ. This relationship is called the **sociotechnical system.**

People have skills, or technological expertise; they also have feelings about such things as dull, routine work, being tied to the logic of efficiency that guides the production line, their chances of being replaced by machines, and so on. People and machinery interact. The effects of the technology on the workers and of the workers on the technology also need to be considered when developing the organization design.

Subunit Designs. Up to this point we have examined the organization as a single system with certain technological characteristics. But within the large organization there are subgroups that also need to be considered from a design standpoint. To the extent that technology differs among subunits, the organization design of each unit might vary accordingly. In organizations composed of subgroups that perform substantially different functions, it is unlikely that a single organizational plan can be imposed throughout the company. Further, it is possible that even among

IF WE MANAGED THE WAY HE DID THEY WOULDN'T HANG OUR PICTURE, THEY'D HANG US.

divisions doing the same kind of work, different outside variables might require the setting up of different designs.

Environmental Forces and Organization Design

Environmental forces that can affect organization design might include such factors as the political-legal climate, the sociocultural norms, the economic situation, the geophysical setting, and the ecological considerations of the locale. In addition, the environmental forces must also be examined in terms of their relationship to one another; for instance, the rate of environmental change versus the degree of political or economic stability, the economic and sociocultural consequences of opening a large company in a small town, and so on. In considering all of these variables, a number of students of organization design have come to the conclusion that if internal states and processes are consistent with external demands, then the organization will be more effective.

Like the studies of the effect of people on organization design, many studies conducted a number of years ago are just now being recognized. The impetus for reexamining these early findings is tied to the increasing degree of change in the environment and the increasing interdependence and complexity of the environment and the organization.

The research of Emery and Trist disclosed that the environments of organizations are changing at an increasing rate (as a result of technological invention, for one), and that it is therefore essential to understand the environment surrounding an organization to fully understand the organization itself (11). Terreberry also found that organizational environments are increasingly turbulent, and she noted that such turbulence, or change, is making formal organizations less and less independent (12). In fact, many external forces are brought to bear by other organizations. According to Terreberry, internal organizational change is largely externally induced, and those organizations that learn to adapt to changing external environments will be the most successful.

The basic idea that has emerged from all these studies is that there is no one organizational form that is the best in all situations. Rather, the best organizational structure is the one that most closely reflects the environment of the organization. This basic idea can be further expanded to include the thought that the more stable the environment the more efficient will be the rational model of organization, whereas in a turbulent or changing environment the most efficient structure will be one that is loose and easily adaptable. Burns and Stalker called the two extremes of organizational structure **mechanistic** and **organic** (13).

In an important study by Lawrence and Lorsch, Burns and Stalker's ideas were substantiated and extended (14). These researchers examined firms in the plastics, container, and food industries to determine whether the organizational structures of high- and low-performing companies differed according to environmental conditions. Differences were found in both differentiation (division of work) and integration (coordination). For example, it was found that the effective plastics firm, operating in a dynamic and diverse environment, had the most highly differentiated organizational structure whereas the top-performing container firm, operating in a stable and a homogeneous environment, had a classic hierarchical organizational structure. By the same token, it was found that the integration and coordination in the successful plastics firms were highly developed into specialized positions, whereas in the successful container companies these functions were centralized in the general manager's position. Both organizations had developed structures in tune with the demands of their environments, and although quite different from each other, both were highly successful.

Organizations as Systems of Contingencies

The theory that optimal organization design and effective managerial behavior are dependent on a variety of diverse factors is known as the **contingency approach** to management. This approach takes into account the fact that the variables of subdivided work, coordinating hierarchy, people, technology, and outside forces are all interdependent. It also states that managers must not only understand a concept but also be able to predict the effects that any combination of variables will have on the entire organizational system.

In contrast to the early theories of organizational management typified by Taylor and Gilbreth's "one best way" to perform a task, the contingency approach is best described by the phrase "It all depends." A contingency in this sense is the effect that one or more variables have on another variable. For example, the unpredictability of human behavior (count as one variable) can render inoperative even the most sophisticated computer system (count as another variable). Or, conversely, people can make terribly outmoded systems run smoothly and efficiently.

This current view of organizations is that they are not orderly arrangements of offices, machinery, and buildings that are static and can be understood by charting them on a graph or by taking photographs. Rather, they are interdependent sets of interacting forces (contingencies) in which all elements influence all others. Seen in this way, *organizations are systems*. A systems approach provides a convenient way of assessing the variables common to all systems that can generally be applied to organization design.

Characteristics of Systems

Since the systems approach views organizations as interwoven sequences of events connected directly or indirectly with all other events, it follows that any change in customary or expected actions of any one variable, or event, is likely to produce effects throughout the system. To understand this concept, one need only imagine the way in which a small stone splashed in a still pool produces ripples across the whole body of water.

The major consideration in organization design then is a knowledge of the ways in which the parts interact with the whole.

Open and Closed Systems. Systems can be ranged along a continuum from totally closed to totally open, as illustrated in Figure 2–2. The degree of openness is determined by the ease with which outside forces are allowed to penetrate the organization. A totally closed system would have an impenetrable boundary, a totally open system no boundary at all. The extremes of the continuum are hypothetical models only and do not exist in reality. Approaching either of these extremes too closely can lead to the demise of an organization. For the most part, organizations are open in that they are connected with other organizations on which they depend for input of resources and to which they send outputs. In this sense, they can be viewed as small-scale nations that, through a balance of trade, depend on one another for their economic survival.

When organizations become too closed to the environment, they cannot satisfy their internal needs; when they become too open, however, they are unable to maintain a favorable balance of operating costs and output values, and eventually they become fused with the environment. The completely closed system (shown at the left of Figure 2–2) is shut off from its environment and will continue to function as a system only until its supply of resources is exhausted. At such time, **entropy,** a random distribution of its elements within impermeable boundaries, sets in and the organization falls in on itself. At the other extreme, the boundaries of the organization have disintegrated and the parts have been absorbed by the environment. A bankrupt business firm whose assets have been distributed among its creditors is an example of the disintegrated organization.

Input-Output Flow. An organization is an open system. Like other such systems, the organization maintains contact with its environment to secure inputs of energy. These energy inputs are the resources the organization needs in order to operate. Employees work with the inputs to create the company's outputs. These outputs may be utilities, goods, or services that are useful and valuable to other organizations or to the public. It is also possible that the operations of a system may produce unintended or nonvaluable outputs, such as water or air pollution. In such instances, the cost of rectifying or utilizing these outputs may have to be borne by some external group in the environment, usually the government.

If a system remains open to its environment, it receives feedback about its operations. If the output is valued by society, the outputs of the organization generate a continued supply of inputs. The outputs of a business firm, for example, are distributed in the marketplace in exchange for funds, which the business utilizes to continue to buy the resources necessary to produce its product. A major distinguishing feature of the business organization is the fact that the disposal of its outputs directly generates

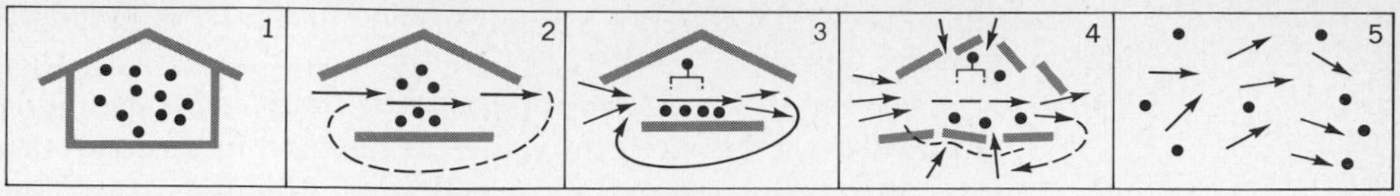

	CLOSED SYSTEM	MOSTLY CLOSED SYSTEM	OPEN, STABLE SYSTEM	MOSTLY OPEN SYSTEM	COMPLETELY OPEN: NO SYSTEM
	1	2	3	4	5
RESOURCES	No access	Limited access	Access to resources needed to survive and thrive	Access unlimited; too many choices	None
PRESSURES FROM ENVIRONMENT	Not susceptible	Sensitive to few	Sensitive to relevant ones, ignores others	Overly sensitive and reactive to too many forces	Pressures flow at random
INTERNAL STABILITY	None: random disorder or entropy; internal units separate from each other	Stable, but in a rut; ossified, inefficient	Stable	Unstable; too many changes and pressures to react to	None; internal elements merged with environment
OUTPUTS	None	Cost of outputs may be low, but outputs may not be valued in environment	Satisfactory relative to inputs, needed in environment	Cost of outputs excessive relative to inputs	None
FEEDBACK	None	Limited sensitivity to effect on environment	Accurate, prompt, relevant	Responds to too many other forces	None

FIGURE 2–2
An open-closed continuum of systems.

funds for the acquisition of additional inputs. Other kinds of organizations rely upon less-direct sources for their maintenance. Educational institutions, for example, do not sell their products (students) but rely for continued existence on both public and private sources, which are several steps removed from actual contributions by graduates.

Organizations, Work Groups, and Environment. Every organization is a subpart of a larger system, or environment. The environment supplies the organization with resources and maintains some control over its operations. If those who supply the resources do not approve of the organization's outputs, they can eventually do away with that organization. As a subunit of society, an organization must be seen as relevant or face the possibility of extinction. Maintaining a dynamic balance internally, preserving a flow of resources from the external environment, and producing a steady stream of valued outputs require managerial competence of a high order.

The environment will continue to permit organizations to operate only if the total, long-term value of their outputs equals or exceeds the total, long-term costs of inputs and work. In other words, the survival of an organization is dependent on its being both **effective** and **efficient.** An organization is considered effective if it satisfies some need of the environment; it is efficient if it satisfies this need in a manner consistent with good business practice—that is, that the value of the outputs exceeds the cost of the inputs plus the cost of doing the work.

Organizations show a tendency, however, to do more than merely equate total costs of operation with total value of outputs. If a business continually operates at a marginal level, where income barely exceeds costs, the survival of the enterprise is uncertain at best. To avoid this condition, there is a constant striving to acquire more resources of value than are minimally necessary so that a reservoir of resources is always available to tide the system over hard times. This **maximization principle,** or attempt to secure more inputs than are used, increases the organization's chances for success. The most obvious example of this principle in use is the business enterprise with large amounts of retained earnings. These reserves protect the company from an often hostile environment and allow it to grow without going outside for funds, which would likely result in a dilution of internal control.

The Role of the Manager in Organizations

We have seen that the complex systems of interrelated activities known as organizations need to be managed by some person or group of persons. And we have stated that one of the chief responsibilities of the managerial hierarchy is the coordination and integration of the various working parts of the enterprise. But exactly how do managers coordinate the work? And what else do they do? The remainder of this chapter examines several different perspectives of the managerial role in order to begin to answer these questions.

The Managerial Process

The word *process* means a proceeding, a taking of steps, or a forward movement over a period of time. Thinking of a manager's role in terms of a process is useful because the work that managers perform in the organization is a continuing, ongoing series of actions that takes place over a period of time. The managerial process occurs on all levels of an organization regardless of its size.

Managing the work of others is quite a different process from performing the work that is managed. Henri Fayol, for one, has distinguished managerial work from such other activities as producing, buying and selling, financing, insuring safety, and accounting (15). And although managers may sometimes help do the work of their departments, when they are doing so they are not managing. Managerial activities are unique functions that must be looked at separately from other activities that managers may perform. Thus, even though the work of managers of engineering firms or accounting departments, for instance, may demand some specialized expertise, managerial skills per se are more or less the same regardless of the type of work being managed. Consequently, unlike technical skills, managerial skills are transferable among specialities.

Administrative Management

Early ideas about the managerial process were contributed by members of the **administrative management** school of thought. Fayol said that "to manage is to forecast and plan, to organize, to command, to coordinate and to control" (16). Luther Gulick amended Fayol's description, saying that the management task consists of planning, organizing, staffing, directing, coordinating, reporting, and budgeting (POSDCORB) (17).

Following Taylor's dictum that workers should do and managers should think, the administrative management theorists viewed **planning** as one of the most critical of a manger's functions. The planning process may be defined as outlining what it is that needs to be done and how to do it. Effective managers do not plunge right in without first knowing what they are going to do and how they are going to accomplish their objectives. The result of a good planning process is a detailed program of what actions are to be taken to accomplish predetermined objectives, how long it will take, and where it will take place.

Once the plan, or program, is finalized, the manager can proceed with the balance of the operations. **Organizing** means building the formal structure of authority and arranging the work of the subdivisions. **Staffing** involves securing, maintaining, and developing a staff of people. **Directing** includes making decisions, communicating the decisions to employees through orders and instructions, and leading the organization. **Coordinating** is the process of interrelating the various parts of the work. **Reporting** is keeping superiors informed about what is going on. And **budgeting** includes fiscal planning, accounting, and control.

The proponents of administrative management were instrumental in providing the first comprehensive view of the managerial role. Of particular help in formulating a theory of management was their postulation that all managers, regardless of their specialty, do about the same thing when they are managing, and that managerial skills are transferable within and across organizations. Although subsequent management theorists extended and supplemented the basic ideas of these pioneers, POSDCORB still seems to be a fairly accurate description of the tasks of managing, and it is remarkable that the people who generated these ideas were administrators in different kinds of organizations in several different nations.

One of the important qualifications of administrative management theory is that managers at different levels of the organizational hierarchy differ in the manner in which they perform their functions. For example, at lower levels, managers are primarily concerned with getting the work out within predetermined budgets and within some fixed time period. Thus their activities are primarily internal to the organization. At higher levels of the echelon, managers typically have a longer time perspective, are less concerned with the details of operative work, and are more likely to be influenced by external, or environmental, forces.

In addition, at lower levels of the hierarchy, managers have less **discretion,** or more rigid constraints on their freedom to make decisions, than do managers at higher levels. Because the quality of managerial decisions is so important to the health of the organization, some theorists see the differential allocation of discretion at various hierarchical levels as the most critical aspect of administrative management, and decision making as the most vital managerial task.

The Manager as Decision Maker

Chester I. Barnard, former president of the New Jersey Bell Telephone Company, set forth in his book *Functions of the Executive,* published in 1938, the basic features of what has become known as the **decision-making approach** to management (18). But because his fresh and novel insights, which were based on his own experiences and from his studies in the behavioral sciences, were couched in the language found in the principles of management and in the Hawthorne Studies, his original contributions did not at first seem as important as they were later to become. It was not until 1945, when political scientist Herbert A. Simon reviewed and extended Barnard's thinking in his book *Administrative Behavior,* that Barnard's ideas finally caught on (19). Simon and a group of scholars at the Carnegie Institute of Technology (now the Carnegie-Mellon University) eventually put forth a comprehensive theory of organization based on the decision-making process (20). They also developed a technique for simulating many kinds of human decisions through the use of high-speed electronic computers, thereby initiating studies that continue to this day. Because decision making is so complex an operation, computers have been valuable in helping researchers test and understand this important process.

The Decision-Making Process. In stressing the importance of decision making in the managerial process, Simon goes so far as to say that decision making *is* managing (21). He maintains that the decision is logically the basic unit of investigation for the organization and that the organization is but a network of communication channels between decision centers (22).

Researchers have found that the managerial decision-making process does not adhere to the logic of the scientific method in that managers do not follow a precise series of steps to reach conclusions. In careful studies of how people actually make decisions, investigators have found that rather than seek the optimum solution to a problem, managers search until they find an alternative that is satisfactory. Simon calls such behavior *satisficing*. Furthermore, the search for a reasonable solution does not follow a logical course. Instead, the decision maker's mind erratically jumps around, searching for information, noting alternatives, comparing standards, searching again, and so on. This kind of hit-and-miss search process is called **heuristics,** and, for the most part, works out fairly well. (These and other decision-making processes will be discussed in more detail in Chapter 13.)

Management Science. Another contribution of decision theorists, which can be viewed as an extension of scientific management, is called **management science.** While Simon and his associates attempted to describe and understand organized systems in terms of the decision-making processes, management scientists were concerned with finding rational techniques for solving specific problems. Through developing and implementing mathematical and statistical methods, and by showing how these tools can help to solve such troublesome problems as inventory control, plant location, or the number of employees necessary to serve a group of waiting customers, management scientists sought to improve the speed, efficiency, and effectiveness of organizational work.

The Manager as Leader

Remember that Luther Gulick divided the directing function of managing into decision making, communicating, and leading, meaning that once a decision is made it must be carried out by first conveying the decision to those who will implement it and then persuading them to do what is asked. This persuasion process may be thought of as **leadership.**

Much has been written about the subject of leadership—what qualities constitute an effective leader, what leaders do, and so forth—but even so, a precise understanding of the leadership process is yet to be formulated. One reason why a definitive theory of leadership has not emerged from the vast body of literature is that researchers have been unable to agree on a single definition of the term and so have developed several conflicting theories, each based on different interpretations of what leadership means. Out of this controversy, however, has emerged one concept, known as the **contingency model** of leadership, developed by Fred Fiedler, which has gained a good deal of support (23). According to the contingency model, leadership is not an abstract quality, but rather is a series of influencing activities, performed by people looked to as leaders within a particular human group or social system. Whether one is successful in leading others depends on the size and composition of the group to be led, the personal characteristics of the group members and the leader, the kind of work to be done, the location of the activity, and a long list of other factors. One of the major points made by this theory is that an important part of the managerial role is leadership.

Mary Parker Follett (1868–1933)

Mary Parker Follett was one of the earliest of the management consultants and among the first to view an organization as a social system of contingencies. Her ideas, published in a series of books between 1896 and 1933, were so far ahead of their time that they are only now being incorporated into the management literature. Her personal life style was also out of keeping with that of other young women of her time. She chose a profession instead of marriage and a family, achieving a prominent place as a professional in a field dominated by men. Both her ideas and her personal life style were precursors of things to come.

Mary Follett entered Harvard Annex (later Radcliffe College) in 1888 and spent her junior year studying at Newnham College of Cambridge University in England. While in England she wrote, and later published, a paper titled *The Speaker of the House of Representatives.* After some years of traveling, Follett was graduated from Radcliffe in 1898 at the age of twenty-nine.

Follett's early efforts were consistent with those of other wealthy young women of the time. She performed charitable activities for children in her home town of Boston; she founded a whole league of debating clubs for boys; and then she established community centers where young people could congregate after school. She was instrumental in setting up a job-placement bureau in Boston, which later was absorbed by the state as the department of vocational guidance. By 1918 Follett had earned a reputation as a writer as well as a consultant to such business leaders as Henry S. Dennison, of the Dennison Manufacturing Company, and Lincoln Filene, of Filene's department store in Boston. Her insights into the management process, which aided these and other executives, were gained only as a result of her experience in organizing and managing the nonprofit organizations with which she had been involved earlier.

Follett was among the first management theorists to maintain that the handling of people is a major problem of modern management, to assert that the ideas that govern management are applicable to almost any field of human endeavor, and to develop a consistent theory of human behavior as an aid to managers. Follett's theory of human interaction is called the *principle of the circular response.* In a social situation, one person acts and another perceives and reacts; the reaction of the second person then influences the perception and reaction of the first. Each influences the other, and the reactions build upon one another. "When the numbers in the interaction multiply, so do the interrelationships between the responses, and it is the totality of all the intervening relationships relevant to a given time and place that constitutes the 'situation.'"

Mary Parker Follett viewed organizations as systems of contingencies in dynamic interaction, and she saw the managerial process as one of interaction and integration. Her work clearly presaged the contingency approach of systems theory and anticipated the findings of the Hawthorne Studies, which were conducted during the last five years of her life while she was living in the United Kingdom.

Source: Elliot M. Fox. "Mary Parker Follett: The Enduring Contribution." *Public Administrative Review*, Vol. 28 (Nov.-Dec. 1968), p. 523.

The Manager as the Interacting Person in the Middle

The contingency theory of leadership suggests that many people affect the managerial role and place pressure on the leader. The typical manager is beset by pressures from superiors, subordinates, the environment, and other parts of the organization. Thus, the manager is the person in the middle. In fact, it might be said that the managerial role was designed to handle pressure—to take it from the top levels of the hierarchy and apply it to the lower levels—so that the individual subunits will continue to work to accomplish existing organizational goals.

The results of three independent research studies investigating managerial behavior all emphasized that managers spend a large percentage of their time interacting with a wide variety of other people. Thus, there is an obvious need for skill in handling interpersonal relations and an ability to deal with ongoing pressures.

The view of the manager as a "person in the middle" is best illustrated by a series of observational studies of managers conducted by Kelly, Sayles, and Mintzberg. The common thread that runs through these studies is that managers spend a great deal of their time interacting with a wide variety of other people. Lower-level managers spend a high percentage of time with subordinates and other managers associated with the work flow (24). Middle managers are greatly involved with horizontal relationships and with staff groups within the organization (25). Top managers spend as much as half their time with people outside the organization and provide the link between the organization and the environment (26).

Not everyone feels comfortable as a manager. The job is one of frustration, compromise, and constant pressure from others. For instance, Mintzberg found that managers have little time to concentrate on any one activity and that the nature of their activities is widely diverse. They seldom have time to think anything through or to complete it thoroughly. But, Mintzberg found, rather than being bothered by these seeming disadvantages, managers have a preference for such scattered diversity (27). They dislike desk work and past history and would rather talk than write.

Mintzberg also examined the ability of the managers to control their own affairs by recording the degree to which they were active or passive during the interactions they had with others. The results were not encouraging: for a majority of the time, the managers were reacting and not initiating. Mintzberg felt, however, that these managers had two important areas of freedom: they made initial decisions that put into effect a chain of long-term commitments and they were able to manipulate their work to serve their own purposes.

These studies of managers at different levels of the organizational hierarchy seem to confirm the view that the manager is a person in the middle. The role requires that he or she maintain equilibrium and concurrently initiate change both in the company and in the surrounding environment in order to accomplish the organization's goals. Following is a brief review of what managers do.

1. Managers interact with others most of the time. These interactions are rich in variety and with approximately half occurring with members of organizational units and half occurring with people in the outside environment.

2. Managers initiate and react. Although a great deal of managers' time is spent responding to the demands of others, the majority of their activities involve initiating action both inside and outside the organization.

3. Managers work in an ambiguous environment in which their tasks are fragmented and their projects incomplete.

Part 2 of this book deals with the arena of the manager and the organization. It opens with a discussion of the goals of organizations and continues with an analysis of how goals are assigned to people, combined into jobs and departments, and coordinated with other goals. Part 3 deals with resources coming from the environment and focuses on how resources are obtained, the manner in which they are allocated, and the ways in which they constrain and determine how work is performed. The activities of the manager are the subject of Parts 4 and 5. These activities are divided into two sections: the first section deals with those activities concerned with directing the organization, from decision making through communication to influence; the second section is concerned with the sequential set of adaptation activities, including planning, controlling, and changing.

Chapter Review

This chapter has presented a historical review of the development of management theory from the eighteenth century and Adam Smith (1776) through Frederick W. Taylor (1911) to the relatively recent work of Henry Mintzberg (1973). The first part of the chapter was meant to develop the reader's understanding of organizations, while the second part attempted to put into perspective some of the major research conducted on the role of managers. The order in which topics were presented in the chapter anticipates the organization of the remainder of this book and represents an initial statement of ideas that will be further discussed, developed, and updated in the chapters that follow. The major thoughts that have been highlighted in this chapter are outlined below:

1. Organizations exist because they can produce work more efficiently and effectively than can individuals acting alone.

2. One of the reasons organizations are efficient is that they permit the specialization and division of labor. Specialists concentrating on a limited number of tasks can become increasingly more efficient (Adam Smith).

   a. If work divided among specialized employees within organizations makes each more efficient, then it follows that if the work of society is divided among specialized organizations, each can become more efficient.

   b. If trade among organizations and nations is free of governmental restraint (laissez-faire capitalism), the work of all will be more efficient; the wealth of all will increase.

3. Specialized and divided work can be made more efficient through careful study and analysis (Frederick W. Taylor and scientific management theorists).

4. The coordination of specialized tasks requires an administrative organization (administrative management theorists).

5. The administrative organization is hierarchical in form. If the relationships among managers and their employees are diagramed, the resulting chart looks like a pyramid made up of authority levels or echelons; a hierarchy (administrative management theorists).

6. In designing an organization, human behavior, technological considerations, and environmental forces must be considered, along with an efficient division of work and an orderly arrangement of offices. People, technology, and environment temper the logic of efficiency and order.

7. Employee behavior is motivated by many forces besides wages, including employees' sentiments, past experience, hopes, and associations with other people (the Hawthorne Studies).

8. Technology—physical tools, such as implements and machinery, and human tools, such as knowledge and method, dictate the arrangement and flow of work to some extent and thus affect organization design (Perrow and others).

9. Environmental forces, such as political-legal, economic, sociocultural, and natural, influence organization design (Lawrence and Lorsch and others).

10. Organizations can be viewed as open systems of interconnected forces (contingencies) that secure resources from the environment and contribute outputs to it.

11. The managerial role can be examined as a series of:

    a. **POSDCORB processes**—planning, organizing, staffing, directing, controlling, coordinating, reporting, and budgeting (administrative management theorists).

    b. **decisions** (Barnard, Simon *et al.*).

    c. **leadership behaviors** (Fiedler and others).

    d. **actions, reactions, and interactions** based on pressures from all directions. The manager is the person in the middle of continual pressures and forces that require action (Kelly, Sayles, and Mintzberg).

12. Managers work in an ambiguous environment in which their work is fragmented and their projects incomplete.

Discussion Questions

1. Describe the general characteristics of the administrative management model of organization.

2. Define the terms *specialization, division of work,* and *free trade.* How are these ideas helpful in understanding the nature and purpose of organizations and their management?

3. Explain the main ideas of scientific management.

4. Are all organizations hierarchical structures? Must they be?

5. Compare and contrast scientific management, administrative management, and management science.

6. What were the major factors leading to the emergence of the human relations movement in management? What was the impact of this movement on organizations?

7. Debate the following statement, taking either a proponent's or an opponent's view: "There is no best form of organization."

8. Diagram an input-output model of organization. Is this an open or a closed model? Why? What is the usefulness of this model?

9. Managerial activities have been defined as (a) the POSDCORB processes; (b) decision-making processes; (c) leadership processes; and (d) interactive person-in-the-middle processes. Compare and contrast these four versions. What are the similarities among them? What are the differences? Which is most likely to be the "correct" version? Are all equally correct?

10. What is the manager's job from a systems viewpoint? How does it compare with the picture of the manager in the administrative management and human relations models?

Involvement Activities

1. Either talk to a manager or consider your own work as a manager and answer the following questions about the organization in which you or the manager works:

    a. How is the work divided?

    b. What would the authority hierarchy look like in a diagram?

    c. How is the work coordinated?

2. For the organization you are examining, find out and describe how the people, the technology, and the environment have affected the working relationships (that is, the organization structure or design).

3. Which of the following terms best describes the actual work the manager does in the organization you are examining? Explain your answer.

    a. POSDCORB.

    b. Decision making.

    c. Leadership.

    d. Person-in-the-middle.

    e. All of the above. How?

    f. Some of each. Which?

2

Work and Organization Design

Just as athletes need a thorough knowledge of the field or court on which they play, managers need a precise understanding of the arena in which they operate. This arena is the organization. The reader should keep in mind, however, that unlike an athlete's playing field, an organization is not a static entity nor one that the manager cannot alter. Organizations are dynamic and constantly changing, and managers may be the designers of these arenas as well as the chief players within them.

An organization is a socially contrived body that is established to accomplish some purpose or goal. Thus the first major part of a definition of an organization is that it is purposeful. An organization also has a structure. The reason for organizing is simply that people can accomplish more by working together than they can by acting alone. Further, when people are brought together in an organization, each person does a specialized part of the overall task. A structure enables all these different people with their various skills to work together harmoniously and productively. This is where management enters into organizations. One person or a group of people must coordinate the efforts of all the people to see that everyone is pulling in the same direction.

Almost any group of people brought together for any purpose will exhibit the characteristics of specialization and managerial coordination. Even a bridge group, for instance, will coordinate its efforts so that some people bring refreshments, others furnish the playing cards, and so forth. Also, someone is usually in charge of seeing that everyone does his or her job so that when the group meets to play bridge all tasks will have been completed. Student groups do the same thing. Organizations are simply formalized systems that more clearly and specifically define the goals, tasks, and jobs of the group and those who are its members.

Part 2 of this text is intended to develop the reader's understanding of how an organization is structured. We have used the symbols of a triangle and arrows to represent an organization in its most basic state — that of a purposeful system striving toward a common objective, or goal. This is the subject of Chapter 3. In Chapter 4 we begin to break down the overall goal into smaller units, which is the assignment of work to individual members of the organization. Here there are many arrows, all pointing in the same direction. Chapter 5 examines the ways in which the work assignments are recombined to form jobs. This process is represented by arrows that have been grouped together. In Chapter 6, we see how jobs are combined into larger organizational units called departments. This process is called departmentation and is represented by groupings of arrows above and below each other such that a hierarchical arrangement of groups is formed. Here we see the beginning of the organization chart. Finally, in Chapter 7, this part of the text is completed by focusing on the coordination aspect of the organization. When all the relationships in the organization are clearly defined and connected to one another as a result of coordination, the symbolic arrows are arranged into a formalized organization chart.

3
Goals

Organizations are systems that are designed by people to accomplish some purpose or to achieve some goal. A good place to start explaining the nature of organizations, then, is with a discussion of goals and how they are formed. The topic will be introduced by an examination of the nature of goals and then further developed by a discussion of how organizations strive to achieve a number of goals simultaneously. The chapter continues with a consideration of how managers set goals, the ways in which goals change in organizations, and how goal achievement can be evaluated.

The most basic element of any organization is the goal or set of goals toward which the organization strives. For this reason, we have chosen the symbol of three arrows within a triangle to illustrate the fact that organizations are purposeful; they are designed to accomplish some goal (see Figure 3–1). This chapter will focus on the right-hand portion of the model—the area concerned with outputs—because it is here that organizational goals are realized.

Goals are an elusive and complex concept. We take for granted that people and organizations set and seek goals. Yet if one were to ask individuals or managers of organizations to explain their goals, the chances are good that they would have a hard time clarifying them. But it is important that goals be clarified—both in the minds of those who seek them and in the minds of those who are directly or indirectly affected by them. For without clear and concise definitions of goals, the work directed toward their accomplishment cannot be effective or efficient.

The Nature of Goals

Organizations may be thought of as tools for attaining desired goals.[1] People establish organizations to accomplish specific purposes of their own or to benefit from serving the purposes of others. If organizations were static

---

[1] It is interesting that the words *organization* and *work* are derived from the same Greek word *ergon*, meaning work or action. The word *organon* means an implement, tool, or instrument useful in doing work; thus the word *organization*. Through centuries of use, *ergon* became *wergon*, then *werg*, then *werk*, then *work*. Thus an organization is a tool used to do work.

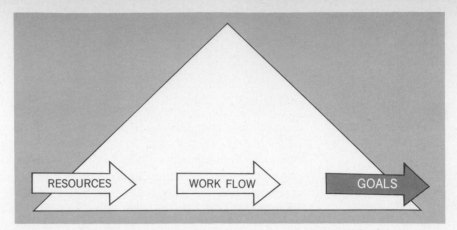

FIGURE 3–1
The place of goals in
the organization.

Our basic model of the organization (the triangle) shows three arrows—one for inputs, or resources, one for the work performed in the organization, and one for outputs, or goals. The shading of the right-hand arrow indicates the emphasis in this chapter on the goals of the organization.

objects that one could see, hear, feel, or smell, they, and the purposes they were built to serve, could easily be described—much as one would describe a house. But organizations are not tangible; rather, they are complex bodies of people, work, activities, and interactions that defy physical description. An attempt to hold them still to get a clear picture of what they are leads simply to illusions, such as an assumption that they can be defined by a chart showing a hierarchy of work groups and managerial levels, or by a photograph of the buildings in which the activities occur. In fact, organizations really exist only when they are at work in the process of attaining ends, objectives, or goals. And to understand what they are, one can only describe the parts and functions utilized in this process. Because goals are what give organizations meaning and direction, it is appropriate to start our inquiry into organization design with a discussion of the nature and characteristics of goals.

**Characteristics
of Goals**

Goals are defined as desired future states of affairs.[2] But not all desired future states of affairs are goals. True goals must contain the characteristics of *time, value*, and *specific state*, or *condition*. If a certain desire for something lacks one of these properties, it may be a wish or an intention, but it is not a goal.

Time. By definition, goals always lie sometime in the future. They are catalysts for present and future activity, and provide guidelines for performing the activity. Goals can be either short-term or long-term; that is, they vary along a time dimension with very short-term goals (say an hour

[2] Throughout this book, many words are used interchangeably with the word *goals*, such as: aims, objectives, ends, planned outcomes, purposes, and so on. They all refer to desired future states of affairs.

or so) at one extreme and very long-term goals (ten or more years, perhaps) at the other extreme. "Sometime in the future," however, is not a sufficient definition for a true goal. Regardless of how long-range the goal is, it must be stated in a relatively specific time dimension.

Once goals have been reached they are called **accomplishments** or **achievements,** the historical result of past action. If an organization has been established to work toward a specific short-term goal and that goal has been accomplished, the organization no longer has a reason to continue its existence. Examples of this type of organization can range from school dance committees (which disband once the dance is over) to congressional investigating committees (which disband after the investigation is completed and the final report drawn up). For an organization to survive, then, its goals need to be accomplished repeatedly. A bakery, for instance, repeats its goals (a supply of breads and pastries) daily and continues its existence until there is no longer a demand for its products.

Value. The example of the bakery brings us to the next goal characteristic, which is that it must be of some value—either to those who work to accomplish it or to someone else. If people benefit directly from goal accomplishment (such as students who work toward a degree that will enable them to pursue a career) then the goal itself will be enough to secure their commitment to the work. If people strive to achieve a goal that is intended for someone else, however (such as teachers who help students obtain a degree), the workers must obtain some goal satisfaction of their own through the process of satisfying the primary goal. These other goals may be wage compensation, the opportunity to do research, the prestige of being associated with a well-known university, or the like. The organization then (in this case, the university), comprises many different goals, each of value to some portion of the employees.

Specific Condition. In order to serve as guides to behavior, goals must be described in specific terms. Before starting to make a refrigerator, workers need to know the size, weight, and other characteristics of the finished product. Without specified conditions of quality and quantity, there would be no way of determining whether the goal had been accomplished; in fact, there would be no goal. For example, what does an office employee do when the boss orders, "Clean the place up" and then departs? Does the manager want the wastebaskets emptied, the papers on the desks piled more neatly, or the floors swept? Similarly, if no specified time for goal accomplishment is set, then there is no real goal. Consider the non-invitation "Let's get together one of these days." Because no meeting has actually been arranged, there is nothing to accomplish. The vague desire to get together is a non-goal.

Operative and Official Goals

Real, or **operative,** goals can be used to guide actions; they look like those that have been described above. They are called operative because by defining a precise future condition they set in action a series of operations by which the goal can be attained. In an organization, operative goals are worked out by managers and employees. These goals commit people to their work and guide day-to-day working relationships and interactions with other parts of the organization. Goal statements that refer to nonspecific outcomes or that have no particular value to people, or that are to be achieved at some vague and unstated future time, are more properly called ideals. An example of an ideal goal statement might be, "Someday I'm going to fix up the back yard."

Official Goals. Official goals are general, often vague, statements that express a purpose or reason for being of a group or organization. These statements are usually ideals and sound something like, "Our goal is to provide the best possible product at the lowest possible price," or "The goal of this firm is to maximize profits." Neither of these statements says when the goal is to be achieved, who will value the outcome, and what the conditions will be when the goal is reached. Such statements offer no form of guidance for obtaining a result. What, for example, would an employee, a manager, or even an owner of, say, a retail clothing store be doing next Thursday to maximize profits or provide the best service at the lowest cost? At best, the answer to the question will be vague. When an organization is first established, official goals may guide operations to some extent because everyone concerned has a general idea of what is expected. But as organizational roles expand, such official goal statements provide increasingly less guidance for operations. Official goals do serve a purpose, however. They represent a general philosophy of the managers who make them and provide an overall rationale for the existence of the organization. But they are primarily tools for public relations and not guides for specific behaviors.

Multiple Organizational Goals

As noted earlier, in the example of the university, organizations have more than just a single goal. A hamburger stand, for instance, would seem to have as its goal the provision of hamburgers for profit. But the owner of the stand might declare that the goal is to have a chain of restaurants across the country. The manager of the stand might claim that the goal is to provide the most efficient service in town. And the cook might maintain that the goal is to serve the best-tasting hamburgers. Each person in, or each part of, an organization sees, and works toward, a different goal. The goals are not in conflict because each supports the continued existence of the operation. All organizations, even simple hamburger stands, have an overall goal of remaining in operation and subgoals that relate directly to the work of the people and groups within the organization.

Subgoals differ both vertically and horizontally within the organization. Similarly, at any particular level of the organization different func-

The Growth and Multiplication of Goals

Most organizations start with a single purpose and expand both in size and goals if they are successful. The Truck Plaza in Portland, Oregon, is an example. In 1947, two brothers, Jack and Robert Burns, opened a truck stop, which today is the second largest in the United States and is one of four owned by the Burns brothers. In 1977 the firm expects to gross $30 million.

Trucks and automobiles form the basis on which the business maintains its identity, but the operations go considerably beyond trucks and automobiles. The Burns truck stops are miniature communities. Restaurants and motels are available, repair services, shops, grocery stores, and even office spaces are for rent within the truck compound. Services to truckers have expanded to include provision of

tires and snow chains, and the advent of campers, particularly the large motor homes, has opened other opportunities, such as clothing stores, barber and beauty shops, CB sales and service, Western Union, and so forth.

The goals of the Burns brothers now extend beyond expansion into new products. They are looking into ways and methods of reducing gas consumption. And most significantly, they see their employees as the most important part of their growth. The Truck Plaza can expand only as the capabilities of its employees expand, and that is why working for the Burns brothers is often a family affair. Some employees are children and grandchildren of former employees, and one family has five members working at the Truck Plaza.

Source: *The Oregonian*, July 24, 1977.

tions have different goals. These different functions in turn lead to different perceptions of the organization as a whole. When one considers how many different perceptions might exist in any one organization, it becomes clear why sales, production, and finance departments are often at odds with one another.

Specific goals within organizations are not mutually exclusive, however; they are characterized by overlap and interdependence. One approach to understanding how multiple goals interact is illustrated in Figure 3–2. Segment 1 of the figure represents the environment that is external to the organization. This segment provides the framework within which organizational goals operate by establishing the organization's opportunities and constraints. Segment 2 indicates the goals associated with the input of resources into the organization; segment 3 represents the output goals by which the organization is indentified, and segment 4 shows the variety of goals associated with internal operations. The arrows between the segments indicate the interactions that take place between the goals.

The Environment   The environment poses constraints on existing goals and provides opportunities for new ones. Arrow 1 of Figure 3–2 indicates external relationships, or the interactions among parts of the environment. We live in a time of rapid and unprecedented change. It is no longer sufficient simply to "mind the store and let the rest of the world go by." Environmental changes more often than not directly or indirectly affect even the smallest

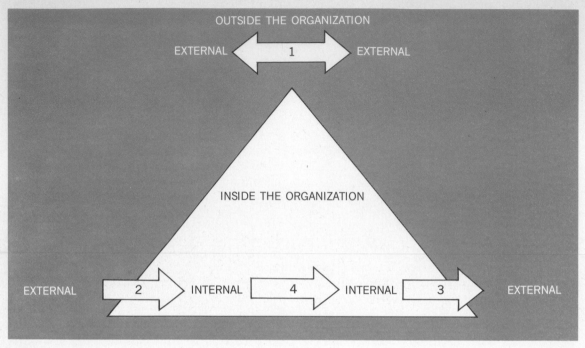

FIGURE 3–2

The organization and its environments: four types of relationships. (1) Outside: external-external links; (2) input: external-internal links; (3) output: internal-external links; (4) inside: internal-internal links among subunits.

organizations (such as our hamburger stand). Consider, for instance, the changes brought about by passage of such bills as equal opportunity legislation, truth-in-packaging requirements, and the proposed Equal Rights Amendment. How do such factors as the energy shortage and environmental safety provisions affect organizational goals? These are but a few of the hundreds of environmental forces that to greater or lesser degrees affect what organizations may and may not do.

These pressures come from a variety of sources, including the economic, political, social, technological, geophysical, and ecological environments. Although these various environments will be discussed in detail in Chapters 11 and 12, we will preview them quickly here to see how their interactions might affect an organization's goals.

Economic. Economic conditions may affect organizational goals by influencing the supply of resources or the extent of markets. For example, if the manager of a bookstore wants to increase inventory to meet demand, he or she may find that money is in such tight supply that suppliers will not increase the credit limit and banks will not permit short-term loans.

Political. From the political sector, laws, rules, and regulations pour forth regularly. Some laws, such as those prohibiting the sale of goods below cost, prescribe what *not* to do. Others prescribe what *to* do. For instance, the National Labor Relations Act requires that employers bargain with unions in good faith. Still other laws provide opportunities. Some tax laws provide shelters, or forms of investment, that free current income from present tax payment.

Social. The mores and customs of a society are as binding in setting standards of conduct as are formally written rules and regulations. For instance, when only men wore pants, Levi Strauss & Co. wisely did not try to sell its products to women. But as custom changed, a new market demand created a whole new women's pants industry — and, in turn, complementary industries of belts, shoes, blouses, and so on.

Not only changes in custom, but revisions of socially accepted conduct have far-reaching consequences on goals and on the actions taken to reach them. Where once various forms of bribery were standard operating procedures for large industries dealing with governmental agencies, those same practices today are often punished by jail terms for those attempting to employ them. In the United States, a beer producer, trying to enlarge its market, advertised its beverage as a "high-class" drink and not only failed to appeal to the elegant market but also lost its "common" one.

Technological. As yet, modern technology precludes economical interplanetary travel, conversion of sea water into fresh water, and electricity tapped directly from the sun. But these goals may be future realities. Technology creates new markets, products, and services. Xerox and IBM have recently flourished from revolutionary breakthroughs in copy-reproduction and computer technology. In addition, the high technological level of agriculture and manufacturing allow the United States to devote many of its resources to service-oriented activities.

Geophysical. The natural environment both provides and limits business opportunities. Resorts that promote snow skiing do well in winter, provided there is plenty of snow and a means for skiers to reach them. Copper mines serve the needs of industry and the public for copper tubing and wiring, until the ore runs out.

Ecological. The ecological environment consists of the network of interdependent living systems (the ecology) that furnishes, for example, food and lumber. Growing and converting living things into useful products provides many organizations with a reason for existing. Getting rid of insects or bacteria that damage crops, animals, or people provides goals for other organizations. Ecological conditions also limit possibilities. If pesticide-resistant insects flourish, they may destroy the main crop in an area. Ecological systems also depend on geophysical conditions. Floods, earthquakes, droughts, winds, and other natural phenomena may interfere with the delicate ecological balance. In similar fashion, all of the environments with which an organization interacts create a complex web of forces that continually alter one another and in so doing change the conditions under which the organization must survive.

Resource Inputs

It may seem odd to think of the need to secure adequate inputs as an organizational goal, but since no organization can survive without maintaining an adequate and uninterrupted influx of resources, such a goal is requisite to the organization's existence and is illustrated by arrow 2 in Figure 3–2. One measure of success of an organization is *efficiency*; that is, the difference between the cost of resources and the income from the finished product or service. In fact, it may be that this is the only completely measurable goal of an organization, for it certainly indicates its ability to survive.

At any one time, the organization's ability to undertake new products or to increase production is directly dependent on its available resources. In modern organizations, many resources take the form of technology, made available by a large capital investment in machinery and equipment. Once an organization has sunk its assets into expensive machinery, the only way to recover the investment is to keep the equipment running over a long time period, perhaps many years. Thus, any such organization will need to produce the same product (or at least only products that can be manufactured by that machinery) for a fixed number of years. Fixed resources lock an organization into a restricted set of goals, not only because the equipment must be made to pay for itself, but also because no excess funds are available for alternative ventures. For example, oil companies cannot easily convert their refineries to the production of pet food.

Resources other than capital include land and its products, people, and information. Maintaining a steady supply of funds, materials, workers, and information is an important function of any organization and represents the specific goals of some individuals or departments. Procurement (purchasing) and recruitment (hiring) departments are concerned largely with activities that result in the acquisition of resources. Some say that the prime organizational concern, or goal, is maintaining the ability to renew itself through securing an adequate supply of inputs (1). It does seem valid to say that no matter what else happens, any organization must maintain a steady flow of energy inputs to stay alive.

Organizational Operations

Input and output goals connect a system with its environment, but various subsystems within an organization also have goals, as illustrated in Figure 3–2 by arrow 4. Internal goals can be classified either as operative work goals assigned to employees and groups, or as *informal* goals that develop spontaneously from the interactions of people at work.

Work Goals. The diversity of internal goals is based in part on the division of labor, which accounts for a horizontal division of goals; and in part on hierarchical position, which leads to a vertical division of goals. Planned work goals are concerned with the conversion of resources into outputs, and with the coordination or integration of work-group goals by managers at various levels of the hierarchy.

Work goals may range from policies and objectives to procedures and rules. They are operative goals because they not only specify outcomes but also often dictate the methods to be used in attaining them. These goals may become dysfunctional when external conditions change without a corresponding adjustment of procedures. For instance, internal procedures that once kept minorities from certain job positions are now illegal.

Informal Goals. Coexisting with official work goals in an organization is a complex set of implicit personal goals and informal group goals. Each subunit within an organization, whether one individual, an informal group, a task force, or a whole department, has its own set of goals toward which some activities, interactions, and decisions are directed. People have goals, sometimes called "wants" or "aspiration levels," which they try to achieve within the framework of the larger organizational goals. These personal goals may or may not be consistent with work goals; and the methods for achieving them are derived in accordance with the person's or group's own systems of rituals and taboos.

Informal goals may be necessary to get the work done, even though they appear to be dysfunctional. Individuals are motivated to satisfy such personal needs as those for affection, status, achievement, or power; they are rarely motivated solely by formal organizational goals. Thus, to satisfy organizational goals, employees must simultaneously be able to meet some of their personal needs.

The shared informal goals among groups of people provide an organization with an unplanned communication network and workflow system that may help, or might even be essential to, the accomplishment of planned organizational goals. For example, formal relationships are rarely established between departments with different functions, such as accounting and sales. But accounting clerks and salespeople often establish an information-exchange system about customer invoices and accounts that benefits the operational goal objectives of both groups.

Outputs and Goals

An organization is merely one small segment of the grand network of environmental relationships. Organizations are tied to the environment on the input side (arrow 2 of Figure 3–2) because they depend on inflows of resources for their own preservation. They are also tied on the output side (arrow 3) because the environment absorbs what the organization creates.

Looking at organizations from the outside, we can see that their goals are to create something useful to the environment by securing, maintaining, and manipulating resources (inputs), and then producing and distributing outputs to obtain more resources and repeat the process. From this perspective, goals are planned outputs intended to satisfy the needs of clients or customers in the environment. Outputs may be sold directly to users or they may be provided to clients who pay for them indirectly, through taxes, or through an intermediary system, for instance. Outputs thus lead directly or indirectly to continued organizational functioning. From the perspective of those outside it, then, the organization's goals are to provide them with goods or services they can use to reach their own goals. In this sense, the goals of one organization create the input for another. And as long as the organization satisfies its clients at a reasonable cost, it will remain in operation.

Sometimes output goals are called the **mission** of the organization. The term mission implies the overriding importance of providing something vital for others, and also suggests that members undertake their tasks with zeal. No doubt, when an organization is first formed its founders are enthusiastic and have a clear idea of the mission to be accomplished.

Either the organization is established to satisfy the needs of its members directly, as a softball team might be, or indirectly, by providing a service for some outside client or customer who will reimburse the system for the goods or service provided. If the organization is successful in fulfilling its initial task, it generally will continue to try to provide the same product or service. Frequently, the system will seek new goals as well. Multiple output goals are common features of successful organizations.

The Managerial Process of Goal Setting

In theory, the first task of managing is to set goals for the organization. This task is part of the planning function and involves arranging a hierarchy of organizational goals according to level of importance. However, this procedure implies that goals are predetermined, unchanging, and planned objectives, and we have seen that such is not the case. Thus, the managerial task of goal setting is really an ongoing process of mediating among the various organizational goals and integrating the goals of different units, both inside and outside the organization, into a coherent and efficient whole.

The Complexity of Goal Determination

Ready-made assortments of goals do not exist. Often goals become confused with the methods and means for obtaining them. And general statements of ultimate purpose may give little guidance for dealing with day-to-day operations. Measurable outcomes that do exist may set one internal department against another. Or short-term values may be achieved at the expense of long-run commitments. To guard against these or other dysfunctional consequences, managers need to be sensitive to the interrelationships among goal-seeking activities both inside and outside the organization. An examination of the goal concerns of managers in terms of the four goal arrows presented in Figure 3–2 will help clarify the goal-related activities necessary to each segment.

The External Environment. The forces entirely external to an organization have little direct effect on goal setting in the short run. This tempts managers to concentrate on their defined jobs and ignore what is happening outside in terms of how it might help or hurt the organization. Because of this tendency, some organizations set up special departments to scan the environment. Such departments may include marketing research, to find new markets and products; research and development, to design new and better products; or economic forecasting, to try to predict trends. Top managers and specialist groups in large organizations may not only seek to discover relevant new environmental events, they may even try to influence or initiate such events. For example, powerful organizations often buy out or absorb smaller companies; they influence legislation by keeping lobbyists at work in the capitol; and they engage in public relations programs, advertising, or other activities that are only indirectly related to putting out the product.

Determining Input Goals. Managers who deal with the external environment from the input side of the organization compete for resources with their counterparts in other organizations. They must maintain good relationships with the investing public and with bankers, with sales representatives, and with those whose knowledge will help them keep abreast of new or more economical resources as they become available. Because the satisfaction of input goals has costs in terms of time, effort, skill, and money, managers need to state them in explicit terms.

Determining Subgroup Goals. A prime responsibility of managers whose main focus is on the internal organization is the division of organizational goals into person- and department-sized pieces so that work can be accomplished. This dividing procedure takes the form of work assignments at various managerial levels in ways that best integrate and coordinate the various goal-directed activities. Because the formal and informal systems are inseparable once the activities, interactions, and decisions of the organization's work are in process, coordinating or integrating the many internal goal systems is one of the most difficult and important aspects of a manager's work.

We have already noted that to accomplish its ends, every subunit of an organization requires resources. But because the resource pool is always limited, every allocation decision is likely to appear unsatisfactory to one or all of the subgroups. Thus, one of the many tasks of management is to moderate and control seemingly irreconcilable differences and conflicts over resource allocation. Such conflict is especially common between the production and marketing departments of a business firm.

Salespeople want a diversity of products designed to meet their customers' needs more effectively than those of competing firms. However, making a variety of specialized products is costly. Production people can produce more efficiently a standardized and limited variety of goods. The longer the production run and the less frequent the shutdown time, the lower the unit cost. Low production costs are immaterial, however, if the finished goods cannot be sold. General management, charged with the responsibility of selling the product at a profit, cannot let either the salespeople or the production staff "win." Effective managers are experts at mediating a compromise between marketing and manufacturing, and between many other naturally conflicting departments as well.

Determining Output Goals. Planned outputs are probably the most clearly defined of all goals. Managers who are responsible for releasing the output into the external environment must concern themselves with goals that have to do with product acceptability. Marketing or client service involves receiving information from the environment and adjusting internal operations in order to continue to create a product or service that is environmentally relevant. To achieve this goal, it is also necessary to send information out in the form of sales promotion or publicity to help build and maintain demand for the output.

Factors Affecting Goal Determination

In addition to the special needs of people in each of the four goal segments, several other factors also affect goal setting. These include the needs to: (1) suboptimize goals; (2) accommodate change; (3) think of goals as constraints that limit choice; and (4) balance or harmonize diverse objectives.

Suboptimizing Goals. From the point of view of employees in the above-mentioned production and marketing departments, compromise forces **suboptimization,** which means a lowering of standards of excellence. Salespeople know that they can improve sales with a more varied product line; production employees know they can further reduce unit costs by increasing standardization and producing an even more limited product line. Thus the integration of subsystems is essentially a matter of suboptimizing the goals of each in favor of higher-level organizational or environmental goals.

Accommodating Change. When change occurs in any segment of an organization or its environment, all other sectors are likely to be affected in ways that are sometimes unpredictable. As the rate of environmental change increases, the manager's task of adapting and coordinating becomes more difficult. For instance, to accommodate the increasing demand for highly technical products, organizations have been hiring large numbers of engineers and scientists. The presence of these professional people in previously nonprofessional organizations initiates a need to protect the substantial investment in this human resource by assuring that there will be a continuing need for ever-more-complex products. Thus a circular need arises: Technology demands professionals; they, in turn, produce higher degrees of technology, which demand even more professionals.

Thinking of Goals as Constraints. At any given time, the sets of real goals toward which organizations and their subsystems work constrain, or limit, the way work is done and the achievement of other goals. The choice of any one activity or goal restricts the ability to enjoy the advantages of other possibilities. In economics, the price paid for giving up such advantages is called the "opportunity costs." Thus it is appropriate to talk of organizational goals as constraints, or sets of restrictions, imposed by the organization's chosen role. Goals channel resources in one direction and away from others. For example, if a retailer decides to sell hardware and assembles appropriate resources for this purpose—inventory, a store, clerks, counters, capital—not much will remain for, say, opening a new restaurant.

As organizations interact with their environments at both input and output points, they develop customary routines of behavior. Custom, as much as the investment locked up in resources to accomplish present goals, further constrains behavior and restricts the freedom of choice managers have to strike off in new directions.

Consider the student who has always underlined important passages in studying textbooks and who has always earned the grades (goals) desired. To this scholar, underlining is the only way to study. If someone suggests that speed-reading or outlining might be preferable, the student will probably reject the idea. Organizations develop similar routinized behavior patterns that, while they assist goal attainment, also constrain or limit alternative behaviors that might prove even better.

Balancing Diverse Objectives. In a very real sense, survival of an organization depends on serving everybody's needs. This is not an easy task because, as we have seen, the various subunits are not cohesive and have diverse and conflicting interests. To complicate matters further, each group or individual has multiple interests that are not necessarily compatible. These individual and small-group goals must somehow be made to mesh with organizational goals.

Organizations exist because they can satisfy human needs better than can individuals acting alone. Not only are they more efficient than individual action because they make possible a specialization of talent and division of labor, but also because they are designed to satisfy the human needs of their organizers. And through output goals, they also satisfy some goals of people in the external environment (clients and customers). This ideal model of an organization, in which the private needs of members and organizers and the public needs of clients are wholly integrated, is oversimplified, but to a certain degree it is an operating fact. And the ideal model serves as a goal toward which most organizations work.

The model best fits the informal social system that develops whenever people work together to engage in activities that are meaningful to members. But problems of integration exist even in this situation. Members may originally be attracted to the group activity because of mutual unsatisfied needs, but when these needs are satisfied, or fail to be satisfied, the members may drift away to satisfy other needs through other groups. To maintain adequate membership, new activities must be introduced and new goals developed. As activities become formalized, the group becomes an organization. If goals or activities become incompatible to different cliques, the group may divide. For example, college sororities and fraternities grew from informal groups of friends into large-scale international organizations.

Fraternities and other friendship groups are primarily concerned with satisfying internal needs—those of their members. Most organizations, however, are established to satisfy the needs of clients outside the organization and as a result have even more severe problems in integrating organizational and member goals. In formal organizations, members (employees) are hired to do a job for which they are paid. Implicit in this arrangement is the understanding that "In return for working toward our goals, we will provide you with a reward (salary) that will enable you to satisfy your own needs elsewhere."

This point of view may sound callous, and certainly it is not popular. Recent management investigations have been based on the premise that the needs of employees can be made compatible with organizational goals, that the need for affection or achievement, for example, can be satisfied as people work to turn out such items as cars or budgets. The results of these investigations have indicated that a good portion of human needs can indeed be satisfied on the job, to the benefit of employees, managers, and the organization. It seems unlikely, however, that *all* individual and organizational goals can be simultaneously realized, or that they will ever be fully integrated.

The separation of ownership from control that exists in most large businesses illustrates the problem of satisfying the needs of many interests. The owners of large, publicly held corporations are rarely in a position to exert direct control over managers because any one person or group owns only a small percentage of the outstanding stock. Since top management is also the board of directors and controls the proxies, this group is, in effect, a self-perpetuating body because they can simply elect themselves into office. Owners of corporate common stock are most likely to sell their shares when they become dissatisfied with management. Even so, management must keep the stockholders happy either through payment of adequate dividends or by increasing the value of the stock. At the same time, management must keep the employees sufficiently satisfied to ensure continued work. Suppliers of materials must be paid for their goods; the customers must be satisfied enough to continue to purchase the products; and the government must remain convinced that the actions of the organization are within the law. Thus, while the management of the corporation has no one group that they must account to directly, they have many groups whose demands must be kept at least partially satisfied.

To summarize, goal determination is a process of integrating diverse interests within the constraints of the real goals that people in each segment are pursuing. As goal setter, the manager is negotiator and integrator, trying to keep clients and supporting agencies satisfied; preserving, maintaining, and protecting the operating work groups; and at the same time accommodating environmental changes. Goals are the consequences of patterns of interaction between internal, output, input, and environmental forces. Each segment develops a role that defines its relations with other systems and that acts as a set of constraints on behavior within the segment. Managers may have some choice over the selection of organizational goals, but the alternatives are limited. And to implement the choices that are available, managers are required to do a complex bit of negotiating.

The Dynamic Nature of Goals

To say that managers have only limited choice in setting goals is not to imply that goals are fixed. On the contrary, goals are in a constant state of flux as a result of the patterns of activity, interactions, and decisions of people associated with the organization. Three major causes of goal changes are **goal displacement, goal succession,** and **goal multiplication.**

Goal Displacement   Goal displacement occurs when a new goal or set of goals diverts resources away from the real, preplanned goal. This kind of substitution seems to occur in all organizations, and results, in part, from the process of assigning work. Once employees are armed with work to do and resources to use in doing it, they may substitute their own personal goals for organizational ones, or come to look on prescribed activities as ends rather than as means (2).

Personal Versus Organizational Goals. Personal goals become a problem when employees seek to maintain or improve status in the organization or come to value their relationships with other employees in ways that disrupt or impair organizational goals. The most obvious example of troublesome attempts to satisfy personal goals is the flagrant use of status symbols, such as carpeted offices or keys to the executive washroom. Status symbols use up organizational resources and make little measurable contribution to goal accomplishment. Other potentially disruptive personal goals include the need for power, influence, and control in excess of that necessary to accomplish the assigned work.

Satisfying the need for friendship on the job leads to such dysfunctional behavior as output restriction. The research of Taylor and of Roethlisberger and Dickson noted the tendency of employees to collaborate with their friends to put an upper limit on production (3). More often, rather than a conscious or malicious collusion, employees will simply engage in nonproductive conversations to the exclusion of their regular work. The number of cartoons about people loitering around a water cooler amply supports the truth of this observation.

Means as Ends. Goal displacement also occurs when the methods of doing work (the means) become substitutes for the output (ends)—in other words, the means themselves become ends. This kind of displacement occurs, for instance, when rules rather than goals come to govern behavior (4). Rules are established to specify what kinds of behavior are necessary and acceptable, and to govern deviations. But there is always the possibility that certain rules will be taken too literally and create friction, at best, or work contrary to the intended goal, at worst. Consider the following examples.

A foreman ruled out smoking in a foundry, where the use of fire was

FUNNY BUSINESS   By Roger Bollen

essential to melt metals, on the grounds that a lighted cigarette was a fire hazard. A heart-disease patient went into her local pharmacy to refill her life-sustaining prescription. The pharmacist telephoned the patient's health insurance company for payment approval. The insurance clerk refused to authorize the prescription because the rules required written request. When informed that the patient was likely to die without the medication, the clerk finally but grudgingly gave approval, on condition that the appropriate forms be mailed at once.

Ceremony, custom, or routine may also become valued as ends in themselves. In the armed services, for example, the extreme deference paid to rank may become an end goal rather than a means of securing discipline and making certain that someone competent is in charge. A group of office workers who proclaim, "We always go to lunch at noon," imply that their lunch schedule is more important than any work that might need to be done at that time. Or a sales clerk in a clothing store may keep on stocking shelves even when customers are waiting. The familiar joke about "red tape" is one of the most extreme examples of goal displacement: the desired end is obscured by the mountain of forms to be filled out and managers to be consulted. When means become ends, employees may take an inappropriate attitude toward the very people they are meant to please, such as when a sales clerk is domineering, or a welfare worker coldly impersonal.

The confusion of means and ends illustrated in the foregoing examples means that observing rules and behavior "rationally" gradually takes precedence over adapting to change. In turn, this confusion limits the growth of organizations because they become less flexible and more vulnerable to competition from younger, more dynamic firms.

Organizations as Ends. A special case of means-ends reversal is the organization that becomes an end in itself. Organizations are tools for accomplishing human purposes. But as soon as they are established they become ends to many people associated with them. The German sociologist Robert Michels noted this phenomenon in his book *Political Parties* (5). In his studies of labor unions and socialist political parties, Michels noted that these organizations violated their proclaimed goals of democracy and socialism. The leaders became self-perpetuating rulers of hierarchical bureaucracies, rather than elected representatives of the communities they were meant to serve. Michels considered this tendency, which he called the Iron Law of Oligarchy, to be in direct conflict with avowed goals. Similar to the tendency toward oligarchy, which means that the power to rule is held by a few persons, is the tendency of organizations to adopt survival as their primary goal.

Survival as a Goal. This form of goal displacement is the attitude of "survival-at-all-costs." Once this position is adopted, the people who believe in it come to value the organization not for what it does but simply because it exists and because they have a role in it. Many governments contain an array of boards, bureaus, and standing committees whose reasons for existence have long since disappeared and whose functions are obscure even to those who are members. Similarly, many business firms, school districts, religious bodies, and volunteer groups continue to operate, often at great expense, merely because their one pervasive goal is survival. To survive, any organization must cover its total costs of operation in the long run. A business firm must sell its products at a price that returns enough to cover costs. Firms that cannot so dispose of their outputs will seek to reduce costs of operation, increase prices, or try to get some other organization to support them. When pressed, business people will turn to the government for help through subsidies, tariff protection, fair-trade acts, and cost-plus government contracts.

Business firms find political power helpful. Other organizations, whose clients do not pay directly for the services they receive, may find it almost essential. Universities, for example, depend for their survival on support from public agencies or on voluntary contributions from alumni and benefactors because most students are unable to afford the full costs of their education. Thus, university officials or their representatives lobby with governments to pay for scholarships, research funds, and tax breaks for those who donate large sums of money.

To keep themselves going, charitable organizations, whose existence depends on public contributions, may bend their programs to be more acceptable to the general public—often with some sacrifice of their initial mission. For example, a drug-counseling center founded during the turbulent 1960s by a group of radical students who volunteered to help their friends in trouble, is now a "crisis-counseling" center run by professional employees and supported by the community.

Throughout the discussion of goal displacement runs a negative note, as if personal goals, means-ends confusion, the tendency toward oligarchy, and organizational survival were somehow wrong. But when an organization is viewed as a complex series of interactions among diverse elements, a good argument can be made that goal displacement is not a disease, but a natural and necessary phenomenon. For example, in an earlier discussion we indicated that people try to satisfy their personal needs at work. To secure their contributions, organizations may find it essential to provide employees with such opportunities.

It is true that the confusion of means with ends may lead to inappropriate behavior. On the other hand, the ends of one segment of an organization may be the means of another. The goal (end) of a stockroom manager in an office is to keep stationery and other supplies on hand. From the point of view of office personnel, however, the stockroom is a means to their ends of producing letters, reports, and so on. And from the point of view of the owner or general manager looking down the hierarchy, the ends of each of these work areas are his or her means for generating output that will, in turn, result in more input.

BERRY'S WORLD

© 1968 by NEA, Inc.   John Berry

The existence of a self-perpetuating set of leaders in a bureaucratic organization could be dysfunctional if the leaders abused their power, or otherwise diverted the system from its professed goals. On the other hand, an oligarchy might provide the stability and efficiency needed to attain ultimate goals, including even political democracy and socialism.

If an organization serves a new mission well, its survival is beneficial to at least some groups or some individuals. Many organizations do fail; but those that have not have persuaded their supporting public that they serve some desirable purpose.

Goal Succession

Goal succession means seeking new output goals when old ones have successfully been accomplished or when they cannot be reached. Replacing an old goal with a new one is another instance of making survival the supreme goal. Almost by definition, an organization is unnecessary once its end is accomplished or when goal achievement is found impossible.

Organizations do not shed old goals without some difficulty. Occasionally companies seem to prefer to die rather than to change with the times, as did many of the manufacturers of horse-drawn carriages. Changing goals can be a traumatic experience, especially for members of an organization dedicated to preserving certain standards of excellence in one particular endeavor. Yet in these rapidly changing times, organizations may be able to thrive only if they change their goals to accommodate new demands.

David L. Sills provides a dramatic example of goal succession in his classic study of the Foundation for Infantile Paralysis, which appears in his book *The Volunteers* (6). This organization, informally called the March of Dimes, comprised thousands of volunteers who for more than twenty years instituted a war on the dreaded disease polio. Millions of dollars were collected from households across the nation, eventually leading to research that produced the Salk vaccine. Then, its goal realized, the Foundation kept its organization virtually intact by switching to a new goal—the prevention and healing of birth defects.

An opposite example of goal succession is that of an organization unable to achieve its ends. Consider, for instance, the number of religious orders that have developed during the last 2000 years expressly to greet the Messiah; or those established on the belief that the world will end on a predicted date. Although many of these sects eventually disband in discouragement, some survive as churches to nourish the perennially faithful (7). "Temporary" committees may also have a tendency to continue with a new mission after they accomplish their initial assignment. And a threatened business organization sometimes successfully employs goal succession when the odds are against its survival. The Heublein company, producer of Smirnoff vodka and other distilled spirits, kept itself going during Prohibition by concentrating on its other product, A-1 Steak Sauce.

Goal Multiplication

Goal multiplication is different from goal succession in that it adds new output goals without dropping old ones. Most organizations have multiple output goals either by design at the start or through necessity later on. In most universities the goals are to produce research *and* educate the students; most shoe stores carry shoes *and* a large line of accessories; and so on.

Goal multiplication is both a cause and a result of organizational growth. The new or small organization is primarily concerned with survival, but if it weathers its first few years, its purposes are likely to increase and to become more complex. One reason why this happens is that successful organizations are generally able to build a cushion of resources in good times as a hedge against bad times. Because organizations increase in size as capital accumulates, decision makers will be encouraged to seek new ways to employ the larger supply of organizational resources.

The Evaluation of Goal Attainment

One very important aspect of a manager's job is to evaluate the degree to which goals are reached. If an organization had but one clear and measurable end to accomplish it would be a simple matter to determine whether

Durable Denims—The Levi Story

Levi Strauss & Co. has built a business empire on one of the most unlikely products—blue jeans. A combination of sticking with a good product and taking advantage of the trends in the marketplace has created one of the most successful firms in the field of apparel manufacturing, a field that is characterized by rapid change of fashion and fad.

Levi's were developed by accident in the days of the California Gold Rush. Levi Strauss, attracted to the West by gold fever, arrived in San Francisco with a stack of dry goods, including canvas for tents and wagons. The canvas was not needed for tents but the miners were very much in need of heavy-duty pants, which Strauss proceeded to manufacture from the canvas material. These pants, later called Levi's, eventually became the symbol of quality work pants for both children and adults throughout the country. Today the name is a generic one and can be found in the dictionary as synonymous with blue denim work pants.

While Levi's are still the mainstay of the company's product line, Levi Strauss & Co. has expanded into shirts, jackets, boys' and women's clothing, and even shoes. The company keeps track of new trends by sending representatives out among the youth to such places as football games and the Florida beaches during spring vacation.

The trend toward more casual clothes is not unique to the United States. Recently, people all over western Europe and even in the Soviet Union have begun clamoring for Levi's.

Source: Richard D. James, "Durable Denims: Levi Strauss Builds Its Success on a 'Fad' That Has Not Faded," *The Wall Street Journal*, Feb. 7, 1977, p.1.

the goal had been attained. But if organizations have complex networks of interrelated goals, and if goals are constantly changing and multiplying, the evaluation process is naturally much more complicated. In this section, we will review two important and interconnected aspects of evaluating goal attainment: effectiveness and efficiency. An organization is *effective* if it reaches its real goals; it is *efficient* if the costs of inputs are equal to or less than the value of its outputs.

Effectiveness

Effectiveness is the degree to which an organization is successful in acquiring and using resources to accomplish its real goals (8). Built in to this definition is the idea that effectiveness refers to the satisfaction of output, input, and subunit goals. Also implied is the notion that effectiveness means environmental relevance. Thus, any measure of effectiveness must include a reckoning of how well the goals of each segment in Figure 3–2 are achieved.

Adapting to a Changing Environment. Whether an organization is flexible enough to adapt to a turbulent and often adverse environment is a major managerial concern. Few organizations, however, have operational goals to determine flexibility. One reason for this lack is that the future is so unpredictable that goal succession and multiplication—as well as the overriding goal of survival itself—can only be understood in terms of *attempts to maintain* adaptability. The questions "Adapt to what?" "When?" and "Why?" are never completely answerable.

But managers can set two real goals to help maintain adaptability. First, they can establish specific procedures for assessing problems and opportunities in the environment and charge individuals or departments with the mission of regularly reporting their findings. Second, they can set up procedures for continually reevaluating existing procedures, policies, and objectives. People in organizations have a tendency to become locked in to tried-and-true methods and objectives that worked in the past but that may not be satisfactory in the present or future.

Maintaining Resource Supplies. Those responsible for maintaining an adequate supply of material, human, and financial resources sometimes have specific goal targets, but often they do not. Because the effectiveness of an organization depends on maintaining a regular supply of inputs, it is essential to be able to anticipate changes in the amount of inputs needed, at least in the immediate and near future.

Preserving Essential Internal Operations. The goals of individuals, groups, and departments within an organization coexist in a complex network of interactions. To maintain a steady output of contributions

NOW WHAT?!!

from internal subunits requires at least two common measures of effectiveness. One is an estimate of **productivity** relative to specific objectives of each subunit. The other is a measure of **satisfaction,** or the degree to which human goals are met in the process of working toward organizational ends. Although productivity and satisfaction are not necessarily related, they undoubtedly work together, because some personal and group goals must be satisfied if productivity goals are to be reached. Productivity as a measure of efficiency will be considered further in a later section. Satisfaction has so many dimensions that it will be discussed at length in Chapter 8 and Chapter 10, which deal with human behavior in organizations.

Planning Output Goals. Planned output goals are generally the most specific of all goals, and the degree of their attainment is therefore easily estimated. The more precise the goals are, the easier it is to determine whether they are accomplished. Not quite so easy to ascertain, however, is the degree to which planned outputs are likely to remain relevant if the environment changes radically. Once again, special effort must be made to assess changing environmental requirements and opportunities.

One environmental requirement that is becoming increasingly important is that organizations assume responsiblity not only for planned outputs but also for those unplanned and unwanted effects that mar the landscape, destroy ecological systems, or harm the land, waterways, or atmosphere. Such unplanned outcomes are called *externalities* because they occur outside the organization that creates them, usually as a by-product of something that does serve environmental needs.

Although unintended outputs are not "goals," the operation of organizations leads inevitably to unplanned results. These may have positive value, like a salable by-product; neutral value, such as the discharge of pure water or carbon dioxide; or negative value, such as pollution. Unplanned negative outputs lead to economic, social, and organizational problems for other organizations and for the environment. For example, government agencies spend a great deal of money trying to reduce air pollution by demanding that automobile manufacturers not only control the discharge of production waste but also install smog-control devices on the cars they make.

Measuring Effectiveness

As we have seen, different organizations have different goals; most single organizations have multiple goals; and every subunit within an organization has goals that to some extent differ from the goals of all other subunits. Some goals overlap, others are in conflict. Although overall effectiveness is difficult to measure, some aids are available.

Goal Statements as Performance Standards. One way to aid the measuring process is to make sure that all goals that could possibly affect the organization are stated in clear and operational terms. A second way is to evaluate each goal in terms of the importance of its contribution to specific work and output goals. And a third way is to estimate the degree of overlap and conflict between goals so that each unit can be allocated enough resources to contribute to the general mission without impairing the ability of other units to function. Through these procedures, goal statements can then be used as performance standards by which to measure organizational effectiveness.

While this procedure makes good sense, it is not easily accomplished. Organizations are adaptive and in constant motion, making a review of what has happened not only difficult but often irrelevant. The problem of using goal statements as performance standards by which to measure organizational effectiveness is compounded by the necessity to add many outside constraints. In addition to the need to suboptimize subordinate units, internal and external standards of performance will differ, long-term and short-term standards will differ, and the explicitness with which the standards can be stated will depend on the nature of the compromise on which they are based.

Quantitative Measures of Performance Objectives. Quantitative data provide management with seemingly objective criteria and leave little room for argument and interpretation. Thus there is a tendency to quantify whatever can be put into numbers. Quantitative measurement, however, is subject to many problems of manipulation and interpretation. Furthermore, a great many goals defy quantification. Attempting to measure such qualities as "high morale" is difficult if not impossible, and consciously trying to measure such elusive attitudes may actually lower the morale that does exist (by making people self-conscious about their "attitude").

Even in situations in which measurement is possible, there are problems of comparing and applying values to different data. For example, how does one compare a million-dollar accounting profit with controlling 60 percent of the market? Is a 10 percent increase in sales worth the doubling of labor turnover? It can be seen that the weighing and comparing of quantified goals is essentially a subjective activity.

There is also the danger that quantifiable goals will be used as the sole or major judgment of organizational effectiveness. Many "control" efforts in organizations represent an overemphasis on simple and quantifiable measures of effectiveness. This tendency is particularly dangerous if the measured goals are not the critical ones. Concentration on those variables that happen to be measurable can misdirect attention to items that are not really important to effective performance or that are not within the control of the individuals concerned with them.

The same problems of measuring organizational goals are also true for measuring job goals. But appraising the performance of individuals includes a host of other problems as well. One of these is the fact that people want to be told how they are doing, but only if what they are told is positive. Negative feedback does not motivate people; rather it precipitates defensive behavior that often worsens performance (9). Managers, as well as teachers and parents, frequently overlook this fact. It is common for a manager to ignore adequate, acceptable, and even superior performance but to be quick to comment on mistakes. At the other extreme is the manager who will not accept responsibility for performance appraisal and automatically gives all employees superior ratings. This behavior has as bad or worse an effect as negative feedback.

Another problem is that the employee and the manager may disagree about what behavior is actually goal-oriented. For example, employees may believe that their clothing and hair styles are irrelevant, whereas managers may honestly think that their judgment of what is good taste in such matters is of paramount importance in running tidy and efficient operations. Such discrepancies in perception adversely affect the intent of performance appraisal and cause conflict.

Performance appraisal based only on goals imposed on employees by high-level managers may mean little to those being evaluated. But appraising performance of actual work-group goals that resulted from interactions among peers and immediate supervisors is relevant and meaningful. Clearly, if managers and employees were made to negotiate to set goals and performance standards, then the result would be more realistic goal statements and better performance.

In summary, the measurement of performance requires that managers help in the determination of realistic goal statements and then mediate among all relevant sectors of the organization to balance attainment. The balance of goals should be such that it maintains goal-oriented behavior in each segment without impairing the effectiveness of others.

Efficiency

We have seen how the effectiveness of an organization can be measured by the degree to which it reaches its real goals. And we have discussed how its efficiency is measured by the ratio of costs to benefits (that is, the ratio of input plus work costs to the value of outputs). Since these two are different measures, an organization can be effective without being efficient and efficient without being effective.

If an organization reaches its goals, it is effective; but if it does so at excessive cost, it is not efficient, or at least not as efficient as it could be. Perhaps any activity can be more efficient than it is. The common complaint about the alleged waste of resources in a large-scale bureaucracy, such as the armed services or other governmental agencies, is a case in point. But business organizations may not be efficient, either, if they can pass on excess costs in the form of higher prices. Competition might lead to greater efficiency, but it might not prevent inefficiencies.

An organization, or a part of it, can be efficient without being effective. For example, in one firm, two common measures of efficiency used in a credit department were "cost per account" and "percentage of credit sales collected." The manager kept costs low by regularly replacing experienced credit managers with less expensive trainees, and kept collections high with a tough approach to credit approvals and collections. Whether it was desirable to let experienced people go or to lose credit sales was not at issue because the performance of the department was evaluated according to the two measures of efficiency. Because the measures were clear and easily evaluated, there was a tendency to substitute efficiency measures for effectiveness measures. This approach led to a means-ends reversal in which "looking good" in terms of efficiency distracted attention from the need to evaluate effectiveness.

Efficiency Measures and Time Period. Efficiency is measured in a number of ways, but each has in common the notion that value of output in the long run must exceed, or at least be equal to, the costs of inputs plus work flow activities. To be a useful operational guide, however, input-output ratios must be calculated for specified periods. Daily, weekly, monthly, quarterly, and annual calculations of costs and profits focus attention on immediate problems of inputs and outputs. What creates an efficient measure in the short run may lead to negative ratio in the long run; on the other hand, the price for perpetuation of a workable system may be consistently negative short-term ratios.

We could hypothesize that the longer the time period over which efficiency is measured, the greater the chances for the organization's survival. The reason is that managers who operate in such a way would be challenged to undertake long-range planning and to make immediate ends subordinate to longer lasting ones. Unfortunately, most organizations fail to act on this probability. Rewards tend to be given for short-term performance, and managers who don't "produce" are quickly replaced. Perhaps many current problems, ranging from a large number of business failures to a sorely damaged ecological environment are due in part to an exclusive insistence on short-term results rather than on long-term relevance and survival. It is true, though, that it is much easier to measure monthy performance against explicit cost, output, and profit standards than to measure such an elusive quality as "long-term relevance."

Profits, market share, and return on investment (ROI) are the best-known examples of efficiency measures. But though they have the advantages of objectivity and measurability, they also have the disadvantages discussed above. Also, they are not always so specific a measure as they appear. Profits, for instance, may vary considerably depending on the definition given that term and on the accounting practices of the particular organization. In fact, this lack of specificity led Tilles to call these measures "oversimplified deceptions" (10). Thus, while these measures of organizational efficiency are necessary, they should be recognized as relatively nonspecific and should be applied with caution.

Profit Maximization. Because of the common assertion that "the purpose of a business is to maximize profits," a special word about profit maximization seems in order. For several reasons, profit maximization cannot be a goal. First, it is not specific enough to direct activity. Although it may be stated in terms of a time period, and presumably has value to someone, the term is too vague to serve as a real operational guide. One cannot maximize profits any more than one can maximize happiness; in both cases it is impossible to tell when the value has been "maximized." Second, the calculation of profits is always relative, not absolute. In other words, profits in one quarter or in one year may in fact be higher than they were the previous quarter or year, but there is no way of telling whether they are at their *absolute* maximum. Third, as pointed out above, profits are calculated according to various accounting standards and therefore differ depending on which method of, say, inventory valuation, is used. Fourth, profits are measures of efficiency, not effectiveness, and like other measuring devices they cannot (or at least should not) be ends in themselves. If one feels chilly in a room (wonders how the firm is doing), one might check the thermostat (the income statement). But the goal is warmth (money, or income) not the thermostat reading (the income statement). One can feel chilly even when the thermostat registers 78°. Huge profits might be earned if, for example, the firm sold its assets, but such action might threaten survival if it impairs the company's ability to reach output (effectiveness) goals. Profits are goals, but only to people, such as owners, in certain specific segments of an organization. They do not drive all employees. And even owners compare profits with other time periods, with other organizations, and with alternative investments, to determine how well their goals are being met.

Chapter Review

This chapter has focused on the arena in which managers work—the organization—with emphasis on organizational goals, the purposes for which organizations exist. Key points from the chapter are listed below.

1. **Goals** are desired future conditions. The three distinguishing characteristics of goals are **future time, value,** and **specific condition.**

2. Organizations have **multiple goals.** These include **environmental** goals, **input** goals, **work** goals, **informal** goals of individuals and groups, and, of course, **planned output** goals. For an organization to thrive, all of these goals must, to some degree, be satisfied.

3. The managerial task of goal-setting is a complex and ongoing process of balancing the divergent objectives of people both inside and outside the organization.

4. Organizational goals are always in a state of flux. Some are in constant danger of being displaced either by survival goals or personal goals or by the means of their attainment. Other goals are succeeded by new ones or supplemented with additional ones.

5. The evaluation of goal attainment is based on an ability to determine goal **effectiveness** (the degree to which the goal is reached) and goal **efficiency** (the cost of reaching the goal relative to its value when accomplished).

Discussion Questions

1. What is a goal? Must all organizations have goals? Must an individual?

2. Describe the three characteristics of goals.

3. Define the goal of a business organization from the points of view of the following people:
   a. managers
   b. employees
   c. stockholders
   d. customers
   e. suppliers
   f. the general public

4. Distinguish between *operative* and *official* goals. Are official goals really goals?

5. In what sense do organizations have multiple goals? Why are planned output goals not the only kinds of goals that need be considered?

6. How do organizations arrive at the goals they have?

7. How do managers set goals? Describe the process of goal determination and discuss the variables that affect this process.

8. Define and discuss goal displacement, goal succession, and goal multiplication.

9. Define organizational effectiveness and efficiency. How are goals related to these two concepts?

10. What advice would you give a manager who is trying to improve the quality of his or her goal-setting techniques?

11. How does *profit maximization* correspond to an operative goal of a business organization?

12. One critic asks of managers, ''Whom do you represent?'' What does this question mean? How would you answer it?

Involvement Activity

Consider an organization you belong to, such as a college or university, a company you work for, a club, or even your family, and respond to the following statements and questions.

a. List the environmental, input, subunit (work group, informal group, individual), and output goals of the organization in question.

b. Describe how each of these goals is set.

c. Discuss the current state of flux of each set of goals. Are they in the process of changing? If so, how and why are they changing?

d. How is goal attainment determined and evaluated? Who makes the evaluation? When? How?

4

The Assignment of Work

The purpose of this chapter is to describe the process by which work and goals are divided into basic units, that is, the assigning of work to individual employees. Combining specialized task goals leads to job goals; the coordination of job goals leads to an administrative organization that can be diagramed as an organization chart. Operative tasks are arranged horizontally with the work flow; managerial tasks are arranged vertically to coordinate the flow of work.

This chapter is devoted to a discussion of the assignment of work—the process of dividing specific task goals among employees. The topics that are covered include: work assignments, the variables affecting work assignments, the effects of work assignments on organizational structure and on people, and the methods of assigning work.

A major task within the manager's area of responsibility is to translate goal statements into group or individual activities called **work assignments.** For example, an organizational goal of "a new product in the next six months" is a clear goal statement. But what does such a statement mean for individual salespeople, production engineers, machinists, or office workers? These people, and others in the organization must be given detailed task assignments with specific deadlines in order to know what to do, how to do it, and in what time period it needs to be done. Without such instruction, employees' activities would likely have no appreciable effect in accomplishing the goal.

Managers, then, must evaluate their groups' abilities and resources in terms of the overall goal, determine subgoals, and organize and mobilize individual work stations in order to satisfy the goal of "a new product in six months." Goals focus on the planned output; tasks focus on the specific activities that are carried out to accomplish goals. This chapter deals with the intermediary process of designing work assignments for individuals and groups. This action involves both subdividing goals and establishing the tasks that constitute the parts of a job. Figure 4–1 represents the subdivision of goals into multiple tasks all heading toward the same

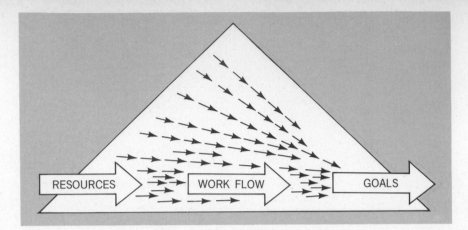

FIGURE 4–1
An organization as a collection of work assignments to accomplish specific goals.

general goal. In contrast to the diagram in the last chapter, which had only three arrows, and the focus on the right-hand one, this diagram has a host of arrows indicating that the various subunits of the organization all have their own goals. All arrows point toward the organizational goals because the purpose is to create a system in which all the subunits contribute to the overall organizational goal.

Assigning Work

As we saw in Chapter 1, work has both an external and an internal aspect. Externally, work is viewed in terms of the outputs created (the organization's goals) and the resources needed to accomplish the goals. Internally, work consists of the activities, interactions, and decisions required to transform the resources into the desired outputs.

An External View of Work

From the outside, the assignment of work is concerned, first of all, with determining *what* the manager wants done. This "what" may be thought of as a goal statement in that it specifies the nature of the desired output and the time in which it is to be completed. The statement, then, has three aspects; an end state (output), of a given quality, at a certain time.

End States. Clear statements about the desired end state are obviously necessary for any assignment of work. Such statements may include such instructions as: "Type a form letter explaining price changes to all our customers," "Turn out 1000 subassemblies," "Give a penicillin injection to the patient," and any number of other, equally precise, statements. End-state directives include either a material output (letters, subassemblies) or a service (injections) and an indication of number or quantity desired.

Quality Standards. All statements of desired end states assume a level of quality. The machinist's subassemblies are not of any value unless they can be used in following production stages. Inferior quality impedes effective goal accomplishment. But quality can also be too high. For example, a perfectionist who will not let the product proceed to the next stage until he or she is entirely satisfied that each aspect of it is flawless, may hold up the entire production sequence and invalidate the time deadline. Excessively high quality is inefficient.

Quality standards may not always be spelled out in an assignment of work, but they are always implicit. A secretary does not have to be told that letters must not contain typographical errors; this is an implied quality standard for all letters. In fact, for the majority of assignments, there is an implicit quality standard that is understood by veteran employees. For this reason, managers must take care to explain any variations in these implicit standards that may be required of a particular end state. For instance, a series of letters going to the board of directors might well require special attention to ensure the highest possible quality.

Time Requirements. The time dimension is also inherent in any work assignment. A goal is just a dream until a time for accomplishment is put to it. Goals may vary in time span from a few minutes to twenty or more years. In any goal that encompasses many tasks, the major problem is coordinating and timing each function so that they all intermesh in such a way that all tasks are accomplished on time.

People vary considerably in the way they handle the time dimension. Some people need the pressure of short-term goals in order to work well; others are more comfortable when they know they have plenty of time to work at a relaxed and steady pace. Matching the time requirements of goals with the idiosyncrasies of the various workers is a matter of combining or dividing work assignments. If a manager assigns a long-term project to an employee who is most comfortable with short-term goals, then he or she may want to subdivide the task into separate functions and make the completion of each function a goal in itself. Teaching is very much this way. If you show fourth-grade students what sixth-graders are doing, they look at it and say they will never be able to do that. But by taking it bit by bit, they easily master the sixth-grade subject matter almost without realizing it. Jaques claims that it is this time dimension in jobs that gives employees the feeling of responsibility. The more time that elapses before a person's work is reviewed the more responsibility he or she feels (1).

A more difficult problem is what to do with the person who has the ability to undertake goals with a longer time duration. The manager can combine tasks in such a way as to increase the time dimension, but this is only feasible when the time constraints on the manager's own work allow it. The organizational hierarchy imposes its own time limits. Each level is limited by the time dimension allotted to the level above. A person whose ability to handle goals of a longer time duration than his or her hierarchical level allows is, according to Jaques, ready to be moved up the organizational ladder (2).

Providing Resources. Another aspect to consider in the external view of work is the assignment of resources. And since people are a major resource, matching the person to the job is an important managerial task. Different types of work require different skills, and people differ measurably in the skills they possess. For instance, one machinist may be very fast and able to get work out in a hurry. Another machinist may be very accurate but considerably slower. Each machinist can do the job, but each possesses skills in a different area. It is the manager's responsibility to assign work to the two machinists on the basis of whether speed or quality is the most important goal.

Providing the proper tools and materials is also the manager's responsibility. This function may or may not present a problem depending on whether the type of work assignment is regularly repeated or new and different. For repeated tasks, the tools and materials ordinarily are readily available. A special work assignment, however, requires additional advance planning to secure and make ready the necessary materials.

Providing information is an area in which managers often perform inadequately. For an employee to carry out work in an interdependent situation, he or she needs to know the nature of the larger task and how the assigned work fits into it. Imagine, for instance, the frustration of a manager who is charged with the responsibility of hiring people for jobs on a secret project, the nature of which even the manager does not know. The manager not only is unable to describe the job to the applicants, but cannot determine whether the applicants' qualifications are appropriate for the job.

An Internal View of Work

The internal view of work focuses on *how* the work is done. Being specific about what is to be done is almost always beneficial, but a description that is too detailed regarding how work is to be done is often both inefficient and ineffective. Thus, in this section the discussion will center on the degree to which it is functional to spell out the activities, interactions, and decisions of work. A more thorough description of these elements themselves is reserved for the next chapter.

Activities. Most of us associate work with a set of physical activities, or things to do. So there is a tendency to spell out the activity aspect of a work assignment much more than the interaction and decision aspects. When employees are well qualified for their jobs, detailed instructions in how to do the work are not functional. First, the employee knows how to do the work so instructions are redundant. Second, it is demeaning to the employee to be told exactly how to do something that he or she already knows. The employee may feel untrusted and in turn develop hostility toward the person assigning the work. Third, detailed instructions preclude the possibility of the employee's making any necessary or useful adaptations within the context of the assignment. When the situation is too completely spelled out and the circumstances require an alteration of the instructions, the person either proceeds as originally directed, which will prove dysfunctional, or has to go back for new instructions. Employees who are unhappy with their managers or the organization have been known to retaliate by "working to rules"; that is, doing exactly as instructed regardless of the situation.

Describing how things are done is necessary to some extent, of course. Certainly full descriptions are called for when employees are new on the job, when assignments are in some way novel, or when certain aspects of the task are of critical importance. Another important exception has to do with instructions about how *not* to complete a task. For instance, when certain methods of task completion are in conflict with other organizational work, the manager will need to draw the employee's attention to the ways in which the task should not be handled. An example might be a salesperson who often sells to customers who are a credit risk. In attempting to meet sales goals, this employee jeopardizes other organizational goals.

Interactions. Although the nature of interactions frequently is not spelled out when work is assigned, the interactions that take place among employees may significantly affect work accomplishment. At each work station in an organization, resources of materials and information flow in and out. Most of this flow takes place through human interaction, particularly information flow. Employees may accomplish their own work well but may create problems further down the line by not communicating important information about what they have done and how.

Other people may communicate too much. These employees have such an interest in interaction that they frequently have little time left over for getting their work done. Still other people become quite expert in interactions. They can help get the work done because they know where things are, such as materials that are not being used or people with skills that fit the task.

Decisions. Each assigned task requires that decisions be made. Decisions become more operational and specific as work is assigned to individual work stations. There is no work that requires no decision making. If a person were never required to make a decision, he or she would have no feeling of responsibility for anything and this becomes unbearable (3). The human ability to make decisions is obviously treasured by society because if it were not, we would not pay high salaries to decision makers.

The more that work is assigned and distributed down the organizational hierarchy, the less it affords the opportunity for individual discretion. This phenomenon is illustrated in Figure 4–2. The discretion allowed in carrying out the work progressively narrows as it moves down the pyramid. This fact ensures that behavior at lower levels is in accord with overall organizational goals.

The progressive narrowing of discretion happens as managers assign work to those under their jurisdiction. No employee can have a greater area of discretion than has his or her immediate supervisor. At the bottom of the hierarchy, the employee occupying a position in a work station has only his or her own actions over which to exercise discretion. These individuals can assign certain ways to complete the work to themselves. Once the available discretion has been exercised, however, the employee may become bored with the work (4). Often, employees find different ways to perform their tasks not to increase efficiency but simply to reduce boredom.

A manager who supervises a number of organizational levels may either prescribe action for only the immediate level below or for all levels below. A direction or order that prescribes activities for all levels below is called a **contraction order.** Such an order takes away the discretionary powers of the manager(s) of lower levels. An example of a contraction order would be a "No Smoking" dictum by the plant manager applicable to all employees. A **noncontraction order,** on the other hand, would direct all lower-level managers to examine the danger of smoking in their own areas and issue appropriate statements (5).

Contraction and noncontraction orders have important implications in the area of employee accountability. With a contraction order, employees can be held accountable only in terms of whether the order was carried out properly. The employee cannot properly be held accountable for the effect of the decision making. Thus, if the contraction order "No Smoking" causes problems in morale and labor relations, it is the plant manager who should be held accountable. If the noncontraction order causes the same problems, it is the lower-level managers who can be held accountable for the faulty exercise of discretion.

FIGURE 4–2
The narrowing of discretionary area as work assignments move down the organizational hierarchy.

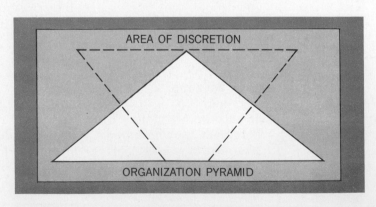

Variations in Work Assignments

We have seen that work assignments vary according to content; that is, in terms of *what* is assigned and *how* to do it. In this section, we will see that work assignments also vary in terms of form, or the *manner* in which work is assigned.

Specificity and Vagueness

In the last section we stated that repetitious work assignments need not be spelled out in great detail. The what and time aspects are more likely to be described than are the how and quality aspects. Often, however, even these latter aspects are not specified until the employee actually starts to work. At such time, the employee is told "how it is done around here," or "I really want you to do it this way."

The Argument for Specificity. Logic and empirical evidence indicate that the more specific the work assignment the better the quality of the work. This does not mean that it is necessary to remove all discretion from the job, but it does mean that it is important to make clear what the expectations and constraints are of a particular situation. The individual has the security of knowing what actions to take under which circumstances. Further, it is unreasonable to hold people responsible for results when the goals have not been clearly specified. Studies have shown rather consistently that productivity of individuals and groups is higher when specific goals have been set (6). Knowing what to do and how to do it saves the employee from having to search around for the goal and for the methods of attaining it. The amount of activity that is not goal oriented is thereby reduced, and the responsibility for goal accomplishment can be accurately delegated.

The Argument for Vagueness. To some degree, vagueness in goals is inevitable. Managers simply are not able to predict all the possible variables and how they will affect goal accomplishment. Thus, the more complex the situation, the more general the work assignment must be.

Further, there are several reasons why vagueness is desirable to some degree. First, vagueness permits employees more flexibility to adapt the work to changing conditions and it encourages the use of initiative. Second, vagueness permits employees more freedom to make their working conditions less repetitive and boring. It also allows them to escape the feeling that their every move and thought is regulated like clockwork. Third, vague work assignments leave room for compromise settlements in the event of an employee's dissatisfaction with a particular task or a disagreement between two or more groups assigned to the job. Organizations depend on internal cooperation and collaboration. According to Gross, insistence of technical precision in work assignments can easily set one group against another, which can lead to an expenditure of organizational resources to settle conflicts rather than to accomplish the work (7).

Degree of Difficulty   Probably one of the most important variations in work assignments is the degree of their difficulty. On one end of the continuum are work assignments that are impossible to complete. At the other extreme are assignments that can be accomplished without any significant expenditure of energy or skill. Note, though, that the degree to which difficulty is perceived is a subjective experience. Whether a task is "hard" or "easy" can only be decided by the person doing the work: what seems "difficult" to the manager, may be "effortless" to the employee, and vice versa.

Activation Theory. One way of looking at the difficulty dimension of work assignment is through **activation theory** (8). This theory suggests that the degree to which the brain is activated determines the extent of activity. Assuming that the degree of difficulty in work assignments is related to increasing levels of brain and behavior activation, the relationship between the two phenomena would look like the curve that appears in Figure 4–3. Easy work assignments have little impact on performance because there is no challenge. Over time, easy assignments are performed by rote. They are simply activities that occur habitually, and the people performing them do not have to think about what they are doing. Assignments that are difficult require conscious effort on the part of the person because they contain the element of chance or failure. They push employees to try a little harder than they have in the past: they are challenges. Unreasonably difficult work assignments have nearly the same effect as very easy ones—people ignore them. What appears to happen is that the individual feels defeated at the outset and so has no motivation to attempt an assignment that affords little chance of success. Because the goal is seen as unattainable, it has no activating power.

Goal aspiration is closely associated with past experience. People who have in the past experienced success in achieving goals are motivated by reasonably difficult work assignments. People whose past experience is characterized primarily by failure are easily distressed by difficult assignments. They anticipate failure even before they begin (9).

FIGURE 4–3
Activation level and varying degrees of work difficulty.

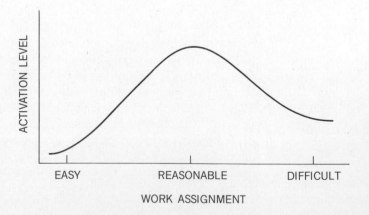

Ideals. Unattainable goals may have certain value if the person is not necessarily expected to fully meet them. Such goals are **ideals** to be sought after. The ideals of a true democratic state, of peace on earth, and of universal love, are goals that are probably unattainable, but they motivate people to reach for them nonetheless. And by doing so, people improve the quality of life. In the same way, people strive to "perfect" their tennis game or their ability to learn a foreign language, and so on.

Quantitative-Qualitative Dimension

A third variation in assigning work is the quantitative-qualitative dimension. Assignments stated in quantitative terms are those that are expressed numerically. Examples include such statements as: sand 105 castings today; sell 5000 units by March 31; hold turnover to 10 percent this year. Quantitatively termed assignments have a very clear advantage —they can be readily measured in terms of goal attainment. The employee is always aware of how far away the goal is and when it has been reached. Further, most communication networks in organizations are designed to handle and accommodate quantitative information. Accounting systems are excellent examples.

But not all work assignments can be expressed in quantitative terms. For instance, an assignment to produce a quality product, or to keep up morale in the plant, or to maintain good public relations with the community cannot be measured on a quantitative scale. These assignments are qualitative in nature. And often, qualitative assignments are far more important for the organization's goals. With qualitative assignments, the *how* rather than the *what* is usually unclear. The end state of such an assignment normally is apparent once it has been reached, but the means for achieving it often are difficult to determine. In addition, it is hard to know how far away one is at any point along the way and whether one is even proceeding in the right direction.

Given these problems of qualitative work assignments and the attractiveness of quantitative ones, the tendency to focus upon quantitative goals at the expense of qualitative goals is not surprising. But the effect of concentrating on quantification can lead to an inappropriate concern with aspects of goal attainment that are not really useful. One way to avoid this tendency is to develop quantitative substitutes for qualitative goals. For instance, one could concentrate on turnover rate as a way of improving morale among workers, or on customer complaints as a way of increasing product quality.

Matrix of Goals

Jobs vary greatly in the number of work assignments they contain. Occasionally, one assignment is enough to accomplish a goal. But more often, one goal requires several work assignments. When this is the case, each assignment within a job should have its own goal. Thus, any given job can be seen as a **matrix** of interlocking goals. This idea of a matrix is very useful because goals focus the person's attention on the specific activities that help meet the goal. Aspects of the job not included in goal statements tend to be ignored and not accomplished.

It should be pointed out, though, that this matrix of goals can also be a hindrance. For one thing, the situation may be made so complex that the employee cannot handle it; for another, if the goals are not complementary, or if they are inconsistent, the employee will become confused. In addition, the dimensions of quantity and quality almost always carry an inherent contradiction, and when the dimension of time is added, the problem becomes even worse. For example, *incentive systems* pay people for the quantity they produce in a given time period. But these systems invariably contain elaborate quality-control programs to keep employees from focusing solely on the number of products they turn out. Thus, any particular work assignment must be made with an eye to both the desired end state and the other assignments already inherent in the job.

Integrating Work Assignments

The assignment of work cannot be considered an isolated activity. It is integrally related to many other organizational functions. Thus, before assigning work, the efficient manager will be aware of other ongoing work throughout the organization and will integrate work assignments with other organizational areas, in particular the reward and communication systems. The manager must also take into account the person who will be performing the task. As mentioned earlier, matching the work with individual goals and skills is important in obtaining an employee's commitment to the desired end state.

The Organizational Structure

Figure 4–4 presents a simplified diagram of how the assignment of work based on the accomplishment of one goal is filtered down through the organizational structure. A major organizational goal (G_0) originates at the top of the organization. In order to accomplish this goal, three people (G_1, G_2, and G_3) are assigned work with specific subgoals. For these people to accomplish their work, a further subdivision of goal assignments is created on the next organizational level. This level, in turn, creates another subdivision, and so on, until it is no longer practical to continue subdividing work. The last unit of subdivision theoretically would be the individual employee, but often, in modern and complex organizations, it is not possible to carry the process this far.

When you consider that, in reality, organizations have a number of goals that are simultaneously being pursued, rather than just the one as illustrated in Figure 4–4, you begin to understand the potential for complexity and confusion. To help reduce this mass of confusion into workable assignments, the following guidelines have been suggested.

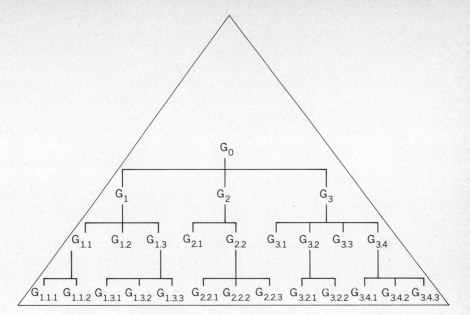

FIGURE 4–4
The subdivision of goals throughout the organizational hierarchy.

Dimensions of Work Assignments. One way to reduce confusion is to rely on the dimensions described in the previous sections. For instance, the time dimension can be varied. Ideally, a person would have some short-, medium-, and long-range tasks to perform. Having only short- or long-range tasks would lead to frustration and an inability to budget time well. Consider, for instance, the student as a person with a number of "bosses," each one assigning work. At the beginning of the semester, typically only a few assignments are given. By the end of the year, however, the student is swamped with preparing term papers and studying for final exams. This leads to very erratic expenditures of effort. Everything is clumped together, both in terms of time and complexity of tasks. The best situation is one in which the person has a mix of complexity in work assignments, ranging from relatively easy assignments to reasonably difficult ones.

Group Assignments. In complex situations that require people to work closely together, it is often helpful to assign goals to the group as a whole rather than to individuals. A good example is the way coaches instruct athletic teams. Although each player may have a particular task, the overall goals pertain to the whole group. Players are thus reluctant to let their individual tasks take precedence over group goals for fear of jeopardizing the team's chances of winning the game. One drawback to this method of work assignment is that strict focus on group goals can create problems for the individual in terms of personal commitment.

**Means–End
Hierarchy**

The subdivision of goals represented in Figure 4–4 may also be viewed as a **means-end hierarchy.** In other words, at each organizational level, managers examine the work to be done and distribute it among their employees. This constitutes each person's assignment of work. The manager is thereby developing the means by which the goals assigned to the unit will be accomplished. From the manager's point of view, an employee's assignment is a means to an end.

To the employee, however, the assignment is not a means but an end, or goal. It is not upon the organization's goal, or even the manager's, that the employee focuses, but upon the completion of the work assignment. Thus, employees need not look to the organization's goals to evaluate or verify their behavior but only to their own work-assigment goals.

The importance of any one work assignment (and often any one employee) to the manager is simply a means to an end and very impersonal. But to the employee, the importance of the work is seen as central to his or her place in the organization. The individual at the bottom of the hierarchy may look up and see some general managerial goals that are so broad that the ones way up at the top may not even be visible. But when the person at the top looks down he or she sees only one goal with a complicated set of means to attain it.

The argument as to whether the ends justify the means takes on a different light when all means are also seen as ends. A particular example is the extreme task specialization of the assembly line. As a means to an end, assembly lines are very successful in creating high levels of productivity. But as providers of goals, or ends, they have generally failed. Efficiency has been accomplished, but the jobs lack the necessary discretionary powers to provide interesting and challenging goals for the employees.

Communication

Assigning work cannot happen without some form of communication. But aside from communicating the necessary what and how of tasks, managers also must tell people *why* the task needs to be done. Communication is a necessary means for providing commitment, allowing discretion, and creating feedback.

Commitment. People need to know how their individual goals fit into the grand scheme of things in order to feel good about what they are doing. In addition, employees will commit themselves to tasks that make sense to them much more readily than they will to tasks that have no apparent purpose. Students, for example, tend not to try as hard in required courses that appear to bear little or no relation to their major area of interest.

Commitment to one's work can be strengthened beyond just communication of goals. For instance, employee participation in setting work assignments has been shown to be an effective method of obtaining commitment. In addition, participation is useful because it enables managers to

Where Do You Stand?

You are a middle manager in a medium-sized organization. On the continuum shown below, place an *x* on the spot you see yourself occupying; place a *y* on the spot you think *most* managers see themselves occupying.

Your
Manager _____ Your
Employees

When you have marked the two locations, refer to the boxed insert on page 98 to see where others place themselves.

obtain information about the job from the person who knows it best — the employee. Finally, in our society, participation has a positive value because it is the basic ingredient of democracy.

There are, of course, varying degrees of participation, which can be thought of as ranging along a continuum. At one end is the situation in which the manager makes all the decisions about assignments without consulting employees. Workers are simply informed as to what they will be doing. Consultation prior to establishing work assignments is a first step along the continuum. At this point the manager requests information from employees, establishes assignments, and then communicates the assignments to the employees. The manager would also listen for any reactions the employees might have to their assignments. A further point along the continuum is a condition in which employees are asked to establish their own work assignments while the manager independently establishes work assignments for them. The two sets of assignments are then compared and an acceptable settlement is reached. Finally, at the far end of the continuum is the situation in which employees are able to establish their own work assignments without any involvement on the part of the manager.

It should not be inferred that any of the above positions is necessarily better than any of the others. Each may be useful in a particular circumstance. The tasks involved, the types of people, and the organizational climate are all variables that determine which degree of participation will work best. Because establishing work assignments is a process that involves at least two people, one of the most important variables is the level of trust that exists between the people. Where the trust level is high, a great deal of participation is possible and can result in increased productivity and greater job satisfaction. Where trust is low or absent, more directive forms of assigning work are appropriate.

Discretion. A second reason for explaining to people how their work fits into the hierarchy of goals is to allow them to exercise discretion. If people are to make decisions they must have an understanding of the general context in which their decisions take place. They need to know that

Raymond Miles conducted an interesting study with a group of managers. He found that these managers generally placed themselves right next to their own superior managers and a long way from their employees on the continuum. In addition, Miles found that where the managers placed themselves was in direct accordance with their attitudes about how they felt they needed to manage their employees and how they wanted to be managed by their bosses. They wanted their bosses to see them as resources, their skills recognized and used. As managers, however, they felt they had to use human relations techniques to get their employees to do the work.

Source: Raymond Miles, "Human Relations or Human Resources," *Harvard Business Review*, vol. 43, no 4 (July–Aug. 1965), pp. 115–130.

the best way to approach a particular situation may not coincide with overall organizational goals. Without such knowledge, a sales manager, for example, may develop a sales program that is inconsistent with the advertising program, certain credit restrictions, or the organization's production capabilities.

Feedback. People have a felt need to know whether their actions are "on the right track." In a course for which the entire grade is dependent only upon the final examination, you cannot know if you are assimilating enough knowledge during the semester. So, when assigning work, it is useful to define points along the path toward the goal that employees can use as indications of whether they are "on target."

Furthermore, with feedback employees can work at a more consistent pace. People become very uncomfortable if they move along on a task and have no idea if it is getting done properly. As this tension builds up, the person starts avoiding the task altogether or decides that management does not feel it is very important to complete. Then just before the date when the task is to be completed the person engages in a flurry of activity that is not as efficient as steady progress would have been.

A major problem with feedback, however, is determining the proper recipient. Most control systems in organizations are designed so that an outside group (such as accountants) take the measurements and submit the results upward in the organizational hierarchy either directly to the manager or to the manager's boss. This upward reporting system often results in an incomplete communication loop, unless the manager completes the loop by transmitting the information downward to the individual. It is the manager's responsibility to make certain *all* information is redirected to the employee as soon as possible. The emphasis is on the word *all* because there is a tendency for feedback loops to contain only negative information. When the feedback loop fails to transmit positive information, employees are likely to avoid seeking out information about how they are doing. The ideal feedback loop would be one that stays right with the employees. In other words, employees would have the means for making their own determinations about their progress, such as meeting time or quantity goals, as discussed earlier. In such instances, people know what their goals are and do not need any outside help to determine whether they are being met.

Rewards

In addition to employees having knowledge of what the goals are and about how well they are accomplishing them, they also need to have a reason to pursue organizational goals. The owner-operator of a small business, for example, has no conflict in goal commitment because what is good for the business is good for the owner. But for most employees in organizations, the goals of the organization are not their own goals. They pursue the organization's goals not because they are inherently attractive to them but because they will obtain rewards by doing so. Figure 4–5 illustrates three possible positions that a person can be in with regard to personal versus organizational goals. Position 1 in the illustration represents the owner-manager mentioned above. Here, organizational and personal goals are identical. In position 2, organizational and personal goals are parallel; and in position 3, organizational and personal goals are in conflict. Position 1 is possible only in limited circumstances and for a few people. Position 2 is an ideal situation both for the organization and for the individual. And position 3 is unfortunate for both and should be avoided whenever possible. In reality, most employees are somewhere between positions 2 and 3.

Much of what helps employees move toward position 2 and away from position 3 comes under the general heading of motivation and will be covered in a later chapter. But another useful means for helping employees bring their goals in closer harmony with those of the organization is the use of rewards.

First, specific rewards should be associated with specific goals. For instance, in a piece-rate system, people are paid (rewarded) a stated amount for each unit of production. Second, the rewards offered must be something the person wants. An organization that offers a fine pension

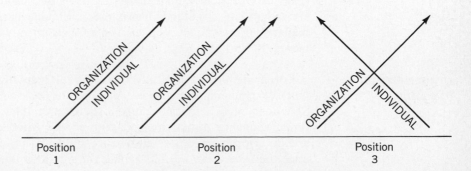

FIGURE 4–5
Personal versus
organizational goals.

program but that employs only people who are young is not matching its rewards with the needs of its people. Third, employees must be able to perceive a connection between the organization's goals and their own goals and needs. For example, an organization that offers merit increases for high performance stands a better chance of obtaining goal accomplishment than one that gives raises solely as a function of time on the job.

Effort Versus Performance. The purpose of feedback, rewards, and participation is to increase the probability that work assignments will be accomplished through employee acceptance and commitment. Acceptance and commitment are quite different from attainment of work objectives, however. Acceptance and commitment lead to effort, but effort is not the same as performance; rather it is one component of performance. There are at least two other components that are necessary before performance can happen. The first is ability. Aside from a desire to perform, the person must have the mental and physical tools that the work requires. Second, the person must have an understanding of what it takes to do the job. Graduates who are starting out in their first job often face the problem of nonunderstanding simply because they lack experience. They are intelligent, they put forth a lot of effort, but they do not yet fully understand their job or the organization. Performance, then, is a function of both selecting the right people and rewarding them properly. These topics will be explored in greater depth in later chapters.

The distinction between effort and performance is often blurred. Managers, professors, employees, and students all have been known to confuse the two. They assume that people who are working very hard must be accomplishing something. This assumption, sometimes called the ethic of busyness, is dispelled when work assignments are well defined and goal accomplishment can be easily measured (10).

Methods of Assigning Work

The final section of this chapter outlines three specific methods that managers use to assign work. The first method is organizationally oriented and takes care of recurring situations by using **organizational programs.** The second and third methods, **delegation** and **management by objectives,** are managerial techniques that can be of help in day-to-day work assignments.

Organizational Programs

All organizations periodically require implementation of new or special work assignments. On these occasions the task of assigning work is a time-consuming activity because it requires thinking through a whole different sequence of activities. Past methods, whether personal habits or computer-programed procedures, are suddenly no longer applicable. But once the tasks have been assigned, the methods that were used to make the decisions ordinarily are written down. In this way, the methods may be used again when similar situations arise. These methods are reusable programs.

Goal Statements. Most organizations try to make their goals known by writing them out in a set of formal statements. Official goals are stated as **general objectives.** These objectives are statements about future desired states that the organization wishes to achieve. There are usually a number of these, depending upon the size, variety, and function of the organization. In other words, a conglomerate, that comprises firms in a number of industries, would have more general objectives than would a firm that concentrates its activities within a single product area. Goal statements are extremely broad, covering total organizational areas of interest and unconcerned with how the goals are to be achieved.

Policies. Once goal statements have been formulated, the next step in specifying work is to develop policies. A **policy** is an organizational statement that defines in broad terms how goals are to be achieved and thus serves as a guide to managers in their decision making. In large organizations, there are policies guiding most functional areas. In the area of personnel, for example, a policy might be to promote or hire strictly on the basis of merit and qualifications. Very often there is a policy manual for each major department. In small organizations, few formal policies are necessary, and the managers can keep them in their heads.

THOU SHALT DO THIS. THOU SHALT DO THAT.

Procedures. A much more restrictive step in determining how work is to be done is the development of **procedures.** These are guides that specify exactly what is to be done and how in any given area of work. For example, a statement about how to fill out an expense report form is a procedure. Procedures are aimed more at employees than at managers. The manager's job is to determine which procedure is appropriate for every task, and the employee follows this procedure in performing his or her activities. The number of procedures tends to grow with the age and size of the organization. Even small organizations are likely to have sets of procedures to keep managers from having to tell employees how to do the work each time the same task is required.

Rules. Ordinarily, work **rules** are specific statements about what sort of deportment is expected of employees. Examples might include rules about what time employees are to report for work and leave, or the way tellers are to treat customers in a bank. Procedures and rules are usually drawn up after some situation has occurred that required special handling and that is likely to occur again. For instance, in a college or university, rules specifying a deadline for dropping a class often are formulated only after large numbers of students drop classes late in the semester.

Bureaupathic Behavior. All of the above guidelines for behavior develop from an experienced need to regulate activity. They are useful to the extent that the present situation resembles the past. Unfortunately, there are times when following these guidelines becomes an end in itself. When managers spend a great deal of time worrying about whether rules are being followed rather than whether the work is getting done, organizational resources are being wasted. This phenomenon, which is often called **bureaupathic behavior,** is the slavish adherence to rules and regulations whether they are appropriate or not (11).

Delegation

Although organizational programs, such as policies, result in very impersonal methods of assigning work, most work assignments are made directly between a manager and an employee on a very personal basis. The characteristics of both people and the relationship between them affects the way in which work is assigned. Assigning work requires that the manager "let go" of the work—delegate it to an employee. However, the manager is still accountable for the results. So unless the relationship between them is positive, there are a number of reasons why managers may not want to "let go" and why employees may not want to accept the delegated responsibility.

"I Can Do It Better." Managers frequently overestimate their own ability compared to that of their employees. As a result, they openly demonstrate a lack of confidence in their employees' abilities (12). In most cases, the employee probably can do as good a job as the manager—even though it may be done differently from the way the manager expects. But more important, the manager is not making the correct comparison. The question should not be whether the manager or the employee can do a particular task better, but which, out of all the tasks needing to be performed, should the manager be undertaking. Managers may decide that they should be doing other tasks even when they know the task will not be done as well as if they had done it themselves.

Lack of Skill in Delegating Work. Some managers just do not have the ability to delegate. This may stem either from improper training or from the personality of the manager. The ability to delegate requires that the manager be able to plan ahead, organize, and communicate to employees. When managers are promoted on the basis of technical skills they often do not have the necessary managerial skills. In the majority of cases, management development training can increase managerial skills, but some people, because of inflexible personality structures, are not able to develop the ability to trust their employees' skill and judgment. The manager, in order to delegate, must be willing to take a risk, to "bet" on the employee's ability to handle the work.

Organizational Difficulties. Delegation is difficult and more of a gamble when there is inadequate control and feedback. Control systems that provide avenues for accurate feedback increase the likelihood that managers will feel good about delegating responsibility for the work. Delegation causes managers to be dependent on employees in that the manager's success or failure depends on the performance of the employees. Thus the manager must have a workable system of control, and the employee must receive feedback before either can adequately carry out the task.

The Information Dilemma. Basically, delegation represents a dilemma to the manager. An important part of the manager's job is the collection and dissemination of information. In order to delegate effectively, the manager must disseminate the necessary information as well as the work. If the information is very complex, the dissemination process may be as time consuming as simply doing the work oneself. In such cases, the manager gains little by delegation (13).

Employee Resistance. Managers are not the only cause of delegation difficulties. Employees often avoid responsibility. It may be easier for them to ask the boss because they fear criticism, they lack the necessary information or resources, they are already overloaded with work, they lack self-confidence, or they are not given enough incentive to take on responsibility.

Note that all but one of these factors, lack of self-confidence, is something associated with the work situation and not with the individual performing the work. McGregor makes the point that people are not inherently lazy (14). They learn to be lazy through their experiences in organizations. Finding it easier to ask the boss through a fear of criticism is a result of the relationship between the manager and the employee that stresses dependency. A lack of necessary information and work overload can be seen as problems in work design. Lack of positive incentives may result directly from the manager-employee relationship, or, more broadly, from the way the organization as a whole sets up the reward structure. Even a lack of self-confidence may, in many cases, result from the person's past experience in organizations.

Management by Objectives

Much of what has been discussed thus far about assigning work is contained in a concept called **management by objectives** (MBO). This concept was first popularized by Drucker in 1954 and, later, by McGregor in 1967. It was made operational by General Electric and others (15). A description of management by objectives constitutes this final section of the chapter.

Performance Appraisal. The original intent of MBO was to reduce some of the negative effects of performance appraisal. Customarily, a performance-appraisal program consists of the manager completing a form rating the characteristics of the employee on a scale from high to low. This rating is then discussed with the employee and suggestions are made as to how to improve the low-rated characteristics. A great deal of ambivalence is created in both the manager and the employee by this traditional performance-appraisal program. Employees want to know how they are doing but do not want negative feedback. The manager feels uncomfortable "judging" others. This leads to a great deal of defensiveness on both sides and restricts the ability of the performance-appraisal process to create a change in the employee's behavior.

Traditional performance appraisal focuses on inputs, not on outputs. That is, performance-rating sheets contain such personal input items as employee initiative, which the manager is supposed to rate. The rationale is that these behaviors lead to greater productivity output. The problem is that the desired outputs are never clearly described, and the individual is not judged by what is accomplished but by what he or she is contributing in terms of personal inputs.

MBO Programs. MBO reverses the focus of traditional performance appraisal: It focuses on goals, participation, and feedback. Following is an outline of the way MBO works and what it hopes to achieve.

1. MBO focuses specifically on what is to be accomplished, that is, on goals. In an MBO program, each person from the top to the bottom of the organization has a set of goals to accomplish over a specified time interval. These goals are not to be stated in vague terms but rather in a spe-

cific (preferably quantitative) and measurable format. Further, goals are to be challenging but clearly within the realm of attainment. This requirement takes advantage of the aspiration levels of employees and their achievement drives.

For instance, a student might set as a goal a grade of B for a particular course. A grade of B is measurable and, for the student, challenging but realizable. After reviewing the course requirements, the student may decide on a series of subgoals, such as always coming to class, devoting at least six hours a week to the course, and always reviewing notes before examinations. Keeping a record of the accomplishment of subgoals, as well as of interim grades on examinations and papers, provides feedback on how well the overall goal is being realized.

2. In MBO, goal setting is participatory. This means that the manager and the employee get together to arrive at a set of mutually acceptable goals. Participation is intended to increase both understanding of and commitment to the goals. This aspect of MBO is often misunderstood. It should be clearly noted that participation does not mean that the employees may decide to do anything they please. Rather, goal setting must be a mutual activity that takes into account both the employee's and the organization's needs. If the manager "comes on strong" regarding the organization's needs, however, the employee usually feels trapped into an agreement.

3. Finally, MBO requires that employees receive feedback about the results of their work. Most control systems are designed to provide feedback to higher organizational levels rather than directly to the operating levels. Thus, a redesign of the control system is usually required when an organization institutes an MBO program. Direct feedback to the operating levels has been shown to improve employee performance.

Problems with MBO. There is little question that MBO is theoretically sound and has produced some significantly positive results. It has not been universally successful, however, and has met with resistance from both managers and employees. Where it has been unsuccessful, the reasons have been attributed to the problems listed below.

1. In the goal-setting stage, problems arise from trying to make goals clear and explicit. Not all situations lend themselves to precise goal statements. The focus on measurable goals tends to exclude qualitative goals, even if they are of great importance. Further, people tend to focus only on those goals that have been clearly defined and to ignore other important but less explicit activities.

2. Participation in goal setting presents the problem of trust and unequal power relations. MBO requires that managers and employees trust one another. But such trust cannot be ordered to happen. If managers use MBO to obtain commitment and cooperation without truly feeling that employees can set reasonable goals, MBO becomes a manipulative

device (16). At best, the participation problem is substantial because of the inherent difference in power between the manager and the employee. The employee has a definite tendency to try to find out what the boss thinks and then reflect back those goals the manager wants to hear. On the other hand, some managers become so nondirective that the employees do not integrate their goals well with organizational goals. Participation presumes that people want to be involved in setting their own goals. But many people still like, or need, to be told what to do.

3. As mentioned above, the control system must be adapted to provide feedback information directly to the employee. Information is often not available, however, or may not be seen as relevant to the employee. This is particularly true when information is of a general organizational nature. Another problem in this area is that the information often indicates that a change is needed in goals. Thus, midway to attainment of certain goals, the whole process may need to be reevaluated.

4. At the beginning of this chapter, work was viewed in terms of what is to be done and how it is to be done. MBO focuses almost entirely on what is to be done. How work is to be completed is important though often ignored by MBO programs. The objective may be reached but in a way that is either inefficient or ineffective. Recently, MBO programs have come under attack for their lack of focus on how work is done (17).

Despite all these criticisms, good MBO programs can be and have been constructed. Successful programs depend on a high level of trust within the organization and a definite commitment by management to the program. Further, managers and employees need to have a clear idea of the complex nature of organizational goals and therefore realistic expectations of their success.

Chapter Review

The topic of this chapter has been the assignment of work. The logic of organization is that each person makes a small and specific contribution to the overall task or goal, making it imperative to subdivide the overall goals of the organization into small segments. These are the work assignments. Important terms and ideas developed in this chapter regarding the assignment of work appear below.

1. **Work assignments** need to be made clear in terms of *what* is to be done and *how* it is to be done. The *what* of work assignments is stated in terms of:
    a. end state
    b. quality
    c. time
    d. resources

The *how* of work assignments is to contain:

    a. activities

    b. interactions

    c. decisions

2. **Contraction orders** are those that leave the employee no choice as to what to do or how to do it.

3. Although studies have shown that work should be assigned in specific terms, real-life circumstances often make this impossible or undesirable.

4. Work assignments should be made challenging but should be neither extremely easy nor impossible to accomplish.

5. Work assignments stated in quantitative terms are more easily measured than those stated in qualitative terms, but they are not always the most important assignments.

6. Work assignments can often be made to a group instead of to an individual.

7. A **means-end hierarchy** is the subdivision of goals as seen from the different perspectives of the manager and the employee.

8. Communication regarding work assignments helps create commitment, discretion, and feedback.

9. **Reward systems** need integration with work assignments by:

    a. offering what the employee wants

    b. connecting performance to reward

    c. connecting effort to performance

10. Effort does not always equal performance.

11. Organizations create several levels of programs about how work is to be performed.

    a. **Goal statements** are broad objectives.

    b. **Policies** are guides for decision making that indicate what work is to be achieved.

    c. **Procedures** detail how work is to be done.

    d. **Rules** indicate correct employee behavior.

12 **Delegation** is the manager's "letting go" of a work assignment and holding an employee responsible for its completion.

13. **Management by objectives** is a program by which managers and employees jointly design *what* the employee is to accomplish in a given time period. The major features are:

    a. measurable goals

    b. participation

    c. feedback of results

Discussion Questions

1. What are the external/internal dimensions of work that need to be considered in assigning work?

2. What advice would you give to a manager who is attempting to improve his or her method of assigning work?

3. What is a contraction order? In what circumstances would such an order be useful? When would it not be useful?

4. "All aspects of a person's work should be clearly defined." Make an argument for and against this statement.

5. What advice would you give to the sales manager who last year doubled each employee's quota and who wanted to get employees to work even harder?

6. How might you go about "quantifying" the following "qualitative" ideals?

    a. Good morale.

    b. A quality product.

    c. Maximum profits.

    d. Improved customer relations.

7. What is a means-end hierarchy? What are its implications for an organization? For a manager?

8. How could you go about integrating organizational and personal goals?

9. What is the difference between effort and performance? Why is this an important distinction?

10. Distinguish between goal statements, policies, procedures, and rules. Give examples of each.

11. List several reasons why it is hard for a manager to delegate responsibility.

12. You are a personnel manager and your boss has requested you to set up an MBO program for the organization. What factors do you need to consider and how will you proceed?

Involvement Activities

1. A course assignment is very similar to a work assignment. So to gain a first-hand understanding of how work is assigned, try to answer the following questions about an assignment you have been given in one of your courses — perhaps this one.

    a. Work assignment

        (1) How well were the *what* dimensions of the assignment described?

        (2) Were the resources readily available?

        (3) Were people matched to their assignments?

        (4) How well were the *how* dimensions of the assignment described?

        (5) Who decided upon the particular assignment — you, the instructor, or both together?

    b. Delegation

        (1) How well did the instructor delegate work to you?

        (2) How applicable are some of the constraints on delegation in this case?

        (3) How willing were you (and other students) to accept the delegation? Why?

    c. Management by objectives

        (1) How well did the assignment of work follow the ideas of MBO?

(2) Can you redesign the assignment in terms of MBO guide-lines?

(3) Would such a redesign be effective? Why?

2. How well do you assign work? See if you can apply what you have learned in this chapter by incorporating the concepts into a simple task assignment. Either think of one on your own or use one of the suggestions below.

a. Send someone (perhaps yourself) to the store to purchase several items, such as groceries, hardware, or household goods.

b. Assign someone (perhaps yourself) the task of repairing the carburetor of the car, baking a cake, cleaning the house or apartment, or setting up the stereo set.

c. Describe in detail to someone how to play a complicated game or a sport with which you are familiar.

5

Job Design

A work assignment and a job are not the same thing. Some jobs contain a single work assignment, but most jobs involve a number of different work assignments. The purpose of this chapter is to explore the ways in which tasks are combined to form jobs.

Some of the factors that must be considered when designing jobs, and which are examined here, include: work specialization; models of work design; job simplification and job enlargement; the sequencing of work; and methods of job design.

Managers are accountable for all of the tasks assigned to their departments, but they do not perform all the work themselves. The work of a department is too "big" for any one person to handle alone. No one has the time or the skills to do all the tasks that are required. Therefore, the manager must subdivide the total job into specialized "person-sized" subunits. It is this process of subdividing that, in effect, creates **specialization** within an organization. Indeed, it creates the organization itself. (Figure 5–1 represents graphically this step in the organizing process.)

Managers must deal with the issue of who is to do what whenever new tasks are added to the work of their departments. They do this by creating new jobs or by adding the new tasks to existing jobs. Because organizations are constantly changing (thus changing the nature of the required tasks), a periodic review of current job assignments is useful as there is a tendency over time for jobs to take on new tasks. The original job description then becomes outmoded and new jobs may exist for which there are no descriptions.

An Overview of Job Design

Work specialization is as old as civilization. People understood very early that many tasks could be accomplished better by two than by one. Later, during the Industrial Revolution, many people, each of whom was proficient at a particular task, were brought together under one roof to form the first large-scale organizations.

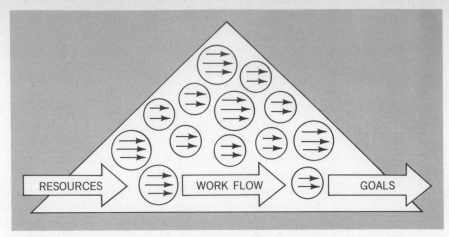

FIGURE 5–1
Organizations as a
series of jobs.

The individual task goals in this diagram have been brought together in similar kinds of groups, with each task designed so that it may be performed by one individual.

Now, almost all the work done in industrial nations is accomplished in large organizations. But even very small organizations divide and specialize work. Obviously, the larger the organization, the further it can subdivide the work. In a two-person shoe store, both people are responsible for many different tasks. In a hundred-person department store, there are sales clerks, accountants, cashiers, stockers, and others, each performing highly specialized tasks for which they have been specifically hired and trained.

It is apparent that the latter is a more efficient operation. Specialists can perform one task better than generalists can perform many tasks. But in the pursuit of greater and greater efficiency, we sacrifice something, too. Before the Industrial Revolution, shoes were handmade by cobblers. Then, as more people moved to the cities, the demand for shoes outgrew the cobblers' ability to supply them. Factories were established for the purpose of mass-producing shoes. Cobblers began to specialize in specific areas of shoe production, and machines were created to do much of the work. Eventually, cobblers were a thing of the past. Quality, care, and pride in craftsmanship were sacrificed to efficiency. But shoes are plentiful, and mass-production, because it is efficient, allows them to be sold at prices everyone can afford.

Although modern-day mechanization and automation are rendering obsolete many traditional skills, the complexity of large-scale organizations requires the services of new kinds of specialists. Engineers, scientists, computer programers, accountants, and many other technologists are responsible for quantum changes in virtually all areas of human endeavor. One need only look at the advances made in medicine and space exploration for a glimpse of how far specialization has taken us in just the last quarter century. But these new specialists also create a dilemma for the organization: That is, how can jobs be designed to fit the particular skills and training of these specialists while simultaneously meeting the needs of the organization? This, plus other considerations in designing jobs, are the subjects of this chapter.

A Model of Job Design

Tasks come in all sizes and shapes. An overall organizational task, such as manufacturing machine parts, is quite different from an individual task, such as driving a truck. Yet both tasks may be performed in the same organization. Even the people who operate the machines each have individualized and specialized tasks. It is easy to see why no one person has the skill to perform all the tasks of an organization. Literally, a single motion by any one person can be considered a task. In fact, a single bodily motion is considered the basic unit of job design.

Task Characteristics

In a typical warehouse organization, the overall task is to unload trucks and store goods. The major subtasks are removing the goods from the trucks and placing them in the proper storage areas. The task of unloading the goods can be further subdivided. Before the actual unloading, someone must deal with the truck driver, take care of office paperwork, and make decisions about how best to proceed with unloading the particular goods. The unloading itself consists of a set of activities involving lifting, transporting, and setting down the materials. Storing the goods involves a further set of subtasks, such as checking the quantity against an invoice, inspecting for damage, and making sure the goods are set down in the proper area and adequately protected.

If this is a one-person warehouse, then all these tasks must be done by a single person. Even if the warehouse is very large, the tasks could still be performed by one individual, but the operation would not be very efficient. If people are hired to staff the warehouse, someone must make decisions about who will do what. Who is going to unload which trucks? Where is all the material to be stored? Are workers going to be crossing over one another to store the goods? Very possibly it would be wiser if some of the employees spent their time unloading the trucks while others were involved only in putting the material away. Besides, unloading and storing require different skills. Who will take care of the paperwork? Pay salaries? Answer the telephone? Keep the building clean and protected against robbery? Quite clearly, there is much to consider.

Each of these tasks has a unique character. Operating a forklift, for instance, involves very different skills from those required to handle a payroll. Thus, tasks may be examined in terms of the **activities, interactions,** and **decisions** they require.

Activities. Activities are the things people do. They are physical and observational in nature. The activity of typing, for example, involves observing (or hearing) a symbol, interpreting that symbol, matching it with a symbol on the typewriter, and pressing the proper typewriter key. Some activities are mainly physical—lifting boxes or driving a truck; and some are mainly observational—reading a bill of lading. Almost all tasks, however, require some combination of both. And the degree to which observation accurately guides actual physical movement is the application of a person's skill.

The activities of a task vary according to **variety, complexity,** and the **time** required to complete them.

1. *Variety.* A task may involve only a single activity or a wide variety of activities. For example, the person whose task is to take boxes off a conveyor belt and stack them six deep for someone else to cart off has a narrow variety of activities to perform. A person doing the warehousing tasks in a small warehouse would be required to perform a wide variety of activities. The fewer the activities involved in a task, the smaller the num-

ber of skills required of the person performing the task. This reduction in variety leads to specialization, which in turn leads to proficiency.

2. *Complexity.* Ordinarily, the more activities there are to perform, the more complex is the task. But this is not necessarily true. For example, a single person performing the whole set of tasks required to operate a small warehouse still does not have as complex a task as an electrical engineer or a computer programer whose task is to design one piece of equipment for a space capsule. Complexity in physical movement has to do with the allowable tolerances. Picking up boxes is not as complex in this sense as is machining parts to 0.001-inch calibration. Complexity in observation has to do with the degree to which a person must be able to distinguish between and interpret stimuli.

3. *Time.* Some activities take only a few seconds to perform; others go on for weeks or even years. An assembly-line worker might have a time sequence of thirty seconds or less to complete an activity, whereas a sculptor may take five years or more to complete a work of art. The time sequence may be related to the attention span of the individual performing the task. If the sequence is shorter than the person's attention-span capability, the individual will feel frustrated. If the sequence is too long, the person loses interest in the activity.

Interactions. People usually interact with other people (and with machines) in order to accomplish their work. In an organization, this is always the case. As discussed in Chapter 1, different tasks require varying numbers of interactions, varying degrees of initiation and response, and varying time restraints.

1. *Number.* Some tasks requre interaction with only a limited number of other people. At a minimum, a person must report to one supervisor. Most tasks also require interactions with co-workers and some tasks, such as those in a personnel office, demand constant interaction with a variety of people.

2. *Initiation.* Most frequently, interactions are initiated with employees by managers, with customers by salespeople, with suppliers by purchasing agents, and so on. Those who want a service performed, or those who want to perform a service, initiate the interactions. Of course, once the initial contact has been made, both parties participate in the initiation and receipt of subsequent interactions.

3. *Time.* The amount of time spent in interactions is also a function of the kind of task being performed. Generally, people in highly specialized tasks, such as piecework operations, spend a minimal amount of time

in interactions. More generalized tasks, such as managing, often require interactions of long duration, as do tasks that necessarily involve long interactions, such as teaching or counseling.

Decisions. Signals must be sent out and observations interpreted before a particular physical act can be performed. In like manner, the interactions between people are interpreted, producing further interactions and activities. These are all mental activities that require decisions. And decisions can be characterized along the following dimensions:

1. *Discretion.* All work has a prescribed and a discretionary content. In performing any given task an employee is constrained by the work that needs to be done and by instructions about how to do it. This is the **prescribed** content of the work. Similarly, every task permits some freedom of choice among alternatives: this is the **discretionary** content. The prescription-discretion continuum is similar to the idea of programed and nonprogramed decisions (1). Programed decisions are those for which an organizational prescription, such as a list of procedures, is available. Nonprogramed decisions require the person to search for alternatives and to exercise judgment.

2. *Time.* Decisions take place within a time period, which may range from a few seconds to many years. The overall task sets the framework for the time dimension, with all subtasks having to be performed within this constraint.

3. *Complexity.* Decisions differ in terms of how many variables need to be processed and the ways in which they must be combined. Consider three kinds of decision situations. The first involves sequential or linear decisions, in which each is *dependent* on the preceding decision — for example, a decision regarding the proper sequencing of tasks necessary to complete a project. The second situation involves a consideration of variables that are *independent* of one another — for example, a decision to change the way work is performed, which involves such factors as the cost, the union contract, the customers, and the suppliers, all of which contain their own requirements. The third situation involves variables that are *interdependent.* Consider, for example, the consequences of changing work assignments. If the employees are unhappy about the change, problems may develop among the employees or between the employees and the managers. These social problems, in turn, may affect the way work is performed, which will have further consequences for managers.

4. *Environment.* In terms of decisions, **environment** refers to the amount of information available. The environment may be rich in information, offering clear and available decision-making guides, or it may be

Distinguishing Between Prescribed and Discretionary Decisions

If "work" is defined as a combination of activities, interactions, and decisions, then all of your behavior is "work." In your activities and interactions, you have a wide range of choice about what to do and how to do it. In other words, the discretionary component of your decisions is fairly large. But many activities are prescribed for you, by your own habits, by social rules of what is proper, and by the other forces in your environment.

Consider several activities and interactions you engage in frequently, such as eating, talking with people, attending classes, playing a game, and the like. Over how much of your behavior in each of these activities and interactions do you have a choice? How much is limited? What is it limited by? Do you think it is always possible to make a distinction between prescribed and discretionary behavior?

relatively barren, making decisions difficult to reach. Alternatively, information may be available, but so ambiguous or so conflicting with other information that decisions are equally difficult.

Separating Task Characteristics

Any task presupposes that someone (or some people) will carry out activities, engage in interactions, and make decisions. And we have just seen that the dimensions of each of these three requisites vary considerably with the type of task being performed. Any task can be analyzed and the dimensions of each characteristic pulled out in detail. These are useful practices when the task is repetitive and continues over an extended period of time. For instance, when a new product goes into production, and it is known that it will remain unchanged for a couple of years, task separation is useful. On the other hand, the more variability and change in a task, the less useful it is to spend a lot of time analyzing its components. The end product of task analysis should be a detailed listing of the activities, interactions, and decisions that constitute the ways in which the task is carried out.

Combining Task Characteristics

When the overall task requires more than one person, the task characteristics need to be divided among the various people in some combination. Figure 5–2 illustrates four possible combinations. Person A has an equal balance of activities, interactions, and decisions. An example of such a situation would be a relatively independent and complete task, such as the whole warehousing task described earlier. Person B makes a great many decisions but does little physical activity. This situation is most typical of a managerial position. Person C performs many activities but does little decision making. This is best exemplified by people who do piecework, or assembly-line tasks. Person D participates in many interactions but does

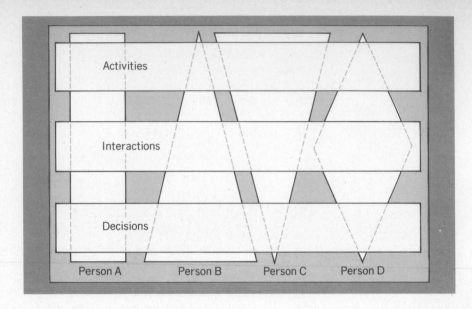

FIGURE 5–2
Possible combinations of task characteristics.

little activity and makes few decisions. This situation is characteristic of people dealing with the public, such as salesclerks.

Job Simplification

Which combination of task characteristics is appropriate depends on both the situation and the people involved. The larger the size of the overall task and the more people needed, the more diverse can be the combinations. If the task requires only one person, the possible combinations will vary according to the methods of assigning work as discussed in Chapter 4. There is still a good deal of controversy over whether jobs should be simplified or enlarged in terms of how many task characteristics they embody.

The Case for Job Simplification

Job simplification can occur in one of two ways. First, the task characteristics can be limited. For instance, Person C in Figure 5–2 has a simplified job because the tasks are almost all in the activities area. The second way to simplify jobs is to limit activities in terms of complexity and length of time. Interactions can be brief and the person a responder instead of an initiator. And decisions can be prescribed, of a short time dimension, linear, and dealing only with known quantities. A number of arguments favor work simplification.

Limitation of Skills. One of the major reasons why work is simplified is that people are unable to accomplish most jobs alone. Even if time is not a factor, few people have either the skill or the strength necessary to complete a job single-handedly. Thus, a major advantage of work simplification to organizations is that people's talents are put to use where they are most advantageous. Each person can concentrate on the portion of the total task most aligned with his or her area of expertise. In this way efficiency is increased.

Learning Time. A person can learn a simplified task faster and more effectively than a complex one. Given the complexity of many jobs, it is not hard to imagine someone spending an entire lifetime learning a skill and still not mastering it completely. From the viewpoint of the organization, simplified jobs require a minimal amount of time to learn, and the organization is then not dependent upon any one individual who has hard-to-replace skills. When one person can be trained rapidly to take the place of another, employees become relatively interchangeable. In a period of full employment, this means that organizations can adapt quickly to labor turnover.

Proficiency. An employee develops a proficiency by repeating an operation. The operator of a bulldozer, for instance, is much more skilled at bulldozing than is a foreman, who might have to perform this task only once a year. To the extent that proficiency increases efficiency, the organization benefits. Proficiency also is personally gratifying. People feel a sense of accomplishment from doing a job well.

Organizational Efficiency. Situational factors also contribute to the efficiency of simplification. For instance, when operations can be standardized, individuals are saved from having to work out procedures each time they are used, or from having to set up machinery over and over again.

Efficiency is also improved when operations can be run concurrently, such as when all the parts of an automobile are made simultaneously and independently and then assembled. In this way, full use of the organization's facilities can be maintained. Additionally, standardization produces goods and services that are uniform in design and quality. Buyers or customers can then depend on consistency: They know what to expect.

The Case Against Job Simplification

Since the days of Fredrick W. Taylor and other scientific management theorists, the trend has been toward work simplification. The arguments for this trend are all around us, evidenced primarily by the production of goods at reasonable costs. Work simplification is effective in a wide variety of industries. Lying behind this impressive efficiency of work simplification, however, is a value framework about human nature and motivation, as well as a rationalization about why simplification is necessary, if not humane.

The Steelworker

When work is simplified too much, organizations may profit and the public may be satisfied with the final product or service, but workers' feelings about what they are doing often reflect the consequences. The following quotation is from an interview with a steelworker and appears in Studs Terkel's book *Working*.

It's hard to take pride in a bridge you're never gonna cross, in a door you're never gonna open. You're mass-producing things and you never see the end result of it. (Muses) I worked for a trucker one time. And I got this tiny satisfaction when I loaded a truck. At least I could see the truck depart loaded. In a steel mill, forget it. You don't see where nothing goes.

I got chewed out by my foreman once. He said, "Mike, you're a good worker but you have a bad attitude." My attitude is that I don't get excited about my job. I do my work but I don't say whoopee-doo. The day I get excited about my job is the day I go to a head shrinker. How are you gonna get excited about pullin' steel? How are you gonna get excited when you're tired and want to sit down?

It's not just the work. Somebody built the pyramids. Somebody's going to build something. Pyramids, Empire State Building—these things just don't happen. There's hard work behind it. I would like to see a building, say, the Empire State, I would like to see on one side of it a foot-wide strip from top to bottom with the name of every bricklayer, the name of every electrician, with all the names. So when a guy walked by, he could take his son and say, "See, that's me over there on the forty-fifth floor. I put the steel beam in." Picasso can point to a painting. What can I point to? A writer can point to a book. Everybody should have something to point to.

It's the not-recognition by other people. To say a woman is *just* a housewife is degrading, right? Okay. *Just* a housewife. It's also degrading to say *just* a laborer. The difference is that a man goes out and maybe gets smashed.

From Studs Terkel, *Working* (New York: Pantheon Books, a Division of Random House, Inc., 1972), pp.1–2.

There are also arguments against work simplification, however. Jobs can be made too simple for people, causing them to become bored and disinterested in their work. There are also a series of dysfunctions that become compelling as work simplification is carried to an extreme.

Need for Coordination in Simplification. One limitation of job simplification is that it creates a high degree of worker interdependence and the attendant need for someone to coordinate the tasks. To produce a product that requires ten operations, either ten workers may each perform all ten operations, or ten workers may perform one operation each. In the former arrangement (job enlargement), the loss of one employee reduces the output by one tenth. But in the latter situation (job simplification), the loss of one employee can reduce the output of the group to zero. While a high degree of work specialization reduces the need for the organization to depend on any specific individual, it increases the interdependence of the parts of the organization by giving any one of the parts the capability of shutting down the whole work flow. To avoid this possibility, a high degree of coordination is required. Increasing specialization therefore results in an elaboration of the managerial structure, which means higher indirect operating costs (2).

Reliability as Rigidity. Another drawback of high job simplification is that employees become inflexible. The more their tasks are circumscribed, the less they are able to focus on overall organizational goals. Individuals come to value and work toward the subgoals of their work group without regard for the effect of such behavior on the total organization. And as pointed out earlier in this book, there are times when the suboptimization of group goals may be desirable, or even essential, for organizational survival.

For work simplification to operate efficiently, stability in a number of areas is required. The volume of work must be consistent. If volume decreases, the organization needs fewer employees and the work simplification among those remaining will need to be redefined. Also, inputs of other resources must be standardized and regularly available. Because the work of each person is interdependent with the work of others, each work station must be filled or operations will stop. The substantial investment in technology, including capital equipment, technological systems, operating procedures, and skills, requires that products not be vulnerable to rapid change.

Use of Employee Skills. Although one of the advantages of work simplification is a better match between individual skills and work assignments, it is often true that simplification is carried beyond the point of a good match. Modern organizations have found it efficient to carry work simplification to such a degree that little of an individual's mental or physical skills are used. The result is that the employee finds work to be without much meaning and best suited for a child (3).

Job Enrichment

Recent theory and research have challenged the logic and the achievements of work simplification. There is currently a concern with the quality of working life in the United States (4). The argument is that people are bored with their jobs and that the boredom has a detrimental effect on their productivity and, ultimately, on all of society (5). Some theorists believe that the way to increase productivity and job satisfaction is through the redesign of work in terms of job enrichment.

In an **enriched job,** the task characteristics (the activities, interactions, and decisions) are balanced. Furthermore, there is a balance of the dimensions within the characteristics. In other words, activities comprise complete sequences and result in an identifiable output; and all the interactions and decisions necessary to complete the output are also a part of the job. In one example of job enrichment, employees had been assembling the top covers of washing machines, which contained forty-six components, by having the cover pass by each work station where employees

The Stonemason

When people take pride in their work, they feel good about themselves. And it doesn't matter whether the job is mixing concrete or sculpting a work of art.

This is what one stonemason has to say about his work. Again, it is from Studs Terkel's book *Working*.

Every piece of stone you pick up is different, the grain's a little different and this and that. It'll split one way and break the other. You pick up your stone and look at it and make an educated guess. It's a pretty good day layin' stone or brick. Not tiring. Anything you like to do isn't tiresome. It's hard work; stone is heavy. At the same time, you get interested in what you're doing and you usually fight the clock the other way. You're not lookin' for quittin'. You're wondering you haven't got enough done and it's almost quittin' time. . . .

. . . So I take a lot of pride in it and I do get, oh, I'd say, a lot of praise or whatever you want to call it. I don't suppose anybody, however much he's recognized, wouldn't like to be recognized a little more. I think I'm pretty well recognized.

From Studs Terkel, *Working* (New York: Pantheon Books, a Division of Random House, Inc., 1972), p. 8.

would attach one or more parts. In redesigning the task, each worker was assigned the entire sequence of tasks so that every work station was responsible for the completion of an entire cover. In addition, inspection and testing were also done by the employees (6).

Making Work Meaningful

Job enrichment has its own logic and value framework. The proponents of job enrichment take the position that productivity and satisfaction at the work place will rise as jobs are designed in ways that allow people to experience a wide range of need satisfaction that is not possible in work simplification. People are more interested in their work when they do a number of operations rather than a few, when the unit they work on "makes sense" in terms of having a beginning, a middle, and an end, and when they have at least some control over what operations they perform and how they perform them.

Is Job Enrichment the Answer?

Research that examines the value of job enrichment has produced mixed results. Many studies have shown that positive results can be obtained by increasing the number of activities and decisions of the individual worker (7). Other studies of job enrichment indicate that it is successful mainly in organizations in which management is really committed to it and particularly where the employees desire it. People who have low skills, who have adapted to simple jobs, or who simply are uninterested in the rewards available from enlarged jobs do not respond positively to job enrichment (8).

What is unquestionably true is that efficiency and work simplification do not enjoy the positive, linear relationship once thought to exist by scientific management theorists. This optimistic relationship, represented as

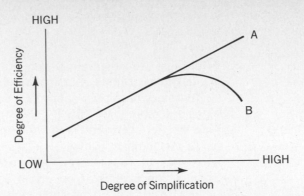

FIGURE 5–3
The relationship between work simplification and efficiency.

Line A in Figure 5–3, is more likely to look like that represented as Line B, where efficiency falls off with high levels of simplification. When organizations fail to recognize and utilize employee skills, workers become bored with their jobs and restrict production.

Work Sequencing

In addition to dividing a total task into subtasks and then reassembling the subtasks into jobs, the **sequencing** of subtasks must be considered. Every task has a predecessor task that supplies some necessary resource and a subsequent task that utilizes its output. The only tasks that do not have both predecessor and subsequent tasks are the beginning and ending subtasks. In order to accomplish the overall task, each of the subtasks must be sequenced so that the output of one subtask feeds into the input of the next, and so on.

Timing the Work Flow

The ideal situation is one in which each subtask is completed at just the time that the next subtask is to begin. Consider the warehouse as an example. The ideal situation would be one in which the time spent to take certain boxes to the storage area would just equal the time spent to stack another set of boxes for removal. Clearly, such precise timing is very difficult to achieve. What is more likely is that either boxes would pile up or a person would stand around waiting for boxes to be stacked. Both situations are, of course, inefficient. Which situation is least desirable depends upon the relative cost of storage for partially finished goods versus the cost of the unused labor. Project-type organizations, such as contracting firms, continually must deal with the problem of timing. Ideal timing for projects occurs when the decline of the first project coincides with an increased demand in the second project, and so on. If one were to spread projects out linearly, then the demand for people would rise and fall, leaving them inefficiently employed. On the other hand, if the projects were squeezed together, the demand for employees would exceed the organization's supply.

Concurrent Operations

Fitting tasks together in sequence does not always result in a single linear line of subtasks, however. A major advantage of work specialization is the ability to perform many subtasks concurrently and then fit them together on an assembly-line basis. But if a single person were producing a radio, for example, one would start with a chassis and then assemble an amplifier, a preamplifier, a tuner, and speakers. Finally, all these would be fit into a cabinet. In an assembly-line operation, the component parts would be built concurrently. Concurrent work considerably reduces the time required to produce a product. However, the complexity of the production sequence and the coordination requirements are increased.

Critical Paths

The addition of concurrent operations turns tasks into a number of interdependent time sequences. The result can look like a mirror maze at a carnival, and the problem is to get the product through the maze (see Figure 5–4). The advantage of concurrent operations is time, and this factor is the key to the maze. Using a **critical-path method,** the time taken to perform each subtask is recorded, and the results are plotted on a graph showing the subtasks in sequence. These are connected by lines, which represent the amount of time taken to complete all the tasks in the sequence. One can then calculate which path takes the longest time from start to finish. Any path feeding into this one that takes less time is said to have *slack* in it. This means that the schedule can slip without affecting the total amount of time required to complete the overall task. Of course, any slippage in the critical path will cause an increase in the total time required to complete the task.

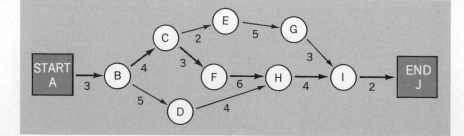

FIGURE 5–4
An example of a critical path for a project.

The circles represent events that are the ending and beginning points of activities. The arrows are activities, and the numbers represent the days expected to complete the activities. There are three possible paths in this sequence. The path with the heavy line represents the critical path because it is this sequence that will take the longest time to complete. The other two paths have "slack," that is, they do not take as long, and if activities in these paths take longer than expected, the additional days will not affect the overall time to complete the project.

Methods of Job Design

Some areas of job design, particularly work simplification and sequencing, have well-developed methods and techniques for applying concepts. Other areas are conceptual and do not have specific techniques. The methods used in job design can be classified as **description, simplification, enlargement,** and **sequencing.**

Descriptive Methods

Written descriptions of jobs serve a variety of purposes in organizations. For example, all of personnel administration (staffing, training, evaluation, and compensation) starts with a description of the job. Employees can use these descriptions as a guide for their behavior, and managers can use them to know what activities and behavior they might expect from employees.

Job Analysis. The first step in documenting a good description of a job is to analyze its various functions. **Job analysis** is a systematic method of gathering and recording information about a job. The information collected on the job varies somewhat with the purpose for which it is intended. The first step in collecting information is to delineate the tasks that make up the job.

The tasks then must be broken down into their various dimensions. This chapter has suggested ways of examining the activities, interactions, and decisions of the task, but there are a number of ways to look at tasks. For instance, the Department of Labor uses a data-people-things approach. Another popular technique is the PAQ (Position Analysis Questionnaire) developed by McCormick. This technique has six categories: information input, mediation processes, work output, interpersonal activities, work structure, and job contact. The method of obtaining this information is through a standardized questionnaire (9).

The most common way to collect information is to interview a job incumbent, the manager, or both, if possible. The interview should be structured in that questions are organized beforehand to make certain the desired information is obtained. Most job analyses of this type are done by job analysts who are concerned with describing jobs for purposes of evaluation and compensation.

Questionnaires can also be used to collect job information. The PAQ has a standardized questionnaire. Some questionnaires are in the form of a checklist, such as the Job Information Matrix System (10). Another method, multidimensional scaling, asks a large number of questions about a position and then statistically analyzes the results to obtain factors that represent the major dimensions of the job. A different approach to job analysis is the **critical incident approach. A critical incident** is any important event, which the manager (or employee) records as it occurs on the job. A record of these incidents is kept for a period of time and analyzed for significant factors (11).

Job Descriptions. The purpose of job analysis is to be able to write out a description of the job that will reflect the behavior that takes place in the performance of the work and the relevant outcomes. In practice, job descriptions can vary from a brief one-page document to a seven- to ten-page minute description of every aspect of a job. At a minimum, the job description should (1) identify the job in terms of a title and organizational location, (2) indicate the major tasks in the job and the percentage of the time spent on those tasks, and (3) state the performance requirements needed for the job.

The last of these, performance requirements, is needed primarily for staffing purposes. The section on tasks is the one that may be expanded considerably as necessary. Jobs that are standard in the society, such as machinist or mechanical engineer, and that are occupied by people who have skills obtained outside the organization, can be quite brief. Jobs that are organizationally specific require more detailed description.

Organization Charts. The ways in which jobs relate to one another can be partially illustrated on an organization chart. The **organization chart** describes the basic authority relationships that exist within the organization. It represents the result of rational thought about relationships and provides at a glance a basic understanding of where each position fits into the overall structure. For example, knowing the particular position a person plays on a football team will tell you quite a bit about the range of activities the player is likely to engage in during a game. But you would have to know much more about this particular player and the other players on both teams, as well as the different plays of each team, before you could predict the player's behavior on any particular play. So even though charts clarify some relationships, they are at best incomplete statements.

An organization chart resembles a pyramid. At the top is the chief executive officer of the organization, on the next level are those people reporting to the top manager, and so on, to the bottom of the organizational hierarchy. Each position is represented by a box that contains the position title (such as, vice-president and treasurer), the incumbent, and sometimes a brief statement of duties. Authority relationships are noted with solid lines between boxes, and other types of relationships, such as staff relationships, are indicated with dotted lines. Positions on the same organizational level are depicted on a horizontal plane. In a small organization, one organization chart will suffice, but for a large organization there are usually many, each representing one organizational unit, with the master chart showing only the major managerial positions.

Work-Simplification Methods

Methods of work simplification are among the oldest and best developed methods of job design. The scientific management movement, which started in the early part of this century, was dedicated to developing ways to make work more efficient. It focused on the development of methods that could be used to simplify jobs. Motion and time study is the most popular of these methods.

Motion and Time Study. For perhaps two major reasons, motion and time study has been used chiefly at the employee level. First, the jobs at the lower levels of the organization are primarily made up of activities, making analysis easier. Second, managers believe that their jobs are not easily subject to this type of analysis and resist such examination, and techniques for observing the decision-making process are still rudimentary.

As you may recall from Chapter 2, motion and time studies subdivide activities into fine units of basic physical movements, such as grasping, selecting, picking up, and setting down. All activities of work are completely catalogued. An analyst observes the motions in which the employee engages and records the movement and the length of time taken to perform the motion. With this information recorded, the analyst takes the information back to his or her desk and determines whether the sequence is correct and whether savings can be made by concurrent operations — for instance, by using both hands at once instead of separately. By adding together the time it takes to complete all the necessary motions, a "standard" time to perform the task can be determined. This method has been used to design jobs and to determine pay rates based on a production-incentive system.

"One Best Way." Motion and time analysis is useful for dividing the component parts of a task among a number of employees and for examining in detail the portion of the task assigned to each employee. Motion and time study tries to determine how work *should* be done. A basic premise of scientific management is that there is "one best way" to perform every operation and every job. This "one best way" can be discovered through a complete analysis of all the movements that take place in the job.

Simplicity is the key in motion and time study. The job should contain the fewest possible operations. And tasks should contain mostly activities and very few interactions or decisions. The greatest efficiency is created when every employee does exactly as he or she is told. These values, as we have seen, have created problems that limit the applicability of scientific management. For example, employee ingenuity is often bent on "beating the system" when the industrial engineer is around.

There has been considerable attack on the "one best way" concept. Studies and observation of employees indicate that there may be a number of different ways of doing a particular task, all of which are equally efficient. Using different methods at different times also reduces the boredom of the task. The "one best way" concept assumes that each situation meets the exact condition of the plan, which is a potentially dangerous assumption because even slight variations can render the plan inoperable.

**Job-Enrichment
Methods**

The idea that jobs should be enriched rather than simplified is a relatively new one, and thus the techniques for implementing job enrichment are not as well developed as are the techniques for simplification. Some of the techniques that are being used at present include **job rotation, group work assignments, job enlargement,** and **vertical loading.**

Job Rotation. The oldest and simplest way of reducing boredom on a particular task is to rotate employees among a number of tasks in a sequential fashion. Job rotation has the advantage of providing a pool of workers who know how to do a number of tasks, which may be imperative in situations in which error rates rise dramatically after a couple of hours on a single task. But job rotation does not take the boredom out of the work itself.

Group Work Assignments. A technique that uses job rotation but that includes enrichment to a greater degree is the assignment of "whole" tasks to a group of people to complete, rather than to a single individual. The group, then, is responsible for the completion of an entire unit, such as a washing machine or the body of an automobile. The tasks that need to be done have not been changed, but the group can get together and decide who is to do what and for how long. Group assignments give employees a feeling of control over their work environment and are useful where a small group can, in fact, be assigned a specified output (12).

Job Enlargement. The most obvious way to enrich a job is to increase the number of tasks that the employee is to perform. As in group work assignments, the idea is to have the person assemble or work on a major portion of a whole unit. Job enlargement is horizontal in nature; it simply adds similar tasks to the original assignment. Enlargement better engages the employee's attention because the variety of activities has increased, the sequencing of activities is now required, and the output is clearly identifiable.

Vertical Loading. Herzberg maintains that jobs must be increased in size and complexity not just horizontally (more varied activities) but vertically (more decision making) as well (13). He claims that what motivates people to do their best on a job are the factors within the job itself. Thus the motivation factors that one should focus on are achievement, recognition, skills and knowledge, responsibility, advancement, and growth. Jobs are enlarged by infusing them with the above factors.

Vertical loading means putting back into the job the responsibilities that have been taken out of jobs and placed in supervisory or staff positions. For instance, a dog-food manufacturer gave responsibility for making job assignments, scheduling coffee breaks, interviewing prospective employees, and deciding on pay raises to an entire work group rather than to an individual supervisor (14). At Volvo, teams of workers are now responsible for producing major sections of a car, including the inspection of the completed units, rather than simply performing the same discrete tasks over and over again (15).

Work-Sequencing Methods

Methods of work sequencing are both old and new. Production managers traditionally have been in the forefront of developing sequencing methods because work sequencing is a major consideration in production departments. Recently, though, with the advent of computers and highly complex research and development projects, newer forms of work sequencing have gained popularity. Two of these methods, one old and one new, will be examined here. These methods help the manager time the work sequencing, develop concurrent operations, and determine critical paths.

Gantt Charts.* A Gantt Chart is used in production to facilitate planning and control. It is a very simple chart whose horizontal axis is stated in whatever time increments (hours, days, months) are most appropriate to the production process. The vertical axis lists all the functions of the production process. In the squares at the junction of time and function, the planned time usage of functions is plotted by filling in a portion of the square. The time actually taken to complete the function is recorded in a different section of the square. The result is a record of planned and actual time taken to complete a particular production cycle. With the addition of appropriate symbols, the reasons for deviation can also be included on the chart (see Figure 5–5).

PERT. The Program Evaluation Review Technique (PERT) was developed by the United States Navy to keep track of progress in its Polaris missile program. It is a sophisticated type of production control system. PERT starts by making a list of activities required to complete a project. Each activity must have a starting and stopping point. These start and stop points are called **events**—the beginning and ending of an activity. Events are represented on a network by circles; activities are represented by lines.

The network is one of event circles tied together by activity lines. Each event is really a double event—the end of one activity and the beginning of the next. Activities are the time- and resource-consuming part of the network, and the lines also serve to indicate the sequence in which events must take place.

The most complex and difficult part of PERT is determining how

* *The Gantt Chart* by Wallace Clark was first published in the United States in 1922. H. H. Albers, in his book *Principles of Management: A Modern Approach* (New York: John Wiley, 1969), has this to say about its popularity: "This book was translated into French, Italian, Polish, Czechoslovakian, German, Spanish, Russian, and Japanese. In Russia alone 100,000 copies were printed, and according to some reports, the first 'Five-Year Plan' was completely plotted on Gantt Charts."

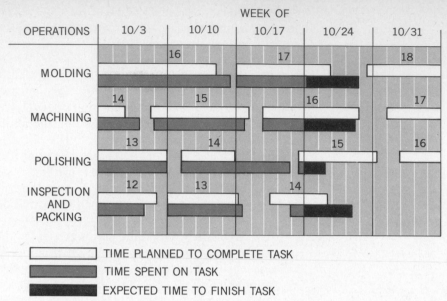

FIGURE 5–5
A Gantt chart for a
foundry organization.

TIME PLANNED TO COMPLETE TASK
TIME SPENT ON TASK
EXPECTED TIME TO FINISH TASK

In this situation, assuming this is October 24, four tasks are in process with tasks 14
and 17 taking longer than planned and one (task 15) taking less time than planned.
Number 14 is late not because of inspection but rather because polishing took considerably longer than planned.

much time activities will take. The reason for this difficulty is that the activities are typically ones that have never been done before and are themselves so complex that there is no way to know in advance how long they
will take. What is used, then, is *estimates* of time. The managers are asked
for estimates of least possible time (everything goes right), expected time,
and longest possible time (everything goes wrong). These estimates are
then treated statistically to arrive at an approximate expected time of
completion. They are then plugged into the network and a critical path
can be plotted through the network (16).

PERT has been used for projects with as few events as twenty or, in
some cases, such as the Polaris program, as many as seventy thousand.
Complex PERT networks are like organization charts in that there is a
master PERT chart containing all of the activities, and then each separate
activity has a PERT chart of its own.

Chapter Review

This chapter has described the ways that tasks are combined to form jobs
in conjunction with people's skills and abilities. The critical issue that has
been addressed is the size of the job; that is, how many tasks should be
contained in the job and how complex the activities, interactions, and

decisions of the tasks should be. The major ideas and terms covered in this chapter are listed below.

1. **Specialization** of jobs occurs because no one person has the time or the talent necessary to do all tasks.

2. **Tasks** occur when resources are acted upon by activities, interactions, and decisions directed toward some organizational goal. **Jobs** are groups of tasks that, when combined, form a unit of work for a single person.

3. Any job may be seen as requiring activities, interactions, and decisions. **Activities** are the physical and observational things people do; **interactions** are contacts with people that are made while performing work; and **decisions** are the intellectual choices that are made in regard to the work to be done.

4. Jobs vary greatly in the number of tasks they include and in the complexity of activities, interactions, and decisions required.

5. **Job simplification** means reducing the number of tasks and the complexity of the activities, interactions, and decisions of the tasks.

6. Job simplification is inevitable because of people's limited skills and time, the need for proficiency, and the organizational efficiency it creates. At the same time, simplification creates a need for coordination and encourages rigid behavior. It also results in poor use of skills and causes work to lack meaning.

7. **Job rotation** is the movement of people from one set of tasks to another; **job enlargement** involves adding more tasks to make the outcome of work a complete unit; and **job enrichment** means making the job more complex by increasing the decision-making characteristics of the tasks.

8. The sequence of jobs in a task is important. Tasks must be put in proper **time sequence** and opportunities for **concurrent operations** explored. **Critical-path methods** outline the activities (tasks), the time it takes to complete tasks, and the sequencing of tasks to determine which events must be watched most closely.

9. **Job analysis** is the activity of studying jobs for the purpose of developing a description. The tasks of a job and their activities, interactions, and decisions are recorded through interviews or questionnaires. The final product is a statement of the job called a **job description,** which contains all the above information plus a statement of needed worker qualifications. This statement is called the **job specification.**

10. **Organizational charts** are depictions of the organizational relationships of jobs in terms of an authority structure.

Discussion Questions

1. Discuss why jobs are specialized within organizations.

2. Distinguish between jobs and tasks. Give examples of each.

3. Describe the activities, interactions, and decisions of a job or task with which you are familiar.

4. What kinds of jobs would contain the most
   a. physical activities and observations?
   b. interactions?
   c. decisions?
5. Why are jobs in organizations simplified? What are the drawbacks of job simplification?
6. Distinguish between job rotation, job enlargement, and job enrichment. Give examples of each.
7. Where and under what circumstances would job enrichment be most likely to succeed?
8. What are the major considerations in work sequencing?
9. Design a work sequence for some activity, such as a party, using a Gantt chart.
10. How would you go about conducting a job analysis? Why would you conduct one?
11. What is the purpose of job descriptions?

Involvement Activity

Think of some task with which you are familiar such as planning a party, overhauling a car, constructing a fence, making a shirt, playing a sport.

Now take that task and divide it up among a number of your friends (mentally of course). Try first doing it with just a few people and then expand the exercise by dividing the task among a large number of people.

a. Into how many units can you break the overall task and still make complete units of work for which the person could identify an output?

b. How do you think the people assigned to these tasks would feel about their work at each stage?

c. What, if any, supervision would you need to provide at each stage?

d. Draw a sequence of the activities that must take place and determine the critical path.

6

Departmentation

In this chapter, the procedures for combining work assignments, which were developed in the last chapter, are explored further. We have seen how specialization develops as a result of the inability of any one person to handle all the diverse tasks of an organization. Here we will introduce the concept of departmentation, which is the combining of specialized tasks into separate work groups, or departments. Departmentation occurs because in any large organization there is more work than a single manager can oversee. Thus it becomes necessary to create a number of specialized departments, each headed by its own manager. The topics that will be considered in this chapter include: methods of departmentation, combinations of departmentation, and vertical differentiation of work.

There is no one way to arrange jobs that is inherently superior to any other way. The proper combination of jobs depends on what is best for the given situation. There are advantages and disadvantages connected to all the various forms of combination, and managers must learn to recognize the clues in each situation that indicate which particular form will be the most effective.

The ability to organize is a skill. It involves insight and foresight. The organizer must be able to look at a whole, complex situation and see its discrete parts, and he or she must then be able to visualize the best way to recombine those parts into a new and different whole.

The task of organizing begins any time after a goal has been decided upon. When a number of people are to be involved in accomplishing a goal, the first part of the task is to decide who is to do what. Much of this process has been discussed in the last two chapters on the assignment of work and job design. But organizing requires more than just breaking apart the overall task into individual jobs. Grouping tasks together into organizational units is an equally important function of organizing. This grouping procedure, called **departmentation,** may be done in many different ways, but however it is done, it must be consistent with the resources, especially the employees' skills, available to the work group.

And still the task of organizing is not complete. As seen in the last chapter, one of the demands of simplification is the need for coordination.

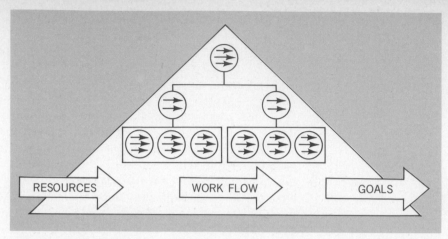

FIGURE 6–1
Departmentation
of jobs.

This figure combines work assignments by grouping related jobs into departments, each under a separate manager.

This need occurs any time there is a subdivision of work. There is little to be gained from work specialization or simplification if the output is not regrouped, coordinated, and combined into meaningful arrangements directly related to goal outcomes. This process of departmentation has been illustrated in Figure 6–1.

Methods of Departmentation

Departmentation begins at the top of the organization and is not complete until the overall organizational task is subdivided all the way downward and through the hierarchy and all the positions are included and identified. The focus is on the management structure in terms of determining the areas of work responsibility to be assigned to each departmental grouping on every level of the organization. Departmentation involves studying the combination of elements that will create the most efficient operation. As a method, departmentation is almost entirely normative; that is, it is assumed to be the correct and proper procedure. But its value has not been tested, and even the criteria it uses are debatable. Nevertheless, the underlying assumption is that the combination of like elements will create a more efficient arrangement of parts. The four major categories of like elements are: (1) the **process** or **function,** such as engineering, medicine, carpentry, stenography, statistics, accounting; (2) the major **purpose** being served, such as furnishing a product, healing people, or educating children; (3) the **persons** or **things** dealt with or served, such as veterans, Indians, forests, mines, parks, farmers; and (4) the **place** where the activities occur, such as Hawaii, Central High School, Boston, the factory.

What is being considered in departmentation is the grouping of elements at a particular level. Different organizational levels may, and usually are, combined differently. Also at one level there might be positions that utilize different categories of departmentation. Observation indicates that there are almost always different categories used from level to level. The four categories can be further condensed by combining persons, purpose, and place, all of which have similar characteristics.

**Functional
Departmentation**

Figure 6–2 is a schematic representation of departmentation by function. Each function or specific type of job is represented by the letters within the circles, with each function under the supervision of a separate manager. The work flow starts on the left of the diagram with resource inputs entering the organization and flowing from one department to another until the final product emerges on the right side of the figure.

Any one manager may have all accountants, machinists, drill-press operators, or any other such specialized grouping of individuals. **Functional departmentation** divides organizations into groups that perform a specialized function that is necessary to accomplish the overall organizational goals. The word *function* encompasses a broad category of possible tasks, including **organizational, managerial,** and **technical** functions.

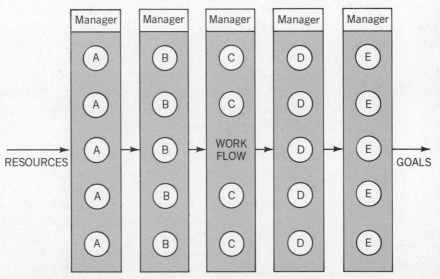

FIGURE 6–2
Departmentation
by function.

The letter symbols in the figure represent different operations. In a cabinet-making shop, for example, the *A* might represent the receiving of lumber, *B* the storing of it, and *C* its requisitioning. Cutting, gluing, and finishing operations are shown by the *D;* storage in the finished-goods warehouse is represented by *E.*

In a large organization, the receiving department, the lumber yard, the inventory-control operation, the manufacturing operation, and the product storage area each might have its own manager.

Organizational Functions. Three major functions of all organizations are to procure resources, to convert the resources into outputs through work, and to distribute the outputs in the environment. In a large business organization the procurement function is often subdivided into finance, purchasing, and personnel departments; the work function is manufacturing; and the distribution function is marketing. The importance to the firm of marketing, production, and finance is often illustrated by the presence of a vice-president of each of these functions. Governmental and service organizations are similarly organized. Hospitals, for example, have admitting and emergency areas as part of their procurement function; nursing, pediatrics, surgery, and other medical departments as their work function; and the discharging of well patients or the output of research as their distribution function.

Managerial Functions. Another approach to functional grouping is organization according to managerial activities. For example, an organization might take its list of functions from the principles of management and set up planning, organizing, resource assembling, directing, controlling, reporting, and budgeting departments. Or managers might look at some other views of managerial work and organize accordingly. The model set forth in Chapter 1, for instance, would suggest an internal–external division. In many organizations, this division is evidenced by a distinction between a department head and an associate department head.

Technical Functions. To produce a product or provide a particular service, certain technical specialties are required. A hospital requires doctors of quite a number of specialties, each of which constitutes a separate department. To build a house, skilled craftspeople in a number of different trades are required, such as carpenters, plumbers, sheet-metal workers, and so on. In a large construction company, the specialists in each trade might constitute a department.

The Advantages and Costs of Functional Departmentation. Functional departmentation is so similar to work simplification that it is subject to all of the same advantages and costs. Departmentation by function essentially takes advantage of the efficiency of specialization. In addition, it provides the individual with a straightforward and easily visible line of promotion and advancement. An accountant in an accounting department, for example, is clearly aware of the possibilities and means of advancement. Another advantage of this type of grouping is that people with common backgrounds and interests form a cohesive unit that enhances internal communication and makes control easier for management.

A study by Marquis indicated that for performing technologically complex tasks, functional departmentation created superior products (1). Other studies indicate that functional departmentation works best in stable environments. Further, it has been found that organizations with firm and stable product lines have stayed with functional departmentation — a good indication that it works (2).

One of the major costs of functional departmentation is that it goes against the work flow, as illustrated by the arrows in Figure 6–2. Because the top-level manager would be the first person concerned with the total product or service, coordination under functional departmentation must be accomplished at higher managerial levels than in other types of departmentation. Furthermore, functionally specialized groups may be interested at times in pursuing their own ends to the detriment of the overall organization. The manager who has come up the organizational hierarchy through a specialist department is uniquely unsuited to fill a position that requires a balanced view of all aspects of the organization. This narrowness of vision is compounded by the fact that functional departmentation encourages, even demands, a centralized decision-making organization. Thus, the training the manager has received is often both too narrow and too shallow for the demands of higher-level positions.

In common with other highly specialized forms of organization, functional departmentation makes coordinating more difficult. While communication and understanding is easier *within* specialized groups, it is more difficult *between* groups.

Departmentation by Product, Person, or Place

Figure 6–3 indicates an alternative method of arranging the same series of tasks as are shown in Figure 6–2. Functions are combined to form a grouping by the products produced, the people serviced, or the place where the activities occur. Members of the organizational unit are identified not by what they do, as in functional organizations, but by their relationship to a product, customer, or location. Inputs starting at the left side of the figure stay within the department as they move from operation to operation until a final product emerges from the department. Departmentation by product, person, or place does not take advantage of work specialization but combines various specialties into one organizational unit. In a sense, the top hierarchical level of organizations is structured this way.

Product or Service. Organization by product or service involves the combining of all activities geared to producing a particular output into a single unit. An example is a division of General Motors, which produces only Chevrolets. Banks are generally organized in this way. For example, such services as commercial transactions, trust accounts, and loans each make up a separate department.

Customer or Client. An essentially similar type of departmentation is organization according to client or customer. Thus, a publishing firm is departmentalized into childrens' books, fiction, popular nonfiction, textbooks, and so on. Similarly, the pediatrics ward of a hospital is a result of organization by client.

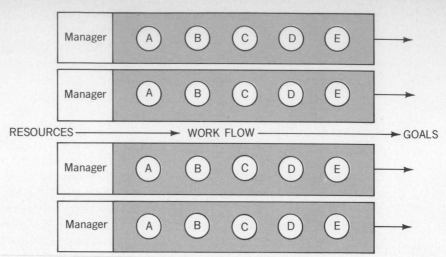

FIGURE 6-3
Departentation by product, person, or place.

In this figure, rather than having one manager for each function, there is one manager for each product, for every person associated with a product, or for each district branch of the organization. For example, a cabinet shop might be organized by the job (product) or by the customer (person). In organizing by the job, one group might process an order for a hundred bookcases, another an order for fifteen tables, and so forth, with members of the work group doing everything from receiving the lumber to storing the finished goods in the warehouse. Very small organizations are ordinarily organized in this manner because they do not have enough employees to permit specialization: everyone must do many tasks. Very large organizations with a diversified product line or with many district branches might also be organized by product, person, or place.

Physical Location. Another form of departentation is grouping according to physical location. This grouping is particularly useful to a company that maintains branch offices throughout the country or around the world. As international endeavors increase, this type of grouping will probably become even more prevalent. Merchandising organizations, such as Sears, Roebuck and Company, often use this form of departentation. A major advantage lies in the organization's ability to react locally to the conditions that exist in a particular area rather than having to make organization-wide changes to accommodate the demands of one locale.

Projects. A final form of departentation that is illustrated in Figure 6-3 is project organization, a method of grouping generally employed by firms that do scientific, construction, or engineering work. In these types of organizations, development or design is a major function, and project groupings allow all or most of the necessary specialists to be assembled under one project director, who handles the coordination of work for the project. Project members may be assigned on a permanent or temporary basis and on a full-time or part-time basis. There are many problems inherent in this type of system, but it has the advantage of providing a coordinated effort toward the solution of a particular technical problem. As product-development activity becomes more important in industry, this type of departmentation can be expected to increase in popularity.

The Advantages and Costs of Product, Person, or Place Departmentation. Product, person, or place departmentation is not work specialization in the same sense as is functional departmentation. The major purpose of departmentation by product, person, or place is to improve coordination. The need for this type of departmentation arises out of the coordination problems inherent in functional departmentation. When coordination problems become too great, managers create organizational levels designed to eliminate the causes of the problems. Indeed, the study cited earlier on the advantages of functional departmentation also noted that product-oriented organizations were associated with better records of meeting schedules and controlling costs (3).

From Figure 6–3 we can see that product, person, or place departmentation is oriented according to the flow of work and incorporates all the necessary elements to complete a task or produce a product. Decentralization of decision making to lower organizational levels is encouraged. Because all necessary tasks are combined, this grouping can be more independent and autonomous than groupings that are functionally organized.

The training of top-level managers is encouraged by this type of departmentation. The person in charge of a product or service must learn to balance many or all functional considerations, a job that only the top level can do in a functionally oriented organization. The organization then is assured of managers who have the breadth to take on top positions.

Product, person, or place departmentation provides employees with an organizational unit with which they can easily identify because there is a definable output. This is a particularly important factor if the job itself does not contain an identifiable output. And definable outputs enable management to better judge whether the job is being done.

Product, person, or place departmentation also has its costs. When there is more than one goal, there may be a struggle for the scarce resources of the total organization. Autonomous groups may and often do engage in activities detrimental to other groups in the organization. For example, a customer-oriented group may adopt the values of the customer at the expense of the organization. This phenomenon shows up particularly in salespeople and others who operate at the boundaries between the organization and the environment.

The specialist, or expert, is often subordinated and lost in this form of departmentation. And avenues for promotion are not always clear. If one is to stay within the organizational unit one must either broaden oneself and forget one's specialty or move to a functional area in the organization. But in order to transfer, one must be doing a "good job" where one is. If the specialist is the contact between functional and product groups, he or she might not be in good standing with either. Another aspect of the problem is the resistance most work groups show to utilizing "advanced methods" developed by specialists. Such help, like most advice, is usually received as criticism, and resentment builds up toward the person offering it.

Combinations of Departmentation

In organization design, there is always a compromise between the efficiency of specialization on the one hand and the need for coordination on the other. This compromise usually leads organizations to use varying forms of departmentation in different parts of the organization and at different levels.

Combinations Within and Across Organizational Levels

Within a given organizational level the structuring of departmentation is usually consistent. However, there are exceptions. An automobile manufacturer can have a basic departmentation-by-product structure and also have an international division to handle all overseas operations. This mixing of strategies within a level is usually a result of a new and expanding function or of one particularly important function that spans existing subdivisions.

Across organizational levels, changes in departmentation structuring are common and responsive to the twin needs of specialization and coordination. Thus a marketing department (departmentation by function) may be divided internally by such technical functions as market research, sales, distribution, and advertising. The sales department, in turn, is very likely to be organized by either product line or geography, and these two structures may alternate for a couple of organizational levels. Each level must be examined to see which need is dominant, specialization or coordination, in order to determine which form of departmentation will best accomplish its goal. In recent years, departmentation by product, people, or place has become more popular, reflecting an increasing complexity of organizational environments and the resultant need for coordination.

Matrix Organization

The ultimate in departmentation combinations is an overlapping of Figures 6–2 and 6–3. The result of such a combination is a **matrix organization.** This style of organization produces a hierarchy that is vertically arranged by functions and horizontally arranged by work projects. As in project organization, the project manager supervises the work of specialists assigned to the project. But here, the specialists are also functionally related to their managers in the vertical hierarchy. Thus, production employees, personnel staff, and accountants may all report to the same project manager and also report individually to the production, personnel, and accounting managers. Figure 6–4 is a schematic representation of a

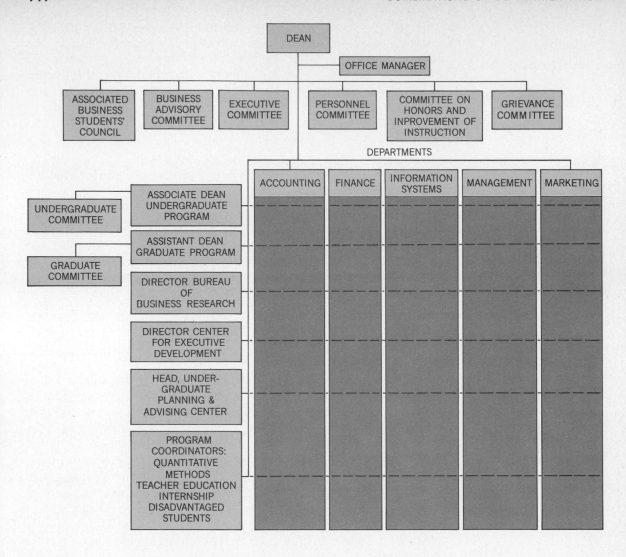

FIGURE 6–4
A school of business administration structured according to matrix organization.

school of business administration structured according to matrix organization. The heads of the departments (shown at the top of the columns) are concerned with the technical expertise of the professors in the functional areas for which they are responsible. The coordinators of programs (shown at the left of the columns) are concerned with the success of particular programs. The professors may be teaching or doing research in one or more programs in a particular specialty.

Matrix organization is a response to the increasing complexity of the environment. The defense industry pioneered this form of organization, but it is rapidly spreading to other industries. The common feature of these industries is environmental uncertainty, as reflected in the introduction of many new products and a shortening of product life.

Depart-
mentation
Within Large
Organizations

Large organizations use a number of types of departmentation in their organizational structures. The large manufacturing firms, such as General Motors or General Electric, which produce a variety of products, generally have a structure much like the following description.

At the top is a corporate staff that is organized by managerial and technical functions, such as industrial relations, legal, marketing, and finance. These are the planners for the organization. The major organizational division is by product, such as appliances, type of car, or kind of food. Within these major divisions there are either further product divisions or functional divisions by marketing, manufacturing, finance, and others. A manufacturing division is likely to be subdivided into specific plants, which may be viewed geographically or by the products being produced. Similarly, a marketing department is most likely to be subdivided by geographical regions of the country or the world.

The advantages of matrix organization are that it can combine the features of specialization and coordination and that it is designed to be temporary and flexible — two prime requisites in an uncertain environment. People can readily be moved about to where they are most needed, and whole projects can be undertaken or discontinued without disrupting the total organizational structure (4).

Matrix organization also has its costs. It looks more complex than other structures, and it is. There are often struggles for power and authority, and the project manager usually is the focal point of considerable pressure. If the project managers have the power to obtain the resources they need, the functional department heads are caught between conflicting demands for more people than they have available. If the project managers do not have this much power, then completion of projects is in jeopardy. Program managers most often do not have as much power, or at least authority, as they need, and they are forced to rely on their personal skills of persuasion and communication to get the job done (5).

Matrix organization often leads to frustration among employees, too. It is not always clear who one's boss is, which can cause conflict when the functional department head says one thing and the project manager says another. The temporary nature of the projects is another cause of frustration. Frequently people are moved to a new project just as they have settled down and become knowledgeable about the one they are working on. In general, the same frustrations that are found in organization by product, person, or place are also applicable to matrix organization.

Vertical Differentiation of Work

Work can be divided both horizontally and vertically. Horizontal division, which occurs among a number of people on the same organizational level, has been discussed in the previous section of this chapter. Vertical work specialization is the assignment of different tasks to people at different hierarchical levels. Vertical specialization suggests that people at different levels of the organization do different things. For example, the closer to the top of the hierarchy a position is located, the more it contains decision-making tasks and the less it contains physical activities. Also, externally oriented tasks become more dominant as the organizational level gets higher, suggesting that the adaptive activities of planning, controlling, and changing take on greater significance at higher levels.

Activities

Scientific management theory took the extreme position that the activities of planning and doing should be entirely separated. Thus it was believed that what is to be done, when, and how are not to be part of the employees' work: employees are only to carry out orders. All planning is to be done at the managerial levels, which also are specialized. Taylor's concepts would reduce employee discretion to a minimum, and managers would be allowed only to organize and plan—not to perform the actual work of the organization.

This idea of the separation of planning and doing is deeply embedded in American culture, more so than can be attributed to scientific management alone. In government, there has always been a similar division of labor. It is the function of the legislature to make laws and set policy; the administration is to carry out, or execute, these laws. In practice, the supposed difference between policy making and administration, or planning and doing, is very hazy. In the government sector, the executive branch interprets the law to such an extent that an entire set of administrative laws has been developed; similarly, the legislature holds hearings that are remarkably like court procedures; and the courts regularly make policy decisions.

The separation of powers in other kinds of organizations is even less distinct. In spite of scientific management, all jobs require that some activities be carried out, and even the most humble work contains an element of decision making. Despite these hazy lines, it can clearly be observed that the majority of physical activity directed toward organizational goals occurs at the bottom levels of the hierarchy.

Interactions

The interactions of low-level managers are vertical in nature. These managers respond to initiations from higher up in the organization. In turn, they initiate interaction with their subordinates. A study by Kelly describes this interaction pattern of first-level managers. He found that these managers spent approximately two-thirds of their time in interaction with others, which was consistent with the findings of almost all observational studies of managers. Of the time they spent in interaction, approximately one-third was with peers, one-quarter was with other managers, and a little less than half was with subordinates (6).

Middle managers have a wide variety of lateral relationships. They are both initiators and responders (7). Katz noted several types of administrative skills employed by managers. One of these, called human skills, he further categorized into leadership skills and group-relations skills. This latter skill is peer oriented and is most important at middle organizational levels (8).

Top-level managerial contacts are external to the organization. Mintzberg indicates that top executives maintain a network of contacts in industry and throughout the community to obtain information regarding the organization's environment. Such information enables the executive both to respond to and to initiate interactions for the benefit of the organization (9).

Decisions

A study made some years ago confirmed the fact that some decision making takes place at all hierarchical levels. One researcher examined decision making in a manufacturing plant at four hierarchical levels. Decision making was compared across levels for time perspective, degree of structure, and patterns of social relationships. It was found that at lower levels, decision making was continuous and rapid. At higher levels, it was discontinuous and leisurely. Lower-level decision making was concrete; higher-level decision making tended to be abstract and nebulous. That is, at higher managerial levels the number of concrete alternatives was lower, more search activity was necessary to find solutions to problems, and cause-and-effect relationships were hard to isolate. The study further showed that while the manager-employee interactions were similar at all levels, horizontal contacts between organizational participants were greatest at lower levels. Furthermore, the higher the level, the less personal were the contacts as evidenced by the fact that there were more notes and memos than spoken interactions (10).

Managers at lower levels need to be able to make quick decisions on immediate problems in a relatively certain environment. Managers at higher organizational levels need to be able to make decisions after deliberation on long-term programs in a relatively uncertain environment. The situations are sufficiently different to question whether the same skills are required of low- and high-level managers.

Differences Among Organizational Levels

Pfiffner and Sherwood described in more detail the distinctions between organizational levels. Following is a summary of their report (11).

First-Level Managers. The first levels of management are concerned chiefly with the work flow through their part of the organization. Thus, first-level managers are (1) involved in day-to-day operations almost exclusively; (2) concerned with coordination in the sense of finding immediate solutions to operating problems; (3) operating within a short time span; (4) subject to influence from outside the unit; and (5) concerned with making primarily concrete, immediate, and highly personal contacts with employees. These managers are truly "people in the middle" inasmuch as they must integrate organizational and personal needs.

Middle Managers. The middle range of management consists of a broad spectrum of positions that require coordination of the efforts of lower levels. To this end, these managers act as channels through which the policies of higher levels are focused on specific tasks and objectives. Middle managers (1) are involved in day-to-day operations; (2) experience coordination as both a major purpose and a major problem; (3) have an intermediate time perspective; (4) experience constraints imposed both by higher-level managers and by company policies and procedures, which require that operations be in phase with those of other units; and (5) make decisions that are less concrete, detailed, and structured than those of first-level managers, but that are not yet abstract or unstructured.

Division-Level Managers. The next higher level of managers are (1) primarily concerned with a particular function or product; (2) heavily involved with integrating their primary task with other parts of the organization and with the environment; (3) able to deal with longer time perspectives, often as long as ten years; (4) operating under general rather than specific constraints; and (5) dealing with rather abstract and discontinuous decision-making patterns but with the help of some guidelines and structure.

Top Managers. Top managers are concerned with (1) the relationship of the organization to its environment; (2) the organization as a whole; (3) the need to integrate and coordinate internal operations with the external environment; (4) decision making over a long span of years; and (5) abstract and discontinuous decision making with few guidelines and little structure.

Board of Directors. The function of a board of directors is to direct and review the work of top management. It exhibits the features of (1) trusteeship, representing the viewpoint of stockholders or the general public; (2) external orientation, in that it views the organization as a whole; (3) policy making in terms of acting as the legislature for the organization; (4) concern with long time spans, possibly exceeding twenty-five years; (5) awareness of constraints imposed by the environment, whether legal or societal; and (6) uncertain decision making with few guidelines and little structure.

Implications. The important point in this discussion of differences between organizational levels is that work changes in kind as well as in complexity as one moves up the organizational hierarchy. It is not a case of more of the same but rather a case of something different at each higher level. The implications of this difference in kind are numerous and only a couple will be examined.

A major difference is that of viewpoint and focus of activity. It is very difficult for managers who have been thinking about long-term planning to

| The Catch-22 of Management Development | The differences between hierarchical levels of the organization require that managers exhibit different types of behavior as they move upward in the organization. Furthermore, the selection standards are different at succeeding levels. At the bottom of the organizational hierarchy the emphasis is on dependable behavior and on the ability to deal with immediate problems. The opposite characteristics are required at the top of the hierarchy; that is, the abilities to deal with long-range problems and to be creative and innovative. Thus, if you show your top-management propensities while at the bottom of the organization you will be ineffective and never reach the top. But if you are a good bottom-level manager there is no evidence that you have top-management abilities and you will fail to be promoted.

Obviously some people do get through the maze. But often it must be done by playing some rather frustrating games. |
| --- | --- |

suddenly reorient themselves when confronted with an employee who comes in with an immediate problem. First-line supervisors complain about a lack of interest in their problems on the part of department-level managers. Department-level managers in turn express the view that it is very difficult to respond to what first-level managers "think is important" when they have just gotten off the phone with a representative of the state capital or the regional office regarding problems of a much broader scope. In large part, the problem is an inability to "shift gears" as rapidly as is required.

Another broad implication of these differences has to do with promotion. If the demands of different organizational levels are different in kind, then the best person to promote is not necessarily the person performing the best job at a lower managerial level. A first-level manager may be very good at dealing with immediate problems but have considerable difficulty planning long-term operations that are a function of middle management. Promoting this manager, who might continue doing what he or she does best, would result in a gap in planning as well as a group of first-level managers whose jobs are usurped by the new middle manager. This mispromotion phenomenon has become popularly known as the Peter Principle (12).

Organization Design — An Illustration and Exercise

Organization design often changes over time and, in particular, with the growth of a firm. It is therefore instructive to investigate how such changes might take place with the growth of one organization. Imagine a small shoe store (the Fashion Shoe Store) located in a downtown shopping area of a fairly large (and growing) city. The organization chart of the Fashion Shoe Store at this stage is extremely simple. The chart is

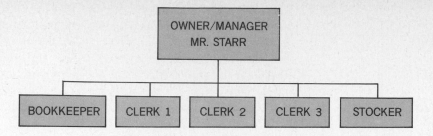

FIGURE 6–5
Fashion Shoe Store,
stage 1.

represented in Figure 6–5. The owner/manager does all managing, including performance of such critical functions as marketing, finance, and personnel. He is also the buyer and an occasional clerk, spending much time on the floor attending to customers. His employees are differentiated by function, but not by a great deal because everyone must help out at whatever task needs doing at any particular time.

Mr. Starr, the owner/manager of the store, is an expert in women's shoes. And although he runs a fairly successful operation, he has begun to notice that women often ask whether he carries children's shoes and that there are a lot of men walking by the store. Mr. Starr decides to expand his line to include children's and men's shoes.

1. What alternative forms of departmentation are now available to Mr. Starr?
2. How might he proceed to engage in work specialization?
3. What will happen to the clerks and the bookkeeper shown in Figure 6–5?
4. What will Mr. Starr be doing now?

Mr. Starr decides to set up a number of departments by type of shoe sold, with each department headed by an expert in the product area. The organization chart now looks like the one illustrated in Figure 6–6. Differentiation is by customer and product type. Although the chart does not

FIGURE 6–6
Fashion Shoe Store,
stage 2.

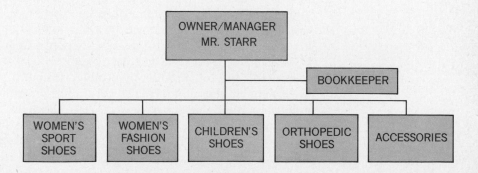

show the succeeding hierarchical level, it would have the same clerks and stocker as the stage 1 illustration in Figure 6–5. Actually there is an interesting choice at this level. The clerks could be assigned to each specialty area thereby increasing their expertise and improving service, or they could be left under Mr. Starr and allocated as needed to the specialty areas. This latter has the advantage of reducing the probability of clerks standing around in one department while customers are left unattended in another department.

Note the appendage as the bookkeeper moves into a staff position. At this stage, Mr. Starr has relinquished any purchasing chores to the departmental experts and spends his time on marketing, finance, and personnel. Although he finds his job challenging, he misses the opportunities he once had to sell to the customers and he has a feeling of being away from the action.

We are now going to make a rather large jump (one that was rather traumatic for the Fashion Shoe Store and for Mr. Starr). The changes we will note occurred as a result of dramatic changes in the environment. As with many cities, action began to move away from the downtown area. Shopping centers started to spring up in the suburbs, and Mr. Starr looked around for new business opportunities. The result was a chain of stores in several suburban locations.

In order to obtain the needed capital to finance these stores, Mr. Starr incorporated Fashion Shoe Stores and sold stock to the public.

1. What do you think the organization chart should look like now?
2. What should the major form of departmentation be?
3. What would you do with experts in each type of shoe?
4. What will happen to the bookkeeper? What about other organizational functions?
5. What will Mr. Starr do now?
6. What problems do you think Mr. Starr encountered along the way?

When the number of stores increased to twenty, the organization chart looked like the one depicted in Figure 6–7. Now organization is by location. Only some of the stores are represented in this figure, but each one looks internally much like the store in Figure 6–6. There are some differences because the demands from different locations vary, making some departments irrelevant. So the organization now has two major levels; one organized by function and one by geographical area in which the store is located. The organization-by-product structure still exists under the buyers at both the central office level and the individual store level. A few other important changes have occurred. There are now vice-presidents for finance, marketing, and personnel, and there is a board of directors to whom Mr. Starr reports (although he is also chairman of the board).

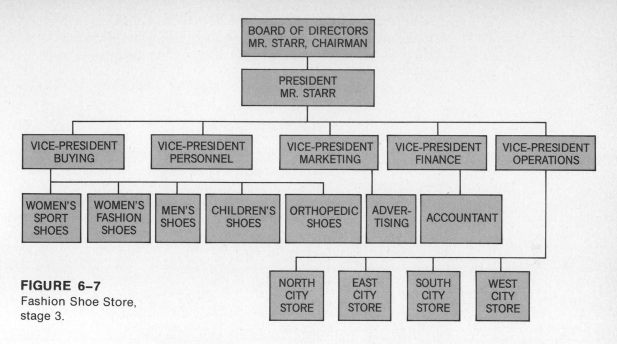

FIGURE 6–7
Fashion Shoe Store,
stage 3.

Although the organization is running well now, there was a time when there were some problems. When the suburban stores were first established they resembled Figure 6–5, not Figure 6–6, except for the downtown store, which had already progressed to stage 2. And because there was not yet a vice-president of operations, each store manager reported directly to Mr. Starr. The problems arose from two areas. First, as the number of stores increased, Mr. Starr could not look after them all, and some were badly mismanaged before he was aware of the problems. Second, the buyers all had influence over the store managers. Each store carried only what was decided upon by the downtown buyer. Again, losses occurred, this time because the downtown buyer did not understand local suburban demands. This led to tremendous frustration (and turnover) among store managers. Conditions improved once store managers were given more autonomy and local buyers were hired. But these buyers find themselves even today caught between the demands of the store managers and those of the vice-president in charge of buying.

Meanwhile, what is Mr. Starr doing now that he has delegated all the functions he originally performed? His primary job is that of coordinating between the functional specialists and the stores. He also must spend a large proportion of his time dealing with people outside the organization. There are industry people, government officials, investors, and many others that he sees and talks to regularly. But the task he finds most exciting and most frustrating is planning where the organization is going to go in the future.

1. In what possible ways could the Fashion Shoe Stores expand now?
2. What effects would your planned expansions have on the organization chart? On Mr. Starr's job?

This illustration could continue considerably further. One sequence might have Mr. Starr, Jr., who takes over from his father, diversifying the organization by buying out apparel shops, hardware stores, and other shops located in the various shopping centers. He also may integrate backward by purchasing firms that manufacture shoes. Whichever way you care to pursue the expansion, it is clear that organizations change. Their base of specialization, their organizational departmentation, and their methods for designing jobs all evolve in ways that accommodate current prevailing conditions in the environment.

Chapter Review

This chapter has extended the discussion of how work is organized by exploring the ways in which jobs are combined into organizational units under a specific manager. This is the process of departmentation. The two basic methods of departmentation are by function and by person, product, or place. The former has the advantage of specialization whereas the latter has better coordination. The proper type of departmentation for any organization will depend on the particular needs and circumstances of that organization. Each method has its own advantages and drawbacks that need to be weighed in terms of the requirements of the organization. The major ideas and terms developed in this chapter are outlined below.

1. **Organizing** as a managerial activity consists of:
    a. **subdividing** goals into work assignments.
    b. **combining** work assignments into jobs and jobs into departments.
    c. **coordinating** the specialized activities created by the processes of subdividing and combining.
2. **Departmentation** is the combination of jobs on the basis of like elements.
3. **Functional departmentation** is the combining of jobs that are similar in terms of the activities or skills they require. It is done on the basis of organizational, managerial, or technical functions.
4. **Departmentation by product, person, or place** combines jobs on the basis of organizational output, customers, or physical location.
5. Every organizational level usually has a dominant form of departmentation.
6. A **matrix organization** is one that has a functional hierarchy as well

as a horizontal organization by project. In this system, people report to both a functional manager and a project coordinator.

7. Work at succeeding organizational levels differs in nature as well as in quantity.

a. Activities are carried out mainly at the lower organizational levels, and decisions become more important at higher levels.

b. Interactions are primarily vertical at the lower levels, horizontal at middle levels, and externally oriented at the highest level.

8. Decisions are immediate, continuous, and certain at low levels and proceed to long-term, discontinuous, and uncertain at the top levels.

Discussion Questions

1. Describe the managerial activities involved in organizing.

2. Consider several organizations with which you are familiar. Describe and discuss their bases of departmentation. Do they experience the advantages and drawbacks discussed in the text? In what ways? Do you think they are organized in the best way for the type of work they do? What suggestions would you make to their managers?

3. What is functional departmentation? Under what circumstances would you use this form of organizing?

4. What do you think would be the major form of departmentation in the following organizations? Why?

a. An international company operating in twenty-five countries with a limited product line.

b. An engineering-design organization that designs large projects, such as oil fields or airports.

c. A medium-sized manufacturing company with a single major product.

d. A large consumer-products organization selling throughout the United States.

5. What is the advantage to the public of different forms of departmentation?

6. Why organize by product, person, or place?

7. In terms of the concepts discussed in this chapter, describe the ways in which a job would change as an employee moved from the position of first-line manager to chief executive of a corporation.

Involvement Activity

All organizations of any size have departments. The titles and activities of these departments depend upon the goals of the particular organization. For each of the following organizations see if you can figure out what departments there would be:

a. A local television station.
b. A local branch bank.
c. A grocery store.
d. A hospital.

1. What form of departmentation are the units you have described?

2. Can you think of an alternative way to structure these organizations? Which form would work better? Why?

7

Coordination of Work

With this chapter we will complete our discussion of how separate organizational tasks are transformed into a structured, well-functioning whole, as represented by an organization chart. Once jobs have been grouped into departments (as seen in the previous chapter), the management hierarchy can be designed and coordinated. The methods by which work is coordinated and fit into the organization structure is the subject of this chapter. The specific topics to be covered include: methods of achieving coordination; vertical coordination in the management hierarchy through chain of command, authority, unity of command, and span of control; horizontal coordination in the management hierarchy through coordinative positions and staff-and-line positions; and variations in the management hierarchy through decentralization.

When the work of an organization is divided and assigned to specialized subunits, the inputs and outputs of these subunits must mesh. The synchronization of input and output activities within subunits is called **coordination.** If the methods of work assignment, job design, and departmentation, described in the last three chapters, were completely developed and perfectly carried out, and if the effects of resources, which will be discussed in Part 3, could be ignored or held constant, then the process of managing would be reduced to the tasks of setting goals, assigning work, and organizing. We would then have a perfectly designed organization. Each part would mesh exactly with all other parts, necessitating little further work for managers. In reality, of course, no such perfect organization can exist. Not only is the ability to organize far from perfect, but also organizations, resources, and environments are dynamic and not static. This constant process of change and adaptation makes coordination a major managerial task.

As a managerial activity, coordination involves (1) integrating the organization with the environment and (2) integrating organizational subunits so that outputs consistently move toward the accomplishment of organizational goals. The work activities, interactions, and decisions of people must also be made to fit with one another and with the nonhuman elements of technology and work flow. Coordination must occur between: organizations; organizational subunits; people performing different work; and people, technology, organizations, and environments. Coordination, then, occurs on both vertical and horizontal levels and across a wide spectrum of the work milieu.

Circumstances dictate the type and extent of coordination required, with the **degree of interdependence** being the primary factor. For instance, a department made up of subunits in which the output of one is the input of the other will require close coordination. Thus, coordination between production and sales departments is likely to be more in evidence than it is between production and finance departments.

Because coordination activities are expensive, they usually are implemented only when necessary. Too little coordination can result in situations ranging from an overlap of work to work that is not assigned to anyone. Too much coordination can result in enormous costs and severe morale problems. Figure 7–1 shows how coordination begins to be achieved through the organizational hierarchy.

Achieving Coordination

Coordination is not a single activity. It is achieved through a number of sources and is applied through a variety of techniques. Those we will consider here include **cultural conditioning, social interaction, managerial activity,** and the **organizational hierarchy.**

Cultural Conditioning

The most apparent, and often least considered, source of achieving coordination is cultural conditioning, or socialization. People grow up in association with others, in both formal and informal situations. They learn how to react toward others, how others are expected to act toward them, and what to expect from organizational associations. And as long as the individual's expectations are consistent with organizational requirements, no particular coordination effort is needed. Thus, to some extent coordination may be considered internal to the individual. Barnard and Simon stated that this internal coordination or socialization leads to a **zone of indifference** or **zone of acceptance** in the individual. This means that there is a range of actions that employees will perform without question or thought because the requests are both expected and acceptable (1).

McGregor agrees, saying that there is an **implicit contract** or **agreement** between the organization and the individual. The employee agrees to perform certain activities and give a certain amount of time in return for certain rewards—monetary and otherwise. And as long as the

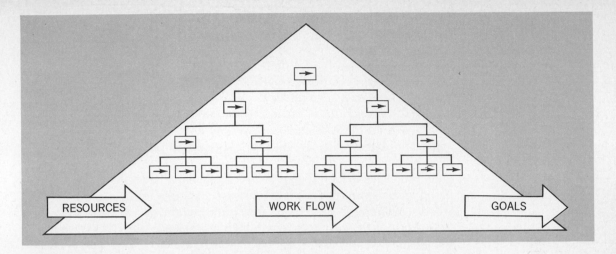

FIGURE 7–1
An organization chart. This figure now closely resembles the illustration of an organization in Chapter 1. All the jobs have been grouped together into departments, and the departments have been connected in a hierarchy to ensure the coordination of activities toward goal accomplishment.

required activities are within the employee's capability and are consistent with the agreement, they will be carried out (2). Thus a stockroom clerk orders the supplies and keeps an inventory. He or she might also change burned-out light bulbs, if asked. But if the manager asks the clerk to come in and paint the building on Sunday, he or she will probably not do it, unless the person's zone of acceptance is particularly wide.

The culturally learned characteristics of the individuals in an organization can make coordination either easy or difficult depending on the fit between the organization and its cultural surroundings. Problems occur when managers and employees have considerably different cultural backgrounds. American managers of companies with branches in foreign countries quickly become attuned to the differences in expectation that native-born employees have toward management, organization, and work. In our own country, particular groups within society, such as the underprivileged or the highly educated, also require special consideration (3).

Social Interaction

Another implicit source of achieving coordination is through social pressure on the job. Many interactions among employees that seem to be social are actually attempts to coordinate their work. Because organizations rarely provide formal descriptions of how employees are to gear their activities to fit in with those of others, workers often develop their own means for doing so. The assumption typically made by management is that employees will carry out their work without regard for the effect of their labors on others. (Individual incentive systems in organizations are representative of this assumption.) But people generally are not so individually oriented. They tend to seek out informal relationships in order to get the work done, although these informal relationships usually extend considerably beyond interest in the work alone. This area of coordination is considered more closely in the discussion on groups in Chapter 10.

Activity *within* organizations resembles the level of activities that take place *between* organizations. As seen in Chapter 1, organizations engage in exchange relations; so also do people and subunits within organizations. These exchange relations are much looser arrangements than the economic transactions of organizations, but they are just as real and necessary. Again, these relations are simply not included in most work assignments, but employees quickly learn that to get the work done they need to engage in reciprocity. For instance, campus bookstores often grant privileges to faculty that are not available to students. The reason is based on reciprocity. Teachers must assign books for classes, and bookstores need to be given book requests considerably in advance of the start of the term if they are to regulate their work load. The bookstore needs the cooperation of faculty members, and they know that they are more likely to receive such cooperation if they offer the teachers special privileges (4).

Managerial Activity   Managers constitute a major tool for the purpose of coordinating work. They engage in a number of specific activities that are especially designed for this purpose. For instance, they can directly intervene to ensure coordination takes place. (These and other managerial activities are the topics of Part 4 of this book.)

WHAT WE NEED IS A LITTLE ORGANIZATION AROUND HERE!

The Managerial Hierarchy

A final form of coordination, the managerial hierarchy, is similar to cultural conditioning and social interaction in that it is more implicit than explicit; that is, the manager does not confront employees and take action. But management does plan working relationships, which implies that coordination of work through the managerial hierarchy is much more conscious than is socialization. The organization structure, particularly the managerial hierarchy, can be specifically designed to improve the chance of good coordination. These design considerations involve the vertical flow of information, both up and down the hierarchy, and the horizontal relations that are established across the organization. The underlying assumption is that if prescribed methods or principles are followed, then coordination of effort will follow as a matter of course.

All organization theory deals with both work specialization and the attendant problem of coordination. The remainder of this chapter will consider some of the structural recommendations proposed by organization theorists, define the techniques employed, and examine the effects of certain determinants. The techniques are divided into those that aid in the determination of the vertical nature of the managerial hierarchy and those that affect the horizontal nature of the hierarchy. A final section of the chapter will be concerned with a contemporary issue that touches upon the problem of coordination in large, complex organizations: the problem of decentralization of decision making.

Vertical Coordination

Work flows across an organization, essentially across the bottom levels of its hierarchy, through a number of subunits and people. Between these bottom levels and the top, where there is just a single person or a small group of people, reside a series of positions to be arranged in an optimum manner for accomplishing the organization's work. One aspect of the arranging of positions has already been considered — the grouping of positions into organizational units (departmentation). This section focuses on the arrangement of vertical relationships for the purpose of transmitting communications for directing the organization's work.

Chain of Command

In any large organization there are a number of managerial levels. There flows through these levels a chain of reporting relationships — the **chain of command.** The line running vertically through the organization chart in Figure 7–2 illustrates the direction of this chain of command. A **reporting relationship** is the connection between two or more people that is established for purposes of accountability for one's work. Who is accountable to whom can be determined by starting at the bottom of the chain of command and following it upward.

An extreme interpretation of the chain of command would allow interaction to take place only within the established reporting relationships.

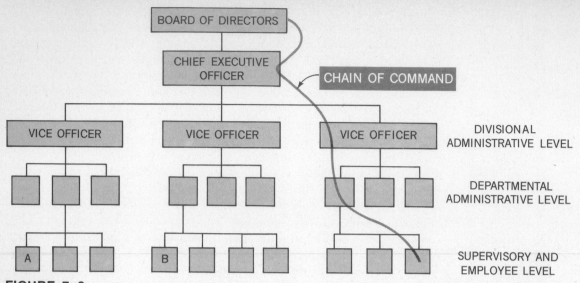

FIGURE 7–2
An organization chart showing the chain of command.

But this extreme is obviously impossible and inefficient. Work-flow relations must be maintained, and many problems are not sufficiently serious to warrant "going through channels." For instance, any problem between A and B at the supervisory level in Figure 7–2 would have to go to the chief executive's office and involve seven people if A and B could not simply talk to each other. Horizontal, or lateral, interaction is clearly a necessity unless the problem is of considerable magnitude.

On the other hand, neither the upward nor downward function of the chain of command can be entirely ignored. "Going over the manager's head" is usually viewed as a serious action by employees and implies a problem with the immediate supervisor. At a minimum, the communication channels are severed and important information may not reach the necessary level. The same is true in by-passing managerial levels from the top down. An upper-level manager, such as a division manager, who goes directly to a first-level manager, causes the lower levels to question the competency of the department manager. In turn, the department manager is left in the dark about matters that are directly his or her concern.

Lateral contacts may initiate similar problems. Upper levels of management, say the managers of the production and sales departments, may get together to work out a particular problem. Their solutions may prove satisfactory for their own departments, but may have a negative impact on the finance department.

Authority

Authority is the glue that holds together the chain of command. Although there are many power bases for people in organizations, such as money and recognition, perhaps the most forceful is the knowledge that the higher one is in the chain of command, the more readily are one's decisions accepted. Thus, the closer to the top of the hierarchy, the greater the expectation that one's commands will be obeyed. It is because this power of authority is so widely accepted in society that workers obey managers, motorists stop when they are signaled to by a police officer, and students turn in assignments more or less on time. In each case, the person who obeys a command does so because he or she recognizes and accepts the authority figure's right to direct certain behavior.

Definition of Authority. There are many definitions of the word *authority*. The meaning ascribed to it in this book is very narrow, even among management theorists. However, it is consistent with the definition of one group of theorists and useful for the purposes of this discussion. Authority is an institutional or legal right to influence, or attempt to

Climbing the Corporate Stairway

There would be no way to mistake your position in the organizational hierarchy if you happened to be employed by this West German insurance firm. Each story of the building represents a progressively higher standing in the company, from typists and clerks, who occupy the ground floor, all the way up to the top, where the firm's president sits alone on the twelfth floor. According to Heinz G. Kramberg, the company president, the unusual design of the building is meant to "encourage ambition and provide a visual image of [the] organizational structure."

What do *you* think of this idea?

Courtesy of Lufthansa German Airlines.

influence, the behavior of individuals or groups in a goal-oriented direction. Authority is essentially an organizational concept as opposed to a personal concept because it is the position or role the individual occupies, not the individual personally, that carries the authority. In other words, if the role occupant were to leave, the next person to occupy the position would assume that authority: "The King is dead, long live the King." Not all bases of influence stay with the roles, however. Expertise, for example, which carries its own power, strictly follows the individual. (A discussion of the full range of influence and power is reserved for Chapter 16.)

Acceptance of Authority. Barnard pointed out that authority is only useful if it is accepted. Thus, looked at from the bottom of the hierarchy up, the base of authority lies in its acceptance by those upon whom it is imposed. It can be said, then, that authority is an accepted right as well as an institutionally based right. Employees do not question every order because of their culturally conditioned notions of what is acceptable, as discussed earlier. But clearly, this bottom-up view of authority accentuates the fact that it works only when it is exercised within the acceptable limits of the cultural environment in which it is tried. Note, however, that neither the organization nor the individual manager is a passive agent willing to agree on whatever the employee judges to be an "acceptable" exercise of authority. The individual's zone of acceptance may be either too wide or too narrow to suit the needs of the organization. Organizations are able to shape employees' acceptance levels by offering or withdrawing rewards. In this sense, certain organizations that are lacking in rewards, such as volunteer agencies, are unable to create wide zones of acceptance. An important part of the work of all managers is keeping the zone of acceptance wide enough that organizational work can be accomplished (5).

Up to this point, authority appears to be a very satisfactory device for creating coordination. The use of authority certainly contributes to, and is supported by, all of the bases of coordination touched upon earlier in this chapter. It is a simple, easily understood technique that is built in to the chain of command. But despite all its advantages and usability, authority creates considerable argument. The argument is not, however, a question of kind but of degree.

Uses and Limitations of Authority. As we have seen, the use of authority as a means to ensure coordination is supported by the socialization process that conditions the acceptance of authority as a legitimate method of influence. This is not to say that authority is an all-powerful or even a useful method in all circumstances. To a certain extent, authority, conceived as hierarchical, is antiequalitarian and undemocratic. It is generally a fact, for example, that rich people have more authoritative power than poor people; and that individuals exercise authoritative power for self-serving purposes. Too, a particularly strong power conflict exists between hierarchically ascribed authority and the authority derived through power of expertise. This conflict grows stronger as the managerial job is further specialized and the organizational environment becomes more complex (6).

Managers tend to rely on their authoritative power too frequently simply because it is so easy to use and so readily available as a means of ensuring compliance. It is so much easier, for instance, to say, "because that's the way I want it done," than to offer a descriptive explanation of why one way is better than another. Also, managers tend to internalize the goals and values of the organization more strongly than do other employees. As a result, they often view their use of authority as being more legitimate than do their subordinates. This difference of opinion regarding the validity of one's authority shows up, in extreme instances, in an outburst of righteous indignation when one's authority is challenged or in vigorous arguments about "management prerogatives" at the collective bargaining table. The conflict lies with the individuals' perceptions as to the utility of authority and to what extent its use is necessary to achieve coordination.

The overreliance on authority is an example of the overemphasis placed on the chain of command. At the same time, excessive adherence to the chain of command is considered **authoritarian.** Both have the same effect: a reliance upon rigid forms of behavior even when they are inappropriate. Authoritarianism can be viewed both as characteristic of roles and as a characteristic of the personality of the individual.

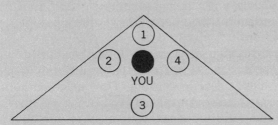

You are the manager in the middle. The other circles represent some of the other managers in the organization. Over which managers would you expect to exercise authority? Who would exercise authority over you?

Chances are you said that Manager 1 exercises authority over you, and you exercise authority over Manager 3. This is an almost universal view of authority as perceived in Western societies. People in powerful positions are equated with height or elevation. Even God is "up there."

But there is another possible view of authority. Some American Indian tribes view their gods as residing in the four corners of the world and thus on the same elevation with humans. What problems in developing an organizational structure might an Anglo-American or European encounter in societies with this view of authority?

Note that Managers 2 and 4 above are on a parallel level with you. Even if you do not have authority over them nor they over you, all three of you must interact to accomplish your work. So, even in organizations with vertical authority structures, some horizontal relationships exist that have the possibility of developing authoritative characteristics.

Source: Walter B. Miller, "Two Concepts of Authority," in Harold J. Leavitt and Louis R. Pondy, *Readings in Managerial Psychology* (Chicago: University of Chicago Press, 1964), pp. 576–577.

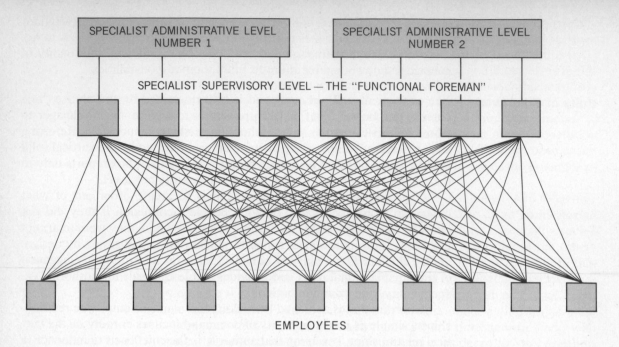

EMPLOYEES

FIGURE 7-3

A sample of an organizational structure based exclusively on managerial expertise: a functional or staff system of organization.

quate to explain or control all the behavior in organizations. Observational studies indicate that managers spend a majority of their time dealing with horizontal interactions connected with work flow (13). Sayles has commented that these lateral relationships are the most neglected areas in the study of management. Because unity of command is unable to include lateral relationships, and to the extent that these relationships are important in a given organization, the concept is inadequate (14). Kahn and his colleagues have also noted that rigid or authoritarian personalities rely greatly on such simplifying concepts as unity of command, and to the degree that they are able to freely use it, they impede essential lateral relationships within the organization (15).

In summary, unity of command is intended to assist coordination by reducing an employee's vertical relationships to a minimum. Although it appears to have great "face" validity, and it surely is one of the most accepted ideas in management, unity of command is subject to some valid criticisms. Organizations simply do not and cannot operate totally in the manner prescribed by unity of command.

Span of Control

Again referring to Figure 7-2, it can be seen that while each box reports upward to only one other box, looking downward, all boxes have a number of other boxes reporting to them. The number of people reporting to any one manager (box), then represents the person's **span of control**, a concept introduced in Chapter 2. This structure creates a means whereby managers can coordinate the work of their employees by limiting the number of their own interactions. Because no manager has unlimited time or ability, he or she can effectively manage only a limited number of interactions at the same time. Thus, the span of control addresses the issue of how many employees a manager can efficiently direct.

Through mathematical calculations, it can be shown that as the number of employees increases in arithmetic progression, the number of possible relationships increases geometrically. The following formula shows how this equation works:

$$C = N \left(\frac{2^N}{2} + N - 1 \right)$$

where C' is the span of control and N is the number of employees. The substitution of a few different numbers for N shows that the number of relationships does indeed rise dramatically. For instance, when $N = 3$, the span of control is 18, for 5 it is 100, and for 10 it is 5,210. Therefore, if coordination is to be achieved, one needs to limit the number of employees under each manager's control to some minimal number.

Management theorists have prescribed specific numbers, or ranges of numbers, of people that constitute an optimum span of control. Davis suggested three to nine for top-level managers and up to thirty for first-level managers (16). Urwick suggested four for executives and eight to twelve for lower-level managers (17). Both these suggestions assume that the work of employees interlocks in such a way that all possible relationships need direction.

But observation does not support these prescriptions. Woodward notes that the span of control for lower-level managers ranges from twenty-three to fifty in successful organizations, depending on the technology utilized (18). Worthy showed that wide spans of control, exceeding twenty, were successful for Sears, Roebuck and Company and was one of the factors responsible for an improved level of employee satisfaction (19).

Evaluation of the Span of Control. This discrepancy between prescription and practice indicates that the situation is more complex than the mathematical formula given above allows. Following are a number of other considerations that need to be taken into account when deciding upon an optimum span of control for a given situation.

1. *Interlocking Work.* Although management theorists correctly emphasize the interlocking characteristics of organizational work, it is unlikely that all work can interlock in such a way that every possible permutation must be accounted for. In addition, the assumption that the manager must direct every interaction between employees can be challenged. It is possible that any one manager can successfully supervise a large number of employees whose work is related but independent, such as a group of salespeople.

2. *Outside Interactions.* On the other hand, managers may have to direct activities that are not under their immediate command. Among the most important relationships that managers must maintain are those with peers in other departments, with their employees, with higher-level managers outside the chain of command, and with representatives from the outside environment. Since managers are, in effect, connections between the work group, the organization, and the environment, the span of control inadequately deals with all required interactions by focusing only on interactions with employees. The desirable number of employees may be as few as two if "outside" interactions are many and critical.

3. *Employee-Manager Relations.* The nature and strength of the relationship between managers and their employees is important in determining the optimum span of control. The manager's attitude toward subordinates will materially affect the intensity and the amount of direction and control needed. A manager who wishes to see only "the results" can probably manage more employees than one who insists on directing each stage of the task. The attitude of employees is equally important. For instance, highly trained employees can be left much more on their own than can employees who are being trained or who do not wish to accept responsibility.

4. *The Work Group.* The nature of the work group also influences the determination of the span of control. For instance, if the goals of peers within the work group are consistent with organizational goals, the manager can allow the group to exercise control over individuals through its norms and sanctions. If group goals are incongruent with organizational goals, the manager must spend a great deal of time working with and controlling the group and the individual relationships within it.

5. *Technology.* The type and amount of technology used will affect the span of control. As Woodward points out, the optimum span of control is considerably different for different technological situations. For instance, in process industries (such as oil refineries) where control is extremely important because the operations run continuously, the optimum span of control is very small. Other technological innovations, like assembly lines, for instance, often serve to replace managerial control, making wider spans of control possible (20).

6. *Job Design and Departmentation.* The organizational structure itself is another major determinant of span of control. As seen in the last two chapters, the way in which work is organized to a great extent determines the amount of coordination needed. The more interrelated the work, the greater the possible number of interactions required to accomplish the task. Thus, the span of control will be narrow. In addition, the more a group's work interrelates with other parts of the organization, the

more time the manager must spend dealing with these other groups and the less time he or she has for the immediate group. Again, the span of control must be narrow.

In summary, it may be said that although there is a limit to the number of interactions a manager can handle successfully, no set number of employees can be specified as optimum. To determine how many people a given manager should directly manage, it is necessary to have considerable knowledge of the capacity of the manager, the interaction pattern among the employees, the need to directly control interactions, and the number and intensity of interactions that the manager must maintain outside his or her own direct command. Studies have shown that most managers are responsible for more than the suggested optimum number of employees, indicating that the situation is more complex than the concept of span of control proposes. Further support for the idea that outside relationships limit the span of control is provided by studies showing that the span of control narrows at higher organizational levels where outside contacts become most important.

Varying the Span of Control. The span of control is not necessarily a passive or static feature. Managers can consciously vary the span of control and thereby affect other organizational conditions. The most obvious effect of the relationship between span of control and organization structure is the span of control's influence on the managerial hierarchy. If spans of control are small, the managerial levels within the hierarchy will be many; thus, the pyramid will be tall and narrow. A broad span of control will create a flat, wide pyramid. The shape of the hierarchy, either tall and narrow or short and wide, in turn affects communication. A short, wide hierarchy means information travels faster because there are fewer levels to traverse.

The span of control can be used by the organization to enforce preferred methods of managing. For example, a wide span of control literally forces managers to delegate responsibility and employees to accept it. Managers simply are unable to take charge of everything within their broad range. By delegating some of their responsibilities, managers' jobs are made easier and employees' jobs are enlarged.

Horizontal Coordination

The function of vertical coordination is to translate external environmental requirements into organizational activity and then to integrate this activity with overall organizational goals. The function of horizontal coordination is to integrate the work flow within the organization as a whole and between organizational subunits in particular. Some of the methods of horizontal coordination have already been described in previous chapters, particularly those of assigning interactions and organizing by product, person, or place. These will be briefly reviewed here, and other methods of horizontal coordination will be introduced, including developing coordinative and staff positions.

Assigning Coordinative Responsibility

The purpose of individual and group interactions is to integrate the various work assignments of the organization. People can either be left to determine the necessary interactions for themselves, or managers can state very specifically what employee interactions should be. Certainly if interaction is important to the job it should not be left to chance. Spelling out the necessary interactions is important when the need for coordination with other work in the organization is high. Unfortunately, many organizations often neglect this fact.

Telling people to coordinate through interaction and getting them to do it, however, are two different things. Such assignments might be analogous to telling a brother and sister to "get along with each other." Subunits of organizations, because of their different goals and outlooks, often find it impossible to realistically and fruitfully interact with one another. Occasionally they do not even "speak the same language."

Many scientific researchers, for example, find it impossible to account to financial analysts for the money they spend—often millions of dollars. When it becomes clear that two groups are unable to interact directly with each other, an intermediary, or "go-between," is often used to complete the interaction. The intermediary thus acts as a **coordinator** to integrate the work flow between the two groups. Coordinators must be able to understand the needs and problems of both groups. The job titles for this position vary among organizations; some common names include expeditor, liaison, and project coordinator.

Lawrence and Lorsch found that the need for coordinator or integrator positions rises proportionately with the complexity of the organization. These researchers also found that effective coordinators are those whose own goals, time perspectives, and interpersonal orientations lie somewhere between those of the two subunits with which they deal. Coordinators need to be able to focus on the goals of both groups impartially. And they need to have a time perspective between the two. For instance, coordinators between research (long time perspective) and production (short time perspective) are effective if they maintain a median time perspective. Interpersonal orientation, in this study, refers to a distinction between task- or person-oriented groups. Again, the effective integrator is one who operates between the extremes of the conflicting subunits (21).

Designing Coordination into an Organization Structure

An advantage of organizing in ways other than functional departmentation is greater coordination. For instance, in product departmentation, all the responsibility for getting out a particular product would reside in one person, the product manager. The matrix organization, with its many project managers, is an even clearer example of organizing to increase coordination.

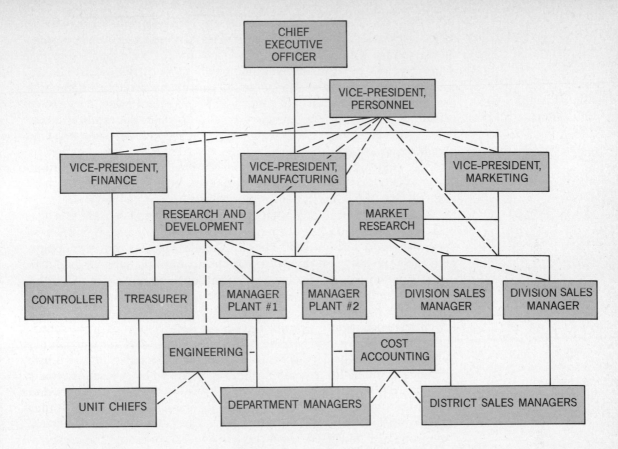

FIGURE 7–4
Line-and-staff organizational structure.
(The dotted lines indicate direction of functional authority.)

However, coordinating the work flow with product or project output creates another sort of coordination problem. In product and project organizations the functional specialties will need to be coordinated. Financing, personnel, accounting, purchasing, and legal procedures must be consistent among subunits, or functional coordination problems will arise. For instance, if two or more product departments kept their own accounting reports and each used a different system of accounting, there would be little way to compare performance levels between departments. One way to avoid this problem is to develop special staff functions within the organization.

The diagram of the managerial hierarchy in Figure 7–2 represents a **line organization.** That is, all positions are directly related through a *lineal* chain of command. A more complex form of organizational structure is the **line-and-staff organization.** This type of structure is diagrammed in Figure 7–4. Relationships with staff groups (represented by the dotted lines) cross over the chain of command and complicate the organization. This structure begins to take on the features of the structure shown in Figure 7–3 (the representation of functional foremanship), which is appropriate since the ideas of Taylor are the basis of line-and-staff organization.

Line-and-Staff Organization. The use of staff people is intended to increase a manager's sphere of influence and is a response to an overload of interactions within a manager's span of control. With staff assistance, managers can extend themselves and handle more activities and interactions than otherwise would be possible. This phenomenon is often noted in the extension of the span of control of the president through a concept called the **presidency.** The president is an individual, but the presidency consists of a large number of people who represent the president and who extend his or her influence and ability through their individual expertise. Staff personnel represent a division of labor within the managerial job. They provide a degree of efficiency through specialization and coordination that would be impossible for any one manager to achieve alone.

In simple organizations that are departmentalized by function, the basis of organization is the chain of command, which is accompanied by a narrow span of control. All work in this model consists of line functions with each subunit representing a particular specialty, such as manufacturing or selling. When organizations increase in size and complexity, this functional form of organization becomes impractical and the span of control must be increased.

With the change to a product, place, or person form of organization, and an increasing span of control, **staff** units appear. When organization is by product, place, or person, there is a need for specialists to coordinate functions throughout the organization. Managers who have spans of control that are too wide to be effectively supervised can either turn over part of their areas to new managers or extend their spans of control by setting up staff positions to handle some functional parts of their managerial task. For example, all managers supervise personnel. In a simple line organization, each manager recruits, trains, promotes, discharges, and retires employees. In a line-and-staff organization, many of these specialized personnel functions are centralized in a personnel department. Each manager's job would have a portion of its personnel function carved out of it (22).

The existence of a staff complicates the authority and influence structure within the organization. If a staff has authority and influence over a specialized part of managerial work, the organization chart would look more like Taylor's functional organization (Figure 7–3) than the clear chain of command (Figure 7–2). One way to handle the confusion is to assert that the role of staff is to aid and support the manager and to provide information and advice when necessary, but that it is not to include the authority to make decisions. The typical line-and-staff organization chart shows the staff as horizontal extensions located outside the authority pyramid. Line personnel often speak of the staff as "administrative overhead," indicating that line functions are those that deal directly with the objectives of the organization. The purpose of staff, on the other hand, is to service the line positions by providing advice only.

Some argue that since staff is not central to the organization's purpose, staff work is not as necessary as line work. This is an oversimplification and is generally used as a rationale when there is an employee cutback in the organization. Staff positions are carved out of the line manager's job, so the addition or removal of staff does not change the manager's responsibility; it only affects the location of the work. The elimination of personnel jobs, for example, does not mean that less personnel work will be done; it simply means the execution of it will revert back to the line manager. Thus, it cannot be said that staff work per se is less vital to the organization, only that staff personnel may be found unnecessary.

Distinguishing Between Line and Staff. Distinctions between line and staff functions are clearer in theory than they are in practice. Distinction by function depends upon organizational purposes. For example, personnel work is clearly a line function in an employment agency; however, as noted in the example above, personnel work can be a staff function in another type of organization. Thus, we cannot classify particular functions as line or staff without knowing the context in which they operate.

Where staff units are limited to "advice only," their ability to influence is limited to persuasion and logic. If management were always responsive to logic, these tools would be sufficient. But many managers, in common with certain other groups of people, resist changes proposed by "outsiders," no matter how logical or well presented these changes may be. In fact, the more logical a proposal, the more resistance it is likely to meet.

It has been observed that staff groups simply do not act as they are supposed to. Although the "advice only" dictum is appealing in theory, it is satisfying neither to the staff nor to top management. The purpose of staff units is to coordinate some functional area of the organization. Top management may want staff groups to do much more than just give advice and so assigns to a staff such tasks as auditing and control to ensure consistent outcomes. Personnel departments, for example, may review all firings, particularly if there is a union contract, and finance departments may check expenditures of certain funds. Clearly such reviewing and checking go beyond simply giving advice.

Studies by Myers and Turnbull and by French and Henning found that, depending on the needs of the particular organization, the functions of staff groups fall into slots along a continuum (23, 24). At one end of the continuum, the line group has full responsibility for the functions, and the staff group has responsibility only for giving advice. (Neither study found many staff groups that operated at this extreme.) At the other end of the continuum, the staff group maintains full decision-making authority within its specialized area. (This extreme was found to be equally rare.) Ranged along the continuum, the majority of staff groups were found to hold joint decision-making responsibility with line groups, and varying degrees of staff control were observed.

Staff units do perform certain functions that are intended to aid line managers and that therefore contribute to organizational goals. As mentioned earlier, the function of providing *advice* is based on the expertise of the staff. Some staff units provide a *service,* such as a typing pool. In these instances, expertise takes the form of specific utilitarian functions that increase efficiency. Staff advice and service areas are responsive to requests for aid from the line manager. Staff also *audits* and *approves* the activities of line managers at the request of top management. Auditing involves having the staff review what has happened to see if it is in accord with stated plans, policies, and procedures. Accounting has the most extensive auditing function. "Approval" might be considered a preaudit function when the line manager must seek staff permission to proceed with a particular action. For instance, a line manager, particularly in a unionized company, may have to check with the personnel department before firing an employee. In this case, approval is sought to ensure that the action is consistent with the terms of the union contract.

Conflict Between Line and Staff. Given the confusion in distinguishing between line and staff functions, it is not surprising that there exists an extensive body of research on line-staff conflicts. One important study found that conflicts between line and staff were likely to be based on such factors as: differences in perceived mission and in education and social behavior; pressures on staff personnel to justify their existence; fears by line personnel that staff members would undermine their authority; and the fact that staff experts must rely for promotion on line executives (25). Whether true or not, a common belief is that the road to the top of the hierarchy is through the line, not the staff. At the root of the presumed conflict may be the fact that technical experts do unquestionably remove part of a line manager's work and influence organizational behavior.

The staff specialist undercuts the authority of the traditional line manager. To the extent that line managers have relied for their effectiveness on the authority of their position, they no doubt resent attempts by experts to influence their employees. Influence by authority may be in direct conflict with influence by expertise. As organizations become more complex, the power of expertise increases at the expense of the power of authority. Staff groups are thus becoming increasingly more powerful and will surely have even more status in the organizations of tomorrow.

One way to alleviate line-staff conflicts, and indeed to reduce conflict between any two groups, is for management to make explicit the real organizational role of each group. Typically, line managers are given the mixed message that although they have "full authority," staff managers will "coordinate" certain functional activities for them. So when the staff managers try to coordinate the activities, the line managers consider this an infringement upon their authority. A full and detailed description of the work of each group, which clearly outlines both the prescribed and discretionary content, can greatly minimize this type of conflict.

Decentralization

A final aspect of coordination has to do with where in the management hierarchy decisions are made. The more spread out decision making becomes, the greater the possibility for diversity in subunits. However, information and expertise are not all located at the top of the organization. And, if all decisions were made at the top, they would be unlikely to be the best possible decisions. Thus as organizations become more complex, the contradictory forces of central coordination and local expertise create a tug-of-war between centralization and decentralization.

A Definition of Decentralization

Decentralization means the assignment of decision-making responsibility to the lowest practical managerial level in the organization. The concept does not necessarily have anything to do with diversification, either in terms of goals or of location. Just because an organization may be diversified, or may have many goals and products, or may be physically dispersed throughout the country or the world, does not mean that decisions will be decentralized. Diversification can lead either to centralization or to decentralization. Decentralization of decision making can lead to more effective coordination *within* work groups, but this pushing down of decisions to lower levels can also lead to less coordination *between* work groups. The more autonomous that work groups are, the more they are flexible, adaptable to local environmental changes, and needful of strong and capable managers. But autonomous work groups mean that the organization is represented differently by each work group, and outsiders who deal with more than one group often consider the organization's policies inconsistent if not bewildering. Uniform policies and record keeping, central information systems, and consistency in general are promoted by centralized decision making, which occurs in top levels of the managerial hierarchy.

Organizations themselves are not centralized or decentralized, but organizational functions are. Thus, personnel decisions may be decentralized to local plants while capital expenditures may be made only by the top executive. The lower in the organization that decisions about a particular function can be made, the more that function is decentralized.

Decentralization and Organization Structure

Although decentralization addresses itself to the area of decision making, it nevertheless has a major impact on organization structure. By the same token, a particular organization structure will have an influence on the degree of decentralization that exists in the organization.

Departmentation. In order for decentralization to be effective, organizational units must be independent and able to operate on their own. Product, person, or place departmentation, in contrast with functional departmentation, creates relatively autonomous organizational units. Product, person, or place departments operate as independent organizations, maintaining control over their own output. One current trend in decentralization is the **profit center** concept, which means that central controls are of a financial nature. The manager of each profit center is evaluated on the basis of measurable results, such as the return on investment or the amount of profit earned, rather than on the basis of decisions or behavior. In this approach all functions other than finance are decentralized.

To employees, decentralization can mean job enrichment. The greater the degree of delegation, the more individual employees can coordinate their own tasks. Most successful job enrichment programs have been carried out by decentralizing most functions of the manager's job. A basic trust in the abilities of employees and managers is a prerequisite of decentralization. Such trust must come from the top of the organization and permeate all levels of the hierarchy. Each level of managers must have enough decision-making responsibility to pass on. It is impossible for managers to give employees decisions to make if they themselves have little decision responsibility.

Functional Staff Managers. Because decentralization encourages departmentation by product, person, or place, there is a trend in decentralized organizations to have a large functional staff at the top of the organization. This structure complicates the unity of command, but the line and staff have quite different functions. The staff is responsible for the areas of planning and control. They stay away from daily operations, concentrating instead on decisions regarding the future direction of the organization and on ensuring that the various subunits produce results that are consistent with these plans. In addition, the staff is the major agency of control in a decentralized organization. The line organization, in contrast, carries out the operations of the organization (26).

Rationales for Decentralization

Certainly one reason for the recent trend toward decentralization is that it is currently fashionable among management theorists. But that is only part of the explanation. The trend goes much deeper than that.

Cultural Values. Decentralization is rooted in the cultural values of the United States, which may explain its continuing popularity even in the face of high-speed electronic computers that can greatly aid centralization. Decentralization spreads out the decision-making process among many people. It is, in a way, democratic, or at least it appears to be. It requires a trust that people can manage their own affairs with a minimum of restrictions and overseeing, an attitude that lies at the base of democracy. Decentralization does not create a democratic organization, but it does reflect democratic values and operating procedures.

Quality of Life. To the extent that decentralization and job enlargement are similar phenomena in organizations, decentralization has responded to a societal concern for the quality of working life in the United States. This concern mounted as more and more studies revealed the extent of alienation that the majority of employees experience on the job. Attempts to enlarge jobs to decrease worker dissatisfaction have had positive results in improving productivity and product quality and in reinforcing the belief that society works better when people are given some control over their work environment.

Management Training. Decentralization also provides high-quality training for executives. Potential managers learn to handle a full range of activities because they are given responsibility for balancing all the functions necessary to make an organization run. (Recall that decentralized work groups contain all the elements of a miniature organization.) This factor may be of critical importance because predictions indicate a future shortage of managers (27).

Flexibility. A final rationale for decentralization is that it enables the organization to remain flexible. And in times of rapid change, flexibility is important. Organizations need to be able to respond rapidly to changing environmental conditions. Small organizations have always been noted for their ability to adapt rapidly and to take advantage of new opportunities. In a large organization, in which a maximum of functions have been decentralized, the decision-making process approaches that of several small organizations.

Problems with Decentralization

Decentralization is not a cure-all for organizational problems. Like most ideas about how to structure organizations, decentralization has drawbacks as well as advantages. Some of these drawbacks are lack of management talent, unwillingness or inability to delegate responsibility, and unreliable or invalid control devices.

Management Talent. A decentralized organization requires managers who are willing to accept high degrees of responsibility, who are able to work on their own, and who are able to effectively delegate responsibility to others. It is no easy task to find many people with these qualifications, and the number of students who are attracted to these challenges is declining (28).

More critical than the availability of such people is the problem of how to develop people's skills in these areas of management. Generally, lower organizational levels are not allowed broad areas of decision making unless decentralization is taken very seriously all the way down to the bottom of the organization. Thus, by the time upward-moving managers reach a level that allows them to make important decisions, they have not had sufficient practice to enable them to adequately deal with their new responsibilities.

Delegation. It is also difficult to develop the paradoxical skills of an easy acceptance of responsibility and a willingness to delegate responsibility. The temperament of many managers, combined with the organizational climate, often causes employees to be viewed in an instrumental fashion, with their abilities underestimated. This short-range managerial view is concerned with getting the job done now rather than with developing the next generation of managers (29).

Control. Unquestionably, the biggest cost of decentralization is in the area of control. Once having delegated responsibility, how does the manager keep track of what is going on? Unfortunately, there is no ready answer to this question. There is still too little known about what goes on in organizations or about how to describe and develop precise measuring devices. Although sets of measurement devices are plentiful, they are usually developed in response to particular operating problems rather than for purposes of accurately describing all relevant organizational behavior. Accounting records, for example, are prepared primarily to please stockholders and conform with tax laws, not to keep track of how well the organization is functioning.

In the last analysis, prevailing conditions in the environment, in organizations, and in the local work groups will continue to have a determining effect on the locus of decisions. Freedom to centralize or decentralize will still be sharply limited by these conditions.

Chapter Review

This chapter completed the discussion of the nature of organizations by examining the method by which coordination is built into the organization structure. Many of the basic ideas of the administrative management theorists have been considered along with the advantages and costs of each of the methods. The major ideas and terms that have been developed in this chapter are outlined below.

1. **Coordination** is a managerial activity designed to bring diverse organizational activities in line with overall organizational goals. This is accomplished through:

    a. **cultural conditioning,** by which people behave and react in accordance with what they have learned is right and acceptable;

    b. **social pressure,** by which people behave in ways that are expected by their peers;

    c. **managerial activities** that direct employee activity; and

    d. the **managerial hierarchy,** by which coordination is built in to the organization through set procedures and principles.

2. **Chain of command** is an imaginary vertical line connecting people

in an organization in such a way that each person is accountable to the next higher person in the vertical structure.

3. **Authority** is an accepted right, inherent in a position, to influence others; it is an expected characteristic of certain organizational relationships.

4. Authority should equal responsibility, but because it rarely does, managers must rely on other forms of power.

5. **Unity of command** means that each person has only one other person to whom he or she is accountable.

6. **Span of control** refers to the number of people any one manager can supervise effectively. There is no optimum number of people that should be in a manager's span of control, but the following factors will exert some influence:

    a. interlocking of work;
    b. outside interactions of the manager;
    c. employee-manager relations;
    d. the work group;
    e. technology; and
    f. job design.

7. **Horizontal coordination** is needed to maintain an effective and efficient work flow. It involves assigning work and interactions in order to integrate the various organizational tasks.

8. **Staff positions** are functional subdivisions of the overall managerial job; they are created to increase a manager's span of control.

9. Staff influence may range from simply giving advice to making decisions. In a typical organization, staff people provide services and give advice to all levels of managers, and provide only auditing and control functions for top management.

10. **Decentralization** is the delegation of decision-making responsibility to the lowest organizational level that is practical.

11. Organizations with many decentralized functions tend to have a large central staff, which performs planning and control functions.

**Discussion
Questions**

1. Define *coordination*. What factors make coordination necessary in organizations?

2. In what ways may coordination be achieved? How successful are these methods?

3. Define *authority*. How useful is it? Why?

4. Comment on the following statement: "To hold a group or individual accountable for activities of any kind without assigning to him or them the necessary authority to discharge that responsibility is manifestly both unsatisfactory and inequitable."

5. Distinguish between *chain of command* and *unity of command*.

6. Are unity of command and coordination always consistent? Why?

7. Describe *span of control*. Is it a valid concept? Why?

8. What factors influence the maximum possible span of control? What effect does the span of control have on other concepts of management?

9. What is the nature of *staff* and *line* work? Describe the problems in trying to distinguish between the two.

10. List several reasons for staff-line conflict. How might these problems be resolved?

11. Evaluate the concept of *functional foremanship* (include as many of the aspects of structural coordination in your analysis as you can).

12. What is *decentralization?* Why is there confusion about its definition?

13. Describe the advantages and problems of decentralization.

14. You are the president of a chain of markets. You feel that it is important that a maximum amount of discretion be in the hands of the individual store managers. Structurally, how can you obtain this level of discretion? What advantages and costs would ensue?

Involvement Activity: An Exercise in the Coordination of Work

Organizations differ considerably in the amount of coordination required, the methods used to achieve coordination, and the use of coordination techniques within the managerial hierarchy.

For each of the organizations described below, indicate: (1) the degree and level of coordination required; and (2) the characteristics and relative usefulness of:

a. Chain of command.
b. Authority.
c. Unity of command.
d. Span of control.
e. Coordinative positions.
f. Staff positions.

1. This organization produces a single product line. The market is well established and the technology is simple, stable, and widely dispersed throughout the industry. No significant new products or technologies have appeared in the past five years.

The organization is structured functionally, containing production, finance, and marketing departments. The president is a hard-driving person who knows the plant and the industry well. There are approximately 500 people employed in the company.

2. This organization produces various but similar products. The product line is subject to constant change as some products become obsolete and others gain popularity. The products are highly complex technologically, and require the services of many technical specialists.

The organization is structured functionally, containing research, engineering, production, and finance departments. The president is an inventive and hard-driving individual with a strong reputation in the industry. There are approximately 500 people employed in the company.

3. This nationwide organization is engaged in retail trade to the general public. It provides a broad range of household goods and does little or none of its own manufacturing. Competition in the past few years has been fierce

as older firms have become more competitive and newer but more special-ized firms have taken over a portion of the total product line. Although the product line remains fairly constant, the specific items typically change every year.

The organization is structured territorially with a large central staff that is organized functionally. There is considerable decentralization of operations to the various areas to take advantage of local conditions. The president has been with the company for 30 years and has been able to maintain a company growth rate equivalent to the growth in the economy during his five-year term as president. The company employs approximately 25,000 people.

4. This organization is a municipal government of a fairly large city. The range of services provided is very broad and typical of most modern cities in the United States. The past few years have seen a continual demand for more and newer services caused by (1) growth of the city and (2) demands from the state and national governments.

The organization is functionally oriented, but the functions vary greatly in their degree of sophistication; they range from trash collection to complex engineering problems. The city has a strong city-manager plan, and the present manager is young, has a strong political base, and has been on the job for five years. The city employs just over 5,000 people.

3

Determinants of Organization and Work Design

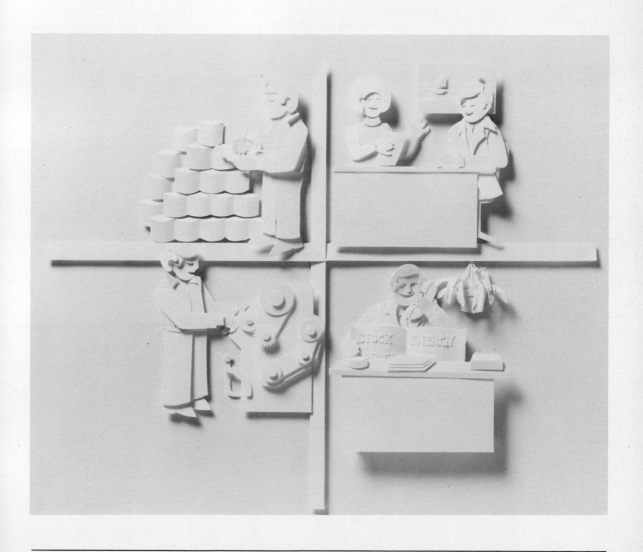

The five preceding chapters, which constituted Part 2 of this text, were concerned with the managerial processes involved in designing an organization structure. It was shown how the managerial task of designing and organizing work is complicated by the people who do the work, the technology available to do it, and the environment in which the organization exists. In this unit, people, technology, and environment will be explored in depth to show how each influences and affects the organization and how each influences and is influenced by managerial activities.

Because people are the most valuable, costly, and perplexing of all organizational resources, the first three chapters in this unit are devoted to an inquiry into the nature of human behavior. Chapter 8 explores some of the psychological and physiological determinants of behavior and includes a discussion of what managers can learn about employee motivation. Chapter 9 focuses on personnel methods, with emphasis on the ways in which managers recruit and develop employees, match positions and individuals, and compensate people fairly and effectively. In Chapter 10 we depart from the view of people as resources and examine humans as members of groups within the organization. Group characteristics and dynamics are explored, and group behavior is discussed in relation to its effect on organization design. All three of these chapters on human behavior stress the point that people affect the way work is done, the way organizations are designed, and the way managerial activities are conducted.

In Chapter 11, the focus shifts away from people and toward the technology people employ to carry out their work. Technology includes both the resources secured from the environment and the tools and talents available within the organization. Technology, like people, has a considerable effect on how and where work is performed, on the ways organizations are structured, and on the types of managerial activities that are necessary.

The final chapter in this unit, Chapter 12, addresses itself to the environment of organizations. It will show how the environment exerts monumental demands on managers' time and attention and how environmental pressures from many quarters contribute both opportunities for, and limitations to, the organization's operations.

8

People: Behavior in Organizations

People are the primary resource of all organizations. In fact, without people an organization cannot exist. People represent both a challenge and a frustration to managers and constitute a major constraint on, and a source of opportunity for, the accomplishment of the organization's work.

The purpose of this chapter is to help the reader gain an understanding of the ways people behave in organizations. It will describe theories of human behavior that will serve as a framework for the discussions that follow, both in this and the next chapter. In particular, two theories of work behavior will be described, expectancy theory and exchange theory.

The chapter will go on to examine the roles of perception and thought in influencing behavior, and close with a discussion of the ways managers can develop skills for better understanding human behavior in the work setting.

Millions of people work in organizations all over the world, and every person is unique. Each has a particular combination of genetic structure and learning experiences that are different from anyone else's. Yet people are alike, too. We all develop physiological and mental processes in similar ways and respond predictably in certain situations. This combination of uniqueness and individuality often creates problems for people who want to be able to control others' behavior.

Managers would like employees to behave predictably and "fit in" with the work of the organization. But employees often behave upredictably and in ways that appear incompatible with organizational goals. Managers attempt to minimize "people problems" in two ways. First they try to refine their recruitment, selection, and training procedures so that they hire and keep only those people who fit the jobs. Second, they try to motivate people in such a way that their behavior is consistent with the work of the organization. This latter attempt is the focus of the discussion in this chapter; the former will be considered in the next chapter. The focus on people as resources is illustrated in Figure 8–1.

FIGURE 8–1
How the variables of human behavior, technological change, and environmental pressure affect the flow of work in an organization. The emphasis in this chapter is on people.

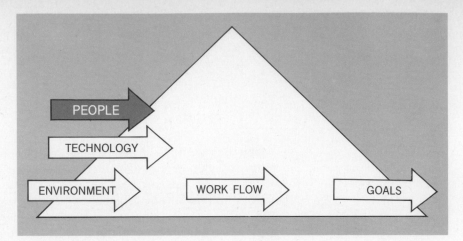

Management and Human Behavior

Taylor and his scientific management movement provided the initial impetus for the scientific study of people in organizations by contending that job requirements must be matched with human skills and abilities. Scientific management developed tools for measuring jobs but left to industrial psychologists the task of measuring people. These scientists did some pioneering work during the early years of this century in the study of such subjects as fatigue and boredom, but the impetus for substantial research grew out of World War I. During that time, the need to match large numbers of people to jobs resulted in the development of psychological testing and measurement instruments. During the 1920s, industry became interested in these testing devices. Although success was mixed, psychological testing is still used as a major selection tool (1).

The Hawthorne Studies of the late 1920s and early 1930s made it clear that people problems were much more complex than simply matching employees to jobs in the best way possible (2). A search was initiated for a model of motivation that could be applied to the work environment. But the search is still underway, and a comprehensive model has yet to be discovered—those presented here are, at best, only partial. Models are incomplete because the forces affecting human behavior in organizations are numerous and difficult to isolate. Furthermore, each organization, and each group of individuals within it, exhibits such unique properties that even the best models can explain only general behavior and very little specific activity.

Managerial Perspectives of People

In order to deal with the human resource, managers develop concepts of what makes people "tick." For the most part, such concepts are based on their own lifelong experiences with people. In this sense, they reflect the individual manager's personality more than they do any objective theories of personality. Thus, if a manager's relations with other people have been positive, the concept that develops will be reasonably optimistic; if the relations have been negative, the manager's way of dealing with others is likely to be pessimistic (3).

At one time, most managers reflected the view that all human behavior was economically oriented; that is, that people tried to maximize gain and minimize loss. This concept was apparently true enough to be useful in eras when behavior was highly regulated, such as in the Middle Ages when feudalism reigned, or in other times when the bulk of humanity lived at bare subsistence levels, such as in the early years of the Industrial Revolution. But this view of people has proved less and less valuable as industrialized nations have become more affluent and the work force has come to include more people with varying cultural norms. How much times have changed is exemplified by the true story of a worker at General Motors Company who, when asked why he always missed one day of work each week, answered "I can't make it on three."

Managers as Motivators

The managerial role in motivating behavior is complex. Managers have available to them a number of means to help individuals satisfy their needs. But different employees have different needs. Thus, because money is a means that can satisfy a broad range of needs, it is the one most frequently used as a motivator. Managers, however, must examine the range of other means available and learn to use them in ways that will produce the biggest payoff to the organization and to the individual.

Management does not activate individual behavior; the individual does. Managers can manipulate the inputs around the individual and thus hope to obtain different outputs, but they cannot determine what goes on inside the person. So while the behavior models presented in this chapter cannot provide complete instructions for understanding the nature of human motivation and behavior, they can at least help current and future managers learn a little more about what makes people "tick." It should be noted, however, that even though one may come to partially understand human behavior, the translation of this understanding into practice requires extensive personal skill that is grounded in both practical experience and, perhaps, in some skill-building courses.

A General Model of Behavior in Organizations

The basic ingredients of all organizations are people and work. So the model of behavior in organizations illustrated in Figure 8–2 has as a base the interaction of a person with the work to be done and on how these two aspects of an organization affect each other.

Personal Determinants of Work

One of the first considerations on any model of behavior in organizations is to determine how personal factors affect work factors. Three determinants have been isolated: skill, knowledge, and effort, as illustrated in Figure 8–2.

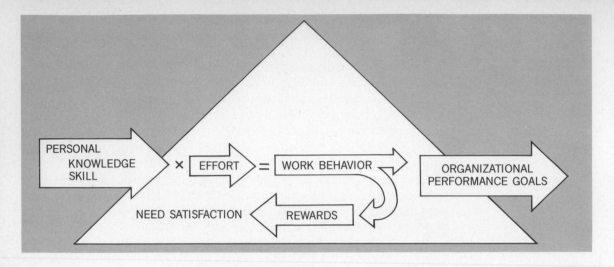

FIGURE 8–2
A model of human
behavior in organiza-
tions.

Skill. First, the person must be capable of doing the work, both physically and mentally. A warehouse worker must be able to lift boxes; a secretary must be able to type; a design engineer must be able to draw accurately and to do mathematical equations; and a salesperson must be articulate. These are all skills that require learning. And until such skills as are necessary for the job are acquired, the person cannot adequately perform the work.

Knowledge. Knowledge may seem synonymous with skill, but it encompasses a broader area. For instance, an individual might have the skills to be a draftsperson but not know the type of work being done by a particular organization well enough to do the job without some study and training. Even if the person did know the work, he or she would also need to understand how the particular organization operates. Policies, procedures, and methods of arranging work differ somewhat between organizations, even those engaging in very similar activities.

Students often experience a lack of specialized knowledge. A student has the skill to be a student, but different courses and professors require different application of student skills. And each course contributes to the overall body of the person's knowledge of how to be a student. Some courses teach the student how to retain information, others teach how to write papers, and still others teach ways to contribute to class discussions or give speeches. Knowledge, in this sense, means being properly trained for the context of work.

Effort. All the skill and knowledge in the world, however, are of no avail if people do not put forth an effort to apply their skills and knowledge to the specified tasks.

Effort is an expenditure of energy directed toward completion of the work task. It is critical to accomplishing work, but it does not guarantee results. A futher distinction must be made between effort and performance. In other words, if you put in a lot of hours studying, playing a sport, mixing ingredients for a cake, or tinkering on a car, you have put forth effort. If you get an A in a course, win a tennis match, bake a delicious cake, or get your car running, your effort has resulted in a good performance. The combination of effort, knowledge, and skill produces good performance. When one of these components is missing, the chances for effective performance are considerably reduced.

Work Determinants of Behavior

People put forth effort if they perceive they will get rewarded for it. In order to look at the relationship between effort and reward, it is useful to complete the model started earlier. Work has two aspects—an external one and an internal one. The external aspect is concerned with outcomes, that is, performance; the internal aspect deals with the behaviors that constitute performance. One way to view effort, then, is to say that it will be expended if it is related to performance and if performance is related to rewards. Thus, as shown in Figure 8–2, people exchange their knowledge, skills, and effort in performing their work for rewards that lead to satisfaction of their personal goals. In other words, people do what the organization wants because they see the exchange as equitable.

March and Simon suggest that a further explanation of why effort is expended is that it is the outcome of *decisions* to participate and to perform. These decisions are based on factors internal to employees and to variations in the patterns of rewards offered by the organization (4). For example, students ask themselves whether they should participate in their classes and to what extent they should perform once they have decided to participate. One decision they make early in a term is whether to drop a class or stay in it. This is a participation decision based on whether the course is "worth it." Once the decision to stay has been made, the next question is whether to drift through or work hard. This decision is related to whether the student perceives that effort will be rewarded by a needed high grade, by status, or by recognition.

Satisfaction

A major issue in organizational behavior is the relationship between job satisfaction and productivity. The issue of job satisfaction was first approached by early human relations theorists, who maintained that job satisfaction is a necessary condition for high productivity. "Happy workers are productive workers" was the theme. They hypothesized that job satisfaction is a moderator variable that lies between motivation and productivity. Recent studies, however, fail to support this proposed relationship, although Vroom's research did indicate that satisfaction and productivity may be related in some other ways. Vroom found a consistently negative relationship between job satisfaction and the probability of resignation, absenteeism, and accidents. If for no other reason than this, job satisfaction would be a worthy concern of managers (5).

In addition, Porter and Lawler noted that while the relationship between job satisfaction and productivity was not high, it was shown to be slightly positive overall in the studies that addressed the issue. Thus, while the relationship is slight, it is consistent (6).

By turning the relationship around, Porter and Lawler developed the theory that satisfaction occurs when performance and rewards are linked to an individual's expectations. Referring to Figure 8–2, we can see how this relationship fits into the behavior model. Thus, job satisfaction becomes a measure of the ability of the organization to satisfy an individual's expectations and of the degree to which it is able to reward productivity.

This relationship might result in any of four possible situations. In the ideal system, high productivity would result in a continuing series of rewards commensurate with each person's real needs and expectations and would therefore be associated with high satisfaction. Second, the organization might demand high productivity and provide needed rewards but do so in a way that does not meet the person's expectations. In this case, productivity is high but satisfaction is low. Third, the organization might not relate productivity and rewards but meet expectations anyway. It would be fun to work in this organization because satisfaction would be high. However, productivity would be low and the organization might not survive. Fourth, an organization might be found that fails to provide needed rewards and does not meet people's expectations. In this situation, there will be low satisfaction and low productivity, and the organization will most certainly not survive.

Expectancy Theory

To the manager, obtaining effort is a matter of motivation, which is why managers are always asking the question "How can I motivate employees?" The answer is that managers cannot motivate employees because they are already motivated. But if this is true, a manager might legitimately wonder, "Then why aren't they doing what I want them to do?" The fact is that although people *are* motivated, they are not necessarily motivated toward organizational goals. The question that should be asked, then, is, "How do we direct people's motivation toward organizational goals?" **Expectancy theory** can help answer this question. It assumes that people will seek things that are attractive to them, avoid things that are painful to them, and ignore things that have neither characteristic. Thus, organizational goals need to somehow be made attractive to people.

Basically, expectancy theory has three major variables—a reward variable and two different expectancy, or probability, variables. The reward variable, called **valence,** has to do with the attractiveness of an outcome. Outcomes can range in attractiveness from positive, for those that are preferable, through indifference, for outcomes that are neutral, to negative, for outcomes the individual does not want at all. Thus an offer of a $100 bonus for working Saturday night might have positive valence for someone who needs money, indifferent valence for someone who doesn't need the money, or negative valence for someone who not only does not need the money but has plans to go on a special trip for the weekend.

The other two variables, from which the theory derives its name, are expectancy variables. **Expectancy** in this sense is the degree of belief a person has that one thing will lead to another. Like the reward variable, expectancy ranges from a belief that both things are positively connected, through no connection, to a belief that both things are negatively connected. The expectancies that are relevant here are (1) a belief that productivity will lead to reward, and (2) a belief that effort will lead to productivity.

Expectancy theory further states that motivation and behavior in a given direction happens as a result of these three variables operating together. Thus, in Figure 8–2, effort leads to performance and performance leads to a desired reward. Imagine, for example, a young woman who is about to graduate from college and is looking for a job. She receives two job offers. The first offer has high attactiveness; it is in an industry that has always been of interest to her. On the other hand, the field is overcrowded with women and she sees little possibility for advancement. In addition, her school experience makes her doubt her ability to perform the work well. The other job offer is in an industry that she strongly dislikes; it has low attractiveness. However, the field needs women, she knows she has the competence to perform well, and she has good prospects of doubling her salary in a few years. Here we have the extremes of expectancy theory. Neither choice is able to offer a combination of the

... BUT THEIR SALES RECORD IS TOPS IN THE COMPANY!

three variables that will lead to motivation. In the first choice, high attractiveness is not supported by a belief that productivity will lead to reward or that effort will lead to productivity. In the second choice, there is a belief in the latter two variables, but there is no support from the attractiveness variable.

Rewards

The basic premise of all motivation theories is that people will behave in a given way if they can obtain something they want or need by doing so; that is, if they are rewarded. The premise is very simple, but it poses great problems for organizations because different people want and need different things. And clearly, organizations cannot provide all things to all people. What is considered a reward by a manager, for instance, is not necessarily the same thing that is considered a reward by an employee. For instance, promotion into the higher managerial ranks, which is clearly attractive to a manager, may be neutral or negative to an accountant. And the employee who is independently wealthy surely works for rewards other than money.

Therefore, in any organization, whatever an employee perceives as relevant or desirable becomes a reward to that person. And the total number of possible rewards in any organization is great indeed. Dubin found that people have more than one hundred different attachments to work that are important enough to be considered rewards (7). These items may be categorized and dealt with in groups. For our purposes here, one of the most useful categorizations is the distinction between **extrinsic** and **intrinsic rewards** (8).

Extrinsic Rewards. This category includes those rewards that surround the work and are provided by the organization. Pay, working conditions, supervision, and status are examples of extrinsic rewards. They are built in to the structure and practices of the organization, and individual employees do not have much control over them. Control extends only to whether the individual perceives the reward as attractive.

Intrinsic Rewards. These rewards are an integral part of the work and are derived from actually performing a task. Examples of intrinsic rewards are a sense of accomplishment, involvement, and recognition. These are not rewards that the organization can offer to a person. Rather, the individual experiences them internally through a personal set of criteria about what makes work attactive. The best that management can do is set up the conditions under which the person can experience these rewards. Job enrichment, for instance, is an attempt by management to increase the intrinsic rewards available from work.

Needs

Rewards, regardless of the type, are not ends in themselves. People seek rewards as a means to satisfy their needs. Needs are clusters or sets of partially unsatisfied physiological-cognitive-emotional conditions that are out of equilibrium and that consciously or unconsciously make themselves known to the individual. At any given moment a person's behavior is directed by a particular need or by several competing needs. Right now, for example, you may be getting sleepy, or your mind may be wandering to what you will be doing next weekend, or your attention may be diverted to an attractive member of the opposite sex who just walked by. But somewhere in your mind, too, is the thought that you would like to pass this course.

When one need becomes stronger than others, it begins to dominate your attention. Such a need is said to be in *tension,* which means that it demands satisfaction. Conflicting needs propel a person in several different directions, but eventually one need becomes stronger than the others, and at this point the individual is aware of a disturbance. The unsatisfied need elicits effort along a path leading to the goal of satisfaction, or alleviation of the tension. In humans, this goal is called a *want.* If the want is not satisfied by the effort expended, the individual becomes frustrated. Frustration leads to trying new and different paths to reach the goal, and the cycle is repeated.

Hierarchy of Needs. There are many ways to conceptualize the ways in which needs operate in individuals. But the theory developed by Abraham Maslow was readily accepted by many students of human behavior, including management theorists, because Maslow proposed the concept based on a lifetime study of normal human behavior. The heart of his theory is that people's needs can be categorized and arranged into an ascending order of importance, creating levels, or a hierarchy, of needs (9). Maslow's hierarchy of needs is illustrated in Figure 8–3.

1. *Physiological Needs.* On the bottom, or most basic level, are the physiological needs—those that are necessary to maintain and reproduce life. Among these are the needs for air, water, food, sex, and sleep. Humans cannot exist for long without air, water, or food. Individuals can survive without sex, but the human race cannot. Prolonged lack of sleep causes severe emotional and physiological problems, and if put off indefinitely, may result in death.

FIGURE 8–3
Maslow's hierarchy of needs.

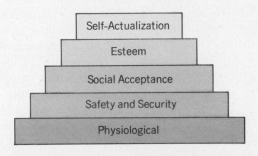

2. *Safety and Security Needs*. The safety needs are those that are secondarily related to staying alive, such as the needs for clothing, shelter, warmth, and so on. Security needs also pertain to staying alive, but not quite so directly. They are the needs to be emotionally safe, such as knowing there is somewhere to go when you need help.

3. *Social Acceptance Needs*. These needs, originally called the love needs by Maslow, have to do with the search for acceptance, love, and affection. Once the basic survival needs are met, the individual's behavior is directed toward satisfying the social acceptance needs.

4. *Esteem Needs*. Esteem needs refer to those desires that have to do with wanting to be well thought of by oneself and by others, and with wanting to know that those whose opinions you value think you are all right, too. The desire for esteem is natural and common to all people. This desire, however, is different from the excessive need for approval often exhibited by people with an extreme lack of self-confidence.

5. *Self-Actualization Needs*. The need for self-actualization is somewhat more complex than the others. Maslow believed that what a person *can* be, he or she *must* be. This means that people have a full range of potentials (talents, knowledge, emotions, and so forth) that must find expression. When people begin to actualize their potential, they begin to perceive themselves, others, and the environment creatively, spontaneously, and appreciatively.

Physical and Psychological Needs Contrasted. The first two needs of the hierarchy, the physiological and the safety and security needs, are basic to physical survival and well-being. Humans hold these needs in common with other animals. The remaining three, however, have to do with people as social creatures. They derive from the social and cultural conditions that set humans apart from most other species.

The most important thing to know about needs is that a satisfied need does not motivate behavior. The person who has just finished a large meal will not be motivated by the promise of another meal. Maslow's theory is that people do not have the time or energy to satisfy higher-level needs while they are still seeking to satisfy the lower-level needs. Even when lower-order needs are well satisfied most of the time, the person's ability to become self-actualized can never be completely fulfilled. The very striving for actualization encourages the quest for more and different personal and interpersonal goals.

The way the hierarchy of needs operates is more complex than the preceding discussion might imply. Physiological needs, for example, must be satisfied over and over again. And no one need must be entirely extinguished before the next higher-order need becomes important. At any one time, a person may be driven by a combination of needs from all levels.

But the needs at the bottom will be fulfilled even if doing so means sacrificing the ones toward the top. The need to survive is powerful indeed, and people are capable of anything when their lives are at stake.

Socially Derived Needs. Certain needs arise out of interaction with others in the process of living. McClelland classified some of these as affiliation, power, and achievement needs (10). Affiliation needs are very similar to Maslow's love, or social acceptance, needs. The power need is very much associated with the managerial task because it involves the need to manipulate and control others. Through this controlling, the individual gains a feeling of superiority over others. Because this need carries some negative cultural connotations, it is often ignored or its importance denied (11). Nevertheless, the need is a real one and one that can be satisfied through a managerial position. (This need will be discussed in more detail in Chapter 16.)

The third, and most studied, of McClelland's need categories is that of achievement. The person with a high need for achievement has a number of distinctive characteristics. The first of these is a desire to take moderate risks. These risks are achievable but not easy; they provide a challenge but are not discouraging. The second trait of high achievers is the requirement of immediate feedback. The person must be able to see progress toward the goal. Third, the high achiever finds the task itself, as opposed to the reward, intrinsically satisfying. The path is as important as the goal. The fourth, connected to this latter aspect, is a preoccupation with the task. The high achiever keeps after things until they are done right.

Contrary to popular opinion, and our secret desires, the achievement drive is not widespread in the population. A specific kind of early environment seems to lead to the development of this need. Children who are raised to be independent and who are rewarded for such behavior, while having clear-cut and reasonable demands placed upon them, tend to have this achievement need. Since it is socially derived, the achievement drive, while not high in all people, can be learned. In fact, McClelland has developed a course designed to increase a person's need for achievement (12).

Implications for Managers. What is the relevance to the manager of these theories about rewards and needs? For one thing, they indicate that individuals are complex creatures who are striving for many things simultaneously. There is a great temptation to assume that a manager needs to know the specific level of need satisfaction on which each person is working in order to motivate employees. But this is not true; it is not even possible. Individuals themselves cannot even say for sure what combination of needs is driving them at a particular time. And even if they could, needs are always changing.

Thus directing behavior toward organizational goals must consist in part of dealing with the environment around the person. By establishing a situation that is positively reinforcing and that provides feedback, the desired behavior can usually be secured (13).

For most people in contemporary American society, physiological needs are relatively well satisfied. Even without working, a person can survive. And for many people, there is a broad range of jobs to choose from in order to make enough money to satisfy the basic physiological needs. Thus, motivation aimed only at satisfaction of these survival needs is not going to be particularly effective. The approach of promising more "bread and butter" or threatening unemployment is usually inadequate.

This straight reward and punishment approach, while simple and appealing, is too restrictive. The past thirty years have seen dramatic changes in views toward employee motivation. First came a consideration of and planning for social needs both on and off the job—such things as physical layout and recreational facilities. Lately, there has been considerable interest and discussion about job enrichment and other changes in the work itself. These implementations are intended to increase the availability of intrinsic rewards, such as a sense of accomplishment, involvement, and a chance for growth (14). In this sense, it may be said that the methods of motivation have progressed up the hierarchy of needs during the past thirty years.

Individual needs may be compared to organizational goals in that both are multiple rather than singular, and both may be satisfied through a number of different avenues or means (paths). At any given time, individuals and organizations may be striving to satisfy one need or goal by many separate means, or one particular means may be intended to satisfy several different needs or goals. It would be an impossible task to coordinate the entire range of needs/goals and possible means/paths so that individuals and organizations could be mutually supportive at all times. It is rare when such harmony is achieved even for a short time.

This brings us to the use of money as a motivator. Money is a useful, all-purpose motivator because it can be traded for an almost endless variety of need satisfiers. It is clearly a means to achieve fulfillment of the physiological and safety needs, and it also has direct connections to the paths leading to psychological need satisfaction, particularly esteem needs. Money is the most obvious indicator of success that industrialized societies have available. This multiple-path feature of money helps to make managers' jobs easier because, through a paycheck, they can simultaneously satisfy a whole range of individual needs.

Individuals substitute means for ends as do organizations. Psychologists have long known that a means to an end will, after a while, be treated as an end in itself. Scott and Mitchell noted that individuals develop a series of derived needs that originally were means for satisfying some basic need but that now require satisfaction for their own sake (15). Some examples of these derived needs are power, opportunity, recognition, communication, and independence. And money, of course, is the most common example. Many individuals seem to have a need to accumulate

"I don't want a raise, Mr. Harlingen. I just want bouquets and accolades and tokens of esteem and bravos and huzzahs and a piece of the action."

money that extends far beyond any conceivable use it may have as a means to satisfy other needs.

Effort,
Performance,
and Reward

According to expectancy theory, in addition to supplying rewards that satisfy needs, the manager must also attempt to connect effort to performance (E → P) and performance to reward (P → R). These connections, E → P and P → R, are **probabilities**. That is, either one may be *consistently* connected (a probability of 1.0), *sometimes* connected (a probability of, say 0.75), or *rarely or never* connected (a probability of 0.10 down to 0.00). These probabilities, however, are subjective in nature because they stem from personal observation. But management can, depending on the way the reward system is structured, make the probabilities more objective. For instance, an incentive plan, which ties the units produced to payment, is a much more objective situation than a merit increase system, which depends on managers' judgments of an individual's performance.

Three variables determine whether a person will perceive a relationship between $E \rightarrow P$ and $P \rightarrow R$. These are the actual situation, past experience, and personal attitudes (16).

1. *Actual Situation.* Obviously, if effort does not lead to performance, or performance to reward, then it will be hard to make the connection. But even when there is a connection, it may not be perceived by the person. A major influence in this perception is other people, particularly ones who are influential. If co-workers believe that performance leads to reward, then the person is also likely to believe the relationship. For instance, if an expert, such as a coach, tells a player that he or she is capable of a certain performance, then that player will try very hard to perform at that expectation level.

2. *Past Experience.* A major influence on whether a person believes in $E \rightarrow P$ and $P \rightarrow R$ is whether it has happened in the past. If an employee has worked hard and achieved, and this achievement has led to promotion, then he or she is likely to believe that the same relationships will hold in the present situation. Past experience adds a degree of objectivity to the subjective probabilities. There is a warning here for managers. When setting up a new reward structure, people are going to be skeptical if their past experience tells them that effort does not lead to performance or performance to reward.

3. *Personal Attitudes.* Faith in one's own opinions, or self-esteem, has a great deal to do with whether a person perceives the $E \rightarrow P$ and $P \rightarrow R$ relationships. Rotter measured the internal-external control dimensions of people with the conclusions that internally controlled people believe that they influence the world, whereas externally controlled people believe the world controls them. Internally controlled people are much more likely to perceive the connections of $E \rightarrow P$ and $P \rightarrow R$ than are externally controlled people (17).

Developing the connections of expectancy theory is not easy. Performance is the critical variable because it enters into both expectancies, yet it is difficult to define in the organizational setting. Where performance can be measured, such as units produced or dollar sales volume, then the connections are made more easily. But for the majority of jobs in organizations, such measurement standards do not exist. At best there is performance appraisal, which is not a measurement of output but a judgment of worth often based on inputs. In these circumstances, the connections are harder to make objective.

The E $\rightarrow$ P connection is also complicated by the fact that effort is only one variable in performance. Where skill and knowledge are sufficient and equal, the E $\rightarrow$ P connection is more likely to be perceived. In schools, graduate students are more likely to see the E $\rightarrow$ P connections than are undergraduates because the selection process is more rigorous and the group of people more homogeneous in skill level.

In addition, the P $\rightarrow$ R connection is sometimes obscured by the fact that rewards are often consciously or unconsciously provided for factors other than performance. For example, if maintaining a consistent work force is an organizational goal, people may be rewarded simply for staying with the organization. The section that follows explores this organizational emphasis on participation.

Exchange Theory

Another perspective on the reasons why people behave in certain ways in organizations is offered by **exchange theory,** which states that in any interaction between two or more people, and particularly between people and the organization they work for, some form of exchange occurs. A number of behavioral scientists have shown how organizational behavior can be examined in terms of an exchange situation (18).

The Exchange Situation

The basic form of exchange that takes place in organizations is no different from any other economic transaction. Two parties, each with something the other wants, agree to make a trade based on mutually acceptable terms. In the employment situation, the parties consist of the employees on one hand and the managers representing the organization on the other. Where there is a union, the bargaining is formalized between the union and management representatives. Exchange works because each party receives something it needs and provides something the other needs. The employee receives money and other rewards and provides time, effort, and skills. The organization receives help in achieving its goals and provides salary and other forms of compensation.

While the basic idea of exchange is very simple, the operation of an equitable exchange is complicated by a number of factors.

Power. Where one party in the exchange has more power than the other, the terms of the exchange may not be entirely fair. The organization generally has considerably more power than the employee. A major reason for unions is to equalize this power relationship.

Perception. Each party in an exchange views the transaction somewhat differently. These differences are not only inevitable but desirable. If both parties were to put the same value on that which is being traded, an exchange could not take place. Thus if an employee values his free time

Vive la Différence   Crozier reports on a situation he came across in a bank in Paris. Apparently some of the clerks in the bank were dissatisfied with their salaries. Upon investigation, it was discovered that there were no differences between the jobs of those who felt dissatisfied and the jobs of those who were satisfied. It was, however, discovered that the dissatisfied people were all born and raised in Paris. While management could see that this difference distinguished the two groups, they did not see it as relevant in establishing pay scales. The Paris-born clerks, however, considered a Parisian upbringing an asset for which they should be additionally rewarded.

Reported in J. S. Adams, "Toward an Understanding of Inequity," *Journal of Abnormal and Social Psychology*, vol. 67, no. 5 (Nov. 1963), pp. 422–436.

more than he values the need for money (or the satisfaction derived from working in the organization), no exchange will occur. Similarly, if the organization values (or needs) cash resources more than it values (or needs) the services of the employee, no exchange will occur.

Another difference in perception is that one or the other party may see something in the exchange that the other does not. In order for something to be a part of an exchange, at least one party must *recognize* it and consider it *relevant*. The closer the two parties come to considering the *same* factors relevant, the higher the probability that the exchange will be regarded as fair by both parties.

Specificity. The employment exchange is not generally well spelled out. Some aspects, such as hours of work, production standards, and pay rates and benefits, are usually quite clear. But other factors, such as the organization's expectations of loyalty, commitment, adherence to behavior norms, and the employee's expectations concerning status, achievement, and recognition, are rarely made clear in advance. Thus the discrepancy regarding these expectations may be great. The high turnover rate of new college graduates is often caused by this discrepancy in expectations (19). From the employee's viewpoint the employment exchange means receiving rewards for making contributions. These rewards include a wide variety of extrinsic and intrinsic factors. The importance of employment to the person is related to how well these rewards satisfy his or her needs. Work provides not only monetary rewards but a number of other important rewards as well. In particular, work provides a means by which the individual finds a place and status in society. But the importance of employment in satisfying human needs can be overemphasized. Satisfaction of all human needs is not available through work. And if employees expect total satisfaction they will be disappointed and unhappy with the exchange.

In order to obtain rewards, people must make a contribution to organizational goals through their effort and by applying certain of their abilities. But organizations usually require many more contributions than this minimum as stated in the exchange agreement. Also, people tend to see themselves as contributing more than the organization either requests or is even aware of. For instance, indirectly related job experiences are often used in the job but are not recognized or rewarded by the employer.

Time. The employment exchange is ongoing. People are paid at specific time intervals in exchange for the work they have done, but the exchange is not completed each time a pay period ends. While both parties are reasonably satisfied, the exchange remains in force. And the longer the exchange is in force, the greater are the expectations of both parties. For example, an employee who has been with the organization a long time expects to receive extra considerations—such as not losing his or her job during a period of staff cutbacks. A professional may not expect immediate recompense for working long hours of overtime, but he or she will view this extra work time as contributing to future advancement considerations. On the other side of the exchange, the manager may expect employees with long tenure in the organization to work harder than newer employees during especially busy times. The expectation is that older employees have a greater degree of commitment to the organization.

Exchange Comparisons

People continue to take part in an exchange as long as it is "worth it" to them. This indicates that there is an ongoing comparison of contributions and rewards. However, since it is difficult to directly compare contributions and rewards, people in organizations typically compare their *ratio* of contributions and rewards to that of other employees, especially to those who work in similar jobs. When information needed to make such comparisons is not available, people may look outside the organization in an attempt to know whether their exchange is equitable.

When the exchange is thought to be equal or fair, the person will perform as required. But when the comparison is seen as unfair, the person seeks to equalize the exchange. This may be done by asking for a raise, working harder or not as hard, seeking to change the rewards given to, or contributions made by, the person with whom the comparison is made, or reevaluating the worth of the contributions and the rewards. If all equalizing attempts fail, a last resort is to terminate the exchange. The method that an individual uses to bring the exchange into line with his or her expectations will depend on the particular situation (20).

Implications for Managers

Developing an equitable exchange is a different process from connecting effort to productivity to reward. Because the compensation program of most organizations is geared more to fairness than to expectancy theory, a fair exchange is usually easier to achieve than is a direct effort-performance-reward connection. This does not mean that organizations can achieve only low levels of performance. The manager can define the expected levels of behavior quite high and provide high levels of reward to make it equitable. In general, organizations obtain the level of behavior they ask for and give rewards accordingly.

The perceptual nature of the exchange indicates that managers need to keep open the lines of communication between the organization and the employees. Organizations often offer rewards that managers are not aware of but that employees feel are important. For instance, most public utility companies provide stable and secure employment for their work force. Security is a very important need to many individuals and security-minded people are attracted to utility companies. Despite this fact, however, most executives of utilities deny that their employees are security-minded and refuse to acknowledge this advantage in their recruitment efforts.

People's reactions to inequity vary with the alternatives they perceive are open to them. Good economic conditions and low unemployment encourage people to look elsewhere for a position when they feel their present exchange is inequitable. High levels of unemployment encourage people to reexamine their comparisons. When the exchange is seen as positive by the employee, he or she will move toward increasing the zone of acceptance, making new contributions possible. A marginally acceptable exchange narrows the zone of acceptance and makes the employee inflexible.

Perception and Thought

From the expectancy and exchange theories of motivation, it is clear that people are not automatic responders. Rather we are thinking beings whose behavior is subject to change depending on how we perceive the world around us at any given moment. The world exists as we perceive it exists, and our perceptions are then subject to complex interpretations through our thought processes.

Perception: The Filter for Behavior

Sensory organs are constantly sending impulses to the brain about the information they receive. Because the brain receives far more information than it can handle, it automatically sorts out what is relevant. This sorting process is called **selective perception.** Relevant information is usually that which is related to need satisfaction and also that which is consistent with past experience. Information that does not meet these two criteria is not perceived unless it is at a high enough level of intensity to be unavoidable. In other words, familiar and/or relevant information can enter the sensory organs at a lower level of intensity than can unfamiliar, disturbing, or irrelevant information (21).

Problems in Perception. Responses to stimuli may be distorted or may deviate from the anticipated or expected response in a variety of ways and for a number of reasons.

1. *Overreactions*. A stimulus may cause a greater reaction than was intended. Overreactions typically result from a stimulus that is immediately associated with a number of past situations. For instance, a person may not only remember having received that particular stimulus before, but may also remember all the feelings and emotions it provoked. Thus the next time the stimulus is experienced, a whole range of positive or negative feelings will accompany the response.

2. *Unintended Reactions*. A stimulus may contain elements that are unintended or that are not seen by all observers. People listen to *how* something is said as well as to *what* is said. For instance, a person may respond negatively to words that are meant to convey something positive if he or she notices a particular tone or gesture that is interpreted as meaning the person is lying. Unintentional or nonverbal forms of communication are often more powerful stimuli than are intentional, verbal forms.

Although unintended stimuli often convey hidden clues about the sender's message, they just as often provoke a **projection** reaction on the part of the receiver. This means that the receiver ascribes to the sender motives or intentions that are not there at all. **Perceptual errors** — seeing or hearing something inaccurately — can lead either to different behavior from what is expected or to additional behavior that was not meant to be brought forth.

3. *Mistaken Signals*. One stimulus may be mistaken for another. When this happens, inappropriate behavior is quite likely. This form of error has to do with the individual's discriminatory ability. Discriminatory ability is partly a function of sensory ability. If the person has defective eyesight or hearing, for example, discrimination will be poor. Also, if the surrounding circumstances hinder or confuse adequate sensory perception, the stimulus can easily be mistaken.

Probably a stronger cause of poor discrimination is lack of training. Small children do not react to written orders because they cannot read. In organizations it is important to be certain that the individuals to whom information is addressed can understand the meaning of that information. A problem in this area is the special language developed by occupational groups, such as computer programers. In communicating outside the group it is extremely easy to be misunderstood. Education, in this light, is a process of increasing the individual's sensitivity to different stimuli so that correct responses are made.

4. *Closure*. If stimuli are consistent, people's perceptions can fill in what may be missing. Thus, we not only pick and choose among stimuli, but, having chosen, we proceed to fill in the gaps with what we think should be there. This process is called **closure**; and, in a way, it is how we create order from a chaotic array of disconnected stimuli. For instance, when we watch a film, what our eyes perceive is really a series of discrete

images closely connected. Our brains fill in the gaps to create the impression of a continuous, "moving" picture. Ordinarily, closure is a positive phenomenon. But when we make connections that are different from the reality of the situation, we operate with an incomplete or incorrect model of the world.

Past Influences on Perception. What has been experienced and learned in the past acts to create the "pictures of reality" that we carry around in our heads. These images of reality create models for the way we perceive the world and for how we think things ought to be. And they serve as a context for understanding stimuli. For instance, the word "orange" is understood in different contexts by (1) a small child who has never seen the fruit called orange nor played with orange-colored crayons; (2) a person who has only seen either the color or the fruit but not both; (3) someone who has seen both the color and the fruit; and (4) someone who has seen both and whose school color is also orange. Images of reality constantly change as we continue to have new experiences. Each significant event in our lives changes our perceptions to the extent that it influences the response that is evoked by a given stimulus.

Attitudes and Values. As mentioned earlier, the images that we carry in our heads are not only descriptive ones regarding *what* the world outside is like, they are also **prescriptive,** indicating what the world *ought* to be like. **Attitudes** are similar to "oughts." They are preconceived notions, beliefs, or feelings about specific objects or conditions. They are subject to change as the person has new experiences. **Values** are more enduring and harder to change than attitudes. They are strong emotional responses to ideals or institutions that are based on learned concepts of good and bad or right and wrong (22).

Because attitudes and values result from an accumulation of past experiences and learning, it is easy to see why human behavior varies so greatly. It is unlikely that any two people would have exactly the same experiences that would produce the same set of attitudes and values. The total, cumulative environment of every person is different from that of every other. Even identical twins who have been raised together and thus have as similar an early environment as possible have different environments because each has the other as part of the outside world. The totality of attitudes and values of an individual, along with many other emotional, physical, and mental traits and characteristics, constitute the personality. And although attitudes and values are internal, they may be viewed by others through the behavior of the person. As the person is observed over a period of time, his or her reactions to people, objects, and situations can begin to be more or less predicted. Thus, an outside observer can make inferences about the person's attitudes and values.

What is perceived and how it is perceived are functions of the attitudes and values we hold. In this sense, present behavior reflects past experience. For the manager, then, changing an employee's behavior may involve having to change the person's attitudes and values. This evokes the old argument of whether attitudes change behavior or behavior changes attitudes. Both are true. Current attempts in organizations to eliminate prejudice (an attitude) can and do proceed from both directions. One approach is to legislate against discrimination (a behavior) and assume that the results will change attitudes. Another approach is to deal directly with prejudicial attitudes in training programs and assume that a change in attitudes will eliminate discrimination.

How the Future Influences Behavior. People's behavior is also influenced by what they expect will happen in the future. In other words, to the extent that people have goals or make predictions about their future needs, their behavior will be affected accordingly. Few individuals do not strive for some future goal or aspiration. And, often, people have long-range goals that require a great deal of planning. Each new level of goal attainment toward which a person strives is called an **aspiration level.** Past success at reaching an aspiration level will encourage a person to try for an even higher level. And the greater the success, the higher the future goals. Failure, however, can break this upward spiral. One or several setbacks generally cause people to readjust their current and near-future goals downward. Continuous failure may lead to a reconsideration of the whole forward-reaching chain of goals, and, in some cases, may result in a drastic reconsideration of the present and near-future situation. Case studies of the unemployed, both at the unskilled and executive levels, clearly confirm this process of downward reconsideration (23).

Success breeds success, and failure breeds failure. The best way to "develop" employees, "teach" young people, or "raise" children is to give them praise for what they do well. Positive reinforcement of functional behavior is a stronger motivational tool than reprimand and punishment. Fear and the threat of punishment elicit compliance in outward behavior but discourage individual growth and do not promote internal motivation. In fact, these negative reinforcers may elicit rebellion or organizational sabotage.

Thought

All humans are born with a genetic heritage that, in addition to determining physical characteristics, supplies certain predispositions to act and react in particular ways. But compared with animals, humans have a very limited set of inherited instincts, or "programs," that predetermine behavior. Almost all human behavior is learned. Our large brain gives us the ability to think and make choices, to contemplate the past and to wonder about the future, and to have an awareness of self. The human brain also houses an inconceivably vast reservoir of memories. It is thought that all experiences of importance are stored in the brain and extinguished only with difficulty. Thus, even though we cannot ordinarily retrieve the bulk of this information, it is there nonetheless and represents what Freud called the **unconscious.** According to Freud and his followers, the unconscious mind contains material of which the self, or **ego,** is unaware but that nevertheless is capable of influencing our conscious thoughts and behaviors. It is because of this influence that we do not always know why we do what we do: We are often motivated by thoughts we do not know we have.

The Role of Language. Thinking involves a mediation between the self and the environment. The senses perceive stimuli and send messages about them to the brain. The brain then compares these messages with information that is stored in memory to come up with an explanation of what is being sensed. Language helps greatly to organize impressions and express experience. People think in language and receive and deliver messages in the language of their experience. For this reason, people who use different languages may react differently to the same stimuli. Often less apparent is the fact that people who seem to use the same language sometimes do not experience word messages in the same way. Every subculture, for instance, develops its own way of expressing its common experiences. Many generation gaps, misunderstandings between ethnic groups, and labor-management conflicts are caused by the absence of a common language.

Part of the problem is that people learn to respond to words as if they were events. Words are merely symbols used to express thoughts and emotions. What happens, though, is that certain words, over time, become value-laden. We learn to attach some emotional significance to them. Thus, if one group uses words that signify something different to members of another group, reaction can be out of proportion to the intended meaning. By the same token, words can be purposely used to elicit an emotional response. Politicians and advertisers have developed this phenomenon to a fine art. Managers need to be aware of the subtleties of language if they are to lead and respond with understanding.

Reason and Emotion. The nervous system is a complex, constantly active network that sends messages to, and receives messages from, all parts of the body. Closely connected, but separate, from this system, is the **endocrine system,** which controls the functioning of the body's glands. The glands produce hormones, which, among other things, regulate behavior. Thus, physiological, cognitive, and emotional processes are so fused and interconnected that they are nearly inseparable. The combined functioning of these complex, interacting systems often leads to behavior that is termed "emotional." Managers must learn to deal with emotional reactions with sensitivity and acceptance.

Equilibrium. A part of the brain called the **hypothalamus** is responsible for regulating the internal bodily functions, such as heart rate, hormone secretions, temperature, and so on. This regulation process is the body's way of maintaining a balance, or **equilibrium,** between internal functions and external stimuli. When stimuli represent a stressful or fearful situation, the body begins to prepare to cope with it. Heart rate and breathing increase to provide more oxygen, muscles tense, blood rushes to where it is most needed, and so on. The body is doing what it can to maintain equilibrium. We also have mental and emotional tools to help maintain equilibrium. For instance, when we get bored we may try to maintain a level of interest by seeking stimulation; when we are angry, we "blow off steam." In an organizational setting, managers need to be aware of the environmental conditions that may lead employees to engage in nonproductive or disruptive activities to restore equilibrium. (For a different view of equilibrium, refer to the discussion in Chapter 19.)

Managerial Skills in Understanding Behavior

Once managers truly understand that there is no real distinction between "mind" and "body," and that people behave in complex, often nonrational ways that result from a myriad of factors, they can begin to be more effective in dealing with their employees. People respond, not to some objective "reality," but to their private interpretation of whatever field of forces surrounds them. As a manager, it is best to work from the premise that all behavior is reasonable and goal directed. What may appear irrational to one is perfectly logical to another. Those managers who discover how others perceive the situation are likely to be more effective than those who try to use their own perceptions as the only measure of reality.

If managers wish to understand why employees act as they do, they must somehow try to experience the world from others' perspectives. The ability to "put oneself in another's shoes," called **empathy,** is not easy. Empathy requires managers to set aside their own values and try not to immediately evaluate or judge what the other person says and does. Empathic listening takes practice, patience, and time. And most managers would complain that they are too busy. It could be, however, that spending time building empathic listening skills is the most important and valuable thing a manager can do to keep the organization viable and relevant in a rapidly changing environment.

No matter how empathic a manager may be, however, the fact remains that organizational goals and the work requirements based on them will at times be incompatible with one another and with the personal needs of the employees. When their path to personal goal achievement is blocked, individuals will try to find substitute ways of reaching their objectives, restoring equilibrium, or neutralizing the source of stress. In these attempts to satisfy their needs and to retain equilibrium between the forces within and the pressures without, all persons will behave defensively at times.

Blocking need satisfaction creates a feeling of frustration within the individual. Frustration, in turn, creates some degree of aggression. Interestingly, aggression can take an internal and external form. External forms of expressing aggression generally are not allowed in most areas of society and certainly not in organizations. They are not recommended here as an effective recourse for dealing with frustration.

Internal expressions of aggression involve turning the anger or frustration on oneself. Its external symptom is that of **apathy.** Apathy is a major method used by employees to deal with blockage of their goals on the job. But it is self-defeating and an ineffectual means of coping with frustration. Managers need to look at the underlying causes of apathy rather than try to deal just with the symptom.

How deep the division is between the organization's goals and the individual's needs is the subject of continuing debate. Argyris and Presthus contend that the division is large indeed. Argyris claims that as individuals mature, their needs and competencies change. They develop many skills, have longer attention spans, want more depth, and become more independent. His observations indicate that organizations often thwart these new developments by keeping the individual in a condition of dependency. Presthus finds that a majority of people in organizations may be classified as *indifferent*. They do not agree with the organizational goals but have quit fighting them. All they want is to be given their check on payday (24).

The cost to an organization of indifferent people is great. They become inflexible. And as a result, they refuse to change when external conditions require it. Nor are they creative or innovative when their skills are needed. Perhaps the worst part is that the whole cycle leads to a **self-fulfilling prophecy.** That is, people act apathetic because they do not expect much from the organization. Management then designs jobs for apathetic people, which reinforces, or fulfills, people's low expectations and creates more apathy.

Chapter Review

People are an organization's most important resource. But they are also the most frustrating and complex resource that organizations have. The models of human behavior that are available are partial at best; however, they do provide managers with guidelines for creating an atmosphere conducive to motivating employees toward organizational goals. The purpose of this chapter has been to examine these models so that managers can better understand and use these available methods. The specific ideas and terms that have been covered are outlined below.

1. All people are both different and the same.
2. Managers cannot motivate employees; they can, though, establish conditions whereby human behavior is directed toward the accomplishment of organizational goals.

3. Human behavior in an organization is a combining of the factors of **skills, knowledge,** and **effort.**

4. Satisfaction is *not* necessarily connected to performance but it has been shown to be connected to turnover and absenteeism.

5. **Rewards** are valued outcomes that result from behavior. **Extrinsic rewards** are external to the work and provided by others; **intrinsic rewards** directly result from performing the work.

6. **Needs** may be described as a disturbance in an individual's equilibrium. Need categories according to Maslow include:

   a. **Physiological needs,** which pertain to the basic life-preserving functions;

   b. **Safety and security needs,** which are concerned with secondary preservation of life and with security;

   c. **Social acceptance needs,** which have to do with wanting love and affection;

   d. **Esteem needs,** which derive from wanting to be well thought of by self and others and that lead to positive self-regard; and

   e. **Self-actualization needs,** which drive people to become the best that they can be.

7. **Socially derived needs** result from human interaction. Some of the more important are **affiliation, power,** and **achievement.**

8. **Expectancy theory** posits that behavior is a function of offering rewards that satisfy a person's needs; connecting performance to rewards; and connecting effort to performance.

9. **Exchange theory** says that behavior is caused by a perceptual comparison of contributions and rewards.

10. **Selective perception** is the process by which stimuli are filtered through the brain to sort out what is relevant. Perception can be inaccurate as a result of **overreactions, unintended reactions, mistaken signals,** and **closure.**

11. **Attitudes** are preconceived notions, beliefs, or feelings about things; they create predispositions to act in certain ways. **Values** are enduring emotional responses of good or bad and right or wrong about ideals or institutions.

12. People are a combination of physiological, emotional, and cognitive processes that operate together in an attempt to maintain **equilibrium.**

13. **Empathy** is the ability to "put oneself in another's shoes," to experience another's feelings and behaviors from his or her point of view.

Discussion Questions

1. Explain the implications of the questions:
   a. Will I participate?
   b. At what level will I participate?

2. Evaluate the statement "Good managers are those who can get people moving."

3. How do skill, knowledge, and effort relate to job performance?

4. A manager throws up his hands and says, "People are just irrational." Does this statement make sense? Why?

5. Describe the relationship between job satisfaction and productivity.

6. Your boss (and owner of the company) has just come back from lunch with friends convinced that the way to raise productivity is through a profit-sharing plan. Explain your response to this proposal in terms of expectancy theory.

7. Why is the study of needs relevant to a course in management?

8. Describe Maslow's hierarchy of needs. Where do you see yourself in this hierarchy?

9. What are the main variables of expectancy theory and how do they interact?

10. How does exchange theory operate?

11. Why is the study of perception relevant to understanding human behavior in organizations?

12. What advice would you give to a manager who wants to move beyond a knowledge of human behavior into having effective personal relationships with others?

Involvement Activity

1. Write a paragraph or more about a class that you did exceptionally well in by your standards. Describe why you think you did well and explain how you felt about the class as an experience.

2. Write a paragraph or more about a class that you did very poorly in or that was "a waste of time." Describe why you think you did poorly and explain how you felt about the class as an experience.

3. To what extent did each of the following factors influence the two situations described above?

Set 1	Set 2
Achieving	The administration of the course
Being recognized	The instructor
Learning something	The relations between you and the instructor
Being responsible	Class physical conditions
Advancing	Relations with others in the class
Growing	Not knowing how you are doing
	Grades and grading standards

(Set 1 is adapted from Herzberg's list of motivator factors and is most likely associated with the first situation you wrote about. Set 2 is an adaptation of Herzberg's hygiene factors, or dissatisfiers, and is most likely associated with the second situation you wrote about. In terms of this chapter, Set 1 contains mainly intrinsic factors and Set 2 contains primarily extrinsic factors.) (25)

4. Compare your paragraphs with those of others in the class and discuss the relative influence of the factors in Sets 1 and 2.

5. If Herzberg is correct, people are motivated to perform at high levels when motivator factors are present and when hygiene factors have been stabilized and accepted. How would you design a course structure that maximizes the use of motivator factors? What difficulties might you encounter in designing such a course?

9

People: Personnel Methods

Just like any other resource, people have to be brought into the organization and maintained. But unlike maintaining other resources, maintaining people requires the organization to engage in a continuing and flexible exchange relationship that balances the needs of the organization with the needs of the employees.

The purpose of this chapter is to introduce the reader to the range of personnel methods used to help attract people to, and maintain them in, the organization. The methods that will be examined here include: staffing—the activities that bring people into organizations and match them to their jobs; development—the activities associated with adapting human resources to the ongoing changes in work within organizations; and compensation—the activities associated with obtaining employee effort through adequate rewards.

In this chapter, people will be viewed as an organizational resource. The major consideration will be how to best use these human resources to accomplish the work of the organization. The place to start, of course, is **staffing.** The function of staffing is to match the skills, knowledge, and effort potential of the person with the requirements of a particular position. Once the right person has been recruited, personnel activities focus on **developing** the person's knowledge about the specific work environment. Finally, procedures for **rewarding** the person in ways that maximize effort must be implemented.

Methods for best matching people and jobs in organizations constitute a major portion of the courses and books in personnel administration. This chapter obviously cannot cover this subject in depth. What it can do, though, is present an overview of the ways in which personnel activities interact with the motivation models presented in the last chapter and consider the impact of personnel methods on other managerial areas of activity. Since this chapter deals with methods of people management, Figure 9–1 is the same as Figure 8–1.

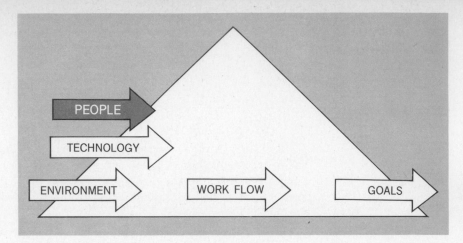

FIGURE 9–1
How people affect the
work of organizations.

Staffing

The traditional approach to staffing operates under the assumption that the nature of the job determines the skills and characteristics required of the person who fills it. A search then ensues for someone whose skills and characteristics best match the job requirements.

In this model, the job is the constant and the person is the variable. People are chosen to fit jobs. The advantage of this approach is that organizations can design coherent and logical arrangements of jobs that best suit the work to be done. As long as there is a large and diverse labor market, the chance of finding people who match the jobs is good.

A major drawback to this approach is that it fails to utilize the full range of a person's abilities. We have seen in the last chapter that people are not all alike. So to lump a large group of people together in the same type of job and expect each person to behave like all the others is not realistic. Some portion of the work group will probably be stretching very hard to keep up, and others will be bored because they do not feel challenged. Teachers face this problem all the time: how can they keep the top students interested without losing the slower students?

Another disadvantage of adhering strictly to the job design is that it creates a **negative selection system.** This means that everyone in the organization who is involved in the hiring decision has the opportunity to say "no," and only one person has the authority to say "yes." It is really a wonder that anyone ever gets hired at all. From the clerk at the front desk through all stages of the personnel department, all have the authority to turn back an application. Only the manager for whom the applicant will be working has the power to make a positive decision. Thus, the selection process becomes one of finding faults with or negative information about prospective employees in order to turn them down. This negative selection system is reinforced by the fact that people tend to place greater weight on negative information than on positive information in selection decisions (1).

An alternative approach to staffing reverses the procedure by asking, "What can this person do?" not "What is it this person can't do?" This approach assumes that jobs are flexible to the extent that they can be made to accommodate individual differences in talents and interests. In this way, organizations make fuller use of human resources. The cost, of course, is that it requires flexibility on the part of management, and that jobs cannot always be designed in such a neat and orderly fashion. At the extremes of the labor market this alternative strategy is particularly useful. Organizations do not usually design jobs for professionals, such as doctors, scientists, and lawyers, with rigid, predetermined requirements. Rather, organizations tend to design these jobs in accordance with the interests and particular areas of training of the professionals. At the other end of the labor market are the chronically unemployed, whose skills are either minimally developed or of little use to most organizations. For this group, jobs need to be specially designed to take advantage of whatever skills the person does have.

Affirmative Action Considerations

Organizational staffing is currently undergoing a revolution created by new laws in the area of equal employment opportunities. The revolution was begun by the Equal Pay Act of 1963 and was extended by Title VII of the Civil Rights Act of 1964 and the Equal Employment Opportunity Act of 1972. The thrust of this legislation was to eliminate discrimination in all personnel decisions on the basis of race, religion, color, sex, or national origin.

Initially, the assumption of equal opportunity legislation was that if employers were forbidden by law from consciously discriminating against minority-group members and women, then these people would begin to appear in the wide range of jobs suddenly made available to them. But this assumption was inaccurate. It turns out that discrimination is so deeply entrenched throughout the whole system that it cannot be eliminated simply by making laws that deal with overt hiring practices. For instance, in one celebrated court case it was learned that blacks had been denied employment on the grounds that they did not have a high-school diploma, which was required for the particular job. However, the company could not show how or in what way a high-school diploma was a necessary requisite for performing the job. It was ruled that the company cease to require a high-school diploma as a selection criterion for that position (2).

The additional assumption that great numbers of minorities would begin to apply for positions proved untrue. They simply did not believe the statement at the bottom of the advertisement that claimed "equal opportunity employer." Years of practice are not undone by simply saying one is going to change. Positive action was needed. The organization had to go out and actively seek minority-group people and assure them that it did indeed have jobs for them. In many cases this meant convincing people that they were qualified and could do the job. This problem is particularly evident in the case of women moving into managerial positions. Because women have been socialized from youth to take a secondary role and not to be aggressive, positive programs are needed that not only change the organizations' attitudes but also change women's attitudes about themselves. Women must truly believe in the falsity of the bias they have accepted before they will try for managerial positions.

Attempts to deal positively with discrimination problems are called **affirmative action** programs. Rather than simply removing the obstacles to employment and advancement, an affirmative action program seeks ways to actively recruit women and minority-group members for positions in the organization. In many cases this program has led to the establishment of employment goals. This means that organizations attempt to maintain a certain set number of minority-group people and women in positions on all levels of the organizational hierarchy. The Equal Employment Opportunity Commission (EEOC) has been established for the purpose of investigating and prosecuting cases of noncompliance with affirmative action legislation. Although the Commission is understaffed and handles only major cases, the cost of settlements is already several millions of

The Truth About Women?

Write *agree* or *disagree* next to the following statements and then compare your responses with the facts provided below.

1. American women work just for pin money.
2. Women would not work if economic reasons did not force them into the labor market.
3. Women are more concerned than men with the socio-emotional aspects of their jobs.
4. Women are more concerned than men with the hygiene aspects of their jobs.
5. Women are less concerned than men that their work be self-actualizing.
6. Women are more content than men with intellectually undemanding jobs.
7. Women are less concerned than men with getting ahead on the job.

FACTS

1. Over one-third of working women are sole or major wage earners.
2. A lower percentage of married women than men would not work if they did not have to, but there is no difference between men and single women.
3. The only difference is that women tend to place somewhat more importance on having friendly and cooperative co-workers.
4. Yes, to some degree. Women place more importance on physical surroundings, convenient travel, and good working hours.
5. Men and women share equal concern with having meaningful work.
6. Neither sex likes undemanding jobs.
7. Women are just as interested in promotion as men *when they feel* they have a chance for promotion.

Source: J. R. Crowley, T. E. Levitan, and R. P. Quinn, "Seven Deadly Half-Truths About Women," *Psychology Today*, vol. 6, no. 10, (March 1973) pp. 94–96.

dollars. Affirmative action is not something any organization can afford to ignore these days (3).

Affirmative action provides the organization with a good opportunity to create a truly effective personnel program. The goals of affirmative action are essentially to have all positions occupied by the people who can best perform the job. In pursuit of this goal, many of the current personnel practices, particularly psychological testing, have been called into question and found wanting. Out of this questioning, however, are arising staffing procedures and techniques that are far more valid than those used in the past.

Supply and Demand Considerations

The process of matching people and jobs necessarily depends on supply and demand. The demand is unfilled jobs and the supply is available people. Unlike many other areas of the economy, organizations have not had to concern themselves much with planning ahead for staffing needs because rarely does the demand exceed the supply. And in the few times that it does, organizations are able to adjust both the supply (people) and the demand (jobs) to take care of the problem. Excess supply is of little concern to individual organizations, and the problem is left to government to handle. The approach by government has been to try to keep demand high by stimulating the economy and providing relief to those who cannot find jobs.

It is likely that personnel planning will become more important in the future. As more people develop specialized skills that organizations need, the labor market changes from a single entity to a number of separate entities—each comprising people with a certain set of skills. Shortages in these specialized markets can then cause demand to exceed supply, and organizations will need to be able to predict such eventualities. Furthermore, affirmative action programs make it more difficult than in the past to fire people, and hiring decisions need to be carefully thought out in terms of future needs.

Job Specifications

In order to implement the traditional staffing approach defined earlier, it is necessary to define and describe jobs to determine what qualifications are required of the people who will perform them. Job descriptions and specifications are the end products of job analysis. (Job analysis and descriptions were discussed in Chapter 5.)

Job specifications are statements of the qualifications needed to perform the job tasks and they constitute the major tool used in staffing. Job requirements can be determined in two ways. First, the job analyst can observe people already performing the tasks and note the skills that they use to carry out the job. Second, for newly created jobs that are not yet staffed, the job analyst can determine what skills are required by analyzing the tasks that need to be performed. In the first method, one might observe an engineering aide using algebraic equations and determine that a knowledge of algebra is required for the job. In the second method, one would look at the nature of the problems to be solved and come to the same conclusion.

Once the job requirements have been defined, the organization then searches for the best-qualified applicant. But this still leaves open the meaning of the word *qualified*. In Western society the idea of merit or ability is strongly ingrained into people's thinking. It is so pervasive in fact, that we resist all other bases of qualification on the grounds that they are inefficient. Affirmative action programs are based on the belief that merit is the only valid criterion. But merit is often defined in terms that are too broadly stated. In other words, merit should be made to apply only to the specific position, not to the general labor market. Misunderstanding of this point leads to overselection and underutilization of human resources. This is a "more is better" philosophy. Suppose, for instance, that an organization has determined that it takes an I.Q. of at least 95 to perform a particular drafting job. The organization then administers an intelligence test to all applicants and ranks the applicants according to their scores;

the highest I.Q. scores are ranked at the top. If the highest-scoring applicant is chosen for the job, the organization may not necessarily (or even probably) be placing the best-qualified person in the position. If the optimum I.Q. for the drafting job is, say, between 100 and 110, a person who scores 135 on the I.Q. test is undoubtedly overqualified for the job and may soon grow bored. Overselection and underutilization produce a number of problems, such as high labor turnover, bored workers who may experience a variety of personal problems (alcoholism is common), trouble-makers, or most important, underutilization itself. If superior talent is available and unused, the organization is failing to take advantage of its human resources. It may need to examine its job design with the idea of upgrading its positions.

Another error in using merit as the only criterion in selection is that current behavior tends to be confused with the requirements of a different job. This is the error noted by the Peter Principle, or the rule of incompetency (4). This rule says that people are selected for higher-level positions based on how well they perform their present job. But as discussed in Chapter 6, different levels have different demands. When people are no longer considered "promotable" they have reached a level beyond their best performance, or one level above their level of competency. Thus the organizational hierarchy is staffed, by definition, with people who have reached their "level of incompetence."

Recruitment

Recruitment is the next step in staffing after the job requirements have been determined. Recruitment starts with obtaining a list of people who are qualified for and interested in the position(s) to be filled. From this list, a search is instituted for the person or persons who are most interested in participating in the organization on the terms and conditions that are extended and who are basically qualified to do the work.

Recruiting Specifications. The job specifications used in recruiting can vary considerably. At one extreme, only a broad definition of the skills required is identified, such as "must have initiative and be a mechanical engineer." In this case, the job will be fitted to the person. At the other extreme, the job is clearly defined and the requirements are extensive and limiting, such as "must have five years' experience in the design of servo-mechanisms," meaning that the individual(s) selected must meet the specifications exactly.

Which approach is used by an organization depends on both the degree of structure within the organization and the prevailing conditions in the labor market. These two factors can be in conflict. An organization that has definite organizational roles and rigid specifications for those roles will have a difficult time recruiting in a tight labor market. It will have to look extensively to find the individuals who fit the well-defined roles that have been established. Furthermore, the organization may have to offer higher rewards to ensure getting the people who are available.

Recruitment as Potential Exchange. The exchange model provides a useful framework for examining recruitment. In the terms of the exchange model, recruitment can be viewed as offering rewards for contributions. The ratio, of course, depends on a number of forces. As mentioned earlier, one force is the perception of relevancy by the prospective employee. Another is that there must be a positive balance between rewards and contributions. Both the organization and the individual can affect this balance of rewards and contributions. For instance, if the rewards are low, the organization may require fewer working hours. If the contributions are less than anticipated, the organization may lower the rewards.

These adjustments may be theoretically open, but a complicating factor is the outside environment, particularly current economic conditions. An individual's perception changes with the economic tides. When the economy is down, opportunities are fewer so the organization's rewards look better. Conversely, when the economy is good, and people have a scarce skill, they can very easily upgrade the value they place on their contributions. During the past ten years, for example, engineers and scientists have found their skills in demand at one time, and in oversupply at another. Both the intrinsic and extrinsic rewards expected by these groups are higher than those of many other groups in industry. The reasons are that for years there has been a high demand for their services and they have enjoyed high professional status in the community. However, when there is a surplus of engineers or when there is a cutback in a federal program, a very different set of perceptions is evident.

Recruitment Sources and Techniques. The purpose of recruitment is to try to attract qualified people to the organization. In order to do so, the organization must first locate these people and then decide on the best manner of attracting them. Recruiting is an expensive activity so it should start as close to home as possible.

1. *Inside the Organization.* The first place to look for people is inside the organization, starting with personnel records of who is employed and what they are capable of doing. Finding out who is in the organization usually does not present a serious problem except in very large organizations, but knowing what people are really capable of doing is very difficult.

Some organizations attempt to maintain a **skills inventory** so that a knowledge of human resources is always available to them. However, such inventories are typically very limited in scope and operation. One reason for the limited use of inventories is that many managers are not eager to have the whole organization know about their good employees. Another reason is based on the fairly common assumption that people at lower organizational levels have few suitable skills except the ones they are currently using on the job. But affirmative action programs are now trying to combat this assumption by making it necessary for organizations to know more about their employees by keeping up-to-date and accurate personnel records (5).

One of the most persistent problems of recruiting from within the organization is that there is more negative information available about employees than about applicants from outside the organization.

2. *Outside the Organization.* Labor markets can be defined according to both skill and geography. When recruiting outside the organization, the first thing to do is discover where the people are that are needed. If an organization can expect to find sufficient clerks in the nearby community, it is not efficient to advertise all over the state. If the search is for new college graduates, a nationwide canvass of college campuses is the logical place to start. A careful effort must be made to define the labor market when the organization is seeking people with specialized skills.

3. *Interviews.* Recruiting ordinarily involves interviewing people. The purpose of the recruitment interview is twofold. One is to collect information about the person, and the second is to give the person information about the organization. The first interview is usually preliminary; that is, if mutual interest is established, the person is usually called back for a second interview. In recruitment interviews, the criteria are often so general that the determination of whether a person is qualified is very subjective. In fact, while interviews have a good deal of "face" validity, their empirical validity and reliability has proved to be quite low (6).

Selection

Selection is the final staffing activity and consists of making the choice of the right person for the right position. Selection involves analyzing all the results from recruitment activities and then choosing the one person who best fits the requirements of the position.

Strategy. Selection, like staffing in general, can focus either on the job or on the individual. Focusing on the job is an organizational strategy based on the work to be done. Focusing on the individual is a vocational guidance strategy intended to place the person in the best possible position. In practice, most selection strategies are some combination of these two strategies. An attempt is made to hire the best possible person for the job, but there is also the expectation that the job will be modified somewhat to accommodate the person's individual skills and personality (7).

In a loose labor market (when unemployment is high) managers have more power to determine the content of the job in advance of selection. In a tight labor market (when unemployment is low) job definition is a more bargainable issue and is more likely to be jointly determined by the manager and the individual. Another alternative for management is to realign the jobs in terms of the availability of personnel in the particular market.

For instance, an engineering design task might be accomplished by a small number of high-level designers or by a large number of beginning designers and draftspeople. The decision as to which way to go would depend upon the availability of the various skills both inside and outside the organization.

Sequence. Selection puts together the two kinds of information gathered thus far in staffing. The first is information about the job in terms of human requirements needed to perform the tasks. This information constitutes the criteria for selection. These criteria are then converted into a group of **predictor variables.** That is, if a manager observes that the draftsperson is using algebraic equations, the job requirements will reflect a knowledge of algebra. In turn, a grade of C or better in second-year high-school algebra or a passing score on a math placement test is a predictor variable for a knowledge of algebra. Typically there are a number of predictor variables for any one job.

Second, there is information about a number of candidates who appear to meet minimal organizational requirements and who are interested in joining the organization. These people are expected to vary in the degree to which they possess the attributes of the predictor variables. Two things need to be said about this list of candidates. First, it is not complete. As indicated earlier, recruitment is expensive. At best it contains only some portion of the people who *could* do the job. So any selection activity involves picking from a limited population. The more important the job, the more there will be an attempt to draw from the largest possible population.

Second, how good this selection process is will depend not only on the number of people generated but on the number of people needed. As an example, assume an organization has been able to establish a list of one hundred people. If two people are needed, the organization can be very particular. If twenty-five are needed, the organization is still able to maintain very high standards. But if sixty or more people are needed, organizational standards are going to be quite low. If the organization arrives at the point where the number of applicants and positions are exactly equal, the strategy employed is unlikely to lead to placements that best use the skills of the applicants (8).

The purpose of selection is to compare the qualifications of the applicants with the predictor variables. If there is a single variable, then all people may be ranked according to the degree to which they have that variable. Selection would then consist of picking from the top down on that list. Thus, in the example used earlier of a knowledge of algebra as a predictor variable, the applicant with the highest math grades or the one who had completed the highest-level college math courses would be the first choice. It would be easier, however, to use scores on a mathematical placement test because all applicants would be competing on a standardized measure. Also, the test could be designed to reflect the type and extent of math knowledge needed for the job and would be a better predictor variable. But in either case, there is still the problem of defining "best qualified" as discussed before. For example, those at the top of the list may be *over*qualified rather than *best* qualified.

Very few selection decisions are made on the basis of a single predictor variable; rather a number of predictor variables are commonly used. Furthermore, people do not rate the same on all these predictor variables. Thus, a weight must be placed on each predictor variable to indicate the strength of its contribution to the overall decision. All candidates are then rated on each predictor variable and a composite score is calculated according to the varying weights. This process assumes that all predictor variables can be reduced to a numerical score. When these conditions cannot be met, and usually they cannot, the weighting and comparisons must be made in the decision maker's head, using subjective judgment.

Reliability and Validity. So far, this discussion of the selection process has assumed a direct relationship between predictor variables, criteria, and eventual performance on the job. But such a perfect relationship does not exist. The usefulness of a predictive variable is measured by its **reliability** and **validity.** If a measurement technique is **reliable,** it is consistent; that is, it will give the same results every time it is used. A math test is not useful if the same person scores in the tenth percentile one day and the sixtieth two days later. So the first standard a predictor variable must meet is reliability.

A measurement technique also must meet the standard of validity. A **valid** technique is one that measures what it is supposed to measure. A math test that does not adequately reveal a person's knowledge of math is not a valid test, and it will not predict future performance accurately.

Psychological tests have come under considerable attack in the past few years by the EEOC because there are very low correlations between test scores and performance and because organizations have no information about the validity of their tests. This questioning has cast some doubt on the value of psychological tests for employment purposes. However, even where tests are not used, the validity of the process may not be high. The EEOC is currently examining the whole selection process, and extensive changes are expected to be implemented in testing, interviewing, and other selection techniques (9).

In summary, staffing is the series of activities by which the organization attempts to match people and jobs. It is a predictive process in the sense that the organization is guessing, from limited information, how well the individual will do in a prescribed set of future circumstances (the job). The process is imperfect. The validity of the predictive variable is, at best, low and is often unknown. The process has rigidities that tend to select out qualified people, and it is incomplete in its ability to even determine who is "best qualified."

Only as Good as His Skin Test

Market research has moved into television news in a big way. Fresh from victories in the deodorant and pantyhose wars, the social scientists of the supermarket are now busy measuring our emotional reactions to on-air news personalities.

News programs are big profit-makers for the network O&O stations (owned & operated). Each network is limited to five such stations and they battle for ratings like demons in the three cities—New York, Chicago and Los Angeles—where they compete head to head.

Last spring, the CBS O&O in Los Angeles—KNXT—was having serious ratings problems with its news shows. So it hired a San Francisco firm called ERA Research to round up a hundred typical viewers, who were paid $20 apiece to attend a special screening at a hotel. Once seated, these volunteers had electric sensors attached to their fingers—two metal plates were bound to the pads of their index and ring fingers on one hand. Their GSR (galvanic skin response) was about to be measured.

Skin reactions are a standard part of lie-detector tests. When people are calm, their palms stay dry. But when they get emotionally turned on—frightened, angry, guilty or just sexually aroused—their sweat glands open up, the skin gets wet and its resistance to an electrical current passed through the fingers is lowered. When you measure resistance, you are measuring emotion—or so the researchers claim. And emotional response to TV performances tends to bring viewers back for more.

When the audience had been wired up, the houselights were darkened and the show began. It consisted of video tapes of newscasters, most of them from the Los Angeles market. During each segment, ERA meters traced the skin responses on graphs. When each tape was finished, the lights came on and the audience answered questions about their feelings. Word

columns filled the pages of the questionnaires and the viewers were asked to circle the words most closely describing the newscaster they had just watched. Friendly, cold, warm or distant? Shifty or believable? Attractive, plain, familiar, dull? Good diction, syntax and vocabulary? Then on to the next tape, the next newscaster.

Three months later the test results were delivered to CBS management in Los Angeles and New York. The next day, handsome KNXT anchorman Patrick Emory was fired. Two days later, pretty co-anchor Sandy Hill was called into news director Bob Schaefer's office and given the same bad news. Over the next few weeks about two dozen on-air reporters and supporting players suddenly found themselves out of work.

ERA skin testing is showing up all over the country. There is talk that sweat glands are being measured at KING-TV in Seattle, WBBM-TV in Chicago, in Minneapolis and in Denver. Recently in St. Louis, CBS used ERA on its KMOX-TV newscasters.

George Putnam, veteran Los Angeles anchor personality and award-winning journalist, voices the feelings of many less outspoken newspeople. "This ERA thing is frightening," he said. "I'm sure if they showed Adolf Hitler up there on that screen, the needle would jump right out of the glass. But that's no reason to hire Adolf to anchor the 5 o'clock news.

"Skin tests leave out the most important element—a person's ability over the years to do the job of electronic journalism. I can see a time coming when actors and actresses who want to be anchorpeople will just buy themselves a set of skin sensors and practice getting their friends and family to react emotionally."

Development

While the staffing process involves a determination of the individual's present skills and abilities, the development process deals with what the person could be at some future time. The advantage of people over machines is their flexibility and ability to grow and change. Development seeks to make the most of these human traits. It is a second approach to staffing that grooms and prepares the current work force for future job needs. The choice, however, is not between development and staffing but between the size of the role that each plays in the management of human resources. At a minimum, development activities must be capable of providing the employee with specific knowledge of the organization and of the position that extends beyond the more general skills and abilities needed to perform the job.

Internal Development Versus External Staffing

Most organizations employ a mixed strategy, doing some internal development and some selection from outside. Obviously some selection from outside is always needed to replace those members who leave the organization. A strategy question then is the level at which people will be recruited to enter the organization.

Limited Entry Points. Some organizations have only one or two levels at which people may enter. The military service is a clear example of this extreme. This alternative creates a clear-cut career ladder for employees. They know what they must do to progress and are secure from outside intervention. They also know with whom they must compete. From the organization's standpoint, such a system would support a neat and orderly organizational structure and clear delineation of jobs. The danger lies in rigidity and inbreeding; reliability can easily turn into rigidity, or means can quickly become ends in this system. The "ideal type" bureaucracy developed by Weber is the model of this type of organization. As organizations grow larger they generally take on the characteristics of a bureaucracy, including that of limiting entrance to the lower levels only (10).

Open Entry Points. At the other extreme, people are recruited for all levels from outside the organization unless a present employee is clearly best suited for a particular position. This second alternative provides a maximum degree of flexibility for the organization. But in some ways this too is a dangerous policy. It places the organization at the mercy of the environment. The cost of obtaining qualified people may be high in a tight labor market, both in terms of salaries and recruiting costs. Further, one could expect less loyalty on the part of people within the organization if they know there is little chance for advancement, or if they have to compete with outside people for every opening. It can be expected that the individual will reciprocate by dealing with the organization strictly on a

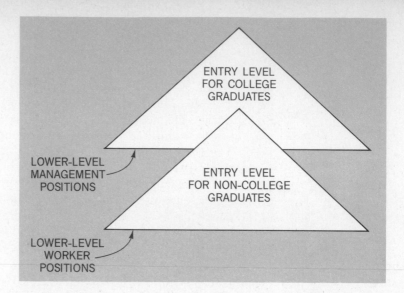

FIGURE 9-2
Double pyramid of career ladders in a dual-entry organization.

competitive basis, and have no qualms about moving to another firm when offered a better future. Thus, flexibility is gained at the cost of stability.

Most organizations do not operate at either of these extreme positions. Rather, there is generally a policy that favors one or the other practice. As the organization moves toward the first alternative, that of a closed entry system, development becomes more important, especially if the entry level is low in the organizational hierarchy. More typically, organizations allow entry at two places: in a lower-level management position for college graduates, and in a worker-level position for the nongraduate. This practice creates two separate career ladders with very little overlap, especially in larger organizations. The double pyramid of career ladders caused by the two-place entry system is shown in Figure 9-2. The entry level for the nongraduate typically has fewer levels and terminates at a level or two above the entry level for college graduates.

Developing Skills and Behavior Patterns

Organizations view development as a means to create needed skills and knowledge for the purpose of accomplishing the work to be done. Individuals view development as a process of continual adaptation to a changing environment.

Becoming Open to Change. People are motivated to change if they see their present strategies for satisfying their needs as ineffective or if they anticipate that a change will result in better methods of need satisfaction. Children change and adapt easily because they have not developed routines and because they anticipate the future with enthusiasm. Older people frequently become locked into familiar strategies and often must experience some kind of upending experience before they again become open to learning new modes of behavior. Human growth and development is essentially a process of people developing increasingly workable strategies for satisfying their needs. The primary task of growth is to produce an adult who is capable of living creatively in a complex social framework. In general, people have a positive thrust toward growth. When thwarted they will become frustrated and defensive, which leads to dysfunctional behavior both to the person and to the organization.

Learning. Learning is a vital yet frustrating part of every person's life. People need to change and adapt in order to grow, but the desire to grow is often grounded in a feeling of dissatisfaction with the present. In terms of expectancy theory, a person has a need that he or she seeks to satisfy. When a certain learning activity is perceived as the path to this need satisfaction, the individual will engage in that activity. Thus a person who wants to become a lawyer will attend law school and study and take the bar exams.

Types of Development

Organizations engage in a wide assortment of development programs, which vary according to the particular needs or circumstances of the company. These programs range from orientation procedures to skill- and basic-training techniques.

Orientation and Socialization. When people first come into an organization they need to know "how we do it here." This is a process of organizational socialization. The same thing occurs as people move to new positions laterally or vertically in the organization. They need to learn the appropriate values, attitudes, and other nondescribed aspects of the job they are undertaking. For the new employee, organizations develop orientation programs to dispense such information. The manager or a group of employees usually provides specific job-related information. In many cases there are what could be considered initiation rites, which are designed to acclimate the person to his or her place in the group.

A great deal of management development is an attempt to get the individual to internalize organizational values. Such internalization reduces the need for the organization to develop external rules and regulations that define desirable behavior. This type of training aims for reliability of behavior without the external signs of bureaucratic control. On the other hand, indoctrination can be dysfunctional if the individual resents such manipulation and rebels or simply loses trust in the organization and in the manager (11).

Skill Training. Organizations often design jobs for which no one in the labor market qualifies. For these special jobs, the organization must develop employees' skills. At other times, the organization may find the labor market too expensive. In either case, the organization may undertake skill development. Development may be for physical skills, such as

Training of the Hard-Core Unemployed

Many programs for the hard-core unemployed start, not by defining the job and selecting people, but by bringing in people, testing them to see what they can do, and then designing the jobs around current skills. The more successful programs have recognized that socialization is a major development problem. Chronically unemployed people have usually dropped out of the educational system and live in subcultures with very different value systems than exist in the mainstream of American life. These people do not have the same views about coming to work at given times five days a week, staying at their tasks until done, getting along with others, or deferring gratification in the same manner as do the majority of the work force. Assigning a "buddy" to the hard-core trainee is one technique used to alleviate this problem. The buddy's job is to show the trainee how the organization works.

When the hard-core unemployed must be developed for specific organizational jobs, basic training is usually required. This has often proved easier than once imagined. For instance, one program found that teaching potential truck drivers to read was an easy task once the material used consisted of bills of lading, maps, and street signs instead of "The Adventures of John and Mary."

Skill training turns out to be the most traditional aspect of training the hard-core unemployed. Two major requirements for positive results are an instructor who understands the people and an absence of the traditional classroom situation. The latter requirement stems from the fact that most of these people have previously experienced failure in the classroom, and the fear of failing again will inhibit their ability to learn in the present situation. Finally, if the supervisor has had some form of sensitivity training, he or she is more likely to be able to empathize with the group members and help them merge with the existing work force.

electronic assembly techniques, or for mental skills, such as a knowledge of procurement regulations and how to apply them. Skill development may also include training in interpersonal skills, which have to do with getting along well with other people.

Basic Training. Underlying job skills are *basic* skills. For instance, underlying the drafting skill are the basic skills of mechanical drawing and a knowledge of algebra, among other things. Basic skills are most often taught in the education system and not at the job location. However, when demand is high for certain basic skills, on-the-job training may be necessary. On-the-job training is useful when employees are no longer needed in their present jobs and have some of the basic skills necessary for a new job. Thus for new drafting positions, it may be useful to develop the mechanical drawing skills of a group of aides who already have the basic skill of algebra.

Development Programs

Development programs should be devised so that they incorporate the ideas on motivation discussed earlier. Development is the learning of new patterns of behavior. And people have to recognize that these new patterns will benefit them before they will commit themselves to participating in such a learning program. This is one advantage a business organization

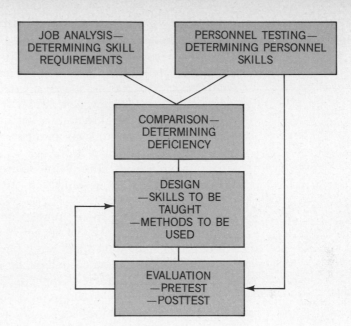

FIGURE 9–3
Development program sequence.

has over an educational institution. The business organization can show the person clearly what the gain might be, such as the possibility of a better job or a higher salary in the present position. Development, in common with all learning, occurs when the person experiences a *need* for learning new skills or behavior. The sequence is illustrated in Figure 9–3.

Job Analysis. The first step of a development program is the same as the first step in the selection process: job analysis. The purpose of the analysis is also the same, that is, to determine the skills that are required to perform the job.

Testing. The second step begins to mark a difference from the selection process. The same testing or examination of people occurs as in selection, but the purpose is to take an inventory of skills rather than to rank or rate the skills. A comparison of person and job also occurs, but here the purpose is to provide a list of job-related skills that the person does not yet have.

One of the major difficulties in development is that some employees will be almost ready for the new job at the beginning of training while others will require extensive skill development or even basic training. Putting together a single development plan is very difficult when there is such variability among program members. Where possible, the best approach is to establish a personalized system of instruction in which people are tested separately and a plan of action is developed that fits individual needs. This type of instruction is aided by programed learning techniques, which are described in the following section.

Methods of Instruction. Once the discrepancy between present knowledge and desired knowledge is ascertained, a training program can be developed. In general, if the organization is trying to dispense information, then lectures and films are efficient and fairly effective. The value of these techniques decreases as one moves toward other goals, however. Acquisition of knowledge is best accomplished where there is interaction and feedback, such as through discussions and programed instruction. When the goals are to change attitudes, such techniques as sensitivity training, case studies, and role playing, which involve the person as an active participant, are best. In developing problem-solving skills, active participation works well, as in simulation settings, games, programs, or case studies (12).

Note that in these more complex tasks of development the most useful techniques are those that are active and that require a great deal of feedback to the individual about his or her behavior. It is one thing to be able to listen to others and to understand the logic of a concept, but it is quite another thing to be able to apply it. The ability to apply concepts is a skill in itself, which also needs to be developed. Furthermore, feedback encourages the person to set short-run and intermediate goals and to develop a sense of accomplishment and success along the way. The problem with active learning is that it often appears erratic and hard to control.

Feedback and Control. The design of a development program should also include methods of measuring its effectiveness in terms of the behaviors for which the program was established. One of the reasons why knowledge of the effectiveness of different training techniques is sketchy is that criteria for measuring success have not been established. Thus organizations find themselves in the middle of an argument. Proponents of some training programs maintain that the programs are good because they work; critics argue that they are no good because they don't work. But neither side spells out clearly the criteria by which an objective judgment can be made.

Compensation

Developing skills and knowledge still does not ensure that needed behavior will be obtained from people. Organizations must also make certain that people put forth sufficient effort and maintain continuity of membership in the organization in order for goals to be accomplished. As discussed in the last chapter, people put forth effort in return for rewards. Thus, the development of an adequate compensation system is crucial to an organization's success.

Goals

The last chapter contained two models of motivation. The first emphasized the connection between rewards and desired behaviors. To the extent that employees are qualified, perceive the connections between performance and reward and performance and effort, and actually desire the reward, they will strive to accomplish the organization's work. It may be said, then, that one goal of compensation is to initiate and maintain goal-directed behavior; that is, to *obtain performance*.

The second model of motivation is that of exchange. This model emphasizes that organizational rewards must be in balance with employee contributions. Another way of stating this is that the exchange must be perceived as fair and reasonable. The second goal of compensation then is to provide an *equitable distribution of rewards*.

A final part of the overall model of behavior in organizations is satisfaction. Satisfaction is directly related to turnover. People who are satisfied stay with the organization. And turnover is expensive. It can cost upward from $10,000 to hire a highly skilled employee, and the cost of losing one can easily be $50,000 in lost investment. So maintaining *continuity of membership* is the third goal of compensation.

Although these three goals are often compatible, they can be at odds with one another. Equity goals take on organization-wide significance when jobs are compared across hierarchical levels for the sake of establishing equitable rewards. At the same time, connecting rewards and productivity on an individual basis often produces results that are at variance with the established wage scale. There must be an opportunity for the person to increase the amount of his or her rewards by increasing the amount of output he or she produces. But if the increase is too drastic, organizational equity is jeopardized. This situation is common in sales departments, where the salesperson works on a commission basis and the sales manager is on a salary. The successful salesperson can make more money than the manager — a situation that is perceived as inequitable in most organizations.

Strategies

Every organization must bargain for its resources in the marketplace on a competitive basis with other organizations seeking the same resources. And human resources are no different. For most organizations, people are an expensive, if not *the* most expensive, resource. It is important that the organization obtain the quantity and quality of people it needs but not spend too much time or money doing so.

While human resources are important to all organizations, they are more important to some than to others. The goals and structure of the organization make a considerable difference in the type of compensation strategy it employs. For instance, an organization that produces a fairly simple item, like pencils, on a mass-production basis using low-level skills, can compensate its employees without much regard to the compensation goals discussed above. On the other hand, an electronics engineering organization that designs and produces aircraft navigational equipment has a highly complex staff of experts and the organization's reputation rests with the services of its staff. This organization will undoubtedly be very much concerned with compensation goals and pay its employees accordingly. In broad terms, there are three possible compensation strategies that organizations use.

Under the Market. The first strategy is to stay below the market. This strategy seeks to minimize human resource costs by paying minimum wages. For the organization that makes pencils this might be a useful strategy. The advantage, of course, is that costs are kept to a minimum and the competitiveness of the organization in the product market is enhanced. The cost of this strategy is high turnover and employee dissatisfaction. But if the labor market is loose and rewards and contributions have been directly related, the costs of turnover may be minimal.

With the Market. A second strategy is to be a market follower. This means that the organization offers compensation that is competitive and that is fair to its employees. This strategy is probably the one used by most organizations. Almost all government agencies make the statement that they will endeavor to pay "prevailing wages in industry." The emphasis in this strategy is on equity. It is an appropriate policy for organizations in which human resources are important but not as critical as in the example of the engineering firm described earlier. A major drawback of this strategy is that the organization does not have control over the environment and thus is subject to wide economic fluctuations. It is a reactive stance, and the organization may find itself offering bigger rewards than it can afford or than are really necessary.

Market Leader. The third strategy is to be the market leader in offering rewards. The advantage of this strategy is the likelihood of attracting and retaining the best human resources. For the engineering organization, such a stance would be critical to maintaining the competitive edge of expertise and service. Obviously such a strategy is costly, and so it is most appropriate for organizations that can easily pass the costs on to the customer, such as service organizations.

To a great extent, the strategy that is employed will reflect the manager's perception of people. If the manager holds an economic view of people—that they respond to rewards and avoid punishment—then the chances are good that the under-the-market strategy will be used. A self-actualizing view of people—that they are growing, changing beings, striving to fully develop their skills—will tend to promote a market-leader strategy.

Administration of Rewards

A major contribution of behavioral scientists to the area of compensation has been increased awareness of the variety of rewards available in organizations beyond purely economic compensation. Money, while still the most flexible of rewards for providing access to many avenues of need satisfaction, is not the only reward that people find important. Some innovative companies have rearranged the forty-hour work week to extend their employee's weekends. And, as discussed in the last chapter, organizations are beginning to offer more intrinsic rewards in the form of job enlargement and enrichment.

The systems for administering extrinsic and intrinsic rewards differ from each other. Extrinsic rewards, such as salary, job security, good working conditions, medical insurance, and so on, are determined by organizational policy and are often under the province of such specialists as wage and salary administrators. Another area of extrinsic rewards is under the jurisdiction of the departmental manager. These rewards depend upon the understanding the manager has of human nature. They involve such things as trust, openness, casual versus formal relationships, and emphasis on competency rather than conformity. A manager's attitude toward his or her group can make the workplace either a pleasant experience or a battleground. Since intrinsic rewards center primarily around the job and the work, the way jobs are designed and the extent to which job involvement is encouraged are the systems through which these rewards are administered (13).

The appropriate combination of extrinsic and intrinsic rewards will depend upon the needs of the particular employees and the prevailing conditions in the environment. For instance, people operating on the lower end of Maslow's need hierarchy will want a greater preponderance of extrinsic rewards. Highly skilled, well-paid employees will require more intrinsic rewards as well.

The success that employees will have in bargaining for better or different rewards shifts with the conditions of the labor market. In times of low unemployment, the employees' bargaining position is good, and they can easily get extrinsic rewards. Once these are attained, bargaining begins for intrinsic rewards, although it is often not clearly marked as such. In times of high unemployment, of course, the employees' bargaining position is poor.

A problem with bargaining for intrinsic rewards is that it is often hard to verbalize the need for them. Employees may not know exactly what to ask for, and management may wonder whether the demands are legitimate. Thus in many recent teachers' strikes, the issues that were hardest to settle did not concern wages at all, but rather such seemingly inconsequential grievances as whether teachers had to stand watch on the playground during recess.

Methods

The methods for compensating employees are directly related to the goals of compensation. The method of job evaluation is tied to the goal of equitable distribution of rewards. The methods of performance appraisal and incentive systems relate to the goal of obtaining performance. And the method of offering fringe benefits is associated with the goal of maintaining membership continuity.

Job Evaluation. Equity can be summed up by the phrase "equal pay for equal work." Organizations develop elaborate systems for matching rewards (particularly monetary rewards) with the value of the job. This method, known as job evaluation, starts at the same point as do staffing and development — with job analysis. The information obtained from job analysis is set forth in a job description, and the description is then weighed against prescribed criteria that define pay levels in the organization. An example of this process appears in Figure 9–4.

In this hypothetical organization there are six pay levels and four job categories. Jobs are examined first to determine which category they belong in and then to determine what pay level is appropriate. The vertical lines in each job category indicate the pay levels used for each category of jobs. Job evaluation is made by comparing the job description with a given set of criteria (a description of each job level or a rating of job factors) and then making a judgment as to where within the range the particular job belongs. Each job would be rated according to the degree to which it possesses each factor, and the total number of points would give the relative standing of the position.

Performance Appraisal. Everyone regularly evaluates and is evaluated by others, so performance appraisal occurs naturally and spontaneously in all organizations. A more formal appraisal happens whenever managers assign work or take any personnel action, such as a promotion, transfer, or termination. A performance evaluation system, on the other hand, attempts to formally record judgments as to the quality of an employee's performance. Performance appraisal is often the instrument through which specific salaries are determined. Positions are not assigned precise rates of pay by job evaluation; rather they are placed in a **pay range.** Based on performance appraisals, people may then be given merit increases within the pay range for their position. While the system seems reasonable, it has some serious problems.

One major problem with a formal performance appraisal system is that it is often not related to output. That is, people are judged on such characteristics as initiative and cooperativeness, which are not outputs but inputs and which management hopes are connected to performance. These subjective judgments are a source of discomfort both to the employee and the manager. No one likes to give or receive negative feedback about personality traits.

Another problem with performance appraisal is that its goal is to both change behavior and reward behavior. This double-edged goal presents a conflict. For instance, the person knows that a reward rests on the outcome of the appraisal. Thus, any negative information he or she receives will be greeted defensively. But defensiveness is exactly the wrong attitude for being open to suggestions regarding behavior changes. Furthermore, even a change in behavior may not place a person's performance within the rewardable range. The manager then is faced with the dilemma

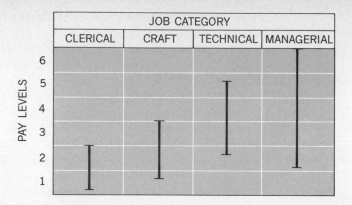

FIGURE 9–4
Model of a job evaluation system.

of whether to reward the change even though performance is still low (a problem of equity) or to tell the employee to keep trying, which will probably discourage the person and halt further change.

Incentive Systems. A second way of obtaining performance through compensation is through an **incentive system,** which offers direct rewards for specific behavior. For example:

1. People are paid a given rate for each unit of output they produce.
2. A standard day's output is defined and then people are given the option of receiving extra pay for all units produced above that standard or leaving when finished.
3. A standard production cost is determined, and any saving in this cost is shared with employees.

For incentive systems to work effectively, outputs must be measurable and complete.

The conditions for establishing an incentive program are based on expectancy theory, and they are quite demanding. First, the incentives must be something the employees want and need. It is also necessary to make certain that rewards are not in conflict. In particular, social rewards from group cooperation may be in conflict with incentives offered for individual effort.

Second, the person must be able to perceive the connection between performance and reward. Often, incentive plans are so complex that the employee does not understand what is being rewarded.

Third, incentive systems must tie effort to performance. This requires that people have control over their behavior. It is not functional to set up an incentive program that pays people for the number of units produced when the number of units produced is controlled by a machine. There must be some independence to the person's work, such as is more typical of a salesperson than a production-line worker. Where jobs are highly interdependent it is more reasonable to establish a group or company incentive program. The point is to match rewards with effort. Incentive systems only work when the employee can see that his or her efforts are directly connected to the output that is rewarded.

Fringe Benefits. Employees expect to be rewarded for more than their performance on the job. They also expect certain rewards for being members of the organization. These additional rewards are usually classified as fringe benefits and include such things as retirement programs and health or life insurance coverage. When the value of these fringe benefit rewards varies, it is usually as a result of the length of time the employee has been in the organization (seniority). Pension programs are a good example of how seniority can affect the value of these rewards.

Although people want, even demand, a complete package of fringe benefits from the organization, in the long run these rewards may trap people in the organization. The more that is invested in such programs as pension funds, the more expensive it becomes to move on to any other organization.

Chapter Review

This chapter has reviewed the methods used by organizations to attract and maintain employees. We have seen how people are brought into the organization and matched to jobs—the methods of staffing. And we have examined the ways in which development procedures seek to increase the value of the person to the organization and how compensation methods attempt to provide incentive and equity. The major ideas and terms developed in this chapter appear below.

1. **Staffing** is a process of matching people and jobs. In most organizations, people are matched to the requirements of the job rather than vice versa.

2. **Affirmative action** is a program established by law that requires organizations to hire, promote, and compensate employees on the basis of merit. This program includes nondiscriminatory personnel procedures as well as active involvement in ensuring that affirmative action goals are met.

3. **Job analysis** is an activity concerned with examining the contents of a job, including tasks, activities, interactions, and decisions. A staffing outcome of job analysis is a list of specifications or criteria for selecting people to fill the jobs.

4. The *best* qualified person for a job is not necessarily the *most* qualified person for the job.

5. **Recruitment** is the activity of developing a list of eligible applicants for positions within the organization.

6. **Predictor variables** are measurement devices that correlate job criteria with future performance.

7. **Reliability** is the quality of consistency of a predictor variable; **validity** is the degree to which a predictor variable measures the criterion it is supposed to measure.

8. **Development** activities are those that help employees achieve personal growth and obtain professional skills.

9. **Internal development** and **external staffing** are alternative strategies for filling jobs.

10. Development methods include: **orientation,** which socializes people to the organization and the job; **skill training,** which develops specific skills required for the job; and **basic training,** which develops general skills that underlie the job.

11. The purpose of **compensation** is to reward people equitably, for performance, and for staying with the organization.

12. **Job evaluation** is the activity of comparing jobs with preestablished standards to determine the relative worth of the jobs to the organization.

13. **Performance appraisal** is used to allocate rewards within a given salary range.

14. **Incentive systems** attempt to relate rewards directly to performance.

15. **Fringe benefits** are forms of compensation not directly related to the job but that are intended to attract people to and keep them in the organization.

Discussion Questions

1. Which personnel methods are associated with the work accomplishment determinants of skills, effort, and knowledge?

2. Why do organizations design jobs and then seek people to fill them instead of the other way around? What would happen to organizations if they first selected people and then designed jobs?

3. Distinguish between equal opportunity and affirmative action.

4. Think about being interviewed for a job. What would you like to know about the job? How would you like to be treated? Now think about being an interviewer for a company. What would you like to know about the person? How would you like the person to behave? What differences between the two situations do you see? How might you reconcile these differences to create a compatible interview situation?

5. Because of the low validity of personnel tests, some experts have suggested that they be discarded. What do you think of this suggestion? Why?

6. What are the advantages and drawbacks of hiring new employees on only the lowest levels of the organization?

7. What are the stages of the learning process? Which stages are hardest to get through?

8. Determine goals and methods for the following development situations:

a. bringing in a new group of college graduates;

b. retraining accounting clerks to be keypunch operators; and

c. assuring a supply of managers who can fill vice-presidential openings in a bank.

9. What are the goals of compensation programs?

10. Make an argument for being *under, over,* and *even* with the market in terms of the compensation programs offered by an organization.

11. Research the ways in which each of the following methods of job evaluation operates:

a. ranking;

b. classification;

c. point; and

d. factor comparison.

(See David W. Belcher, *Compensation Administration,* Prentice-Hall, 1976; or J. D. Dunn and Frank M. Rachel, *Wage and Salary Administration,* McGraw-Hill, 1971.)

12. Discuss the conditions for establishing incentive systems. How do they work? How can they go wrong.?

Involvement Activity

You are a recent graduate of State University and have just been hired as the personnel director of Golden Stores, Inc. Golden Stores is a chain of retail stores specializing in gifts, decorations for the home, and bath supplies. There are currently over fifty stores in shopping centers throughout the Southwest, and plans are being formulated to extend the chain to the rest of the country.

Golden Stores employs approximately four hundred people. A small group of employees is located in the company's headquarters. This group is responsible for purchasing, general management, accounting, and financial control. In addition, a series of regional warehouses is also controlled from the company's headquarters. The remainder of the employees are spread throughout the stores; these people are the store managers, assistant managers, and clerks. Each store has about five employees.

You are the first personnel manager. Until now, the district managers have handled personnel matters as a part of their jobs. The reasons for establishing a separate personnel department seem to be a result of:

a. complaints to EEOC by two female employees regarding wages and denials of promotion to assistant manager positions;

b. overtures by the Teamsters' union made to the warehouse personnel in the regional locations; and

c. problems of turnover among store managers.

Your first task is to organize and develop your own job. To this end, write a job description that covers:

1. the major tasks that will be carried out;

2. the policy areas to be considered and developed; and

3. the interrelations with other parts of the organization, specifically:

a. regional managers;

b. store managers; and

c. headquarters staff (accounting and payroll).

(Remember the discussion of staff and line in Chapter 7.)

10

Groups in Organizations

The purpose of this chapter is to explore the dynamics of groups in organizations and the ways in which groups affect organization design and managerial work.

Groups will be defined and discussed in terms of their degree of formality, member attachment, and influence. A model of group behavior will be developed according to how groups are formed and how they function. Properties of group culture will be defined in terms of norms, cohesiveness, roles, status, and leadership. And finally, we will explore the managerial response to groups and the ways groups can be used as training devices.

Because one employee seldom has a job assignment exactly like that of another employee, much of the work in organizations happens on an individual basis. Thus, managers need to know something about individual motivation and behavior, the subject of Chapter 8. But not all behavior in organizations is based on the personal characteristics of individuals. A considerable amount of activity results from the dynamics of and interpersonal relationships within small groups. Organizations hire individuals, but once people start to work they interact and soon become allied with others. Some of these alliances are **formal** work groups, which are assembled to get a job done. Such formal groups are part of the required system of organizations. Other groups are **informal,** developing spontaneously as people become involved with one another. Some groups facilitate the accomplishment of organizational goals, and others are formed more to meet the personal goals of their members. Therefore, some of the "group" arrows in Figure 10–1 point toward organizational goals and others diverge. Groups significantly influence organization design and the way work gets accomplished. Thus, if managers can understand the dynamics of these social relationships, they will be in a better position to positively affect the workings of the organization.

A **group** can be defined as a collection of two or more interdependent people, psychologically aware of one another, who have or develop a

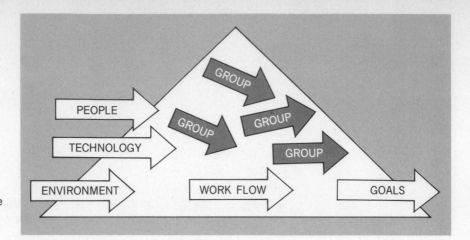

FIGURE 10–1
How groups of people affect the work of organizations.

shared goal. A group potentially exists wherever and whenever people associate with one another or are put into a situation in which they must interact. Over time, their activities, interactions, and decisions tend to develop a characteristic pattern that distinguishes one group from another. Whether inside or outside a formal structure, this pattern makes each group something like a small-scale organization. The interdependent members have roles (work) to carry out, they draw resources from the environment, and they value the processes and outcomes of the group's work (1).

A Classification of Groups

Not all groups in an organization are the same. Each organization is made up of many interacting and overlapping groups, and any one person may belong to a number of groups, both inside and outside the working organization. Each group has a different meaning for, and influence upon, the individual, the organization, and the manager. These overlapping groups can be categorized according to the three characteristics shown in Figure 10–2: degree of formality, degree of member attachment, and degree of influence.

Degree of Formality

One distinguishing characteristic of groups is their degree of **formality**, which has to do with how well defined the tasks and other activities are; how specific the leadership communication patterns and other interactions are; and how programed the decisions are. Organizations are made up of a number of formal subunits designed to carry out various parts of the total work output. One way to look at groups, then, is to examine their functions, or the kind of work they do, and specify the similarities and differences between various departments, such as production, accounting, sales, and so forth. Another way is to classify them according to their particular internal relationships, as did Leonard Sayles (2).

Formal Groups. Sayles identified two kinds of formal groups, **command groups** and **task groups. Command groups** are the most typical type of group in a formal organization. They consist of a manager and workers. A manager is a member of two such groups, as a leader of one and a follower in the other. Because the expectations of subordinates may differ substantially from those of superiors, the manager of a command group may experience a considerable degree of internal conflict.

Task, or **project, groups** are assigned a specific goal by an organization, and then may be allowed to develop their own methods for carrying out the assignment. Such industries as aerospace and construction organize work primarily on a task or project basis.

Informal Groups. Sayles also described two types of informal groups, **interest groups** and **friendship groups. Interest groups** may develop within organizations around some common bond, such as professional interests or shared experience, even though the members may belong to different command or task groups. For example, there may be a group of cost accountants from seven different production departments who lunch together. Or members who have worked for the company for at least twenty years may have weekly "Twenty-Year Club" meetings. Interest groups may also take the form of pressure groups, whose purpose is to influence top management to adopt certain policies or procedures. Some professional interest groups may even evolve into craft unions.

Friendship groups are similar to interest groups except that, in addition to shared interests, members have strong positive sentiments toward one another. In most large organizations, these groups command a person's allegiance more strongly than does "The Company" or "The Corporation."

Informal   Formal
Low _____ High
                          DEGREE OF FORMALITY

Primary   Secondary
Low _____ High
                     DEGREE OF MEMBER ATTACHMENT

Weak   Strong
Low _____ High
                       DEGREE OF GROUP INFLUENCE

FIGURE 10–2
Group classification according to degree of formality, member attachment, and group influence.

Formal and Informal Organization. For many years after the Hawthorne Studies, it was customary to speak of informal groups and the social relationships of workers and managers as the "informal organization" in contrast with the "formal organization," which was the system of authority and work as conceived by its designers. More recently, discussion of the two kinds of systems has waned. They both exist, to be sure, but not as the separate entities locked in conflict, as was implied earlier.

An organization consists of patterned interactions that take place in order to reach goals effectively and efficiently. Every work group, once established, eventually develops informal characteristics; and every social group develops regular patterns that over time give it an increasingly formal structure.

Human behavior at any given time is a function of a number of forces external and internal to the individual, including pressures from a number of groups demanding allegiance. Thus, in large part, people's behavior in the organization is influenced by the array of subunits acting and interacting within the person's sphere of awareness. For this reason, virtually any attempt to determine which action or set of actions is prompted by "informal" and which by "formal" systems is extremely difficult. The question, then, is not whether an activity, interaction, or decision is "formal" or "informal" but whether it aids in the accomplishment of work.

Managers assign work to the command and task groups, but they cannot prescribe all of the activities, interactions, and decisions that must take place to get the work done. Thus the behaviors that develop as people interact help to fill out the total organizational structure. Some of the unprescribed behavior, especially that which is concerned with holding the group together and keeping it running, provides a major coordinating device and assists in fulfilling organizational demands.

Conclusions About Degree of Formality. Whenever and wherever people are assembled, a group is likely to form. Sometimes managers bring groups together in command or task groups; sometimes people form special interest or friendship groups; and at other times people may just happen to be present when some kind of collective activity is necessary or desirable. When first formed, and throughout its existence, the group develops patterns of activities, interactions, and decisions that can be classified according to the degree of formality—the regularity and predictability of behavior—that exists. Generally, formality depends on how long a group has been in existence, how successful it is in satisfying the needs of its members, and how well it accomplishes its assigned organizational mission.

Degree of Member Attachment

A classification of groups according to their degree of formality is based on a relatively objective and detached analysis. Groups can also be categorized according to how individual members feel about them, or the degree to which they are attached to or affiliated with their associates.

Primary and Secondary Groups. One common way to classify member attitudes is according to whether members view their groups as primary or secondary. **Primary groups** are generally informal and quite small. Interactions are spontaneous, as in friendship groups of teen-agers or in a family situation. Members whose association is primary are dedicated to the group. An individual will make little commitment and dedicate few talents to those groups viewed as **secondary.** In secondary groups social distance among members may be greater, size may be larger, and interactions may be less frequent than in primary groups. Associations are more likely to be based on logic than on sentiment. Secondary groups include professional associations, sports groups, departments in organizations, clubs — such as tennis clubs — and other groups toward which many members feel less than full commitment.

What is a secondary group to many will be a primary group to one or a few members, and vice versa. For example, most groups have a core of dedicated members at their heart. To these people even a tennis club, which may be secondary to most of its members, will be a primary group. Likewise, a member on the fringes of a primary friendship group may consider the group secondary. The primary-secondary classification should be viewed as two ends of a continuum; members usually identify with a group somewhere along a line between these two extremes. Even a secondary group requires a certain amount of positive sentiment in order to progress efficiently toward its goals. On the other hand, families, clubs, and professional groups often have planned and prescribed interactions, and the sentiments are not always positive. The more completely a group satisfies personal needs, the more likely it is that one will view a group as primary.

A characteristic common to all groups on the primary-secondary continuum is the core of dedicated, high-status people at the center. To marginal members or to outsiders, these core people may be considered part of the "ruling clique." The group leader is often called the "ring leader" by those hostile to the group.

A manager who tries to remove the "bad influence" of the ring leader by discharging or transferring the person might indeed destroy the group, but a more likely outcome would be for the members to "gang up" against the manager, appoint an even more militant leader, and become even more troublesome. Groups that are important to members are hard to destroy. School principals and managers sometimes learn too late that dismembering a group can make it invisible but cannot always make it disappear. Forcing a primary group underground can be very destructive to the organization.

Reference Groups. Reference groups are special kinds of groups on the "degree of member attachment" continuum. They can be any kind of association of persons, inside or outside the organization, with which people identify, but of which they are not, in fact, members. Nonetheless, reference groups influence behavior because the people who identify with them tend to adopt the goals, values, and behavior they imagine the members of the group to have.

A reference group is any collection of people that one admires and hopes to join. A young person might select as a reference group a motorcycle gang, a musical group, a bridge club, an athletic team, or any other such aggregation of people. A worker might develop values from the activities of such groups as organizers of agricultural unions, patriotic societies, boards of directors, or a particular work group. Although reference groups guide people's behavior, they are not always apparent to an observer. Most people, however, will be happy to tell you which groups they admire. A manager needs to be aware of the reference groups of employees in order to avoid unpleasant misunderstandings. Suppose, for example, the reference group of a janitor is a local patriotic society that believes labor unions to be undemocratic. If the manager assumes that the custodian is a believer in the benefits of unions and makes remarks on the basis of this assumption, the janitor may develop a great deal of animosity against the manager.

**Degree of Group
Influence**

One of the most important classifications of groups is based on a group's effect on management. According to one extended study, Sayles identified four types of groups in terms of the degree to which they had an influence on the organizations of which they were a part. Each of the four types, the **apathetic,** the **erratic,** the **strategic,** and the **conservative,** also differed according to its place in the organization as a function of technology and job design (3).

Apathetic Groups. These groups are characterized by (1) few grievances or pressure tactics, (2) an absence of clear leadership, (3) internal disunity and/or frictions, and (4) suppressed discontent. Apathetic groups seem to be those that are not fully formed or developed. From management's viewpoint, these types of groups seem trouble-free because when discontent arises it is not well focused. However, petty jealousies and interpersonal problems are more evident here than in other types of groups. As a result, apathetic groups are neither consistently high in productivity nor fully cooperative. Their internal problems may produce dysfunctional effects. Apathetic groups generally contain people in the low-skill, low-paid areas of the plant. Work crews, in which each person performs a specific and separate part of a total job, may also be apathetic.

Erratic Groups. These groups are often characterized by management as ones from which "you just don't know what to expect." They can change almost overnight from passive to troublesome. Management rightly considers them very dangerous, and they consume an inordinate amount of a manager's time. Sayles indicated that erratic groups (1) are easily inflamed, (2) have poorly controlled pressure tactics and inconsistent behavior, (3) can be quickly converted to a position of good relationship with management, (4) often have highly centralized leadership, and (5) are active in the organizational phase of unionism. Roles are not well defined in these groups, and the group's strength often depends upon outside threat. When threatened they are strong; otherwise they tend to fall apart. Erratic groups are found primarily in jobs where everyone has an identical or nearly identical task.

Strategic Groups. These groups exert constant pressure on management. They are coldly calculating and have a very well planned course of action. Management thinks highly of these groups because their members' behavior is consistent and predictable. However, they are often feared because of their power. These groups are tightly knit and have a small core of highly active and influential leaders. Strategic groups (1) apply continuous pressure, (2) engage in well-planned and continuous grievance activities, (3) possess a high degree of internal unity, (4) often sustain union participation, and (5) generally, but not always, have a relatively good production record over the long run. Strategic groups are found among jobs that: (1) are primarily independent operations and not technologically interdependent, (2) require a relatively high degree of skill, and (3) are comparatively important to the plant and to management.

Conservative Groups. These are the aristocracy of work groups. Overt action on the part of conservative groups is not often necessary because their power is substantial and widely recognized. In general, they have what they want. Restraint is a major feature of these groups, but they can and do take action to gain their ends when they feel it is necessary. The characteristics of these groups can be summarized as (1) restrained pressure for highly specific objectives, (2) moderate internal unity and self-assurance, and (3) activity-inactivity cycles in terms of union activities and planned grievance procedures.

Members of conservative groups generally perform jobs at the top of the promotional ladder. They are almost always individual operation jobs, although members occasionally might work on a repair or maintenance crew. They hold their power position because of the importance of their work to the organization and to the work flow.

Conclusions About Group Types

At any given time, a group can be classified according to its degree of formality, degree of member attachment, and degree of influence on the organization. Using the classification scheme represented in Figure 10–2, managers can develop profiles to describe the various groups around them in order to understand and deal with them more effectively. Managers also can profit from having a model of group behavior. From the model, managers can learn the structural properties of groups and gain insight into the ways in which groups can influence the organization.

A Model of Group Behavior

One of the results of research on small groups has been the development of models of group processes. The intent of these models is to improve understanding of group behavior and to observe the similarities and differences among groups. The model discussed here is derived from that of George C. Homans (4).

Group Formation and Development

A group is a social system that embraces three separate yet interdependent behaviors: *activities, interactions,* and *decisions.* These three parts interact to form an **internal system.** At the same time the behaviors are all influenced by the external environment. This **external system** acts as a constraint on the internal system and may be called the **required system.**

The Required System. The required system consists of tasks that the organization (or the group) assigns to members. To carry out their jobs, people must take action, interact with one another, and make decisions. They are thus thrust into a social system by their work roles and job assignments. This social system is the formal group.

The Emergent System. As they work together over time, people form relationships that lead inevitably to the development of group characteristics, which were not necessarily part of the original work design. In other words, the external system brings the people together and specifies the organizational requirements of their activities, interactions, and decisions. Although constrained by the external system, the internal system is formed by these three kinds of behavior. This development is called the **emergent system,** because it "emerges" as an unplanned result of group process over a period of time. The emergent system is akin to the informal group. It develops as people modify and expand upon work methods and try to satisfy personal needs on the job. Emergent behavior makes it possible for people to satisfy their needs for security, social acceptance, and esteem. These needs do not disappear when people are working, so it stands to reason that people, wherever they happen to be, will try to satisfy them. Some needs can be satisfied better, or only, through accommodation or cooperation with others. Such adages such as "In union there is strength," or "Two heads are better than one," express this idea (5).

Some managers might wish that some aspects of emergent groups in their organizations, with their chatter and other "frivolous" behavior, would go away. They won't. The emergent system exists, and it is inevitable. Because it develops in response to the unsatisfied needs of its members, it unites powerful forces that have substantial effects on persons and on organizations. These effects can be functional, dysfunctional, or neutral both for individuals and organizations. The manager who understands the emergent system and who learns to work with it may be able to capitalize on its potentials.

Not all members of a department or work group will be a part of the emergent system. Some may be social isolates, who get their satisfactions in some other way. Nor are all relationships harmonious in the emergent system. People may not get along, or rival groups may form within the same department. Some "joiners," people who join everything around, may belong to several groups, each of which exerts demands on them. The network of relationships is hardly simple. Managers can better assess the impact of groups on the organization when they have a model for studying emergent group behavior that details the structural properties of groups.

Analysis of Group Process

An analysis of group process could begin with any part of the internal emergent system or with the external, required system. A complete analysis, however, requires an examination of all parts of the system as they interact within, and as they are influenced by, the external system.

Activities. Activities are the things people do, such as walking, typing, playing a piano, sitting, thinking, writing, or dictating. In the work situation, required activities refer to the actions the person must take in order to complete the tasks that have been assigned. But assigned activities are not the only ones a person engages in while on the job. "Horseplay" does not get the job done (although it may satisfy needs). As group formation proceeds, a wide variety of activities that serve the emergent system and not the required system become evident.

Interactions. Interactions are the contacts people make while carrying out activities. As people interact, a communication network develops that can become quite elaborate. The links that connect people are partially planned by the required system, partially established by the emergent system to get the work done, and partially developed by the participants to enjoy the companionship of one another.

In a sense, the communication network defines the structure of the organization. But it would be impossible to totally plan the network because no one in an organization can know in advance what kinds of problems will arise that will require specific kinds of interaction. The network is dynamic, always humming with messages, and is constantly undergoing changes that reflect changing work requirements, changing members, and changing external demands.

Not every person is tuned in to the entire network. Managers have a system that they might try to keep private. Indeed, there may be more than one managerial network. And other members may also have private or "closed" systems. When a number of relatively closed communication systems exist within one organization, varying amounts of effort may be expended as members of one group try to find out what is going on in other groups. Sometimes management unwittingly contributes to this state of affairs by promoting rivalry and competition between departments and by trying to suppress disapproved networks. Those managers who learn to work with, rather than against, the labyrinth of communication networks are in a position to keep the systems open and to make certain that all concerned have factual information to spread around. The communication network works rapidly and well and cannot be easily suppressed.

Social groups develop communications systems when they are first formed. Open primarily to members, these systems are determined by the content of the messages; by the routes they take; by the attitudes and feelings people have toward one another; by work and social behavior; and by the direction, frequency, and duration of interactions. One can learn a good deal about groups by observing who contacts whom, about what, how often, and for how long.

Individuals who interact *frequently* often do so because their tasks require interaction. Frequent contact usually leads to the development of strong positive sentiments. The *duration* of activities is equally important. For instance, interactions requiring a long time period are seen as more important than those that take a short time. The third category is *direction*. We have seen that in any interaction there is an initiator and a responder. Leaders, or those with considerable influence in group matters, will more often be initiators than responders.

Decisions. The third behavior of groups is decision making. Every person in a group makes decisions to join, to remain a member, and to participate with some degree of enthusiasm — or lack of it. These decisions, as well as those about the activities in which one will engage and the people with whom one will interact, are partly required and partly emergent as members of the group develop and change their characteristic ways of behaving. Whether designated a leader by members of an emergent group or appointed a leader in a command group, the person in charge is expected to make decisions (6).

It's a Wise Organization

In one organization that made a change to automation, a group of workers who had previously been in close physical proximity where considerable interaction was possible suddenly found themselves widely dispersed. Interaction became very difficult and, as a result, the coordination of their activities became very difficult. Management found that it was wise to install a telephone system so that interaction among the workers could occur while they were on the job and to allow them to come together on coffee breaks to further increase interaction. This solution led to a much more stable internal system and one in which management was able to get the needed coordination of activities.

Source: F. E. Mann and L. R. Hoffman, *Automation and the Worker* (New York: Henry Holt and Co., 1960).

**Performance
Within Groups**

Sentiments. People who are the actors in the interplay of activities, interactions, and decisions bring with them their own unique combination of emotional or internal states. These feelings, attitudes, and values, which are called *sentiments,* influence the behavior of group members. Conversely, the activities, interactions, and decisions a person engages in affect his or her sentiments. Homans makes the generalization that the higher the interaction rate between two people, the higher the *liking* rate between them. On the other hand, if two people *dislike* each other, they will try to reduce the frequency of their interaction. The external (required) system influences the internal (emergent) system through sentiments as a result of the values, beliefs, and attitudes people bring with them to the group (7).

Multiplier Effect. Once the required system is set in motion by management, there is a kind of **multiplier effect.** This means that the required activities and decisions lead to interactions, which in turn lead to sentiments of liking or disliking. Where sentiments of liking occur, there is an increase in interactions beyond those prescribed by the required system. These extra interactions again lead to further activities and decisions, which also are not requirements of the external system. These extra activities, which are meant to accomplish the goals of the emergent system rather than those of the organization, lead to yet another elaboration of interactions and sentiments.

Equilibrium. The set of activities, interactions, and decisions described by the model will tend toward equilibrium. Thus, the elaboration of activities and interactions does not go on forever. Barring change in the external system, the internal system would settle down and remain stable. In fact, the external situation does not remain stable, and neither does the internal one. However, since the internal system is always heading toward equilibrium, people in it will fight against any changes in the external system that have an adverse effect upon the stability of the group.

The manager who makes changes in the required system without considering the emergent group is usually in for a surprise. Things do not go as expected. The group may resist, often in seemingly irrational ways, and changes cannot be effected as planned. A total **systems analysis** involves looking at both the external system and the internal system and examining what effect changes in one system will have on the other. Furthermore, the manager must deal with the consequences of these changes.

Group Culture

Once people in groups start acting, interacting, and making decisions, unique features develop that make it possible to distinguish one group from another. Over time these distinctive characteristics tend to become so regular that each group can be said to have its own **culture.** The culture of a group refers to the members' shared ideas, customs, and technologies. For this reason, the features of one group are never exactly like those of another, and each has its own cultural atmosphere. Thus one group may seem exciting, another dull and lifeless, and still another crackling with anger and suppressed hostility. An understanding of the cultural characteristics of groups can help managers deal with both the unique and the similar patterns of behavior in all the groups with which they come in contact.

Included in the unique culture of each group, and each organization also, is a belief system, an internal economic system, differentiated social status, a political and reward system, and such overt features as symbols, rituals, and taboos. The culture of a group is based both on the work to be done to achieve goals and on the outside cultures brought into the group by each member. The culture of an organization is therefore both a reflection of the external environment and a combination of the members' internal expectations.

The greater the ability of a group to satisfy the needs of its members the greater will be the commitment of its members. The organization that satisfies the economic, social, political, and belief needs of its members is therefore likely to draw a considerable amount of commitment from its employees. But the culture of most organizations in industrial nations is quite shallow, and as a result, people tend to compartmentalize their commitments into many different arenas.

To summarize, people belong to many groups, each with a different culture. Outside the work organization one may identify with the customs of a nation, a region, a societal class, a political party, a religious group, or many types of social associations. Within the work organization one may also be a member of several social groups, including a command or task group in the required system or one or more groups in the emergent system, such as a special interest group. The culture of each group helps individuals define their position and determine appropriate patterns of behavior. The more strongly affiliated a person is with one culture, the more likely he or she is to act out its values or adhere to its norms.

Norms

Norms are shared standards of thought and action that are both accepted by and expected from group members. Norms encompass a whole range of attitudes and behaviors, including emotions, values, customs, interests, manners, and so forth. All together these norms constitute a code of rules and regulations that members are expected to obey if they are to remain in good standing.

The norms and values of a group or culture are expressed in **symbols.** One set of symbols includes the special language, or jargon, of the group. Every human group develops a language similar to the prevailing language of its environment but with its own key words and accents. Words are only one kind of symbol. Conduct, or behavioral tendencies, constitutes another. Special handshakes, winks, manner of dress, and other ritualized kinds of behaviors convey considerable meaning without a sound. Other kinds of symbols may include such material items as flags and pennants, ornaments, insignias, custom-made clothing, and so on. Symbols often take on highly emotional significance. A flag, for example, can stand for a complete set of beliefs and values, and attacks on a flag can inflame deep passions.

Development of Norms. Interaction normally leads to liking. Not everyone likes everybody else, of course, but in general the more people interact the more likely they are to find and to share a common experience. And the more common experiences people share the stronger will become their affection for one another. As group members come to value one another, they develop customary ways of relating. Over time, these customs become **codes,** which communicate messages about what behavior is correct. An assemblage of behavioral modes becomes the group's norms. These norms give members' interactions stability and permit the continuation of the group, even though its membership shifts. Because norms often regulate a substantial segment of one's total behavior, members of certain groups can often be recognized by their appearance, language, or expressed values or beliefs.

A Special Type of Norm: Output Restriction. A particular phenomenon that has been observed in some organizations is a group norm that prescribes output quotas for members. The purpose of this norm is to put a ceiling on productivity. Owing to any number of reasons, members of the group may try to establish what they feel to be a "fair day's work." Anyone producing more than the output quota will be punished by other group members. The quota that is established may or may not be consistent with management's notions of what should constitute a day's work.

The Pressure to Conform

S. E. Asch ran a study of a group's ability to influence perception. Using four individuals as stooges and one as the subject, he asked the group to identify which of four lines was the longest. Each person was asked in turn, the subject being the last to be asked. The four stooges gave consistent, but incorrect answers. In this circumstance about one-third of the subjects also gave the incorrect answer that the group had given. They went against their own perceptions to side with the group's erroneous report.

If this much force can be applied to individuals just by bringing them together with other persons, the possibilities for pressure by an established group which is highly valued by its members should be considerably greater.

Source: S. E. Asch, "Effects of Group Pressure Upon the Modification and Distortion of Judgments," in H. Guetzkow, *Groups, Leadership, and Man* (New York: Russell and Russell, 1963), pp. 177–190.

When the group's standards are congruent with those of management, the group takes over much of the policing or control necessary to get the work done. When a group's standards are lower than those of management there is usually conflict between management and the workers. There are innumerable examples of work groups operating below management-established standards, in accord with their own norms. Frequently, particularly when a piecework system is involved, management has been unable to understand why the workers are satisfied with the lower wages they make. Such incomprehension represents the fallacy that wages are always a more important reward than social gratification. In this case the social needs of people take precedence over their economic needs. To be effective, managers must try to first understand and then influence the standards and norms of the group. Fighting them may not produce positive results.

A Special Type of Norm: The Taboo. In addition to norms that require behavior, groups also have norms that forbid behavior. These norms are called **taboos.** For example, most groups forbid members to let outsiders know their secrets. Lists of prohibitions are often explicit and made very clear to newcomers, and penalties for violations may be quite harsh. Most taboos are initiated for a sensible reason, usually as a protection for members. If everyone who eats pork gets sick, it makes sense to outlaw pork, as did the ancient leaders of the Hebrew culture. But cultures tend to retain taboos long after they cease to be relevant. Thus, certain conflicts between young people and their parents often stem from the youths' belief that parentally imposed taboos are obsolete.

Enforcing Norms. The group has considerable power to force members to obey its norms because people do not want to lose membership in groups that are important to them. The social need to belong is one that a group can directly satisfy. Groups enforce their norms by increasing pressures on those who do not comply. In a situation of noncompliance, several measures can be taken. First, the group members will discuss the pros and cons of the situation using persuasion and rational argument. If this tactic fails, group members will be friendly and joke about the situation. The butt of the joke, of course, is the nonconformist. Should this approach fail, group members apply psychological pressure or, depending on the situation, physical force. If force does not work, the group will use its ultimate weapon, social isolation. Most people find that being excommunicated from their peer group is the harshest form of punishment (8).

Teaching Norms to Newcomers. When new people join an organization or group they have to "learn the ropes." All organizations and groups subject newcomers to some kind of indoctrination process, similar in intent to the pledge period of a fraternal organization.

The more important the group is to its members, the longer and harder is this initiation period. Inside organizations, these initiation and membership rituals range from having a new stock clerk look all over for a left-handed letter opener, to office parties and training programs. Certain management-training programs for college-educated recruits are often simply initiation rituals rather than the on-the-job training programs they are claimed to be. How well the individual can cope with work "beneath the dignity of a college graduate" may tell more about the person than a grade-point average or a thousand interviews.

The rite of entry is but one of many rituals in a group culture. Baseball pools, office parties, collections to honor a new marriage or baby, and company softball games are just some of the hundreds of rites that reinforce the norms and values of groups. Rituals often impede efficiency, as when a company closes all of its plants on the birthday of its founder, or when a college teacher finds classes empty because of such occasions as an all-campus party, a rally for a winning team, or a political demonstration. All festivals that occur with some regularity are rites. And attempts to abolish them are foolish, for they have intense meaning to many persons and will go underground if formally stopped. Often, the best a manager can do is to try to keep rituals from causing damage to property and persons.

Group Cohesiveness

Groups differ considerably in their ability to enforce norms. The degree to which they are able to do so is referred to as the group's **cohesiveness.** A highly cohesive group is one in which all the members "stick together." It is usually one in which the interactions, activities, and decisions are clearly defined and stable. Both personal needs and characteristics of a group help to determine how cohesive it is.

Personal Needs. What makes a group cohesive? People will follow the norms of a group for the same reason they will follow the procedures of an organization, because doing so will satisfy their personal needs. Individuals will be attracted to a group if they find group members to be personally attractive. They may also like what the group does. For example, people who like to play softball may join a company team. Group goals are another source of attraction. Thus, people may join a group that is trying to put pressure on management to set up a cafeteria. Inherent in all these reasons is that the individual will find some personal satisfaction in belonging to the group. Some groups are found desirable because they offer status. Simply being a member in good standing affords a sense of power or accomplishment.

Another factor that contributes to group cohesiveness is the extent to which the individual is dependent upon the group. If the group fills a need that no other group can satisfy, then cohesiveness tends to be very high. Families often tend to be very cohesive because they satisfy certain unique needs that cannot be fulfilled elsewhere. During the teen-age period, though, family cohesiveness may break down because teen-agers find that peer groups can satisfy many of their new needs, such as the needs for independence and close friendships, better than the family can. One could expect, then, that a group whose participants are members of quite a number of other groups would be less cohesive than one in which the members belonged to that group only.

Characteristics of the Group. There are a number of factors about the group itself that tend to affect its cohesiveness. These include *size, environment, technology, group composition, group status, competition,* and *conflict*.

Size. A fundamental aspect of groups is that all members be able to interact with one another. Obviously, as the number of people in the group becomes larger, full interaction becomes more difficult because the number of possible interactions grows even more rapidly. Generally, studies have indicated that large size has a negative effect on group cohesiveness. What tends to happen as groups become larger is that subgroups form, which reinstate the small size necessary for cohesiveness.

The work *environment* often makes interaction very difficult. The more barriers there are between people, the fewer opportunities there will be to interact, and the less cohesion there will be. Barriers are typically such physical factors as spatial distance, partitions, and general background noise. Interaction is difficult when the noise level hampers even required interactions.

Technology. The tools, implements, and other technological means used by members of a group also tend to set it apart from other cultures. Every group uses its tools a little differently. An analysis of such artifacts reveals much about the culture, for they are reflective of both technology and behavior.

Group Composition. Members of a work group share similar skills and consequently have much in common. Commonality of interests and abilities also contributes to group cohesiveness. When people engage in similar activities they have many reasons to interact with one another. Of course, in some ways, a group whose members have diverse interests has an advantage, too. Group goals are often better served when members have a variety of skills and opinions to offer. Discussion groups, for example, would not be very interesting if all members held the same views. But it is important that the various members be able to recognize and appreciate the contributions of other members toward the group's goals if cohesiveness is to remain intact.

Group Status. Generally, high-status groups have high cohesiveness. When individuals aspire to join groups of higher standing than the ones they are in, they are more likely to adhere to the norms of the desired group than to the norms of the group they hope to leave. It is true that those who move "upward" socially tend to forget their old friends and associates. The same phenomenon is apparent in hierarchical organizations.

Those who are moving up in the managerial ranks must adopt the codes of their new associates and discard the norms of lower levels. There may be considerable truth in the saying that "He was a nice guy until he got promoted," or "She was a fine woman until her new position went to her head." On the other hand, people who are not upwardly mobile create a very cohesive group because they substitute social gratification for ego or status needs.

Competition. Rivalries within a group damage cohesiveness and lead to negative sentiments. These attitudes tend to reduce interaction among group members and may also lead to such destructive activities as name-calling or work sabotage. Managers can design jobs in such a way that individuals who must interact do not have to compete. Where cooperation is required, competition is not appropriate.

Competition *between* groups has a very different effect, however. One of the best-known ways to pull members of a system together is to rally their support against a real or imagined threat from outside. Rulers of nations, managers of organizations, and leaders of groups may create an outside "cncmy" when they are beset by internal troubles and strife. One study reports that cohesiveness within groups increased significantly when competition between groups was instituted. Cohesiveness was particularly strong during the competition itself. This phenomenon is best observed in athletic teams, which are more competitive during interschool games than during practice sessions (9).

When groups are in a win-lose situation, cohesiveness in the winning group tends to be high. Internal conflict is at a minimum. Group members feel that the group has attained a high status; it is definitely the group to belong to. The losing group often has trouble with cohesiveness. The degree of tension, anger, and competitiveness among members may be high. If members internalize these feelings of bitterness, the attack will shift from other groups to fellow members. At this stage there is a good possibility that there will be a change in group leadership. If, however, group members accept the situation without blaming one another, the group may maintain or even increase its cohesiveness. There are many examples of athletic teams on a losing streak that retain or increase their cohesiveness because members need one another for support and understanding.

Conflict between cohesive groups that exist in the same area may be inevitable, especially when the social and psychological boundaries that separate them are relatively impermeable and when members of each define the others as "undesirable." School-group cliques that are formed primarily on an ethnic basis are good examples. The resulting battles between such groups can be viewed as a clash of norms.

Culture Conflict. If the values and behavioral requirements of the groups to which we belong are consistent with one another, then we will experience little or no cultural tension. But some of us are members of several different groups, which have divergent and incompatible values.

For example, the family and religious groups may disapprove of premarital sexual experiences, but the peer group may require such behavior. If people want to remain members in good standing with all three groups, then either they must be willing to say "no" to one or more of the groups and hope for the best or they must be hypocritical. Whether people choose the latter path or decide to jeopardize their standing in one or more groups, some internal conflict is bound to be experienced. And if enough individuals experience such conflict there may be open warfare between different groups. Thus churches may attack schools for teaching an ethic they feel to be corruptive and exhort their members to withhold donations and vote "no" on tax issues until the schools "clean up the mess."

Culture Shock. When an individual moves out of one culture into another with different values, he or she may experience **culture shock.** For example, a person from a rural area may have trouble dealing with the cultural expectations of the people in the urban office where the individual now works. The same kind of shock awaits the person who receives his or her first assignment overseas. The values of other cultures may seem merely odd, or they may be viewed as downright terrifying. People who want to get along with a group with which they have no previous experience would do well to find out what is expected of them before they make some irreversible error. Members of the dominant culture expect newcomers to adopt prevailing codes. People must be prepared to suspend both their judgment and their personal value system when entering a new culture.

Organizations mirror the broader cultural environment. Managers can expect, therefore, to be confronted with many of the same cultural problems that exist in the larger society. For example, they may have to deal with employee drug abuse, attacks from members of militant interest groups, alcoholism, or collapsing marriages.

Intergroup conflict can be reduced within organizations if steps are taken to ensure that communication remains open between groups. Management can help to keep the emergent systems open by shifting work assignments, mixing memberships, and creating organizational structures that make it necessary for people to belong to several groups.

Cohesiveness and Morale. A problem with attempting to alter group cohesiveness, however, is that morale tends to be high in cohesive groups. When norms are shared and internalized, people develop a feeling of group identification that leads to involvement in the activities of the group. Such esprit de corps is not only very satisfying to members but helps them better achieve group goals.

The phrase *high morale* is used to describe the feeling tone, or atmosphere, in a group where the attitude of its members is positive and the group involves members deeply. Morale seems to be high when the group is cohesive, when the values and beliefs of members are in agreement, and when traditions have had a chance to develop and flourish. Some researchers have spent a good deal of time and effort trying to devise methods for developing high morale in groups. But like any feeling, high morale is quite impossible to deliver on demand. It is, of course, possible to lay the groundwork for the development of high morale. The problem for most managers is that its nourishment and growth requires such a commitment to group members and their activities that other demands are sidetracked.

High morale in a group is not an unmixed blessing, however. People who are unacceptable to the group may become alienated. They may even be driven out or attacked. A group with high morale tends to become closed and inflexible. Thus it may be resistant to change, hamper creativity and innovation, and become increasingly less relevant to the needs of its environment.

Cohesiveness, Productivity, and Satisfaction. At least one study has shown that productivity is greater in cohesive groups. One would also expect satisfaction to be higher. The group that can achieve its goals is in a much better position to help individual members achieve their own personal goals. The result is satisfying both to the individual members and to the group as a whole (10).

It should be noted, though, that whether a group is productive is a matter of viewpoint. A group may be highly satisfied and feel that it is achieving its goals even though these goals may not be viewed as productive by outsiders. For instance, when one of the goals of a group is production restriction, the group may not look very productive from management's viewpoint. On the other hand, a group that is highly competitive internally may lack cohesiveness and consider itself unproductive but may, by management's standards, be producing at a very high rate.

Similar statements can be made for satisfaction. Satisfaction is high for those members whose needs are being met by the group. But not all members of a group may be experiencing the same need satisfaction. Status or location within the group structure tends to be associated with satisfaction. In studies of small groups put together for the purpose of studying communication patterns, it was found that satisfaction was primarily a function of the centrality of the person within the system. Those who held a central spot in the information flow felt the most satisfaction. Those on the periphery were least satisfied (11).

Ethnocentricity. The more cohesive a group is, the more ethnocentric it will be. **Ethnocentricity** is the tendency on the part of people who share compatible attitudes and who act alike to view outsiders in terms of their own standards or norms. They also tend to think more highly of themselves than of people whose norms are different. When groups are very cohesive and self-centered, they tend toward becoming closed, separating themselves from other groups by boundaries that are difficult for outsiders to cross. Members of ethnocentric groups may be scornful of those who do not belong and may even attack those whose norms are different from their own.

Roles

Groups are characterized by some kind of division of work among members, and **roles** are the resulting differentiations. The group may formally assign functions to members, or a member may be allowed to assume a necessary role. Because roles are not always prescribed from outside the group, members of groups are likely to have more influence in determining their group roles than their organizational roles. Groups are not necessarily more equalitarian than organizations in task division, but they often permit their members to have more influence in decision making.

Many variables affect a person's choice of what role to play. The degree to which the group is satisfying a person's unfulfilled needs will do much to determine whether he or she occupies a central or a peripheral position within the group. A person's skills and talents that are useful to the group will be of some influence. If a role needed by the group is unoccupied, the person may ask or be asked to fill it. Work assignment, the length of membership in the group, the degree of adherence to group norms, and the strength of other pressures, such as the desire to succeed or the pull of other groups, will also affect the person's choice or acceptance of a particular role.

There are three major categories of roles that are evident in groups: **task roles, building and maintenance roles,** and **personal roles. Task roles** are those that are directed toward helping the group to select, define, and achieve its goals. **Building and maintenance roles** include activities that help the group continue to function by altering it, regulating it, strengthening it, and perpetuating it. **Personal roles** include behavior directed toward satisfying the needs of individuals, irrespective of the needs of the whole group (12).

These roles are not rigidly assigned to particular people, for roles in groups are flexible and easily changed. A person can play a task role at one time, a maintenance role at another time, and a personal role at still another time. It is probably true that within the group everyone will play a personal role at one time or another. Most people, however, find it much easier to play either the task role or the building and maintenance roles, as these seem to require different emotional styles.

Two styles that are conducive to the task role are the **strong achiever** and the **logical thinker.** The **strong achiever** is one who is comfortable with strong emotions, such as aggression and anger, and uncomfortable with such tender emotions as love and affection. People with this orientation can play a task role well because they are able to deal easily with the kind of conflict situations that often arise in goal-achievement activities. The **logical thinker** is one who is uncomfortable with emotions, period. This person relies instead on logic, knowledge, and facts for getting things done. To this person the task role is the only relevant role to be played in the group (13).

A personality style that is more relevant to the building and maintenance role is that of the **friendly helper.** This person is more at home with
the tender emotions and is uncomfortable with the tough emotions. He or
she tends to be sensitive to the feelings over which the other two types
have run roughshod in attempting to complete the group's mission. The
friendly helper plays a group maintenance role by expressing these softer
emotions.

Those who play personal roles in groups on an ongoing basis are concerned more with their own needs than with the group's needs and tend to
become social isolates.

Status

Status is the amount of esteem one receives in a group. Some members of
a group are held in higher esteem by their peers than are other members.
This is another way of saying that a hierarchy exists in peer groups just as
it does in other human systems. Thus, members are differentiated from
others on the basis of their status, as well as on the basis of their roles and
emotional styles.

Status Differences. Watching a group in action can provide the observer with a number of clues about an individual's position within the
group. Status in groups depends partly on the role a person plays. If the
group is one that requires high commitment to a particular task, then task
roles are going to be seen as high status. On the other hand, if the group is
more social in nature, then building and maintenance roles may command
higher status.

Interactions within the group also lead to differences in status.
Those people who are contacted frequently usually have higher status
than those who are rarely contacted. The isolate is usually at the bottom
of the group's status ladder. In addition, a person whose role is not well
designated within the group tends to have low status. The newcomer is an
example. The social group tends to put a great deal of emphasis on seniority. As time passes, the newcomer gains status through involvement in the
group's activities and through a clearer definition of his or her role.

Status and Activity. Status is also a major factor in determining the
role the individual will play in the group. As mentioned earlier, in many
groups the newest member is required to do many of the menial duties,
such as going for coffee. Once seniority is established and status rises, the
person is offered a choice of other activities.

People engage in a number of different roles, all carrying somewhat
different status. This adds some complexity to the situation since the
status of one role tends to carry over to other roles. For example, if the
company vice-president is a member of the employee-formed nature club,
he or she is likely to have the highest status in the nature club. Those who
have the highest-paying jobs in the group are most frequently the group
leaders.

Sociograms as a Means of Showing Status

The relative standing of members in a group can be depicted by means of an organization chart, but status shows up better in a **sociogram** of relationships. The sociogram is usually based on the responses members of a group give to a few questions, such as "List the three persons you respect most in the group" and "List the three individuals you would most like to work with." Now picture the group as a collection of members within a circle of permeable boundaries. Assume that those who have highest status receive the most choices, and put them near the middle of the circle, placing those with next highest status around them, and so on. Connect those who interact with lines, using arrowheads to indicate the direction of choices, and you will have drawn a status sociogram. Although everyone who is truly a member of the group will be connected with at least one other person, those with high status will have more arrows directed toward them than away from them. Social isolates will be chosen by no one. Sociograms, such as that pictured below, provide a clear and simple picture of the vertical specialization within the group, and they give some indication of the communications network. Another way to develop such a picture is to observe who talks with whom over a considerable period of time.

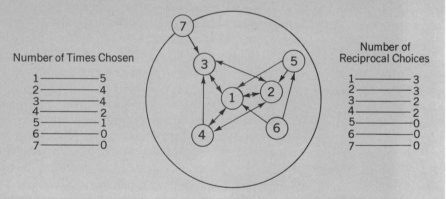

Number of Times Chosen		Number of Reciprocal Choices	
1	5	1	3
2	4	2	3
3	4	3	2
4	2	4	2
5	1	5	0
6	0	6	0
7	0	7	0

Source: J. L. Moreno, "Sociometry," in *Who Shall Survive?* (Washington, D.C.: Nervous and Mental Diseases Publishing Co., 1934).

Status Incongruency. Another complexity is that of **status incongruency,** which means that one may have high status with group peers in, say, a bowling league, but have low status in the organization. This can be a very uncomfortable position both for the person and for his or her associates. It is hard to treat people as though they have high status one moment and low or equal status the next. The professor who goes to a social group meeting with students often finds that students are unable to turn off the "teacher" image; they cannot accept the inconsistency between the roles of professor and peer.

On the other hand, the individual may wish to be treated consistently

—that is, in accordance with his or her highest-ranking position. For example, one who has high status within the community because of family ties and service may find it difficult to accept a middle- or lower-level managerial post, which accords only a modest status level. These kinds of status incongruencies can result in inappropriate behavior when in different groups. The person who on weekends has a high-level officer's position in a military reserve unit and during the week has a low-level staff job will be in considerable trouble if behavior on the job matches that of the duties of an officer. But the person who changes behavior to suit the situation may also be in trouble: He or she may be viewed as hypocritical or two-faced.

Status incongruence, as between the required and emergent systems, can be quite pronounced. Because standards for establishing status in the two systems are considerably different, it is ineffective for the manager to deal with status in informal groups by using the standards of the formal system. Status in the organization many times leads to isolation in the emergent group. The "rate buster" who exceeds normative production quotas is an example. Managers need to be aware of the status ladder of the groups with which they come in contact and which they wish to influence. They can quite inadvertently create status incongruency by bringing people into the work group who do not fit the status level of those who are already there. The college graduate trainee placed in a clerical unit might be an example.

Leadership Roles

The status hierarchy of an informal group organizes and patterns the members' interactions. The result is that some people have a better grasp of what is going on than do others. Over time, those with high status come to occupy leadership positions. Leaders contribute to the group's continuance by directing the members' behavior toward the accomplishment of group goals. They do this through exercising power and making decisions. In any one group only a few can play leadership roles. Most group members play fairly passive roles, as do most people in organizations.

Multiple Leadership Positions. The leadership role in a group is not always as definite a position as it is in an organization. Because both a task leader and a maintenance leader are needed for the group to achieve its goals, and because the two types of roles require different styles, the same person often cannot play both roles adequately. Thus, leaders are likely to change with the changing requirements of the group, especially when the group is new or undergoing change.

Who Group Leaders Are. Group leaders are generally those who are most involved in group activities and who are most committed to the group and its goals. As a consequence, group leaders follow the norms of the group more closely than do other members. In fact, they often become the guardians of group norms. On the other hand, they may be able to change norms more readily than others because their opinions are especially valued and their commitment is unquestioned.

How Leaders Secure Compliance. The group leader, unlike the organizational leader, cannot depend on authority in order to maintain the leadership role. But there are available a variety of other techniques for ensuring compliance. These can range from the use of physical coercion, as in street gangs, for example, to the use of expertise, as in technical groups. None of these bases of power has the stability of authority, however. In more primitive times and cultures, the struggle for leadership in groups usually entailed a dramatic physical confrontation. In modern social groups the battle typically is rather subtle and complex, but it is just as intense.

The Role of the Leader. The group leader is ordinarily the focal point of interactions. He or she is involved in more interactions, of longer duration, and is most often the initiator. The person to whom the group means little, or whose membership is marginal, has fewer interactions, of shorter duration, and is primarily the receiver. Some members are focal points for certain types of interactions. A logical thinker, for example, would make a much better initiator than receiver. As a receiver, the logical thinker is likely to be uncomfortable because of the feared possibility of receiving unwanted emotional content. The friendly helper, on the other hand, would rather receive than initiate. And the strong achiever is able to both initiate and receive interactions well.

Managerial Response to Groups

One way to look at organizations is to picture them as a mosaic of groups. The question for the manager is not whether groups will exist in the organization, but rather how to react to and deal with them. Managerial reactions to groups may range from negative through neutral to positive.

Negative Reactions

Negative reactions to groups that exist in the organization are quite common among managers. This reaction is understandable when group norms are antagonistic to organizational rules or goals. Managers also may react negatively to friendship groups. Despite existing research that indicates that people work better with people they like and are friendly with, some managers believe that friendship in the work situation leads to "goofing off"—a supposition that in fact is often accurate. When managers perceive groups as negative or threatening, they may try to break up the group by transferring some key members or even firing some. They may also try to discourage the group by attempting to control the number of interactions among people and by reducing the number of emergent activities. The result of the latter move may be that the manager must spend a good deal of time supervising and controlling employees to ensure that directives are carried out.

Such tactics may be successful, but they are also rather costly in terms of morale, satisfaction, and productivity. These tactics are oppressive and indicate a lack of trust in the workers. At a surface level, workers may appear to accept attempts to restrict group activities, but they are not likely to be very dedicated employees. In fact the results may be even more negative. Attempting to destroy a group may lead to its going "underground," a situation that creates a secret society and often strengthens group cohesiveness.

Neutral Reactions   A second type of managerial reaction to groups is a lack of reaction. That is, managers simply ignore the group and work with individuals instead, refusing to admit that a group exists. Again, this is a fairly common response by managers, sometimes through ignorance and sometimes as a result of personal style. Some people find it easy to deal on a one-to-one basis with another individual but find it very difficult to deal with a group of people.

A neutral reaction has the advantage of simplicity. It assumes that what is ignored does not exist. However, like the negative approach, this one too leaves managers alienated from the group. In this case, at least,

they may or may not be seen as the "enemy," but in any event, these managers lose considerable predictive and control ability. By ignoring the group, they are ignoring some of the major forces that influence people at work. If managers ignore the effect of groups on individuals, they are very likely to view some worker behavior as irrational. In addition, managers who ignore the group fail to see the possibilities of using it to help control and direct behavior toward organizational goals. By failing to influence group norms positively, managers can only hope that the norms of the group will not be antagonistic to organizational goals.

Positive Reactions

Behavioral scientists have emphasized the fact that managers can profit by working with groups as well as with individuals. Rensis Likert expresses this idea as follows:

> Research in organizations is yielding increasing evidence that the superior's skill in supervising his subordinates *as a group* is an important variable affecting his success; the greater his skill in using group methods of supervision, the greater are the productivity and job satisfactions of his subordinates (14).

Managers using this approach take an active group role. They establish conditions that may lead to a highly cohesive group and increased *teamwork*. These managers may try to be more than just the required leader; they are also attempting to be the leader of the emergent group. When successful, they are able to influence the group norms toward a congruency with organizational goals.

This approach is not an easy one. Managers who take an active role in the group process must be willing to deal not only with the formal or task requirements of the work group, but also with the maintenance or emotional content of the group. They must have a concern for the group members as people, not simply as instruments for getting the work out. This approach assuredly adds a whole new complexity to an already burdened job. For one thing, managers must place themselves in the uncomfortable position of being members of two groups with conflicting demands.

Using the Group to Help Manage

The purpose of this chapter has been to provide knowledge of groups for the manager's aid in understanding, observing, and taking action.

Understanding. In order for managers to use the group to help them manage, they must first understand the nature of groups. If managers begin by understanding that the formation and development of groups is a natural and inevitable process, then they have a good chance of being able to turn some of the energies of these groups into a positive force in helping to accomplish organizational goals. Without this positive attitude, "using" the group becomes a form of manipulation that usually backfires.

1. Activities	Who does what? Are the activities part of the job?
2. Interactions	Who contacts whom? How often? For how long? About what?
3. Sentiments	How do people feel about others? How do people feel about the work group? The organization?
4. Norms	What are they? Are they productive or counterproductive?
5. Power	Who are the powerful group members? What are their sentiments? What pressures do they put on others? How effective are they?
6. Cohesiveness	Is the group cohesive? Why? Should there be more or less cohesiveness?
7. Roles	Who plays what roles? Who are the group leaders? Under what circumstances? Who has status? Why?

What kind of effect is the group able to have on management?

FIGURE 10–3
A checklist for group observation.

Observation. The next step for the positive-action manager is to move beyond a general understanding of group behavior to a specific understanding of the particular group with which he or she is involved. This step requires careful and objective observation. Figure 10–3 lists a series of questions to guide the observation of a particular group. It is important that the observer examine the group with an open mind, withhold judgments about "rights" or "wrongs," and simply record occurrences and the reasons for them.

Positive Activity. After a specific understanding is gained through observation, the manager is prepared to take an active role in the group. Based on his or her position in the required system, the manager might be able to take a high-status leadership role in the group. The easiest role to assume is the task-oriented leadership position because it is likely the one that workers expect; group-maintenance roles may be left to others. In such cases, however, the manager must realize that some leadership functions are being handled by others. Working closely with those who have powerful positions in the group often consolidates both the manager's position and that of the other group leaders. As the representative of the required system, the manager has resources that can either consolidate or disrupt the group. In handing out work assignments, for example, the manager needs to consider such things as not giving important tasks to low-status members. Obviously the manager needs a good understanding of the members' strengths and weaknesses. If the manager is not highly task oriented, he or she may wish to turn over the task role to others and focus on group-maintenance activities instead.

The Group as a Management-Training Device

The approach described in the preceding paragraph requires more than just a knowledge of individual and group behavior. It requires a set of skills in recognizing and acting upon the needs of the group and of the individuals within it. Dealing with a group requires a certain knowledge of oneself and how one affects others. These skills are neither innate nor inherited; they are learned.

One technique that has been used to help managers develop these skills is called **sensitivity training** or **T-group** sessions. Its purpose is to develop in managers an awareness of themselves, of others, of group processes, and of group culture. Typically, the method brings people together in a small group of, say, twelve to fifteen members, which purposely lacks the structure to which an individual may be accustomed. The point is for participants to establish their own structure. Thus, individuals can simultaneously observe and participate in the establishment of the group and its decision-making structure. During the process, individuals are afforded the opportunity to take a look at themselves, both through their own eyes and through the eyes of others. Ultimately, participants are able to explore their values and their impact on others; to determine if they wish to modify old values and develop new ones; and to develop awareness of how groups can inhibit as well as facilitate human growth and decision making. The goal of sensitivity training is to enable people to be more aware of themselves and of their relationships to other people and the environment around them (15).

Few training techniques have created quite the stir and controversy that this one has. To proponents it has become almost a religion. To opponents it is a dangerous practice. But despite all the fervor, the results of sensitivity training are not clear. For the majority of people who participate in a sensitivity-training group, a behavior change occurs at the time and in the group. However, carry-over to the day-to-day environment may not be very great. To a degree, sensitivity training is conducted in a vacuum: the environment of the group is set apart from the pressures and anxieties of the workplace. Thus, when people go back out into the "real world" they find themselves retreating to the old behavior patterns that proved adequate before. In some cases sensitivity training may lead to frustration for managers. They may become aware of their ill effects on others but, owing to a variety of personal and organizational reasons, may not be able to behave differently. Many experts in the field suggest that sensitivity training must begin at the top of an organization. The organization's leaders must not only think it is a good idea but also must be made personally aware of the effects of the process. Without such first-hand knowledge and experience, top management is unlikely to be able to encourage the rest of the organization to adopt sensitivity-training techniques and attitudes (16).

To some critics sensitivity training is seen as an invasion of privacy. They feel that to have people attend sensitivity-training sessions that deal with people's personality structures is a matter outside the scope of an organization's legitimate concern. A similar line of argument is that sensitivity training is a form of therapy and should not be undertaken unless the individual desires it. A third argument is that some people who have a shaky psychological balance can be harmed by sensitivity training. Doubtless, some people probably should not engage in sensitivity training. They are not ready to look at themselves seriously. A fourth criticism is that sensitivity training sensitizes people to a set of variables that may not be the important or controlling factors in the work situation. For instance, if managers turn their attention to individual or group problems when the trouble lies in the organizational structure, they will be wasting their efforts and camouflaging the real problem. Finally, untrained or technically qualified but incompetent leaders may cause a good deal of damage. Sensitivity-group situations are so unpredictable that even a leader who has proved competent in one instance might be a failure in another (17).

Despite these criticisms, however, sensitivity training continues to be used both in industry and in other areas of society. Properly used and administered, it may have a place in management training. It is not, however, the only form of human relations training, nor is it necessarily even desirable. The evolution of management training in the last few years indicates a change in focus toward building decision-making as well as interpersonal skills. In the final chapter of this book, we will discuss a relatively new training process called *organization development*. This technique for implementing organizational change has developed a substantial following in the last decade and seems to be one answer to some of the critics of sensitivity training.

Chapter Review

In this chapter we have seen why and how managers must learn to work with people as members of groups. Group behavior has been explored in terms of its influence on goal accomplishment as a result of its effect on individual employees. Groups have been examined according to their types, their development, their culture, and their effect on managerial behavior.

The specific concepts and terms that have been developed are listed below.

1. **A group** is a collection of two or more interdependent people, psychologically aware of one another, who have or who develop a shared goal.

2. Groups can be classified according to their degree of **formality,** degree of **member attachment,** and degree of **influence.**

3. **Formality** refers to the regularity and predictability of behavior. Formal groups consist of **command** and **task groups:** the former is made up of a manager and his or her employees; the latter is a group assigned a specific organizational job.

4. **Informal groups** consist of **interest** and **friendship groups.** Interest groups are oriented around shared activities; friendship groups are oriented around mutual attraction.

5. **Member attachment** refers to the degree to which members are affiliated with the group, with its processes, and with its norms.

6. **Primary groups** form spontaneously as people interact; **secondary groups** are those formed for more rational and logical reasons. Whether a group is primary or secondary depends on the attitude of each member.

7. A **reference group** is one that an individual admires; a person may identify with a reference group without actually being a member.

8. **Group influence** refers to the degree that groups influence organizations. **Apathetic groups** have little impact; **erratic groups** are unpredictable; **strategic groups** have well-planned courses of action; and **conservative groups** have substantial and widely recognized power that is of primary importance to the work flow of the organization.

9. Groups form spontaneously whenever and wherever people have an opportunity to interact. **Spontaneous groups** are a part of the **emergent system** rather than the **required system** of work assignments and job description.

10. The emergent system is sometimes called the **informal organization.** Because emergent and required processes are virtually inseparable, however, it is very difficult to make a distinction between the formal and informal organization.

11. Groups perform **activities,** engage in **interactions,** and make **decisions.** Activities can serve both the required and emergent systems, but as groups develop, activities may tend more toward serving the emergent system. Interactions can be classified according to their **frequency, duration,** and **direction.** Decisions in a group are often made by designated leaders.

12. **Group characteristics** include **norms, cohesiveness, roles, status** and **leadership. Norms** are shared standards of thought and action that are accepted by and expected from group members. **Cohesiveness** is the degree to which groups are able to enforce norms. **Roles** are the positions that result from the division of work among members of a group. **Status** is

the amount of esteem one receives from other members of a group. And **leadership** roles in a group are assigned, over time, to those members who have the highest status and who best embody the group norms.

13. Managerial responses to groups can be **negative, neutral,** or **positive.** Learning to supervise employees according to their group affiliations can be an aid to the managerial process.

14. **Sensitivity training** is a controversial method of training people to understand group processes and their own behavior as members of groups. Many organizations use sensitivity training and other development programs as aids to overall organizational effectiveness.

Discussion Questions

1. What is a group? How does a group differ from an organization? How are the two similar?

2. What is the informal organization? How and why does it form? What are its functions?

3. Give examples of command, task, interest, friendship, primary, secondary, and reference groups. Where does each fit on the formality, member attachment, and influence scales? Why? Can any of the groups you mention be listed under more than one category? In what ways do they fit each category?

4. "For the individual, and especially for the newcomer in an organization, the informal patterns of behaviors may be at least as binding and constraining as the behaviors described in the official handbook of duties." Comment on this statement and discuss it in light of the material in this chapter.

5. Describe and differentiate between required and emergent systems. In what way is the emergent system related to the informal organization?

6. Do classes have group norms? What are they in your class? Where do they come from?

7. How do groups enforce behavior norms?

8. Describe some of the rituals of groups you belong to. In what ways are these rituals helpful to the group? How are they harmful?

9. As a manager, how would you go about developing strong group cohesiveness among your employees? Would such cohesiveness be advantageous to the organization? Why?

10. Should managers strive for competition or cooperation among groups and individuals? Why?

11. What is status? Why is it important to individuals? How does it affect behavior?

12. Suppose your boss thinks that all first-line supervisors (including you) should attend a sensitivity-training session to improve their interpersonal skills. What would be your reaction? Why?

Involvement Activity

Anyone can make a study of the characteristics and dynamics of any group, whether group members are employees of an organization, a class, or a friendship club. Your task is to select one such group and make a sociometric analysis of it.

First, secure the permission and cooperation of all members of the group or organization you are studying.

Second, ask each member to answer three questions on a sheet of paper. All respondents must identify themselves; list the names of one, two, or three (but not more than three) members of the group in response to each question; and list the names of other group members in rank order. The questions are these:

1. List the names of the one person, or two, or three persons, you like the best in the group.

2. List the names of the person or persons (not to exceed three) that you would most like to have as leader of a work group to which you belong.

3. List the names of the person or persons (not to exceed three) that you would most like to party with.

Third, set up three separate matrices on three separate pieces of paper, using arithmetic graph paper or accounting paper. List the names of all respondents on both the horizontal and vertical columns. The horizontal column is the "chooser" axis; the vertical column is the "chosen" axis.

Fourth, take each respondent's answers to the first question. Reading across the row bearing his or her name, put a "3" in the column under the name of the first choice, a "2" in the column under the name of the second choice, and a "1" under the third choice. Do the same for every person. Repeat the process on a separate sheet of paper for each question. Now add the columns: you can see at a glance who is best liked, who is/are the leader(s), and which members are the most social. (Refer to Figure 10–4.)

Fifth, secure a large enough piece of paper so that the name of every member of the group can appear in a small circle inside a larger one. Go through the answers again, this time drawing a line between the chooser and the chosen, with an arrow pointing at the chosen end. Use different colors for the three questions. If a choice is reciprocal, draw an arrow at both ends of the line. This pattern of relationships is the beginning of a sociogram, which you may refine if you wish by putting the name of the person chosen most often near the center, those chosen next most often in a cluster around the

FIGURE 10–4
A sociometric check sheet.

CHOSEN AS LEADER					
CHOOSER	Alan	Evelyn	John	Mary	Steve
Alan				3	
Evelyn	3			2	
John				2	
Mary	3	1			
Steve					
TOTALS	6	1	0	7	

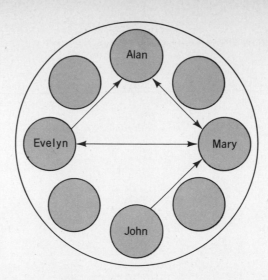

FIGURE 10–5
A sociogram.

center, those chosen least frequently or not chosen at all toward the outside as isolates, and so on. (See Figure 10–5 for an example.)

Now answer these questions about the group you have examined.

1. How cohesive is the group? How do you know?

2. Who is (are) the leader(s)? Why?

3. Is the group structured properly to accomplish its goals? How would you restructure it? Why?

4. If the group now elected formal leaders, do you think your sociometric analysis would predict who they would be? Why or why not?

5. What has your sociometric analysis told you about the group?

6. What important features of group dynamics has your sociometric analysis omitted? How would you discover the missing information?

11

Technology and Organization

The purpose of this chapter is to examine the ways that the technology of an organization—the physical tools and human skills and knowledge it employs—can influence the organization's work and structural design. The major topics include: the nature of technology; the factors that affect the choice of technologies; and the effects of technologies on employees, managers, and organization design.

The Nature of Technology

The three preceding chapters have viewed a manager's freedom to assign work—to set up an ideal organizational structure—in terms of the constraints imposed by the people in the organization and by the groups to which they belong. Unrestrained flexibility in assigning work is further limited by the technology used to do the work and by the advances in technological know-how in society. Technology is so instrumental to the work of modern organizations, and is such a vital part of the lives of all people in complex industrial societies, that it has been called an *imperative,* a commanding power that constrains, controls, and directs social behavior (1). Because technology is used by people to do work to accomplish human ends, it is inextricably linked with human behavior. Thus an organization is properly viewed in terms of both the social structure and technological content of its work system, or as a **sociotechnical system** in which people and technology together influence organization design (2).

This chapter extends the view thus far presented of management in organizations by including technology as another factor of vital importance to managers (see Figure 11–1). Looking at an organization as a sociotechnical system emphasizes that it is an open system with strong and mutually dependent social and technical aspects of work groups. Organizations are systems for getting work done. And in the process, they employ various techniques in order to change materials, symbols, and people. In a sense, then, the techniques employed—the technology—are

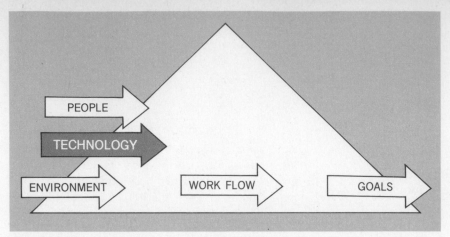

FIGURE 11-1
The effect of
resources on the
organization.

The shaded technology arrow indicates the emphasis in this chapter. The fact that the arrow is both inside and outside the organization (like people) implies that technology has both internal and external characteristics.

the defining characteristics of organizations (3). When organizations are discussed in terms of the work they do, which is the basic orientation of this book, it is appropriate to examine the means by which the work is accomplished.

Technology and Its Uses

In its broadest sense, **technology** refers to the tools people use in doing goal-directed work. Physical tools, such as implements and machinery, and human tools, such as knowledge and skills, are all manifestations of technology.

Physical Tools. When people think of technology, they often picture elaborate machinery and equipment or envision some new technological breakthrough in scientific research. Advanced mechanical implements are, of course, of great value in doing work. Simpler tools, such as hoes, pencils, and screwdrivers, are also of critical importance. These physical tools, the implements and machinery developed to do work more efficiently, are the most obvious elements in technology. Less obvious, but at least as important as hardware, are the human tools.

Human Tools. Human technologies include knowledge, abilities, attitudes, and organizations. The knowledge and know-how that people develop is of prime importance in doing work. Knowledge and wisdom about the human condition and about the environment that accumulate in a society are passed on through the formal educational system. Know-how, expertise, and specialized methods of doing work are passed on in schools of higher learning, in trade or vocational schools, and in organizational training programs.

The abilities and skills that people develop are methods, or programs, for doing their work with increasing efficiency. Attitudes are also important human tools, for they affect work behavior and, consequently, how well the work gets done.

Organizations are special kinds of tools. They make it possible to accomplish efficiently and effectively what for a single individual acting alone would be difficult or impossible. Groups and organizations rely on human collaboration to accomplish ends, and effective management of these cooperative systems is itself an important human technology.

Technology as an Active Concept

Intricate machinery and equipment and huge computer installations are impressive; so may be the credentials of a person who has a wealth of degrees and experience. But to be worth anything, the equipment, degrees, and experience must be put to use to reach goals. Technology, therefore, is an *active* concept. It involves the people who use the means, the actual work they do, and the goals they seek to accomplish. People use means to do work to reach goals, as shown in Figure 11–2.

Technology as an Interactive Concept

Technological means are also *interactive,* meaning both that they are subject to human selection and that they influence the people, the work, and the goals. The knowledge, skills, and procedures that people acquire are affected by the prevailing culture, and vice versa. Similarly, the specific activities, interactions, and decisions that take place as people do their

FIGURE 11–2
People, aided by changing means, do work to reach goals.

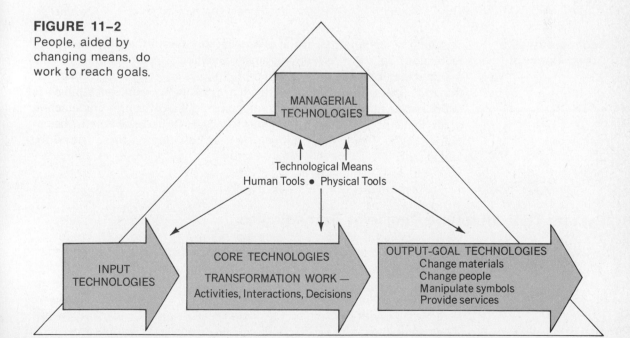

MANAGERIAL TECHNOLOGIES

Technological Means
Human Tools ● Physical Tools

INPUT TECHNOLOGIES

CORE TECHNOLOGIES

TRANSFORMATION WORK —
Activities, Interactions, Decisions

OUTPUT-GOAL TECHNOLOGIES
Change materials
Change people
Manipulate symbols
Provide services

work influence the goals, means, and other people that exist in the environment, and vice versa.

The goals of technology are to alter materials, to change people, to manipulate symbols, or to provide services. The winemaker changes grapes (material) to wine; college students (people) are changed into knowledgeable graduates; and mathematical formulas (symbols) are transformed into answers to tangible problems. The availability of technological means determines whether goals can be reached; the goals, in turn, specify who will use what means and engage in which activities, interactions, and decisions.

Technology as a Changing Process

Technological means are constantly changing. New technologies regularly appear that make old methods and old machinery obsolete. For example, the electrostatic copying machine has substantially altered many office procedures and greatly increased the volume of available information. Equally important is the rapidly expanding base of knowledge, including new information — and ensuing debates — about practically every subject imaginable. In the last few decades, for instance, ideas about how to teach have changed as dramatically as have ideas about how to manage. And the debate about method continues to flourish in both fields.

Rapid changes in means present new challenges and opportunities for managers. The opportunity exists to do better work with better tools. The challenge is to figure out what to do with obsolete equipment that no longer pays for itself or obsolete practices that people are reluctant to alter.

Technology as a Broad Concept

It should be apparent from the preceding discussion that the concept of technology covers a very broad range of elements. Although much of the material that follows centers around such topics as mechanization and automation, the sphere of human knowledge, know-how, and social skills is every bit as important to the technology bank of a culture or organization as are high-speed electronic computers or blast furnaces. There is a technology for providing entertainment just as certainly as there is one for making steel.

Factors That Affect the Choice of Technologies

Managers have some degree of flexibility in choosing among technologies. However, their freedom of choice is limited by goals, by the work itself, by the technological means available, and by the people who will use the tools. The factors to be considered in choosing a technology can therefore be grouped under four major segments: goals, work, means, and people. The technology must be carefully chosen so that it is suited to each.

Technology Suited to Goals

It would be a mistake to think that an organization had but one technology or that the description of one major technology could define an entire system. Technologies differ even in the primary production or work system of an organization. They also differ according to the hierarchical level in the same organization, and they differ greatly among different kinds of organizations. Technologies differ between and within organizations as a function of the goals that are being sought. Furthermore, even where goals are similar, technologies may differ according to the particular path that is chosen to reach the objective.

Goals of Organizations. Technologies differ among organizations according to the different goals each pursues. Clearly, a service organization, such as a university, has a very different technology than that of a manufacturing plant. One way to classify organizations by type of goal is to array them along a continuum, ranging from those that are primarily concerned with providing a service to those that concentrate their efforts on producing materials. This continuum takes into account the fact that all organizations have some kind of service, human, symbolic, and material output.

Goals of Subunits. Individual units within organizations also vary in their technologies because the primary aim of each subunit is different from that of other units. Technologies differ both *horizontally,* in line with the major flow of work, and *vertically,* through the managerial hierarchy.

1. *Horizontal Technologies.* Work-flow or core technologies, shown in Figure 11–2, are those concerned with fulfilling a primary organizational goal (4). In the core of an organization, work flows horizontally from the input sections, where materials are received, through the work and conversion sections, to the output sections. And technologies differ in each segment (5).

Often when people talk of the technology of an organization they refer to the conversion or work system with its accompanying machinery and equipment. In modern industry, conversion processes probably attract the most attention because they are the most technologically advanced and because the size, speed, precision, and cost of sophisticated equipment is most impressive. A high degree of specialization, division of work, and mechanization characterizes the conversion activities of large-scale organizations that mass-produce most of the products used in modern, industrialized societies.

Input processes, those activities directed toward securing resources of people, materials, money, and information, are also necessary, and each has its own appropriate technique. *Output* processes, such as storing, dispensing, and delivering, also require unique technologies. These processes usually do not lend themselves to the kind of routinization possible in production systems because of the requirement of dealing with the environment (6).

2. *Vertical Technologies.* Just as different segments of the performance core use different technologies, so do different groups in the managerial hierarchy. Various managerial groups use technologies that differ markedly not only from those of the performance core, but also from one another. The activities, interactions, and decisions required to integrate or coordinate the output of various work stations obviously require different kinds of technologies than those involved in performing operations on materials. The technology of a managerial segment also differs according to its distance from the conversion system. The farther removed an echelon of managers is from the work-flow core of the production system, the longer its time perspective, the more uncertain its environment for decisions, and the greater the need to keep the organization relevant in its environment. The farther means are from the production system, the more important become human tools and the less important become physical tools.

Goals and Size. The technology selected for a subunit of an organization, or for that matter, the core technology of a whole organization, depends not only on the purpose of the system but also on its size. The size of an organization or subsystem influences the technology because the smaller the unit the fewer are the technological options. Workers or managers must have the *time* to use technology effectively, the *skills* that are required, and enough *volume* of activity to spread the cost over a good deal of productive activity. For example, managers of many small organizations have bought computers only to find that they had insufficient skills to be able to use the computers' full capabilities and too little work to justify their cost. Under such circumstances, the computers are idle or only partially used much of the time and represent an unnecessary drain on limited resources. So the smaller the organization, the simpler the appropriate technology.

Small   Large

SIZE

Technology Suited to the Work

In choosing a technology, a manager needs to consider not only the goals of the unit but also the *characteristics* of the work itself. Three characteristics will be considered here: the degree to which the work is differentiated, the extent of integration required, and the extent to which outcomes of work are predictable.

Degree of Differentiation. As noted before, the division of work into similar and simple tasks can lead to more efficient performance. The extent to which work can be, and is, divided will influence the choice of technology. The more specialized and repetitive the work, the easier it is to design a machine to do the job. To some extent, the degree of differentiation of work, or the degree to which tasks are broken up into specialized units, is subject to a managerial choice between simplification and enlargement. Simplification aids mechanization by making it useful to substitute machines for people. On the other hand, simplification makes the organization's technological system rigid and unable to cope with change.

Low   High

DEGREE OF DIFFERENTIATION OF WORK

Degree of Integration Required by Task Interdependence. If work is divided into its elements and a specific technology is developed for each, then coordination or integration is necessary. Traditionally, the managerial hierarchy has been considered the coordinating technology, but other kinds of integrating tools also are available. In addition to the cultural conditioning, social interaction, managerial activity, and organizational methods discussed in Chapter 7, machine controls, production schedules, and line-item budgets, are also examples of integrating technologies.

The need for integration varies according to the degree that one task depends on other tasks. Thompson notes three types of interdependence: **pooled, sequential,** and **reciprocal** (7). In a situation of **pooled interdependence,** each unit is autonomous and separate but contributes to and draws

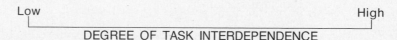

Low   High

DEGREE OF TASK INTERDEPENDENCE

from the total pool of resources. Branch banks are examples of pooled interdependence. **Sequential interdependence** is the common situation in which each work unit depends for its input on the output of some other part. Assembly-line production is a case in point; if one part of the system fails, the entire line must shut down. In a situation of **reciprocal interdependence,** the outputs of each unit become the inputs for all the others.

For example, an aircraft maintenance unit depends on the need of the aircraft for maintenance; and the craft depends on the maintenance unit for its effective functioning (8).

Degree of Predictability of Outcomes. Another dimension of work that influences the technology selected is the degree to which one can predict outcomes. If one were to beat fresh cream, first it would whip and then become butter: the technology of beating cream is quite predictable. Also predictable are the outcomes of the appropriate use of a lawn mower, a drill press, or a ruler. Less predictable are the technologies associated with employee selection or market research. The closer to the performance core, the more predictable are the technologies and the more likely one is to obtain the expected results. The farther away one is from the performance core, the more susceptible are the technologies to the risks and uncertainties of the environment, and the less predictable they are.

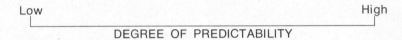

Low   High

DEGREE OF PREDICTABILITY

These characteristics of work—differentiation, integration, and predictability—are probably not mutually exclusive, but they illuminate some of the considerations necessary in selecting an appropriate technology for different kinds of work.

Technology Suited to the Means

Technology should also be selected in accord with the means of technology currently available. A given technology need not be selected simply because it is available, but managers do need to keep up with innovations that might be helpful. For example, few managers use mathematical models to help them make better decisions, yet such models have been available for many decades. The manager who knows how to use such models might gain a critical competitive edge. The three variables related to the means of technology that will be discussed here include (1) the extent of mechanization, (2) the extent to which the means are adaptable to other kinds of work, and (3) the degree to which appropriate technologies are available.

Mechanization. Mechanization refers to the extent to which physical tools and machinery are used to help accomplish work. Often the term implies the replacing of human or animal labor with machines. When work formerly done by humans is mechanized, some people are displaced. This process may seem cold-hearted to some, but if mechanization increases productivity, society might profit in the long run—at least in terms of the goods and services available. The output of goods and services increases and costs are reduced as efficiency increases, and there is no doubt that machines can perform many tasks more efficiently than can humans.

The degree of mechanization of work can be ranged along a continuum. At the low end of the scale, all work is performed by a single individual. Moving along the continuum, the next degree of mechanization would be a group of people who combine their efforts to produce work. Next is the combination of human energy either with animal energy or with physical implements or mechanical tools to get work done. Further along the continuum is the combination of machines to produce work, and the ultimate in mechanization is a single tool that can do everything. This latter situation is of doubtful probability in spite of some science fiction writers' prophecies of an "intelligent" and megalomaniacal computer that takes over the world.

Low   High
Person   Person-Person   Person-Tool   Tool-Tool   Tool
DEGREE OF MECHANIZATION OF WORK

Every step along the continuum toward increasingly complicated technology produces different kinds of person-machine relationships. Each requires a different source of power, dictates differing procedures for processing and handling materials, and indicates the types of control procedures that are most likely to be effective (9). Toward the high end of the scale, human effort constitutes a decreasingly important part of the work. Where the work of a machine, process, or system is automatically controlled by mechanical or electronic devices that replace human observation, effort, or decision, such work is said to be **automated.**

Automation has been a popular topic in recent years. Some people think of automation as a panacea, freeing people from machines, greatly improving output per level of input, and generally bettering the human condition. Others speak darkly of unemployment and social unrest as machines increasingly replace workers in industry. In reality, neither of these extreme views is likely to materialize. The technological systems of various cultures range on a continuum of types from very primitive to advanced, as illustrated in Figure 11–3. Automation, in this view, is but an extension of mechanization.

But whereas mechanization is the extension and/or replacement of human *physical* abilities with machine capabilities, automation involves the extension and/or replacement of human *mental* capabilities. At the heart of automation lies the computer. And to those who worry about such things, the ultimate extension of automation is the factory in which

FIGURE 11–3
A continuum of technological development.

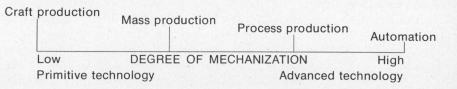

humans are not necessary at all. Clearly, if that state is reached, the nature of management will have changed rather dramatically from that presented in this book.

Adaptability. In addition to considering the level of mechanization when choosing a technology, one must also take into account the adaptability of the technological means. A computer is quite adaptable. It can be programed to control inventory, write payroll checks, solve physics problems, or play chess, among other things. A petroleum refinery, however, is suited only to the cracking of crude oil into various kinds of hydrocarbons. Some kinds of technologies—methods, tools, objects, people—are quite flexible and can be used for a number of different purposes. Others are specific for one or a few tasks. In many organizations, the most adaptable technologies are found at the input and output boundaries where changes are likely to occur in the supply of resources and in client demand. Thus, the managers may need to be more adaptable than the production workers in order to keep up with changing environmental conditions. The more adaptable the technological means, the more likely it is that the organization will survive in a turbulent environment. It follows, then, that if routines are inflexible and the organization has its capital tied up in limited-purpose programs and equipment, the organization will be more vulnerable to sudden changes in the environment.

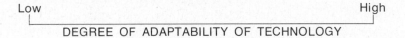

Low   High

DEGREE OF ADAPTABILITY OF TECHNOLOGY

Availability. Technological means also differ according to their degree of availability. Some technologies, such as space shuttles, have been developed but are unavailable to most commercial organizations. Other technologies are unavailable because they are secret, patented, or economically prohibitive. Still others may be possible but, given the present state of knowledge, not yet accessible. For instance, an efficient way may exist to convert solar energy directly into enough electricity to supply all present and future energy demands, but at this writing the means for doing so have not been discovered. The availability of a suitable technology, then, depends on knowledge, accessibility, and cost.

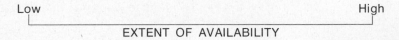

Low   High

EXTENT OF AVAILABILITY

Technology Suited to the People

Another major consideration in choosing a technology is the extent to which it fits the philosophy of the managers and the expectations of the employees. In common with other dimensions of technology, the degree of fit can be ranged along a continuum. Presumably, the greater the degree of fit, the more likely employees will be to use the means to work efficiently and to reach goals effectively. Some technologies, like the lever or surgical skills, are a boon to both users and clients. Others, such as assembly-line production, may benefit stockholders and clients but may alienate those whose working lives are tied to the line. In this case the fit between employee expectations or desires and technology may not be very good. Perhaps the less the fit between technology and people the greater the possibility of resistance or alienation. The effect of technology on people is the subject of the remaining sections of this chapter. They deal in turn with the effect of technology on employees, managers, and organization design.

Low   High

EXTENT OF FIT BETWEEN TECHNOLOGY AND PEOPLE

The Effect of Technologies on Employees

The history of industrialization has been a process of replacing human skills with mechanical tools. Mechanical technologies extend and improve the capacities of humans and in so doing increase per capita output.

"I found the trouble, sir. The big computer is making the little computer do all the work."

Constantly improved mechanical technologies are primarily responsible for the high standard of living enjoyed by the majority of people in the United States. A declining number of farmers can now feed a population well in excess of 200 million, while many less-industrialized societies, with a much larger percentage of farmers, can barely feed fewer numbers of people.

Higher productivity is not an unmixed blessing, however. As more implements and machinery are developed, jobs are redesigned in ways that are not always best for people. Gradually, workers seem to recede more and more into the background as higher levels of mechanization are attained. And as workers' knowledge and abilities become less important, it is likely that their attitudes will become increasingly negative.

Person-Machine Engineering

Because most jobs require both human and mechanical technologies, considerable effort has been spent to design machines with people in mind. This effort represents an attempt to avoid the dysfunctional effects of negative attitudes. Through the use of systems analysis, person-machine engineering considers both individual and machine requirements as variables to be integrated into the design of machines and the jobs associated with them. So far, person-machine engineering has concentrated mainly on the physiological requirements of people. Results have been encouraging, but the analysis will remain incomplete until the psychological, social, and cultural requirements of people are also taken into account.

Another factor that is yet to be considered is that the engineers who design and install equipment may have different values from those who use the machines. Typical of the problems that may result from such differences is an example cited by Walker. The chief engineer of a corporation, applying the best scientific management techniques, came to the conclusion that workers would be pleased to have their jobs described to the last detail. This manager believed that employees would be more loyal to the organization when the engineers proved they knew more about the workers' jobs than did those who actually performed the work (10). Too often the experts who make such decisions make the mistake of believing that people will be content to be fitted into jobs that are defined in terms of mechanistic models of human behavior.

Sociotechnical Systems

A broader view has been adopted by those behavioral scientists who view organizations as sociotechnical systems. In designing jobs, these people take into consideration the individual, the social setting of the work, and the constraints imposed by the physical technology. The results of one attempt at sociotechnical job design are related in the accompanying box about coal mining. In this example, Trist and Bamforth show that if the job design includes individuals, the total social situation in which they work, and the technological innovations necessary to complete the task, then higher levels of both productivity and worker satisfaction can be achieved.

A Study in the Design of a Sociotechnical System

The Longwall Method of Coal Getting

A prime example of sociotechnical systems design is contained in the study of coal mining in England reported by Trist and Bamforth. Before the mechanization of coal-mining methods, pairs of workers worked together with hand tools. These pairs had to be multi-skilled since they carried through the whole process, working largely independently from other groups and from management. Each pair was an autonomous unit, enjoying both social interaction and the pay they received as a team.

"With the advent of coal-cutters and mechanical conveyors, the degree of technological complexity of the coal-getting task was raised to a different level." Mechanization made it possible to work a single long face of coal instead of a set of short faces, as previously worked by the teams. This change in technology created what is called the "conventional longwall method" of coal getting. In this new system the division of labor was extensive, and each worker had an isolated work station. The complete process of bringing a load of coal to the surface took three sets of workers. The first prepared the area, the second dug the coal with machinery, and the third transported the coal to the surface. The process, based on the functional specialization of labor, was seriously dysfunctional in some respects. Each task group tended to go its own way. Instead of cooperating with one another, individuals competed, and coordination became a serious problem. The role of management increased because the workers could no longer be depended upon to coordinate their own activities. Management tried to control the situation through coercion, a difficult means to use in a mine.

Bamforth and Trist, working with management, were able to develop a somewhat different arrangement by specifically considering some of the social factors in the situation and developing an organizational arrangement called the "composite longwall method." The major innovation was not to change the tasks but to view the process as a whole sociotechnical system. The workers, instead of being assigned to a particular task on a particular set, were assigned to a group responsible for the whole cycle or process. Incentive payments were made to the entire group. Individuals enjoyed more variety in the tasks they performed and exhibited more interest in the overall task. The results of such changes were positive in almost all cases.

Technological innovation, with its advantages of efficiency and speed, was retained; and the workers once again were permitted to enjoy teamwork and collaboration. Trist and Bamforth thus suggest that managers, in introducing technological change, must redesign the social as well as the technical systems.

Source: E. L. Trist, and K. W. Bamforth, "Some Social and Psychological Consequences of the Longwall Method of Coal-Getting," *Human Relations*, vol. 4 (1951), pp. 3–38.

The Effects of Mechanization on Attitudes. Employee attitudes are likely to be more positive through the middle range of mechanization and more negative at the extremes. In other words, at very low levels of mechanization, people are struggling for subsistence, and work provides no pleasures other than economic survival. At very high levels, people are tied to the machines they use and feel they have no control over their situation. This latter condition is that of work simplification, which has been discussed previously (see Chapter 5).

In an extensive study of worker reactions to technology, Walker questioned and observed automobile line workers (11). His major conclusion was that automobile workers detested their jobs. They stayed only because they were afraid to leave and lose their seniority and retirement benefits. They also stayed because of the good pay they received, which was interpreted as payment for being bored.

Other findings in Walker's study are also relevant. The quality of work observed was poor, and any control over the quality was removed from the worker. Whenever possible, auto workers avoided work. The absenteeism rate was extremely high, especially on Monday and Friday. Workers cheered whenever the line broke down. Further, workers showed a variety of nervous reactions to their work even when off the job, including alcoholism and family problems.

Installing or changing the technology may not affect all employees in an organization equally, or even all workers in one subunit. Automation is a case in point. The introduction of a computer system has been shown to have little effect on the *average* skill level of jobs. But this is a deceptive statistic and does not mean that the skill level of various jobs has not changed. In fact, what happens is that some jobs in computerized systems require *less* skill and some require *more* skill, leaving the average skill level of the work unit unchanged.

All increases in mechanization need not lead to negative feelings by employees. Studies of computer installations indicate that when time is allotted to train, listen to, and assure employees that their jobs will continue to exist, workers react positively to the change. Taking people into account in designing the system is useful, as suggested by the sociotechnical systems approach. Finally, it should be noted that some employees have adapted to, and enjoy, the simplicity and lack of responsibility present in jobs that are highly mechanized.

The Effects of Mechanization on Self-Concepts. Increasing mechanization reduces the importance of any one employee in the production process and also diminishes individual status in the organization. As roles change, conceptions of self also change. Simon points out this problem in a discussion of a potential "identity crisis" as machines increasingly substitute for human labor and as computers come to simulate human decisions (12). The more we accept that machines can think and learn, the more our feelings of self-worth are threatened. And we may well wonder, "What is left that is uniquely human?"

Workers' self-concepts also suffer because machines make demanding work partners. When a machine does part of the job and a person the other part, the question is Who does what? It may be that workers get the least interesting part of the task. Further, machines do not have the flexibility of humans, and they do not tire. Even though they may break down or occasionally make mistakes, they tend to be rather intimidating in their relentless pace.

The Effects of Mechanization on Groups

Just as machine technologies affect individuals, they also affect groups of people. Physical technologies can either bring people together and require interaction between them, or they can separate and isolate individuals. Thus the cohesiveness of a group can either be aided or hindered by the way mechanization influences interactions, attitudes, and activities.

Mechanization, Group Interactions, and Attitudes. The automobile assembly line is an example of the way mechanization hinders the development of cohesive groups. Each person on the line can interact only with the two or three people in immediate proximity, but no common set of interactions can exist among all (or even a group of) assembly-line personnel. Thus, the interactions necessary to create stable group relationships are nonexistent. "The Case of the Aggravated Cook" offers one example of how technology can influence the interactions necessary for strong group cohesiveness. Managers need to be aware of the influence

The Case of the Aggravated Cook

A rigid status hierarchy exists among employees in restaurants. The highest-status person is the cook; waiters and waitresses are lower; and those who bus the dishes are lower still. Generally, interactions must be consistent with the norms and status structure of the group.

Some years ago, the typical procedure of ordering meals contradicted status requirements of interaction. In most restaurants, the customer gave the order to the waiter or waitress, who relayed it to the cook. Thus the lower-status people initiated work for the higher-status person. This status reversal annoyed and aggravated the cook, and created considerable role conflict for the waiters and

waitresses as well. Negative sentiments built up between the two, creating problems for the restaurant. A restaurant does not thrive with aggravated cooks and confused waiters and waitresses.

What is the solution to this problem?

Technology to the Rescue

The solution to this particular problem was a small bit of machine technology, a device familiar to everyone who has patronized restaurants: a turntable on which the order is attached. The cook no longer has to take verbal orders from lower-status people, and the relationship between the two groups has improved considerably.

Source: William F. Whyte, "The Social Structure of the Restaurant," *American Journal of Sociology*, vol. 54 (1949), pp. 302–310.

that changes in technology have upon social relationships if they wish to minimize resistance to change.

Technology affects group attitudes and sentiments. Positive attitudes are created where the technology surrounds the group and creates their reason for being. Computer installations have this characteristic. Status can be ascribed to machines as well as to people. New machines or more complex ones are seen as requiring more from the people associated with them, whether true or not. The machine's status thus rubs off on those who operate it.

On the other hand, to the extent that technology requires a group of people with diverse backgrounds to come together, it has the potential of producing negative sentiments and considerable friction among employees. When technology changes rapidly, it has a negative effect on group attitudes because the social system never has a chance to fully adjust to one change before it is changed again. The manager must therefore perform many of the coordinating activities that a more cohesive group would do for itself.

Mechanization and Group Activities. The activities of group members both supplement and hinder mechanization, for the relationship between technology and the group is not a one-way affair. One of the major functions of a group is to fill in the undefined portion of the total work system. Technology is not a natural phenomenon; it is a human invention. It is up to the group, the informal organization, to complete the system. Because it is impossible to plan for all the eventualities of a particular technology, the social organization must supply those interactions, activities, and decisions that make the technology work. As a result, the group becomes more important as technology becomes more complex.

A highly complex technological innovation may require a whole group of people just to understand it. Since techniques and machines are often designed by teams of specialists rather than by individuals, they often require equally specialized teams of people to implement or run them. The fact that people must work as a group to accomplish the purposes of the system creates quite a paradox: as technology becomes complex, it demands cohesive group behavior; at the same time, technology sets up barriers to group cohesiveness by requiring physical distance and a wide variety of skills among group members, which limit the opportunities for developing stable interaction patterns.

Machine Technologies and Managers

Mechanical technologies were once limited to the production processes, in which machines took over highly routine manual tasks. The "new technology" in the form of computer systems, however, can now substitute automated operations for the work of white-collar employees (13). Because the effects of the new technology on managers are just beginning to be known, it is rather difficult to be very descriptive when discussing technology and the managerial process. Some research evidence is available, but most of the material in this section will tend to be more predictive than descriptive.

The mechanization of white-collar and managerial work essentially involves the use of computers to assemble and analyze information: in short, the computer has become an adjunct to managerial decision making. Just as operations mechanization has altered the activities, interactions, and attitudes of workers, so has the mechanization of information processing altered the decision-making processes of managers. Thus the topics that occupy the next two sections are the development of computerization and the use of computers in decision making.

Computerization   The computer has opened innumerable new and creative ways to use technology in processing both materials and information, thus extending people's physical abilities to almost incredible limits. Now scientists are working on computer programs that can extend and speed people's mental processes as well. Newer generations of computers may lead to automated thinking as well as to automated production and processing.

HE'S EFFICIENT BUT HARD TO TALK TO

To date, there have been three generations of computers. The characteristic that best separates these generations is the principal electronic component used in their construction. From vacuum tubes to transistors to microcircuits, each succeeding generation has provided more speed, reliability, and compactness than those that have come before.

First-generation computers processed large units of data rapidly. Electronic data processing, or EDP, systems performed the work of battalions of clerks, storing and manipulating huge quantities of data. The major effect of this effort was to cut clerical and paper-work costs. This was no minor improvement; it is estimated that one out of each eight business expense dollars in 1955 went into paper work.

The second generation of computers is generally associated with problem-solving techniques. Not only can these computers organize and arrange information, they can also analyze it. The tools of analysis are called *operations research* (see Chapter 14), which permit the computer to perform operations that indicate to a manager the optimum course of action to follow.

The advance made by the third generation of computers is in the area of time. Large storage capacity and tremendous calculation speed reduce the time lag dramatically. Information is available for decision making almost instantly so that the tempo of both management and the organization as a whole is increased considerably.

The Effect of Computers and Automation on Managerial Work

Automation was defined earlier in this chapter as the use of mechanical or electronic devices to take the place of human observation, effort, or decisions in controlling the work of a machine, a process, or a system. In this sense, computers have the potential to affect all managerial activities.

Decision Making. As seen above, computers can provide more information more quickly and less expensively for improving the rationality of decision making, analyzing more complex problems, and significantly increasing the speed of analysis than can humans. The overall effect of introducing automation into decision making in organizations has been to make it quicker and more rational. The computer is not equally valuable for all types of decisions, however. At present it is most valuable in the area of detailed and repetitive decision making (14). Managers, as a result, can spend their time on less routine tasks. One plant manager, whose decision making became augmented by use of a computer, found himself free to take a look at the plant as a whole system and came up with an idea for change that he felt would represent a savings of at least as much as his annual salary. He also reported that he had more time to spend on human problems, community projects, public relations, and interrelationships of work groups.

Further, with computers, the cycle of decision making is shortened. Whisler found that the computer increases the number and importance of managerial deadlines (15). Real-time systems do not provide for leisurely decision making because there is simply less slack in the system. Computers have also required a different attitude toward information. Management can no longer assume that once a job is designed the information appropriate for carrying out the task will automatically be available when needed. Computers demand large masses of information on a very tight time schedule. Thus the information flow in the organization must be carefully planned. And for this reason, integrating the computer into the organization usually means redesigning the whole communication network.

Computers also affect the question of who makes decisions in the organization. Leavitt and Whisler, for instance, foresaw a trend toward **recentralization.** They argued that as computerization increases the amount of information that top management can digest, decisions that once were made by lower-level managers can now be returned to higher managerial levels (16). This argument is based on the assumption that *if* management can recentralize it *will* recentralize.

An equally plausible argument, however, is that the additional information available will be filtered down to the lower echelons and that decision making will begin to take place on a wider range of hierarchical levels. Thus the decision to use the computer as an excuse to recentralize is clearly one of managerial choice. Decentralization is more than just a strategy for coping with size and complexity; it is deeply rooted in the social values of those who run organizations.

Communication. Although automation does increase the total amount of available information, it also blocks some types of information. In particular, emotional information cannot be handled by a computer. So if the sentiments and feelings of people are important to the system, decisions based only on computer facts may be quite inappropriate.

Computers create groups of computer specialists. As with all specialist groups, computer people have their own language that distinguishes them from other groups. Managers may have difficulty understanding their language, and the specialists, in turn, often fail to understand the managers' language. Because computer specialists deal with the entire range of information in the organization, to be effective they would have to understand the language of all the other groups; a very difficult task indeed.

Influence. "Knowledge is power" is an old proverb but one with considerable truth. It is not surprising that those people who are close to and understand how to use the computer are likely to gain more power than those who do not or cannot use the computer. Certainly the manager who knows how to structure the computer's information system so that he or she is first to get needed information is in the best position to make decisions. In this way the computer can become a power tool.

But computers can also have an adverse effect on the managers' influence. The computer specialist becomes one more staff specialist who impinges on the authority of the line manager. Also, managers often begin to feel that they are simply providers and disseminators of information as their job more and more requires them to handle the increasing flood of information that pours in and out of the computer.

Control. Automation can build control into the system itself so that human interaction is not needed. Not only can electronic controls detect deviations from standards, but in some cases, they can also make actual corrections.

Automatic control is impersonal. In our culture, the values of equalitarianism create dysfunctions when one person controls the actions of another. But when control is built in to the technology, the employee does not feel the same degree of antagonism toward the machine as he does toward the manager. Although workers may feel some dissatisfaction with the machines or with the processes, they are less likely to become hostile or rebellious than when dissatisfaction is attributed to a person or group of people.

The Effect of Computer Technologies on Managers

To some degree, the introduction of automation initiates an identity crisis for managers. Suddenly their work becomes substantially different, and they are faced with having to learn whole new sets of skills and to unlearn others. Computers present the manager with opportunities and constraints. To the degree that managers perceive they can use the computer, their reactions will be positive. But where they perceive the computer as a constraint they will exhibit negative reactions.

Managers are no more rational than any other group of people when their jobs are threatened. Thus a good deal of resistance to automation, particularly to the computer, can be expected from members of the managerial ranks. Consider, for example, the situation in which two similar work groups were combined. One group had used the computer to maintain all its records; the other used a hand-file system. In combining the records of the two groups, it was discovered that the computer had been handling tasks that the manager of the latter group had "proved" was impossible to computerize. In this case, the manager feared the computer system because he did not understand it and, furthermore, had no intention of learning to use it.

The effect of response to automation is likely to be different on different levels of the managerial hierarchy. To first-line supervisors, automation represents just one more restriction in a long line of controls that continue to erode their authority. The only possible bright spot for first-level supervisors is that they have access to more information that might help them to communicate with their subordinates more effectively and to receive more and better information from them.

The effect of computers on middle management is not at all clear. Leavitt and Whisler predicted a disappearance of middle management with their function being taken over by the computer and staff groups (17). But more recent studies seem to show different results, including one that shows middle managers becoming even more important (18). Certainly there is no indication as yet that the computer is effective in handling anything other than those decisions that are quantitative in nature. Situations calling for interpersonal competence will undoubtedly remain within the province of humans.

At this time, few suggest that the decisions of the top-management level are amenable to the computer. The effect of the computer on upper management may be to relieve executives of unnecessary details and to let them concentrate more on planning for the future and on solving unstructured problems. One of the objectives of a computerized information system is to compress data and to provide only "exception" information. **Management by exception** allows the automated system to take over routine administrative matters by processing data from various parts of the organization. Management needs to be involved only when the computer indicates that standards have not been met — that is, when an exception to expectations occurs.

However, all management levels must be able to fully understand the uses and limitations of the computer. Too often, particularly when operations research is involved, the manager is not in a position to know whether the information is valuable. But the information of any computer is only as good as the inputs and the processes used to evaluate the data. If the data or programs are poor, then, in computer jargon, management can expect the phrase "garbage in, garbage out" to apply.

Machine Technology and Organization Design

We have already seen that technology affects the patterns of activities, interactions, and decisions of people in organizations as they work toward accomplishing goals. There is no doubt that technology is a strong influence on the structure and operation of the organization. Technology determines in part where people will work, patterns much of what they do, and indicates with whom they must — or can — interact.

But technology is selected by people and can be changed by people. People can enlarge and enrich jobs, rotate members of the organization between several different kinds of fixed technologies, and select, change, or remove technologies. Because people select the technological devices used, technology is dependent on human decisions. In this sense, technology is best considered an interactive variable in organization design. People, structure, and technology interact and affect one another as seen in Figure 11–4.

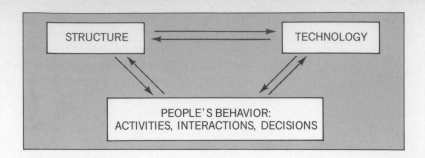

FIGURE 11-4
Technology as an interactive variable.

If technology has an effect on organizational structure, then it is possible that matching the organization form with the patterns of technology can improve the efficiency and effectiveness of goal attainment. Studies of the relationship between technology and organizational structure began in the early 1960s and continue today. Some of the main findings from a few of these investigations are summarized below.

The Woodward Study

During the 1960s, Joan Woodward surveyed one hundred English firms and collected a great deal of information about their structure, products, technology, success, and employee attitudes (19).

Woodward classified the technology of organizations into three major categories: (1) unit or small-batch production; (2) large-batch or mass production; and (3) process production. Unit-production firms fill special-order items and/or provide parts for other, larger systems. The aerospace industry is an example of this type of system, as would be a job shop specializing in repair work, because each unit represents a special order for a particular customer. Large-batch and/or mass production is the most common form of production system in large American organizations; it is best exemplified by the automobile industry. Process-production systems are becoming more common. They are typified by the oil and chemical industries, which rely on highly automated equipment to do their work.

Technology and Hierarchical Levels. Woodward's primary finding was that firms with similar production systems seemed to exhibit similar patterns of organization. Somewhat more specifically, she found that the median number of supervisory levels, or echelons, in the management hierarchy increased from three in the small-batch production firms, to four in mass-production organizations, and to six in the process firms.

Technology and Span of Control. In terms of the span of control, Woodward found that the median number of executives reporting to the president increased with the degree of technological complexity. Thus the median span of control of the chief executive ranged from four in the simplest technologies to seven in mass production organizations to ten in process industries. In sharp contrast with the president's span of control, which grew larger with increasing technology, the span of control at middle-management hierarchical levels became smaller. Therefore, process industries, with very small spans of control at intermediate levels, had long chains of command. The span of control of first-level supervisors was greatest in mass-production industries, which might be expected in organizations where workers' tasks are tied to the schedule of an assembly line. The median number of workers per supervisor was around fifty. Unit-production firms and special-order job shops were next, with some twenty workers per boss. Process industries, employing comparatively few workers compared with volume and value of production, gave the typical supervisor only ten or fifteen employees to oversee.

Technology, Size, and the Ratio of Managers to Workers. Woodward also concluded that the relative size of the management group is a better indication of organizational size than is the total number of employees. She based this notion on her finding that the ratio of managers to workers is one to twenty-three in unit-production firms, one to sixteen in mass-production organizations, and only one to eight in process-production organizations. This finding is consistent with the finding that the spans of control of middle and lower managers vary according to the type of work done.

She found that the ratio of clerical and administrative workers to production workers was different in different kinds of organizations. Process firms had twelve or so "indirect" workers to every one engaged directly in production. Mass-production firms had many more "direct" workers. And the ratio of direct to indirect labor was highest in firms engaged in unit production.

Technology and Bureaucracy. The degree of bureaucracy in the firms studied was found to be lowest at both ends of the technological continuum. Mass-production firms, in contrast, were highly dependent on rules. Unit-production and process-production firms were found to be similar to one another and different from mass-production firms in other ways. Both had more highly developed primary social groups and more highly skilled workers. Control was not a major problem in either type firm because unit shops relied on craftsmanship and process firms had automatic control devices. Neither showed a very highly developed line-and-staff organization, which is a prevailing organizational mode in mass-production firms.

Technology, Structure, and Success. Woodward's study indicates a clear relationship between production technologies and organizational structure. She suggests further that one particular form of organization is likely to be best suited for each system of production. The practical implications of links between technology, organization, and success include the possibility that a manager can better assess the present structure and plan organizational change to achieve better operative results. One way that Woodward substantiated this idea was to compare the business success of various types of firms according to their spans of control. She found that successful firms were those that had the most common (modal) span of control for their technological type; less successful firms had spans of control that were either larger or smaller than the modal value.

Implications. The major conclusion to be drawn from this study is confirmation that technology is a dominant variable that needs to be taken into account when planning and developing an organization's structure. Thus, approaching organizations as sociotechnical systems has a great deal of validity.

Furthermore, changes in technology must be examined in terms of their effects upon the organizational structure. Woodward noted that "management principles" were most nearly applicable only to the mass-production firms. The usefulness of these principles might be questioned in organizations with other kinds of technologies.

The Aston Studies

Shortly after Woodward published her discoveries, the Industrial Administration Research Unit of the University of Aston in Birmingham, England, conducted a series of investigations to determine the actual characteristics of organizational structure and to assess the relationship between the real structure of organizations and their technologies.

Organizational Structure. The Aston group studied more than fifty different kinds of organizations, including automobile manufacturers, producers of chocolate bars, road-repair departments of cities, schools, large retail stores, and small insurance companies. They isolated three dimensions of structure that marked differences among the organizations studied: the extent to which activities are prescribed, or structured; the concentration of authority; and the extent of personal control of the flow of work (20).

Three major points emerge from this research. First, *size* seems to be an important variable. As firms grow, work tends to become increasingly structured. The control of work flow is less and less in the hands of workers and their immediate supervisors and increasingly dependent on the standing rules and regulations of the organization and on the technological requirements of machines.

Second, organizations tend over *time* to become more structured and to be controlled more impersonally. And third, even organizations that rely primarily on human knowledge and skill (as opposed to those that rely on material production and machine technology) can have *authority* concentrated in an administrative hierarchy. The findings also suggest that there may be differences in *kind* as well as *degree* between materials-processing segments of organizations and people-processing segments.

Technology and Organization. In subsequent studies, the Aston group tried to discover the relationship between the organizational structures they had defined and the operations or core technology used in the flow of work. They isolated three different kinds of technology: *operations technology,* referring to the techniques in the flow of work; *materials technology,* meaning the activities performed on objects and materials; and *knowledge technology,* the knowledge necessary to process the flow of work.

These findings confirmed the Woodward conclusion that operations technology affects the structure of the organization concerned with the flow of work, but that in large-scale organizations the core technology may not have too much effect on the administrative structure in other parts of the organization. Similarly, the smaller the organization, the more completely its structure is affected by the technology of the core work flow (21).

Other Studies

The Woodward and Aston studies spawned a good deal of subsequent research. The unique findings of several of these are worth noting.

Multiple Technologies of Organizations. Charles Perrow defined technology in terms of the actions performed on objects or materials, with or without the aid of tools or mechanical devices, in order to make some change in that object, person, or symbol (22). Perrow specified two aspects of technology: the number of exceptional cases (routineness) and the kind of search process people go through when exceptions occur. Lynch tested these ideas and found that if raw materials are perceived to be unfamiliar, search strategies are nonroutine. Lynch also found that multiple technologies exist within organizations and that different technologies among departments are associated with differences in their structural arrangements. Furthermore, the greater the variety of technologies that exist among departments in an organization, the greater will be the conflict (23).

Worker Independence. Hrebiniak also found significant relationships between dimensions of technology and structure, but he suggested that both concepts are multidimensional and heterogeneous. He found, for example, that worker independence and the extent to which workers were involved in decisions were important in defining structure, irrespective of technological considerations (24).

Routineness. Hage and Aiken indicated that the more routinized technology becomes, the more centralized are policy decisions, the more likely there are to be rule manuals and job descriptions, and thus the more prescribed each job will be. They found that the more professional training workers had, the less routine were the jobs they performed. Where work was routine, managers emphasized efficiency and quantity (25).

Coordination. Routine work, therefore, is coordinated according to the *classical* model of organization, with rule manuals, job descriptions, and a fairly rigid authority hierarchy. In small organizations, and in situations where professionals perform the work, personal coordination replaces coordination by authority and rules. In process organizations, control is built right in to the technology.

Regardless of how one approaches the subject, everyone seems to agree that technology is a critical variable in organization design. One can decide for oneself whether technology determines organization design, whether the system of organizing determines the utility of technology, or whether each supposition is accurate depending on what the particular situation calls for.

Chapter Review

In this chapter we have examined how technology affects the design and performance of organizations. Technology includes both the human and the mechanical tools that assist in the performance of work. Although managers select technologies, their freedom of choice is constrained by goals, by the kind of work to be done, and by the technological means available. Once installed, technology has a variety of effects, both on employees and on managers. Evaluating an organization as a sociotechnical system—considering human social needs in the selection and use of technologies—can moderate some dysfunctional consequences of technological change.

Several studies have been cited that suggest that different kinds of technologies require different types of organization designs. There seems to be no one best way to structure all organizations, but there may be better ways to organize around different kinds of technologies. In this sense, technology may well be the defining characteristic of organizations.

The specific concepts and terms that have been developed in this chapter are listed below.

1. **Technology** refers to the tools people use in doing goal-directed work. Technology includes **human tools,** such as knowledge and skill, and **physical tools,** such as machines and pencils.

2. Factors that affect the choice of technologies are those listed below.

a. The **goals of the organization** or its subunit. Technologies suited to goals differ *horizontally* in line with the major flow of work —the **core technologies**—and *vertically,* according to managerial level.

b. The **characteristics of the work,** such as the degree of *differentiation* or specialization, the degree of *integration* or coordination required by task interdependence, the degree of *routineness* of work, and the degree of *outcome predictability*.

    c. The technological **means,** such as degree of *mechanization*, degree of *adaptability* of the technology, and the extent of its *availability*.

    d. The degree to which the technology is **suited to the people** involved.

3. Routine work requires different technologies than does nonroutine work. In general, the more routine the work, the greater the possibility of mechanization.

4. In spite of the higher productivity achieved by machine technology, employee reactions have not always been favorable. Although some attempts have been made to design technologies around people (person-machine engineering) or groups (sociotechnical systems), much mechanization seems to have had an adverse effect on employee attitudes, especially on the sentiments of assembly-line workers.

5. Unfavorable employee attitudes toward mechanization seem to be based on:

    a. damage to individual self-concepts and lower job satisfaction from performing routine, machine-paced work; and

    b. breakdown of informal group processes.

More favorable employee attitudes develop when technology facilitates group formation and development and increases individual job satisfaction.

6. **Automation,** the use of mechanical or electronic devices to control work, relies on computers.

7. Computer technologies have affected managerial work by:

    a. increasing the speed and quality of decision making;

    b. centralizing information in the computer center and thus altering the communication network;

    c. reducing managerial influence;

    d. increasing the need for planning; and

    e. assisting in the control process.

8. **Organizational structure**—the patterns of activities, interactions, and decisions of people in an organization—is affected by machine technology, which determines where people will work, influences what they do, and patterns their interactions.

9. Different technologies seem to require different kinds of organizational designs. The particular form of organization that is selected is likely to depend on whether the system of production is small-batch, mass, or process.

10. The **size** of an organization (the larger, the more bureaucratic), the length of **time** it has existed (the longer, the greater the impersonal controls), and the **technology of each subunit** also are important variables that affect the technology used and the patterns of relationships that will be most effective.

Discussion Questions

1. Does it make sense to you to include human knowledge and skill in the definition of technology? Why?

2. Do differing technologies in different departments of an organization mean that the arrangement of tasks (structure) should be different in the various units? Or should the primary, or core, technology determine the structure of all parts of an organization?

3. Discuss how differences in the following factors affect the technology selected. (Use specific examples to illustrate your answers.)

   a. The goals of a department or organization.
   b. The size of a department or organization.
   c. The hierarchical level in an organization.
   d. Characteristics of the work, such as the degree of differentiation, task interdependence, routineness, and outcome predictability.
   e. Technological means, such as the degree of mechanization possible, the degree of adaptability of technology, and the extent of availability of technology.
   f. The fit between technology and the people who do the work.

4. Distinguish between mechanization and automation. Which is likely to have the greatest effect on the worker? On the manager? Why?

5. What is meant by the term "sociotechnical system"? Of what value is the concept to managers?

6. How do workers usually react to increasing mechanization? How do managers typically react? Why?

7. What are the likely effects of increasing mechanization on the status of jobs? Which jobs will be likely to grow in status? Which jobs will decline? Why?

8. Discuss the statement "The manager of the machine in continuous-process technologies is no longer primarily the supervisor of people, but rather is the supervisor of the technology."

9. Discuss the implications of the statement "As humans produce machines that can think and learn, people cease to be uniquely capable of complex and intelligent manipulation of the environment."

10. How do different technologies affect the following variables:

    a. Number of hierarchical levels.
    b. Span of control.
    c. Ratio of managers to workers.
    d. Bureaucratic organization.

11. Discuss the implications of the statement "Organizations have multiple technologies."

Involvement Activities

1. On a sheet of paper, list the ten most important technologies you use in your life. Include your skills, attitudes, and knowledge, as well as the physical tools you own or have access to (such as a sewing machine, a bicycle, a car, a stereo, a tennis racket, and so on). Identify the goal(s) each of your technologies helps you achieve. Use a format like the following:

Technological Means	Goals

Then write out, discuss in a group, or make an oral statement answering the following questions:

 a. What is the relationship between your technologies and your goals? Do your goals determine your technologies or do your technologies determine your goals?

 b. Do you have adequate technologies for reaching all of your goals? Discuss. If some technology is missing, what do you do about it?

 c. Do your technologies affect your personal relationships? How? Do the structures of your personal relationships affect the technologies you try to acquire or develop? Discuss.

2. After completing activity No. 1 above, interview a manager in an organization. Use a form similar to that above and list the ten main technologies the manager uses, including the human technologies of the manager and his or her employees and the physical tools available to them. After each technology, list the goals that it helps these people reach. Then answer the following questions:

 a. What is the relationship between the organization's goals and its technologies?

 b. Are the organization's technologies suited to its goals? Are better ones available? Are the technologies overutilized or underutilized? How can you tell?

 c. How do the organization's technologies affect its structure?

3. Describe a new and better technology for accomplishing the organization's work. (Be imaginative. Even if no better technology currently exists, try some scientific fiction.) How might the work and structure of the organization change if the new technology were introduced?

12

The Environment of Organizations

The purpose of this chapter is to examine the interrelationship between the organization and its environment and the impact that one has on the other. The chapter opens with a discussion of the nature of environments and continues with an exploration of the many environments of organizations, including natural, economic, political, and social environmental systems. The interactions that occur within and among the environments are then discussed, as well as the effects of these interactions on the organization. The remaining sections include discussions of the social responsibility of organizations; the organization as an environment for internal subunits; and the influence the environment has on organization design.

In previous chapters we have seen how the behavior of individuals, the activities of groups, and the demands of changing technologies all impose certain restrictions that limit the ways in which managers are free to design an ideal organization. In this chapter we will see that pressures from the environment further constrain managers' flexibility in terms of how they may assign work and establish a structure. As with the other determinants we have examined, this relationship is illustrated in Figure 12–1.

Organizations depend on their environments for the resources they need and for the clients they serve. And to the extent that they use environmental resources and serve environmental needs, organizations mirror outside conditions and reflect prevailing social, political, and economic forces. Studies have shown that those organizations that operate in a manner consistent with outside pressures and that best reflect their environments are the ones most likely to be effective (1).

Perhaps there was a time when managers could concentrate their energies solely upon the internal workings of the organization because they accepted environmental forces as stable and relatively certain. But if this time ever existed, it has long since passed. The rapid rate of change in today's environment requires that managers in organizations remain ever alert to outside forces that are sure to affect their organizations. Failure to

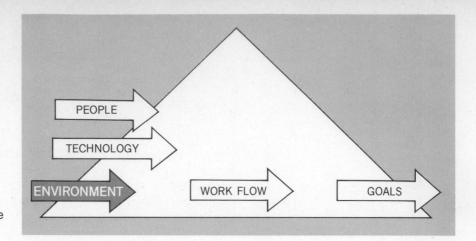

FIGURE 12–1
The environment as an organizational input that affects the work and goals of the organization.

recognize the need for change can lead to organizational ineffectiveness; an ability to detect unexplored opportunities, on the other hand, can lead to growth and success. Organizations, therefore, must be constantly ready and able to adapt to the larger context in which they operate.

The Nature of Environments

The **environment** refers to the assemblage of things, conditions, and influences that exist outside the unit under consideration. In terms of an organization, it includes *all forces outside* its boundaries, including incoming variables (resources), interactions that take place between organizations or between the organization and any other person or group of people, and other phenomena not directly related to the organization itself.

Figure 12–2, which was first used in Chapter 3, depicts an organization in its environment. It shows four types of relationships that can directly or indirectly affect the organization and its managerial process. The first area is outside the organization and consists of all forces and interactions in the environment. Thus it is labeled the **external-external** area. Whether these forces have any direct or immediate relevance to the organization, they invariably have certain long-run implications for managers.

The other three areas are directly related to the organization. The second section is the **external-to-internal,** or input, section, where resources and information flow into the organization. Third is the **internal-to-external** segment, in which outputs flow back into the environment. And fourth is the **internal-internal** section. In this segment relationships between subunits of the organization are the subjects of attention, and the organization itself is considered "the environment." In the remainder of this chapter, each segment will be discussed in turn, followed by a

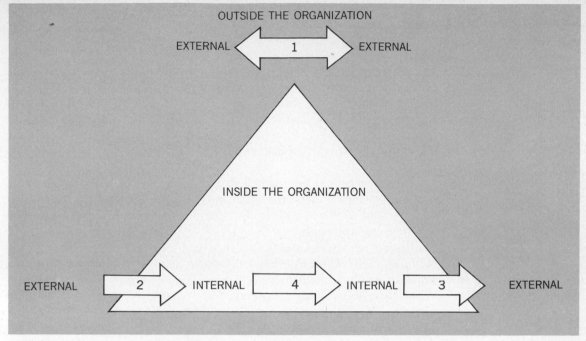

FIGURE 12–2

The organization and its environments: four types of relationships: (1) outside: external-external links; (2) input: external-internal links; (3) output: internal-external links; (4) inside: internal-internal links.

concluding section, which explores the effect the environment has on organization design.

The Many Environments of Organizations

In the environment of any organization are conditions, forces, pressures, and interactions that do not directly or immediately affect it but that may represent trends, opportunities, risks, or disturbances that may have long-run implications. Even if environmental interactions were never to have a direct effect, the "fallout" from them would likely be felt in some way. The forces in the environment that seem most important for an organization can be grouped into four categories: the **natural,** the **economic,** the **political-legal,** and the **sociocultural.**

The Natural Environment

The natural environment can be divided into two subsections, the nonliving, or **geophysical** part, and the living, or **ecological,** part.

     The Geophysical Environment. The physical environment of organizations consists of the naturally occurring elements within, upon, and above the earth. Included are the geographical features, such as the amount of arable land and the existence and condition of bodies of water and mountain ranges, and the geological situation, such as the availability of minerals and ores and the weather conditions.

To the managers of some organizations, the availability and quality of geophysical resources is of immediate importance; to others it may be of only casual interest. Sooner or later, however, as the twin pressures of population expansion and industrialization deplete resources and lead to more waste dumped into the natural environment, geophysical factors are likely to be of direct relevance to everyone.

The Ecological Environment. The ecological environment consists of the complex web of interrelationships between all living things. In biology, the term **ecology** refers to the relationship between living organisms and their environment.

Living resources from farms, seas, and forests support human needs for food, shelter, and clothing, and supply needed derivatives of organic products, such as medicines. The availability and quality of animal and vegetable resources are clearly relevant to all consumers and to many organizations.

Not so apparent, but of equal importance, is the life-support network itself. All living organisms, from a one-celled plant to a human being, are connected to one another in a complex system of relationships. Some ecologists fear that as humans destroy one species of life after another, we will weaken the life-support system for many other organisms and eventually endanger the fragile ecological balance of the entire planet. Others consider this a somewhat radical and ill-founded view.

"I really hate the idea of the physical universe winding down, don't you?"

Some Forces and Factors in the Environment of Organizations

A Checklist for Managers

THE NATURAL ENVIRONMENT

A. Geophysical factors
1. Outer-space problems and opportunities
2. Atmosphere
   a. Climate: weather patterns and changes
   b. Ozone layer
   c. Air quality and composition
3. Land
   a. Geographical problems
   b. Location and extent of minerals and ores
   c. Fossil fuels
   d. Land use
4. Waterways: streams, rivers, lakes, and oceans
   a. Quality and condition of water
   b. Availability of water

Who should own or control scarce geophysical resources?

B. Ecological factors
1. Living resources: farm, field, forest, air, and sea
2. Ecology of life-support systems

Who should own or control life-support systems?

The Economic Environment

It is one of the functions of ecologists to assess the factors that allow organisms to live, grow, and prosper in a particular area. Ecologists also study the competition that occurs among organisms for the limited supply of resources. In the sense that they both study competition, the work of ecologists and economists seems similar. In fact, both words are derived from the Greek word for house, *oikos*. Ecologists study the houses, the habitats or environments, of organisms by examining the relationships among them; economists study the houses, or environments, within which wealth is managed—whether they are organizations or nations—by examining the monetary transactions within and among them.

The economic environment consists of the money value of natural resources (land), human resources (labor), financial resources (capital), and information. Economics also is concerned with the allocation of these scarce resources to and within nations and organizations, the production of valuable economic outputs, and the distribution of these outputs among the owners of the means of production.

Organizations are affected by changes in the economic environment. Managers deal daily with budgets and costs. Those who buy are concerned with the costs of inputs; those who sell, with the values of outputs.

The impact of the economic environment that does not directly affect the organization is difficult to evaluate. Thus some organizations employ economists or retain private economic consultants to keep up with changes that might affect them. Others maintain little direct contact with the economic environment. To many managers of small businesses, balance of payments problems, unbalanced national budgets, prime interest rates, commodity futures, and other such phenomena seem remote. But

WITH A WORKING ENVIRONMENT LIKE THAT, THEY'RE REALLY GOING TO GO PLACES.

because these factors affect the money supply (and thus the price of goods and services), trends in such economic variables may be of considerable importance to these people and to their organizations, whether they know it or not.

Some Forces and Factors In the Environment of Organizations

A Checklist for Managers

THE ECONOMIC ENVIRONMENT

A. Resource allocation and the market system
 1. Trade barriers and comparative advantages
 2. Concentration of wealth and power: rich versus poor
  a. Vertical
  b. Horizontal
  c. Conglomerate
 3. Public sector
  a. Space
  b. War
  c. Government cost
 4. Economic impact of illegal (underworld) operations
 5. Administered prices versus market prices

B. Measurement of economic activity
 1. Reckoning of production—Gross National Product
 2. Economic development and economic dependency
 3. Stock, money, and commodity markets
 4. The costs and values of growth

C. Economic theory and the trade channel
 1. Economics of distribution of goods
 2. Economics of promotion of goods and services
 3. Economics of communication
 4. Economic imperialism

D. Economic organization
 1. Market systems
 2. Oligopoly, monopoly, cartel, and combine systems
 3. Centrally planned systems
  a. Socialism
  b. Marxism
  c. Sovietism
  d. Utopianism

How can one measure the quality of life?

Economic information is readily available in government publications and in business and economics journals, in the newsletters of reputable economic services, and in the pages of most newspapers. On the basis of this information, and from talks with local bankers and economists, most managers are able to obtain or piece together fairly sensible forecasts of national, regional, and local economic conditions. From these they can forecast the cost of future inputs and work-flow processes and the value of prospective outputs.

The Political-Legal Environment

The political-legal environment of organizations contains governments at all levels: local, regional, national, and international. It also includes the activities of legislatures and the laws they pass, the execution of laws by administrative agencies, and the administration of justice through the court systems.

Organizations, like the rest of us, are subordinate to the laws of the land. And many managers, like many other citizens, spend a good deal of time complaining about the ever-increasing tangle of legal constraints that contain and control their activities. There is no question that the political sphere is increasing in influence, size, cost, and importance. The expansion of political controls over organizations may be due to the increasing number of organizations and to the fact that the number of relationships among organizations increases far more rapidly than does the number of organizations alone. Laws are passed to resolve situations that legislators consider to be problems. And managers must understand the laws that affect their organizations sufficiently well to be aware of advantageous rulings and to avoid legal entanglements. Large organizations usually employ full-time attorneys or retain legal consultants for counsel and aid. Organizations without such legal assistance may suffer if they do not know specifically how laws restrain their behavior or the kinds of opportunities that may exist for expanding their sphere of operations.

Assistance to Organizations. Governments assist organizations as well as regulate them. In the United States, government agencies provide a number of services. Incorporation laws make it possible for citizens of cities, members of nonprofit associations, and owners of business firms to limit their liability, through incorporation, only to the amount of money invested. Government advisory services offer advice to farmers, small businesses, householders, and many others. Data-collection bureaus provide a wealth of helpful information with little direct cost (although eventually these services are paid for through taxes). Governments provide police protection for commerce. Subsidies, tax relief, and tariff protection are common for many kinds of organizations. And, perhaps most important, governments provide ways for people to form productive organizations and furnish laws and agencies to protect the contracts, commerce, and interactions that take place between them. Furthermore, the courts provide an orderly means of settling disputes.

Some Forces and Factors
in the Environment of Organizations

A Checklist for Managers

THE POLITICAL–LEGAL ENVIRONMENT

A. Government
   1. On the governance of people
      a. Sources of power
      b. Government by the elite?
      c. Industrial-commercial-military influence
      d. Political campaigns
      e. Political corruption
      f. Intelligence, intrigue, espionage
      g. Planning and development
   2. Importance of superordinate goals: war and peace

B. Comparative government
   1. Democracy
   2. Republic
   3. Oligarchy
   4. Dictatorship
      a. Industrialized regions
      b. Semi-industrialized areas
      c. Agrarian regions
      d. Regions of poverty
      e. Nationalism

C. Executive and administrative functions
   1. Bureaucracy
   2. Decision-making locus
   3. Information collection and control
      a. Censorship
      b. Accuracy of information
      c. Disclosure: full and partial
         (1) Disclosure to whom?
         (2) Informed populace and apathy
   4. Efficiency
   5. Promoting the general welfare
      a. Education
      b. Health
      c. Welfare
      d. Insurance: social security, life, annuity, casualty

   6. Agencies of administration

D. Judicial function
   1. Equality before the law
      a. Justice
      b. Wealth; poverty and the administration of justice
      c. Equity
   2. Definition of crime
      a. "Crimes" against self
      b. Crimes against property
      c. Crimes against persons
      d. Crimes against systems: organizations, the state
   3. Underworld organizations
   4. Prisons

E. Legislative functions
   1. Campaigns and their costs
   2. Governmental regulations
      a. Common law
      b. Statutory law
      c. Laws aiding business
      d. Laws hindering business
   3. The legislative process
   4. Influence
      a. Lobbyists
      b. Elites and political tradeoffs
      c. The press
      d. The public

F. General issues
   1. Leadership
   2. Space race: nationalism and cost
   3. "Military-industrial complex"

G. International relations
   1. War, peace, and the military
   2. Political imperialism
   3. United Nations
   4. World government

Is government necessary?

Controls on Organizations. The ways in which governments control and constrain behavior are well known. Governments impose taxes, prohibit or control a wide range of practices, set prices for their services and for some public utilities, employ inspectors to monitor such factors as unsafe working conditions, determine minimum wages, and do so many other things that the face of government seems to appear everywhere. Laws follow problems; but problems follow laws as well.

Managerial Response. Managers can profit by keeping in touch with the political-legal environment. Attorneys are helpful, but even better are personal contacts with government agencies. It helps to get to know important regional and national politicians and to participate formally or informally in the processes of government. If such activities are in the public as well as in the private interest, they build goodwill for the organization. Managers who cannot maintain such personal contacts can contribute to these activities by paying dues or fees to trade associations or to lobbyists. But there may not be a comparable substitute for direct personal contact.

The Sociocultural Environment

Cultural values in the environment, together with social trends and problems, affect organizations either directly or indirectly. In Chapter 10 on groups, some of the effects of culture on behavior were reviewed. In this section these ideas are assembled, and others added, to illustrate the effect of the sociocultural environment on organizations.

Society includes all forms of social organization and interaction. Social trends consist of both the physical movement of people and the changes in their behavior. Students of these trends (sociologists) are interested in examining collective human behavior in all its forms, including social deviation, organization, mass movements of populations, and occupations and professions. Social movements may appear to have little to do with the managing of organizations, but managers who are interested in keeping their organizations alive will know about and have respect for the potential importance of all collective human behavior.

Culture refers to the norms, values, economic conditions, social status, systems of governance, language, rituals, and artifacts of a society. Every social system has its own culture. Thus it is as important for managers to know what members of a group do and how they think as it is for them to know that the group exists. The study of culture is the province of cultural anthropology, but its insights are intricately involved with sociology. Because the cultures of some groups are alien to the cultures of others, there is often little interaction between them. For instance, few presidents of automobile companies empathize with the values of the workers on their assembly lines, much less meet with them. It is little wonder that the ideas and problems of each seem remote and unreal to the other.

Within certain of the current sociocultural trends lie opportunities for some present and future organizations and the seeds of demise for others. Knowledge of social trends is both valuable and easily accessible. Newspapers, magazines, books, and radio and television programs are filled with such information. To be sure, newspaper editorials and authors of books and magazine articles have their particular bias, and there are few objective guidelines for assessing social trends. Even experts can rarely forecast the sociocultural future with much success. Nevertheless, managers must learn to tune in and to guess with some degree of accuracy when to change with the times. A broad, general education and a tendency to keep abreast of current events may help to sensitize one to sociocultural variables. The paradox, however, is that time spent in studying trends reduces the amount of time one can spend in maintaining personal contact with individuals in the economic, political, and industrial environments.

Because the sociocultural sphere is the broadest, and therefore the fuzziest aspect of the environment, many "important" present trends will die shortly, without creating much impact. It is difficult to know which will die and which will create long-lasting effects. In addition, it is often very hard to imagine the ways in which the world will be different. All we know for certain is that things will change.

Examples of Change in the Sociocultural Environment. Examples of change abound. For example, during the last one hundred years in the United States, the population steadily moved away from the rural areas and into the cities. Recently, however, this trend appears to be reversing. Another reversing trend is that conservative churches, with their emphasis on strict interpretation of the Bible, are gaining in membership and support. And formerly popular liberal social and political groups are losing members. Women are demanding and making progress toward equal rights. The one-parent family is becoming increasingly acceptable and viable as divorce rates climb and more mothers seek work outside the home. Consumer advocacy, planned parenthood, and conservation groups are but a few other growing social movements.

Culture Shock. Each major sociocultural trend has a potentially critical bearing on managerial processes. Of particular importance is the shock that people feel when they interact with members of other cultures. Every person develops a set of behaviors and expectations suitable in the "home" culture. When thrust into a different environment, in which people behave differently, the outsider does not know what to expect or what to do. Left without familiar behavioral guidelines, the foreigner may become disoriented, anxious, or otherwise "culture shocked." This often results in dysfunctional behavior, such as retreating to a settlement of people from home, or dysfunctional attitudes, such as stereotyping the natives as peculiar (2).

Some Forces and Factors in the Environment of Organizations

A Checklist for Managers

THE SOCIOCULTURAL ENVIRONMENT

A. Society
1. Social stratification
2. Social problems
   a. Family nucleus
      (1) marriage
      (2) divorce
      (3) one-parent homes
      (4) communes
      (5) working adults and delinquency
   b. Drugs (including illegal drugs, non-prescription drugs, "ethical" drugs, alcohol, etc.)
   c. Mobility, rootlessness, anomie, alienation
   d. Discrimination and prejudice
   e. Education
      (1) cost
      (2) discriminatory?
      (3) background and language barriers
   f. Information
      (1) TV and other media
      (2) bias and other restrictions
      (3) overload?
   g. Consumption society
      (1) energy addiction
      (2) productive versus consumptive orientation
      (3) auto addiction
   h. Mass society
      (1) mass production
      (2) technology
   i. Complexity
   j. Prisons and decriminalization
   k. Sex, sexual aberration, pornography
   l. Venereal disease
   m. Birth control
   n. Liberation movements: poor, black, Chicano, women, gay
   o. Loss of confidence; escape routes
   p. Gambling, prostitution, pornography, and crime
   q. A nation of spectators?

Are national morals collapsing?

B. Culture
1. Superordinate cultural goals
   a. Protestant ethic
   b. Social ethic
   c. Diverse, divergent value systems
2. Ethics, morality, values, and religions: philosophy of life
   a. Pluralistic ethics
   b. Moral decay?
   c. Religion, fad religions, magic
   d. Effect of religion on cultural change
   e. Money as a value
3. Cultural determinants of attitudes: literature, the performing arts, spectator sports, television
4. Determinants of group culture
   a. Norms and values
   b. Tools and techniques
   c. Life styles
   d. Economic, political, and social organizations
5. Culture shock
C. Future shock
1. Utopias: Are more nearly perfect conditions possible?
2. Doomsday theses: Are we approaching the end of the dream?
3. Reality focus: Where do we go from here?

Why are business people so often condemned and ridiculed in books, plays, movies, and on television?

A Special Case of Change: Multinational Operations. Representatives of the United States government span the globe. Members of nonprofit organizations, such as the Red Cross or various religious orders, are found in countries throughout the world. Managers of firms are also transacting their business or setting up branches of plants and offices in countries far removed from home base. These are called **multinational corporations,** or simply **multinationals.** The number of firms with foreign branches or subsidiaries has increased dramatically in the past ten to fifteen years. Doing business abroad requires dealing with a number of cultures, some vastly different from ours. And the problems that organizations face in adjusting to different cultures have been varied and numerous.

One of the most common areas of difficulty concerns the different values held by people in the work force. American managers often make the incorrect assumption that workers in foreign countries are motivated by the same needs and adhere to the same value structure as do American employees. This attitude is mirrored by managers' surprise when people who have been trained in certain skills work for a while, then suddenly disappear, to be seen again only when they run out of money. What these managers do not realize is that in most developing countries, workers for American enterprises (who may be earning more money than they ever thought possible) simply do not have the need for such high, steady incomes. In addition, they tend to live much more in the present than in the future. Consequently, when the money they have earned accumulates to the point where they do not have an immediate need for more, they simply quit work until they run out of funds.

American managers must either "socialize" native workers into the American value structure or accept the differences and train enough people so that there is a reserve of able employees to take up the slack when some quit.

Another problem faced by multinationals is that most modern organizations require a wide range of skills among their employees. Yet in many preindustrialized nations the needed skills have not been developed. Many farmers, for example, have never even seen a tractor, let alone have the skills to repair one. Thus, while top managers and unskilled workers may be readily available, people with technical expertise are often difficult to find.

Further, many of our concepts of organization design must be altered considerably when in other cultures. For instance, our notions of a vertically structured organization are not very acceptable in societies that view authority as a horizontal concept (see Chapter 7). In addition, one of the basic hiring tenets of American organizations is to select people for jobs on the basis of merit. In some societies, however, bonds of kinship take priority, and hiring practices may be based on an applicant's social class or on his or her relationship to people already employed in the organization.

Interactions in the Environment of Organizations: External-External Interactions

Referring back to Figure 12–2, we can see that there are four types of relationships that exist within the sphere of the organization's environment. The first relationship, called external-external, was described earlier as those interactions that take place outside the organization itself. These external-external relations are in a constant state of flux. When people from one culture interact with those from another, both groups change in the process. Change is also the constant variable in all other relationships in the environment. The economy rises and falls. Political power changes hands regularly. New laws are made while others become obsolete. Sociocultural systems are transformed almost daily. Season follows season—some placid and some filled with natural disasters. Indeed, all that exists in the present is connected to an infinitely long chain of past and future events.

Viewed from this perspective, every event is a composite result of a complex network of other events, and every action leads to a bewildering array of consequences. Thus, any action that a manager takes has the same effect as a stone thrown into a pond. From the point of impact, ripples extend to the shore, and then turn back upon themselves. The manager's job, then, is to identify which ripples are dangerously rocking the boat, discover where the source of disturbance lies, and learn how to predict and control future waves.

Environmental Interactions

To make sense of these complex relationships in the environment one needs certain tools or theoretical frameworks. Sociologists point out that organizations strive to maintain equilibrium with the forces in their environment. And within organizations, people react to pressures that threaten this balance by making adjustments to maintain or restore equilibrium. For example, when confronted with the possibility of new restrictive legislation, managers may pay legislative advocates to lobby against the legislation and simultaneously hire attorneys who will offer suggestions as to how to cope with the new law if it passes.

The idea that organizations just "naturally" adjust to environmental pressures suggests that the behavior of managers is determined by external events rather than by internal and deliberate control. In fact, both conditions occur. Managers simultaneously affect and are affected by their environments. Some interactions are consistent with the organization's equilibrium and can be considered **cooperative,** while others disturb the equilibrium and can be called **competitive.**

The development of the automobile industry offers a good illustration of cooperation and competition over time. At first, a large number of small firms competed in the market. Many failed until only a small number of large companies remained. Of those that failed, many turned their attention to supplying parts or adjunct services. Thus, a mutual dependence developed between the many small supplying firms and the major automobile producers, resulting in a mutually profitable, cooperative relationship.

Strategies for Maintaining Equilibrium

Managers can work out relationships through a series of conscious processes ranging from conflict to cooperation. Figure 12–3 depicts some of the managerial strategies for maintaining equilibrium.

Destructive Competition. Destructive competition, a win-lose situation in which one or the other organization will not exist after the competitive struggle is over, is not common. **Extreme rivalry** is ordinarily destructive to all participants. This type of competition, exemplified by price wars between business organizations, is specifically made illegal in the United States by antitrust and other laws.

Continuous Competition. A step toward cooperation is continuous competition in which both parties continue to compete over an extended period of time. Galbraith describes this situation as **countervailing power,** which means that organizations that compete with one another are equally powerful. No one can pre*vail* over the other, so they *counter* each other (3).

In instances of competition in which no one organization is powerful enough to destroy the other, the share of resources each receives is determined in accordance with some previously agreed-upon set of rules. A continuing game of competition between organizations is not only acceptable in this society but is viewed as the most proper kind of relationship between businesses.

FIGURE 12–3
States of conflict-cooperation between organizations.

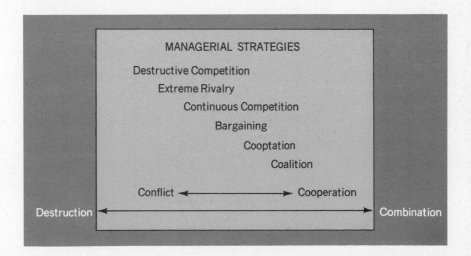

MANAGERIAL STRATEGIES

Destructive Competition

Extreme Rivalry

Continuous Competition

Bargaining

Cooptation

Coalition

Conflict ⟷ Cooperation

Destruction ⟷ Combination

Competition, particularly ongoing competition, is usually a very uncomfortable situation for managers. They, like others, wish to maintain a higher degree of certainty in their lives than competition affords. It is very likely, therefore, that organizations will continually seek ways to move closer to the cooperative end of the scale and thus reduce the amount of competition they face.

Bargaining. Bargaining, the first really cooperative step along the continuum, is the working out of contractual relationships. A contract sets forth the mutual responsibilities of the parties to an exchange in which each party promises to supply the other party with certain resources. A **collective bargaining agreement** is an example of this kind of contract. Here, the workers agree to engage in specific kinds of activities under certain conditions guaranteed by the employer. At this stage of cooperation a great deal of conflict and competition seems to take place in the process of setting the terms of the contract. While some cooperation occurs, each party retains considerable independence. The contract spells out the terms of interdependence. In all other respects, each organization is separate from the other.

Cooptation. A further step along the cooperation line is that of absorption, or **cooptation.** Cooptation is a term applied by Philip Selznick to a phenomenon he found while making a study of the Tennessee Valley Authority (TVA) (4). Selznick discovered that when certain pressure groups threatened the TVA, the TVA simply incorporated the threatening elements into its own structure. Thus, when certain farm groups presented opposition to TVA plans or proposals, the TVA put the leaders of these dissident groups on its governing board or in some other way gave them a voice in its affairs.

Business organizations may help to maintain or increase their credit by coopting a banker for their boards of directors. Similarly, students may be coopted by universities when they serve with faculty members on policy committees.

Cooptation, or absorption, presents some dangers. The coopting organization may find that when competing elements are absorbed, external conflicts become internalized. It may have coopted a particular organization in order to influence it, only to find that it has been influenced by the organization that it has coopted; interaction is reciprocal.

Coalition. The final stage along the cooperation line is **coalition,** or combination, in which organizations that were formerly separated are united. For example, two local grocery store owners may decide to combine their assets and merge into one large supermarket. The former competitors are now partners. At the collaborative end of the continuum, as well as at the rivalry end, federal antitrust laws restrain certain business activities. The Justice Department would file suit to stop the combination of, say, all steel companies into a single firm (collaboration), just as it would not permit General Motors to force other automobile companies out of business by keeping their prices so low that Ford and Chrysler would go broke (destructive competition).

The Need to Maintain Equilibrium

Managers do not attempt to control their environment merely because they want to be more powerful, although the desire for power may be some inducement. Managers attempt to control the environment primarily because organizations have a need for stability and predictability. Especially in need of these factors are those organizations with large sums of money tied up in capital equipment or those with substantial task specialization. These organizations need to maintain equilibrium with their markets in order to spread the cost of the machine and human technologies over many units of production. To give an extreme example, telephone companies would hardly be enthusiastic if telepathy became available to their customers. The result would cost thousands of people their jobs and make billions of dollars' worth of equipment worthless. In his book *The New Industrial State,* Galbraith argues that the modern American corporation, particularly through advertising, does a pretty good job of influencing the environment. He finds also that an organization's desire for stability is so strong that it must go out into the environment to ensure that it can and will have a market for its products (5).

Interactions Between the Environment and the Organization: External-Internal and Internal-External Interactions

People whose work assignments place them at the input and output boundaries of the organization often experience conflict. They must maintain their loyalty to the employing organization and at the same time stay on good terms with the organizations and people in the environment with whom they interact. Stressful situations frequently occur for those "marginal" people spanning the boundaries of two or more groups. They must accommodate the demands made on both sides — even when those demands are contradictory. Some who work at organizational margins often have trouble with their allegiance. For instance, salespeople identify with their customers as well as with their employers; at times they must defend the attitudes and behaviors of one to the other.

Boundary-spanning personnel commonly serve an important function as buffers for the employing organization. They absorb many pressures from the environment. They protect such vulnerable interior parts as the performance core, which must maintain a high degree of stability. In many organizations, for example, customer complaints and demands are many, but the boundary personnel filter out the bulk of these and pass on only the most critical issues.

External-Internal Interactions: Input Relationships

The input area, shown as the second relationship in Figure 12–2, is the site where environmental resources and pressures flow into the organization. It is through the protection provided by boundary-spanning personnel who operate in this area that managers of internal areas are able to maintain fairly good control over the forces at work in the inner parts of the organization.

Managers in the input areas have less control because the resources and pressures that exist in the environment usually lie outside their full command. These managers are forced to take a more **reactive** role. They may have little choice other than to learn to identify the sources of resources and pressures and to adapt to them. Resources flow in as materials, labor, and money. Pressures flow in either as information, which consists of organized and useful facts, or as data, which are disorganized bits and pieces of facts. Input-area managers develop considerable skill in receiving, interpreting, and evaluating information and data.

Most resources are scarce, so organizations must develop strategies for acquiring them. At the same time, it is incumbent upon agents within the environment to develop ways to fairly allocate the scarce resources. For instance, in the United States much of the acquiring of resources occurs through open competition in the marketplace. However, this market system is often imperfect, so the government steps in with rationing or with taxes. But these interventions sometimes create their own problems. Rationing, for example, often leads to black markets; and higher taxes adversely affect the poor more than the rich. The allocation problem is complex and potentially inequitable whether the government is involved or not. In other cultures, allocation of resources may be determined by tradition or by the political system, but these means also carry inequities and tend to work imperfectly.

Material Resources. Problems connected with determining the need for, the acquisition of, and the proper flow of resource inputs are more properly the concerns of books dealing with the financing of organizations, personnel administration, procurement, and purchasing. It is sufficient to say here that managers who deal with suppliers have the responsibility of maintaining and preserving adequate sources to meet organizational needs.

Information Resources. Organizations cannot operate in a vacuum. They need information about what is going on in the environment around them. But they must also avoid data overload. Managers need to regulate the information flow to get rid of surplus data while ensuring that needed information reaches the right place at the right time.

Two sources for obtaining environmental information are available: inside sources and outside sources. Every manager, indeed every person in an organization, is in regular contact with the outside environment. These contact points can provide a steady input of data, both useful and nonuseful. Because everyone in an organization potentially has valuable information, the organization will profit by making itself receptive to internal sources of external news.

Of course, valuable information is also available from a number of outside sources, including suppliers, customers, placement agencies, politicians, bankers, competitors, trade associations, government agencies, and many others.

Internal-External Interactions: Output Relationships

Organizations not only react to the environment, they also influence it. Managers who serve at output boundaries attempt to control the environment so that it will be predictable and benign. At the output side of organizations, shown as the third relationship in Figure 12–2, managers have an active, or **proactive** orientation. Proactivity means taking positive steps to influence events.

Output personnel concentrate their activities on supplying goods or services to the marketplace. These outputs are the planned, or intended, results of production efforts. However, as noted earlier in this book, organizations also produce unplanned, or unintended outputs. For example, no one set out to pollute Lake Erie; it happened as a side effect of the planned operations of the many organizations that share their environment with Lake Erie. Fortunately, not all unintended outputs have such negative consequences. Indeed, intended and unintended outputs can be considered positive, neutral, or negative, depending on who is doing the evaluating.

Intended Outputs. Intended outputs consist primarily of goods and services, valuable byproducts, and information and data considered valuable by other organizations and individuals in the environment. Because outputs were discussed in detail in Chapter 3 on organizational goals, this section will be brief and will approach the topic from a different perspective.

Understandably, one of the primary functions of intended outputs is to maintain a clientele for the organization. Business firms need customers, hospitals need patients, public service agencies need recipients, and so on. A century ago, when nearly all goods and services were in short supply, most organizations had little difficulty recruiting and keeping clients. But things are very different now. Rivalry among organizations for clients has never been greater. And modern electronics has provided a means for intense competition through radios, telephones, computer consoles, and television sets.

For those who work at the output boundaries of organizations, the complexity of the modern environment means acquiring different and new coping strategies. Current and future clients now must be courted with offers of quality and economy, or they will move swiftly to patronize other organizations. Public outrage, justified or not, can quickly undo an organization that has prospered with distinction for many years. And rapidly

changing fads and fashions create and destroy organizations almost overnight.

Some of the strategies that managers use to cope with these relatively
new developments include marketing campaigns, public relations programs, customer service (or special unit) departments, and research and
development programs.

Marketing campaigns include advertising, personal selling, and sales
promotion. Marketing strategies are proactive when they consist of creating a demand for the product or service by convincing people of its desirability. Reactive marketing programs involve questionnaires or surveys to
discover client needs or demands in order to set about serving them. It
takes time, skill, and money to develop adequate marketing strategies, but
the rewards usually more than offset the expenditure.

Public relations (PR) programs are designed to persuade the public
that the organization serves the public interest. Public relations personnel
deal almost exclusively with the general environment. Their functions are
diverse, yet in almost all cases they try to either positively influence or at
least to neutralize public opinion toward the organization. Another major
function of public relations programs is to create a favorable environment
for the organization's products or services. For example, many PR groups
maintain constant contacts with all levels of government regulating agencies in order to make sure the legal environment is hospitable to the
organization's output. Public relations departments are likely to increase
in number in the future as more organizations recognize the need to
present a desirable image to an increasingly concerned public.

In recent years many large organizations have established **special
units** for dealing with the environment. These units are variously referred
to as Department of the Environment, Customer Service Agency, Ecology Center, and so forth. Depending on the size and nature of the organization they may or may not replace or include public relations personnel.
It is the function of these departments to issue special news releases and
brochures that explain the actions of the organization, inform clients of
any change in the organization's products or procedures, and generally
solicit support and acceptance.

Research and development programs are geared toward promoting
organizational growth. The purpose is to gain more power, capture a particular market, or serve more diverse sets of clients with new products or
services so that the loss of any one group will not drastically hurt the
organization.

Unintended Outputs. Unplanned and unintended outputs are inevitable consequences of production technology. But unintended outputs
are not limited to waste products or other observable phenomena. Many
organizations, particularly very large ones, find that one of their unplanned outputs is a negative public image. Because it is easy to misuse
power, many people tend to distrust organizations that are perceived as
having a disproportionate amount of influence. It is not uncommon for

large organizations with negative public images to invest a great deal of money and energy into advertising or public service campaigns aimed at reversing, or at least neutralizing, their unpopular images.

In addition to unintended outputs that are clearly negative—such as pollution—and those that are unmistakably positive—such as the accidental discovery of certain medicines, there exists a whole range of outputs whose desirability is open to interpretation. For example, the effect of burning natural gas is the creation of carbon dioxide and water vapor. Because these two compounds occur naturally in the atmosphere, most people might consider them of *neutral* consequence. Horticulturists, however, know that carbon dioxide is beneficial to plants, and they might view this unintended output as *desirable*. Still others, perhaps farmers whose crops require a dry climate, would consider excess water vapor *undesirable*.

It can be seen, then, from this fairly innocuous example, that judging whether outputs (planned or unplanned) are harmful or beneficial is dependent on one's point of view.

The unintended damage an organization causes to the environment is called an **externality.** If the organization that creates the external problem does not pay for correcting it, the damage is called a **social cost.**

Who pays for social costs? Everyone agrees that externalities are undesirable, but an argument rages over who should pay for them. The solution is not as apparent as one might suspect. In nature, the waste of one organism is the fuel for another; all life exists in a complex system of relationships. For many thousands of years, humans, as part of the natural order, have used the air, the waters, and the land as waste dumps. Nature has obliged by converting relatively small quantities of this organic waste into fuel for other organisms. Natural processes, however, can no longer accommodate the wastes of densely populated industrial cities. Too much is disgorged too fast. Futhermore, much of the current waste matter is synthetic and does not disintegrate or degrade into natural, usable components.

Organizations are willing to pay for the cost of their inputs and for the cost of disposing of their direct wastes, but they fear they cannot sustain the cost of paying for all their externalities. A smelting company in a city in the West disgorges sulphur dioxide gas into the atmosphere in quantities considered unsafe. When combined with water vapor in the air, the gas becomes a corrosive acid that eats both metal and stone. The local city council ordered the firm to clean up its emissions. Managers responded that the cost of doing so would force them to close the plant. They explained that competing companies faced no such restrictive regulations, and that if they raised their prices to accommodate the costs of cleaning their emissions, they could no longer compete in the marketplace. Because several thousand people would have lost their jobs, the city backed down. The social costs of this firm are now being paid by residents of the community in the form of medical bills, repair costs for corroded pipes and scarred buildings, and shorter life expectancies. But the city figures these costs are offset by the thousands of people who remain employed and by the millions of dollars per year it collects in taxes from the organization.

Another problem with "who pays" is the difficulty of figuring out who creates the externality. For instance, who is responsible for cleaning up the atmosphere fouled by automobile exhaust: the owners of the cars, the petroleum companies, or the automobile manufacturers? If all are partly responsible, who pays what portion?

Social Responsibility. The question of who pays is part of the larger question of social responsibility, which asks to whom and for what an organization should be held accountable. All major institutions — governments, schools, labor organizations, the military, churches, businesses — are being asked to solve social ills (6). Schools and housing developments must integrate their populations, professional associations and clubs must accept women and minority groups as members, and so forth. But the major emphasis in affixing social responsibility has been directed at business firms. The reason is that businesses employ the most people, manufacture almost all products, and in general make the biggest impact on the environment.

Traditionally, the business organization has been expected to return a profit to its owners by creating and selling a product or service at a price higher than cost. And at least one economist, Milton Friedman, takes the view that the only social responsibility a business has is to increase its profits (7). Friedman goes on to say that if executives allocate corporate funds for purposes other than profits, they have in effect imposed taxes on their employers, the owners, and decided how to spend the proceeds as well.

Others argue that businesses function by public consent, and that their basic purpose therefore is to satisfy the needs of society as the people define those needs. In its report on the responsibilities of business corporations, the Committee for Economic Development (CED) states that

> The great growth of corporations in size, market power, and impact on society has naturally brought with it a commensurate growth in responsibilities; in a democratic society, power sooner or later begets equivalent accountability (8).

From this point of view an organization is considered responsible to all the people with whom it deals, including owners, customers or clients, employees, suppliers, and community neighbors. And even beyond these direct relationships, since members of organizations interact with a wide variety of other groups, such as competitors, labor unions, special interest groups, educational institutions, the press, government, and many more, they are responsible in some ways to these people also. Thus managers are seen not merely as profit-hungry employees of irresponsible organizations, but as trustees who are charged with balancing the interests of many different groups that are often in conflict (9).

If business is to be held accountable for such social responsibilities as establishing equal opportunities, ending discriminatory hiring practices, abandoning corporate concentration, making jobs more interesting, preserving and protecting the natural environment, serving the needs of consumers, and so on, how will it find time to accomplish its primary goal of producing products or providing services? And how will the costs of these improvements be paid for? Measuring the precise cost of meeting social obligations is difficult if not impossible, although some professionals are beginning to develop applicable auditing techniques. Allocating costs equitably is even more difficult. And collecting might be harder yet. With all these factors to consider, how will managers find time to concentrate on their main mission?

At least one author is not concerned about managers being overly distracted. Earl Cheit sees in the social responsibility doctrine a conservative response by managers to a changing environment, intended to protect the organization. The goal, as he sees it, is not to become "socially responsible" but to adapt a new ideology to the organization's own private interests (10).

The question of what constitutes the proper concern of an organization is an ethical problem. And whether a given set of activities, interactions, and decisions is seen as ethical depends on the values of the people who are asking the question. In a society such as exists in the United States, which accommodates millions of groups with differing values, dispute will continue to rage over what organizations should and should not do. There are few absolute ethics to guide the harried manager. Perhaps there are none. The best prescription is to urge the manager to understand the pressures and to try to balance them equitably while continuing to accomplish the primary organizational purpose.

The Organization as Environment: Internal-Internal Interactions

Because the whole of this text is really about the organization, this section will concern itself only with two major points. These are (1) that the organization acts as a constraint on itself and (2) that for most managers the organization is in fact the most immediate environmental pressure facing them.

The Organization as a Constraint

In Chapter 1 we pictured the manager as a person in the middle, who balances the demands of internal organizational forces against the demands of external environmental forces. From the manager's viewpoint, then, the organization is one more set of factors to accommodate in the balancing act. Much of what has been said previously regarding accommodation is applicable to this view of the internal organization. The manager assumes a proactive stance by changing the organization or a reactive stance by changing the work group. So whether the manager is seen as proactive or reactive depends on whether one is inside or outside the group.

This chapter has focused on the collection of data about the environment as an aid to managerial decision making. There are implications here for the internal organization. Managers must be sure they collect sufficient and accurate information about what is going on inside the organization in an orderly and planned manner. It is not just curiosity that leads top executives out of their offices and on seemingly casual strolls through the plant. Managers need more than the cut and dried reports they receive on their desks; they need the texture and feel of the organization that is available only through first-hand observation or participation.

The Organization as an Environment

For all managers other than top executives, the organization itself is the major environment with which they must deal. A middle manager's day is spent with subordinates, peers, staff specialists, and occasionally some superiors. All these groups want something from the manager, and he or she in return needs something from them. The organization is a complex of interactions, with each manager having to both react to and demand behavior from others. In Part 2 of this text the vertical relationships and some of the horizontal work-flow relationships were covered in detail, and in Chapter 16 a more complete categorization of horizontal relationships will be presented. For the present, the major idea is that *all* managers, regardless of level, must deal with an environment. The nature of that environment will be different on every level of the organization and in conjunction with the type of work being performed, but the demands and requirements on the manager are the same.

The Environment and Organization Design

An organization's structure consists of the patterns of relationships among internal groups and the interactions that occur between boundary-spanning groups and the external environment. As environmental forces change, the strategies managers use to cope with and adjust to the changes inevitably affect the organization's design. This section of the chapter reviews some of the research that has been conducted to discover the precise effects of environmental pressures on organizational structure. The primary conclusion is not surprising: The more nearly the design of an organization fits the requirements of the environment, the more effective the organization is likely to be. The studies reviewed here include those reported by Chandler, Stinchcombe, Lawrence and Lorsch, and Burns and Stalker.

**Chandler:
Structure and
Coping Strategies**

From his study of the effects of the environment on four large corporations in the United States—DuPont, General Motors, Standard Oil of New Jersey, and Sears, Roebuck and Company—Chandler concluded that organizational form is dependent on the strategies that managers develop to cope with a changing environment (11).

Decentralization. Chandler found that in their early period of growth the organizations he studied found it most efficient to have a highly centralized structure. Even as they became fairly complex internally, their external goals remained more or less uncomplicated. Changes in purpose eventually occurred as the companies developed new strategies, diversified their product lines, and deployed the products farther geographically. Gradually, top managers became increasingly incapable of running the entire organization from one central location. The coping strategy at this stage was decentralization. In some cases, as at DuPont, decentralization came about as a rational, conscious decision. In others, as at Standard Oil, the decentralization that occurred was almost totally unplanned and unconscious. Indeed, formal decentralization may have been stalled for a number of years because management did not recognize the already changing strategy.

Policy and Administration. Chandler also noticed that policy, or strategy, development tended to be separated from day-to-day operations, or administration. When the top managers were finally freed from the daily operational problems and allowed to concentrate their energies on developing new strategies, they were able to see clearly the relationship between strategy and structure and make the necessary adaptations to the environment.

**Stinchcombe:
Structure and Age**

Stinchcombe studied several organizations to determine whether there was a relationship between the times they started and the structures they adopted (12). His results were positive. He found that after many years their structures remained similar to one another even though all had changed from their original patterns. Stinchcombe attributed much of this similarity to the fact that the social environment at their beginning required organizations to structure themselves in specific ways.

**Lawrence and
Lorsch: Different
Environments,
Different
Structures**

Lawrence and Lorsch studied a number of firms in the plastics, packaged foods, and standardized container industries (13). In each industry the researchers identified high-performing and low-performing firms and came to the conclusion that the most effective organizational structures were those that mirrored their particular environments. The environment of the container firms was quite stable; the internal structure of effective organizations in this industry resembled a classical hierarchy, with authority and control at the top. The environment of the plastics companies, on the other hand, was changing rapidly. The internal structures of effective organizations in this industry were less formal, with widely shared centers of influence.

All the organizations were found to function best when authority and influence were located in the hands of those with the most relevant knowledge. Thus the researchers suggest a *contingency theory* of organization: since organizational variables are in a complex interrelationship with one another and with the pressures from the environment, organizations whose internal designs are consistent with external demands will be most effective in dealing with their environments.

Burns and Stalker: Mechanistic or Organic Structure?

Burns and Stalker, who studied electronics firms in Scotland, suggest that types of organization design vary along a continuum (14). Highly **mechanistic** organizations occupy one end of the scale, highly **organic** ones the other. A **mechanistic organization** has a bureaucratic structure, with a stable authority hierarchy, well-defined jobs, and definite rules, policies, and procedures to control and limit behavior. Each person has a specialized skill and performs within the constraints of his or her assigned job. The organization chart is a useful tool to determine relationships in this kind of structure.

In comparison, the **organic organization** appears almost disorganized. Managers in organic systems sometimes take pride in not having an organization chart. Jobs are not well defined. Skills and abilities are considered more important than roles or positions. People are expected to find out what they are to do rather than wait to be told. Few rules and regulations exist, except in the form of general policies. The organic organization can be both challenging and frustrating.

Each type seems to have its place. If the product is standardized, if the major problems are those concerned with production, and if markets are well defined, then the best type of organization would seem to be mechanistic. If the market is not well defined and if the main problems are those of marketing and development, then the organic form of organization would appear to be better. Mechanistic organizations apparently cannot make the rapid changes necessary to keep up with changing conditions.

Managers have some choice in organization design, but the pattern they choose needs to be appropriate to the conditions and forces that prevail in the external environment. The organization design also needs to be constructed around a changing technology and conditioned to the desires and expectations of the individuals and groups that do the work.

Chapter Review

In this chapter we have examined many of the environmental forces that affect managerial work and that influence organization design. As the pace of environmental change accelerates, wrestling effectively with outside pressures is likely to become an increasingly critical part of the job of all managers.

The specific ideas and terms that have been discussed in the chapter are summarized below.

1. The **environment** refers to all things, conditions, and forces that exist outside of the organization or organizational subunit under consideration.

2. Four environments have been modeled: the **external-external,** consisting of relationships among units entirely outside a given organization; the **external-internal,** or input section; the **internal-external,** or output segment; and the **internal-internal** section, consisting of relationships among an organization's subunits.

3. The external-external segment contains the **natural,** the **economic,** the **political-legal** and the **sociocultural** environments.

  a. The **natural environment** consists of the nonliving, or **geophysical,** and the living, or **ecological,** parts.

  (1) **Geophysical forces** include **geographical** features, such as land or mountains, and **geological** conditions, such as weather and the supply of minerals and ores.

  (2) **Ecological factors,** the complex web of interrelationships between living things and their environments, exist in a delicate balance that, if upset, may endanger the life-support system itself.

  b. The **economic environment** consists of such scarce resources — which, being scarce, are often valued in monetary terms — as the **land** and its products, the **labor** of humans, **capital** or financial investments, and **information.**

  c. The **political-legal environment** includes all branches of government — the legislative, executive, and judicial — and what they do.

  d. The **sociocultural environment** includes the cultural values of a society and its social trends and problems. **Society** includes all forms of social organization and interactions; **culture** refers to the norms, values, rituals, status systems, economic conditions, and government relationships in a society.

4. **Multinational corporations,** or **multinationals,** are business firms with branches or subsidiaries in countries outside the home nation. The number of these organizations is increasing rapidly. Managing international organizations presents special problems associated with doing business in natural, economic, political, and sociocultural environments that are unfamiliar.

5. Managers react to changes and attempt to keep their organizations in tune with the environment with a variety of coping devices. These range from **combination** with other units, through **cooperation, coalition, cooptation, bargaining,** and **continuous competition,** to **extreme rivalry,** or **destructive competition.**

6. External-internal, or input, relationships between an organization and its environments require that managers who span an input boundary maintain a relatively passive or **reactive orientation** in procuring material and informational resources.

7. Internal-external or output relationships between an organization and its environments require that managers spanning the output boundaries maintain a more **proactive** orientation by taking positive steps to influence external events. Output personnel, such as a sales force, concentrate on such activities as supplying goods and services to clients or customers and maintaining public support.

8. Organizational outcomes that are generally considered undesirable, such as pollution and waste, are called **externalities** or **social costs.** The question of who should pay for such outcomes is part of the question of **social responsibility,** but defining to whom and for what an organization should be responsible is complex, difficult, and debatable.

9. Environmental forces affect an organization's structure in some of the following ways:

a. Organizational form is dependent on the strategies that managers develop to cope with a changing environment.

b. Different environments require different structures; stable environments seem to accommodate hierarchical bureaucracies with centralized authority; rapidly changing environments require more flexible, informal, and organic control systems with diverse centers of influence.

c. The **contingency** theory of organization stipulates that organizations will be likely to be effective to the extent that internal relationships are consistent with external demands because organizational variables are in a complex interrelationship with one another and with forces from the environment.

Discussion Questions

1. In what ways does government aid businesses? How does it hinder businesses?

2. How can managers of organizations obtain information about what is going on in the world outside?

3. Describe the effects of the following on management actions and decision making:

a. suppliers of financial capital

b. government agencies

c. customers

4. What is culture? Why is it useful for managers to understand cultures? What differences might you find in organizational structure in different cultures? Why?

5. As the personnel manager of the XYZ Corporation, you have been concerned with civil rights. Acting upon this concern you have bent the entrance requirements and have hired a number of minority-group members. Now you are receiving complaints, not about the performance abilities of these new employees, but about their work habits being "out of step" with

the organization's demands. What is the nature of the problem? What steps might you take to correct the problem?

6. What are some special considerations for managers of multinational corporations?

7. To what degree can a business organization influence its environment? To what degree *should* it exert influence? Why?

8. Discuss the strategies managers might employ to maintain the equilibrium of their organizations.

9. Compare and contrast the work of managers who span the boundaries of an organization with the work of those whose jobs are mostly internal. Would the marginal role require different skills than the internal one? Discuss.

10. What are externalities? Who should pay for them? Why?

11. What effect do different environmental conditions have on organizational structures?

12. Discuss the likely effects of the following on organization design:
    a. stable environmental forces
    b. rapidly increasing internal complexity
    c. separation of policy making from administration
    d. the length of time the organization has been in existence
    e. rapidly changing environmental forces

13. What relationships does the manager maintain within the organization that constitute an *internal* environment?

Involvement Activity

Select for study an organization with which you are familiar and from which you can secure detailed information. Any organization will be satisfactory: a club, a university or a department within it, a small business firm, a government agency, a hospital, and so forth. (Probably a small organization is better than a large one, however.) Then make an analysis of the organization as directed below.

1. Draw a diagram, or organization chart, showing the intended relationships between the various jobs.

2. Describe in a general way the work goals of the overall organization and of each specific job within it.

3. Define the boundaries of the organization. Is your definition subject to debate?

4. Which employees in which jobs interact most with "the environment"? Which interact least? Why?

5. List the specific external-external forces that are likely to affect the organization in the long run (during the next ten years). Consider:
    a. the natural environment
        (1) geophysical factors
        (2) ecological factors
    b. the economic environment
    c. the political-legal environment
    d. the sociocultural environment

6. Who are the input personnel? What kinds of relationships do they have with environmental forces?

7. Who are the output personnel? What are the effects of their work on the external environment? Be as specific as possible.

8. How do each of the environmental factors influence organization design? Be specific. If you think the environment does not influence internal working relationships, explain why and defend your answer.

9. Identify and describe the types of internal relationships individuals and groups have with one another.

Write out your analysis, or give an oral report of your findings. In particular, assess the impact of the environment on the organization and the effect of the organization on its environment.

4

Managerial Activities of Directing

In the last two sections we have considered the design of organizations and work and the managerial task of organizing. But managers do more than just organize—they also run the organization. Therefore, the remaining two units of this text will address themselves to the study of how managers act to accomplish the work of their organizations.

Work in an organization has been defined as the activities, interactions, and decisions undertaken to reach the designated performance goals. Operative work involves the activities, interactions, and decisions of those employees who work directly with the resources being processed: with making, buying, or selling goods; teaching students; transacting loans; or performing any of the other myriad tasks that constitute the organization's performance core. Managerial work, on the other hand, consists of the activities, interactions, and decisions engaged in by those who *supervise* the operative work. These tasks include decision making, communicating, influencing, and leading (the subjects of Part 4), as well as the adaptation activities of planning, controlling, and changing (the subjects of Part 5).

Because no managerial activity is more important than decision making, two chapters are devoted to this activity. In Chapter 13 we discuss how decisions are made and note some of the variables that affect the process. Chapter 14 continues this discussion with the focus on managerial decision-making styles, the ways people formulate their views of the world, and some of the behavioral and quantitative techniques that aid the decision-making process.

Decisions are only as good as the effectiveness of their implementation. The processes of communication, influence, and leadership are the means by which managers carry out the decisions that have been made. Chapter 15 explores the nature and importance of communication and some of the problems involved in creating and maintaining an effective communication system. And since communication represents an attempt to influence people, Chapter 16 is concerned with the ways managers use resources to get others to do what they want them to do. The degree to which influence is successful depends on the relative power position of people in a social situation; thus, the chapter contains sections on how power is obtained and used and what the results of its use are on those being influenced.

Leadership combines the activities of communicating and influencing into a vehicle for accomplishing the manager's purposes. Chapter 17 develops a model of leadership and several theories of how and why people become leaders. It concludes with a general discussion of the role of leadership in the overall managerial task.

13

Decision Making: The Activities and the Environment

The concern of this and the following chapter is decision making — perhaps the most important of all managerial activities. It is through the making and carrying out of decisions that organizational activity is translated into goal accomplishment. In this chapter the focus is on models of decision making, the varieties of decisions made in organizations, and the environment in which decisions occur. In the succeeding chapter the focus will be on the decision makers — their styles and methods.

Recently one of the authors stopped in to talk with a friend who is a manager. On the manager's desk were the following items:

- An appointment calendar listing a 10:00 A.M. appointment with a bank officer, a lunch engagement with a colleague in another organization, and a 2:30 P.M. meeting with two subordinate managers.

- An in-basket containing letters from
    - a company salesperson regarding a late shipment
    - the headquarters financial vice-president about a change in return-on-investment standards
    - the chamber of commerce requesting a donation for their economic growth committee's operations
    - a high-school shop teacher requesting permission to bring a group of students through the plant
    - the company lawyer pointing out that the firm has only fifteen days left to comply with new air-pollution laws

- Telephone messages from
    - a customer wanting a discount in return for a large purchase

- a college friend who handles commercial real estate and may have an opportunity for a new building for the plant
- a neighbor who complains about the noise of the machinery

- A note about a broken casting, which is the subject of the 2:30 P.M. meeting.

A quick perusal of these items left no doubt that this manager maintains steady contacts with a wide variety of people both in and out of the organization. A conversation with the manager friend about these interactions indicated that each of these situations would require at least one, and probably several, decisions. The manager went on to say, "People always seem to be asking me to make a decision."

The model of managing presented in Chapter 1 shows the manager as a mediator between the pressures of the outside environment and the internal demands of the organization. To be successful, managers must know how the organization works internally and what outside forces may pose threats to, or create opportunities for, the organization. But this knowledge alone is insufficient. Managers are more than receivers and processors of information; they also must initiate actions based on the information they have. In this sense they are decision makers, negotiating between the environment and the organizational work groups in an attempt to keep the organization moving steadily toward its goals. This section of the book deals with how the manager directs organizational activities, starting with making decisions, as pictured in Figure 13–1. How decisions are made and the context that surrounds the decision-making process are the subjects of this chapter.

Ways to Study Decision Making

The term **decision making** has been used and interpreted in various ways. For the purposes of this chapter, decision making is defined as all the thoughts and actions that lead to a choice, including the choice itself. In other words, decision making is viewed as an activity. The concept will be broadened in the following chapter, in which decision making will be examined in terms of the behavioral and quantitative techniques that also are involved in the process.

Because activities that constitute decision making occur within a human, or social, environment, the process is constantly modified by what is perceived or recognized by the decision maker as relevant. And what decision makers see as relevant is determined by a combination of their history and their present situation. Thus, decision making is a dynamic rather than static process, affected by forces within both the individual decision maker and the environment. The decision to build a new plant,

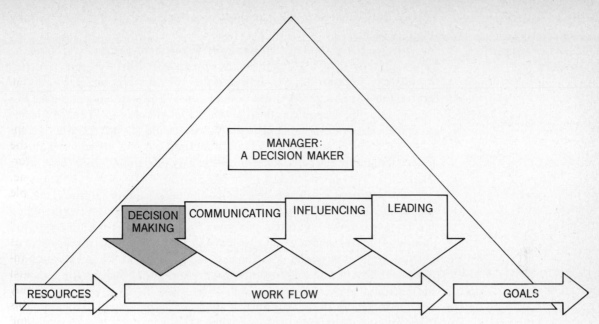

FIGURE 13–1
Managerial activities
of directing.

This figure illustrates those managerial activities that are performed mainly inside an organization. Their purpose is to help others do their jobs so that the organization's performance goals are realized efficiently. Decision making is an important managerial function. But once decisions are made, they must be implemented. Communicating, influencing, and leading are three additional functions managers perform in helping others to carry out decisions. The four functions overlap because they are not mutually exclusive: almost any action is based on decision, involves some kind of communication, and may be an example of influence and leadership as well.

for instance, is influenced by projections of product demand, competitive pressures, management desires, money markets, and many more conditions. And it is up to the decision maker to interpret and integrate these factors in order to decide whether building a new plant is the right course of action at that particular time.

The initial step for managers in any decision-making process is to become aware of the ways their own perceptions and interpretations limit or extend the information that is available for helping them make the decision. Some information is so obvious that there is little chance it can be ignored or misinterpreted. Other information must be searched for and interpreted carefully. Simon calls the process of searching for information **intelligence activity.**

The second step in decision making is to assess all the alternatives that are available. This step involves developing and analyzing courses of action, and Simon refers to it as the **design activity** of decision making. The third important step is the **choice activity,** which refers to actually choosing the appropriate alternative (1).

Prescriptive versus Descriptive Decision-Making Models

The **scientific method,** which is the framework for all scientific inquiry, suggests basically that problems can be solved rationally by progressing through a series of predetermined steps. These steps generally involve the following activities: (1) define the problem; (2) state the objective; (3) formulate a hypothesis; (4) collect data; (5) classify, analyze, and interpret the data; and (6) draw conclusions. The scientific method has greatly influenced people's ideas about decision making. Primarily it has led to the assumption that decision making can and should be effective if it follows the above steps. The scientific method offers a **prescriptive model** of decision making; that is, it suggests the way decisions *ought* to be made (2).

As it happens, however, few decision makers adhere to the prescriptive model. The decision-making process includes more complexities than this linear sequence of activities allows for, and it does not take into account the limited abilities of most decision makers nor the rapidly changing environment in which decisions occur. March and Simon pointed out that the ability of humans to act on a purely rational basis is limited. For this reason the prescriptive model of decision making gives way to a **descriptive model,** which describes what *actually* occurs as people go about making decisions (3).

Complexity. One of the major limitations of the prescriptive model is that the complexity of the real world makes it impossible to assemble all the facts or to know all the possible alternatives. All the variables that might somehow bear on a given situation are too numerous to collect within the limits of the time, money, and skills generally available. Even if resources were adequate, the variables would change between the time that the information was collected and the time that it was analyzed. Furthermore, there are too many alternatives; and if the values to be maximized are many, the number of variables that would have to be juggled by the decision maker would become too great to handle. However, it is possible for decision makers to alleviate some of this complexity by using mechanical assistance. For relatively uncomplicated problems, simply making lists of all the variables may help. As complexity increases, computers are useful. But some problems are beyond the scope of computer capabilities. Computers, for instance, cannot assess such human variables as emotions and attitudes (4).

Emotions. Emotional reactions are factors that not only impede computers but that limit human decision makers as well. People cannot totally separate their rational capabilities from their emotional reactions. Information from the environment may be objective, but when perceived and interpreted through the human organism it takes on the values of the decision maker. Further, most information reaching the decision maker is not objective; it already has been biased by the values of those through whom the information has filtered.

Programs. Programed behavior is another way in which the prescriptive model is limited. Habits, conventions, procedures, and rules lead one to use learned "solutions" or programs that have been successful in the past. Even when the situation demands new behavior, some managers continue to use familiar old ways. Habits inhibit experimentation; programs constrain organizations in similar ways. Other programs include unconscious motivations and the values, attitudes, and prejudices of the decider.

Limited Choices. The search for alternatives is limited by time, skill, and cost constraints as well as by inadequate resources, previous commitments, unavailability of certain information, and the laws and customs of society. Considering the number of restrictions on choice presented to the decision maker, the wonder is that decisions get made at all (5). Yet they do, even though the decision maker often must simplify the situation in order to make a choice. Although prescribed functions and constraints do restrict managers to relatively few values or alternatives, they nevertheless have available certain systematic methods of making choices that can increase the number of variables within these limits (6).

Types of Rationality

Within the confines of objective thought and knowledge, decision makers are rational. But the type of rationality they employ depends on the situation that surrounds the decision-making process. **Objective rationality** is most closely obtainable in a laboratory situation, where it is often possible to control all the variables. This kind of objectivity is rare in organizations, except perhaps when dealing with such tangible problems as the number of cubic feet needed to store twenty refrigerators. **Subjective rationality,** on the other hand, is reasoning based on the search for maximum results, given the available knowledge. This type of rationality is most frequently employed in human decision making. **Conscious rationality** implies consciously making an adjustment in the means and ends of goals to accommodate reality. Other types of rationality include **organizational rationality,** which is concerned with reaching organizational goals, and **personal rationality,** which may or may not be conscious and which has to do with obtaining personal goals.

Decision-Making Models

In this section we will examine three separate scenarios dealing with decision making. These three illustrations represent the ways in which decision makers act. They are intended to be descriptive rather than prescriptive; that is, they attempt to show how people normally proceed to make decisions rather than to offer ideal models of how decisions *ought* to be made. In all three scenarios the major variables are the same—information, image of the world, search, alternatives, and choice—it is the combination and sequence that change.

The Short Sequence

Figure 13–2 illustrates the fastest and simplest decision sequence. In this situation the individual receives information from the environment (step 1), which is then compared with his or her image of the world (step 2). If the information and the image are congruent (step 3), the information is simply stored in memory (step 4). If the information and the image are not congruent (step 5), a problem exists (step 6). Search for a solution then begins by checking the memory (step 7). When found there, the alternative is immediately adopted (step 8), and action ensues (step 9).

This decision sequence may be exemplified by the foreman who has just been told that the old milling machine has broken down again. Since the machine has broken down a number of times in the past, the foreman is sure he knows what the problem is and how to fix it. He immediately issues the appropriate orders and the machine is repaired.

The Long Sequence

The second scenario (Figure 13–3) is identical to the first up to the point where the problem is compared with memory (steps 1–4). In this longer

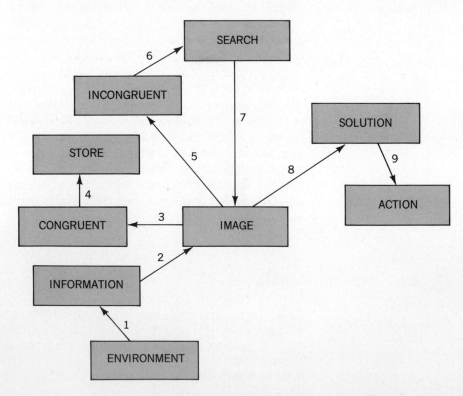

FIGURE 13–2
A short decision sequence.

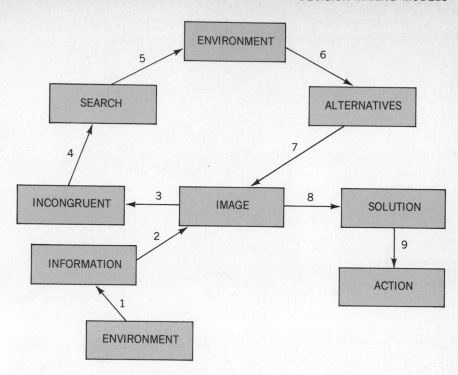

FIGURE 13-3
A long decision
sequence.

sequence, the person finds that no alternative is suggested by past experience, and the individual must turn to the outside for more information that
will produce other alternatives (step 5). As alternatives are found in the
environment (step 6), they are compared with the image (step 7) until a
satisfactory alternative (step 8) is adopted; and then action may com-
mence (step 9). An elaboration of this scenario involves separate judgments about several alternatives, which are then compared to produce the
optimum choice.

A sequence that involves this development and comparison of alternatives may be exemplified by an investment decision. Suppose the financial officer of an organization finds that the company has $100,000 in cash
that it will need in six months but that it does not need at present. This is a
common situation in this company, and after some thought, the financial
officer decides that a 6 percent return with good safety would be a satisfactory investment. She proceeds to contact a bank, which offers 5.70
percent interest on the money, and she then contacts a savings and loan
association, which offers 6.75 percent. She accepts the latter offer. The
more extended scenario would have the financial officer also contacting a
broker in government securities to find out what the return on treasury
notes or other short-term security rates would be and then withholding a
decision until all possible alternatives are laid out in front of her.

AND THIS, GENTLEMEN, IS THE BOARD
THAT MAKES ALL OUR DECISIONS.

The Complex Sequence

The third scenario follows from the second one but varies again in the search situation. This sequence is depicted in Figure 13–4. The critical idea here is that an alternative cannot be located in the available time period (steps 1–5). When the search thus fails, the person returns to the image (step 6) and changes the comparison standards (step 7) to make them compatible with the alternatives already assembled (step 8). The individual then adopts the best alternative (step 9) available at that time (step 10), and action proceeds (step 11).

This final scenario may be illustrated by a selection decision. Imagine, for example, that owing to a new affirmative action program, a personnel manager is searching for a female purchasing agent with four years' experience in administration of government contracts. Initial search turns up a candidate with three years' experience, and the personnel manager feels lucky to have found her. In this instance, the standards were changed to accommodate the available choices.

In the sections that immediately follow, a discussion will be presented of each of the major stages of the models just described.

The Image

At the heart of the decision-making model is the *image*. Everyone carries around in his or her head pictures of what the world *is* like and what it *should be* like. These images cover a multitude of topics from physical data (such as what an eclipse is), through social data (opinions on poli-

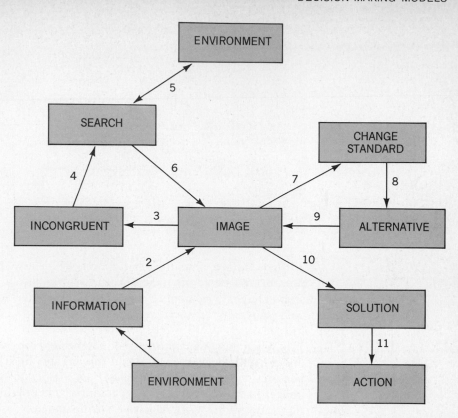

FIGURE 13–4
A complex decision
sequence.

tics), to emotional data (feelings about another person). In totality the
image is our memory of past events, feelings, values, and attitudes (7).

Small children have very limited images because they have not had
much experience. Older people have extensive images, but often they are
somewhat rigid and difficult to adapt to new situations. And young adults
have relatively large images that tend to be fairly easily adaptable.

Testing Information Against the Image. All of us are constantly
bombarded with stimuli (data and information) from the environment,
which our brains nearly simultaneously compare with stored information.
This comparison between incoming and stored information sets the stage
for decision making. There are three possible consequences of this comparison: there will be nothing stored in memory that offers a comparison;
there will be comparison information, and this information will create
either a congruent or incongruent state between image and information.
Figure 13–5 diagrams these three possibilities.

When information is received for which there is no existing comparison, the individual usually ignores it. Many managers, for example, ignore
the information sent to them each month by the accounting department
because they do not understand the basics of accounting. It is likely that

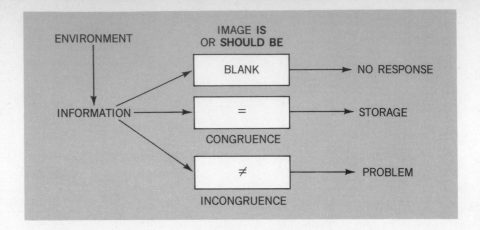

FIGURE 13–5
Alternative states of
information–image
comparison.

at some future time this inattention will cause problems, but in the present, the person is unable even to formulate a problem because the stimuli have no meaning. Persistent stimuli, when attached to consequences, eventually create memories for the person. This is how images are formed.

When incoming information matches existing perceptions, the result may be called **congruence.** Again this creates little or no response in the person. Congruent information serves simply to reinforce already held images and is stored in memory. Continued congruence between perceptions and information leads to a strong image.

It is possible, however, for information to be congruent with one part of the image and incongruent with another. The clearest example of this is when the images of *is* and *should be* are not in agreement. For instance, the speed limit is 55 miles per hour, but many people believe it ought to be higher. For these people, driving at 65 miles per hour is congruent with their beliefs but incongruent with the law they know to exist. A problem occurs if they are stopped by a police officer and issued a citation.

A decision situation exists when incoming information is **incongruent** with existing images. Examples of incongruence include such situations as a return on investment of 6 percent when it was supposed to be 12 percent; turning the key in your car and finding that nothing happens; or discovering that employees are taking longer than the ten minutes allotted for a coffee break. Each of these examples has an *expected condition* that did not occur and an *actual condition* that was not expected.

Determining whether a problem exists is itself a decision-making process. Any variation from expectations may be a symptom that something has gone wrong. But the deviation does not explain *what* has gone wrong or *why*. In organizations it is often difficult to isolate the causes of deviations from expectations because the number of variables is usually great and there is little possibility of setting up a laboratory condition in which variables can be isolated. It is true, though, that physical problems having to do with such matters as inventory control, equipment maintenance, or accounting forms are easier to solve than human problems because the operative variables are more precise.

The Problem with Problems. Another difficulty that exists in the pre-decision-making stage is defining what is and what is not a problem. In the first place, the image is not totally conscious. A person often "feels" something is awry before really knowing what exactly is wrong. The more fully aware one is both of the external realities and of the internal forces at work on one's perceptions of those realities, the easier it is to define the problem. This leads to the interesting observation that individuals often think they know more about something than they really do. This fact is made clear when a person who is faced with having to specifically define an existing problem (if any) discovers that it is impossible to do so.

The more accurately a person is able to observe a large number of variables in the environment the better he or she is able to isolate the existence and nature of the problem. For example, people who know very little about the operation of an automobile are unlikely to be able to make very many meaningful observations about what is or is not wrong with their cars. The garage mechanic who observes more variables is able to locate and define the problem with a great deal of accuracy.

People run into trouble in their decision-making attempts when they try to define problems before they have gathered enough information. Their haste may cause them to solve the wrong problem or to constantly redefine the same problem. Studies conducted by Kepner and Tregoe have shown that most people spend very little time collecting information beyond the original symptoms that brought the problem to their attention in the first place (8).

People also need to learn how to correlate the image with the information from the environment. Knowing how incoming facts are related to certain parts of one's image is not always an automatic process. The relationship between information and image can be obscured by the diversity of information received or by the existence of an incomplete or biased image. The result is a greater difficulty in perceiving incompatible information and a tendency to pay attention only to information that reinforces the existing image.

A car that does not start or a body temperature higher than 98.6° F are clear indications that a problem exists. But these indications are not themselves problems—they are *symptoms* of problem states. In order to start the car, the mechanic must find and correct the underlying difficulty. To lower the body temperature to normal, the doctor must locate and treat the cause of the fever. Treating symptoms, while sometimes temporarily expedient, rarely solves the problem. Thus it is important to be able to distinguish symptoms from problems.

Problems versus Symptoms

Try to distinguish the following problems (p) from symptoms (s):

1. a. engine won't turn over
   b. dead auto battery

2. a. 104° temperature
   b. congested chest
   c. pneumonia

3. a. poor performance
   b. invalid selection tests
   c. payment on the basis of time only

4. a. sales below estimates
   b. low profits
   c. costly production

ANSWERS

1. a. s   2. a. s   3. a. p   4. a. s
   b. p   b. s   b. s   b. p
              c. s   c. s   c. s

Search Procedures	It should be clear from the foregoing discussion of symptoms and problems that the need to search for information is an important step in the decision-making process. And a vital part of this search involves seeking alternatives. A totally rational model of decision making assumes that all alternatives are neatly laid out before the decision maker at the time the decision is to be made. Unfortunately, this assumption is not generally the case. Since all possible alternatives are rarely knowable, the question for the decision maker is how long to continue the search. Search is costly in terms of time, effort, and money, so after obtaining a few good possibilities it is usually not practical to look further.

The first place to look for alternatives is in the image. If the situation has come up before, people will usually institute the same solution that worked in the past. When the sequence has been completed enough times, the person is no longer even conscious of making the decision; the sequence becomes a habit. Most organizations, to achieve consistency and efficiency, rely on this historical approach. The image is stored in the heads of the organization's members through socialization and training programs, or it is recorded in procedures manuals.

Habits and procedures are programs. They save managers an immense amount of time and energy in making decisions because they enable many decisions to be made automatically. Every once in a while, however, programs create their own problems. For example, when the problem does not exactly fit the program, or when the environment has changed, the program will not be effective. Suppose, for instance, you are driving to school along the route you always take. It is so familiar that getting to school is automatic, a habit. Even if there is a blockage in your usual route, any detour you take is also likely to be an automatic response. This time, however, all the roads with which you are familiar are blocked off, and the detour has taken you into unknown territory. Your program for handling this decision process is no longer effective.

The most expedient thing to do would be to pull over and look at a map or to stop and ask someone how to proceed. In either instance you would be going through a sequence of finding an alternative and comparing it with the problem to see if it fits. If it does fit, you would select that alternative; if not, the search would continue.

Observations of people making decisions suggest that alternatives are considered sequentially rather than all together. That is, the decision maker examines each alternative in sequence to see if it meets some minimally acceptable standard or criterion as determined by the image. If it does, then one might go a little further than simply choosing the first alternative that is acceptable. One experimenter observed a situation in which a group of students were making job decisions. He found that he could predict the job the individual would choose before the person made a selection. Through interviews he was able to establish the criteria each student would use in making job choices. Independently, the experimenter then applied these criteria to the alternatives that appeared and came up with the same choice as did the student. He also found that students would go somewhat beyond the initially acceptable alternative, but not very far. Thus, students might wait two or three weeks after the first acceptable offer, looking around for a better alternative, but if none appeared they would then accept the first offer. Even though this sequence is rational within bounds, it is a search process for acceptable alternatives to **satisfice**, or to get by, rather than to maximize outcomes. Searching for maximal alternatives seems to be a process that occurs infrequently among all groups of people (9).

Reevaluating the Problem. Determining that a problem exists and then defining the problem pushes the decision maker to search for solutions. This relationship has reciprocal characteristics. That is, as one searches for alternatives, the nature of the problem necessarily changes to adapt to the alternatives found. In fact, finding a good alternative is often an excuse for redefining the problem. In a recent class discussion, the following sequence took place when a student described how her bicycle, which was her only means of transportation to and from school, had broken down on the way to class. As she saw it she had two alternatives: repair the bicycle or buy a new one. These alternatives, in turn, could be broken down into a series of subalternatives. For instance, repair the bicycle herself, ask a friend to repair it, or take it to a bicycle repair shop. As the discussion progressed, it was suggested that she take the bus to school. Although this is an acceptable alternative, it addresses itself not to the central problem of repairing the bicycle, but to the problem of getting to school. This interaction between search and problem is continuous: when alternatives are not readily available, the problem continues to be redefined until a satisfactory solution is found.

Rational Search. So far in our discussion of search procedures, there is no indication that a complete search for the best alternatives is ever carried out. Actually, systematic searching activity does occur in certain instances. But because such activity is costly and time consuming, when it is undertaken the problem is typically very important. For example, when a company is attempting to enter a new market or in some way to change its basic organizational structure, a thorough search for optimum alternatives is probable. The more commonplace and operational the decision, the greater the likelihood that the satisficing model will be utilized.

Evaluation Procedures

The evaluation of alternatives is ordinarily not a separate activity from the search process. Rather, evaluation occurs simultaneously and automatically with the discovery of alternatives. And whether the alternatives are evaluated quickly in the mind of the searcher or analyzed through rational search by teams of experts or by complicated computer programs, the method of evaluation is essentially the same. That is, they are measured according to the probability of their chances of solving the problem and their value to the decision maker. Of course, the prerequisites to the evaluation process are that the decision maker has a clear notion of what the criteria are, that he or she has a means of determining the relative value of the outcome of each alternative, and that the probability of the outcome occurring as predicted can be measured.

Probability. Every alternative has some probability of being able to solve the problem. And since different alternatives are likely to vary in probability, it is necessary to calculate probabilities for each alternative considered. Where the problem has arisen many times in the past and a set of alternatives has been tried, the calculation of probability is fairly easy and is called *objective* probability. The decision maker can calculate the percentage of time the alternative has worked in the past to estimate the probability of its working again. For instance, if increased advertising has produced a jump in sales in three out of four past slump periods, there is a 0.75 probability of an increase in advertising boosting sales in the present slump period. Of course, that assumes that the current sales problem is a result of the same factors that caused the previous problems and that the current and future conditions are the same as they were then.

It is possible to obtain probability statements even when past information is unavailable. The best way is to ask experts—people who have been in similar situations in the past. This is *subjective* probability. The accuracy of subjective estimates depends on the experience of the estimator and, again, on the similarity of current conditions to past ones. The way to improve the accuracy of subjective probability is to obtain probability statements from several experts. If they agree, the probabilities can be accepted with confidence. If they do not agree, then the reasons they differ may be instructive (10).

Utility. Some alternatives are preferable to others regardless of their probability. In other words, the value of a particular alternative to the decision maker is higher than is the value of all other alternatives. Value in this case is a measure of the usefulness of the results to the decision maker, and all alternatives can be ranked by their usefulness. This utility rating of alternatives multiplied by their probability of solving the problem results in an overall judgment of the worth of the alternatives. Choosing then becomes a matter of picking the one with the highest overall worth.

Applying utility to an alternative is complicated by the fact that decision makers typically have more than one utility to consider; indeed, there may be quite a few. In an investment problem, for example, one may wish the greatest return with the least amount of risk. However, as investment return rises, the risk factor increases. Thus the decision maker must weigh the different utilities against one another. Utilities include factors concerning the nature of the problem as well as elements derived from the personal values of the decision maker. Neither of these components can be ignored when evaluating alternatives. Consider, for example, a college graduate seeking a job. The objective is to earn a good salary doing the kind of work he or she has been trained for. But if the person is offered a job that meets these requirements in a company that produces products or engages in activities that are antithetical to his or her values, then a new alternative must be sought. The best alternatives, then, are those that have a high probability of occurrence, solve the problem well, and are satisfying to the individual in terms of his or her values.

Selection Procedures

Once the criteria for choosing an alternative are determined, the utilities ranked, and the probabilities of various outcomes determined, the act of selection itself is rather routine. The decision maker merely multiplies the probability by the value of the outcome for each alternative and selects the one that obtains the highest score. Sometimes this sequence is so automatic that the decision maker is not consciously aware of having gone through the process. Other times the selection is based on comprehensive analyses of a multitude of data and the decision maker feels a great sense of accomplishment at the conclusion of the sequence.

Because there are so many elements in the selection process that cannot be directly compared with one another, good choices often require the kind of judgment a person acquires only after substantial and successful experience. Choice may be relatively subconscious when the selector determines what factors are important and what utility to put on them.

Entoven (11) describes three kinds of judgments. The first is *likelihood* or *probability* judgment, in which the decision maker must assign some probability to an alternative even when it is unknown. A second kind of judgment is *value* judgment, which involves the person's goals and his or her sense of whether what is being done is correct. And the third kind of judgment involves *estimating results* where the processes are too complex or not well enough defined to know what the variables are.

The use of judgment is inevitable and may be what managers are paid to exercise. But telling someone to "use your own judgment" is not a license for haphazard thinking. Managers should be able to state with a fair amount of clarity the bases on which their decisions were made.

Variations in Decision Making

In the previous section, decision making was shown to vary considerably depending on the particular decision to be made, the decision maker, and the specific circumstances in which the decision occurs. In this section, we will discuss the major variations in the parts of the decision process and how these variations influence or determine the decision sequence that will be used.

Programed and Nonprogramed Decisions

The first type of decision variation has to do with whether the problem is a common one and has been dealt with before. In other words, is there a satisfactory alternative that has already been used? If so, the decision maker simply uses that alternative, which is now a *program,* and the decision-making procedure is like the short sequence described earlier. When there has been no previous decision situation similar to the present one, there is no program and the decision is said to be *nonprogramed.* In this instance, the decision-making sequence will resemble the second scenario.

Programed Decisions. Organizations and the people within them need reliable behavior for goal accomplishment. They obtain efficiency partly from the availability of reusable problem-solving programs. In fact, one of the ways in which organizations are held together is through the development of systematic procedures for solving problems and performing work activities. These methods ensure reliable and efficient behavior within the organization and save a considerable amount of time and energy.

Organizational programs take the form of procedures, methods, techniques, and other regularly used sets of actions that are part of a job. These programs, though usually not as complex or rigid, are analogous to computer programs that have been designed to solve problems or analyze data. Every manager, when given certain tasks to perform, is also given (or must devise) some approved organizational programs to use in accomplishing those tasks.

Managers must be wary, however, of using programed decisions in situations that call for new solutions. They must also take care to choose the proper program for the situation with which they are dealing. Often a decision-making condition resembles one for which there is an existing program, and not until it has been closely scrutinized is it found to be different.

Nonprogramed Decisions. Nonprogramed decisions are those that occur in novel situations. They tend to happen primarily on higher organizational levels and generally involve goal decisions rather than work-accomplishment decisions. Nonprogrammed decision making takes much more time than does programed decision making because it is a more thoughtful, rather than an automatic, process. The long-sequence scenario, described above, is called into action only after the decision maker realizes that there are no alternatives readily available and that some search outside the area of past experience is required.

A major problem for managers is finding the time to engage in nonprogramed decision making. By its nature the nonprogramed decision diverts time and energy away from the steady flow of day-to-day activities. Simon points out that there is a sort of Gresham's law involved here, which says that programed decision making drives out nonprogramed decision making. Managers are so caught up in the ongoing demand for routine decision making that they are reluctant to take the time to make the really important decisions that constitute the heart of their jobs (12).

Balancing Programed and Nonprogramed Decision Making. Early management theory suggested that all policies and general plans are determined at the top of the organization and then passed down to others to be carried out. In this sense, all nonprogramed decisions would occur at the top of the organization and all programed decisions would occur at the bottom. In fact, while this is an approximation of what actually happens, rather than an absolute separation between programed and nonprogramed decisions, there is a gradual decline in the amount and magnitude of nonprogramed decisions as one moves downward through the hierarchy. If one assumes that the number of all decisions made at each level of the organization is approximately equivalent, then a distribution of programed and nonprogramed decisions would look something like that shown in Figure 13–6.

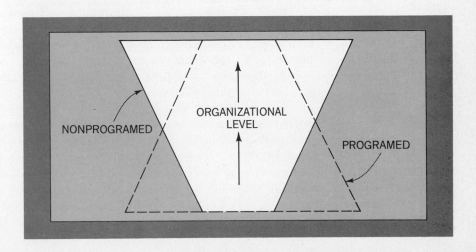

FIGURE 13–6
Distribution of programed and nonprogramed decisions in an organization.

**Linear and
Heuristic Decision-
Making Search**

A second type of decision-making variation has to do with the type of search method that is called for. A predecision decision must be made regarding where to search for alternatives and in what order alternatives should be considered. At one extreme is a systematic or **linear** search method and at the other is a **heuristic,** or "rule of thumb," method.

Linear Search. "First things first" is a fairly accurate description of linear search. The manager starts by looking systematically at those alternatives that are closest at hand. If these prove fruitless, then he or she moves outward to other parts of the environment. Computers often work in this fashion. Suppose, for instance, a manager wants to find a person to fill the position of sales manager. The criteria include a college degree in business, five years' experience selling the company's products, and a knowledge of the East Coast. The computer would be programed with this information and would then search through the company's computerized personnel records. It would first identify all employees with a degree in business, then, from that group, identify those with five years' selling experience with the company, and finally, from the remaining group, identify those who have lived and worked on the East Coast.

Linear search is a very appealing method but a difficult one to carry out if you are not a computer. When the search area is small and the decision important, it can be quite successful. A systematic search is likely to uncover alternatives that otherwise would be missed. But it is also clumsy and time consuming. Further, the more complex the environment the more difficult the search. In the above example, the computer search was no problem because all the personnel records had been previously programed. Even in a very large organization, say one that employs more than 100,000 people, this procedure would not be difficult. But consider the amount of time and degree of chaos involved in conducting the same search manually in an organization even one-tenth that size. The task would be overwhelming.

Heuristic Search. From observations of people making decisions, the indications are that decision makers are not very systematic. People are more likely than not to take shortcuts in the search sequence. Try to remember a time when you misplaced something you needed. How did you go about searching for the lost article? If you are like most people, you probably proceeded much like the man in the following example.

Jack sat down at his work bench and discovered that his hammer was not in its customary place. His first thought was that perhaps his wife had taken it to use somewhere in the house. He looked around in a few of the most likely places, but he could not find it. He then went into the backyard to see whether his daughter had taken it to use in her tree house. When it was not there, he went next door to see whether his neighbor had borrowed it. Finally, Jack sat down at his work bench and after a few moments discovered the hammer beneath a pile of rags he had inadvertently dropped on top of it.

The type of search procedure Jack followed to locate his hammer is called a **heuristic** approach. It means that one attempts to solve a problem by applying rules of thumb based on past experience. Jack knew that his wife, daughter, and neighbor sometimes used his hammer, so he began his search based on the assumption that such was the case this time. A heuristic problem-solving approach is a logical method, but it is not very systematic. It often saves time, but, as illustrated in the above example, the best alternative is often overlooked. If Jack had taken the time to think about the problem linearly, he most likely would have remembered where he had last placed the hammer and would have looked under the pile of rags.

Environmental Considerations in Decision Making

Decision makers find and judge alternatives based on information that comes in from the environment. But the environment is constantly in flux, and information is not always accurate. In addition, some types of information are more certain than others. The conditions surrounding the information and the sources through which information is obtained create a continuum of uncertainty that affects the decision-making process.

Certainty. A condition of certainty exists when the manager has sufficient knowledge of the environment to say that an alternative definitely will or will not solve the problem. Certainty carries a probability of $+1.0$ or -1.0. An environment that fosters certainty usually contains physical data or objects, such as inventory control records or available merchandise. Problems relating to production, inventory control, or finance, for example, may involve a large number of variables, but all can be measured. If the probability of all alternatives is $+1.0$, selection involves simply choosing the one with the highest value. Only under conditions of certainty can a decision be purely rational and produce maximal results.

It is not difficult to see why examples of decisions made under conditions of total certainty are hard to find. But such conditions do exist in certain circumstances. Consider, for instance, a decision regarding what type of material to use in the manufacture of a certain product. The choices include plastic, steel, wood, and aluminum. The decision maker first subjects all four materials to a rigorous physical testing program and establishes, with reasonable certainty, that each is equally suitable for use. The only consideration left then is cost, so the decision is easily made on the basis of which material is the cheapest.

Risk. A condition of risk exists when the probability is less than 1.0 but can still be calculated. This condition makes decision making more complex; the evaluation of alternatives must include both probability and utility. Depending on differing future conditions, alternatives may have considerably different probabilities attached to their outcomes. Further, the process of assigning probability statements carries its own degree of uncertainty, especially when the probabilities are subjective in nature.

TABLE 13–1

Probability Estimates in a Risk Condition*

| | Profit Margins | | | |
MATERIAL	IMPROVING ECONOMY (0.25 probability)	STABLE ECONOMY (0.50 probability)	DECLINING ECONOMY (0.25 probability)	EXPECTED VALUE
	$	$	$	$
Plastic	2.50	2.00	1.50	1.99
Steel	2.00	1.80	1.60	1.80
Aluminum	3.00	2.00	1.00	2.00
Wood	2.75	2.25	1.50	2.17

* The alternative with the highest expected utility can be estimated by multiplying the profit margins for each material by the probability of each economic condition and then summing the rows across the page. The answers are in the right-hand column. In this instance, wood would provide the highest expected return given the probabilities of the future economic conditions. Different probabilities, of course, would produce different results.

Decision making under risk conditions may be illustrated by continuing the example of the manufacturer started above. Suppose the manager has calculated the costs of each material and has arrived at an accurate estimate of the profit margins that would derive from the product units manufactured in each of the types of material. But a further variable to be considered is that the future market is dependent upon the condition of the economy. If the manager calculates the probabilities of an improving economy at 0.25, a stable economy at 0.50, and a declining economy at 0.25, a new estimate of the profit margin for each type of material under each economic condition can be made. Such an estimate would resemble the figures shown in Table 13–1. Since future economic conditions cannot be estimated with certainty, it can be seen why this situation represents a risk condition.

Uncertainty. Organizational decisions often are made under conditions of uncertainty; that is, where such subjective probability cannot be estimated. Although many factors affecting the decision are known, some key variables are either unknown or are so complex that the manager is unable to assign a probability statement to the outcome of any of the alternatives. In this situation the decision maker is forced to take a trial-and-error approach to problem solving. Because this approach is the least systematic of all decision-making procedures, certain guidelines have been developed to help managers make the most of what they have to work with.

One of these guidelines involves having decision makers classify outcomes according to the attitudes they have about them. If there is no way to determine whether one alternative is more likely to work than another, then selecting the one that would produce the best results if it worked at all might be the best choice. This criterion presupposes that the manager is *optimistic* and will pick the alternative with the highest utility.

A similar form of selection, but one that takes an opposite point of view, is the *pessimistic* approach. That is, the decision maker has a negative attitude about all the alternatives but chooses the one whose consequences, if nothing works right at all, will hurt the least. A third approach under uncertain conditions is for the decision maker to choose the alternative whose possible outcomes will *minimize regret*. The possibility of future regret can be measured by weighing the difference between the results one will receive from the various alternatives against the results one might have received had the best possible certain condition existed.

To see how these approaches might operate in a real situation, let us assume that the manufacturer in the above example was not able to obtain good probability estimates of future economic conditions. If the manufacturer is an optimist, he or she will scan Table 13–1, find the overall highest profit margin, and proceed with that alternative. In this case the decision would be to go with aluminum. If the manufacturer is a pessimist, he or she will take the alternative with the highest profit margin in the worst possible condition, which in this case would be steel, since it does not go lower than $1.60.

The criterion of regret is somewhat more complex and involves compiling a different set of figures. The manager would have to estimate the greatest possible loss for each type of material in each of the possible economic conditions. The result would resemble the figures shown in Table 13–2. In an improving economy the manufacturer experiences a loss of $0.50 for plastic, $1.00 for steel, no loss for aluminum, and $0.25 for wood. Similar calculations are made for the two other economic conditions.

In this case wood would be chosen as the least regret that could be experienced because $0.25 is considerably lower than the other alternatives.

TABLE 13–2
Estimates of Regret in a Risk Condition*

	Reductions in Profit Margins			
MATERIAL	IMPROVING ECONOMY	STABLE ECONOMY	DECLINING ECONOMY	AMOUNT OF REGRET
	$	$	$	$
Plastic	0.50	0.25	0.10	0.50
Steel	1.00	0.45	0	1.00
Aluminum	0	0.25	0.60	0.60
Wood	0.25	0	0.10	0.25

* Profit margins are those expected or estimated for each material under each economic condition. The reason for the decline in steel in a declining economy might be because steel prices do not fall. The decline in profits for aluminum as conditions improve might be the result of increased competition.

**Utility
Considerations in
Decision Making**

In addition to the differences among utility values discussed earlier, there are other dimensions of utility that can create variations in the type of decision-making activities that occur. These variations include the number of utilities that exist for any one alternative, the quantitative-qualitative characteristics of each utility, and the discrepancy between the desired utility of an alternative and its actual utility.

Number of Utilities. When there is a single purpose or utility that an alternative is meant to serve, decision making can proceed in a relatively linear fashion. The manager would simply rank alternatives according to each one's probability of meeting the utility goal. One way to do this would be to develop a scale of minimum utility requirements and then match each alternative against this standard. A graduate school of business, for example, might set a requirement of a 3.25 grade point average as the minimum standard for admission on that particular utility dimension. Admissions personnel would then compare applicants' academic records with this standard to determine whether they may be accepted.

When the number of utilities that an alternative must serve increases, the complexity of decision making increases proportionally. For instance, if acceptance to the graduate school also depends on students' scores on an admission test, adding the test scores to the grade point averages to determine qualification makes the task more difficult. If a student's test score and grade point average both fall above or below minimum standards, the decision is still relatively easy. But when the two scores diverge, the decision becomes more complex. In this situation a sliding scale is often used: the lower the grade point average the higher the test score must be and vice versa.

If at this point a third utility dimension were to be added to the admission decision, such as an undergraduate degree in business administration, the decision would become still more complex. When decisions become this complicated, certain techniques, such as linear programing, may be utilized, which make the manager's task easier. These techniques will be discussed in the following chapter.

Quantitative-Qualitative Characteristics. Although with the addition of each utility requirement the decision sequence becomes more complex, there are clear-cut methods of dealing with this complexity as long as the utilities can be measured on a quantitative basis. The worst that can happen is that the various utilities will cancel one another out and no alternative will be satisfactory.

In situations that demand qualitative utility requirements, however, the decision process is more complicated. Suppose, for instance, that admission to the graduate school also depends on such qualifications as having a keen mind, getting along well with others, and having perseverance. Now in addition to the problems of comparing candidates on the quantitative standards, the decision maker also has the problem of comparing candidates on these more subjective standards. Even the most sophisticated computer techniques cannot handle subjective decision making, so the judgment of the decision maker must be relied upon here. Fortunately the human mind (often subconsciously) is very good at this kind of mental juggling.

Desired Versus Actual Utility. The degree to which one must search for alternatives will depend in part on the standards of utility that have been established and how far above present standards the desired state is. If the graduate school in the example above is willing to accept applicants with a 2.5 grade point average and a 50 percent score on the admissions test, it will not have to search far to find new students. But if they set their standards at a 3.5 grade point average and a score of 80 percent on the test, it will have a much narrower field of applicants from which to choose and the recruitment personnel may have to do a considerable amount of searching to find qualified future students.

The more discrepancy there is between the standard that is set and the existing standard, the more likely it is that the complex sequence of decision-making models, described earlier, will need to be employed. A major drawback of setting expectations very high is that one may end up settling for an alternative that is worse than ones previously rejected. For instance, if the school sets its admission standards too high, not enough students may qualify. Finally, when the search is extended, the school may find that the next-best-qualified students have already enrolled in other schools.

The Environment of Decisions

Decisions are not made in a vacuum. To begin with, a considerable amount of information must be processed when a decision is made. This information, even if processed unconsciously, comes from the environment. The search for alternatives and the implementation of the final choice also occur within an environmental context. Further, it is often the case that decisions are made by groups of individuals rather than by a single person. Thus, for the manager as a decision maker, there are external, organizational, and group considerations that influence his or her decision-making activities and the eventual choices that will be made.

The concluding section of this chapter is concerned with the ways that groups and organizations influence decision making and how decision making, in turn, can affect the functioning of groups and organizations.

Group Decision Making

The increasing complexity of most organizations often requires that a number of people with different areas of expertise work together to arrive at decisions. Because major decisions, such as moving a plant or opening a new branch office, typically affect a large part of the whole organization, the people who will be affected often are asked to be part of the decision-making process. In addition, the organization will probably seek the people who can offer advice about labor, material, and transportation costs, make analyses of the financial and environmental impact, and many others who can contribute to the decision. Bringing people together in a group decision-making situation appears to be a common and highly visible characteristic of modern management (13).

Committees. One of the major organizational vehicles for group decision making is the committee. Some committees are temporary, or ad hoc, organized expressly for the purpose of making a single decision; others are standing committees with continuing responsibility for decisions in a particular area. Most major corporations have a management committee, as a subunit of the board of directors, which meets regularly to make ongoing decisions about the operation of the organization.

Many management theorists and members of organizations greatly dispute the use and value of committees. There is little argument that committees are costly, both in money and time. A meeting of five executives whose salaries average $50,000 a year costs the organization nearly $150 per hour, and this does not include the loss incurred by time spent away from other activities. At these prices the committee had better be producing some significant results. Often, however, the task direction of the group is diverted by maintenance functions—waiting for all members to arrive, reading minutes, and so on—or by personal affairs and role-playing tactics.

But despite the drawbacks of time and money diversions, committees do produce positive results. In situations where no one person has all the information or knowledge required to make a decision, committees are virtually indispensable. And studies have shown that groups make more accurate decisions than do individuals acting alone (14). Also, when implementation is likely to cause major problems, a group decision has a better chance of gaining acceptance among diverse factions of the organization than does a one-person decision (15).

Increasing the Effectiveness of Group Decisions. Two phenomena that tend to decrease the effectiveness of group decision making are **domination** of the group by an individual and **groupthink.**

Groups are better than individuals at making decisions because group members share information and provide feedback to one another on the ideas that are generated. But if the group is dominated by one person, these advantages disappear. Domination occurs through the use of one or more of the power bases suggested in Chapter 16; following are some examples:

1. One member talks continuously, overriding all interjections until everyone else is worn down.

2. The boss is chairing the meeting and opens the discussion by saying, "This looks good to me, how does the group feel about it?"

3. One person is sent to the committee meeting with instructions from the boss to get a certain point of view adopted.

The problem of domination cannot be entirely removed, but certain actions by group members can lessen its effects. If you are the chairperson it is wise not to let your preferred solution be known at the beginning; or better yet, come to the meeting without a preconceived best solution and keep an open mind. Being a good listener and drawing others out so that all members participate is a second way to reduce the possibility of domination. A third way is to indicate a strong interest in having the group come up with a good solution (16).

In Chapter 10, in the discussion of group cohesiveness, it was demonstrated how people who work together closely or who have adopted the norms and values of the group typically begin to think and act alike. When group members continually reinforce one another's thinking regarding certain issues or decisions in order to avoid disunity, a degree and type of cohesion is created that destroys the group's ability to freely exchange ideas. This type of decision making is called **groupthink.**

One of the most famous examples of groupthink is that which produced the decision to invade Cuba in 1961, and which has since come to be known as the Bay of Pigs disaster. The Kennedy administration was just under way, and the group (consisting of select members of Kennedy's staff, the CIA, and the military) was anxious to prove how well they all agreed on basic policy. Also, since the power position of everyone present was considerable, no one was inclined to voice any negative sentiments he may have had about the plan. Consequently, the decision escalated in certainty although biased by scanty and inaccurate information. The result of the decision was extremely costly and nearly disastrous.

One way to avoid groupthink is to make certain the communication channels are open to the outside, solicit and accept negative information, and be objectively critical of proposals once they have been formulated. Kennedy learned a valuable lesson from the Bay of Pigs decision. In subsequent group decision-making sessions he always appointed someone to take the role of devil's advocate, to search out other information and question the direction being taken. This technique produced a much more accurate decision in the case of the Cuban missile crisis (17).

Decision Making and the Organization

Organizations exert influence on decision-making procedures in many ways, but in the largest sense they do so because they constitute, for the most part, the environment in which decisions take place. At the same time, decision making influences the organization because it is through decisions that the organization is created and infused with direction and structure. How well managers perform the decision-making task determines how well the organization accomplishes its goals. The extent and nature of goal accomplishment, in turn, determines the type and magnitude of decisions that need to be made.

Organizational decision making is a flow of events or activities intended to institute action toward certain goals. Decisions represent the link between thought and action; they are the activities by which ideas are translated into prescriptions for behavior. Decision making breathes life into the organizational structure by joining today, tomorrow, and yesterday together through a continuing sequence of action. And through decisions the organizational structure is both differentiated and integrated.

Differentiation. As pointed out in earlier discussions, decision-making responsibilities closely follow the line prescribed by the formal organizational structure. But the two do not always run exactly parallel. The formal structure is a basis for determining work relationships and activities. Decision making may be viewed as a pattern of overlays that modify this structure (see Figure 13–7). From this perspective it can be seen that decision-making patterns help emphasize the horizontal and diagonal relationships within the structure and not just the vertical, hierarchical relationships. For instance, there is a considerable emphasis on work-flow (horizontal) relationships in any examination of organizational decision-making sequences.

One of the most pronounced differences between the decision-making structure and the formal organizational structure has to do with the use of the specialist. Authority in the organization typically resides in line managers. And the higher up the manager is in the line, the greater is his or her authority. Specialists are usually in staff positions or in subordinate, nonmanagerial roles. But in increasingly complex organizations, line managers cannot make all the necessary decisions. The result is that more

FIGURE 13–7
A decision overlay.

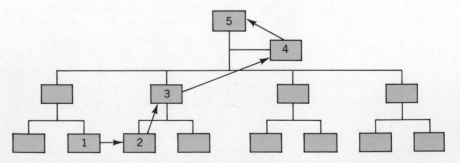

Positions 1 and 2 might be subunits of engineering and production. These employees get together on a product adjustment and send their decision to the marketing executive (3), who in turn takes it up with the president's administrative assistant (4), who in turn takes it to the president (5).

and more decisions must be made by the people who have specialized knowledge. This situation creates increasing tension between the authority figures as designated by the organizational structure and the specialists who carry the power of expertise (18).

One way that organizations are likely to resolve this tension is by restructuring the organization to better accommodate the specialists. A model for this type of reorganization might be the collegial structure, in which authority is diffused throughout the system and located in groups that have expertise in their given field. Administration in this case becomes a support function for expert groups. The project, or matrix, form of organization is a further example of this trend (19).

Integration. A somewhat opposite approach to viewing decision making is that it may be seen as an integrator of the many forces both internal and external to the organization. Much of this integrating function of decision making was covered, from a slightly different perspective, in earlier sections dealing with search procedures and environmental considerations. Too, we have seen how people from various departments within the organization are often integrated into one or more decision-making groups. Since the consequences of decisions can have far-reaching effects on nearly every area of an organization—from determining what goals to seek, to allocating resources, to producing the final output—it is easy to see why decision making is considered a major integrator of organizational activities.

How the Organizational Structure Affects Decision Making. Earlier in this chapter it was stated that nonprogramed decisions typically are made near the top of the organizational hierarchy and programed decisions are made at the bottom. While this is generally true, there are other aspects of the organizational structure that also bear on who makes what kinds of decisions. These aspects include technology, organization design, and managerial style.

Computer technology often increases the separation of programed and nonprogramed decisions by centering nonprogramed decision making in the upper regions of the organization and relegating programed decision making to the lower echelons. But it is also the case that the computer makes more information available throughout the hierarchy so that more decisions can take place on the bottom levels. The pattern of centralization or decentralization in the organization also has significant impact on where in the hierarchy decisions are made. In one sense, decentralization means that nonprogramed decision making is delegated to lower hierarchical levels. Recent studies indicate that decentralization is the most effective organizational structure in environments that are turbulent. And since the environments surrounding a great many organizations seem to be heading toward increasing change and diversification, it is possible that more and more decisions will take place on lower levels of organizations.

Decision-making responsibility is also influenced by the type of work roles assigned to the various organizational groups. Where the staff function is to give information only, line managers (who have formal authority) make all the decisions. But where staff experts are given decision-making authority, the responsibility for decisions will be shared. In many complex organizations it is difficult to distinguish between line and staff because as information becomes more centralized the staff people that control information become decision makers for the line.

In organizational structures that have boundary-spanning positions, such as salespeople, recruiters, and purchasing agents, decision-making responsibility may also be decentralized. In a benign and stable environment the voices of boundary-spanning personnel may not need to be heard very loudly; everyone understands and knows what the environment is like. However, in highly dynamic environments where there is constant tension between external and internal forces, these positions take on increased importance and those who hold them often have the power to affect decision making.

The way the organizational structure channels information flow also determines who will make decisions. For instance, the manager who gets the information first is the one who will make a decision about it. Also, the manager who has access to the *most* information is usually in the best decision-making position. Thus, in setting up an organizational structure for channeling the flow of information, one is also creating the organization's decision makers.

On the other hand, if managing is a process of decision making, then as more and more people are given decision-making responsibilities, the organization may end up with more managers than employees. Too, every manager may find that it is necessary to check with every other manager before making any decision or taking any new course of action. If approval is required from a number of other sections, the manager will probably discover that while any one of these groups can say "No," none can give an unqualified "Yes." Even when approval is obtained, it means only that the manager may proceed to the next phase of the operation before needing to seek approval again.

Such fragmentation not only leads to frustration for the manager, but also to conservative decisions. The more people who must add information or approve the process, the more people there are who have to be pleased and the more unlikely it is that the decision will depart from tradition. The advantage of fragmentation is that it can work fairly well as a control device. The chances of mistakes or bad decisions are reduced if a manager is required to seek the approval of many others before he or she can proceed with implementation (20).

The Frustration of Fragmentation

A friend of mine came in just before noon and said, "Let's go to lunch."

"Fine," I said.

When we were finally seated and had our food in front of us, my friend surprised me by stating, "I just quit."

"Why?" was my immediate response.

"Well, a lot of things I guess. But it all boils down to a general atmosphere. Let me give you a primary example. Eighteen months ago I was asked to study and revise the promotion form for managers. Now that is really a big deal. But I didn't realize how big until I began. I spent six months just trying to find out who used the form and what they did with it. No one wanted to tell me.

"Revising the form took very little time, but then it really got tough. I tried to 'sell' my new form. No one, not even the head of industrial relations, can approve that form on his own. I had to go back to each user and get approval. Each one wanted changes that the others then needed to approve.

"I haven't done anything else during the last six months but work on that form. This morning I got the last approval and told the boss 'I quit.' "

Chapter Review

This chapter has introduced the topic of managerial decision making, described models for three different types of decisions, and outlined a general model that suggested how most decisions actually are made. Taken into account were several variations in the decision-making process and the effects of the environment surrounding the decision maker. The specific terms and ideas developed in this chapter are as follows.

1. **Decision making** is defined as all the thoughts and actions that lead up to a choice, including the choice itself.

2. Few decision makers follow the **scientific method,** which is a **prescriptive model** for making decisions, because rationality is bounded, or limited, by complexity, emotion, programed behavior, and limited choice. Rather, people make decisions based on **descriptive models,** which are descriptions of the behaviors that actually occur as decisions are made.

3. In addition to **bounded rationality,** four other types of rationality are identified:

a. **objective,** where all variables are available and measurable;

b. **subjective,** where people search for the best results possible given available resources;

c. **conscious,** where means and ends are consciously adjusted to one another;

d. **organizational,** concerned with reaching organizational goals; and

e. **personal,** concerned with reaching personal goals.

Note that these types of rationality are not mutually exclusive.

4. Three models of the decision-making process are the short sequence, the long sequence, and the complex sequence.

    a. **The short sequence**
- Environment supplies information;
  information tested against image.
- If congruent with image,
  store information.
- If information is incongruent,
  search image for stored alternative or program;
  adopt programed solution; make a choice; and
  take action.

    b. **The long sequence**
- Environment supplies information;
  information tested against image.
- If information is incongruent with image,
  search for alternatives;
  incorporate relevant alternatives into image;
  adopt an alternative as a solution; make a choice; and
  take action.

    c. **The complex sequence**
- Environment supplies information;
  information tested against image.
- If information is incongruent with image,
  search for alternatives.
- If search process fails,
  change image so it is compatible with alternatives;
  adopt satisfactory alternative; and
  take action.

5. The **image** consists of a person's world view, containing the totality of one's memory of events plus feelings, values, and attitudes.

6. Everyone constantly *tests* or compares information, received as stimuli, against the image. Comparisons that are incongruent are defined as *problems*.

7. **Problem definition** is difficult for several reasons
    a. the image may be partly subconscious
    b. information may be incomplete or inaccurate because observations have not isolated all the relevant stimuli
    c. the image may not be sufficiently accurate to permit relevant observations
    d. symptoms may be treated as problems

8. **Satisficing** is searching for and finding alternatives that are acceptable enough to achieve satisfactory outcomes. Most decision processes attempt to satisfice rather than to maximize.

9. **Evaluating alternatives** is a process of assessing the *probability* of occurrence of the outcome desired and measuring its value or *utility*.

10. **Selecting an alternative** involves making judgments about likely results, probability estimates, value judgments, and choice.

11. **A program** is an alternative that has previously achieved results. Programs include problem-solving techniques, procedures, methods, and other regularly used sets of actions.

12. A **programed decision** involves the choice of a stored program; an **unprogramed decision** involves the choice of new alternatives through the long sequence or complex decision process. Generally, the higher the managerial level, the more nonprogramed decisions are required.

13. **Linear search** for alternatives involves following a systematic, step-by-step path; **heuristic search** involves an unsystematic, random, trial-and-error search.

14. Whether or not an alternative can solve a problem depends on the degree to which its effects on the environment can be predicted. There are three conditions of environmental predictability:

   a. **certainty**, which means there is a 100 percent chance that the alternative selected will lead to predicted results

   b. **risk**, in which there is less than a 100 percent chance that a selected alternative will lead to predicted results

   c. **uncertainty**, which means that the variables are either unknown or so complex that no probability can be assigned to an alternative

15. **Group decisions** can be improved if no one individual is allowed to dominate the group and if **groupthink** is avoided. Groupthink means that members carry out decisions more in the interest of group solidarity than in accordance with sound decision-making practices. Dissonance is avoided in favor of maintaining cohesiveness.

16. Factors that affect who makes what kinds of decisions include:

   a. the **hierarchical position** (the higher the postion, the less programmed the decision)

   b. the **technology** (the greater the technology, the more likely it is that decisions will be centered in this technological core)

   c. *organization design* (the conscious decentralization of decision making or the assignment of integrative work to specialist groups)

17. The **fragmentation** of decision making (which means that many must approve an action but any one can veto it) acts as a control against mistakes; it also slows decisions and assures traditional behavior.

Discussion Questions

1. Comment on the implications of the following statement: "I shall find it convenient to take mild liberties with the English language by using 'decision making' as though it were synonomous with 'managing.'"

2. How do the prescriptive and descriptive models of decision making differ from each other?

3. What is meant by bounded rationality?

4. Describe the short, long, and complex decision-making sequences. Give examples of situations in which each sequence would be used.

5. How does the image affect one's ability to define problems and make decisions?

6. How are alternatives evaluated? What is the role of probability in evaluation and selection procedures?

7. Give examples of programed and nonprogramed decisions that you make in your everyday life.

8. Distinguish between linear and heuristic search procedures and give an example of each.

9. What does it mean to say that a condition of certainty exists in a decision-making environment? A condition of risk? A condition of uncertainty?

10. In what situations would you use a group to make a decision? Why? How would you avoid "groupthink"?

11. How can decision making create differentiation within the organizational structure? How does it create integration?

Involvement Activity

1. How well do you think you make decisions? Complete the test below, answer the questions that follow it, and then fill out the score sheet and see how you do.

Lost on the Moon

Your spaceship has just crash-landed on the moon. You were scheduled to rendezvous with a mother ship 200 miles away on the lighted surface of the moon, but the rough landing has ruined your ship and destroyed all the equipment on board, except for the 15 items listed to the side.

Your crew's survival depends on reaching the mother ship, so you must choose the most critical items available for the 200-mile trip. Your task is to rank the 15 items in terms of their importance for survival. Place number one by the most important item, number two by the second most important, and so on through number 15, the least important.

_____ Box of matches
_____ Food concentrate
_____ Fifty feet of nylon rope
_____ Parachute silk
_____ Solar-powered portable heating unit
_____ Two .45-caliber pistols
_____ One case of dehydrated milk
_____ Two 100-pound tanks of oxygen
_____ Stellar map (of the moon's constellation)
_____ Self-inflating life raft
_____ Magnetic compass
_____ Five gallons of water
_____ Signal flares
_____ First-aid kit containing injection needles
_____ Solar-powered FM receiver-transmitter

2. How did you decide on a ranking order for the items?

a. Did you have any criteria that helped you decide which items were useful and which were not? What were the criteria?

b. Did you mainly compare the items with one another or did you compare them against developed criteria?

c. Did you set up any methods for proceeding with your decision (such as ways of determining the most and the least important items)?

d. Did you change either your criteria or your methods as you went about making the decisions?

e. How confident are you that your answers are correct?

3. Before checking your answers, take the test again with a group of at least four other people. The group must reach consensus on the ranking of each item. Do not take votes but proceed by discussion until all participants are satisfied. Now look at how the group proceeded to make decisions by again answering the five questions listed above. Which answers, individual or group, do you think will be more accurate?

4. Fill out the scoring blank below and discuss the results with the other group members.

LOST on the MOON

Items	NASA's Reasoning	NASA's Ranks	Your Ranks	Error Points	Group Ranks	Error Points
Box of matches	No oxygen on moon to sustain flame; virtually worthless	15				
Food concentrate	Efficient means of supplying energy requirements	4				
Fifty feet of nylon rope	Useful in scaling cliffs, tying injured together	6				
Parachute silk	Protection from sun's rays	8				
Solar-powered portable heating unit	Not needed unless on dark side	13				
Two .45 caliber pistols	Possible means of self-propulsion	11				
One case of dehydrated Pet milk	Bulkier duplication of food concentrate	12				
Two 100-pound tanks of oxygen	Most pressing survival need	1				
Stellar map (of the moon's constellation)	Primary means of navigation	3				
Self-inflating life raft	CO_2 bottle in military raft may be used for propulsion	9				
Magnetic compass	Magnetic field on moon is not polarized; worthless for navigation	14				
Five gallons of water	Replacement for tremendous liquid loss on lighted side	2				
Signal flares	Distress signal when mother ship is sighted	10				
First-aid kit containing injection needles	Needles for vitamins, medicines, etc., will fit special aperture in NASA space suits	7				
Solar-powered FM receiver-transmitter	For communication with mother ship; but FM requires line-of-sight transmission and short ranges	5				

Total ———   ———

Error points are the absolute difference between your ranks and NASA's (disregard plus or minus signs).

Scoring for individuals:
0–25 = excellent
26–32 = good
33–45 = average
46–55 = fair

56–70 = poor
71–112 = very poor, suggests possible faking or use of earth-bound logic

14

The Decision Maker: Style and Method

In this chapter the subject of decision making in organizations is continued, but with emphasis on the person rather than on the process. We will explore the variety of decision styles and methods used by decision makers and develop some decision-making models in an attempt to show which methods work best in which situations.

The chapter begins with a discussion of how the image is formed, particularly the prescriptive, predictive, and descriptive models for decision making, and how theories develop. It goes on to describe different decision-making styles, especially how information is gathered and utilized, and finally, there is a comprehensive discussion of behavioral and quantitative decision methods.

The meeting in the bank's conference room was breaking up. The participants separated into twos and threes and went their different ways, some hurrying and some walking in a leisurely fashion. Two who were not hurrying were Jane Thompson and George Hernandez, the chief loan officer and the operations officer, respectively. These two have been with the bank a long time and are the senior managers directly below the executive vice-president.

George: "They really put it to us today."
Jane: "They sure did. That plan was very complete."
George: "You mean you understood what they were doing?"
Jane: "Not really; I can understand what they are driving at but not how they are going to do it."
George: "I can't figure out at all what they are doing to the f
Frankly, I don't trust that computer. How do I know w
doing or what Fred and his assistant are putting into i
Jane: "Well, it certainly sounded impressive. You sure
though, when you brought up the public relations a
seemed to stop them for a while."

George: "Yes, they just don't have a good feel for the whole situation. I guess we are going to end up doing it their way, but I still don't understand how they got there."

Going off in a different direction at a more lively pace were Fred Bonelli, the comptroller, and his assistant for operations analysis, Peggy Asher.

Peggy: "You said those people would be tough and you were right."
 Fred: "I sometimes think that Jane and George are scared to death of anything that is systematic. They seem to be able to come up with solutions but they don't think about how they got there."
Peggy: "That's true, but it really caught us cold when George brought up the public relations aspect. We hadn't planned for that in our analysis."
 Fred: "You know, George does that in meetings quite often. It's as if he sees the world differently from everyone else. I wonder how he does it? He sure keeps me on my toes."

Arthur Davis, the executive vice-president, mulled over the meeting as he went into his office. "I get the feeling that those people have a terrible time just talking to one another and I'm sure that no one understands what the other is saying," he mused to himself.

This chapter is about the musings of Arthur Davis. It shows that people approach decision making differently and that each uses different techniques and methods to arrive at decisions. No one style is necessarily better or worse than another—they are simply different. And it is these differences that make it hard for people to understand and trust one another (1).

Differences in decision-making styles and methods have become more pronounced in the past twenty years owing to the development of the computer and to the sophisticated decision methods that have grown out of computer technology. Most of these methods are highly structured and analytical in character. But the interest in methods has expanded to include not only these technical aspects but the behavioral methods and styles of the decision maker as well. This chapter will look first at the style of the decision maker and then at some of the behavioral and quantitative methods of decision making. The manager as a decision maker is illustrated in Figure 14–1.

Image Formation

Because decision making is a human activity (even computers rely on humans for their programing), it is not surprising that decisions are made in a variety of different ways. As seen in the last chapter, one of the major

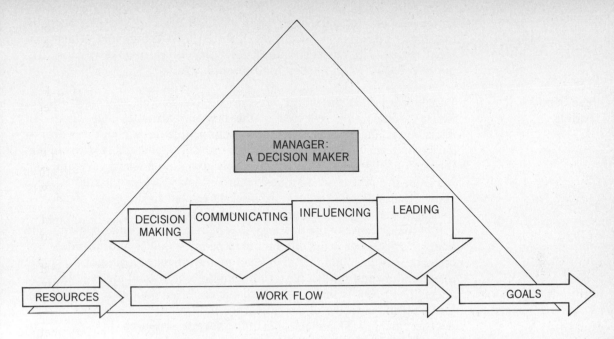

FIGURE 14–1
The manager as decision maker engages in decision making and carries out the decision through communicating, influencing, and leading.

causes of these differences is the different images, or mental models, that people have for viewing the world.

No two images are exactly alike. From birth, each of us continually experiences events that are recorded in the mind and recalled later as a means of interpreting the present. Education and training are methods of increasing the efficiency of experience because they enable people to draw on the cumulative experiences of others. Nevertheless, even these "second-hand experiences" are interpreted and understood through the person's own image. Images allow us to understand the nature of the world (descriptive), to predict events (predictive), and to develop ideas about how the world should be (prescriptive). These different parts of the image consist of ideas and feelings that represent, but that are not in fact, the world. One way of thinking about images is to consider them as models of reality. There is, then, a descriptive, predictive, and prescriptive model of reality in each person's mind.

A **model** is any representation of some aspect of reality whose purpose is to describe or explain why and how things are as they are. As a representation of reality, the model is always less complex than the total situation from which it is extracted. The best models are those that are simple enough to work with yet complete enough to accurately reflect that portion of reality that is desired.

Most mental models are **analog** models, which means that the object or symbol used to represent reality is not a copy of the original but is analogous to it. Diagrams (such as the boxes on an organization chart, which in no way resemble the people they represent) or verbal models (like the word telephone), are examples of analog models. This book is also an analog model because it substitutes words for the actions that occur in managing. The analog model is well suited for the studying of management because its subject matter, the behavior of people, is most frequently described and understood through words.

Prescriptive Models

People learn what the world *ought* to be like as well as what it *is* like. These "oughts" are reflected in the person's attitudes and values. In decision making, **prescriptive models** help people determine the worth of various alternatives by serving as comparison standards. For example, the person who values freedom highly is going to choose a very different job from the person who values security highly. Research studies have shown that individual values are directly related to the types of choices that managers make in all areas of their jobs (2).

A major cause of the difficulty that people have in understanding one another's decisions is the differences in people's values and attitudes. For instance, Porter found that high-level managers place a greater emphasis on autonomy and self-actualization than do middle- and lower-level managers. The result is that top-level managers often complain that those in lower positions in the organization are not willing to take risks in their decision making (3). Values also differ between cultures. In which countries of the world do you think people would be most likely to make decisions that resemble those made by people in the United States? Which cultures are likely to be very different?

Prescriptive models are popular in management theory because they indicate the "proper" way to manage. Thus, when a certain span of control is suggested as optimum for a particular situation, the theorist is offering a prescriptive model. Prescription is inevitable and desirable, but difficulties may occur when the models are based on incomplete images. For example, a prescription as to how to motivate employees based on positive results with retail salesclerks may not be valid when applied to engineers or production-line workers. Not only does one have to be careful about generalizing models across situations, but the model maker must also be aware that a prescription that worked in the past may not work in the present. Motivational techniques, for instance, are different today than they were fifty years ago as a result of changes in the composition of the work force, altered cultural values, and other factors. Fifty years from now, the motivational techniques of today will no longer be valid.

Predictive Models

A **predictive model** helps the decision maker determine which of a number of alternative actions will work best. The use of models to predict what will happen if certain changes are made is extremely helpful to managers as they try to determine appropriate courses of action. Decisions made without predictive models lack foresight and have no rationale. Managerial action is based on a certain amount of planning, which includes estimates of the future outcome of the action.

A major difficulty with predictive models is that they sometimes assume a simple or unilateral relationship between variables rather than a complex system of interaction. Thus when a manager tries to apply the model, he or she finds that predictions may be incorrect because some important interaction has been neglected or its significance underestimated. A further difficulty with predictive models is that they often do not "look like" the reality they are intended to predict and are therefore hard for the person to understand. For instance, supply and demand curves are not good descriptions of what the world of commerce looks like even though they are good predictors of future behavior within that world.

Descriptive Models

A **descriptive model** of the world is an image a person carries in his or her mind of what the world looks like. This image is based on observation and classification of real-world phenomena and serves as a way of enabling the person to understand the ways that seemingly diverse pieces of the world fit together in some logical patterns. Descriptive models can be useful in explaining managerial behavior and in suggesting ways in which various aspects of managing can be investigated and measured. They do this by laying out in a systematic way precise descriptions of the variables that operate in given situations. We have seen how this works in the decision-making models described in the previous chapter.

It is difficult to make a decision if there is no existing image related to the decision-making situation. For instance, a new employee, although possessing the specific skills to perform the job, may be unable to make effective decisions until an image has developed of the organization.

On the other hand, decisions are also made difficult by an image that is too complex. When a simple decision is called for and the person immediately sees all the possible ramifications, action becomes nearly impossible. Descriptive models may be seen as ranging along a continuum. At one end is the image held by the technical specialist, which is deep but not broad. This person's decisions are technically accurate but fail to provide for the consequences to other parts of the organization. At the other end of the continuum is the "academic" person's image, which contains much information and awareness of so many consequences that the person is unable to make any decision at all. To be effective, then, managers must be able to operate somewhere between these two extremes. They must have a wide-range view of the consequences of a decision but be able to know when to cut off information gathering and proceed to make the decision (4).

Comparing Models

The differences between descriptive, predictive, and prescriptive models are synthesized in Figure 14–2. As an example of the relationship that exists between these three models, consider the descriptive statement "People working together over time tend to form informal social groups." On the basis of this statement, a manager could predict that if he or she assigns an assortment of people to a task that involves working together, an informal group will form. Further, if the manager wanted to create a greater degree of cohesiveness among employees, he or she might apply the prescriptive model and assign people to work on a group task.

FIGURE 14-2
Descriptive, predic-
tive, and prescriptive
models.

Description: A→B (condition A leads to outcome B)
Prediction: If A, then B (if A exists, then B will follow)
Prescription: If B, then A (if B is desired, do A)

All three of these models are part of the manager's image, and in decision making they form the comparison against which alternatives are evaluated. The manager is often unaware of using one or another model because thought sequences are often unconscious. It is to try to develop managers' consciousness about how and why these models work that the following material is presented. For without knowledge of when and where to use the models, managers cannot make their decisions clear to others—and often, not even to themselves.

The Image as Theory

In many ways the words *model* and *theory* are interchangeable. People do not learn by their experiences alone; they learn by analyzing their experiences. And to analyze efficiently and effectively they must have rules for analysis. This is theory building. You can see how the relationship between theory and action works by referring to Figure 14-2. Theory is descriptive of relationships that can, or do, exist; it is predictive and it can also be prescriptive. Theory and experience are two phases of the same cycle of learning and problem solving, and each relies on the other to complete the cycle. Without theory, experience has no meaning; and without experience, theory has no relevance (5).

A **theory** is a set of statements that describes and explains behavior in ways that help one understand, predict, and control action. This is the basis of scientific inquiry. Insofar as a theory is descriptive of actual relationships, it is factual (or accurate) but it is not itself a fact. The steps in building a theory are to identify the facts, relate them to one another, and test the relationship to see if it is factual.

Identifying Facts. A **fact** is an empirically verifiable observation based on the careful examination of events and stated in such a way that any person who observes the occurrence can confirm the fact. Examples of facts are such statements as "Birds fly," "People work in organizations," and "The interest rate has risen in the past five years." Statements of fact must be precise so that others can verify their accuracy. Because of this preciseness, theories are often expressed in the form of mathematics or in other kinds of scientific notation. Words are also used, but both the words used and the order they follow must be as precise as a mathematical notation.

Discovering Relationships Between Facts. Theories are statements of relationships between facts that are ordered and classified in such ways that they represent a body of knowledge. These relationships are then subjected to repeated tests to determine whether, and under what conditions, they hold true. An example of a theoretical statement based on one of the facts noted above would be "People work in organizations in order to satisfy their financial needs." In order to be an accurate theoretical statement of relationships, however, all of the terms used must be clear and concise. In the above example "work" and "needs" are particularly vague terms and are open to varying interpretations. The statement also implies causation; that is, in order to get people to work, organizations must satisfy people's financial needs.

The theorist starts by putting an observed relationship into words. For example, a theorist interested in motivation may observe that some people engage in a considerable amount of activity directed toward organizational goals while others exhibit a minimum of such goal-centered activity. The observer may have some notions that explain these differences (from his or her image), but at present the notion is very general. It does, however, suggest some possible relationships. The next step, then, is to further define the relationship by making statements of observed behavior that might be associated with motivation. For example, "People who exhibit a great deal of organizational-goal-directed activity find that this activity satisfies their personal needs." These kinds of expanded statements are known as **hypotheses;** statements that clearly describe the proposed relationship.

Because these proposed, more specific relationships are deduced from the general relationship, the act of defining them is called **deductive reasoning.** To continue the example used above, the general relationship may be stated as "People will behave in a given manner if they perceive that such behavior will be rewarded." Deductive reasoning may produce the more specific statement that "A wage incentive program would be effective in motivating employee behavior."

Testing Relationships. When all the key words have been defined in measurable, or operational, terms and the relationships stated, the final step is to test the hypothesized relationships. If they are tested and not disproved, they may be called a theory. In the above example, an investigator would have to find ways to test whether people who are working in organizations satisfy their financial needs or, conversely, if when people's financial needs are *not* satisfied they stop working for the organization.

Although some attempts have been made to follow the research methods of the physical sciences, behavioral hypotheses have been tested more effectively by utilizing specially designed techniques that allow for the complexity and the unique problems associated with using people as subjects. In general, research designs for testing hypotheses in the behavioral sciences can be classified as the **observational,** the **survey,** and the **experimental** methods. The nature of the hypothesis provides a tentative explanation of the phenomena to be explored and directs the investigator toward the most appropriate kind of research.

1. *Observation.* The **observational method** of research design involves careful and objective gathering of data to produce an accurate description of what is observed. No attempt is made to control or manipulate the variables. This technique has simplicity as its major advantage both in design and in execution, and the researcher can often draw conclusions based on observed cause-and-effect relationships. However, because observation is in-depth exploration of one particular case, generalizations cannot be made and applied to other cases. A second difficulty is that every person, depending on his or her image, sees different things in a situation. The image biases the study to the extent that the investigator "finds" the data that fit the hypothesis. In addition, the observer inadvertently changes the situation just by being there. The observation method is used primarily in exploratory research and in preliminary investigations to clarify relationships.

2. *Surveys.* The **survey method** collects data through questionnaires, patterned interview forms, or other instruments that are prepared in advance of the study to permit the systematic collection of specific information. This technique is a relatively simple method for collecting a large amount of data and permits considerable quantification. It can be used to test hypotheses regarding associations but gives no clues as to causal relationships. Furthermore, it measures the perceptions and attitudes of respondents rather than their actual behavior. Too, because the survey usually involves a sample of a population rather than the entire population, the results may be generalized to the population only if the sample is representative. Other potential distortions may arise from interviewer bias, a lack of accuracy and clarity of the instrument, or the unwillingness or inability of the respondents to reply accurately and honestly.

3. *Experiments.* The one research technique that can determine the relationship between cause and effect is the **experimental method,** or laboratory experiment. The experimenter controls the environment in a test area, varies certain independent variables, and notes the changes that occur in other, dependent, variables. The drawback to this method is that in creating the experimental conditions, the investigator must put people into artificial situations and assume that they behave there as they would in the real world, an assumption that is not altogether accurate. Furthermore, subjects are hard to find for these kinds of experiments, so the social researcher often must resort to the use of animals or college students over which the experimenter has some form of control. The transferability of findings from these special experimental conditions to the world of formal organizations may be dubious.

As the manager observes relationships about specific phenomena, he or she incorporates the findings into theories through a logical process known as **inductive reasoning,** or reasoning that progresses from the specific to the general. The processes of science involve a continual elaboration of concepts through induction; through the deduction of hypotheses from the developing concepts; through testing descriptive hypotheses by means of an appropriate research design; and through the incorporation of newly tested hypotheses into a theory.

**Management:
Science or Art?**

Science is an approach to observing the world that leads to verifiable statements about relationships. No matter how systematic a body of information may be, it is not a science if it begins with "self-evident" propositions and ends with deductions from these; nor is it a science if its aim is to gain converts for a cause. The primary purpose of scientific investigation is rational understanding of things, events, and behaviors.

The function of a science of management would be to empirically examine the behavior of managing and to assemble the knowledge so gained into sets of statements that would help managers make more effective choices. Making the choices and implementing them is practice, and there is indeed art involved; but the sets of expectations that provide the criteria for making the choices derive from theory based on careful scientific investigation.

Management, then, is both a science and an art. The problem with the present stage of development of management theory is that there is a host of competing, overlapping, and occasionally vague notions that confound the data and sometimes conflict with one another to the extent of canceling themselves out.

JOHNSON HAS A REAL FLARE FOR DECISION MAKING, DOESN'T HE?

Decision-Making Styles

People differ in their decision-making styles partly as a result of individual differences in images discussed above and partly as a result of the variations in the decision situation discussed in the previous chapter. Thus, different people will tend to emphasize different steps in the process, or implement the steps in a variety of ways. The following discussion is intended to highlight these differences and to indicate the conditions under which one style may be more appropriate than another. This discussion will follow the three stages of decision making indicated by Simon: intelligence activity, design activity, and choice.

Intelligence Activity

Intelligence activity involves observing what is going on and searching out information about what has been observed. For example, much of the educational process is aimed at helping students observe more variables in the environment so that they will be better decision makers. What happens, though, is that because knowledge is so specialized, a student of chemistry "sees" much more in a chemical reaction than does a psychology student. The psychology student, in turn, will observe many more variables operating in a group situation than will the chemistry student. Expertise, whether in chemistry, psychology, selling, or any other field, is partially a matter of knowing what to observe. In an organization filled with many different types of experts, it is inevitable that people will observe phenomena quite differently.

Collecting Information. Some people are much more concerned with collecting information than are others. In organizations, it is generally the staff groups that are information collectors. Accountants, for example, are good collectors, as are other personnel charged with auditing or controlling another group. Some people enjoy the information-collecting stage; in fact, some people would rather collect information than do anything else. Some researchers and scientists, for instance, spend a lifetime collecting information and leave the application of their findings to others. In most organizations, where success depends on utilizing information, the collectors must be able to know when to stop gathering and start processing what they have learned. As mentioned earlier, it is often the case that the more information one has, the greater the feeling that any action at all could lead to undesirable outcomes.

Research into information gathering and processing shows that people have an inverted-U-shaped curve for handling information. By looking at Figure 14–3, we can see that the complexity of a person's response increases as information becomes more complex, but only to a certain point. When the complexity of information reaches very high levels, be-

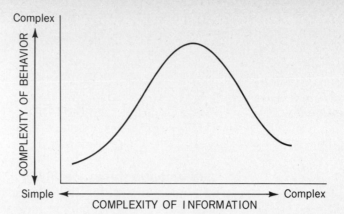

FIGURE 14–3
Information-response
curve.

havior becomes increasingly simple because the person is overloaded and unable to act (6).

Categorizing Information. Making sense out of information is at least as important as collecting it. People learn to interpret information through experience, education, and training. Thus, the chemistry student not only will notice the variables at work in a chemical reaction but will attach meanings to these variables as well. In organizations, the advantage of having experts who are trained to interpret data in specific fields is that complex problems can be solved by collaborating and pooling knowledge. No one person can acquire the expertise necessary to handle the entire range of information that most organizations deal with.

The way in which information is brought together will vary considerably depending on the type of information, on the ability of the person or group, and on the nature of the required outcome. Figure 14–4 illustrates three possible sets of connections that can be made in categorizing information. In Level 1, a simple serial connection is made between A, B, C, and D. In Level 2, the person must relate B, C, and D to A. And in Level 3, the person must interrelate all four variables.

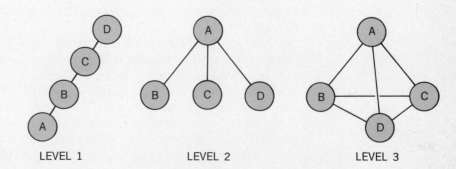

FIGURE 14–4
Three levels of information structuring.

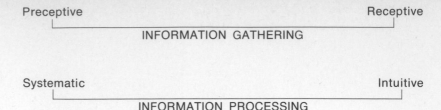

FIGURE 14–5
Information gathering
and processing styles
in decision making.

Information-Gathering Styles. McKenney and Keen have developed a model of decision styles that includes two dimensions: how individuals gather information and how they process it. This model, illustrated in Figure 14–5, further categorizes the styles into two types of information gatherers, the **preceptive** and the **receptive,** and two types of information processors, the **systematic** and the **intuitive.** In common with other continua in this book, these are idealized extremes and not necessarily descriptive of any particular individual (7).

Preceptive persons use *concepts* to filter information as it is received. They look for consistency with or deviations from their mental concepts (image). In this way the preceptive gatherers are able to quickly identify problems. Receptive individuals are more open to information that does not fit their existing image. They collect it for later processing rather than filter it as it is received. Both styles have their advantages and their faults. Preceptive persons often miss important details, and receptive individuals may fail to see how the information they have fits with other concepts.

Design Activity

The design-activity stage in the decision-making process is concerned with evaluating information. It consists of using the information to define the problem and to develop alternatives for resolving it. Design activity requires critical judgment in order to develop, evaluate, and reduce the number of alternatives.

People differ substantially in the way they evaluate information. Some of those holding staff positions in organizations largely ignore evaluation. Either they are asked for information only, or they are not knowledgeable enough about operating problems to make an evaluation. In these instances it is the line manager's responsibility to evaluate information.

Among those who do evaluate information, there are, as mentioned earlier, systematic processors and intuitive processors. Systematics have well-organized minds with clear methods of approaching the problem. They are likely to proceed logically through a series of steps until they have an answer. Systematics come closest to using a rational, scientific approach to decision making. Intuitives, on the other hand, tend to use a trial-and-error approach. They simply select the most obvious alternative and test that one first. If that fails, they move on to the next, and then the next, and so on until a satisfactory approach is found. Intuitives find it difficult to describe their methods since they often change from one technique to another when making decisions (8).

McKenney and Keen go on to show that different styles of information processing and evaluation are appropriate in different parts of an organization. For example, a preceptive-systematic approach is more suited to the areas of production or statistics than is a preceptive-intuitive approach, which is appropriate to the position of sales manager. An auditor may be a receptive-systematic; a salesperson, a preceptive-intuitive. Often these two types of people have trouble communicating. Intuitives may distrust systematics, and systematics think intuitives are much too sloppy in their methods (9).

Choice

People also differ according to the extent to which they are willing or able to make choices. The act of choosing requires a commitment on the part of an individual, and to many people, commitments are uncomfortable. As the time for choice nears, this discomfort often leads to vacillation among alternatives or to a postponement of the decision (10). Procrastinators will put things off as long as they can. Others may rapidly select a convenient alternative and put their choice into immediate action. As with anything else, the extremes on either side of this dimension are to be avoided. Choosing an alternative should not be so traumatic that decisions never get made, nor should it be so hasty that the wrong decisions are made.

Behavioral Decision Methods

Decision making is a behavior, and like all behavior, it can be changed and improved. Attempts to improve people's decision-making techniques generally have proceeded in two directions: examining the existing problem-solving sequence and suggesting ways to make it more effective; and developing new methods of problem solving by increasing people's use of creativity and inventiveness. DeBono has described traditional decision methods as characterized by **vertical thinking** and creative or innovative methods as representative of horizontal or **lateral thinking.** Both are necessary thinking processes, but each has different purposes. Vertical thinking proceeds systematically and logically to a conclusion; horizontal thinking is often not direct or logical, but it inspires imaginative and diverse solutions to problems (11).

Problem Solving

A *problem* has been defined as the difference between the existing and the expected state. But rarely do people stop to clearly describe the *nature* of the problem. And while the focus is on problem *solving,* it is often problem *finding* that is the more difficult endeavor and the one that requires the greatest amount of time. The complete problem-solving sequence is illustrated in Figure 14–6. The sequence is divided into two

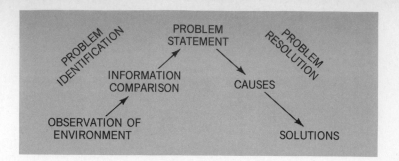

FIGURE 14–6
The problem-solving sequence.

major parts: **problem identification,** which consists of observation and comparison and which leads to a problem statement; and **problem resolution,** which proceeds from the problem statement by first determining the cause of the problem and then finding a solution by choosing among alternatives. Each of these steps involves methods that can increase the effectiveness of the entire sequence.

Receiving Information. The first step in problem identification is becoming aware of the variables that are involved. This process is not as easy as it may seem to be. As discussed in Chapter 8, all incoming stimuli are filtered by the brain to sort out those that are relevant. The guide for this filter is the image. Those signals that are foreign, contrary, or upsetting to the image tend to be ignored unless they are exceptionally strong. People who have especially keen powers of observation, such as those ascribed to Sherlock Holmes in the boxed insert on pages 380–381, are able to identify variables that others will miss. Some of the ways to improve information gathering appear below (12).

1. *Withhold Judgment.* The major reason observations fail to be recorded in the image is that they are prejudged as nonuseful. One technique for recording information without judging it is to ask, "What is this information useful for?" rather than, "Is this information useful?" Imagine the difference in the type of information that will be received by two managers who start investigating a situation with the following statements:
Manager One: "What happened here?"
Manager Two: "Whose fault is this?"

2. *Ask "Why?"* One way to obtain information is simply to ask for it. But it must be asked for objectively, as seen above. While this seems to be a fairly obvious prescription, many people fail to ask for the information they need because they do not want to appear ignorant. Students rarely ask questions in class even when they do not understand the material because they are afraid they will be considered dumb. Even when the information is known, asking "Why?" can produce more data or a different

view of the situation. The point is that a questioning attitude produces information while a knowledgeable attitude blocks off information.

3. *Use the Image.* Rarely does the situation organize itself in a manner useful for analysis (events occur chronologically and not by category). The image helps relate data to one another and to fit discrete bits of information into recognizable categories.

Comparison. Once received, information is compared with the image. The purpose of the comparison process is to clearly and concisely specify the problem. A comparison can lead to one of three situations:

1. *Development of Further Facts.* Secondary or related information is often derived as a result of comparing facts with the image or with other sources. For instance, observations of a balance sheet lead to the development of financial ratios. These ratios are then interpreted to determine whether a problem exists.

2. *Congruence.* When the expected and actual situations are seen to be in alignment, the person perceives no problem.

3. *Incongruence.* If the facts deviate from the image or from the expected state as set forth elsewhere, a problem is recognized and the person must then find out its nature.

One useful approach to defining and specifying problems is to make the degree of incongruence explicit. Some kind of checklist, such as that shown in Figure 14–7, might be helpful. The first step is to state explicitly one's expectations, images of what ought to be, or standards (column 2), by noting what is expected; where, when, and how it is to occur; and who is to be involved (column 1). The next step is to determine actual outcomes (column 3), compare them with the standard, and note deviations (column 4). A summary of each deviation (column 5) will then help to clarify the situation.

1 Dimensions of the Standard	2 Statement of the Standard	3 Actual Outcomes	4 Nature of Deviation	5 Problem Statement
What				
Where				
When				
How				
Who				
Why				

FIGURE 14–7
A problem definition checklist.

An Excerpt from "The Cardboard Box"

by Sir Arthur Conan Doyle

In choosing a few typical cases which illustrate the remarkable mental qualities of my friend, Sherlock Holmes, I have endeavoured, so far as possible, to select those which presented the minimum of sensationalism, while offering a fair field for his talents. It is, however, unfortunately, impossible entirely to separate the sensational from the criminal, and a chronicler is left in the dilemma that he must either sacrifice details which are essential to his statement, and so give a false impression of the problem, or he must use matter which chance, and not choice, has provided him with. With this short preface I shall turn to my notes of what proved to be a strange, though a peculiarly terrible, chain of events.

It was a blazing hot day in August. Baker Street was like an oven, and the glare of the sunlight upon the yellow brickwork of the house across the road was painful to the eye. It was hard to believe that these were the same walls which loomed so gloomily through the fogs of winter. Our blinds were half-drawn, and Holmes lay curled upon the sofa, reading and re-reading a letter which he had received by the morning post. For myself, my term of service in India had trained me to stand heat better than cold, and a thermometer at 90 was no hardship. But the morning paper was uninteresting. Parliament had risen. Everybody was out of town, and I yearned for the glades of the New Forest or the shingle of Southsea. A depleted bank account had caused me to postpone my holiday, and as to my companion, neither the country nor the sea presented the slightest attraction to him. He loved to lie in the very centre of five millions of people, with his filaments stretching out and running through them, responsive to every little rumor or suspicion of unsolved crime. Appreciation of nature found no place among his many gifts, and his only change was when he turned his mind from the evil-doer of the town to track down his brother of the country.

Finding that Holmes was too absorbed for conversation I had tossed aside the barren paper and, leaning back in my chair, I fell into a brown study. Suddenly my companion's voice broke in upon my thoughts.

"You are right, Watson," said he. "It does seem a most preposterous way of settling a dispute."

"Most preposterous!" I exclaimed, and then suddenly realizing how he had echoed the inmost thought of my soul, I sat up in my chair and stared at him in blank amazement.

"What is this, Holmes?" I cried. "This is beyond anything which I could have imagined."

He laughed heartily at my perplexity.

"You remember," said he, "that some little time ago when I read you the passage in one of Poe's sketches in which a close reasoner follows the unspoken thoughts of his companion, you were inclined to treat the matter as a mere *tour-de-force* of the author. On my remarking that I was constantly in the habit of doing the same thing you expressed incredulity."

"Oh, no!"

"Perhaps not with your tongue, my dear Watson, but certainly with your eyebrows. So when I saw you throw down your paper and enter upon a train of thought, I was very happy to have the opportunity of reading it off, and

Source: *The Complete Sherlock Holmes* (Garden City, N.Y.: Garden City Publishing Company, 1938), pp. 1043–1046.

eventually of breaking into it, as a proof that I had been *en rapport* with you.''

But I was still far from satisfied. ''In the example which you read to me,'' said I, ''the reasoner drew his conclusions from the actions of the man whom he observed. If I remember right, he stumbled over a heap of stones, looked up at the stars, and so on. But I have been seated quietly in my chair, and what clues can I have given you?''

''You do yourself an injustice. The features are given to man as the means by which he shall express his emotions, and yours are faithful servants.''

''Do you mean to say that you read my train of thoughts from my features?''

''Your features, and especially your eyes. Perhaps you cannot yourself recall how your reverie commenced?''

''No, I cannot.''

''Then I will tell you. After throwing down your paper, which was the action which drew my attention to you, you sat for half a minute with a vacant expression. Then your eyes fixed themselves upon your newly framed picture of General Gordon, and I saw by the alteration in your face that a train of thought had been started. But it did not lead very far. Your eyes flashed across to the unframed portrait of Henry Ward Beecher which stands upon the top of your books. Then you glanced up at the wall, and of course your meaning was obvious. You were thinking that if the portrait were framed it would just cover that bare space and correspond with Gordon's picture over there.''

''You have followed me wonderfully!'' I exclaimed.

''So far I could hardly have gone astray. But now your thoughts went back to Beecher, and you looked hard across as if you were studying the character in his features. Then your eyes ceased to pucker, but you continued to look across, and your face was thoughtful. You were recalling the incidents of Beecher's career. I was well aware that you could not do this without thinking of the mission which he undertook on behalf of the North at the time of the Civil War, for I remember your expressing your passionate indignation at the way in which he was received by the more turbulent of our people. You felt so strongly about it, that I knew you could not think of Beecher without thinking of that also. When a moment later I saw your eyes wander away from the picture, I suspected that your mind had now turned to the Civil War, and when I observed that your lips set, your eyes sparkled, and your hands clenched, I was positive that you were indeed thinking of the gallantry which was shown by both sides in that desperate struggle. But then, again, your face grew sadder; you shook your head. You were dwelling upon the sadness and horror and useless waste of life. Your hand stole towards your own old wound and a smile quivered on your lips, which showed me that the ridiculous side of this method of settling international questions had forced itself upon your mind. At this point I agreed with you that it was preposterous, and was glad to find that all my deductions had been correct.''

''Absolutely!'' said I. ''And now that you have explained it, I confess that I am as amazed as before.''

''It was very superficial, my dear Watson, I assure you . . .''

Frequently, once a problem statement is formulated it points out another problem, which in turn points out another problem, and so on. When this happens, the manager may be able to group all the statements together into a common category. These groupings help to distinguish symptoms from problems, a distinction that was discussed in the previous chapter.

Causes. Problems result from changes. To discover the specific causes of the problem being investigated, the manager again must ask "Why?" But the purpose of "Why?" at this stage is to narrow the field, not to broaden it. A well-defined problem statement narrows the search for causes down to those factors directly involved in the change. Extraneous factors can be sifted out using the worksheet described above.

The image can both aid and hinder the process of discovering the specific causes of a problem. When the problem has occurred previously, the image gives the manager a fairly good idea where to look. Thus, when there is a problem of employee grievances, the manager will probably start the search by looking at those people who have a history of troublemaking. This is a heuristic search pattern.

When two or more previous events have not been linked together or when the image is incomplete, the manager will have difficulty making the proper connections. Further, the cause may be well hidden and not identifiable by one of the obvious connections.

A useful technique for isolating causes is the **reversal method.** This process involves turning the situation around so that the variables in the field are looked at as potential problems rather than as probable causes for existing problems (13). The advantages of this method are that the situation is looked at in a nonstandard fashion and information is exposed that would otherwise not be seen. The result is a provocative rearrangement of information that often produces a restructuring of relationships.

Solutions. Rather than having a *single* solution, problems usually have a *range* of possible solutions. Kepner and Tregoe suggest the following categories of solutions (14):

1. Interim action: Putting a temporary repair on a machine rather than overhauling it.
2. Adaptive action: Developing a training program to provide technicians in a situation in which hiring technicians is prohibitive.
3. Corrective action: Eliminating a defect in a product.
4. Preventive action: Making sure that machines are properly inspected on a regular schedule.
5. Contingency action: Having a line of credit at the bank.

For any given problem, any one of the above may be a usable solution. The amount of time available is obviously one consideration, and cost is another. When some action must be taken immediately, interim action is called for. Corrective or preventive action assures an optimum solution with no, or just a few, dysfunctional side effects; but often these solutions are not feasible. When the existing conditions make the situation a dilemma, adaptive action may be the only possible alternative.

A common mistake in the solution stage is to take off with the first reasonable alternative. Suggestions for preventing this occurrence usually involve having the decision maker generate a specified number — or quota — of alternatives (15). Then the person must increase the number of alternatives by trying to repattern the problem and look at it from a variety of perspectives. This approach calls for inventiveness and creativity.

Creativity

Being a good problem solver does not necessarily mean that one is creative. And creative people are not necessarily good problem solvers. The two are different — and equally useful. Most of the emphasis in education and in management development is on problem solving. But organizations need innovation and creativity as well. Creativity is a skill that can be developed by breaking traditional thought patterns and by learning to think laterally or creatively.

As mentioned earlier, the image is made up of a series of descriptive, predictive, and prescriptive models and of methods for relating these models to one another. The patterns in the image develop over time, and once established tend to keep information flowing along familiar paths (16). These pathways constitute a system for handling information. The purpose of learning to think laterally is to challenge this system so that information gets channeled in new directions. When this happens, the person is forced to make different kinds of interpretations in his or her image, which lead to new ideas and unusual thought patterns. Lateral thinking can be encouraged by morphological, association, and modeling techniques.

Morphological Techniques. Morphology is the study of form or structure. In the sense that it is used here, morphological techniques are methods that can be used to alter the thinking process. Some of these techniques follow:

1. *Attribute Listing.* This approach calls for the person to list the attributes (or characteristics) of a situation; list a number of alternatives for each attribute; combine the alternatives in a variety of different ways; and evaluate each of the combinations. Suppose, for example, a manager wishes to redesign the package currently used for one of the company's products. All the attributes of containers, such as types of material used, methods of loading the containers, and the printing that appears on them, would be listed. Then all possible alternatives to these attributes would be listed and combined at random to see which, if any, combinations were the most practical and useful. The advantage of this technique is that the recombination of the various aspects of a situation can lead to novel and ingenious solutions (17).

2. *Input-Output Reversal.* In this technique the desired outcome is listed in clear terms and the various ways one could get there are then described, listed, and evaluated (18). Developing ways to arrive at the desired outcome is the critical phase of this procedure. What is wanted is quantity, not necessarily quality. The purpose of "brainstorming" sessions, for instance, is to generate as many ideas as possible—regardless of how far off the track they may seem—in order to increase the number of possible alternatives. In an atmosphere free from criticism or judgment, people often come up with creative and innovative ideas.

Two things to look for in implementing this technique are **dominant ideas** and **crucial factors** (19). In thinking about any problem, one's thoughts are automatically dominated by certain ideas. The idea that an automobile is *pushed* by the wheels leads to rear-end-drive cars. Changing that dominant idea to the notion that cars can be *pulled* leads to front-end-drive cars. A crucial factor is one that dominates because it always must be considered. Dominant ideas organize the way one thinks about a situation while crucial factors reduce the mobility of thought by acting as an anchor. That automobiles are vehicles to provide transportation might be considered a crucial factor.

3. *Fractionation.* This technique involves separating the problem into parts, somewhat similarly to listing attributes. For example, the problem may be broken into its two main aspects and these into two more and so on. The units developed are not necessarily independent, but each can be examined separately for alternatives to their attributes and then recombined in new ways. Often this technique leads to a redefinition of the dominant ideas or the crucial factors (20).

Association Techniques. Association techniques are based on suspending judgment so that people are encouraged to generate lots of ideas in a short time.

1. *Brainstorming.* This technique, described above, involves a group of people brought together specifically to come up with as many alternatives as possible in a given time period, the emphasis being on quantity of ideas. The session is formally organized and includes a chairperson and a recorder. The chairperson promotes ideas and squelches evaluation or criticism, while the recorder writes down all ideas.

Evaluation is allowed only after all ideas have been listed. Some ideas will be useful. Others will need to be examined to see how their basic concepts can be utilized. And many ideas, which may not seem useful as stated, often contain rudiments of solutions that can be developed.

2. *Synectics.* This technique is a complicated version of brainstorming in which criticism is allowed. It consists of three basic procedures: problem definition, analogy, and solution definition (21). This approach, which also involves a group of people acting together, starts by an accep-

tance of the fact that the problem as stated by the leader will be different from the problem that is understood by the participants. Thus the first operation is to reduce the discrepancy between the problem as given and as understood.

At the heart of the approach is the use of similes or metaphors or analogies to enable group members to clearly see and understand the nature of the problem before offering possible solutions. Analogies are simple stories or situations to describe the problem situation. Because they are symbolic representations of real-life situations, they encourage—in fact, demand—the use of imagination, thereby stimulating the participants' lateral thinking ability. And in creating analogies, decision makers often develop new models for solving problems.

Several types of analogies have been found useful in developing lateral thinking. A **personal analogy** has to do with a person, or a person's behavior, in comparison with the problem situation. This type of analogy encourages identification of the problem. A **direct analogy** is a statement that is directly parallel to the problem, and one in which the facts and comparisons can be directly compared. A **symbolic analogy** is one that compares the problems to an objective or impersonal object or situation but that is not directly parallel. This type of analogy is sometimes hard for people to grasp at first. Finally, a **fantasy analogy** is a comparison with some wild ideas in a person's imagination.

Modeling Techniques. Morphological and association techniques for developing creativity depend on the use of verbal models of the world. Other types of models, some more and others less abstract than verbal ones, also can assist creative thinking.

1. *Visual Models.* When people draw pictures of solutions to a problem, they often gain new insight. This is a very good technique to use with children because they have more picture images than word images. Many adults, too, tend to think graphically about the world.

People who are not used to visual models may resist this method. Most people feel they do not draw very well and are reluctant to try. Furthermore, many topics are difficult to describe visually.

2. *Mathematical Models.* These models are more complex than visual ones and require a prior knowledge of mathematics. But many problems can be easily solved through mathematical equations that otherwise would take a considerable amount of time.

Quantitative Decision Methods

Managers have always used quantitative data in decision making. But never before have quantitative data and the methods that have been developed to analyze them been as abundant and available as they are today. As testimony of this phenomenon, a whole field called **management science** has emerged in order to deal with the development and application of mathematical techniques in the area of organizational decision making. Two major areas within the field of management science are **statistics** and **operations research** (OR). Statistics is a mathematical science that has been around for a long time but that in recent years has seen many advances. Operations research is a newer area that has developed partly in conjunction with the advent of the computer.

Statistical and OR techniques about to be described are not applicable to every kind of problem. Their misuse could be as dangerous as their correct use could be helpful. They are most useful under conditions of certainty and risk, where the variables are limited and measurable. Attempts to use such models for problems in which some key variables are unknown or unmeasurable often are not satisfactory. The enthusiasm of management science theorists and proponents may lead managers to expect results when, in fact, much of the data needed to make sound decisions are not amenable to quantitative analysis. One of the goals for the future study of management science is a merger of behavioral analysis and quantitative decision analysis.

TABLE 14–1

Enrollments in Management Classes
Fall 1967–Fall 1978

	BASIC MANAGEMENT	PERSONNEL MANAGEMENT
Fall 1967	174	63
Spring 1968	227	65
Fall 1968	195	64
Spring 1969	138	67
Fall 1969	241	46
Spring 1970	210	49
Fall 1970	215	80
Spring 1971	242	85
Fall 1971	241	81
Spring 1972	225	48
Fall 1972	242	88
Spring 1973	304	104
Fall 1973	392	116
Spring 1974	330	149
Fall 1974	397	126
Spring 1975	356	119
Fall 1975	476	133
Spring 1976	396	124
Fall 1976	492	102
Spring 1977	430	103
Fall 1977	529	96
Spring 1978	499	121
Fall 1978	531	120

What do you think these enrollment figures mean?

The discussion that follows is not intended to make the reader an expert in the use of quantitative techniques; rather, the intention here is to place these techniques in perspective and to indicate the kinds of decision situations that would most likely benefit from their application.

Statistics

Statistics is used in all scientific areas and in many other fields of endeavor as well. In business, it is a basic method of data analysis. Statistics provides the decision maker with a set of prearranged rules for determining the meaning of the data being analyzed. Some of the more common of these rules are discussed below.

Descriptive Statistics. Quantitative data often arrive at a manager's desk in raw form as undigested bits and pieces of information. To be meaningful, data must be collected and arranged. Descriptive statistics provides a variety of means for arranging and displaying data to make them easier to understand. *Tables* organize and categorize data in a systematic way, as illustrated in Table 14–1 or Table 14–3. But tables of numbers, if very extensive, can be confusing. *Charts* and *graphs* are therefore used to display data visually. The enrollment data of Table 14–1 can be plotted in a *time series*, as shown in Figure 14–8. Years are noted

FIGURE 14–8
A time series of enrollments in management classes, Fall, 1967–Fall, 1978 (from Table 14–1).

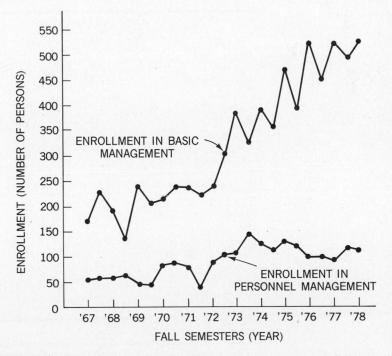

Do time series divulge more information than a table of raw data, as in Table 14-1? Interpret these two time series. What do they mean to departmental administrators? To students? Would an annual average of enrollment be clearer than a semester-by-semester plotting? Why?

on the horizontal axis, with the earliest year on the left; the number of students enrolled is shown on the vertical axis. Customarily, all time series are arranged in this way, with numbers on the vertical axis and years on the horizontal axis.

Another way to glean more information from raw data is to convert the figures to *index numbers*. Index numbers are derived simply by taking one bit of data as a "base" and dividing all other numbers by it to arrive at a percentage figure. Index numbers can help people make sense out of such complexities as the growth of the national debt, seasonal unemployment, and fluctuating stock prices. Table 14–2 shows how the raw enrollment figures can be converted into index numbers. Note that the enrollment for Fall of 1978 is 305 percent of the enrollment eleven years earlier in the basic management course but that the increase in the personnel course in this example is only 190 percent.

Another very useful tool of descriptive statistics is the **frequency dis-**

TABLE 14–2
Index of Enrollments in Management Classes
Fall 1967–Fall 1978
(Fall 1967 = 100)

	BASIC MANAGEMENT	PERSONNEL MANAGEMENT
Fall 1967	100	100
Spring 1968	130	103
Fall 1968	112	102
Spring 1969	79	106
Fall 1969	139	73
Spring 1970	121	78
Fall 1970	124	127
Spring 1971	139	135
Fall 1971	139	129
Spring 1972	129	76
Fall 1972	139	140
Spring 1973	175	165
Fall 1973	225	184
Spring 1974	190	237
Fall 1974	228	200
Spring 1975	205	189
Fall 1975	274	211
Spring 1976	228	197
Fall 1976	283	162
Spring 1977	247	163
Fall 1977	304	152
Spring 1978	287	192
Fall 1978	305	190

Interpret these index numbers. What trends do they indicate?

If these index numbers were plotted on a times series, how would the curves differ from the curves of the raw data shown in Table 14-1?

tribution. Much of statistics is based on the notion that phenomena occur with varying rates of frequency. Thus, to determine the frequency rate of any given phenomenon, the statistician groups or ranks all phenomena within the field of observation into a frequency distribution. For example, if an instructor wants to grade students on the basis of class comparisons, he or she would first have to itemize all the scores from Table 14–3. If the maximum possible points was 400, the lowest score was 283, and the highest score was 393, the frequency distribution would be calculated on

TABLE 14–3
Raw Data of Grades and Total Points
Management Class, Section 11, Fall 1978

Student Number	Test I	Test II	Paper	Test III	Final	Total Points
1.	50	50	96	50	147	393
2.	50	44	99	50	131	374
3.	41	41	91	41	134	348
4.	41	38	74	45	110	308
5.	47	50	95	47	114	353
6.	44	44	92	44	142	366
7.	35	38	65	45	142	325
8.	38	35	81	44	142	340
9.	44	47	76	44	145	356
10.	47	47	97	47	145	383
11.	38	41	78	38	102	297
12.	44	44	85	44	120	337
13.	50	47	100	50	145	392
14.	35	35	94	44	142	350
15.	41	43	80	41	145	350
16.	45	41	83	47	134	350
17.	41	50	86	41	139	357
18.	47	44	87	47	120	345
19.	44	38	89	45	118	334
20.	50	41	98	50	137	376
21.	44	35	90	44	126	339
22.	35	50	66	35	112	298
23.	47	38	75	45	128	333
24.	35	47	70	35	145	332
25.	50	38	93	45	145	371
26.	44	50	84	44	150	372
27.	38	44	67	38	142	329
28.	50	35	77	44	126	332
29.	35	41	68	35	104	283
30.	38	47	82	38	145	350
31.	38	50	72	38	115	313
32.	35	44	69	35	107	290
33.	38	38	73	45	145	339
34.	44	41	71	44	99	299
35.	41	35	88	44	126	334
36.	41	38	79	45	123	326

TABLE 14–4
Frequency Distributions of Total Points
(from Table 14–1)

Array of Total Points, Management Class, Section 11			Frequency Distribution
393-/	353-/	329-/	380-400- 3
392-/	350-////	326-/	360-379- 5
383-/	348-/	325-/	340-359-10
376-/	345-/	313-/	320-339-11
374-/	340-/	308-/	300-319- 2
372-/	339-/	299-/	280-299- 5
371-/	337-/	298-/	36
366-/	334-//	297-/	
357-/	333-/	290-/	
356-/	332-//	283-/	
		36	

What is the *mean* score? How is it calculated?
What is the *median* score? How can you find it?
What is the *modal* score? How do you arrive at it?

the basis of where scores fall between these two extremes. Table 14–4 ar-ranges the total points for the class, shown in Table 14–3, in a frequency distribution. The instructor would need to determine the *average,* or most representative score in order to come up with a grading system. The cen-tral point around which most of the scores are observed is called the **meas-ure of central tendency.**

The three possible ways of obtaining a measure of central tendency are the *mean,* the *median,* and the *mode.* The **mean** is the arithmetical middle of all the scores being ranked. The measure is obtained by adding together all the scores and dividing the sum by the number of people in the class. The mean of the total points in Tables 14–3 and 14–4 is 340. The **median** is the score that falls physically in the middle of the frequency dis-tribution equidistant from both ends. This measurement is obtained by ranging the scores along a continuum, as in Table 14–4, and then counting in from either side. The median of scores in Table 14–4 is between 339 and 340. The **mode** is simply the score that occurs with the most fre-quency, in this case, 350.

In order to assign letter grades to the students' scores, the teacher would select one of the above measurements (usually the mean) and as-sign a grade of "C" to those scores that group around this average. The remaining grades would then be assigned according to where they fall above and below the average.

In most cases, given large amounts of data, certain phenomena occur more frequently than others—that is, they center around the mean. If this type of distribution is plotted on a graph, it might look like the illustration in Figure 14–9. Here, the grouped scores from the frequency distribution

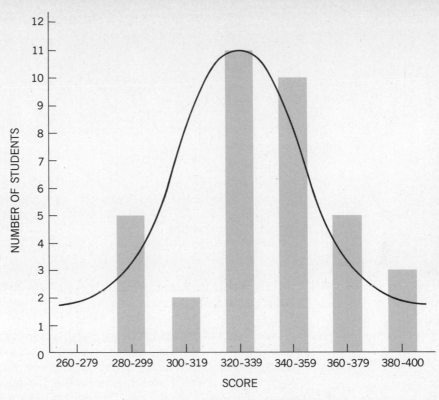

FIGURE 14–9
A bar chart of summary frequency distribution (from Tables 14–3 and 14–4).

If this class had had many more students, the scores might have arrayed themselves more "normally" and smoothed out over the range of a "normal" distribution, as shown by the curved line. The scores in this class show a relatively narrow "spread" or dispersion, with most scores in the middle range. Thus the distribution is steep.

in Table 14–4 are drawn as a bar chart. If this class had had many more students, the scores might have arrayed themselves more smoothly, as shown by the bell-shaped curve. This is called a **normal curve** because it represents the most common type of distribution: most occurrences cluster around the average, with a few extreme cases in either direction.

A normal curve does not necessarily have to look like the one pictured in Figure 14–9. It can be taller and narrower or shorter and wider, depending on the way the scores are dispersed, as shown in Figure 14–10. The different slopes possible in a normal curve indicate that the **dispersion** of scores differs. This dispersion can be measured in a number of ways. The **range,** or **spread,** is the distance between high and low scores. In the example in Table 14–4 the range is from 283 to 393 points, a spread of 110. A distribution can also be broken up into points at which various percentages lie above or below a given point. If a score lies at the 99th **percentile,** it is higher than 99 percent of the others. If a score lies in the top

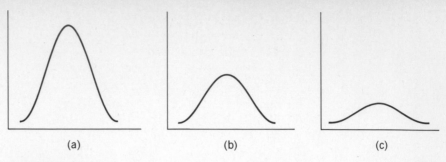

(a)   (b)   (c)

FIGURE 14–10

Different kinds of normal curves. (a) A tall distribution, narrow spread, low dispersion. The mean is very important. (b) A "normal" normal distribution based on probability. (c) A flat curve, with wide dispersion. The averages are not too meaningful.

25 percent, it is in the top **quartile.** It is also possible to measure the **deviation** of scores from the mean, but we need not pursue the measurement of average and standard deviations here.

Measures of central tendency and dispersion are very useful for comparing observations. Suppose, for instance, that a manager finds that the number of units produced in the last month was 1,572, whereas the average number was 1,650. It is important to know whether this is a significant variation from normal. To calculate whether a change in variables is significant, one first has to know what the probabilities are of that change occurring by chance. These types of calculations are governed by the rules of **probability theory,** which is the basis of **inferential statistics.**

Inferential Statistics. Descriptive statistics provides valuable tools for observing data; inferential or inductive statistics provides the means whereby the researcher can interpret and draw conclusions from the data that have been observed. The odds of getting heads or tails when flipping a coin is 50/50. So what would it mean if in 100 tosses tails turns up 54 times? or 75 times? Is it chance, or is it a **significant difference** that needs further examination? Statisticians have devised methods for determining the probabilities of chance occurrences. For example, if the odds of getting tails on a single toss is 50/50, or one in two, then the odds of getting tails on two consecutive tosses is half that amount, or one in four. The more times the coin is tossed, the lower the probability of continuing to turn up tails. If the odds against an event's occurring by chance alone are 1 in 20, then any occurrence of that event can be viewed as significant and will bear looking into.

Thus, the production manager in the example above will need to calculate whether a 78-unit decrease in production during the month can be attributed to chance before knowing whether a problem exists.

In statistics three types of associations occur between events. **Mutually exclusive events** occur when one outcome prevents or precludes the occurrence of another one. Tossing a coin has mutually exclusive outcomes: heads *or* tails will occur, but not both.

Independent events occur independently of one another, and the occurrence of one does not affect the occurrence of the other. For example, whether a shipment will arrive on time is independent of whether it will meet specifications. Both or neither may occur. **Dependent events** occur together and each influences the other. Cause and effect are involved. Thus, if the shipment has to be hurried to meet its arrival schedule, quality may be affected and specifications not met.

Correlation. Correlation provides a means of determining the degree of association between interdependent variables. The degree of association can be estimated visually by plotting both variables on a graph, with the dimensions of one variable on each axis, and observing the pattern of the resultant dots. If, for example, college admissions officials expected that students' scores on standard aptitude tests would predict their performance in college as measured by grade point average (GPA), they could plot the GPA of each student enrolled against that individual's test score. If there was little association, the dots would form no particular pattern, as shown in Figure 14–11(a). If the association was fairly substantial, a pattern like that in Figure 14–11(b) might form.

Plotting variables visually is a convenient way to assess the degree of relationship between them. But statisticians have also developed more

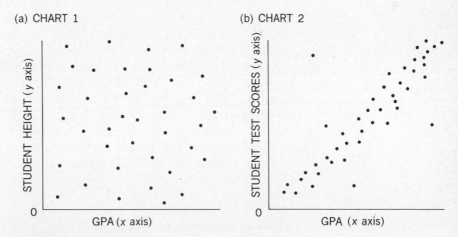

FIGURE 14–11
Examples of two correlation situations. (a) Chart 1 shows little relationship between the variables plotted on the *x* (vertical) and *y* (horizontal) axes, as the dots are spread all over the graph. (b) Chart 2 shows that as either *x* or *y* increases, so does the other variable.

precise mathematical techniques to measure the degree of variable association. We need not belabor the mathematics here, but if the relationship is perfect and positive, the correlation is +1.0; if perfect but negative, with the variables moving in opposite directions, the correlation is −1.0; if no relationship exists, the correlation is 0.00.

Whether visual or mathematical, correlation does not show cause and effect, nor even that variables are dependent upon one another. The association shown in Figure 14–11(b) does not indicate that test scores lead to effective performance; it merely suggests that they are associated. The results might be accidental, or each could be associated with some other variable not considered in the correlation analysis. (Estimating mathematically the kinds of associations that exist is called **regression analysis,** of which correlation is one outcome.)

Many other kinds of inductive statistical tools are available, all of which are useful aids in solving a number of special types of problems. Still other tools for helping decision making have been developed by operations researchers.

Operations Research

Operations research, or OR, is a set of decision-making techniques that were developed to aid in making complex programed decisions. They provide a means for devising a mathematical model of the situation, putting the measurement into the model to determine an optimum solution, and implementing the results. The techniques were first developed during World War II as a means of ensuring that personnel, materials, weapons, ships, air support, and so forth got to the right place at the right time from stations all over the globe.

Operations research is very much like scientific management in that both seek an optimum solution to problems in a wholly rational way. The results of both methods have been similar, too, and occasionally rather spectacular. OR has made it possible for managers in a wide variety of situations to make rational decisions not previously possible. But in common with all programed decision-making techniques, operations research can be misapplied. It is most useful in situations where the decisions to be made involve *quantifiable* variables and where the goal is to develop a programed course of action. In cases where *qualitative* variables are important, attempts to use OR have not been very successful. In fact, among some people in organizations, OR is about as popular as time-and-motion studies. Below are some of the better-known operations research techniques.

Linear Programing. Linear programing is useful in allocating organizational resources in terms of a given goal (22). Consider, for example, a situation in which three separate products are produced by using a number of different machines, and each product has cost and profit margins. A linear programing model can indicate the best combination of machines and inputs for producing the three products at the lowest price. The inten-

Linear Programing: Simple to Complex

Some problems of the type that linear programing can solve are so simple that no special technique is needed. If, for example, there are surpluses of freight cars at two cities that are required to meet shortages in two other cities, one can easily determine how to redistribute these cars so as to minimize the costs of hauling empty cars. Assume that City A has a surplus of 10 cars and City B a surplus of 12 cars. City C and City D require 11 cars each. It costs $80 to send a car from A to C, $100 from A to D, $90 from B to C, and $70 from B to D. The problem can be pictured as:

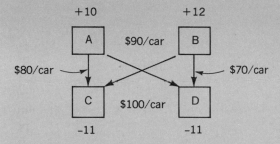

In this problem, it is obvious that it will be least expensive to send all 10 cars at A to C and that one additional car is needed to be sent from B to C, while the balance of 11 at B should be sent to D. (Even on this simple problem, however, if one were to calculate all feasible solutions and to find the cost of each, 11 different shipping plans would have to be examined.)

But if, instead, one had to solve a similar problem involving three origins and five destinations, with a total of 20 cars to redistribute, the answer no longer would be apparent by inspection. If one were to list and evaluate all feasible solutions to this relatively simple problem, the number of solutions to be considered would be in the order of 10,000,000. Linear programing can provide the solution in not more than six or seven steps.

If the problem involved 50 to 100 origins and destinations and several thousand freight cars, the number of possible solutions would be beyond counting, and the linear programing solution would only be possible if one used a high-speed electronic computer. Fortunately, standard solutions to linear programing problems have been programed for most of the computers in use, and with such a program the computational time is cut to a very short period.

tion of linear programing is to either maximize some value or minimize some cost. It is particularly useful where there are a number of constraints. For the above example, the equation would have a number of statements, such as "Not more than ten units per day can be processed on machine number 2." The object is to find the best value that meets all the constraints. The natural limitation of linear programing, as apparent from its name, is that all the variables must be linear, or in a straight-line relationship. That is, if it costs $10 to produce one unit, ten units cost $100. Where these conditions cannot be met they can often be approximated or the range reduced to accommodate linearity.

Dynamic Programing. When the conditions of linear programing cannot be met or approximated, dynamic programing may be a useful tool. The difference is that in dynamic programing the problem is taken apart and the sections dealt with sequentially. It is most useful in time-dependent situations. In these instances the useful course of action in the first time frame is determined, carried forward to the second and analyzed there, and on through a number of time frames until the best solution is obtained (23).

Queuing Theory. Queuing theory is a mathematical method of solving waiting-line problems, which have to do with providing a service to meet an irregular demand. These problems result in over- and under-demand for facilities and resources. Rather than being an optimizing technique, this is a balancing technique. It is based on the probability of arrival of the person or item to be dealt with over a time period. The result is a balance between costs of waiting and costs of unused resources. For example, queuing theory can help determine the number of checkstands to have open at a grocery store during different times of the day, with implications regarding how many people are needed and at what times. The problems handled with this kind of technique often can be extremely complex. One can see why many airline reservations and maintenance systems are handled with queuing theory programs (24).

Modeling and Simulation. The advent of the computer has enabled management scientists to bring together greater amounts of information than ever before possible and to better understand the relationships between the variables at work in a large number of situations. All this makes it possible to develop very sophisticated mathematical models of large parts of reality. For example, before new airplanes are tested in the sky, they are "flown" millions of miles through computer models to test out their configurations. The same thing is true of economic models developed by governments and universities, which attempt to simulate all the relevant data regarding the economy. In businesses, such factors as changes in technology or new product lines can be "run through the program" to determine their impact before they are brought out on the market.

Models can be built in two ways. One is to put all the possible data into the computer and let the relationships be determined by past behavior. The other way is to specify the relationships and then introduce data to verify or modify those relationships. In either case the purpose is to simulate some aspect of the "real world." The computer model allows the situation to be manipulated so that the manager can find out what would happen under different conditions. That is, different sets of data can be added or subtracted and different values can be assigned to the variables in an effort to describe the reality under given sets of conditions. In effect, the decision maker can rapidly run the model through different possibilities of future time periods. The use of simulation has increased greatly in the last few years and, because of its flexibility, appears to be one of the

most useful current aids to decision making. It has also proven quite effective as a teaching device. Simulation games have become very popular
in courses that focus on managerial decision making, particularly in policy
areas.

Chapter Review

In this chapter we have continued the discussion of decision making, concentrating primarily on the different decision styles of people and on some
of the methods that are used to aid the process. The specific terms and
ideas developed appear below.

1. Different people make decisions differently and use different techniques in doing so.

2. **Images** are world views stored in the mind as memories, which
help us to understand (descriptive images), predict (predictive images),
and decide how things ought to be (prescriptive images).

3. Images are **models.** A model is not reality, but it is a representation
of some parts of reality.

4. A **theory** is a model that describes or predicts relationships between facts.

5. To test hypotheses about management, researchers may use the
observational, survey, or **experimental** methods. Observation requires
careful description, data gathering, and classification; surveys utilize
questionnaires or patterned interviews; experiments require carefully
controlled laboratory conditions and are the only means whereby cause-
and-effect relationships can be determined.

6. **Inductive reasoning** is the process of drawing general conclusions
from specific observations. **Deductive reasoning** proposes specific relationships based on a general theory.

7. Ideas about improving decision-making behavior have been developed by examining the *problem-definition* and *problem-solving* processes
or by suggesting techniques to increase *creativity* and inventiveness.

8. **Problem definition** is a process of comparing information against
the image. Sometimes information is congruent; sometimes additional information is necessary. When information is incongruent, a *problem*
exists.

9. The *causes* of problems are difficult to isolate. The **reversal**
method, looking at possible causes as problems, helps to rearrange causal
information.

10. **Creativity** can be increased by means of several techniques:

  a. **morphological techniques,** methods to alter thought processes. These include listing the characteristics of a situation, clearly

noting desired outputs, and describing how to get there; or *fractionating,* which involves dividing the problem into its main components.

b. **association techniques,** methods used to help people suspend judgment. These include *brainstorming* and *synectics,* the use of analogies of the problem to isolate alternative solutions.

c. **modeling techniques,** methods other than verbal language to isolate problems. These include *visual models,* such as pictures or line diagrams, and *mathematical models.*

11. **Management science** is a field of method that uses mathematical techniques to facilitate managerial decision making. Two branches of management science are **statistics** and **operations research.**

12. **Descriptive statistics** displays data to make understanding easier. **Inferential** or **inductive** statistics helps a researcher interpret the meaning of data.

13. **Operations research** consists of a variety of techniques useful in making complex, programed decisions. Such techniques are mathematical models of reality and include such methods as **linear programing** (for allocation decisions), **dynamic programing, queuing theory,** and **simulations** of the way things might work out, given alternative solutions.

Discussion Questions

1. Describe the difference between the descriptive, predictive, and prescriptive mental models of the world. How is each useful in decision making?

2. How is a theory developed? What is its role in the decision-making process?

3. Identify and describe the three types of research designs used in the behavioral sciences. What are the advantages and disadvantages of each?

4. What is the difference between deductive and inductive reasoning?

5. Describe the different types of decision-making styles in terms of the preceptive-receptive and systematic-intuitive continua.

6. What is the difference between vertical and lateral thinking? What role does each play in decision making?

7. Describe the problem-solving sequence.

8. How would you go about increasing the number of alternatives to consider for a particular problem situation?

9. Suppose the product being produced in your factory suddenly showed an increase in rejection rate of 25 percent. What behavioral decision techniques would you employ to find out what is the matter?

10. What is descriptive statistics? Why is it useful to managers?

11. Identify and give examples of three measures of central tendency.

12. Describe three types of relationships between events. Why should managers be able to determine correlation?

13. Describe a situation in which linear programing could be used; one in which it cannot be used.

14. What are the advantages of modeling and simulation?

**Involvement
Activity**

For each of the following situations, indicate:

    a. what behavioral and quantitative methods might be applicable to the solution of the problem and in what way;

    b. what information would be needed in order to apply the techniques; and

    c. what decision style(s) would be appropriate and why.

(Note that you are not asked to solve the problems, only to answer questions a, b, and c.)

1. You are the supervisor of a small machine shop. It is 4:00 P.M. on a Thursday afternoon and you have just returned from a long meeting. Immediately, a special customer calls to say she is sending over a truck to pick up the order you promised to have ready this afternoon and which she needs for her first production run tomorrow morning. You check on her order and find that the parts are not ready because of a six-hour machine breakdown. The machines have been repaired, but none of the three machinists can work overtime to complete the job this evening.

2. You have just been promoted to division manager of consumer products at General Industries, Inc. Your mission is to "get the division back on its feet." During the past five years, and particularly during the past two, sales have steadily declined. But profits and return on investment have held up nicely, at least until now. An inventory of capital equipment, however, has shown that no new equipment has been purchased in the past four years. Also, the product line has remained unchanged while competitors have more and newer models and products on the market.

3. You are the administrative assistant to the president of a firm employing about fifty people. You know that short-term financing has always been a problem, adversely affecting weekly cash flow. The company uses accounts receivable as collateral for a line of credit at the bank. The bank has just informed the company that the interest rate is going to rise 2 percent as a result of a slowdown in collections. The president wants you to look into the situation.

15

Communication

Once a decision has been made, the first step in implementing it is to tell others in the organization what needs to be done. This step involves communication. Managers communicate almost constantly—it is the biggest part of their job—not only about decisions but about a host of other things as well. Because things do not go right when communication is inadequate, the purpose of this chapter is to present ideas that, it is hoped, will improve the manager's ability to communicate effectively.

The chapter opens with a discussion of how the communication process works—how information is received and transmitted and what can go wrong. It continues with an explanation of how the organizational structure influences communication and how different communication networks, in turn, affect organization design. Finally, there is a discussion of the role that communication plays in all aspects of the managerial process, particularly the design of management information systems.

Typically, managers spend as much as 60 to 80 percent of their time interacting and communicating with others. Even when by themselves they spend a good deal of time involved in some aspect of the communication process, either digesting communications that have been received or preparing messages to send out. In a way, the thought process itself, by which people develop an image of themselves and their environment and make sense out of their experiences, may be considered a form of intrapersonal communication. Thus, with the exception of purely physical reactions, all behavior—to greater and lesser degrees—involves some sort of communication. Figure 15–1 shows how communication relates to the other managerial activities discussed in this unit.

The Communication Process

Effective communication is so important in any organized endeavor and in all interpersonal relations that whenever problems occur they are often characterized as "breakdowns in communication." And the most

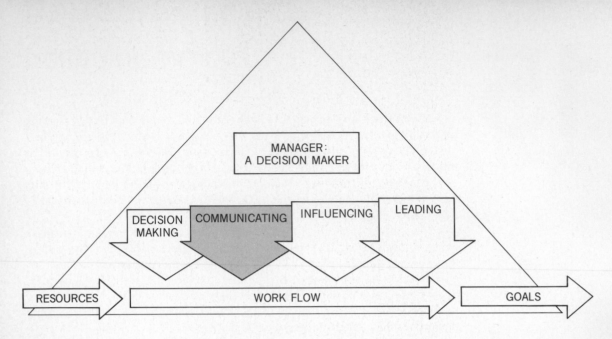

FIGURE 15–1

A manager communicates in order to aid the flow of work toward performance goals.

frequently suggested remedy to these problems is "improve communications"—advice that is not always easy to follow. To communicate well, people must have an understanding of what is being communicated and of the people to whom they are communicating, as well as a knowledge of the technical skills required to get the message across. Usually we do not think about how (or even whether) we are communicating. It is simply something that is taken for granted—a part of ongoing, everyday behavior. Like breathing, its importance becomes obvious only when we cannot do it (1).

For all its universality and importance, communication is not easy to define. The word is used loosely to include a broad range of activities, including conversation, other types of verbal discussions, all forms of media, all written messages, and so on. But certain elements are common to all these activities. For instance, all involve some kind of message, sent by a person or by groups of people to another person or group. Whether or not technological assistance is used in sending the message does not alter the fact that it is a form of communication. The intent of every communication is to transfer an idea or image from the sender to the receiver. If the attempt is successful, the receiver will form in his or her mind the same idea or image that the sender transmitted. It may be said, then, that *communication is an attempt to influence, enlighten, or elicit a response from a receiver.* If the receiver gets some idea other than that intended, or responds in some way other than what was expected, the communication attempt has not been fully successful. Thus, *successful communication can be defined as the transfer of an idea or an image from a sender to a receiver that leads to an intended reaction* (2).

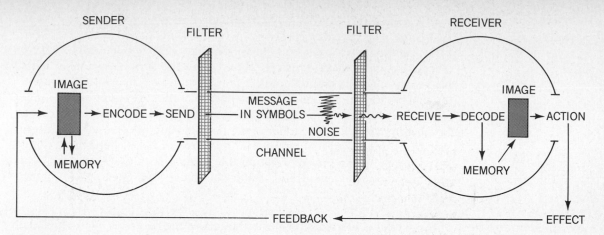

FIGURE 15–2
A model of the elements in the communication process.

Figure 15–2 shows the essential elements in the communication process. These include a sender with an image, a message, a channel or route by which the message is sent, and a receiver with an image. In addition, both the sender and receiver have filters for screening incoming information. These filters, plus the fact that the images contain different sets of memories, which may or may not be compatible with the other person's, often prevent communication from being successful.

How Information Is Received

As we learned in Chapter 8, of the millions of phenomena that exist in the outside world, people receive and retain only those that most closely relate to their needs. This means that we filter out all events that we do not perceive as relevant. Perceptual filters protect us from being inundated with information we cannot use; but they may also block out information we can use simply because we do not see it as relevant.

Receptors. Information enters the brain through receptor organs, which are the senses of sight, hearing, smell, taste, and touch. But even when functioning at full capacity, our senses are limited. For example, people cannot see X rays or hear sounds above and below certain frequencies. And it is possible that we can receive information that does not enter through the usual channels. The growing body of research into parapsychological phenomena, for instance, has attracted a good many followers in recent years.

Reception. Not all information that is handled by the receptors is recorded and used. The restrictions that were discussed in Chapter 8 regarding perception, and those in Chapter 13 regarding the image, are operative here. As indicated in these earlier discussions, all information is compared with the person's current memory. Those things that are congruent are recorded along with other signals that are very stong. Mildly incongruent signals tend to be ignored. In this way our perception is selective, seeing those things we wish to see and ignoring others.

A major consideration in reception is *relevancy*. A class presentation that is not well prepared is often viewed by students as "irrelevant." But the presentation may also be seen as irrelevant if the students do not have a broad enough data base, or image, to receive the information. This might be the case if an instructor tried to teach monetary theory to a group of students who did not understand basic economics. It is not always possible, however, for the person listening to know the value of the information being received. The student may need certain information for future situations that at present is beyond the scope of his or her image. Thus reception is blocked to information that is now seen as "irrelevant" but that later may be very useful. Educators have long been aware of this dilemma.

How Information Is Transmitted

If the sender is to create the desired effect in the receiver, he or she must first formulate a good idea or image of what that effect should be. The next step is to determine the best way to produce the reaction. To make this determination, the sender must understand the receiver's point of view.

Considering the Receiver. The receiver, like the sender, is wrapped in a personal perceptual field that contains a unique combination of receptors, images, and memories. Any information that enters this perceptual field must meet certain requirements if it is to be understood as sent. Thus, although the effectiveness of communication rests with the receiver (because it is this party who either understands and accepts the communication effort or fails to do so), it is the responsibility of the sender to make certain the information meets the specifications necessary to pass successfully through the receiver's field.

If the sender ignores the needs and the conditions surrounding the receiver, the communication attempt is likely to fail. Even if the message is perceived as relevant by the receiver, he or she is not likely to be receptive to everything the sender has to say. As a result, both current and future communication may be hampered.

People fail to understand one another for a variety of reasons, many of which have been described in earlier chapters. Perhaps the most common reason is that people tend to insulate themselves from people, ideas, and surroundings that are unfamiliar. Our social and work groups are predominantly made up of people who think and act the way we do. The newspapers and books we read tend to support our own ways of viewing the world. And we often tune out communication attempts that are initiated by people we do not perceive to be like us. But if we continue to remain insulated, cut off from those who are different and ideas that are novel, we never learn anything new and we never teach anything of what we know to others. Those who are in a position of influence, such as managers, have a particular responsibility to try to make themselves open to the ideas and concerns of others and to try to help others become better able to receive their messages.

Helping the Receiver Perceive. One of the first requirements of effective transmission is to send the message on a level of understanding that is appropriate for the receiver. For instance, talking beneath the receiver's ability to understand either makes the receiver think the sender does not understand the situation very well, or worse yet, demeans the receiver by conveying an attitude of superiority. Talking above the receiver's level of understanding has equally adverse effects. If the receiver feels that the sender is trying to impress him or her with long words, jargonistic language, or abstract generalities, he or she will form a negative impression of the sender and tune out the message.

The ability to see the world as another does is called *empathy*. It requires a lack of prejudgment and a willingness to let go of stereotypes. This is not an easy task. But it is a requisite to effective communication. Managers can help employees receive messages by creating an empathic environment in which receivers feel at ease and are assured that their needs are understood (3).

Another way to help receivers perceive is to send messages that have neutral emotional value. Concentrating on the problem situation rather than on the person prevents people from becoming defensive. For example, the message "Sales are really down this last month, what do you think the problem is?" is likely to be much better received than the message "How come the sales force fouled up?" Another way to invoke trust is to send straightforward messages that do not contain hidden meanings. If people feel they are being manipulated or threatened, they are not very likely to be receptive listeners.

Other means for helping receivers perceive messages effectively include avoiding an attitude of finality and repeating the message in different ways to ensure comprehension. By avoiding an attitude of finality, it is meant that the sender should leave room for modification and discussion of what is said rather than stating the message in such a way as to preclude any further conversation on the subject (4).

Redundancy or repetition, when used carefully, can avoid the possibility of confusion on the part of the receiver. When the receiver indicates a lack of understanding, the sender must resubmit the message, perhaps reshaping it so the receiver can understand it better. Senders can either change their perceptions of the receiver, alter the channel and the symbols used, or deal with other problems before repeating the message.

Encoding. A significant part of the transmittal process is putting the communication in a form that the receiver can understand. This requires translating the idea or the image into symbols, which is called **encoding.** A symbol is anything that is used to stand for or represent something else. Symbols can be words, mathematical equations, pictures, musical notes, a flag, a hand gesture, or any number of other things. Should the sender use word symbols, he or she still must decide between several choices. For example, would "shop talk" be better than standard English? Is formality better than a loose, familiar style? Once the sender has decided upon the appropriate symbols, the next step is to select a medium for the message.

Selecting a Medium and a Channel. A **medium** is a means of transmission. Many media (or mediums) are available. The sender may use oral transmission; tape or videotape recordings; or written transmissions, such as memos, bulletins, letters, telegrams, and so on.

The **channel** is the route through which messages flow. Certain media carry their own channels and leave the sender no choice; for example, radio and television stations must use the airwaves available to them. For other media, there are choices to be made. If the message is to be delivered orally, should the sender use the telephone or speak in person? If the message is to be written, should it be hand delivered, mailed, or telegraphed?

The sender's knowledge, abilities, and attitudes will influence his or her choice of symbols, media, and channels. Some people, for example, dislike using the telephone so much that they will walk a considerable distance to engage in face-to-face communication.

Effectors. Information leaves the organism through effector organs or cells, such as the vocal chords and the muscles. This is a purely physiological means of transmission, which is vital to the communication process but not the only consideration when sending messages. The following section describes some of the problems involved in transmitting information.

Communication Problems

Problems can occur at any stage in the process of preparing and sending messages. Many of these have been discussed in the preceding section. But communication problems also occur at the receiving end, in the channels, and in the symbolic code of the message itself.

Receptor Problems. As we mentioned earlier, the success or failure of communication rests with the receivers. Either they get the messages or they do not. The receiving process is the reverse of the sending process. Receivers filter messages, receive some or all of the content, decode or interpret the messages, check them out against the images and memories, and then decide what to do about them. Misinterpretations can occur at any one of these steps.

A great deal has been written about communication from the standpoint of senders, but very little has been said about the responsibility of receivers in aiding communication. The principal act of receiving is **listening**—an activity that requires more skill than one might imagine. Research studies have indicated that most people listen with only 25 percent capacity and that when managers (and others) are trained to listen better, their overall effectiveness, especially their ability to get along with people, increases dramatically.

One major barrier to effective listening is the tendency to evaluate. To the degree that the receiver prejudges the sender before hearing what he or she has to say, listening will be restricted. Other listening barriers include: labeling the subject uninteresting; criticizing the delivery; faking attention; avoiding difficult material; reacting emotionally; and letting oneself wander off into reveries. This last requires further comment. Most senders talk at about 125 words per minute; but most receivers can listen and absorb at a rate of about 400 to 500 words per minute. So unless the receiver actively participates in the listening process, he or she will quickly grow bored. Active listening means thinking along with the sender, anticipating the next point, identifying the important elements, making mental summaries of what has been said, and thinking about the immediate and potential impact of the communication (5).

When messages are written, receivers must be able to read and comprehend the communication with the same skills required of listening. Effective receiving of written messages means identifying and understanding the important points and determining what, if anything, needs to be done by way of a response. Receivers must also be able to understand physical and behavioral symbols if they are to get the message intended. At the same time, it is important to avoid "reading" a message where none exists. For example, a manager who fails to say "Good morning" may inadvertently be sending a message that the employee is out of favor.

Where messages are not sent covertly and where people have learned to correctly interpret symbols, communication will be most effective and least likely to be misunderstood.

Channel Problems. Direct, person-to-person oral communication minimizes the chances for misunderstanding and has the added advantage of permitting nonverbal gestures and inflections to help smooth the process. The further away one moves from personal contact, the greater are the chances for misunderstanding. More planning must go into the proper working of written communications than of spoken communications. Professors' lectures are rarely as well planned and organized as are their books. But books are not as flexible as lectures because they cannot adapt to changes in the environment or to different receivers. Written communications, therefore, cannot be made as specific as oral communications. On the other hand, written communications are essential where records of action are required or where time and distance are factors. Personal communications are less likely than written ones to bridge the time barrier.

Channels that permit interaction are less likely to distort messages. All participants in face-to-face communications can be both senders and receivers. Feedback is instantaneous, and messages flow back and forth regarding what is being received. Indications of understanding can range from the receiver's reporting back what the sender said to a gleam of recognition (or lack of it) in the receiver's eyes. Feedback may also occur at a later date. In a classroom, for example, the professor may not know until the results of an examination are in whether the students understood the message. In two-way communication, a second feedback channel, which goes back to the sender, allows a give-and-take reciprocity between sender and receiver.

Although most managerial communication does permit some feedback, the quality or timing of the message may be such that it approximates one-way communication. Where there is a choice between the two channels, managers might consider the relative advantages of each. (1) One-way communication is faster, implying that a memorandum distributed to all employees is quicker and less costly than talking to each person individually or in groups. (2) Two-way communication is more accurate. In one experiment it was found that only 20 to 30 percent of the people asked to perform a simple task via a one-way communication got it right, whereas more than 80 percent got it right when two-way communication was allowed. (3) Receivers have more confidence in a feedback situation. Because their response is solicited, they are likely to feel more positive about the message. (4) Senders often feel less confident in a feedback situation. By allowing room for discussion they may feel that their messages will be undermined by complaints or by other expressions of dissatisfaction. Thus, messages about which no feedback is required or wanted often get sent via one-way communication. (5) The feedback method tends to be disorderly and noisy. For those who value a smooth-running operation, feedback is not always desirable. It upsets planned patterns and takes more patience on the part of the sender, who often receives more feedback than he or she wants. In general, the time spent on each type of communication is about the same. More planning is required *before* sending a one-way communication, and more time is taken *during* a two-way communication. Thus, the channel selected is usually determined by how much feedback is required or wanted (6).

Another factor to be considered when selecting a channel is the amount of distortion or confusion (called *noise*) that will be created. Noise can be a function of the channel itself or of the physical conditions surrounding the channel.

The more noise the receiver has to filter out, the less attention he or she will give to the message. And if the message is not particularly interesting, the noise will provide a welcome distraction. Communication requires that the receiver be able to distinguish the message from the background noise. If the physical surroundings are such that the senses of the receiver cannot clearly pick up the signals, communication will be hindered.

Symbol Problems. The symbols in which the message is coded can lead to problems if they are not well understood by the receiver. The receiver may make more out of the message than the sender intended, as when an employee "reads" the mood of the manager as well as listens to

From **Through the Looking Glass**

"I don't know what you mean by 'glory,'" Alice said.

Humpty Dumpty smiled contemptuously. "Of course you don't—till I tell you. I meant 'there's a nice knock-down argument for you!'"

"But 'glory' doesn't mean 'a nice knock-down argument,'" Alice objected.

"When I use a word," Humpty Dumpty said, in rather a scornful tone, "it means just what I choose it to mean—neither more nor less."

"The question is," said Alice, "whether you *can* make words mean so many different things."

"The question is," said Humpty Dumpty, "which is to be master—that's all."

Alice was too much puzzled to say anything; so after a minute Humpty Dumpty began again. "They've a temper, some of them—particularly verbs: they're the proudest—adjectives you can do anything with, but not verbs—however, *I* can manage the whole lot of them! Impenetrability! That's what *I* say!"

"Would you tell me, please," said Alice, "what that means?"

"Now you talk like a reasonable child," said Humpty Dumpty, looking very much pleased. "I meant by 'impenetrability' that we've had enough of that subject, and it would be just as well if you'd mention what you mean to do next, as I suppose you don't mean to stop here all the rest of your life."

"That's a great deal to make one word mean," Alice said in a thoughtful tone.

"When I make a word do a lot of work like that," said Humpty Dumpty, "I always pay it extra."

"Oh!" said Alice. She was too much puzzled to make any other remark.

Taken from *The Annotated Alice* by Lewis Carroll, illustrated by John Tenniel, with an introduction and notes by Martin Gardner. Copyright © 1960 by Martin Gardner. Used by permission of Clarkson N. Potter, Inc.

the message. Also, senders and receivers may attach different meanings to the same symbols.

Symbols can be easily misunderstood, or not understood at all, depending on what meanings are attached to them. Thus understanding requires that both sender and receiver assign common meanings to the symbols used. We have seen in earlier discussions how a shortage of shared symbols sometimes hampers communication between specialists and managers in the same organization. Both parties often have trouble finding, or do not try to find, a set of shared symbols. The result is that communication comes to a standstill.

If the meaning of symbols is descriptive and objective, that meaning is called a **denotation.** If symbols have a subjective or emotional impact greater than the simple denotation of the word, such meanings are called **connotations.** Words such as *communism* and *democracy* not only describe two forms of government but to many people also indicate a "bad" or "good" form of government. Senders must be careful of the emotional impact of the symbols they use. If one wishes to be rational and informative, one will abstain from using emotionally charged words. If one's purpose is to arouse emotions, then the sender must be willing to accept the ensuing reactions.

Although the possibilities for potential problems in communication are numerous, the fact is that communication is generally effective, as evidenced by the abundance of thriving organizations everywhere. But managers can aid the process and limit impediments to the work flow by familiarizing themselves with the considerations discussed above and by becoming aware of the trouble areas in their own work groups.

Communication and Organizational Structure

Communication is by definition an interpersonal event. And like most such events it has a form and structure. The difference is that the form and structure of communication change according to the arena in which it occurs. For example, the type of communication that takes place at a formal dinner party is quite different from that which occurs at a baseball game. Organizations, too, impose certain formalities on the communication process. Imagine the chaos that would result if there were no established channels for sending and receiving information. Some people would almost never know what was going on while others would be bombarded with so much information they would never have time to get their work done.

Organizing effectively reduces the number of possible channels a message must go through while ensuring that every person in the organization receives (and has an outlet for) the information that is pertinent to his or her work responsibilities. The fewer the levels through which a message must travel the greater its effectiveness. A flat organizational structure with few levels, or a decentralized structure with broad decision-making authority assigned to the first few management levels, would be best when communication is of vital importance to operations. Where these kinds of structures do not exist, management needs to take extra care in assuring that communication is understood and accepted at the employee level of the organization while also maintaining open pathways for an accurate upward flow of messages.

The Direction of Communication

Sometimes the form and structure of the organization impose such constraints on communication that real barriers develop. This is particularly the case where role and rank hierarchies are strictly defined, and communication between different hierarchical levels is discouraged. Supervisors may feel they will lose status if they are seen talking with subordinates, and employees may be too intimidated by status differences to attempt to communicate with managers. On the other hand, if the organizational structure is too loose, communication may be equally hampered. Thus, if same-level employees are assigned to do a job, problems may result from the fact that no one is in charge. People may jockey for power positions within the group by withholding information or by assuming an inappropriate leadership role.

Downward Communication. Downward communication follows the chain of command. Messages from the top receive attention because they carry the weight of their initiators' authority. Although a great deal of this type of communication takes place only between two or a few people, there are still many instances in which it flows from one to many. The major functions of downward communications are to describe and assign work by means of policies, procedures, and job instruction, and to coordinate and monitor employee performance.

Although downward communications are often quite general when they are initiated, they become increasingly specific as they move down the hierarchy. The reason this happens is that the people at the top of the organization are concerned with long-range strategy and those at the bottom are concerned with day-to-day implementation of that strategy. Thus, messages that start out as general strategy proposals become specific, workable procedures for implementation as they pass through the hands of each succeeding level of management.

The way that managers translate general proposals into specific work orders is by adding to the content. The "what" and the "how" must be spelled out and described in detail. The "what" usually does not require too many words, but the "how" is often the subject of thick procedures manuals. The more detail these manuals contain, the less chance there is for error; but if they are too detailed, people generally won't read them.

The function of the hierarchical organizational structure in terms of communication is to ensure that each level has the opportunity to add its particular bit of knowledge to the overall body of information and that everyone is informed about what is going on. For the most part, this system works fairly well; but certain dysfunctions are built in to the hierarchical communication channels. For instance, because there is little direct contact between top and bottom levels, people at the bottom often have the feeling that those at the top are not very real. Thus, when directives are issued by top management that reach bottom-level workers without intervention by immediate supervisors, employees may not take these messages very seriously. On the other hand, going through all the levels of the hierarchy takes time, particularly if each supervisor on every level must reinterpret the message. Chances for misinterpretation, unfortunately, are excellent. All the senders and receivers in the chain filter the message in accordance with their personal needs and perceptions. Consequently, top executives often skip levels to deal directly with the people who do the work. When top managers send out a notice to "all employees" they remove the discretionary power allotted to the intermediate managers. This action may be irritating to the subordinate managers and may result in a good many problems, but in certain instances the need for effective communication makes it worthwhile. Of course, the size of the organization plays a major role in determining the best way to handle downward communication.

Upward Communication. Upward communication is the means by which managers are made aware of the condition of various parts of the organization and of how downward communications have been received. In addition, it is an essential channel through which employees can have a voice in the operations of the organization.

There are a number of barriers in the way of effective upward communication that often frustrate employees. For example, because it is the reverse of downward communication, it is primarily a many-to-one communication situation. Instead of a message being expanded, it must be contracted as it moves up the hierarchy. In this upward process, managers will remove, if possible, any inkling that anything is wrong. In addition, they will take out parts of the message that they perceive as unimportant. On both counts, messages about feelings and attitudes are likely to be eliminated. The message that finally gets through is often quite different from the one that is originated. To counteract this phenomenon, top managers may periodically distribute elaborate questionnaires asking employees to provide information about their attitudes and about the work situation. But the results of these are time-locked and so may not reflect important aspects of the working organization.

Upward communication involves low-status, low-power people communicating to higher-status, higher-power people. Since the intent of communication is to try to exert influence, upward communication is not always very effective. Resulting employee frustration may explain to some degree the appeal of unions, which enable employees to communicate with management from an equalized power base.

Where unions do not exist, power differences and resulting frustrated communication attempts lead to some dysfunctional consequences. For example, employees unless required to do otherwise tend to transmit only information favorable to themselves; only what the boss *wants* to hear, not what he or she *should* hear; and only information favorable to their boss or peers. These employee-devised rules seem to guide upward communication under a variety of circumstances. For instance, one researcher found that *mobility aspirations* and *trust* are two important variables in the accuracy of upward communications (7). In other words, the greater the mobility aspirations of an employee, the less likely he or she is to communicate anything that is negative. Conversely, trust between sender and receiver acts to improve the accuracy of communications. But if mobility aspirations are very high, trust will not overcome the felt need to initiate only favorable communications.

Horizontal Communication. Horizontal communications present a dilemma to a hierarchical organization. It is absolutely necessary that communications move horizontally, but such lateral contacts disrupt the authority hierarchy. Nevertheless, even the administrative management theorists accept its inevitability. Fayol, for instance, proposed a bridge of horizontal communications to enable individuals at the same level of the organization to communicate directly with one another (8).

The need for horizontal communication arises from the nature of the work flow. As noted earlier in the book, much organizational work flows across the organizational structure, not up and down it. Individuals need to deal with others over whom they have no formal authority or status but who control resources that they need to accomplish the job.

Employees involved in the flow of work must influence one another to maintain the operations of the organization, thereby replacing authority relationships with exchange relationships.

Communication Networks

Communication is affected not only by the direction of the communication but also by the characteristics or structure of the channels. Behavioral scientists have done some exploratory research with small groups to determine the advantages and disadvantages of different forms of communication structure. Insights from small-group studies do not necessarily provide prescriptions for setting up effective communication networks in large-scale organizations, but the studies do suggest that alternative strategies exist.

Small-Group Structures. A variety of different kinds of communication networks have been tested experimentally. Figure 15–3 shows four of these: the wheel, the chain, the circle, and the all-channel. In the *wheel*

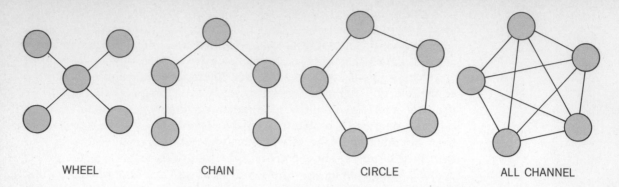

WHEEL   CHAIN   CIRCLE   ALL CHANNEL

FIGURE 15–3
Four types of commu-
nication networks.

structure, the person in the middle communicates with all of the others; they, however, can communicate only with the central figure. The middle role is the most powerful, having access to all information. In the *chain* structure, the person at the top interacts with two lieutenants, each of whom interacts with the top individual and with a subordinate, but not with each other. The people at the bottom interact only with their superiors. The top role has access to most of the information, but information from the bottom is filtered by the intermediaries. In the *circle* form, each member communicates with his or her neighbors only. And in the *all-channel* network, everyone interacts with everybody else. These networks each produce different effects (9).

1. *Satisfaction and Productivity.* To a degree, satisfaction and productivity are opposing forces in these networks. The wheel and the chain structures accomplish a task faster, but the circle and the all-channel networks provide the most satisfaction. Degree of *centrality* seems to have the most influence on personal satisfaction. The most satisfied individual is the person at the center of the wheel, the least satisfied people are those at the end of the chain.

2. *Nature of the Work.* A particular group's ability to handle a task depends to a degree on the nature of that task. Easy or simple tasks are done better using the wheel or chain structures. As tasks become more difficult, however, the circle, chain, and all-channel networks develop advantages. An awkward situation seems to develop in the wheel structure. As the task becomes more difficult, more messages are needed and the person in the center of the group becomes overloaded. The circle can diffuse these messages and appears to be more flexible. The all-channel network is slow and noisy, but provides high member satisfaction. The leader is prescribed in the first two structures but in the circle and the all-channel networks the leader emerges from the group and can be changed with the circumstances.

Based on these findings, which are among the most consistent in the

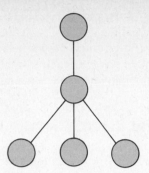

FIGURE 15–4
A simple organization
chart.

behavioral sciences, it seems that the appropriate network of communication for an organization depends on the tasks to be done and the extent to which employees and managers care about satisfaction and productivity. If satisfaction is desired, a circular or all-channel pattern is probably appropriate. If the task is simple, a wheel is good. As tasks become difficult, or as they require flexibility, the chain and circle become more useful structures.

A combination of the wheel and the chain structures, with a little rearranging of positions but not relationships, most nearly resembles the typical organizational structure (see Figure 15–4). The all-channel network, on the other hand, resembles a typical group or committee. Findings from these studies also imply that the person at the top of the structure may not always be the decision maker; rather, it is the person just below the top person because he or she occupies the central position in the communications network.

Informal Structures: The Grapevine. Just as it is impossible to entirely plan the organizational structure, so also is it impossible to completely prescribe the communication networks in organizations. Individuals have many contacts so that an informal communication chain, commonly called the *grapevine,* is created. The primary purpose of the grapevine is to fill the gaps left by the formal networks. If people do not receive all the information they need through formal channels, they will obtain it through informal ones. The grapevine may filter and distort messages, but its continuing existence proves its utility. And its accuracy is probably as good as that of the formal communications system.

The grapevine is *structured* into an identifiable network, but it does not follow the logic of the organizational structure. The individuals in the organization who are most likely to be a part of the grapevine system are those who have a wide range of contacts, such as expert groups, or those who have access to a great deal of information, such as secretaries. As in the formal networks, some individuals are mostly initiators and others are mostly receivers of information. Furthermore, different types of information are carried by different individuals (10).

Managers can make use of the grapevine system to correct misinformation and to spread information informally. For example, they might use the informal network to test reactions to proposed changes. If reactions are positive, then formal announcement may follow. If reactions are very negative, then formal denials can be circulated.

Communication and the Managerial Process

Effective communication is essential to all aspects of managerial work. In fact, without good communication systems the organization could not exist. Managers depend on reliable input data in order to make decisions about the work to be done. In turn, they count on accurate data about the work in progress to help them make decisions concerning the output. In this section the importance of communication to all other managerial processes will be considered.

The Need for Effective Information Systems

Changes during the past few decades have forced management to look more closely at the role that information systems play in the various organizational processes. Managers can no longer take for granted that the right information will be available at the right time. They must plan ahead to ensure its availability. To this end a new discipline called **management information systems** (MIS) has been developed. MIS is concerned with management's need for information and with the techniques that are useful for receiving, storing, and retrieving this information. These systems vary from simply providing information to actually performing the decision-making or controlling functions.

Ways to better process information are also necessary as a result of increasing organizational complexity, the advent of the computer, and the increasing abundance of information available in the environment. Keeping track of what is going on in a decentralized, diversified, and geographically spread out organization is a difficult task. Where facilities are near one another and goals are relatively simple, traditional information processing is sufficient. But old ways are inadequate in large-scale, modern organizations. Economic, political, social, and cultural trends must be considered along with internal matters. Computer technology, while contributing to the complexity of available data, also makes it possible to sort, process, and distribute the information that managers need (11).

Designing Information Systems

The kind of information system an organization develops depends, first of all, on its size and, secondly, on such other factors as the kinds of problems that must be dealt with, the type of information needed, and the extent to which the amount of information needed varies from situation to situation.

The Nature of the Problems. Not all information is needed by all managers. Some information is needed by all, some by a certain group, and some only by one particular manager. The problems faced should determine what information is sought. Because problems vary according to work assignments and hierarchical level, these variables are also important considerations. Obviously, production managers need information about production, accounting managers about accounting, and so forth. Managers at the top of the organization or those functioning in boundary-spanning roles need more information about future trends and other external data than do middle managers, who need more information about policies, procedures, and work flow.

The Type of Information Needed. All managers do need some basic knowledge of overall operations that is presented in understandable terms. And they should know how to "read" this information. For example, if managers do not understand such rudimentary information as a balance sheet or income statement, then making units of a business firm "profit centers" and using "cost-benefit analyses" do little good. Thus the effective utilization of MIS and other techniques may require first that employees are educated in how to use them. However, they do not need to know as much about areas that are not their direct responsibility as do specialists. Too much information only results in confusion. When designing an information system, the questions that need to be asked are "Who needs the information?" "In what depth is it needed?" and "In what form will it best be understood?"

The Amount of Information Needed. The need for various kinds of information changes with the dynamics of the organization and with the environment. It is not an easy task to keep up to date with who needs what. And sending and receiving information is expensive for both parties in terms of time, effort, and money. If one executive periodically fails to put out a regularly scheduled report, and if those who ordinarily received a copy do not complain, the executive will probably stop issuing the report. It is undoubtedly a good idea for managers to take inventory of communication sources at periodic intervals in order to weed out those messages that do not provide needed information and to seek input as to what other types of information should be provided. It may also turn out that some people receive information they do not need whereas others need information they do not get.

The manager also should try to maintain a balanced inflow of information. If too little is obtained, decision making, influencing, planning, and control capabilities are crippled. If too much information is received, the manager wastes energy separating what is needed from what is not. The amount of specific and general information needs to be regulated as well. Managers need enough general information to keep them oriented and enough specific information to help them do their work.

Chapter Review

This chapter has examined the important topic of communication, an indispensable means by which decisions are implemented in organizations. The nature of the communication process was explored along with some of the many factors that can impede effective communication. The workings of upward, downward, and horizontal communication were noted, as were some alternative designs of communication networks.

Following is a summary of the specific terms and ideas developed in the chapter.

1. Successful communication is defined as the transfer of an idea or an image from a sender to a receiver that leads to an intended reaction.

2. People receive information *symbols* by means of their **receptors** (eyes, ears, noses, etc.), *decode* the symbols, and *test* the resultant information against their images (the active part of their minds) and their memories (the passive, storage part).

3. Information is transmitted by means of **effectors**, such as vocal chords and other muscles.

4. To communicate effectively, the sender needs to consider the **receiver**, to be **empathic** — to understand the world view of the intended receiver, to **neutralize** emotional content, to **avoid finality**, and to make sure the receiver understands by **repeating** the message.

5. **Encoding** translates an idea or image into symbols.

6. A **medium** is a means of transmission; a **channel** is the route through which messages flow.

7. Some major communication problems include **reception problems,** such as **attention** (receivers can absorb faster than senders can send); **channel problems,** such as **limited feedback** and **noise;** and **symbol problems,** such as misunderstood **denotations** (meaning) and different **connotations** (subjective interpretation).

8. **Downward communication** in organizations must be expanded from general directives to specific procedures. Because the directive is interpreted and expanded at each level, the chances for distortion are great.

9. **Upward communication** in organizations is usually contracted at each hierarchical level, giving each manager a chance to delete unfavorable information or unknowingly to distort a message in order to reduce the volume of information going upward.

10. **Horizontal communication** parallels the work flow in the production core. This presents special problems in hierarchical organizations because people at the same organizational level do not have authority over one another.

11. Small-group research indicates that different kinds of communication networks may have special advantages. The **wheel** is useful for simple and routine tasks; the **chain** is valuable for more complex tasks in

which work must be further specialized and divided. Chain and wheel networks resemble typical hierarchical organizations: both are efficient. However, where flexibility is desired, participation required, or satisfaction hoped for, **circle** and **all-channel** networks are preferable. These are noisy and inefficient, but permit effective communication.

12. The **grapevine** is an informal communication network in a formal organization that develops spontaneously to fill in gaps in the formal communications system.

13. The new discipline of **management information systems** (MIS) is concerned with the techniques of developing and maintaining a formal information system to deliver to managers the information they need when they need it. Computer technology is an important part of MIS systems.

14. The design of an MIS system depends on organizational *size,* the kinds of *problems faced,* the *type of information* needed, and the *amount* of information necessary for a given situation.

Discussion Questions

1. People start communicating in one form or another from the moment they are born. If "practice makes perfect," we should all be experts by the time we reach adulthood. Why, then, do we find it necessary to study communication processes?

2. In what ways would you communicate differently in the following situations?
    a. Suggesting an idea to your friends or co-workers.
    b. Presenting a proposal to your subordinates.
    c. Outlining a new plan to your boss.

3. What are the comparative advantages and disadvantages of one-way and two-way communication?

4. What is empathy? Of what value is it to effective communication? How can one develop empathy?

5. How would you go about reducing errors in communication? How successful do you think you would be? Why?

6. What is dysfunctional about the "tendency to evaluate"? Can this activity also be functional? Explain.

7. Discuss the functional and dysfunctional aspects of the downward, upward, and lateral communication processes in organizations. How can these dysfunctions be overcome? In what circumstances, if any, might dysfunctional communication be advantageous?

8. What can be learned about organization design from a study of communication networks?

9. In what ways does organization design cause communication problems? How can these problems be minimized?

10. What is the grapevine? How does it operate? As a manager, what would you do about it?

11. What is MIS? What factors should you consider in designing such a system?

Involvement Activities

Effective communication is so important, and the problems involved are so overwhelming, that volumes have been written about it, and millions of dollars have been spent on communications research. In addition, hundreds of communication exercises have been developed to help people improve their effectiveness or to illustrate a point. We have selected two such activities, but you might want to explore the library for other exercises, or even develop some original ones around the ideas discussed in the chapter.

1. Conveying messages through channels.
   a. In a classroom or other setting, arrange everyone present in a circle, either sitting or standing. Divide the circle into quarters, like the face of a clock. Ask the person at the twelve o'clock position to think out a situation involving himself or herself, or the group, or some members of it. The situation he or she develops should be true and interesting to some members, but not too complex. Then the person who develops the story or situation whispers it to the person on the right, who similarly passes it on to the next person, who passes it on to the next, and so forth. Finally the person on the left side of the originator will hear the story, and then will tell everyone exactly what she or he has heard.
      (1) Ask the originator to repeat the original version. How accurately was the message transmitted? What impeded or assisted the communication effort?
      (2) How could the process of conveying the message have been improved? What implications are there for managerial communication in organizations?
   b. Repeat the process, but to simulate the problems of communication in organizations, have three people introduce situations. Ask the people at the three o'clock, six o'clock, and nine o'clock positions each to make a true statement about the group to the person on the immediate right, who then passes it on. After everyone has heard all three stories, ask any one member to repeat all three messages exactly as heard.
      (1) Ask the originators to repeat the original versions. How accurately were the messages transmitted this time? What impeded or assisted the communication effort?
      (2) How could the process of conveying the messages have been improved? What are the implications for managerial communications in organizations?
2. One-way and two-way communication.
   a. Ask some friends or others who have not seen this activity to draw the six retangles in Figure 15–5 exactly as you describe them. They may take as much time as they wish, but may not ask any questions. (If people have seen this activity, use some diagrams they have not seen.) When they have completed the project, collect the papers.
   b. Ask your subjects to draw the six rectangles again. This time, allow full two-way communication, but refrain from showing them the diagrams. Hand back the first set of papers and show everyone the drawings.

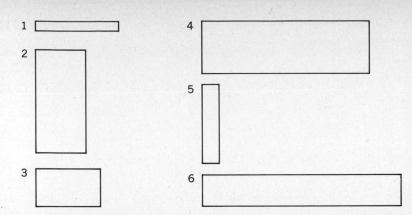

FIGURE 15–5

(1) Which set of drawings was the more accurate? Why?
(2) Was any set of drawings exact? Why or why not?
(3) How could communication about the designs have been improved?
(4) What are the implications for managerial communication?

16 Influence

This chapter continues the discussion of how managers carry out decisions by describing the influence they use to accomplish organizational goals. As we saw in the last chapter, communication is an attempt to alter another person's image through the transmitting of information. In this chapter we describe how managers can influence behavior and attitudes through the use of power.

The chapter opens with a discussion of how the influence process works in terms of the power people have at their disposal. It goes on to describe the roles of the influencer and the influencee and their relative power, with special attention to the ways power can be used to secure compliance. The chapter then continues with a discussion of influence in organizations, considering both the political nature of organizations and the kinds of intergroup relationships that affect the influence process. Finally, there is a discussion of conflict—or what happens when influence does not bring forth the results intended.

Influence sometimes implies the use of rather sneaky or manipulative behavior and conjures up visions of smoke-filled rooms and underhanded tactics. The word also may connote an image of corruptive power strategies. But for the purposes of this chapter, these negative implications will be replaced by a more neutral definition. The word **influence** will be used here to refer to the use of resources in such a way as to secure the compliance of others. Thus, influence occurs when an action by one person reinforces or changes the decisions, interactions, activities, or attitudes of someone else.

The effectiveness of an influence attempt depends on the power of the influencer relative to the power of others. Everyone has some ability to influence others. As members of an organization interact, each influences the other to some extent. The organization in action can be viewed as a network of mutual influence, a political system for governing the activities, interactions, and decisions of people at work.

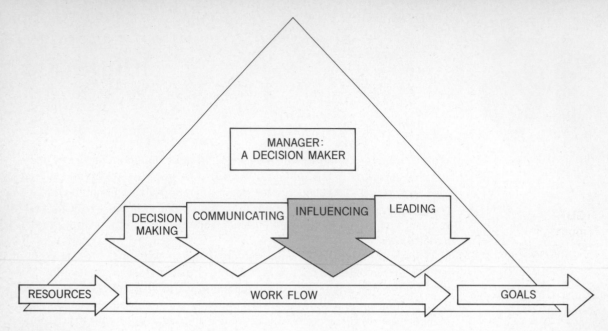

FIGURE 16–1
A manager uses his or her decision-making and communicating skills to *influence* the flow of work toward performance goals.

Figure 16–1 shows influence as the third step in the decision-implementation process. Employees must either ignore, reject, or receive the influence attempts that flow along the communication channels, thereby determining which decisions they will carry out. Since only about 20 percent of employee interactions are likely to be with supervisors, managers need to clearly understand the forces that influence an employee's choice in accepting or rejecting messages.

How Influence Works

A simple model of how influence works is presented in Figure 16–2. The process of influencing is initiated when one person (the **influencer**) sends a message (represented by the solid arrow in the figure) along a communication channel to another person (the **influencee**). The message carries not only information regarding the behavior desired, but also information regarding the force (**power**) that the influencer can apply to obtain **compliance**. Power is represented by boxes of varying thicknesses indicating the relative strength of the power base. The receiver responds either by behaving in accordance with the message or by sending back his or her own influencing message (represented by the broken arrow in the figure).

Because one of the primary responsibilities of all managers is to influence the behavior of others in ways that help to reach organizational goals, it is important that their influence attempts carry more weight than competing messages. However, whether the influencee reacts as the

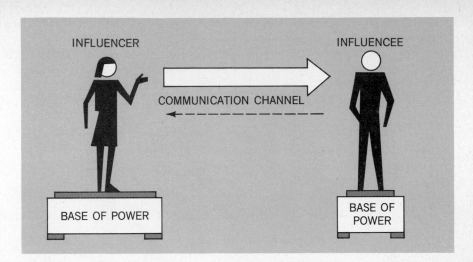

COMMUNICATION CHANNEL

BASE OF POWER

BASE OF
POWER

FIGURE 16–2
A model of the influ-
ence process.

influencer intends depends on a number of variables in the situation, including the effectiveness of the communication process and the willingness of the receiver to accept the message as a guide for behavior. The relative strength of the power base of each participant is a major determinant in the success of an influence attempt. The power base refers to the number of resources a person has available—or that people *think* he or she has available—to use as a means of exerting influence.

Power

Influencing implies an action that is occurring or that has already taken place. A manager has potential influence simply by being an employer, but the degree to which he or she actually influences behavior depends on the employees' perceptions of the manager's power. Power implies the *potential* to influence, rather than the actual influence attempt itself. In other words, power consists of the combined resources others think that one controls.

Whether an influencer actually possesses the resources of power is of less importance than that he or she is thought to possess them. For instance, many people have strong power bases simply because they are close to powerful individuals. Even though their actual resources may never be tested, they continue to exert influence through implied power. Another example is the individual, such as the neighborhood bully, who displays his or her resources only once and then is no longer questioned as to whether they still exist. The bully does not have to punch someone in the stomach very often to establish a long-standing power base.

The resources that constitute a power base are both *organizational* and *personal*. Organizational resources include authority, control of rewards and punishments, control of assets or information, relative status, and function. Personal resources include expertise, contacts, and charisma. These are illustrated in Figure 16–3 (1).

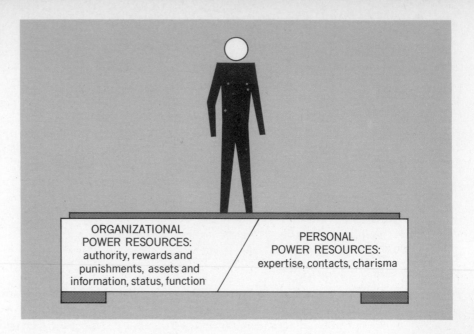

FIGURE 16-3
The resources of a managerial power base.

Authority. Power includes all resources potentially available to an individual in a social system; authority includes only those resources made available to an individual by the official and legitimate channels of an organization. Authority is the power that accompanies a position. By virtue of the legitimate authority that goes with the role, a manager has the right to command and to expect obedience. In Western societies, where organizations with authority hierarchies predominate, this right seems deeply ingrained. Thus, privates carry out the commands of sergeants, students follow the instructions of professors, and employees obey the directions of the boss. However, when sergeants are cruel, professors uncaring, and bosses less knowledgeable than their subordinates, authority may be usurped or undermined.

Because the tools of authority are generally scarce, managers often feel that their responsibility exceeds their authority, which is the means available to accomplish their work. Therefore they try to expand their power so that it will equal their responsibility. One way to do this is to rely on the use of rewards and punishments.

Rewards and Punishments. To some degree, all managers are able to reward and punish employees. As seen in Chapter 8, rewards cover a broad range of both intrinsic and extrinsic factors, some of which are always in the control of the manager, such as praise for a job well done. But different managers have differing degrees of access to rewards and punishments. Organizations need consistency, so the discretion of the manager to offer rewards or to mete out punishment is often restricted.

For example, managers are usually permitted to request salary increases for their employees, but the actual decision may be made by a committee of higher-level managers or by a staff expert. Similarly, managers in unionized organizations may find that their power to fire someone is circumscribed by the union contract.

Managers not only have differing degrees of access to rewards and punishments but they also differ in their ability to use such resources. In Chapter 8 we noted that rewards are superior to punishments. But some managers find it very difficult to praise employees and very easy to find fault. The organization often encourages this negative emphasis by providing sanctions for negative feedback but few for positive reinforcement. However, the manager who regularly makes use of reward power is likely to be a more capable supervisor than one who relies primarily on power gained through punishment.

Resources and Information. Another organizational source of power is control over resources and information. Comptrollers, for instance, derive considerable power from their ability to allocate budgets, as do secretaries and computer-information specialists, who have control over information. Control over resources and information may be a feature of a person's job, or it may be a personal characteristic. Some jobs are closely associated with resources, such as those in purchasing, finance, and personnel, which are at the resource-input position in an organization. Other jobs deal principally with information, such as those of secretaries and coordinators of various kinds. The occupants of these positions distribute resources to others. And the manner in which they do so—or fail to do so—provides them with power. Other people obtain resources and information informally. Some workers seem always to have an extra bit of information or a needed tool. Borrowing such resources comes at a price: the receiver is usually expected to return the favor at some later date. People whose work requires membership in two groups are often powerful because they can provide one group with information learned from the other in return for favors from each.

Information has the power to influence because it provides the holder with something that others need. In return for receiving the information they need, others make themselves subject, in varying degrees, to control by the informer. One consequence of this fact is that people use information as a means of achieving or maintaining power by accumulating as much knowledge as they can and then withholding it until it is to their personal advantage to divulge it.

Managers who like to keep decision making to themselves because they fear that others will usurp their authority are very likely to withhold information. An executive once stated that all the people in his organization eventually get all the information he has, but not at the same time. He apparently felt that as long as no one had as much total information as he, no one could ever replace him. And perhaps he was right to feel this way.

WELL PUT MR. SNEDLY, SIR.

Withholding information may have serious consequences only when people do not have the data they need to perform their jobs well or when the whole atmosphere of an organization is permeated with mistrust and secrecy.

Secrecy in downward communications is a common occurrence in many organizations. Not only is it used as a way for managers to protect their positions, but it also reflects what managers think employees need to know. Managers may, however, have a mistaken idea about what is and is not relevant. When employees feel information is hidden from them, they suspect that management has something to hide. If communicating is influencing, managers who withhold information might actually *decrease* their ability to influence.

Secrecy in salaries is a case in point. Management may keep employees' salaries secret because it considers wage structure to be a private affair between the individual and the organization. But the employees do not always see it this way. They are suspicious about rules that make it "inappropriate" to discuss salaries with other employees, and they suspect that management is not paying equitably for similar work. In a study of the effects of keeping wages and salaries secret, it was shown that people tend to overestimate their peers' salaries and underestimate their manager's. Thus the value of wages as a motivating device is reduced. People incorrectly tend to feel underpaid relative to their co-workers, and they do not understand the income rewards available through promotion (2).

Secrecy may also be manipulative. One may appear to be giving information while at the same time leaving out enough chunks to keep the influencee dependent or to cause him or her to behave inappropriately. Manipulation as a technique of influence relies to a large extent on secrecy. The purpose must stay hidden or the strategy will not work.

Withholding relevant information is a dangerous tool. The costs may be very high both to managers and to the organization in terms of reducing the overall amount of managers' influence. If employees feel mistrusted, they are apt to live up to management's expectations and become untrustworthy. If they are entrusted with at least as much information as is pertinent to their work and with what they are bound to hear anyway through the grapevine, they are much more likely to work hard and loyally toward the organization's goals.

Status. The position of a work group and its manager in the organization may give one group higher status than another. Position refers to the location of a group in the hierarchy, in the work flow, and in the eyes of other members of the organization. Generally, the higher the group in the hierarchy, the greater the power. The more critical the group's importance to the work flow, the higher its status. And the more the group is admired by others, irrespective of its rank in the hierarchy or its position in the work flow, the greater is its power.

Function. People whose work is central to organizational purposes, such as those in line jobs, have more power than those whose work is peripheral or supportive in nature, such as those in staff positions. Thus, people who design new products are more powerful than people who package the products. Sometimes the importance of certain functions changes, which leads to similar changes in the relative power of those who perform the functions. For example, in public utilities, such as telephone companies, marketing groups traditionally have been much less important, and therefore less powerful, than operating groups. But as other firms continue to enter the market to provide competing services, marketing groups take on increasing importance.

Expertise. All of the power resources discussed so far depend on some organizational means that the manager uses to influence others. But managers also have personal characteristics and other nonorganizational attributes that enhance their power. The most obvious of these is the manager's knowledge and skill acquired over time through training, education, and experience. The more expertise one has, the greater his or her power. We have already seen how line managers are becoming increasingly dependent on staff specialists in the area of decision making. As this trend continues—as most likely it will—the traditional power of authority may eventually give way to the power of expertise (3).

The Power of Expertise: "Red" Adair

Being an expert means having power. The greater one's skill, the higher the demand for it; and the fewer the competitors, the greater the power. Consider "Red" Adair. His expertise has made him a millionaire, easily able to surround himself with such luxury items as yachts and expensive automobiles—all in red. And yet he works only about 150 days a year. His expertise: capping oil gushers and putting out oil-well fires.

One day in 1939, Myron Kinley, who invented the business of stopping runaway oil wells, watched as young, redheaded Paul Adair was blown fifty feet into the air by an oil gusher and then calmly picked himself up and returned to work. Admiring such courage, Kinley hired Adair on the spot. When Kinley retired in 1959 he turned the oil well capping business over to "Red." Today, Adair manages a firm of experts at gusher capping, reserving the "impossible" jobs for himself.

In the early spring of 1977, the Phillips Petroleum Company was developing oil wells for Norway in the rich Ecofisk field in the North Sea. One day in April the well called "Bravo 14" erupted, sending a geyser of crude oil two hundred feet into the air. During a week-long series of futile attempts to cap the gusher, five million gallons of crude oil fouled the North Sea. After four unsuccessful attempts to stop the flow, the gusher continued unabated. Finally, Adair flew to Norway from Houston, Texas, and with his crew successfully capped the well. His expertise succeeded where that of others had failed. One of Adair's other feats included stopping a gas-well fire in Algeria that experts expected to burn for a century.

But the job has its dangers. In 1954 Adair's hips were crushed during one adventure, and doctors said he would remain a cripple for life. True to form, he was back at work in four months.

Source: "Taming Bravo 14," *Newsweek,* May 9, 1977, pp. 47–50.

Contacts. Alliances with powerful figures or departments, associations with influential and expanding parts of an organization, and important contacts outside the organization invariably add weight to one's power base. It is a fact of organizational life that people are able to secure and maintain jobs and rise in the hierarchy as a result of whom they know. This practice does not seem particularly fair, and often it isn't; but if you were a manager and two equally qualified people applied for a position in your department, would you hire the one you did not know or the one who came with a letter of introduction from the vice-president of your firm?

Charisma. Charisma is a special quality or characteristic of personality that attracts popular loyalty and inspires devotion and enthusiasm. John F. Kennedy, Martin Luther King, Jr., Elvis Presley, and Billy Graham are a few examples of people who have captured the imagination of the public, or at least a segment of it, with their charismatic personalities. In an organization, a person with charisma can create a high level of loyalty and morale in a work group. But devotion to a person can be a problem for an organization, especially if the goals of the charismatic leader are more personal than organizational. Like the Pied Piper leading the children away from their homes, the charmer may lead employees off on nonproductive tangents. In addition, organizations or departments may run into trouble when a charismatic manager leaves. The successor, no matter how competent, will never be able to live up to the bigger-than-life image of the former leader that remains in the minds of the employees.

The Influencer

We all need to feel that we have some control over our personal environment; and such control comes from being able to influence others. In organizations, those systems in which people must cooperate in order to accomplish work, the influence process determines the priorities of who gets what, when, and where. Managers will be effective to the extent that they are successful in influencing employees to work efficiently toward organizational goals.

The Role of the Influencer. Influencing is much like communicating with someone else. The influencer evaluates the potential influencee, but the influencee may either accept or reject the influencing message. Regardless of how large the power base of the influencer, or how small the

Some Side Effects of Power

To many people, power has negative connotations. But in at least one study it was found that people like to have a powerful manager, and that both their satisfaction and their notions of their productivity are likely to increase proportionally with the power of the manager.

The study in question involved a survey of professors in college departments, which sought the professors' views of the power of their departmental chairpersons. Few managerial-type jobs have less authority invested in the position than do college department heads. Yet even in this role of modest authority, power was found to differ greatly from chairperson to chairperson, even among those heading departments of the same name in different schools.

The study concluded that:

1. The higher the power of the department head, the greater was the likelihood that he or

she could do things to benefit the faculty, and thus the greater the likelihood that the faculty was satisfied.

2. The higher the power of the department head, the more likely was the faculty to think of their department as productive.

3. Variations in the power of the department head explained more of the differences among faculty members in satisfaction and perceived productiveness than did such variables as the faculty member's age, rank, degrees, or years of teaching.

4. The greater the expertise of the faculty member, the less he or she perceived the department head as having power.

Managerial power apparently makes life easier for subordinates: they have more tools and rewards and their jobs are more secure if the boss has considerable clout.

Source: Winston Hill and Wendell French, "Perceptions of Power of Department Chairmen by Professors," *Administrative Science Quarterly*, Vol. 11, no. 4 (March 1967), pp. 548–574.

base of the influencee, the latter is always the one who makes the final choice. Even in the most extreme situations the influencee has alternatives to consider. For example, in the Nazi concentration camps, where compliance with the demands of the captors would seem inevitable, some prisoners chose to die rather than to obey orders that, to them, were beyond human endurance.

In less dramatic circumstances, managers depend on their power as a means of influencing employees to carry out work orders. But the combined power base of all employees is greater than that of a manager, and if the manager's demands are unreasonable, employees may rebel and subvert the influence attempt.

To help avoid the possibility of rebellion, managers need to choose carefully the power resources they bring to bear in the influencing process. Not all resources are equally applicable in all circumstances. For example, the use of authority would be out of place in a committee meeting of equally ranked department heads. Similarly, the use of expertise in a field such as physics would carry little influencing power when discussing the budget with accountants. Different individuals react differently to power resources. Technical people tend to appreciate expertise; newcomers might defer to rank.

The resources a manager chooses to use to influence behavior will depend on the size of his or her power base, the amount and variety of resources within it, and the degree to which the power base is concentrated for easy access. In some organizations, power is concentrated in a few positions. For example, in an elite military unit or a winning football team or a strong and stable business, the power may lie in the hands of one or a few closely associated managers. In other organizations power is diffused or fragmented. To the extent that power is fragmented, employees will be subjected to conflicting demands, all of which have some legitimacy, but none of which overrides the others. The more fragmented an organization's power, the greater the likelihood of its containing opposing political coalitions.

The influencer is always risking his or her power base whenever an influence attempt is made. Where a person exercises power successfully, the amount of influence is increased. But when the person's influence attempt fails, then the power base is diminished. The neighborhood bully may get by for some time on past reputation as a terror, but if he or she happens to pick on someone tougher and gets roughed up, the bully's former followers may desert to the new power figure.

Although everyone seems to need to influence and control others, some seem to have a special, personal need for power.

Desire to Influence. According to the psychologist David McClelland, power is one of the three major socially derived needs of people. Along with the *need for affiliation* and the *need for achievement*, the *need for power* is a vigorous motivating force. McClelland's research indicates that managers have a stronger need for power than do other people, and that effective managers have a stronger need for power than for either achievement or affiliation (4).

Managers with a great need to achieve may have trouble assigning work to other people. They usually want to do everything themselves. Subordinates of such managers tend to think that they have no responsibilities, to report that their boss never praises them, and to believe that things are not very well organized.

Managers with a strong need for affiliation want to be liked and so seek to avoid unpopular decisions. They also have a tendency to let the personal problems of their employees interfere with the tasks to be done. Because these managers focus on people instead of on the work, they may be ineffective in accomplishing organizational goals.

People with a strong need for power have a desire to influence the behavior of others. Becoming a manager is a good way to satisfy such a need, but it may be a bit alarming to others, especially to those who must bear the brunt of its effects. People often fear power, and are particularly leery of those who seem to "need" it. McCelland notes that managers can express their needs for power in two ways: by seeking personal aggrandizement (power over) or by accumulating resources to better accomplish organizational goals (power to). The first expression confirms the reasons why people fear others' needs for power, for it represents a need to have control over other people. The second expression of power is far less threatening and one that organizations often seek in their managers. Through this behavior managers can satisfy their own power needs while performing a superior job both for their organizations and for their employees (5).

Whether a manager with a strong need for power will choose to express this need through personal aggrandizement or through the accomplishment of organizational goals depends to a large extent on the socialization processes to which he or she has been exposed. If an individual's drives have been directed into socially acceptable channels, then he or she is likely to choose organizational expression. Such managers tend to be "joiners" of organizations and to take leading roles in them. They like work, the discipline work entails, and the feeling of accomplishment and pride they get when they see the results. Personal and organizational objectives are often indistinguishable. But problems may arise with these managers resulting from the fact that they have trouble understanding employees who have little desire to work or who seem more concerned with their own needs than with the demands of their jobs. In addition, they may be empire builders who amass resources more for the sake of accumulation than because there is a need for them.

The Influencee

The influencee is like the receiver in communication: the role is to accept the influence attempt. Acceptance in this case is complying with the desire of the influencer. *Compliance* may be defined as the act of yielding to the desires, demands, proposals, or coercive techniques of other people. Compliance is a primary part of the relationship between those who have power and those over whom they exercise it. As said earlier, the effectiveness of an influence attempt can be judged only by the results it obtains. If the attempt produces the intended behavior (that is, if people comply), then the influence is successful.

A Model of Compliance. The basic model of compliance is the same as that of the influence process but from the point of view of the person who complies. The reasons for compliance may be stated in a variety of ways, but what they all have in common is that the influencee believes either that compliance will lead to need satisfaction or that refusal will lead to need deprivation. Those who have power manipulate the means at their disposal so that the influencee finds that following the directive leads to rewards and that refusing to follow the directive leads to deprivation.

Two major factors are at work in compliance. First is the influencee's perception of the power of the influencer to benefit or to restrict the influencee. Some power resources are coercive, or negative, from the point of view of the one who is supposed to comply, such as power to demote, discharge, or withhold benefits. Other power instruments are positive or rewarding. The power to promote an employee or to raise wages are examples of this type. Other power resources are based on shared values or norms. Charisma, status, and deeply valued work are examples of normative power means. These can be represented as a continuum of influencer power from the point of view of the influencee, which ranges from very negative to highly positive, as shown on the left side, or vertical axis, of Figure 16–4 (6).

Second are the attitudes of the influencee about influencer power. These attitudes range from alienated to committed, as shown on the horizontal axis of Figure 16–4. Together these two continua form the matrix of cells indicated in the figure.

An examination of the matrix suggests that the type of power used becomes part of the overall situation that influences attitudes. Cells 7, 5, and 3 are examples of situations in which types of power used and influencee attitudes about compliance are *congruent* with one another. If an imbalance occurs, considerable pressure exists to move toward a more congruent mode. Consider cell 5, for example. A business organization hires a person for pay; the individual accepts the job for pay and a congruent situation exists. But if the employee becomes deeply committed (cell 6) his peers are likely to push him back into a more calculative attitude. Similarly, if managers try normative means to secure compliance (cell 2), such as company picnics, overzealous messages from high officials, or one-big-happy-family sermons, employees with strictly calculative orientations are likely to become alienated (cell 1).

Types of power and types of influencee attitudes are rarely so neatly segmented as Figure 16–4 implies. Powerful figures have many means of

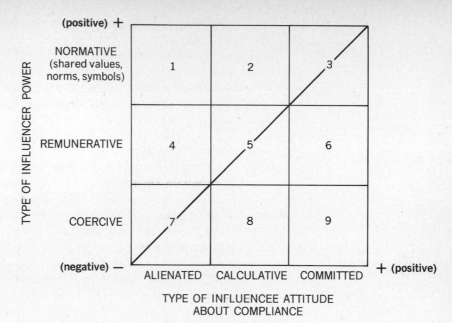

FIGURE 16–4
A model of compliance: A matrix of types of influencee attitudes about compliance based on types of influencer power.

The vertical axis labeled "type of influencer power" is a continuum ranging from negative-coercive to remunerative to normative-positive types of power. The horizontal axis, labeled "type of influencee attitude about compliance," is a continuum ranging from alienated-negative to committed-positive. The exercise of one kind of power or another is likely to elicit compliance in kind: cells 7, 5, and 3 show this type of consistency. Compliance indicated by the other cells is unlikely. Cell 9, for example, indicates that committed compliance is unlikely if the influencer uses coercive power.

influence at their disposal; and attitudes, too, range over the entire continuum. But the matrix does suggest that it might be easier for managers to secure compliance when the means deployed are consistent with employees' expectations.

The Relative Nature of Compliance

In any situation, the power of the influencer to secure the compliance of the influencee is relative to the influencee's view of the other's power and to his or her own power base. The greater the balance of power held by the influencer (in the other's view), the greater the probability of compliance. Furthermore, the greater the power of the influencer to satisfy rather than deny the other's needs, the more readily will the influencee comply, provided that the attitudes of the influencee are consistent with the power used, as explained earlier. If one is alienated, neither expertise, more pay, nor preaching of strong norms is likely to do any good. However, as employee attitudes become more positive, managers can use more positive power implements. By the same token, the use of positive power resources can encourage positive attitudes. Which comes first might depend on the particular situation, but it is unusual for employees to develop positive attitudes under oppressive power conditions.

Finally, it should be remembered that power is relative, and that everyone has some power. When the power of one person is inadequate in a situation, one way to increase that power is to combine with others, all of whom have a little power. Employee unions are one result of such combinations of small power.

Response to Compliance. All managers must depend on their employees to reach organizational goals. But most managers simply do not have the time or the energy to oversee all work personally. Thus a manager has to have some minimal level of trust in his or her subordinates. A manager who habitually employs coercive power techniques, or who is uncooperative or inconsiderate of workers' needs may find that employees will take advantage of the area of discretion they do have.

After all, the influencee has the choice of accepting or not accepting any influence attempt. But even when complying, the influencee can undermine the intended behavior. The most obvious way is with minimal compliance, which may be simply doing a job "as directed" and nothing more. The person in this situation does not use discretion at all. In many cases this action brings chaos to the organization, since almost all tasks are designed for people to use their discretion. But the influencer cannot complain, as employees are "doing exactly what they are told to do."

Employees' knowledge of their jobs is a form of expertise. To the degree that it is hard to replace a particular worker, that person obtains power. For a number of reasons, the longer one stays on the job the more power is obtained. First, the job changes with time to more closely fit the particular person. Second, a successful performance leads a manager to let the person do the job without interference. Third, the person learns his or her way around in the organization, learns whom to contact, where to find information, and what information to transmit to whom. These are all advantages that add to the employee's power base and that can be used to make compliance relative to the type of power used in the influence process. In other words, employees' *zones of acceptance,* discussed in Chapter 7, tend to change over time as they become acquainted with the organization. As they learn the strengths and weaknesses of those who try to influence them, they acquire more understanding and need less direct command. At the same time, their decisions to participate with energy and enthusiasm may become less frequent until they reach some kind of stability between their needs to be part of the organization and their needs to be independent of it. The unsatisfied needs that brought them to the organization in the first place are likely to become moderately well satisfied over time. Somehow managers must be enough aware of the changing nature of worker needs to know what is motivating them; and in addition, they must have the power to help satisfy these needs, whatever they may be (7).

Influence in the Organization

An organization is a social system in that it is composed of people interacting with one another to accomplish shared and personal goals. And every social system is also a political system: it needs to be governed. In this sense, managers are like governors because much of their work is of a political nature.

The political aspect of the managerial task requires the use of power. In all organizations rules need to be made, procedures need to be carried out, and performance needs to be evaluated; these functions are part of the formal political system of organizations. Informal politicking also exists to serve a variety of purposes. Formal and informal political processes are the topics of the first part of this section.

The political power of organizational members is not a function of the political system only, however. Assigned tasks also influence the power base. Therefore, the second part of this section will examine the ways in which various kinds of working relationships influence political processes within organizations.

The Organization as a Political System

The term *politics* has two meanings, both of which have implications for managers. In the first sense, politics means the governance of human associations and includes objective and emotionally neutral functions. In the second sense, politics, especially in recent years, has strong negative implications, connoting artful or dishonest practices. According to the first definition, which may be called **formal politicking,** the manager's job involves the active process of influencing behavior and directing it toward organizational goals. In terms of the second definition, sometimes referred to as **informal politicking,** the manager's job involves undercover power plays designed to improve or maintain personal or group status.

Formal Politicking. The three primary functions of a political system — legislative, executive, and judicial — are the legitimate and formal political processes of an organization.

The *legislative function* in an organization includes determining goals, subdividing work, setting policies and procedures to guide behavior, and securing and allocating the tools of authority. Because the supply of resources (the total power base) in any organization is limited or scarce, someone must decide who gets what. Any allocation decision is difficult. Individuals and groups usually want more, and want to do more, than resources permit. We have seen in earlier chapters how this leads to considerable competition and conflict between people and departments within the organization.

When managers allocate the scarce resources of power strictly in accordance with the precise work needs of a unit, the allocation is consistent with organizational goals. But many factors contribute to a more arbitrary allocation procedure. Members of any unit "politic" for more than their fair share to increase their status, to make their jobs easier, or to provide a cushion for unexpected events. Individuals also politic, or bargain, for greater allotments of personal resources in order to improve their position in the hierarchy (8).

The *executive function* is the process of carrying out, executing, or administering policies in accordance with the rules established by legislative action. Specific activities include coordinating specialized and divided work and leading people to achieve organizational goals.

In any social system, some people break the rules, some do better than expected, some feel slighted, others get into fights, and so forth. The *judicial function* is concerned with adjusting grievances, conferring rewards, administering punishments, and settling conflicts.

In the running of federal, state, and local governments, the three functions are, at least in theory, kept separate and maintained as a system of checks and balances. In business organizations, however, these functions are generally fused, or at least indistinctly separated. Boards of directors are supposed to act as legislative bodies, passing laws to be administered by managers. But in fact, most boards are controlled by the top managers, either because the senior executives own a controlling interest in the firm or because they control the votes of widely scattered and diffuse shareholders. To some degree a distinction between the legislative and executive functions does exist in that senior executives determine goals, set policies, and make general plans, while those at the lower levels carry out operations. But again the difference is often indistinct. Typically, managers at all levels carry out the judicial function in dispensing justice and settling conflict. And although grievances are occasionally handled by judicial procedures established by contract with a union, even then the grievance channels often parallel the managerial hierarchy. Only when a grievance goes to arbitration is there a truly "outside" judicial hearing. In general, managers at all levels of business organizations perform all three political functions.

Pressure from government, from public interest groups, and from labor unions has called into question this concentration of authority, and certain restrictions have been imposed. Business managers more and more are finding their prerogatives (power instruments) limited by such laws as antitrust edicts and antidiscrimination regulations. And in the future there may be even greater challenges to this concentration of power. Domestic businesses in this country are closely associated with those in other nations, and trends elsewhere may soon affect policies at home. For example, in northern Europe, and especially in West Germany, representatives of employees, the general public, and the stockholders share the legislative function of business as they sit together on corporate boards of directors. When policies, procedures, and rules are set by such autonomous legislatures, the authority of internal managers becomes significantly restricted (9).

Informal Politicking. Formal political processes are essential to maintaining the governance of the organization. On the other hand, informal politicking, the activities involved in enlarging one's own power base for personal rather than for organizational reasons, can divert the flow of scarce organizational resources from the work to be done to individuals or groups. This is not to say that informal politicking is either unnecessary or undesirable, however. The history of the rise and fall of empires—and of organizations—is a study in intrigue: novels, movies, and television

Building Power by Politicking

Most managers will tell tales of empire building and power politics in their organizations, but few systematic studies have been made of politicking in organizations. One recent exception is a study conducted by Rosabeth Moss Kanter, a professor of sociology at Yale University.

Kanter defines power as the ". . . ability to mobilize resources to get and use whatever is needed to achieve a person's work goals." In this sense the need for power is not necessarily based on greed, but on the real need to have the means to get the work accomplished. In large hierarchical organizations such as the firm Kanter studied (which she calls Indsco, a fictitious name), only those doing routine jobs had everything they needed to get the work done; everyone else had to work with—and to influence—others.

She reasons that power does not come automatically with the delegation of authority. Managers have to engage in politics to get it. Successful managers in Indsco acquired the power they needed to do their jobs by engaging in the following political activities:

• *doing an extraordinary, visible, and relevant job* (because simply doing a job well is expected and brings neither power nor much notice);

• *being innovative,* making changes, handling crises, managing work so as to gain the favorable notice of others;

• *taking extraordinary risks,* which if successful, bring fame and fortune;

• *maintaining high visibility,* such as being in a boundary-spanning job between the organization and the environment, or between subunits; or being on a prominent task force or committee;

• *engaging in activities considered relevant* in terms of the organization's goals and ideology;

• *developing stable and long-term social connections* outside the immediate work group. Especially important are:

1. *sponsors* in higher management, who fight for their protégés, make it possible for them to short-circuit the chain of command, and endow the protégé with some of their power;

2. *peers,* whom the power-seeker can aid without arrogance (because people do want help but they do not like to feel put down); and

3. *subordinates,* especially those on the way up, on whose loyalty the manager's power depends (and who might some day be one's superior manager).

Kanter questions two assumptions: that successful performance alone leads to power, and that good human relations without the right connections is of any value. One very warm and sensitive manager had his subordinates turn against him because he had no clout with higher administrators.

Source: Rosabeth Moss Kanter, "Power Games in the Corporation," *Psychology Today,* vol. 11 (July 1977), pp. 48–53, 92.

shows reflect the theme. Politicking seems to be a necessary part of the human condition. Although the goals are personal power, influence, and status, rather than the efficient accomplishment of organizational work, management may be able to keep valuable employees only by allowing them to make personal use of organizational resources. In this sense, the diversion of resources to individuals represents payment for services. The results of informal politicking are "bad" only when the costs — however measured — exceed the benefits — however measured. Politicking, though, needs to be carefully controlled.

But control of informal political processes is made difficult by the fact that they are often inseparable from the formal processes. For instance, when a manager promotes an employee, it is not always clear whether it is because the subordinate's work is superior, the manager is playing favorites, or both. People learn quickly how to justify almost any behavior in terms of organizational needs. And the larger one's base of power the more effective — and believable — such maneuvers are likely to be.

An allocation process, like the budgetary procedure, generally is objective enough to ensure that the relatively powerless parts of the system receive at least the minimum resources required to get a marginal job done. But the powerful parts can become rich and complacent, receiving far more than they need to do even the best possible job. And if the imbalance becomes too great, poor areas develop reputations for incompetence and their leaders are replaced. Rich areas can become so sluggish that internal audits are ordered to prune off unnecessary fat. However, even these more or less automatic controls do not always operate effectively. Organizations can and do collapse from poor resource allocation.

Both formal and informal politicking require the building of a power base of resources, the use or administration of these resources, and the ability to make judgments about behavior (means) and outcomes (ends). In the process, people establish coalitions, attempt to influence others, and manipulate resources for personal, group, and organizational ends.

Political activities can be an exciting part of managerial work, or they can be the source of extreme frustration. The same can be said for the kinds of working relationships managers are assigned, for these also develop into political arrangements and affect the power bases of managers (10).

Organizational Relationships

The purpose of the rich variety of interactions in which managers engage is to accomplish the work of the organization or of one of its subunits. Each of the contacts managers make, each relationship established, requires the use of influence and also puts the manager in the position of being influenced. One obvious kind of relationship is the vertical, or supervisory, relationship. Sayles has pointed out that the study of a variety of other kinds of relationships is a neglected area of management research. He suggests categorizing the several kinds of nonhierarchical relationships in which managers, particularly middle managers, are involved in order to understand them better. The character of the relationships that are established determines the degree of influence a manager is likely to have (11).

Vertical Relationships. The first and most obvious set of relationships engaged in by managers is that of vertical, or superior-subordinate interaction. All managers are members of at least two internal groups: the units they supervise and the units on the next higher level of the organizational hierarchy. In this latter relationship, the manager is but one of several people reporting to a higher-level executive. These relationships are depicted in Figure 16–5. In level 1 in the figure, the manager and the workers are shown as constituting one group. All level-1 managers and one level-2 manager constitute the second group. From this perspective it can be seen that managers are the connecting link between all members of the organization (12).

Clearly, authority dominates these vertical relationships. Managers on each successively higher level have authority over all persons in their particular work group. But managerial authority is usually enhanced by other bases of power as well. Higher-level managers have more rewards and punishments, as well as resources and information, to distribute to lower-level managers and employees. There is also the presumption, if the selection process is operating, that higher-level managers have expertise superior to that of their immediate subordinates.

Other relationships are nonsupervisory in nature, but nevertheless influence the power and politics of organizations. Included are work-flow,

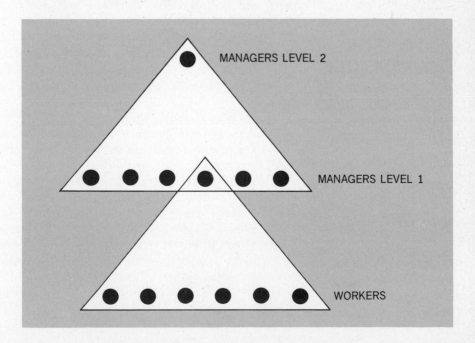

FIGURE 16–5
The manager as linking pin.

trading, service, advisory, auditing, stabilization, and innovation relationships (13).

Work-Flow Relationships. These interactions consist of the input and output transactions of the work group. Such contacts represent coordination attempts and emphasize the interdependent nature of the work process of turning inputs into outputs. Because of differences of opinion that occur about the proper or correct sequencing of work, groups often jockey for positions along the work-flow continuum. Positions at the beginning of the work-flow process are preferable to those at the end because that is where control over resources is centered. The closer to the end, the more constrained the group is by what has already happened. Furthermore, positions at the beginning of the process often have more status than do those farther down the line. The power base involved in work-flow relationships, then, is not authority, but rather the control of resources, relative status, and type of function.

Trading Relationships. These involve the exchanges of goods and services that take place in the process of accomplishing goals. Unlike the relationship between buyers and sellers in the open market, these internal exchanges have no common denominator or price to indicate whether the transactions are equitable. Sayles defined three stages of trading relationships. The first, *missionary work,* involves contacting people to find out what they have or what they might need that would be of value in an exchange. The second stage involves *negotiating* some equitable exchange rate. And the third stage consists of *exchanging information* about the needs and capabilities of each party involved in the trading process (14). Since these arrangements are informal, quite a bit of information needs to change hands so that each party may become aware of any potential problems or risks involved in the transaction. In addition, each party in the trading relationship will want to know what the others need.

Power base elements that are appropriate for trading relationships are resources and information. Other bases would seem inappropriate except for the personal ability of the manager to drive a good bargain.

Service Relationships. Any kind of helping transaction is a service relationship. Some subunits, such as typing pools or mailroom services, are set up primarily to service others. Managers of service units ordinarily have responsibility for setting priorities and schedules. This provides a certain amount of power within the organization because the managers of other work groups will have to depend on these people to help them meet their schedules. This power is based on control of resources and on the function performed. Reciprocity or social exchange helps the manager deal with such groups. Alienating service groups is dangerous, and can deprive a work group of considerable needed support.

Advisory Relationships. In these relationships the function of one group is to counsel another. However, advisory relationships do not always work out as intended. Managers who go to others for advice tend to subordinate themselves by admitting that the advisors are more expert than they. Clever managers of advisory units can manipulate advice-giving interactions so that a particular answer or advised course of action seems to be obvious and clearly the idea of the advice-seeker. In these instances the advisee is usually thankful that the advisor does not take over his or her decision-making role. Advisory relationships are based mainly on the power of expertise.

Auditing Relationships. When one group checks up on another, the relationship is an auditing one. These relationships often appear threatening to the group that is being audited and, consequently, inhibit open communication. The problem is that auditors need the help of the group being audited to get needed information, and the group being audited wants to protect their work and therefore may withhold vital information.

Consider, for example, groups whose work is checked periodically by an auditor who shows up at random intervals. One group may establish a network of informants who signal the auditor's approach so that everyone has time to put his or her work in order. Another group may force the auditor to come around only at prescheduled times, thus accomplishing the same objective. And a third group may actually allow random spot checks but arrange with the auditor an agreement to withhold any negative information until the work is in top order.

Among all the types of interactions, auditing relationships have the highest potential for creating bad feelings between groups. A major contributing factor is that auditors as a group are often unlikely to compromise or to engage in reciprocal or collaborative bargaining activities. The power of the auditor is based to a substantial extent on the power to punish, which explains the negative reactions. Effective dealing with auditors requires keeping and using accurate information.

Stabilization Relationships. These interactions might be called preauditing relationships because they involve seeking approval prior to actions. Examples include checking with public relations people before making a public announcement, and getting clearance from the personnel department before firing an employee. Effective stabilization activities remove some authority and responsibility from the work-group manager, which creates a splintered system of staff groups who have line authority. The purpose of stabilization relationships is to maintain consistent and reliable behavior, so the major power base is expertise.

Innovative Relationships. Directly opposite stabilization relationships in mission are those interactions that occur between special organizational units charged with developing new techniques or with generating new work for personnel in other parts of the organization. These relationships are often difficult at best. Innovation means change, and change is not always viewed positively by those who must do the changing. In order to be effective, groups charged with innovation are better off having a minimum of contact with other parts of the organization and a maximum of internal autonomy. For example, research and development departments are ordinarily kept isolated from other groups. The contacts, when they do occur, may be of critical importance to the organization, for research personnel have many contacts with the broader environment that contains the whole organization. Building easy working relationships between boundary-spanning, adaptive, and the internal production core presents a substantial challenge to the general manager. Expertise is the major power base of innovation groups.

Conflict

One fact that emerges from the preceding discussion is that authority is not the only power tool available to managers. Influence attempts may come from many different sources as a result of the variety of relationships that exist within organizations. Because the demands of potential influencers are unlikely to be consistent, the potential influencee may be in a conflict situation at least some of the time. Therefore, the exercise of power may or may not lead to compliance. And even if the influencee does comply outwardly, such compliance can lead to circumvention, withdrawal, alienation, sabotage, and various manifestations of other forms of conflict. The way in which conflict is expressed depends on the reciprocal power base of the person who is the target of the initial influence attempt.

The remainder of this chapter examines some of the reasons for the occurrence of conflict, the nature of the conflict situation, and the means whereby conflict can be managed. Since conflict in an organization (and elsewhere) is inevitable and, to a degree, healthy, the emphasis will be on managing conflict, not resolving it.

What Is Conflict?

Conflict is a disagreement or a collision between two or more opposing forces. It can also be internal to an individual, as when one is confronted with two alternatives of equal strength and value. Choosing either alternative means sacrificing the other.

Many people have a tendency to classify virtually any kind of clash as an interpersonal problem or a "personality conflict." To be sure, there are people with whom—for no apparent reason—one cannot get along. Often, however, what appears to be a personality conflict is in fact negative feelings that have carried over from other events or, perhaps, from some aspect of the organization design.

Why Conflict Occurs

In organizations, the two main bases of contention are disagreements among people about means and about ends. Conflict about means can be further categorized into two kinds of arguments: *which* means should be used to reach an agreed goal; and *who* should control which means. The first type of conflict refers to disagreement over method. The second has to do with who should control scarce implements of power. Means conflicts develop between members of functional groups with overlapping jurisdictions. The payroll preparation function, for example, involves both the personnel and the accounting departments. Conflicts arise over such matters as times of payment, accuracy of deductions, and responsibility for accuracy.

Conflict is also built in to an organization to the extent that an employee is subject to the influence of anyone other than his or her immediate supervisor. As noted throughout this book, getting the work done requires that every employee interact with many others, and everyone may have a different notion of how the means should be used. Every interaction requires communication, and a great many communication attempts are influence attempts. It follows, then, that everyone is subject to a number of competing influences. An employee is influenced by peers, by supervisors, by staff personnel, and by many others. The idea of the one-person, one-boss rule, or the "unity of command principle" is both a recognition that conflict occurs because of multiple influences, and a suggestion of what to do about it.

Conflict about ends represents the other major basis of contention. Some of this conflict represents inevitable differences of opinion about goals and values, which need to be worked through. But other such conflicts result from the organization design. In the process of dividing and assigning work, individuals and groups wind up with different functions to achieve different goals. Over time, members of various functional groups develop norms and values that center around the kind of work they do. The classic battle between production and sales people fits into this mold. An aim of production personnel is to keep costs low; a goal of sales people is to increase sales. Contradictory strategies are involved in keeping costs low (standardized products and long production runs) and in increasing sales (special orders, small lots, and specially tailored products). The result, of course, is conflict between the two groups.

The Elements of Conflict

Kenneth Boulding has suggested that there are four elements in the conflict situation: the parties involved, the arena or field in which the conflict takes place, the interactions that occur, and the control or resolution of the conflict (15).

The Parties to Conflict. Conflict generally involves at least two parties, which may be individuals, groups, or even organizations. Boulding notes a tendency for conflict to be between individuals and other individuals; between groups and other groups, and between organizations and other organizations. When conflict is not "symmetrical," as when an individual is in conflict with a group, there is a tendency toward equalization of the sides. For example, in the case of the individual versus the group, either one member of the group will become the sole protagonist, or the individual will seek the support of others to bolster his or her case.

The Field of Conflict. The field of conflict does not refer to the place where the conflict occurs, but rather to the conditions that exist at the onset of the disagreement (including the power bases of the parties) and the range of alternative routes that the conflict might follow. The power bases and the alternatives in the field change during the course of the interaction. For instance, both parties attempt to win by using their resources of power. If one party makes significant gains by using certain resources, those resources may be unavailable for use in subsequent "rounds."

The Interactions in Conflict. The activities involved in conflict represent a special case of attempted influence in which two or more parties pit their strength against one another in the hope of winning. The behavior involved in this kind of conflict may be understood in terms of the techniques of game theory (16). The parties to the conflict decide what alternative paths to select—what strategies to use—based on the alternatives they see open to them and on estimates of what they think their opponents will do. These dynamics can be seen in operation in the boxed insert called "The Prisoners' Dilemma." For either team to win, the parties must cooperate with each other—a phenomenon that rarely happens.

The Prisoners' Dilemma

BLUE

		X	Y
RED	A	Both +3	Red −6 Blue +6
	B	Red +6 Blue −6	Both −3

The payoff rates are indicated in each box. The rules are that Red must choose either A or B on each turn and Blue must choose either X or Y. Clearly, if Red always chooses A and Blue always chooses X, both teams would gain something and neither would lose. Although this would appear to be the most logical strategy, it is almost never employed in real-life situations. In open conflict, causing the opponent to lose seems at least as important as helping oneself to win.

Competitors seldom trust one another enough to feel confident that the other will keep his or her part of the bargain. You can see what would happen if the teams agreed to cooperate and one failed to do so.

The Control and Resolution of Conflict. Conflict occurs from time to time during the course of all human interactions. For the most part, there is eventual resolution. The outcomes of conflict are likely to differ according to a number of variables in the situation, including the relative size of the power base of the contestants and, in organizations, the management techniques used to control the episode.

When one party has considerable power over the other, the resolution is often in favor of the stronger party. But whether the defeated member physically leaves or simply suffers, the winner must contend with the effects. If the loser withdraws, the winner is left without the talents of the other. In some instances these talents may be easily replaced, but other times they may not be. If the loser remains, the winner will have to contend with an alienated associate; and to gain further contributions, the winner may have to exert constant pressure of threatened punishment.

When power is more nearly equal, possible resolutions are many, ranging from continued conflict to cooperation to the integration or merging of the contending forces. Which solution is adopted depends on the conflict field and on other dynamics of the situation. As noted earlier, cooperative modes depend on a climate of mutual trust, which may be difficult to attain.

Organizations develop a number of techniques to use in managing conflict. These include glossing over the conflict, buying off the contenders, unifying them under some overall goal, and securing the help of a third party.

The first technique, pretending the conflict does not exist, is often employed when conflict is viewed as an abnormal process. Ignoring causes does not make problems go away, however.

If the conflict is over the means of power, giving the combatants something they want—buying them off—may ease the tension. However, this technique does not deal with the reasons for the tensions, and will not resolve deep-seated differences.

The third device involves focusing the attention of both parties on a larger, *superordinate* goal that takes precedence over the causes of conflict. This technique is quite effective as a temporary measure—especially if the distracting goal is of real and immediate concern to the two parties and requires their joint effort to achieve success. However, once the goal is accomplished, the causes of the original conflict may reemerge.

Where conflicts of major importance arise regularly, the solution process may also be regularized. For example, an outside agent may be called in to help settle the dispute. The outsider may take a variety of roles, ranging from referee to judge. In collective bargaining cases, for example, agencies of the government act as referees. If the case cannot be decided in this way, it may be sent to arbitration where the third party acts as judge and sets the terms of agreement.

Managing Conflict

Although conflict is a naturally occurring phenomenon, people are ambivalent about it. They like the heady excitement of the game, and especially of winning the game. Competition and controlled conflict often build spirit, enthusiasm, and vigor, and result in such positive outcomes as innovation and creativity. But other types of conflict, such as oppression, warfare, and sabotage, are destructive and cause people considerable grief. Managers in organizations need to be aware of the distinction between healthy and destructive conflict and exert necessary controls to prohibit the one turning into the other. The management of conflict, therefore, would seem to require an acceptance of its inevitability with an eye to the desirable outcomes relative to the undesirable outcomes. McGregor suggests that an open discussion of points of contention between contestants, in a climate of mutual trust, might be a very effective way to manage many types of conflict that occur between employees in organizations (17).

Chapter Review

In this chapter we have described the influence process. We have seen that the degree of influence one person has over another is based on the relative power of both parties in the influence attempt. Power is derived from a number of sources, and the ways in which these power resources are used also contribute to the influencer's effectiveness. Especially important, too, are the attitudes of the influencees as they comply, or do not comply, under different kinds of power conditions. The formal and informal political systems within organizations, along with the relationships between organizational members, affect the distribution of power and the use of influence. Conflict, which can be viewed as disagreements about the resources of power, how they should be used, and who should control them, is more or less inevitable, and it needs to be managed rather than suppressed or resolved.

Following are some of the specific terms and ideas developed in the chapter.

1. **Influence** is the use of resources to secure the compliance of others.
2. The elements in the influence process are an **influencer,** an **influencee,** a **communication channel** linking them, and the respective strength of their **bases of power.**

3. **Power** is the potential to influence, and consists of the resources others believe one controls.

4. The **power base** of a manager consists of both organizational and personal power resources.

   a. **Organizational power resources** include authority, rewards and punishments, tangible resources, status, and work function.

   b. **Personal power resources** include expertise, contacts, and charisma.

5. To influence another, the *influencer* needs an adequate power base relative to that of the intended influencee and a desire to exercise power.

6. The influencee is most likely to comply if the influencer's resources are congruent with the influencee's attitudes: alienated employees expect coercion, calculative employees expect pay, and dedicated employees expect such normative rewards as group approval or a personal boost to the ego.

7. *Power is relative.* The greater the balance of power held by the influencer, the greater the probability of compliance.

8. All organizations are **political systems** in which the formal, objective political processes tend to be merged in a single managerial hierarchy. **Formal political processes** include the *legislative* (rule-making), *executive* (policy implementation), and *judicial* (assessment) functions.

9. **Informal politicking** generally revolves around getting or keeping resources in order to preserve or increase one's power base.

10. Different kinds of influence are exerted in different kinds of organizational relationships. *Vertical relationships* are dominated by authority; *work-flow relationships* by control over resources, status, and function (authority plays no role because participants do not supervise one another); *trading relationships* by the exchange of information and other tools of power; *service relationships* by the value of the function and the extent of control over resources; *advisory relationships* by the power of expertise; *auditing relationships* by the power to punish; *stabilization relationships* by their power to maintain orderly, consistent, and reliable behavior; and *innovation relationships* by the power of expertise to bring about change.

11. **Conflict** is a disagreement or a collision between two or more opposing forces either about *means* or *ends*. Conflict over means is based on which methods to use to reach a goal and on who should control which means. Conflict over ends is usually about goals and values.

12. Four elements in a conflict situation are (1) the *parties* involved, (2) the *place* it occurs, (3) the *interactions* that take place, and (4) the *control,* or resolution, of the conflict.

13. Conflict can be managed even though it cannot be eliminated. Means of *managing conflict* include (1) glossing it over, (2) buying off the contenders, (3) unifying combatants under a superordinate goal, and (4) securing the help of a third party.

Discussion Questions

1. Define and make distinctions between the terms *power, authority,* and *influence.*

2. Describe the actors and activities involved in the influence process.

3. Define and describe organizational and personal power resources. How are such resources allocated in organizations? Under what circumstances can managers lose such power? How can they gain more organizational power?

4. Does the withholding of information increase or decrease a manager's power? Why?

5. If you were working for a manager with a strong need for power, how would that manager be likely to act? How do you think you would respond to these actions?

6. Describe the probable results of each of the following situations. (Consult Figure 16–4.)

    a. dedicated employees working for a tough and coercive manager

    b. prisoners supervised by a warm and compassionate warden

    c. unionized hourly employees working for supervisors who are solely interested in paying fairly for a fair day's work

    d. alienated, angry employees working for a boss who tries to get their compliance by offering more money

    e. employees interested mainly in money supervised by a boss who has just completed a human relations training program based on the values of trust, sharing, and group decision making

7. Why do people comply with the influence attempts of others?

8. What are the two meanings of "politics"? Are both kinds essential in organizations? Discuss.

9. Should informal politicking be controlled in organizations? How can it be?

10. What are the bases of power in the following relationships?

work-flow	advisory
vertical	auditing
trading	innovation
service	stabilization

11. What causes conflict? How might managers go about controlling conflict?

12. In the prisoners' dilemma contest, we saw that individuals tend to compete rather than collaborate. Why do you think this is so? What implications does this contest have for power politics in organizations?

Involvement Activity

Although all of us have some degree of power, and thus some influence over others, most of us do not systematically attempt to develop our bases of power. Indeed, those people who do are often considered cold, calculating, and selfish. Nevertheless, much of what we do can be described as unconscious attempts to influence others by building a larger power base: accumulating money, cars, and other assets; getting an education; developing friendships; and so forth.

The following exercise is intended to help you make explicit some of the ways you might increase your power, and thus your effectiveness in influencing others.

Influence is based on the relative power of individuals (or groups) who are parties to a relationship. For each of the relationship situations outlined below, list your power resources, the resources of the other party or parties, and describe how you might build a stronger base of power. Use a format something like this:

Power Resources	Other Party's	Mine	Ways to Increase My Power
Knowledge			
Skills			
Personal characteristics			
Contacts			
Charisma			
Authority			
Rewards			
Punishments			
Other			

Relationship Situations

1. As a student in a management class, you are influenced by your instructor. You also have some influence. Analyze your power position relative to the instructor, then answer the questions below.

2. Consider your relationship with a friend. Based on your analysis of the relative power of the two of you, answer the questions below.

3. If you are a member or leader of a group — such as a club or society — or an employee or manager of an organization, you have some power. Based on your analysis of your power position relative to another or others, answer the questions below.

    a. How might you improve your power position?
    b. What might be your goals in doing so?
    c. What would be the advantages and costs of doing so?
    d. Under what circumstances could you lose some of your power?
In which of the three relationship situations do you have organizational power resources? In which do you not? Explain.

17

Leadership

Leadership is a special type of influence activity. It may be seen in effect in all kinds of social situations, and it is especially apparent where the situation demands that people work together toward common goals. In organizations, leadership is a managerial activity the purpose of which is to direct the employees in one's immediate chain of command toward the accomplishment of work goals. In this chapter we will discuss the factors that influence the leadership role, some theories of what constitutes leadership, and the special role of the manager as leader.

Few areas within the field of management have excited as much interest as has the subject of leadership. Because it is one of the most researched and written about topics in the field, one would expect it to be among the clearest and best understood of all management ideas. Curiously, the reverse seems to be true. One management theorist has noted that "While there have been many studies of leadership, the dimensions and definition of the concept remain unclear. To treat leadership as a separate concept, it must be distinguished from other social influence phenomena" (1). Yet leadership is often not distinguished from such other subjects as influence, communication, motivation, and control. Rather, these topics are frequently combined and treated together under the general heading of leadership, which perhaps helps explain why the concept is still fuzzy despite the volumes written about it.

Figure 17–1 is presented here to point out that leadership and influence are parallel activities that implement the decision-making process. The objective of leadership is to direct people and control their behavior so as to accomplish goals effectively and efficiently. But influence has the same objective. In fact, the entire management process is designed to seek these goals. Then what differences, if any, distinguish the three activities?

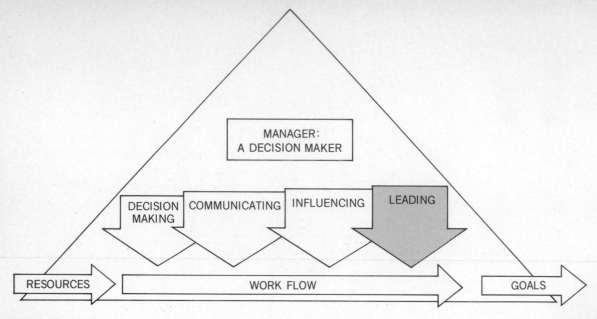

FIGURE 17–1

Managers use their skills in making decisions in order to communicate, to influence, and to lead others toward the accomplishment of performance goals.

The Nature of Leadership

Influence has been defined as the use of power resources by one member of a social system to secure the compliance of other members within that system. Everyone in a social system influences everyone else. But not everyone is a leader.

Leadership represents a combination of behaviors exhibited by one who occupies an elected, appointed, or designated position of influence in a social system. Leadership behavior is therefore officially sanctioned either formally or informally, and the leader is looked to for guidance and direction by those who recognize his or her power.

The term leadership, therefore, can be defined as the exercise of influence in a social situation in which the followers (influencees) *attribute* leadership qualities to the leader (influencer). Leaders are leaders because other people view them as such. The difference between influence and leadership is simply that followers treat leadership actions as acceptable influence behaviors. From this perspective, one may be a leader in one situation and not in another. For example, the star of an athletic team might not necessarily be selected as the leader of a group research project.

Management, in common with leadership, refers to the specific exercise of influence by people who occupy accepted roles. The difference between management and leadership is that management occurs within the specific context of organizations, and managers are appointed or elected expressly to supervise the work of other people in the organization. Leadership refers both to official managerial influence *and* to influence exercised in any other setting by one viewed as a leader. Influence is the all-inclusive term, leadership is a subpart of it, and management is part of both. These differences, and the relationships between them, are shown in Figure 17–2.

As we have seen in earlier chapters, the managerial role involves more than just leadership. Managers have formal duties to perform that are external to the unit supervised. Externally, the manager is recognized as a manager; but from the point of view of superiors, peers, and people outside the organization, the manager is not *their* leader, and is not viewed as such. Internally, from the point of view of employees, the manager is usually a leader, but not necessarily the only one, and his or her leadership role is restricted to the group.

FIGURE 17–2
The interrelationships between influence, leadership, and management roles.

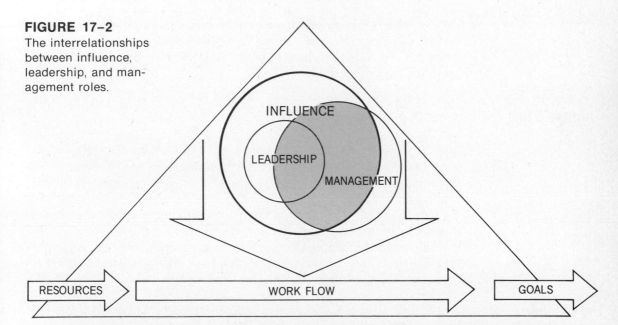

Influence is the use of resources, by anyone, to secure compliance. Because everyone influences others, this role is represented by the largest circle. Leadership is influence exercised by someone approved as a leader by others. Thus it is a subpart of the influence process. Because *management* consists in part of other kinds of work, such as receiving information and planning, part of the "management" circle lies outside the "influence" sphere. The arrow containing all three activities indicates that influence, leadership, and management in organizations are—or should be—directed toward the performance of work.

Not everyone with the title "manager" is a leader. Some managerial positions carry no influence. Such is the case with people who, having made their contribution to an organization, are no longer active in organizational decision making but retain their titles as gestures of courtesy and respect for past achievements. Other managers may lose their influence by default. Some do not like the leadership role and relinquish it to their subordinates or to anyone else who will take it. Such people are often good workers who have been promoted without desiring the role of manager.

Students of management often ask, "If leadership is so similar to managing and to influencing, why study it separately?" For one reason, the idea that managers are leaders is firmly established in everyone's mind — even long before one studies the field of management. To discuss this major managerial role under another topic would be both misleading and disappointing to many people. Some writers even introduce the subject of management with a discussion of leadership, or treat the two topics concurrently (2). Another reason is that leadership research is plentiful, as already indicated, and contains useful information for the student of management. Finally, the idea of leadership can draw together a great deal of what has been discussed earlier in this book. Because it is a broad and often unclear topic, writers have used leadership as an umbrella concept comprising ideas about motivation, group behavior, communication, and influence. Its inclusive quality makes leadership an ideal topic for integrating may of these ideas.

Factors That Influence the Leadership Role

Some leaders are effective; others are not. The differences between people who, in directing employees, motivate them to work hard and with care toward organizational goals and people who provoke neither respect nor inspiration have been the subject of intense investigation in many disciplines. To begin our inquiry, it is useful first to understand the variables at work in the managerial leadership role. These are the leader/manager, the followers, the informal group, the formal work group, the organization, and the outside environment. Figure 17–3 gives a detailed account of these variables and their subdivisions.

**The Leader/
Manager**

The first variable in leadership is the leader, represented in the upper left portion of Figure 17–3. Leaders are people who, like everyone else, have personal needs and hopes. In addition, they enjoy the formal authority of an influential position. The attitudes and sentiments of leaders/managers toward their organizations, work groups, bosses, and employees will have much to do with the way they try to satisfy their needs through participation in organizational work. The type of work, its status, role, and location in the hierarchy are other important variables. The division between

FIGURE 17–3

Leader behavior is conditioned by interrelationships among personal and situational forces. Formal forces, based on the design of the organization, are in the left-hand column. Informal forces, including individuals, groups, and the broader environment, are in the right-hand column.

PERSONAL FORCES	
LEADER/MANAGER	FOLLOWER/EMPLOYEE
Needs and aspirations	Needs and aspirations
Attitudes and sentiments	Attitudes and sentiments
Organization	Organization
Subsystem	Subsystems
Work—status, role location, programed, nonpro-gramed	Work—status, role location, programed, nonpro-gramed
Superior	Manager
Subordinates	Zone of acceptance
Zone of acceptance	Power base—personal, technical,
Power base	informal, organizational
Personal style	Personal style
Personal philosophy	Personal philosophy

GROUP FORCES	
FORMAL WORK GROUP	INFORMAL GROUP
Operational goals	Subsystem goals
Work division	Attitudes and sentiments
Programed–nonprogramed	Organization
Job content	Work
Time	Subsystem
Work coordination	Manager
Level	Informal organization
Type of work	Role and status
Communication system	Homogeneity and cohesiveness
Culture and philosophy of management	Grapevine
Resources	Size
	Culture and philosophy
	Power base
	Norms

ORGANIZATIONAL FORCES	ENVIRONMENTAL FORCES
Goals	Resources
Work division	Clients
Programed–nonprogramed	Industrial
Job content—nature of the work	Other:
Time	Natural
Work coordination	Sociocultural
Form—hierarchical, organic	Political-legal
Status of levels	Economic
Type of work	Technological
Communication system	
Policies and rules	
Culture and philosophy	
Resources	

programed and nonprogramed tasks is another factor likely to affect the willingness of managers to perform at optimum levels. Continuing relationships, transactions, and interactions will, over time, predispose managers to react in characteristic ways when confronted with various kinds of pressures. In short, leader behavior is determined by the relationships between personal characteristics and situational variables.

Personal characteristics include such factors as expertise, contacts, charisma, temperament, appearance, self-concept, and need for power (3). These qualities, plus formal authority, constitute the manager's *power base*. Depending on the nature of the qualities and on the needs of the organization, the factors in the power base will either help or hinder the manager's personal need satisfaction. But the power base itself is necessary for managers to use in getting their work done and in carving a niche for themselves and their work groups in the organization.

These personal characteristics lead to personal styles that either help managers build their resource base or allow what they have to slip away. The *style* of a person in a social situation is a function of the interaction between the individual's personality and the variables at work in the situation. Forces impinging on managers from outside their work groups, from inside the groups, and from within themselves all influence this interaction and create characteristic behavior patterns.

The Follower/ Employee

Leaders can lead only if they have followers. Managers must have employees who will follow instructions to carry out the organizational or group goals. The degree to which employees will follow the instructions of managers is based on a number of factors, including those personal forces noted in the upper-right-hand portion of Figure 17–3. These include their needs, aspirations, and attitudes; their relationships with their managers; the degree to which they are willing to accept work assignments; their personal power bases; and their personal styles and philosophies.

The attitudes and sentiments of employees depend on the nature of their experiences with the organization and with its formal and informal groups. The kind of work performed, whether it is "hard" or "easy," whether it is of high or low status, and where it is done are also important. The degree to which work is programed or nonprogramed is important as well. Some people prefer prescribed work, some like a mixture, and still others prefer to make all their own decisions. All jobs have rank or status in both the formal and informal systems. Attitudes are greatly influenced by where people see themselves in the hierarchy and by the congruence between where they see themselves and how they are treated by others.

Every person has a power base, composed of personal attributes, technical know-how, informal connections, and organizational roles. The broader the power base of an organizational member, the greater will be his or her ability to satisfy personal needs. An employee with considerable power relative to others may feel more or less immune to organizational demands. Personal work habits and ways of relating to others, along with personal philosophy, also contribute to how well employees are able to follow instructions and satisfy their needs.

The Formal Work Group

The formal work group is, of course, concerned with accomplishing operational goals. The subvariations of this factor are shown in the middle-left section of Figure 17–3. Ordinarily these are laid out as quotas or other measurable objectives. The nature of the work to be done in these units is a function of the philosophy of management, the resources available, the imposed constraints, such as time, and many other factors. Job content, whether programed or nonprogramed, enriched or nonenriched, will affect the enthusiasm with which employees go about their work as well as the attitude of the manager. The nature of the work will determine the group's status within the organizational hierarchy; and whether the group is tied officially to important or unimportant executives will have something to do with its success.

The Informal Group

A fourth factor that influences the leadership situation is the informal group, which is represented in the middle-right portion of Figure 17–3. The subgoals of a group, the attitudes of its members, and the group characteristics, such as roles, status, cohesiveness, size, and communication links, will have much to do with determining the willingness of members to be led.

Organizational Forces

The leadership role will also be affected by such organizational forces as its wealth, its market, its profitability, its prestige in society, and its position in the industry. Internally, organizational forces are functions of the culture and philosophy of general management and the aggregate resources available for accomplishing its mission. In other respects, the formal organizational forces affecting worker motivation and leader behavior are much the same as those of the formal work group. These factors are depicted in the lower-left portion of Figure 17–3.

Environmental Forces

Environmental forces directly and indirectly affect leadership; these are shown in the lower-right portion of Figure 17–3. The organizational forces mentioned above are tied to events that take place in the environment, and changes and pressures from the sociocultural, political-legal, economic, technological, and ecological factors in the environment will also have an impact.

A Model of the Leadership Role

Figure 17–4 illustrates how the forces described above impinge on the leadership role. Leadership behavior, shown as an arrow pointing to follower behavior, represents a composite of decision making, communication, influence, and other leadership activities. Leader characteristics — which include the individual's power base — are the foundation of leadership behavior. The leader acts in an interpersonal situation made up

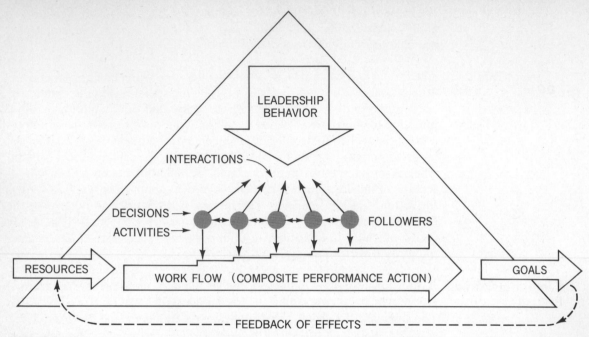

FIGURE 17–4
A model of the leadership situation.

Leadership behavior, a composite of decision-making, communication, influence, and other leadership activities, affects the interactions, decisions, and activities of followers as they engage in collective action. The outcomes affect both the organization and its environment, as shown by the feedback loop.

of others (followers) who are members of both formal and informal groups. Follower characteristics are the basis of follower behavior. Leaders and followers react and interact with one another, as suggested by the arrows pointing from the followers to the leader. In turn, the followers' reactions lead them to make decisions about whether to engage in the activities the leader desires. Each follower makes a separate decision and carries it out, as shown by the activity arrow next to each follower. The cumulative effect of the activities of each employee is shown by the performance, or "composite action," arrow. Collective group action has outcomes that affect both the organization and the environment and that in turn influence the leadership role.

This **situational model** of leadership illustrates the complexity of interaction patterns and challenges the notion that all a leader has to do to obtain the desired response is to find the right stimulus. There are simply too many variables at work to support this thinking. Yet managers continue to search for a tool kit of techniques that will unravel the mysteries of human behavior. Undoubtedly, such a kit would make the manager's life a great deal easier, but to pursue the unattainable is to ignore the real problem of how to deal with the myriad forces that will not respond to simple formulas.

Ideas About Leadership

For centuries, philosophers, politicians, and scientists have been seeking answers to the question of what guides human behavior. More recently, the specific factors that contribute to effective leadership have become a major area of research for social scientists and others concerned with how people behave in interpersonal settings. The situational, or contingency, approach to examining leadership behavior described above is a relatively new development in the study of leadership. This section samples several other ideas about leadership and traces the sources of the situational model.

The Deterministic Approach

Much of human behavior is predetermined. In organizations, this means that many of the duties of the managerial role are prescribed or constrained by forces outside individual control. Personal habits and values established early in life also limit the ways in which people respond as adults. The combined effect of these predetermined forces may mean that a leader's freedom to act is more illusory than real. But this deterministic view has never been particularly popular with management theorists. Rather, the prevalent argument is that the behavior of managers makes the real difference in whether an organization succeeds or fails.

Tolstoy, in his novel *War and Peace,* offered a dramatic challenge to this argument (4). He suggested that the power of administrators and leaders is but an illusion. In times of calm, leaders may persuade themselves that they are indispensable, that only through their efforts does the organization thrive. But, according to Tolstoy, we are all caught in a web of events from the past that move us inexorably from one place to another without our realizing quite what is happening, just as pieces of driftwood float purposelessly on the surface of the ocean. At one time or another, a few pieces of wood may rise to the top of a wave. If these pieces were people in an organization, they might be under the mistaken impression that they had something to do with their being on top, that somehow they had moved the wave. However, like driftwood, they might merely have been thrust up by circumstances outside their control. The movement of the wave controls them, and they can be swept under at any time. A leader is a leader because he or she happens to be in the right place at the right time. So life is vanity, and the best one can do is to cope with it as one finds it, rather than try to change its course.

This view that whatever happens is determined by events outside human control is popular among existential philosophers, although most will acknowledge that within this deterministic framework, individual actions do have consequences for which one must hold oneself accountable.

The "Great Person" Approach

At the opposite extreme of the deterministic theory of leadership are the much more popular "great person" theories, which assert that people have complete control over their own actions and that nothing occurs except by human design. Great leaders are the cause of great successes. Thus, if we want to be rescued from problems that beset us, we need only find the right individual to save us. Or, better yet, with a little hard work, we can become those individuals. The roots of democracy are buried in this belief. The United States came of age believing in the Horatio Alger myth—that any young person (understood to be white and male) could become a great person if he worked hard and patterned his behavior after the great leaders of industry and government. This notion, although somewhat modified during the last decade or so, still influences the thinking of many individuals. In organizations, for example, if things go well, the leaders are praised and esteemed. If things go badly, the leaders are blamed and replaced. Witness how the first to go is the coach when an athletic team does poorly. The inference is clear: leaders are responsible for outcomes.

From a broad perspective, neither the deterministic formulation nor the "great person" theory is very accurate (5). Of course an organization produces leaders and managers. And certainly people in managerial roles can and do make a difference. The apparent conflict between the deterministic and the "great person" theories may be due to a failure to distinguish between prescribed and discretionary decisions and behavior. The deterministic formulation holds that all behavior is programed—an untenable position. "Great person" theories seem to assume that leader behavior is based entirely on discretionary decisions. But all organizations are constrained by forces outside the control of those people who happen to be leaders. Other ideas may be more realistic (6).

Leadership as a Collection of Traits

Similar to the "great person" approach is the notion that the only requirement for effective leadership is a proper assortment of *personality traits*. Those who write articles listing such traits assume that anyone can become a leader if only he or she acquires the right characteristics. Even though trait psychology has been seriously questioned in recent years, many still believe that leadership consists of a collection of personal attributes. One may browse through articles in the popular press, in trade journals, in brochures advertising courses in "personality development," and in the recruitment handbooks many companies prepare, and find lists of traits that, once developed, will enable the reader to "achieve success" in an organization. According to the literature favoring the trait approach, leaders are honest, creative, tolerant, understanding, self-starting, brave, loyal, trustworthy, intelligent, moral, punctual, thrifty, devoted, and so forth. There probably is nothing wrong with exhorting people to exhibit these traits, but one cannot put on a new trait as one does a new pair of shoes. To be sure, new behaviors can be learned, but one cannot easily develop the entire range of requisite traits without changing one's whole personality. And if a person does try to assume a whole new range of behaviors, he or she may develop a great deal of internal conflict or be seen as hypocritical by others. Furthermore, behavior patterns need to remain flexible enough to change along with alterations in the needs of the organization.

Trait theory makes the implicit assumptions that individuals rather than situational circumstances make the difference; that traits are carried around by individuals and operate independently from the situation; and that thoughtful and relevant decision making, communication, and other behaviors will flow naturally from one who exhibits certain personality characteristics. These assumptions, however, are of questionable validity. Indeed, research has shown that no dependable traits can be isolated that reliably differentiate leaders from nonleaders (7). Because trait theories have not proved to be very useful in accurately predicting leadership ability, researchers have turned their attention to an examination of actual leader behavior.

Leadership Behavior: The Ohio State Studies

Acting on the idea that leadership takes place only in a social situation, a group of scholars at Ohio State University in the 1950s conducted a series of studies intended to define and describe leader behavior in different organizational climates. Using scales on a questionnaire called the Leader Behavior Description Questionnaire (LBDQ) to measure follower attitudes toward leader behavior, the researchers were able to isolate two sets of variables; *consideration* and *initiating structure*. **Consideration** refers to the leader's human relations skills and the concern he or she shows for employees' feelings. **Initiating structure** refers to the leader's orientation to the group task, authority, and skills instrumental in achieving the goals of the organization. It was found that these two sets of behaviors exist separately from each other and that leaders vary substantially in the degree to which they exhibit consideration and initiating structure. Repeated studies using the LBDQ showed that some leaders scored high in consideration and also high in initiating structure. Others were high on one scale and low on the other; and some were low on both. The researchers then attempted to determine the relationship between high or low consideration and initiating structure and other organizational variables, such as employee satisfaction and productivity (8).

One might think that a very strong and authoritarian manager would have relatively unhappy employees, but such is not always the case. Although leader behavior seems to be related to employee satisfaction and productivity, the particular relationship between consideration and initiating structure that produces satisfaction and productivity varies among individuals, among departments, and among organizations.

**Leadership
Styles**

Research using the LBDQ continues. Meanwhile, another group of scholars has been trying to identify and isolate different types of leadership styles, a kind of integration of the trait and behavioral views. **Style** in this sense means customary way of acting. The main assumption underlying studies of leadership styles is this: If some leadership styles are more effective than others in accomplishing work goals or in satisfying employee needs, then potential leaders can learn these more effective styles. Or, if these styles cannot be learned, then at least organizational managers can recruit leaders who have already developed the appropriate styles. Leadership-style studies derive from the work of the late Kurt Lewin of the Massachusetts Institute of Technology and his successors there, at the University of Michigan, and elsewhere.

Democratic, Autocratic, and Laissez-Faire Styles. The followers of Lewin classified possible leadership styles under three headings: *democratic, autocratic,* and *laissez faire* (9).

The **democratic** leader seeks employees' guidance in making decisions that affect them, works to get a consensus from them, considers their feelings, shares information, and tries to create pleasant working relationships in a personally rewarding work climate.

In contrast, the **autocratic** leader is organization centered, production oriented, and efficiency minded. This leader gives firm directions, sets controls, and expects compliance. The autocrat makes decisions by right of his or her authority and expects followers to carry them out without questioning their validity.

The **laissez-faire** leader is hardly a leader at all. This person tends to let things ride and seems not to care much about who leads or how things get done. Such a person may seem to be absent even when physically present, for he or she makes little effort to affect the situation.

During the past several decades, hundreds of studies have been conducted to try to determine the extent to which one or another style of leadership is associated with satisfaction and productivity. By and large the results of these studies have been as mixed as those of the Ohio State studies. For instance, although employees generally like a democratic rather than autocratic leader, democrats do not always secure high productivity. On the other hand, not all autocrats secure high productivity. Further, some autocrats seem to be highly regarded by their subordinates. Still, the notion that there is a single and simple relationship between high satisfaction, high productivity, and leader behavior is not easily dismissed from the minds of those who seek such connections. Thus, a number of managers, management consultants, and academicians continue to develop the concept of leadership styles. The idea that managers behave differently from one another is based on common experience. Almost everyone who has worked in an organization has felt the lash of an autocratic boss or the frustration of working for an inept superior. The attempt to pursue an understanding of the effects of different leadership styles seems sensible indeed.

Classification Systems of Leadership Styles. The classification of styles of leader behavior into three discrete categories—democratic, autocratic, and laissez-faire—prompted Tannenbaum and Schmidt to suggest that any leader's style might be placed on a continuum ranging from "maximal use of authority" to "maximum area of freedom" for subordinates. These researchers further maintained that neither extreme is absolute since forces in the manager, in the employees, and in the situation may require varying mixes of autocratic and democratic behavior, as shown in Figure 17–5. Tannenbaum and Schmidt emphasized that managers should be flexible in choosing a leadership style and know which style is most appropriate for which occasion (10). Even the most devoutly democratic leader might find it necessary to give an authoritarian command once in a while, and the most autocratic of leaders may discover the necessity of collaborating with employees in certain situations. Tannenbaum and Schmidt conclude that two important characteristics of a good leader are *sensitivity*, which means accurate understanding of oneself, empathy toward others, appreciation of the forces in the organization, and awareness of environmental variables; and *behavioral flexibility*, which

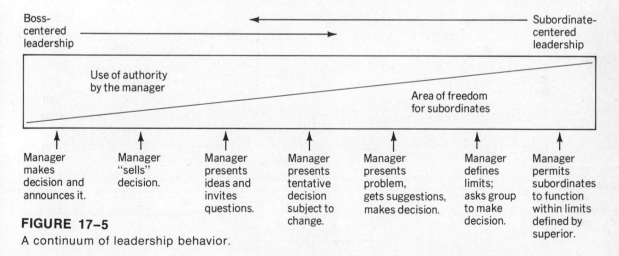

FIGURE 17–5
A continuum of leadership behavior.

"Each type of action [represented on this continuum] is related to the degree of authority used by the boss and to the amount of freedom available to his subordinates in reaching decisions. The actions seen on the extreme left characterize the manager who maintains a high degree of control while those seen on the extreme right characterize the manager who releases a high degree of control. Neither extreme is absolute; authority and freedom are never without their limitations." (Source: Robert Tannenbaum and Warren H. Schmidt, "How to Choose a Leadership Pattern," *Harvard Business Review,* vol. 36, no. 2, March-April 1958, p. 96. Copyright © 1958 by the President and Fellows of Harvard College; all rights reserved.)

means the ability to act appropriately in terms of the changing characteristics of the situation (11).

Blake and Mouton extend the classification system of leadership styles by suggesting that leader behavior does not range along a single continuum running from autocratic to democratic. They propose instead that there are two continua—*concern for production* (which might be roughly equated with the authoritarian style) and *concern for people* (equated with democratic style). There is no essential reason why managers cannot be low in both categories, high in both, or high in one and low in the other (12).

If the two continua are placed at right angles to each other, as shown in Figure 17–6, a Grid® is produced. People-centered leader behavior is shown on the vertical axis and production-centered leader behavior appears on the horizontal axis. By dividing each axis into nine spaces, one can label various combinations of leader behavior. A manager (perhaps evaluated by questionnaires filled out by subordinates) might score a 6 on "concern for production" and an 8 on "concern for people." Such a manager would then be called a 6, 8 leader. A manager who is totally production oriented and not at all person oriented is called a 9, 1. A leader who is completely people centered but not at all concerned with production would be a 1, 9. A person who is concerned neither with people nor with

FIGURE 17–6
The Managerial Grid.

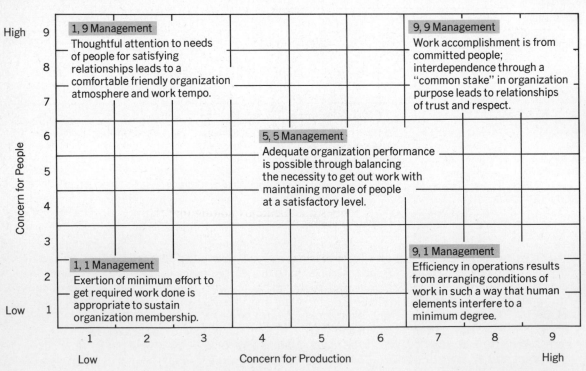

production would be a 1, 1. The optimum kind of leader behavior would be represented by a 9, 9, indicating a maximum concern for people and an equally high concern for productivity. Blake and Mouton purport that most leadership styles tend to fluctuate around the 5, 5 level but that people can be trained to become more nearly 9, 9 leaders than they were before.

It does seem useful to describe various styles of leaders, to measure some of the behavior and qualities associated with different styles, and to examine the varying kinds of organizational outcomes associated with each style. There is a very real danger, however, that descriptions of leader behavior might become prescriptions for how to act, which could have the effect of stifling spontaneity and innovation. Leader behavior develops in response to the needs of people as they interact with one another in the organization. In spite of all the research, no simple relationship has been found to exist invariably between one or another style of leadership and such outcomes as productivity and satisfaction. Determinants of these results are more numerous and probably more dynamic than can be ascribed to a single cause-and-effect relationship.

A leader's style probably *will* change over time, but neither managers nor their superiors can alter it by command. An individual's personal style is deeply imbedded in past experience and personal philosophy, and it is not easily susceptible to change, especially when that style has proved successful over a long period of time. With this in mind, recent research has focused on trying to discover which factors in a situation contribute to what patterns of leader behavior and vice versa. Gradually, research efforts seem to be headed toward an all-inclusive situational model of leadership, concerned not only with leader styles but also with environmental forces, interactions, and the contingencies that affect leader effectiveness.

The Contingency Model of Leadership

Organizational results do not depend only on the leader or on the employees; they are a function of the interactions that take place between them. As mentioned earlier, leader effectiveness is a product of the leader's ability to "read" a situation and to adjust to changing conditions in the environment. The idea of the *adaptability* of the leader stands in opposition to the idea that there is one best style of leadership for all organizational situations (13).

Fiedler echoes this theme by stating that there is no single leadership style that is ideal for every situation. He proposes a contingency model to replace such concepts as leadership style ideas. His model includes more variables than earlier conceptions and suggests that leadership effectiveness depends on effectively matching the organizational situation to the personal style of an individual. Because effectiveness depends as much on the group situation as it does on the leader, almost anyone would succeed in some situations and fail in others. Some of the variables included in the contingency model are: the chances of the situation's being able to satisfy the leader's needs; leader-member relations; homogeneity of the group; the leader's position power (authority); the task structure; the leader's intelligence and technical qualifications; and the leader's personality. Fiedler's studies show that consideration and initiating structure change with changes in the favorableness of the situation to the leader and are not discrete and permanent characteristics. The results also argue against the assumption that leader effectiveness will improve independently of the situation. Improvements in effectiveness are tied to an increase in influence, which is a function of style and power. And style and power must be matched to the situation (14).

The Role of Manager as Leader

The research results discussed in the preceding sections indicate that the leader manages the situation by responding to forces in the environment and engaging in certain behavior that is somewhat restricted by both personal and situational forces. This section continues the discussion of these forces in terms of how they directly affect the manager when dealing with employee attitudes and organizational climate and when acting as

employee director, helper, and representative. Finally, there is a discussion setting forth two views of leadership and a further analysis of the situational approach described earlier.

Employee Attitudes and Organizational Climate

Among the variables that operate in the leadership situation are the values, attitudes, and goals of both the manager and the employees. People respond in accordance with their perceptions and their values. If their attitudes are positive, their responses are likely to be positive, and the social situation will be characterized by a state of high *morale*. Another term for morale—whether it is high or low—is **climate,** or the feeling tone in a social situation. The climate of the situation unites the two concepts of leadership and motivation because it influences the leader's style, which in turn affects employee motivation. Conversely, the leader's style affects the climate, which then influences motivation. These forces are all interconnected and have a circular effect on one another.

Theory X and Theory Y. McGregor theorized that managerial attitudes about how employees become motivated would in part determine the manager's behavior toward the employees and also the employees' responses to the manager. McGregor categorized managerial attitudes as basically falling into several modes, one of which he labeled **Theory X** and another **Theory Y.** Managers who hold Theory X believe primarily that employees are gullible, resistant to change, indifferent to organizational needs, lacking in ambition, and basically lazy. Managers with a Theory X orientation thus see their job in terms of needing to organize, direct, and control people. Employees obviously cannot be trusted, and the manager is there to get things done by pushing, shoving, rewarding, and punishing the employees (15).

Theory Y is a quite different attitude. Based roughly on Maslow's needs hierarchy, it suggests that people do not necessarily resist change, are ambitious, care about organizational goals, and are willing to work hard to satisfy their own and the organization's goals. Managers with this orientation still see the need to perform managerial duties, but they assume that everyone has a potential for growth and that it is part of their job to help people satisfy their own needs while working toward organizational ends. McGregor maintains that people learn to become passive and indifferent under managers who hold a Theory X attitude. They therefore can learn to become active and committed under managers with a Theory Y point of view (16).

Because the Theory Y concept makes good sense, it has been widely taught and enthusiastically received by people in the management field. But in a later book, McGregor voices some concern about the rigidity of those who have been sold on Theory Y, which, he maintains, was a tentative hypothesis and not meant to be a leadership-training method (see boxed insert). He himself is reputed to have encountered some problems in using Theory Y in his experience as a university administrator.

Theory X and Theory Y

Managerial behavior is based in part on the assumptions managers make (or images managers have) about people. Theory X and Theory Y are two different sets of assumptions.

Theory X Assumptions

1. People do not like work and try to avoid it.
2. People do not like work, so managers have to control, direct, coerce, and threaten employees to get them to work toward organizational goals.
3. People prefer to be directed, to avoid responsibility, to want security; they have little ambition.

Theory Y Assumptions

1. People do not naturally dislike work; work is a natural part of their lives.
2. People are internally motivated to reach objectives to which they are committed.
3. People are committed to goals to the degree that they receive personal rewards when they reach their objectives.
4. People will both seek and accept responsibility under favorable conditions.
5. People have the capacity to be innovative in solving organizational problems.
6. People are bright, but under most organizational conditions their potentials are underutilized.

Source: Douglas McGregor, *The Human Side of Enterprise* (New York: McGraw-Hill Book Company, Inc., 1960), pp. 33–57.

Theories X and Y Are Not Strategies

In his book *The Professional Manager,* McGregor says about Theory X and Theory Y:

It was not my intention to suggest more than that these were *examples* of two among many managerial cosmologies [images], nor to argue that the particular beliefs I listed represented the whole of either of these cosmologies. . . .

Theory X and Theory Y are *not* managerial strategies: They are underlying beliefs about the nature of man that influence managers to adopt one strategy rather than another. . . .

Theory X and Theory Y . . . are not polar opposites; they do not lie at extremes of a scale. They are simply *different* cosmologies. . . .

It seems to me to be far less important to categorize and label managerial cosmologies than it is to understand their development, their impact on managerial strategies, and the implications for them of behavioral science knowledge.

Source: Douglas McGregor, *The Professional Manager,* Caroline McGregor and Warren G. Bennis, editors. Copyright © McGraw-Hill Book Company, 1967, pp. 79–80. Used with permission of McGraw-Hill Book Company. Note that McGregor uses the term "cosmology" to mean the same thing as the term "image" we use in Chapters 13 and 14.

Fusion Theory: Personality and Organization. Argyris suggests that managers with a Theory X orientation run their organizations in ways that interfere with human growth. As people mature, he argues, they grow from dependence toward independence, from short-term to long-term awareness, from simple to varied behavior. However, managers in typical hierarchical organizations centralize power and information at the upper levels of the administration and so divide, specialize, and routinize work that they frustrate this human development. Argyris maintains that managers can redesign their organizations by fusing the output needs of the organization with the personal needs of maturing employees, which would thus allow people to grow. Job enlargement is but one possible strategy of organizational redesign that can aid this process (17).

Organizational constraints that interfere with human maturation affect managers as well as employees. Assumptions that managers should (1) concentrate on the objective or task (instead of on human relationships and organizational climate), (2) be rational and leave emotions at home, and (3) motivate with close supervision, minimal rewards, and firm punishments lead to malfunctions in the organization. For example, such activities are inclined to restrict feedback to managers, block their expression of real feelings, hamper their openness, and reduce their risk-taking behavior. These assumptions also tend to interfere with new ideas, retain the status quo, and prohibit negative evaluations. The result is that managers generally have low interpersonal competence. Argyris suggests sensitivity training (see Chapter 10) and organization development (see Chapter 20) as ways to remedy these problems.

Motivation-Hygiene Theory. Based on his studies of motivation, Herzberg recommends work redesign, as we noted in Chapter 5. He says that some reward factors in an organization are *motivators,* or *satisfiers*. These include recognition for achievement and for a job well done, the work itself, increased responsibility, and advancement. To satisfy the needs of individuals on the job while involving them creatively in the organization's work, managers will want to structure the situation so that these need satisfiers are present and available (18).

Herzberg labels another set of factors hygienic factors, or *dissatisfiers,* for their absence can initiate dissastisfaction but their presence neither satisfies needs nor causes motivation. An example would be a clean towel in a public restroom. One doesn't really notice that it is there, but if it is missing, one would become annoyed. In organizations, dissatisfiers are such things as company policy, technical supervision and aid, adequate salary, interpersonal relations, and physical surroundings. Note especially the finding that good interpersonal relations is not a motivator; people *expect* to be on good terms with their associates. On the other hand, regular recognition for a job well done does help build a committed worker. In common with the personality and organization ideas of

Argyris, the motivation-hygiene theory suggests that work should be redesigned to help organizational members satisfy their own needs for growth.

System 4 Model. Likert has combined leadership style theory with employee motivation theory in developing a categorization of four different kinds of management systems, which he calls Systems 1, 2, 3, and 4. System 1 is exploitative and autocratic; System 2 is benevolent, but still authoritarian; System 3 is consultative; and System 4 is participative.

Using an attitude questionnaire, Likert asks respondents to evaluate seven organizational characteristics: motivation, communication, interaction, decision making, goal setting, control, and performance. Employees and managers answer a series of questions about their organizations in terms of these characteristics, including the extent to which they are perceived and desired. When responses are tabulated and grouped, Likert and his associates can determine which of the four systems represents the prevailing managerial attitude. His goal as a research consultant seems to be to help managers diagnose the current system and move toward a System 4 orientation, where all members collaborate to define and solve human and other problems. He reports that these scales have been used with some success in studying and consulting with a number of organizations. System 4 is consistent with the 9, 9 cell on the managerial grid. The results so far indicate that it is a useful research tool as well as an accurate diagnostic instrument (19).

Leadership, Morale, and Motivation

The models presented above have several aspects in common. All are based on the theory that unsatisfied needs motivate behavior. They suggest that typical hierarchical organizations do not adequately satisfy the needs of their members, especially those workers who are relatively low on the totem pole. Managers can help remedy this situation by attempting to provide a climate in which employees may satisfy more of their needs than previously possible. A range of methods is offered. Likert suggests that individuals and groups might become increasingly involved in organizational activities that typically are the province of managers. Herzberg's studies agree that enriching work—that is, assigning managerial responsibilities to employees—might be useful. Agryris, too, recommends system redesign, as does McGregor, who further suggests that managers might consider adopting a more realistic view of worker motivation (20).

Although all these models are based on some real-life experience or research, each tends to shift from describing a real situation to prescribing a "better" one. The bias toward democracy, toward arranging organizations to serve the goals of the maturing persons who are their members, toward humanitarianism, and toward shared decision making is most apparent. Nothing is wrong with such values. On the contrary, they are most appealing. The trouble is that they may not be applicable to any given organization all the time. Furthermore, if the satisfaction of workers were the sole goal of organizations, those who study leadership and motivation could make an even greater contribution than the considerable one they already have made.

But organizations do not exist primarily to serve their employees. Rather, they exist to serve the needs of the environment within the limits of efficiency and effectiveness. The task of managers is to direct employees so that the work is accomplished. If personal needs of the employees can simultaneously be satisfied, so much the better; but that is not the overriding concern.

Missing from some of these formulations is an attempt to understand the *manager's* behavior and needs. Managers are often pictured as the bad folks who have to be retrained, and employees as the compliant workers who will do their best for the organization if only they are treated right. There is, no doubt, some truth is these views. But they remain incomplete to the extent that they do not fully consider managers' needs and behavior, the great commitment of time and energy that managers must make, the need to continually make unpopular decisions to keep the organization going, and the inevitable politicking that is a reality of life. Organizations can be improved, but first they should be realistically examined in all their complexity.

Directing, Helping, and Representing Employees

Many ideas about leadership, as we have seen, are couched in motivational terms. The leader tries to develop certain kinds of employee attitudes and to become sensitive to workers' feelings. But Sayles suggests that such prescriptions omit two elements of vital importance to the managerial role as leader. First, he says that leadership is dynamic. What the leader does is not based on abstract notions of democratic or autocratic leadership modes but rather depends on how things are going in the situation. Second, a most important element in leadership—that of *control*—is neglected. As leader, a manager needs to evaluate the work of subordinates in order to decide where to step in to reduce or control problems (21). From this point of view, the manager's role as leader is to direct the work being done, to respond to both the personal and work-related needs of employees, and to represent employees throughout the organization and in the broader environment. The manager's principal concern is with the work to be done, the primary reason for an organization's existence.

Directing Work. According to Sayles, *direction* is the essence of leadership: the manager is responsible for seeing that the work of a number of employees is produced concurrently. The emphasis is on initiating and superintending the work of subordinates as a *group*. Although important, one-to-one relationships are not sufficient for accomplishing organizational objectives.

Direction, according to Sayles, involves two functions. The first is to intervene when coordinated work efforts are not going according to plan, and the second is to redirect employee effort when environmental circumstances have changed (22). The most important element in giving direction is initiating action. The leader needs to lead, not wait for others to do so. But leaders are not just order-givers; they must know exactly when to intervene and when to maintain distance according to the dictates of the situation. When supervision is too restrictive, employees feel pressured and inhibited; it is also a drain on the manager's energy. On the other hand, to remain remote when employees want direction can cause errors in the work and a feeling among employees that no one cares very much what happens.

Responding to Employee Needs. Managers need to be available and responsive to employees' needs. Some of these needs are work related, such as when an employee needs help in dealing with members of another department or requires some specific technical assistance to get the job done. Other needs are personal. Employees want to know whether they are liked and if their work is good. They want feedback and approval, and they need to understand the formal and informal rules of the organization so they can cope effectively with the environment. They also need support and encouragement.

By responding to employee needs, the manager maintains two-way communication. Managers often need information from employees about their progress and problems, about what is going on, and so forth. Keeping these channels open also helps managers do their own jobs better. For these reasons, managers need to take the time to interact with employees and should not take too seriously those who emphasize the dangers of close supervision. When managers are needed, they should be available.

Representing Employees. Sayles indicates that employees appreciate managers who effectively represent employee views to other administrators. Employees want more than a hearing. They want their leader to represent their viewpoint outside the department, to secure the instruments of power from wherever they are available. Sayles concludes by indicating that managers must represent their groups well or rewards are likely to go elsewhere (23).

The Two Views of Leadership

By focusing on the work employees do in organizations and on the relationships between employees and their managers, Sayles turns the discussion back to the situational view of leader behavior described earlier in this chapter. Clearly, there are really two views of leadership. One, and the one that has been emphasized so far, is that leadership is a social-influence process operating within a number of constraints. The second is essentially a set of prescriptions that amounts almost to a mythology. Pfeffer argues that this second view of leadership is based on certain myths that help leaders keep their power and persuade followers that they can become leaders. Furthermore, the leadership myths lead people to think that leaders make a difference, and therefore that individuals have control, or can have control, over outcomes. Pfeffer came to these conclusions after a review of a good deal of research and writing on the topic. Some of his findings seem relevant—although perhaps a bit disappointing to those who aspire to leadership positions (24). Five of his conclusions are discussed below.

Similarities Among Leaders. In organizations, leaders choose other leaders. This finding suggests that managers will be likely to select as leaders those people whose styles are compatible with their own. In addition, not everyone has an equal chance of becoming a leader: the internal power distribution in an organization sometimes nearly ensures eventual leadership to some while denying the opportunity to others. Finally, leaders, in a sense, almost select themselves by joining organizations in which their personal role meshes with the image of the organization. For these reasons, leaders in an organization are likely to be similar to one another; and to the extent that leaders from different organizations share the same culture, all leaders in the culture are likely to depart little from the norm.

Constraints Imposed by the Organization. Leadership is not so much a cause, as it is often thought to be, as an effect. It results from constraints imposed by the particular situation, by the demands of others, and by organizationally prescribed work and procedures. Leadership is an *interactive* behavior, and as such it both conditions and is conditioned by the people and events that surround it.

Constraints Imposed by the Environment. Many factors in the external environment, such as availability of resources, government regulations, and social movements, are quite outside the control of the leader/manager. Forces inside the organization, such as the authority vested in the managerial position or the company's financial condition, may also be outside the leader's control. Pfeffer cites two studies indicating that managers have little effect on organizational outcomes: leader behavior in these studies was explained primarily in terms of responses to social situations (25).

Preselection of Leaders. Citing some impressive but limited evidence, Pfeffer concludes that succession to leadership positions may be determined by such person-based criteria as social origins or personal connections. One study he cites implies that access to elite universities may be affected by social status and that social status and attendance at elite universities affect later career outcomes (26). To the extent that this information is accurate, teaching leadership to people who have little chance of being selected as leaders seems fruitless. Others apparently do not need such training.

Attribution of Leadership. Finally, Pfeffer argues that leadership is not inherent in people but is attributed to them by others in the situation. He says that "Whether or not leader behavior actually influences performance or effectiveness, it is important because people believe it does" (27). Leaders, then, are symbols, looked up to when action is necessary and considered convenient scapegoats when things do not turn out well. The ceremonies surrounding the hiring and launching of important leaders attest to their symbolic value. From this perspective, successful leaders, as perceived by others in the situation, are those who can separate themselves from organizational failures and associate themselves with successes. Thus we come full circle to the place where we began this chapter: leadership is a process of influence based on the power attributed to one person by other members of a social group. This idea is called the *attribution theory* of leadership.

Chapter Review

In this chapter we have continued the discussion of influence, concentrating on a special type of influence known as leadership. Leadership can take place in any social situation in which a person is acknowledged as a leader by others. Managerial leadership involves directing subordinates to carry out organizational work. Some of the factors that influence the leadership role in organizations are the leader/manager, the follower/employee, the formal and informal groups that exist, and the organizational and environmental forces at work in the situation. We have described several different models of leadership, with special emphasis on the contingency approach, examined the role of the manager as leader and motivator, and discussed several kinds of managerial and employee attitudes, including the effects of these attitudes on organizational climate. Finally, the topic of morale completed this discussion of climate, and the chapter concluded with a discussion of some of the constraints imposed on the directing activities of managers.

Following are some of the major terms and ideas presented in this chapter.

1. **Leadership** is the exercise of influence in a social situation in which the influencees view such behavior as acceptable.

2. Influence, leadership, and management overlap. Since everyone influences others, **influence** is the broadest of these terms; **leadership** is a special case of influence exercised by someone approved as a leader by others; **management** includes all influence and leadership activities, but it also suggests all the other kinds of activities in which managers engage.

3. **Leader behavior** is a result of the interactions of personal characteristics and situational variables. These variables include personal forces

in the leader and in the follower, formal and informal group forces, organizational forces, and environmental forces.

4. Many conflicting ideas about leadership have been suggested.

The **deterministic** approach suggests that leader behavior is predetermined by forces in the situation. The **"great person"** approach asserts that leaders make things happen and that results can be achieved only with effective leaders. The **leadership trait** approach argues that great leaders lead well because of their personality traits and that one can become a leader by developing appropriate traits.

5. Other conceptions have focused on **leadership behavior,** with the idea that what leaders *do* is more important than the traits they have. Two kinds of behavior have been identified as *consideration* — human relations skills, concern for employees' feelings — and *initiating structure*, concern for the tasks to be done. Many students of leadership believe that **leadership style** is an important variable in leader behavior. Styles have been classified in several ways: (a) as *democratic, autocratic,* and *laissez-faire;* (b) as a *continuum of styles* ranging from boss-centered to subordinate-centered; and (c) as a *Grid,* with concern for production and concern for people as separate axes, though not mutually exclusive.

6. The **contingency model of leadership effectiveness** (Fiedler) holds that organizational results depend on the interactions of a number of variables within the particular situation, including the potential of the situation for satisfying the leader's needs, the nature of leader-member relations, group factors, the tasks involved, and the leader's intelligence, skills, and personality.

7. **Organizational-climate** ideas, which include studies of the "feeling tone" in a social situation, unite the concepts of leadership and motivation.

a. **Theory X** and **Theory Y** (McGregor) represent different images or sets of assumptions about people. These assumptions affect managerial behavior and employee responses. Theory X is basically a pessimistic attitude about people, whereas Theory Y is more optimistic.

b. **Fusion Theory** (Argyris) holds that the goals of organizations and those of individuals are antithetical to one another. Management must devise systems that are satisfactory to both; in particular, Argyris suggests job redesign.

c. **Motivation-Hygiene Theory** (Herzberg) holds that some factors, such as recognition and advancement, motivate or satisfy but that others, such as clean working areas, do not motivate if present but decrease motivation if absent.

d. **The System 4 Model** (Likert) is a way of categorizing organizations according to their management systems with the intention of diagnosing and solving problems.

8. According to Sayles, the manager's principal concern is to make sure the work is done. As a leader, the manager is to direct work, respond

to employees' needs, and represent employees in other areas of the organization.

9. According to Pfeffer, the many views of leadership can be reduced to two: (1) Leadership is a social-influence process operating within a number of constraints; and (2) Leadership is a set of prescriptions that amount to a collection of myths. Some of these myths can be compared with reality as follows:

Myth	Reality
• Anyone can become a leader	• Leaders are similar within and between organizations because the process of social selection primarily selects only those who fit in.
• Leaders *cause* outcomes	• Leadership is an *effect* of the dynamic social situation within a group, and of group interaction with forces from the environment.
• Leadership can be taught	• Leadership is based on social origins and personal connections: those who will be leaders need no training; those who will not be leaders cannot benefit.
• Leadership is personal	• Leadership is situational.

Discussion Questions

1. What do you think would be the best kind of leader for an organization facing bankruptcy?

2. Define leadership.

3. Distinguish between an influencer, a leader, and a manager.

4. What factors influence the leadership role in small groups and in formal organizations? How do these factors affect the leadership role?

5. Compare and contrast the following approaches to leadership:
   a. deterministic   d. behavioral
   b. "great person"   e. style
   c. trait   f. contingency

6. Describe the organizational climate likely to exist under each of the following theories of leadership and motivation:
   a. Theory X   d. Motivation-Hygiene Theory
   b. Theory Y   e. System 4
   c. Fusion Theory

7. What does it mean to say that *direction is the essence of leadership?*

8. Defend the idea that leadership depends on the situation rather than exclusively on the leader.

9. Under what circumstances would each of the so-called myths about leadership be a valid theory? Discuss.

10. In terms of the ideas about leadership presented in this chapter, discuss and evaluate the following excerpts from Longfellow's poem "A Psalm of Life."[1]

(Stanza 5)   In the world's broad field of battle,
                        In the bivouac of Life,
                Be not like dumb, driven cattle!
                        Be a hero in the strife!

(Stanza 7)   Lives of great men all remind us
                        We can make our lives sublime,
                And, departing, leave behind us
                        Footprints in the sands of time;

(Stanza 9)   Let us, then, be up and doing,
                        With a heart for any fate;
                Still achieving, still pursuing,
                        Learn to labor and to wait.

Involvement Activity

Read the following short case, then answer the questions at the end.

Leadership at Memorex

Memorex, located in Santa Clara, California, was a glamorous space-age computer equipment company in the 1960s. In the early 1970s it went into a tailspin, and by 1974 was insolvent and headed toward bankruptcy. In 1973 the company lost $119 million, and liabilities exceeded assets by $87 million. The New York Stock Exchange delisted its securities, an act that ordinarily is the kiss of death. Suppliers refused credit sales, employees quit in droves, and the company's bankers were frantic.

Enter Robert C. Wilson as president, a man who was enticed away from Rockwell International for the challenge and potential reward of rescuing Memorex. Wilson, who had already salvaged one company, Collins Radio, set about his task. In rapid order he:

1. Stated specific goals effectively, and then used many communication channels to make sure everyone knew what was going on and that all were working for the same ends.

2. Reorganized the firm by abandoning the haphazard divisional structure, which had no single, clear strategy for growth, and set up profit centers, each with specific work objectives and clear lines of authority.

3. Established financial controls which heretofore had been lacking.

4. Fired seven of the company's nine top executives, along with 125 middle managers, thereby reducing the payroll 10 percent.

5. Brought in fresh managerial talent.

---

[1] Henry Wadsworth Longfellow, "A Psalm of Life," in Leonidas Warren Payne, Jr., editor, *American Literary Readings* (New York: Rand McNally & Co., 1917) pp. 256–257.

6. Started a never-ending series of discussions with employee groups to rebuild morale and enthusiasm.

7. Started to sell rather than lease equipment (to reduce investment in fixed assets).

As a result of these changes, the profits at Memorex improved. Although 1974 showed a loss of $8.9 million, 1975 showed a profit of $18 million, and 1976 a profit of $40.1 million. The company was relisted on the New York Stock Exchange. This may be the first time that any company, once delisted for cause, has ever been returned to the rolls. Some members of the investment community attribute the company's success to the dynamic leadership of Robert Wilson.

His life style is spare. He jogs in the early morning hours, eats only lightly, arrives at work by 7:00 A.M., remains for twelve hours, conducts business over supper, and does necessary paper work at home until 11:00 P.M. In a day's work he meets with divisional groups; analyzes data; maps out his travels to far-flung international branches; handles his mail; confers, talks, and analyzes. But the rewards are good: more than $1,900 for a single day's work plus an option to buy 250,000 shares of Memorex stock for $3.31 a share. Recent price: $27. He has exercised options on 185,000 shares.

Employees come by to thank him for saving their jobs. In 1974, 5,300 were employed; now Memorex employs about 7,000 (28).

Questions

1. Could Wilson teach others to be as effective as he is? How? Would you want to be his student if you could? Why, or why not?

2. Which theory or theories of leadership presented in the chapter best explain Wilson's performance? Discuss how each fits or fails to fit.

3. Why was Robert Wilson's leadership effective at Memorex? Could anyone have done what he did? Why, or why not?

4. What forces in Figure 17–3 influenced Wilson's leadership role? Which forces did not? In what ways did these forces and the relationships between them determine his leadership role?

5. What kind of organizational climate do you think Wilson created at Memorex? How did he do so?

6. What would be the effect on morale of firing so many managers?

5 Managerial Activities of Adaptation

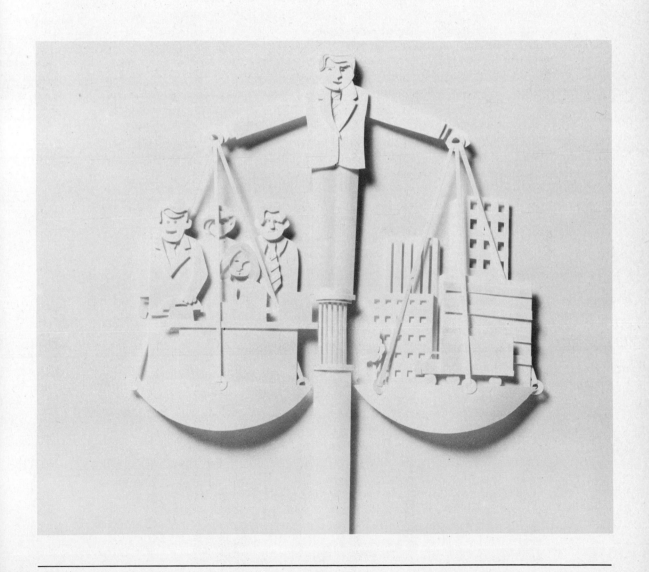

As we have seen in the preceding sections, managerial work consists, in part, of the activities, interactions, and decisions of those who supervise operatives or other workers. In Part 4 we examined four overlapping aspects of internal managerial work—decision making, communicating, influencing, and leading. These internal activities are concerned with directing the day-to-day work of employees toward the accomplishment of organizational goals. Ensuring that goals are reached effectively and efficiently is, of course, a vital managerial function. But of equal importance are the external managerial activities, which are directed toward keeping the organization relevant in a changing environment: these are the functions of planning, controlling, and changing—the subjects of this final section of the book.

These externally oriented functions are called *adaptive* processes because their primary objective is to adjust or adapt the organization to the demands of the environment. Without sound adaptive procedures, even the best-run organizations would wither and eventually die. Keeping abreast of current events, planning for the future, and building change into the organizational structure are crucial to any organization's chances for success.

Chapter 18 examines the *planning* process, the means by which managers try to determine in advance what problems and opportunities await the organization and what strategies they can implement to cope with these developments. In a sense, planning is simply decision making for the long term and oriented toward the environment rather than toward the performance core.

One outcome of the planning process is the establishment of goals, standards, and other measures by which managerial methods and the results they obtain can be judged. Comparing actual events against planned-for events is part of the *controlling* process, the topic of Chapter 19. Another aspect of the controlling process is that managers can compel events to conform to their plans. Some control activities are internal, such as regulating the speed of a production line, but the control fuctions we will be concerned with here are those that continually test the organization's goals and standards to determine if they are remaining relevant to the environment.

Chapter 20 focuses on *change.* We will look at how managers can adapt their organizations, how they can determine when change is necessary, and how they can successfully implement planned change when they decide the time has come for new methods, standards, behaviors, or goals.

The external role of the manager is rather vague and ambiguous. Much has been written about it, but little is really known. Perhaps that is inevitable since the external role is largely concerned with the future, and that is always an unknown. In addition, concern with the environment is a newer major consideration for the manager's attention, making the concepts and methods in this area more prescriptive than descriptive. Nevertheless, it may well be that only those managers who learn to cope successfully with the changing environment will have organizations left to manage.

Planning

With this chapter we begin a three-chapter sequence dealing with those managerial activities directed at adapting the organization to internal and external pressures. The three broad categories of responses are planning, control, and change—the subjects of the final chapters in this book. The goal of planning is to accurately forecast future conditions in order to develop courses of action to meet expected conditions. This activity will be explored here in terms of why planning is necessary, a model of the planning process, types of plans that are possible, human and design considerations of plans, and how managers can organize for planning.

The view presented throughout this book is that the manager is a person in the middle. Managers must respond to pressures from a variety of external and internal sources and in turn exert force back on these sources to maintain an internal organizational equilibrium that allows work to be accomplished. This balance is achieved through the activities of planning, control, and change. There is a cyclical relationship to these activities, as illustrated in Figure 18–1, that moves the manager's attention from planning to control to change and then back to planning.

Because humans do not have instincts to tell them to store food in the summer or to build nests in the spring, they must consciously look ahead and plan for the future if they are to remain safe and secure. Such planning requires an ability to estimate what will happen tomorrow and to take action today to meet probable future conditions.

In most societies great rewards go to those who can predict the future. In primitive cultures, prophets and oracles occupied positions of high status, and their advice was eagerly sought. In more sophisticated societies of today, the content of the predictions may be somewhat different, and predictors are more often called economists, political scientists, or philosophers, but the need for predictions and the esteemed positions of those who can predict the future have not changed very much. If anything, the need to know what to prepare for and how to do it is even greater now than it was in earlier times.

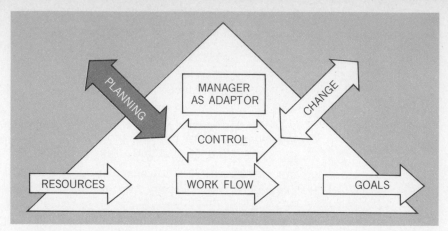

FIGURE 18–1
The managerial
adaptation cycle.

In addition to internal activities connected with accomplishing work, managers must respond to external forces by *planning* goals and methods within environmental constraints, by *controlling* when methods and outcomes do not conform with plans, and by *changing* to keep the organization in tune with changing conditions.

Why Plan?

Although planning for the future is a universally acknowledged necessity, people often avoid doing so because it takes time away from immediate activities, and rewards are often distant and uncertain. Planning is also avoided because dealing with the future is risky. Resources must be put away now on the chance that they will be valuable later, and decisions must be made on the basis of information that, at best, is incomplete. Nevertheless, someone must do the planning because the world does not stay constant and managers need to be prepared for all sorts of eventualities.

For business organizations, the economic environment has traditionally been the single most important environmental force in terms of the need for planning. But even this factor has changed in recent years. The marketplace is more complicated than it used to be, and other forces, such as government controls, also need to be carefully considered and planned for. A major change that has taken place in business organizations is the need to deal with an increasing number of important environmental forces. This multiplication of environmental phenomena has created a need for managers who can recognize and respond to many publics, such as consumers, minority groups, and government agencies. Managers also must plan for ever-changing labor markets and for the special problems inherent in multinational corporations and worldwide markets.

This increasing complexity of the organizational environment has led to greater uncertainty about the future. Uncertainty, in turn, increases the need to plan for the future with greater care. Fortunately, along with these changes have come sophisticated decision-making tools (see Chapter 14) and computer technologies that make it possible for managers to try out many plans in hypothetical future states with little or no cost involved (see Chapter 11). Technology and the demand for it have developed together, and planning has become a highly sophisticated activity.

Most large American businesses maintain plans that extend into the future for as many as twenty-five years. These plans do not provide exact specifications for what will happen, but they do offer general outlines or strategies for handling expected environments. One consequence of this trend in long-range planning is that the plans themselves tend to create the predicted environment. For example, the attempt in 1969 and 1970 to discourage industrial construction and expansion by raising the interest rates was largely ineffective because most major corporations had planned for the eventuality and had already borrowed the money at cheaper rates.

The importance of planning is evidenced by the fact that organizations that have planned ahead have been more profitable and more stable than those that have not planned. What happens then is that greater profitability allows the organization to do more planning to ensure the predicted environment. This trend is true of whole industries as well as of single organizations. The most stable industries are those with large organizations that engage in extensive long-range planning; the chaotic industries are those that are characterized by small organizations that exist almost on a day-to-day basis (1).

Internally, planning is a method for achieving coordination among subunits within the organization. One can get a good idea of how thoroughly an organization plans its activities by examining its subunits to see what does not get done and whether there is an overlapping of duties and authority. In addition to coordinating the organization's work, planning establishes a series of expected behaviors, which in turn are used as targets, or organizational goals. Plans indicate to managers where they need to expend their resources by setting an order of priorities. Planning also is a major part of control systems because plans are used as standards against which performance is measured.

Planning helps managers broaden their overall view of the organization. All people have blind spots or areas they would prefer to ignore. But in planning, managers are forced to think about all aspects of a problem and to understand how they are interrelated; even difficult areas become easier to deal with because plans help them fit problems into the general scheme of things.

A Model of the Planning Activity

Planning is a decision-making process that involves making a determination of what the future will be and then adjusting internal organizational behavior to coincide with the forecasts of external, or environmental, trends. As a managerial activity it can consume an enormous amount of time and resources while demanding information that may not be regularly available from other organizational sources. In brief, planning may be defined as *anticipatory decision making that establishes programs of organizational goals and specifies the methods to achieve them, given the opportunities and constraints of the environment.*

The activity of planning can be thought of as a response to three major questions: (1) Where are we now? (2) Where do we want to be in the future? and (3) How are we going to get there? Represented graphically, these three questions might look like the illustration in Figure 18–2. Bar 1 represents the present situation, labeled x. Assuming that the plan is for acquiring resources, each of the lines across the bar represents a level of current resources. Bar 2 is the estimate of the resources that will be remaining in $x + 5$. Five in this case can represent any unit of time (days, months, years). Bar 3 represents the second question, Where do we want to be (or at what level should the resources be) in $x + 5$? The third question, How do we get there? is represented by bar 4, which compares bars 2 and 3 to come up with the amount of resources that will need to be ob-

HODGKIN'S A GREAT PLANNER... HE JUST GETS CARRIED AWAY.

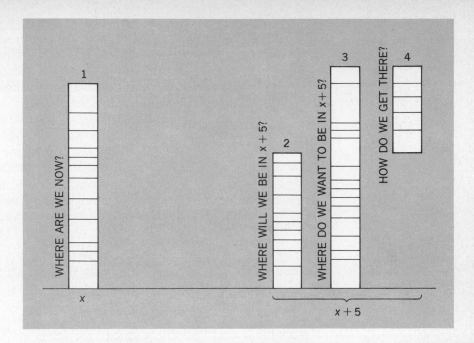

FIGURE 18–2
A model of the
planning activity.

tained. The actual behaviors necessary to obtain the resources become the tactics to achieve the organizational plan. (Tactics are discussed later.)

The remainder of this section will expand on these three questions, which form the heart of planning.

Where Are We Now—Information Gathering

The first step in planning is to assess the present status of the organization by reviewing and analyzing a great deal of data from a variety of sources, including information about the environment, the resources needed, and the organization itself (2).

Environmental Information. The environment, in terms of gathering information for planning purposes, includes a broad range of outside elements. At the top levels of the organization the environment consists of economic, industrial, and supply and demand factors; suppliers; competitors; government and labor constraints; and customers. The information from these sources enables managers to know what they must and must not do in order to survive and grow. This type of information is merely suggestive and requires the manager to make specific interpretations from very general data.

At middle and lower levels of the organization the environment consists of the organization itself. In other words, demands from customers are transformed into work-flow demands. The effect on planning, however, is much the same. The information also tells the manager what must or must not be done, but it is more clearly spelled out than is the information gathered by top managers. Over time, much of this type of information becomes recorded in organizational policies and procedures while other parts of it are learned on the job.

Sources of environmental information were discussed in Chapter 12, "The Environment of Organizations." Some, such as government publications, provide extensive data, whereas others, such as competitors' fact sheets, are not always useful. Often, though, some very useful information can be gathered from easily obtainable and somewhat unlikely sources. For example, census statistics provide information that could have long-range consequences on where an organization decides to open branch locations, which economic and age groups its outputs should reach for, and many other crucial factors that require consideration.

Resource Information. The second area that contains needed information is the resources, including both those presently within the organization and those available in the environment. Resources are found at all organizational levels. At a minimum, the economist identifies as resources land, labor, and capital—land in this sense is broadly interpreted to mean all physical facilities. Other resources clearly available to top management are such things as the labor supply and the marketplace. For middle- and lower-level managers, exchange relationships that provide certain advantages in securing resources within the organization are important areas about which to obtain information. The real significance in gathering knowledge about resources is that the manager can determine most clearly which, out of the full range of possibilities, are the most reasonable courses of action.

Most frequently, resource information is obtained from existing internal records. But again the quality and extent of information varies greatly depending on the resource. For example, data about financial resources are the most readily available, with information about material resources not far behind. On the other hand, knowledge about human resources is often limited. Most organizations can fairly easily supply information regarding how many people are employed and who they are, but far fewer have a comprehensive inventory that furnishes a listing of people's skills (3).

Organizational Information. The third major area of information pertains to the nature of the organization itself. This includes partly tangible information—such as its structure, current functions, and other anatomical characteristics—and partly intangible information—such as the organization's goals, the values and commitments of its members, and a host of other behavioral data regarding how and why things get done as they do. In this area managers at lower levels would appear to have an advantage. As one moves up the organizational ladder, the amount of such information becomes astronomical, and the tendency of the hierarchy is to filter out much of it before it reaches the top. Actually most of this type of information is not even consciously collected. This does not imply, however, that it is unimportant; in fact, it is this information that determines the desires of the organization. Managers must do a considerable amount of introspection in this area because it is their goals and values that carry the most weight in determining where the organization is going.

Organizational Posture. Based on the information gathered from the above areas, the manager makes decisions about current operations. It is necessary to define the current condition or posture of the organization vis-à-vis the environment to determine whether that posture is in line with the environment, the resources, and the organization. Defining the posture of the organization means understanding the interaction that occurs between the organization and the environment. To do this, one must first define the **scope** of the organization; that is, what part of the environment it serves. No one organization can do all things. Even giants like General Motors operate in a limited market area. Thus, to distinguish the market, the individual examines the organization's output, the customers serviced, the types and characteristics of products and/or services rendered, the mix of products, and the basis on which the company competes in the marketplace. Lumped together, these factors identify the **competitive advantage** that the organization is attempting to maintain.

The deployment of resources, when combined with the scope, works to apply impetus in the desired direction and determines the **distinctive competence** of the organization; that is, what it can do well. An organization whose distinctive competence matches its competitive advantage is in balance. A good balance distinguishes one organization from all others in its field. For example, in coming out with the Rambler, American Motors developed a product that was different from other auto manufacturers' products and filled a need for the public without having to compete in an area in which it would surely experience defeat. By examining their resources, the managers of American Motors understood that to gain a substantial footing in the marketplace they would have to offer a product that was significantly different from those of their well-established competitors. The Rambler furnished American Motors with distinctive competence that for a time gave the company a competitive advantage in the auto manufacturing field.

Where Do We Want To Be in the Future? — Forecasting

By comparing the environment, the resources, and the organization, one of two conclusions may be drawn: either there is or there is not a balance between competitive advantage and distinctive competence. When these two factors are not in balance, a clear need for change and planning exists. And even if a balance is discovered, that balance is for today only. The environment must be continually monitored by alert managers to detect changing trends. The boxed insert, for example, clearly indicates that McDonald's maintains its huge edge over other fast-food chains by staying in close touch with its customers and by constantly adapting its products and services to observed needs in the environment.

In order to know where one wants to go it is necessary to have information about what the future will be like. Developing ideas about the future is what forecasting is all about. At best, forecasting is a tenuous activity. The major tool for looking into the future is the extrapolation of past trends. Unanticipated events or a scarcity of past data can make forecasts little better than educated guesses. However, regardless of how inadequate forecasting is, it is all we have. And, as one sage said about life, "Compared to the alternative it's great."

Forecasting is much more complicated an activity than it used to be. For one thing, the number of variables to consider has gone up proportionally with the increasingly complex environment. There is also a trend toward more inclusive planning. Instead of having a series of plans for each function, such as sales and production, planning today must consider the direction of the *total* organization and incorporate all these subplans into the overall strategic plan.

Forecasting requires the planner first to search for information and then to use the information to build a projection of the future.

Keeping on Top

Fast food service is one of the most competitive businesses in the United States, and to stay No. 1 McDonald's must be doing something right. But staying on top isn't easy. McDonald's current hold on the market must be constantly bolstered by adapting to new conditions. And it has proved to be very good at making effective changes.

The days of hamburgers and Cokes only are gone. Today there are fast food firms providing almost every type of food the public desires. The market must be lucrative because the biggest corporations in the country are putting their money and talent into the field. Still McDonald's remains the largest chain of stores in the industry with 4,230 stores and $3.1 billion in sales in 1976 — a 24 percent increase from 1975.

Some of McDonald's success has come from inflation, which has driven the price of groceries up faster than the price of meals eaten out. The result is that going out for meals is financially more attractive than it used to be. Also, McDonald's constantly adapts its menu to keep pace with what its customers want. At least once a year all executives spend a day working in a store to sample customer tastes and reactions.

Recently McDonald's has started serving breakfasts and providing "drive-thru" service in some areas. In addition, it seeks to find the most popular locations in which to open new stores. The stores themselves are being upgraded to appeal to families, and in one of McDonald's more daring ventures, it is now moving overseas. Adopting the idea of fast food service has been slow taking hold in some foreign countries, but McDonald's is hanging in there — as evidenced by advertising posters purchased by students from Germany and Japan.

Source: *Time*, April 25, 1977.

Obtaining Information. This activity, which may be called the securing process, can be done in a number of ways, just as the search process in decision making takes several different forms. Aguilar suggests four possible modes: *undirected, directed* or *conditional, informal,* and *formal* (4).

1. *Undirected Search.* **Undirected search** is simply being receptive to stimuli in the environment without necessarily having anything specific in mind. For instance, a manager may subscribe to a series of government documents just to see if there is anything interesting in them. This tactic is not without merit. Opportunities are often found this way. It is not coincidental that most top executives read several different newspapers on a daily basis.

2. *Directed Search.* **Directed search** is also passive in that the manager receives only whatever information happens to come along, but the difference is that only particular items are looked for. This is analogous to the manager who reads only the financial section of newspapers or selected magazines. This mode is more likely to uncover looked-for information but less likely to spot diverse opportunities.

3. *Informal Search.* **Informal search** is a more active mode of securing particular information, but the activity is limited and unstructured. Informal search, like programed decisions, is limited to those sources that are already well known.

4. *Formal Search.* **Formal search** requires its own plan, first to uncover the likely sources of information and then to engage in a directed search of those sources. This type of search procedure is usually done only when the needed information is of critical importance to the forecast.

Data may range from precise quantitative data to vague, unsubstantiated ideas about what the future holds in store. Quantitative data are ordinarily written down in documents and reports. Qualitative data, on the other hand, often exist only in the heads of experts. And extracting this information may be difficult. One solution would be to use the **Delphi method** (5). The Delphi method involves gathering together a group of experts who all answer questions about future events, such as, "By what date would you expect solar energy to be competitive with coal-produced energy?" The experts then give their answers and the estimates are tabulated and fed back to all the respondents along with reasons for each particular response. The results usually amount to a good central estimate of future events.

Forecast Projections. Forecasts are estimates of the future based on past performance. The three strategies used to make forecast projections are called *deterministic, symptomatic,* and *systematic* (6).

1. *Deterministic Strategy*. A **deterministic** strategy is based on the assumption that the future is a direct function of the past. This is the most commonly used strategy in organizational planning. For example, past turnover rates are used to determine present and future personnel planning projections; materials are ordered in advance of their need based on the average time it has taken in the past for goods to arrive from their origin; and the amount of supplies ordered is fixed by the amount used in the past.

The major drawback of this strategy is that the past may not be like the future. In the boxed insert at the bottom of this page an example is provided of how an outside force, in this case the economy, upset the relationships between past known variables.

The box at the top of page 493 illustrates another problem with the deterministic approach; that is, that the act of planning itself can affect the projections. Sometimes this effect actually creates the projected situation, or, as in this example, the plan creates a situation opposite that projected.

2. *Symptomatic Strategy*. A **symptomatic** strategy uses the present rather than the past condition as an indication of what the future will be. The most commonly used symptoms of current conditions are *leading economic indicators,* which are predictors of changes in the economy, at least in the short run. These present indicators, however, are based on long-term studies of relationships, and they typically are harbingers of either better or worse economic conditions. For instance, a supplier of building materials can predict from current high interest rates that new housing construction will decrease in the near future and that, in turn, demand for building products will also decrease (7).

How Events Affect Plans

One of the objectives of the admissions office of ABC College is to enroll the optimum number of students each year that will most effectively and efficiently utilize the available resources (professors and facilities). The determination of the number of new students to be admitted is based on three variables: (1) the number of returning students, (2) the average number of units taken per student, and (3) the percentage of admitted students who will actually enter the college.

The admissions office keeps very good statistics on these three factors. However, in one recent year almost 3,000 more students were on campus than were planned for. The figures for all three variables were different from the projections. The reason, in retrospect, appears to be that a change in the economic situation within the community made part-time work harder to obtain, thus making it more attractive to students to continue their education and enabling them to take more units than they had planned to. Changing external conditions in this case rendered past data useless.

How Plans Affect Events

In one reorganization, the personnel department became aware of an overstaffing problem. The hiring requirements for one category of employees had been steadily declining, and it was determined that the organization had a surplus condition. An examination of the past turnover rate indicated that the surplus condition would be remedied in six months if no new hiring took place. Consequently, a memo was distributed that prevented any further hiring of this category of employees.

In the next six months not a single person quit, retired, or died. The effect of the memo was to put the employees on guard as to the surplus nature of their occupation and people were hanging on to their jobs. Thus at the end of six months, a forcible reduction of staff was necessary.

This is a good example of how the plan itself actually created the opposite situation from that planned for.

3. *Systematic Strategy*. A **systematic** strategy is a much more sophisticated method of forecasting and requires the use of computers and modeling. The underlying assumption of a systematic strategy is that there are basic regularities in the environment that can be developed into a model of the part of the world one wishes to predict. Consider, for example, an organization of national scope that manufactures a diverse product line. To estimate future needs, the managers of this organization develop a computerized mathematical model of the national economy. The impact of the economy on each product can be predicted by altering the known variables to reflect every possible future condition and then running the computer program to select the most probable condition. Actual conditions are added to the model as they occur to update the program and to increase the accuracy of predictions.

Planning Attitudes. An important variable that forecasts do not project is that of what the planner *wants* to have happen. A forecast does not indicate whether a particular course of action is best or desirable; it simply predicts which events will or will not occur. It is then left to the manager to decide which course of action is most desirable for the organization.

Forecasts can be used in either a passive or an active mode. In a passive, or reactive, mode the environment is viewed as a set of constraints and the planner's job is to steer a course through these projected constraints that will enable the organization to survive and perhaps prosper. For example, projections of new government regulations or pressure-group demands would be used as prescriptions for actions that would comply with these forecasted realities.

In an active, or proactive, mode the planner has a set of goals or an idea of what the organization should be like in the future and uses forecasts to help create the desired conditions. It should be remembered that a forecast does not indicate that a particular event *will* occur; it simply says the event will occur if nothing is done to prevent it. The active planner, then, will look at forecasts in terms of whether they support or hinder predetermined goals and either take action or do nothing, accordingly. Henry Ford's goal was to produce a car that the average worker could afford. But forecasts of the costs of the finished products indicated that they were beyond the means of most of his employees. Accordingly, he raised salaries (which prompted other auto manufacturers to raise their salaries) so that his goal would be realized.

How Are We Going to Get There?—Tactics

Deciding where to go requires a set of plans, but determining how to get there also requires planning. Referring back to Figure 18–2, it can be seen that two aspects of "getting there" are spelled out. The second bar, which represents the loss of resources that will occur between x and $x + 5$ time periods, is the *internal* aspect of the tactical plan. The fourth bar represents the difference between the projections of resource loss (bar 2) and the resources needed to accomplish projected goals (bar 3). This is called the *external* part of the tactical plan because the resources must come from outside the organization.

Internal Planning. The steps to get to bar 2 have already been discussed; that is, determine what the organization's resources are now and then project the loss rate, by using forecasting techniques, over the time period $x + 5$. The only real difference between the forecasting plans discussed above and those employed here is that the source of the information is all internal. Examples of the kinds of information used in internal planning would be the skills inventory of employees, the turnover rate among different groups of employees, the quantity of raw materials in the warehouse, the production schedule of usage, projections of cash flow, and monetary resources versus capital expenditures.

To arrive at bar 3, the goals must be converted into resource needs. If a new product is to be introduced, the resources that will be required to produce and distribute the new product must be projected. It may be found that very little resource change is required or that new resource requirements are substantial. For instance, an appliance retailer who decides to carry a new product, say washing machines, on consignment will experience little need for a change in resource demands; however, if the retailer wants to purchase an inventory outright, a considerable change would occur in the financial resource requirements.

Determining future resource needs requires a high degree of coordination with the plans developed in other parts of the organization. In particular, one would need to carefully examine the marketing plan to find out what products will be sold and in what quantities. From the production plan would come information as to how the production department intends to produce the types and quantities of product to be sold. These other plans now indicate something about the type and level of resources required in five years, months, or days. But this statement is not yet complete. The raw figures must be converted into specific types and quantities of particular resources, which is often a difficult task. For instance, there is no standard way to convert sales and production forecasts into personnel requirements. It is a matter of judgment. There are, however, some ways to improve this judgment and to provide a check on it.

1. *Use Expert Opinion.* One way is to get an estimate by a group of experts. In the case above, the experts might come from personnel, production, and industrial engineering. Their estimates can be improved by using some variation of the Delphi technique discussed earlier. This technique and others like it are not absolutely accurate. They are, however, a significant improvement over outright guessing. The probabilities are good that such a procedure will uncover the major variables likely to affect the composition of the proposed work force.

2. *Use Historical Comparison.* A second method of improving one's judgment is to use historical comparisons. Thus, one would look for similar past occurrences in one's own or in other organizations and study the results. One also would look for trends, which are fairly good indicators of cyclical fluctuations. This technique is closest to forecasting in the deterministic mode.

3. *Task Analysis.* A third method, which is more like the scientific management approach, is to break the total project into specific tasks, analyze all the task components, and then build estimates based on the results of the analysis.

4. *Key Factors.* Finally, one can search for key factors that are correlated with resource requirements. For instance, it may turn out that capital expenditures and work-force requirements are highly correlated. This technique·is akin to symptomatic forecasting strategy.

The end product of the application of some or all of these techniques is a list of total resource requirements in terms of number of people and types of skills needed, total material requirements, and when they must be available.

External Planning. External planning starts by comparing bars 2 and 3 in Figure 18–2 to determine the resources that will be required at future dates and to pinpoint when and where shortages and surpluses will occur. It is on the basis of this step that plans can be made to assure a smooth flow of events.

But there are certain problems in implementing this step. To begin with, the change in demand for resources may not be linear. Often, current and future programs either overlap greatly or have significant gaps between them. This leads to such problems as having a warehouse full of raw material that will not be needed for some time or having an empty warehouse when there is currently a demand. These problems are particularly prevalent in project-based organizations, such as aerospace and construction (see Chapter 5 for a discussion of work scheduling).

Bar 4 is the result of a comparison of bars 2 and 3 and provides a projection of resources needed from the environment. In turn, this projection needs to be compared to the forecasts of environmental conditions. If the comparison results in a positive relationship, plans may move ahead; if a negative relationship is shown, plans may need to be revised. In the case of the retailer mentioned earlier, a plan to move from goods on consignment to outright purchase may require financial resources that exceed internal supplies. The nature of the external financial market over the period of change now becomes central. If the interest rates are predicted to remain constant or to fall, then the plan would be a good one. But if the interest rates are predicted to rise, the plan may prove infeasible.

In terms of the active and passive modes of forecasting discussed above, the retailer can employ one of two strategies. The first is to use the forecasts to accomplish the original goal. Thus, if current interest rates are low but are predicted to rise, then the retailer would borrow immediately. In the second strategy, the retailer would feed the forecast back into the planning system with the information that the environment makes the proposed plan hard to achieve. The result would be to change either the goal or the methods so far developed.

Types of Plans

Forecasting activities lead to a variety of plans. This variety can be categorized along a number of dimensions, which will be considered in this section. The categories of plans that follow are not intended to be mutually exclusive; rather they may be viewed as a multidimensional matrix, with any one plan able to fall into one or a number of the categories discussed.

**Goals—
Strategies—
Operations
Dimension**

Any set of plans that states where an organization is going and how it is going to get there involves a specification of goals, strategies, and operations. These fall along a continuum, illustrated in Figure 18–3, with one directly affecting the other. Goals require strategies to achieve them and strategies in turn need operational plans that set them into effect by specifying the everyday behavior of the organization. The dotted lines

FIGURE 18–3
Three stages of
planning.

running back in the opposite direction show the reciprocal relationship of these three dimensions when behavior affects operational plans, which influence strategies, which influence goals.

Goals. The nature and subdivision of goals was discussed in Chapters 3 and 4 and need not be repeated here. One kind of goal consists of desired future states set forth in terms of outputs. The resources and work activities required are not delineated in statements of output goals.

Strategies. The first step in making goals operational is **strategic planning,** which is intended to integrate the organization with its environment. From forecasts and projections, the strategic planner can see more clearly what it is that the organization is capable of achieving given the resources available and the constraints existing in the environment. The purpose of this comparison is to determine the distinctive competence of the organization, as discussed in the previous section.

A strategic plan not only guides the organization in allocating available resources, but also sets forth steps for seeking out new opportunities. The planner is looking outward toward the environment as well as inward to the organization. Strategic plans specify why and how the development of a unique niche in the environment would be advantageous to the organization (8). Strategic planning can be aided by many of the new decision-making techniques, but it remains a judgmental process in which the entrepreneurial capacity of the planner finds expression.

Operations. Operational plans define exactly how organizational activities can be marshaled to achieve the strategic plan. Operational plans are geared toward keeping the organization running on an even keel over a specified time period, usually of short duration. Most functional plans are operational, whereas the guidelines for establishing them are strategic. Operational planning is internally oriented and defines a specific sequence of activities, usually involving quantitative decision tools.

It seems logical to say that strategic planning occurs at the top of the organization and operational planning at middle and lower levels. Although in general this is accurate, it is also somewhat misleading. All managers operate in an environment, control resources, and have a discretionary area of behavior. Thus all managers are in a position to do some strategic planning. There is no doubt, however, that the impact of such planning is greater at the top of the organization.

Functional Dimension

Another way to look at the different types of plans is to view them as a hierarchical arrangement, much like an organization chart. Figure 18–4 illustrates such a hierarchy. The overall master plan of the organization, a strategic one, is divided into functional plans for each major subunit of the organization, and so on down through the organization until plans are made for individual employees. The plans at the bottom are more likely to

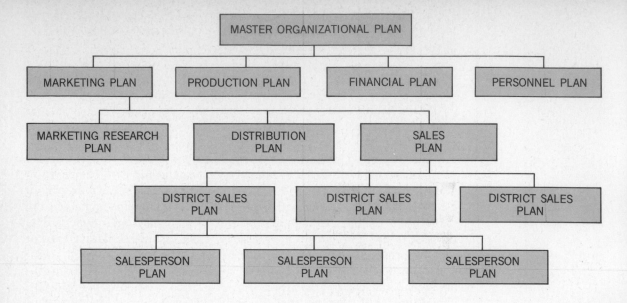

FIGURE 18–4
An organizational
hierarchy of plans.

be operational than strategic, short run rather than long run, and certain rather than uncertain. It is also true, however, that like the double directionality of the three planning stages, planning can run upward in the organization as well as downward.

Master Plans. The master organizational plan is the strategic plan that relates organizational goals to environmental conditions. This plan does not deal in specific operations for each functional area of the organization; rather it focuses on the interrelationships that exist between the functions.

Functional Plans. Each major subunit of the organization has its own set of plans. Subunit plans are drawn up using the master plan as a guideline and constraint. Theoretically, if each unit developed its own plan in a manner fully consistent with the master plan then all plans should fit together. In practice, however, this fit does not work out so neatly. The reason is that each subunit has a differing interpretation of and orientation to the master plan. This makes it necessary for units to coordinate their plans by sharing information. Some plans, such as those for the marketing function, which estimate demand, must be accomplished before others, such as plans for production schedules. It is usually the responsibility of staff departments to coordinate the functional plans for the entire organization.

Some functional plans deal with resources needed, such as money, personnel, and facilities. Other plans deal with activities and are stated basically in terms of time. Each manager needs both resource and activity plans.

Budgets. Plans that deal with organizational resources are called **budgets.** A budget details the resources needed to accomplish an assigned task or goal. The first step in making a budget usually has members of certain staff departments request estimates of resource needs from all operative departments. The next step is for the staff departments to combine and compare these estimates for consistency with the master plan.

Since resources are frequently scarce, the total resources requested usually amount to more than the organization can afford. The process of deciding whose budget shall be cut and by how much is one of the most politicized activities in organizations. Many managers consciously pad their budgets to compensate for the amount they figure will be cut out of it. When the department that makes allocations becomes aware of this tendency, the budget is automatically cut by a standard percentage. The people who end up losing in this game are the managers who do not understand the system.

Most organizations have a budget for each of their major resources. Capital budgets are for purchasing equipment and facilities; operating budgets are for allocating financial resources and supplies; and personnel budgets are for securing human resources. Each of these budgets has a *maintenance* and a *growth* aspect. Because resources are continually used up, they must be replenished simply to maintain the status quo. If the organizational unit is requested to take on new duties, or if it wishes to, then the budget must also include a growth factor.

Activity Plans. Another type of functional plan is the activity plan, which indicates how each organizational unit is going to proceed to accomplish its task. Activity plans are time oriented, indicating when certain activities will take place and in what order. Thus they provide a schedule of events needed to achieve goals. These types of plans have been greatly aided by the use of such methods as PERT and other work-scheduling techniques as discussed in Chapter 5.

Time Dimension

Another way to classify plans is by the length of time they encompass. One can distinguish between short-range and long-range plans, but the distinction is situational. In some organizations, short range would mean a week or a few months; in other organizations, short range might mean a year or more. Similarly, long-range plans may be for one year in one organization and five or more years in another. Generally, the larger the organization and the more stable the environmental conditions, the longer the time span of both short- and long-range plans.

A utility servicing a stable community has a much longer planning horizon than does a manufacturer of children's toys, which is subject to the whims of current buying trends. Both the time frame and the degree of specificity for each of these organizations is different, and the plans each makes will reflect these differences.

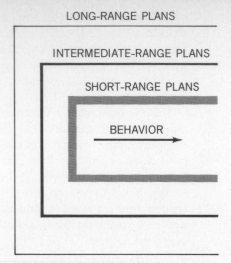

FIGURE 18–5
The relationship between
short-, intermediate-,
and long-range plans.

Short-Range Plans. Short-range plans are specific in nature and detail how activities are to be carried out. The goals are usually included or implied. For instance, a student might sit down on a Friday night and plan out all the study activities that he or she needs to accomplish during the weekend. This delineation can be in terms of time to spend, topics to cover, and what to do on which day. In organizations, budgets are good examples of short-range plans. They rarely extend more than one year and often break the time period down into months, weeks, or even days.

Short-range plans often have long-range implications. Once started, a particular activity gains acceptance and is viewed as a natural part of organizational operations.

Long-Range Plans. The further into the future one looks, the hazier the view and the greater the need for flexibility to adapt to changing conditions. Long-range plans are more general, are ordinarily in the province of top management, and are usually strategic in nature. They provide the framework for short-range plans. In Figure 18–5, the relationship between short- and long-range plans is delineated. Note how the lines become increasingly vague as plans become more long range.

Long-range planning may be one of the most important activities of top managers. It is in this area that one can have the greatest long-term impact on the organization. In general, the higher the organizational level the more likely it is that a manager will devote increasing time to long-range plans and less and less time to short-range plans (9).

**Certainty-Risk
Dimension**

Plans can also be classified according to how likely they are to materialize. Picture a continuum ranging from complete certainty to total uncertainty. At the certainty end of the continuum a plan would be characterized by an assumption of full knowledge of all variables with a single best path shown for goal accomplishment. Such a plan is like a map that has one best route between the starting point and the destination. The advantages of assuming certainty is that planning is simple, costs are lower, and the plan is amenable to the use of operations research techniques. The problem with plans based on certainty is that either the area covered by the plan must be relatively limited or the assumptions made must be somewhat unrealistic. However, many operational and short-range plans assume this certainty condition.

Plans at the intermediate level on the continuum would assume a condition of some risk. The major characteristic of such plans is the inclusion of alternative paths. Such plans allow for contingencies and take into account environmental variability. The intermediate-risk model is a trade-off between the simplicity and lower costs of the certainty model and the total complexity of the high-risk, reality model. The techniques of simulation and dynamic programing are most commonly used to analyze these types of plans.

A more open type of plan is one that assumes uncertainty. This type is the closest to reality and also is the most complex because it must allow for sources of contingencies. A plan such as this is most useful when the results of an error are likely to have disastrous consequences. The general, long-range plans of an organization are types of uncertainty plans. They are usually devised through the use of simulation techniques. Moderately risky and highly uncertain plans allow for alteration and adaptation to changing conditions.

Designing Plans

Plans contain sequences of activities and pertain to a variety of different endeavors, as discussed in the two preceding sections. In addition, there are *design* considerations in plans, which make them responsive to situations, and *people* considerations, which are indispensable since human behavior governs and is governed by plans. These two features are the subjects of this section. It should be emphasized that no plan is ever perfect; but by carefully drawn designs and by allowing for human reactions, managers can considerably improve any plan's chances for success.

Design Features

The design features that will be considered in this section include the repetitiveness, scope, flexibility, and information requirements of plans.

Repetitiveness. Plans vary as to whether they are designed for a particular nonrecurring situation or for the ongoing running of the organization. Plans that are continuing or recurring by nature require continual adjustments to the ongoing situation. Such plans are called **standing plans.** Policies and procedures are examples of standing plans. The advantage of standing plans is that they provide a stable guide for a particular situation whenever it occurs. Standing plans also help to coordinate the diverse parts of the organization.

Organizations that produce a particular product or provide a specific service on a continuing basis, such as oil refineries or banks, will have many standing plans. These plans have all the advantages and problems of programed decisions. One advantage is that they provide useful organizational shortcuts and guides to behavior; one disadvantage is that they can become outdated when the environment changes. For these reasons it is useful to monitor standing plans on a regular basis.

Plans that are developed for a single situation, such as a special project, are known as **single-use plans.** These plans are for a specified time period or for the duration of the task for which they were designed. Single-use plans may run for a very short or a relatively long time period and can be adopted for important new programs or for detailed prescriptions of how to accomplish a given task. Some examples might be building

"I THOUGHT YOU ORDERED THE BARRELS."

and moving into a new headquarters office or developing a new product line. In the latter case, the plans might move to standing plans if the product beomes established. Some organizations, like construction firms, operate almost exclusively on single-use plans.

Scope. Plans also vary in terms of their scope, or the extent of organizational activity covered by the plan. Master plans, strategic plans, and long-range plans all affect a good deal of the total behavior in the organization. Often a single-use plan for a major project will cut across the entire organization and suspend the standing plans for a period of time. In contrast, many standing plans are very narrow in scope. Such plans are called into action only when a very specific situation is encountered.

Keeping the scope of the plan under control is important because there is a constant tendency to broaden the scope of plans and thereby confound their original intention. Plans are formulated with a certain intended scope in order to control environmental uncertainty. The broader the plan, the greater the number of uncertain environmental variables that must be considered, and the more comprehensive and complex the plan must become. In the end, the effort of formulating the plan may exceed its value.

Flexibility. The degree of flexibility of a plan should match the uncertainty of the environment with which it deals. Plans that are too rigid for the circumstances are detrimental to the accomplishment of goals because they will be ignored by those who must carry them out and the people will be left without any plan at all. However, flexible plans are more complex, more costly, and require more discretion than rigid plans. Therefore some trade-off between flexibility and rigidity is required.

Flexibility can be built in to plans in a number of ways, but each way involves making allowances for contingencies. Contingencies, in this sense, are statements that say if *x* occurs, do *y,* but if *a* occurs, do *b*. Some of the ways that flexibility can be built in to plans are described in the three types of plans listed below.

1. *Variable Plans*. These plans state figures in terms of *ranges* to allow for the uncertainty of the environment. For instance, the time estimated to complete a phase of a project might be stated as "three months plus or minus one week." The advantage of the variable plan is that one can easily estimate the effect on the organization of different levels of operation. In the example, the manager could estimate the effects of having the project completed in three, four, and five weeks.

2. *Alternative Plans*. These plans are similar to variable plans in recognizing environmental uncertainties, but in this case the planner sets up two or more entirely separate plans. The plan that is finally chosen is

the one that most closely accounts for the circumstances that arise. This kind of planning requires a careful definition of important environmental factors at the outset, and it is also costly since at least one plan will never be used.

3. *Supplementary Plans.* A third type of flexibility can be obtained through supplementary plans. Although the basic plan may set a firm ceiling on expenditures in a given area, the plan allows for the manager to request further resources should they later be needed. Supplementary plans reduce the constraining effect of the original plan by providing a prearranged appeal channel.

Although each of these plans attempts to create flexibility, perhaps the best way to ensure flexibility is through the attitudes of those guided by the plan. Managers may be encouraged to remember that flexibility is a state of mind and plans are simply representations of reality, not reality itself. People tend to lose sight of the fact that a plan is only a means to an end and often feel that they must use it even if it is not useful. But following a plan that is not going to work creates far more problems than drawing up a revision.

Information Requirements. A final design characteristic to consider in planning is the amount of information required. As was pointed out in Chapter 15 on communication, information does not automatically come to the manager when needed. Much of the information necessary for planning comes from outside the organization and requires specific search procedures to obtain it. Even the internal information required may have been generated originally for other purposes and therefore must be reprocessed and adapted to be made useful to the planner. In common with all decision makers, the planner is both swamped with information and yet often unable to obtain the information that is really essential (10).

Information gathering takes time, money, and effort. It simply may not be efficient to obtain all the information needed. The cost of doing an incrementally better job must be weighed against increased resource expenditures. Typically, it takes more and more resource expenditures to bring in less and less information. Thus cost-benefit analysis is a good tool to apply to the planning process.

Human Considerations

Since plans affect people, people's reactions are important considerations in determining the workability of plans. Three important aspects of this reaction are commitment, aspiration level, and rewards.

Commitment. Plans have a "point of no return" characteristic. For example, a planner can think at length about what needs to be done to alter production processes, but at some point new machinery must be purchased. Once a major expenditure is incurred, the organization and its people must be committed to making the plan work. Plans focus attention on certain goals and actions, which is both good and bad. Focused attention avoids unnecessary and inefficient behavior. All action can be compared with the plan to determine whether it is appropriate and consistent. On the other hand, commitment to a given plan may blind the person to changes in the environment. Negative information, or that which is contrary to the plan, tends to be ignored unless it is exceptionally persistent. Ignoring changing conditions threatens both the plan and the overall adaptability of the organization.

Aspiration Level. A second human aspect of planning has to do with aspiration level. Plans can range from easy to impossible, but both extremes are generally ignored. Plans should reflect goals that are attainable but challenging, and realistic plans will encourage commitment (refer to Chapter 4 for a more thorough discussion of this topic).

Rewards. The final human consideration here is that of building in rewards to ensure getting the expected behavior. It is not enough to design for "what" and "how." One needs to include "why." Expectancy theory (see Chapter 8) indicates that in order to obtain desired behavior one needs to offer rewards that appeal to the person's needs and to make meaningful connections between the rewards and the behavior. These connections must be built in to the plans themselves. For example, one plan might provide bonuses to division managers for exceeding planned levels of return on investment.

Organizing for Planning

As we said in the beginning of this chapter, people tend to avoid the activity of planning. And for this reason, planning, perhaps more than any other managerial function, needs to be consciously programed into the organization. Typically it is only in retrospect that managers realize that they could and should have planned a particular course of action. This tendency to avoid planning stems both from the feeling that there is no time to do so and from the attitude that today's problems are larger and more important than tomorrow's. But these rationales are not always valid. Many of today's problems that take so much time and are of such importance could have been avoided or minimized if the manager had planned for them in advance. In fact, many activities must be planned if they are to be executed at all—in particular, those situations in which events happen sequentially or for which resources must be assembled prior to action. A manager does not decide to change a production line today if new machinery that takes six months to manufacture must be specially built.

Time Management

Finding time to plan is a major problem for most managers. They invariably feel they already have more things to do than they have time to do them and that it is impossible to fit in even one more activity. No hard and fast rules exist, but some aids are available for helping managers find time to plan for the future. One of these is **time management.** The idea of time management is that managers, or anyone else, can become more efficient if they study what it is they do during the day and attempt to organize and evaluate their findings. Time management starts from the twin bases of recording what one is presently doing and what one thinks one should be doing, then noting the differences (11). Finding out what one is doing means simply keeping a complete diary over a period of a week or more, or taking observations at random times during the day. Determining what one *should* be doing is a bit harder. Usually the manager must go back to his or her own goals and rank them in order of priority.

Problems may be demanding and immediate, but if they are not among the most important things to get done they should be laid aside. For managers, many of these time problems can be solved by delegating work to others. Delegation is essential if managers are to accomplish their work, and it must be employed even if they can do certain tasks better than their employees. Managers' time is best spent planning, making decisions, and monitoring their departments. But it is easy under the pressures of the day to slip back into solving every problem as it arises and end up behind again.

Since managers spend about 80 percent or more of their time in contact with others, an important area in which to develop competence is in interpersonal relations. Argyris has shown that when there is an open and trusting atmosphere between employees and managers less time is spent dealing with and solving personal problems and conflicts (12). Similarly, a knowledge of group dynamics allows the manager to understand and handle time-consuming committee meetings in a more efficient manner.

If operations are not properly sequenced in advance, problems pile up so that by the time they reach the manager's desk they are considered emergencies. By taking a step back and planning the proper sequencing of operations, time spent in planning will be saved later by having avoided these problems in the first place.

Who Does the Planning?

All managers plan. But many organizations establish special units devoted exclusively to planning. The advantages of having planning groups are essentially the same as the advantages of having other staff groups. If you bring together people who are experts in planning, the activity should be carried out better. Having experts becomes increasingly important as the techniques of planning become increasingly sophisticated. A planning group also provides a central place where information can reside. It is not efficient for each manager to go out and search the environment for all the information needed. Managers would be duplicating one another's efforts. A planning group can collect needed information and distribute it as necessary. Also, planners' expertise might lead them to sources that a general manager is not likely to find. If a planning group is established, more time will be available to plan. Planning can then be carefully done at a more leisurely pace than is possible on the firing line of day-to-day operations. By establishing an expert planning group, both the planners and the operating managers function in the tasks to which they are best suited.

Planning groups, however, cannot do all the planning. The range of decisions is similar to that of any other staff group. At one extreme the planning group would collect and analyze information, then turn it over to line managers for a decision. At the other extreme, a planning group would develop both general and specific functional plans for line managers to follow. Most planning groups fall somewhere between these extremes, but they are much more likely to be involved in overall strategic planning, long-range planning, and resource planning than in short-range, functional planning. Such groups ordinarily report directly to top management (13).

It is true, though, that planning groups can create certain problems for the organization. The fact that they are physically distant from actual operations, which is useful for providing both time and perspective, can result in a *planning gap*. This means that they may come up with what appears to the line manager as an unworkable plan. Furthermore, the sophisticated techniques of the planner may not be understood by the line manager. Thus the plans may be ignored, subverted, or informally changed to meet the situation in the "real world." Some organizations attempt to overcome some of these problems by rotating line managers in planning assignments. This, of course, negates the advantage of expertise but adds a good reality dimension. Rotation programs have proved useful in assessing the promotability of managers to levels where more time is spent in planning (14).

Participation in Planning

A final issue in organizing for planning is determining how much and what kind of participation managers are going to require of their employees. Participation in planning will increase commitment to the resultant plans. Furthermore, employees may have information that managers need that is not available elsewhere. The only way to secure such information may be to involve them in the planning process. Management by objectives is an ideal way to incorporate employees into the planning process.

The question of who participates is partly a matter of which way the planning progresses in the organization. The most common view is that planning starts at the top with the development of goals. Each level then specifies and makes operational its part of the plan until the employee actually performing the work has very precise, short-range plans from which to operate. But if internal information about the job is a major part of the information needed, then this approach is not workable. It has been noted that planning can proceed from the specific or bottom of the organization to the top and general level of planning. Bottom up planning provides a maximum of internal information but does not take full advantage of environmental information. Bottom up planning involves a maximum number of employees, which does provide good information but that increases coordination difficulties.

The main problem with participation is that employees may cause plans to turn out differently from the way the manager wanted them to be. People bring not only their knowledge to the planning activity but also their needs, values, and prejudices. The plan, as developed, may not look like what the manager had in mind at all. There is always the possibility, however, that it is a change for the better—that it is a more realistic plan and one that the employees are more likely to follow. But no matter how well a plan may satisfy the needs of the work group, it is not workable unless it meshes well with the overall plans of the organization.

Finally, it may be noted that participation should not be used as a technique to obtain commitment unless the manager really believes in or desires the participation of employees. Such a use of participation is manipulative and will be so perceived by employees.

Chapter Review

This chapter has discussed the first of the managerial activities regarding adaptation—that of planning. While planning is one of the most important activities of managers, particularly top-level managers, it tends to be neglected by the pressures of today's problems. Some of the major ideas presented in this chapter are as follows.

1. Organizations that plan are more successful than those that do not plan.

2. Planning as a process consists of answering three questions: Where are we now? Where do we want to be in the future? and How are we going to get there?

3. Organizations must collect information about the environment, the resources they need, and the internal operations. Put together, this information informs the manager of the **posture** of the organization vis-à-vis the environment. This posture consists of the **scope** of the organization (what it does), its **competitive advantage** (what it does well), and its **distinctive competence** (what it can do well).

4. **Forecasting** is the process of predicting future conditions from today's information. It consists of gathering information and building projections based on what is learned. Information can be treated as a constant from past to future—a **deterministic strategy**; as a signal for what will happen—a **symptomatic strategy**; or as a sophisticated model of reality—a **systematic strategy**.

5. Forecasts can be used to *react* to predicted conditions or to *influence* the environment to attain the goals of the organization.

6. **Tactics** refer to specifications of how strategies are going to be carried out.

7. Types of plans may be categorized a number of ways:

a. Goals, strategies, and operations refer to the breadth of the plans. **Goals** are very general directions; **strategies** are ways to adapt the organization to the environment; and **operations** are specifications for completing a task.

b. Plans are also categorized by the functional area that they cover. A **master plan** covers all organizational activity and **functional plans** cover a specific organizational area and integrate into the master plan. **Budgets** are resource plans that project the amount of resources required to accomplish tasks. **Activity plans** indicate the time required to complete tasks.

c. Plans can be categorized as **short** and **long** range. This is an arbitrary distinction depending upon the **planning horizon** of the organization.

d. Plans may also be categorized by the degree of certainty that they assume. Plans that assume **complete certainty** are limited and of short duration. Plans that assume **risk** are more complex and account for a greater degree of reality. The most complex plans assume **uncertainty** because they are the most realistic; they therefore are the most inclusive.

8. In designing plans the following characteristics are important:

a. Considering whether the plan will be used over and over (a **standing plan**) or whether it will serve only one unique situation (a **single-use plan**).

b. Defining the **scope** of the plan, or the area it is meant to cover. The narrower the area the more definite the plan can be, but the more limited its use.

c. Building in **flexibility** to account for changes in future events. Flexibility can be established through **variable plans, alternative plans,** and **supplementary plans.**

9. Planning for human considerations involves obtaining **commitment** to the plan, making the plan match people's **aspiration levels,** and seeing that **rewards** are connected to the planned behavior.

10. **Time management** consists of comparing actual behavior with one's ideas of what one should be doing and taking action to bring the two into alignment.

11. **Planning staffs** have the advantage of knowing how to plan with the use of sophisticated planning techniques, and they have the time to do so. They have the disadvantage of being away from the action and of tending to develop plans that no one understands.

12. Planning can be done either from the **top down** or **bottom up.** The choice seems to be determined by whether internal or external information is most important.

Discussion Questions

1. Why is planning becoming increasingly important as a managerial activity?

2. Explain the planning model in terms of the three major questions it seeks to answer. Devise a study plan using this model.

3. Define and explain the following terms:
   a. distinctive competence
   b. competitive advantage
   c. organizational scope

4. Identify the three strategies used in making forecasts and explain which method or methods would be best for each of the following determinations:
   a. estimating personnel requests from production quotas
   b. estimating sales from new housing starts
   c. deciding if a new product is worthwhile based on a series of economic data

5. Distinguish between strategic and tactical plans.

6. How do resource and activity plans differ?

7. Discuss the characteristics of certain, risky, and uncertain plans. What are their relative advantages and disadvantages?

8. How would you go about designing a standing plan? A single-use plan? What operational and human variables would you need to consider for each?

9. What is time management? What is its importance in planning?

10. Who should do the planning in an organization? Why?

Involvement Activities

Based on what you have learned in this chapter about planning, devise the best possible plan for each of the situations below and then answer the questions that follow.

a. A friend has called and invited you to a party this evening that you very much wish to attend.

b. You are an experienced hiker about to go on a weekend backpacking trip into unknown territory with two people who are eager but novice hikers.

c. You have decided to go on for an advanced degree and must choose which university you will attend.

1. In what ways did the planning activities of information gathering, forecasting, and tactics differ for each of these plans? Why?

2. To what extent did the functional and time dimensions of each plan cause you to develop them differently?

3. Describe the certainty-risk dimension of each plan.

4. What human considerations did you take into account for each plan?

5. On a scale of 0 to 10, how would you rate the workability of each plan? Discuss the reasons for your ratings.

19

Control

In this chapter we will examine the second managerial activity of the adaptation cycle, that of control. Control is the process whereby behavior is compared with plans to determine whether the two are in accord with each other. If deviations are found, either the plans or the behavior must be changed. The ways in which control works to bring about these changes are explored here through a model of a control system, a description of what variables to control and how to measure them, a discussion of how to set perfomance standards, and an overview of how to integrate control into the organization.

In the last chapter we saw how managers can reduce uncertainty and adapt to changing internal and external conditions by planning ahead. The goal of planning is to predict and affect the future environment. Controlling is a companion activity that examines the past to see whether what happened corresponds with what was planned. Further, controlling involves taking action on any deviations that are found between actual and planned occurrences. In this sense, control may be considered a remedial activity. The intermediate relationship of controlling, between planning and changing (the subject of the next chapter), is illustrated in Figure 19–1.

It should not be assumed that because control is remedial in nature it is any less important than planning. The actions and behaviors called for in a plan do not automatically occur simply because the organization has committed itself. Plans must be implemented, which is what most of this book has been about. Implementation is begun by subdividing the plans to make them operational and organizing people to carry them out. Together these two steps determine what behavior is to take place, by whom, and to a large degree, how it is to be done.

Still, there is no guarantee that action will take place or that, if it does take place, it will adequately complete the plans. To this end, managers must be involved actively in the work of the organization as well as at the more detached level of planning and organizing. First, they are the decision makers. They relate the plans to internal and external pressures

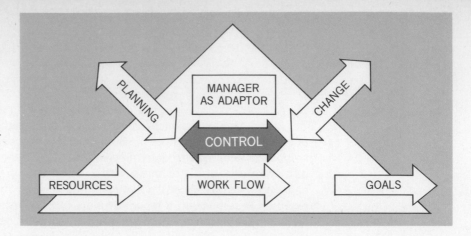

FIGURE 19–1
The manager as a
mediator adapting to
environmental and in-
ternal pressures. This
chapter focuses on
control, which is the
most internal aspect
of the adaptation
cycle.

as they arise. Second, they must communicate the behaviors described in
the plans to the employees. And third, managers must intercede to start
and maintain action through the use of influence and leadership. The final
step necessary to complete the cycle is that of obtaining feedback about
what has occurred and taking corrective action as required. This is the activity of control.

The Basis of Control

Like planning, control depends upon the utilization of information. But
the types of information each activity uses is quite different. Planning
forecasts future events based predominantly on data obtained outside the
organization. Control, on the other hand, measures performance from
data obtained inside the organization.

Data obtained for control purposes typically do not indicate cause
and effect relationships, nor do they indicate what is deviating. To discover the nature of any deviations, managers need to examine the known
data to determine (1) whether organizational performance or behavior is
out of line with the plan or (2) whether the plan is inconsistent with the
(changed) environment. In either case the intention is to restore equilibrium, otherwise known as balance, or **homeostasis.** Any organism has a
tendency to be self-regulating. When disturbed or stimulated in a direction
that upsets the balance, it responds with a series of counterresponses to
regain equilibrium. In most organisms, such as the human body, these
control mechanisms are built in, unconscious, and automatic (1).

Organizations are not quite like organisms, however. It is true that
the organization does have many programed responses that aid homeostasis. These are the procedures and policies of the organization. But
because these responses are not totally adequate, management must
design a control system to supplement these organizational programs.

If organizational behavior is found to be out of line with the plan, then attempts to get the organization back to where it was may work. But even these efforts will be inadequate if it is the environment that has changed. In this circumstance the more proper adaptive response would be to alter the plan rather than the behavior. A major problem here, however, is that changing the plan instead of the behavior generally involves a greater amount of adaptation activity and is more upsetting to people. For this reason it is usually not considered first. In fact, the degree to which this alternative can be considered at all depends on the nature of the control system established in the organization—that is, whether it is an *open* or *closed* system.

The dynamics of control are of considerable interest to scholars in a number of disciplines. To the extent that control involves the problems of balance and homeostasis on the one hand, and those of growth and adaptation on the other, the subject concerns biologists, physiologists, ecologists, mathematicians, chemists, sociologists, and many others. The result of this interest has been the development of a separate field of study called **cybernetics,** a word derived from the Greek word for helmsman, indicating the activity of steering.

Weiner, who coined the term cybernetics in 1948, popularized the notion that there is a comparison to be made between the physiological control systems of living organisms (primarily humans) and the complex mechanical and electrical control systems of computers and other technologies. Essentially, each of these systems needs to adapt constantly to environmental changes. It does so by developing an internal apparatus that processes information and makes any necessary adjustments in operations or behavior. The information provides feedback that compares expected behavior with actual behavior (2).

A Model of a Control System

The writings that have come out of the field of cybernetics vary considerably as to subject matter and level of sophistication. For instance, much of the literature is in highly abstract mathematical form. However, the basic elements of a control system can be distilled from this diverse set of theories. The elements that all control models have in common are outlined in the following discussion (3).

Information Feedback

The first element of a control system is **behavior** or activity. In any organization the amount and variety of behavior that occurs can be staggering. And the larger the organization the greater the diversity of the information. To gain some control over this behavior, parts of it must be recorded and measured by a system called a **sensor.** A sensor takes measurements of behavior and presents the information in readily usable form. An accountant is a kind of sensor. He or she sorts through a mass of daily financial paper work and develops an income statement and balance sheet (usable forms). Note that these papers are not actual financial activities—cash, inventory, and so on—but rather representations of the organization's financial behavior.

The information recorded by the sensor concerns actual activities and outcomes. It also contains assessments of those activities that were supposed to happen but did not. The *decision maker* uses this information to make a judgment about the meaning of what did or did not happen by comparisons of actual behavior with expected behavior. If the actual outcomes are found to be different from expectations, he or she then can determine required *corrective action*.

Corrective Action   Corrective actions may take one of three forms: no further action; change the behavior; or change the standard (or plan). (The original plan—the expected behavior—is called the *standard* because it is the measurement against which all subsequent behavior is compared.) If the comparison shows little discrepancy between actual and expected behavior, usually no corrective action is necessary. If there is a considerable discrepancy, corrective action is needed and a decision must be made as to whether to change the behavior or the standard. Knowing which to change is determined by the information the manager has about both the environment and the organization.

An Example of a Control System. The classic example of a control system is the thermostat (see Figure 19–2). The activity or behavior in this case is air temperature, which is what the sensor (the thermocouple in the thermostat) measures and what the furnace acts upon when so "commanded." The standard is the setting of the thermostat. The decision maker is highly programed in this instance. At a certain point (usually 3 or 4 degrees) below the thermostat setting, the thermostat activates a switch that automatically turns on the furnace (corrective action). The thermocoupler then measures the changing temperature until it is a degree or two above the temperature setting and then turns off the circuit (4).

FIGURE 19–2
A thermostatic
system.

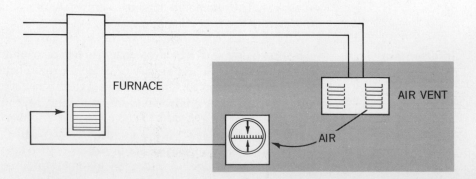

**Open and Closed
Control Systems**

The thermostat is one of the best examples of a closed system because it operates automatically and is designed to perform a prescribed sequence of activities, given a certain environmental state. And it has a complete feedback mechanism. It is called a **closed-loop** control system because it does not discriminate between varying causes of the change in the behavior that it measures but simply reacts to correct that behavior. For instance, a thermostat will "tell" the furnace to go on when the temperature drops, regardless of whether this is the best response (which it is not if the front door has been left open). Thus, the closed loop deals strictly with the prescribed level of activity. It is designed to correct any behavior that is not in accord with the plan, and it ignores all factors except those that it has been specifically programed to account for.

Closed control systems require a simple and stable environmental condition as well as a reliable internal mechanism. The sensor must be accurate, and the decision maker must operate strictly on an automatic basis. For these reasons, closed control systems are not particularly common in organizations. They are most effective when dealing with physical and technological factors. When the system contains social factors, that is, people—who almost never operate fully automatically—the closed system is usually not appropriate (5).

Clearly a closed control system cannot be adaptive to changes in environmental conditions. Also the response time of a closed system may be too long. If the control cycle (discussed below) is not followed, control cannot be achieved.

Open-loop control systems can handle the types of situations for which closed control systems are inadequate. They do so, however, by increasing complexity and disorder. Open control systems admit information and feedback from a great many sources in the environment, requiring that the decision maker use his or her discretion to develop new responses or to change the standards when necessary. The house in which the thermostat is located can be viewed as an open control system. Humans can do a number of things besides turning on the furnace when the temperature drops. For example, they can close the windows and doors, put on warmer clothing, or decide that a cold house is good for them.

Open control systems are learning models. Responses are tried out and used when appropriate, but changing conditions encourage, even require, the development and use of new and different responses. The result is a great deal of experimentation with new behaviors.

In closed control systems, managers' roles ordinarily end once the system is designed. In open control systems, on the other hand, managers continue to play an active role. Since the control sequence in open systems contains nonprogramed as well as programed decisions, managers must exercise judgment. At one level, this judgment is exercised when choosing between alternative responses that are designed to maintain the current level of balance, or homeostasis. On another level, managers are required to make decisions in the form of altering the plans, which disturbs the present equilibrium. This latter response is adaptive. A balance between these two responses is required in any organization. Maintaining equilibrium and following the plan regardless of the situation can threaten the survival of the organization in a dynamic environment. On the other hand, constant adaptation is disruptive to an organization because it makes consistency and coordination impossible.

Finally, managers are actively engaged in the open control system because all the necessary information is not in the feedback loop and it is up to them to provide the closure. That is, they must fill in the holes in the picture and proceed with the information they have at hand. This is an exceedingly important point. Recall from our discussion in Chapter 13 that decisions of any kind are rarely made with all the desired information available. It is simply too expensive, too time consuming, and often impossible.

The Control Cycle

All control systems are feedback mechanisms. They consist of the cycle of events illustrated in Figure 19–3. At the beginning of the cycle, the *behavior* or activity is intended to accomplish organizational *goals*. This behavior triggers a reaction in the *sensor,* who records and *measures* the information. This information is then fed to the *decision maker,* who compares the sensor's data with the *standard* and who, if deviations occur, initiates *corrective action.* The corrective action then stimulates a new series of behaviors, which in turn retriggers the sensor, and the cycle repeats itself. The major variation that occurs, of course, is when the decision maker decides to reevaluate the standard instead of changing the behavior.

The feedback mechanism, or control cycle, is much like the two communications models presented in Chapter 15, which also emphasized feedback. The advantage of the feedback mechanism is that of *redundancy.* Corrective action is taken, results are fed back, and the cycle continues until the behavior and the standard are again in agreement. In this way the control cycle is a major tool for coordination in the organization.

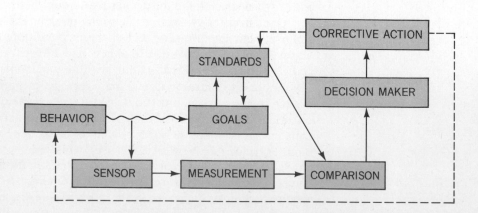

FIGURE 19–3
A control cycle.

To see how this cycle works in a real-life situation, consider the following sequence. In a machine shop, weekly production for a particular product was scheduled to be 125 units, or 25 units a day. According to the daily activity report received by the plant superintendent each morning, production output on Monday and Tuesday was 13 and 22 units, respectively. On Wednesday the superintendent called all the supervisors together to discuss the low output and decided to authorize three hours of overtime. The supervisors paid more attention to output, and the overtime work also led to greater production, so that 38 units were produced on Wednesday, bringing the production output three over quota for this point in the week. However, on Thursday afternoon one of the machines broke down and it took two hours to repair, reducing production that day to 15 units. Faced with the need to produce 32 units on Friday, using a reduced number of machines operated by employees who were tired from working overtime, the superintendent told the supervisors to aim for a minimum of 24 units on Friday. By comparing the actual and expected behavior and reevaluating the standard, the superintendent decided to take corrective action that involved changing the plan rather than the behavior.

Achieving Control

Just knowing what types of control models are available is not enough to attain control. Managers also must know how they are designed (closed control systems) and how to operate them (open control systems). The thermostat again provides a good example. The use of thermostat controls in homes is a relatively new development, having come into popular use within the past fifty years or so. In order to develop such a control system, a decision first had to be made about which activity to measure; in this case the air temperature was chosen. (While this may seem obvious, some heating systems are designed to maintain a constant temperature of objects—including humans—in the area and not a constant air temperature.) Second, a decision had to be made as to *how* to measure the air temperature. The design of the thermocouple solved this question, but left open the problem of *where* to place the control box. If it is situated in the wrong place, parts of the house may be either too warm or too cold. Setting the standard may also pose a problem. What is the proper temperature for a room? People disagree considerably on this point, and in recent years an increasing concern with energy shortage has changed people's attitudes about optimum temperature settings. Standards then are devised from a consideration of both factual and attitudinal factors.

Finally, corrective action will be dependent on making proper decisions. The local climate conditions, as well as the size of the building and its type of insulation, will determine the size and design specifications of the heating unit necessary to achieve the standard. This decision is not wholly technical; it also includes economic, aesthetic, and health consid-

HE'S A GREAT MANAGER... ALWAYS IN CONTROL.

erations. Each of these elements in the control process has its own set of problems that must be solved before control can be achieved.

What to Control   In any organization it would be impossible to control all activity or behavior, and in large organizations this is particularly true. The question then is what to focus on. The most obvious answer in this case is also the most accurate. Focus upon those things that are most important. In 1897, an Italian economist by the name of Vilfedo Pareto noted that the relationship between income and population was greatly skewed; that is, a large percentage of the income was earned by a small percentage of the population. He determined, therefore, that if one wishes to study or affect income, one need only focus attention on that small segment of the population that controls most of the income. This skewed distribution became known as Pareto's Law (6). In organizations the same theory holds true. A small percentage of the employees file the largest proportion of grievances; the majority of an organization's resources is supplied by only a few outside sources; most of the sales are to only a few major customers; and so on. It is not necessary to look at the whole population but only that portion of the population that has the greatest impact on what is being observed. In focusing on the important variables, there are four useful things to keep in mind. These are discussed below.

Control What, Not How. First, control over *what* is being done is more important than control over *how* it is done. Focusing on what instead of how is difficult because most of the information available pertains to the latter. Furthermore, "how" questions usually take up more of the managers' time.

Nevertheless, there are times when focusing on how is very important. For example, if the allowed tolerance for error is very small, such as in the production of certain electronic components, then controlling the how is crucial. One would have to design a working environment that is clean and dust-free and establish other controls to assure accuracy. Controlling the how of work is also important when the cycle of activity takes a long time, such as with a research project. In this case, it may be useful to break down the overall task into components and apply control procedures at the completion of each segment to ensure that errors are not compounded.

Controlling Those Variables That Make a Difference Second, the activities controlled should be those that make a difference. For instance, in a retail department store the control of purchasing may be much more important than the control of personnel transfers, since correct purchasing is at the heart of the department store business. Similarly, large, diversified organizations generally attempt to control the financial aspects of their various divisions because the corporate headquarters is essentially a distributor of corporate financial resources. Drucker suggests a focus on cost points or activities that account for a significant portion of total costs. These costs points are most likely to fall into one of the following four categories: production, support, policy, and waste. Production is the cost associated with getting the product out, and support is the cost associated with directly aiding production. Policy costs are those associated with keeping things from going wrong (management). Costs not associated with any of the above are waste and are therefore not useful (7).

Controlling Changeable Variables. Third, control should also concentrate on factors that are subject to variation. A given variable may be exceedingly important in the work of the organization, but if the variations in behavior or quality of the variable are unlikely to exceed tolerance standards, then elaborate control systems are a waste of time. It is much more important, for instance, to develop an elaborate control system for the disbursing officer of an organization who deals with the cash flow than it is for most other middle managers who do not have an opportunity to misappropriate funds.

Control of Output. The final consideration in focusing on variables has to do with whether input or output behavior is the most important. Theoretically, control can be exercised over each. For instance, in a work group either attendance or the production of the unit can be measured. In practice, though, it seems that control over the inputs is not nearly as useful as control over the outputs. The relationship between inputs and outputs is rarely direct enough to make input control successful. This may explain why it is difficult to develop control systems for governments or other organizations that deal mainly in services. The majority of control systems in government organizations focus on the inputs because outputs are too complex and too difficult to measure. Most performance-appraisal programs have the same problem. The person is judged on a series of traits that, it is hoped, are related to his or her productivity. But productivity itself is not judged because it is very difficult to define.

What and How to Measure

It is one thing to know that you wish to control a certain activity and quite another to be able to measure variations in that activity. For instance, changes in financial conditions are more readily measured than are changes in personnel attitudes because financial resources are quantitative measures and attitudes are qualitative measures. For this reason, organizations keep extensive records on financial activities and relatively few reports on personnel activities. This example points out one of the major problems in control—the tendency to control what can be measured instead of what needs to be controlled. There is no necessary correlation between the measurability of an activity and the importance of controlling it. However, people seem to like to control measurable activities; they are easier to handle because they deal with specific data.

Surrogate Measures. Many activities, however, do not lend themselves to direct measurement. In these cases a **surrogate,** or substitute, measure is required. Thus what one will be looking for is a factor that varies in the same way as does the activity one wishes to control but that is more conducive to measurement. As an example, monitoring employee attitudes may be very expensive and otherwise impractical, but recording employee turnover is easily accomplished and usually varies inversely with positive employee attitudes. A surrogate, then, may be any activity that is highly correlated with the original criterion. However, the relationship between the two activities is not always known in advance, as it is in the example above.

The relationship of a surrogate and the activity to be controlled should be constantly watched. To continue the example, the turnover rate may remain low because of poor economic conditions, while employee attitudes deteriorate. A good way of ensuring against this kind of problem is to have more than one surrogate measure available for the activity.

Focus on the Measurement. The people who are performing the activities being controlled, as well as managers of these people, may focus too specifically on what is being measured. That is, all concerned may tend to focus on the control standards and not on the goals. The dysfunction of this practice is that when the focus is on the control standard it becomes the goal and the real goal may be neglected (8). Perhaps the clearest example lies in the area of wage incentive programs that pay for the quantity of work performed. Maintaining adequate quality of the product becomes a major difficulty when people are paid solely for the number of units they produce.

One final point is worth noting here. While focusing on certain variables may reduce the deviation in those variables, the effect may be to

Dysfunctions of Focusing on Measurement

Organizations are full of examples of people who pay attention only to behavior that is measured and thereby fail to properly carry out their jobs. Consider the following cases:

a. In banks, managers are concerned with the manner in which tellers deal with customers. But tellers know that they are rewarded or punished according to whether they balance their cash out at the end of the day. So it is not uncommon for tellers to keep customers waiting while they straighten out their cash receipts.

b. A standard procedure in one insurance firm was to pay its salespeople commissions on new accounts only. They found out that a large number of customers failed to renew their policies after the first or second year because they were being neglected by their salespersons.

c. Professors are hired to teach classes. But the way to get promoted is to write books and carry out research. As a result, many professors are often unavailable when their students need them.

d. Clerks in retail stores are often paid by the hour and therefore evaluated according to the time they put in rather than by the number of sales they make. Thus they may keep customers waiting while they sort merchandise or even chat with one another.

Source: J. L. Livingstone, "Management Controls and Organizational Performance," in P. E. Connors, T. Haiman, and W. G. Scott, *Dimensions in Modern Management* (Boston: Houghton-Mifflin, 1974).

maximize deviations in variables not under control. Applied to a selection system in an organization, if one maximizes the probability of selecting someone who is able to perform a job by setting up very strict hiring standards, one may at the same time maximize the probability of *not* selecting someone who can perform the job. Many companies now require that applicants for management training programs have a college degree, even when they have no evidence that a degree is essential to good performance. Organizations thus may reject many who could succeed, and they have no way of knowing how those rejected by the standard might have performed.

Performance Standards

Performance standards are plans that describe what is supposed to happen. It is against these plans that behavior is to be compared and deviations noted.

Tolerance Limits. Just as it is impossible to control all activities fully, it is equally impossible to take action on all deviations. Therefore, standards need to be set that allow for some variation and at the same time make it possible to correct any deviations that prevent goal accomplishment. Most standards are defined in terms of upper and lower limits of acceptable behavior. The width of these **tolerance limits** is determined by making a trade-off between the importance of the behavior and the cost of its deviation on one hand and the cost of its control on the other hand.

Instead of controlling all behavior, some leeway is desirable. This suggests that behavior can vary within a certain range or tolerance limit as illustrated in Figure 19–4.

Exception Principle. Control itself should be considered an activity that must be kept under control. Like all activities it vies for organizational resources (time and money). Too much control keeps deviations from occurring but absorbs resources needed for other activities. It also creates its own dysfunctions in terms of stifling individual creativity.

What needs attention are those instances of behavior that vary beyond the tolerance limits. Paying attention only to those behaviors that vary significantly from tolerance limits is called the **exception principle.** It saves the manager a tremendous amount of time and keeps the cost of control within limits. There are some costs, however. In effect, the exception principle means that the manager mainly examines and comments on the negative aspects of a person's behavior. This can be very detrimental to employee morale and motivation. In fact, many psychologists maintain that the exception principle is backward. Positive behavior should be reinforced by rewarding it, not ignoring it. By the same token, negative behavior will disappear if it goes unrewarded and ignored. While it is true

FIGURE 19–4
Tolerance limits on behavior.

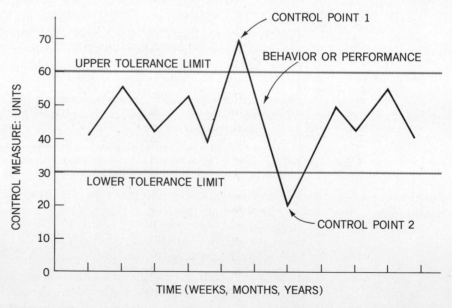

Performance standards are shown as a range of acceptable behavior. Within tolerance limits, performance does not require control. When results exceed expectations (control point 1), the upper limit may be questioned or the causes sought. When performance falls below expectations (control point 2), corrective action is called for or the standard needs to be reexamined.

that punishment has been shown to be effective in extinguishing negative behavior, the problem with punishment is that it does not provide a model of the desired behavior and can result in negative attitudes toward the person administering the punishment.

Setting Standards. Performance standards need to be perceived as realistic by those who must work to their specifications. The salesperson who is given a quota to double his or her sales in a saturated territory is more likely to give up than to work harder. When people are judged by standards they consider unrealistic they feel they are being unfairly treated. This feeling leads people to meet the standard in dysfunctional ways. For instance, managers judged by return on investment often put off needed capital expenditures to keep the return looking good in short-term reports.

Activities vary considerably in the degree to which standards can be set for them and the type of standards that can be used. As we mentioned earlier, the easiest behaviors for which to set standards are those that are easily quantifiable and readily observable. But managerial activities are rarely measurable in quantitative terms (except for the behavior of division managers under profit or ROI—return on investment—programs) and usually very difficult to observe. Very few attempts have been made to establish standards for managerial activities with anything like the precision of the time-and-motion studies used for lower-level employees. This does not mean that hard-to-measure activities cannot have standards. What it does mean is that these activities are likely to have standards that are looser and that are stated in nonquantitative terms.

Multiple Goals. Finally, not all activities have a single goal. Even in a piecework situation the goal is to produce as many items as possible within certain quality constraints. The situation with most other organizational activities is much more complex. Typically a manager is required to keep output or production up, keep costs down, and simultaneously abide by a whole series of constraints imposed by such groups as accounting, personnel, and quality-control departments. In a complex situation, the various goals of each area of behavior should be represented by some set standard—be it quantitative or qualitative. These must then be traded off with one another so that a minimal acceptable level can be achieved in all standards. The ability to maintain a balance in achieving these standards is a requisite for effective managing (9).

Where Controls Originate

As has been expressed many times in this book, the demands and pressures on an organizational participant come from many sources. Although some positions in organizations are established specifically to perform control functions, such as production controller, quality control inspector, and so forth, attempts to institute control can come from any source that needs some specified behavior. From this perspective, most behavior is seen as incomplete or inadequate by at least one person or department. Different groups and individuals have different performance standards. Not everything everyone wants done can be accomplished. Any person being controlled must decide which demands to meet and to what degree. Managers face this problem all the time in trying to satisfy the multitude of external demands made on them by such factions as unions, government agencies, civil rights groups, consumers, environmentalists, safety advocates, and others.

There is also a choice as to where the control point will be. Western societies emphasize external control, meaning there is a tendency to rely on laws, rules, and regulations to govern behavior. But this is not the only approach. Anthropological studies have shown that there are many cultures with few external controls—where cooperation seems to be built in to people's normal behavior patterns through conditioning. All people—regardless of the society—learn their culture's acceptable behaviors and attitudes from birth on. But in very large and highly complex societies there are many different forms of acceptable behaviors, and external controls are necessary to ensure some basic uniformity (10).

In this regard, organizations are much the same as societies. For the most part they, too, rely on both internal and external control methods. Selection procedures are used to eliminate those who do not seem to "fit in." Training programs, particularly management development, contain a great deal of material designed to precondition employees to react in accordance with organizational policy. On the other hand, supervisors, rules, policies, and so forth are all intended to provide external controls.

To rely on internal control is to show faith in people's positive nature and in the socialization process. But the fact is that not many of those in power have a great deal of trust in these functions (11). Thus, rules and regulations are devised. The problem with rules and regulations, however, is in knowing how many to make and the degree to which to enforce them. Internal and external controls must be balanced because neither is sufficient by itself. In a relatively small organization with highly competent employees, managers can and should rely more on people's internal controls. In a large organization, particularly in which heterogeneous groups of people are doing many varied tasks with only partial job knowledge, a high degree of external control is probably needed.

Making Comparisons

A major problem with comparing standards and behavior is determining how to equate the two directly. We have stated that standards are sets of plans committed to paper describing desired behaviors. Actual behavior, on the other hand, is recorded by some measurement device that summarizes behavior in terms of that measurement. Thus in the example of the thermostat, the standard consists of two points on a scale and the behavior is a recorded temperature. In this case both the standard and the behavior are stated in sets of numbers, making comparison an easy task. But what of instances in which the two factors have no such common denominator? For instance, if a hiring policy (standard) states that people will be hired without regard to race, creed, sex, or national origin, what does the behavior (measurement) look like? A series of statistics relating how many blacks, females, Mexican-Americans, and so on, are at what levels in the organization may or may not show that the policy standard has been followed.

This problem of comparability can be improved by careful, consistent advance planning of both the standard and the measurement. In the above case the standard might have been more specific in terms of the percent of women and minority groups expected at each level in the organization. Or the measurement might have been aimed more directly at the selection situation itself to see whether discrimination was taking place in application questions, interviews, and so forth.

Behavior Modification in Business

Behavior modification is not just a clinical or educational technique—it is also a way to manage. B. F. Skinner, the well-known behavioral psychologist, had the idea that behavior is best affected by controlling the environment in which the behavior occurs. Specifically, people will repeat behavior for which they are rewarded and cease to perform behavior that is not rewarded or that is negatively reinforced. The use of behavior modification has spread rapidly in education and is now being tried in industry.

One of the first business firms to use the technique was Emory Air Freight Corporation. Emory's first major experiment was in the Customer Service Department. This department had a goal of responding to any inquiry within ninety minutes. Those in the department, employees and managers, felt that they were meeting this goal. A study of the actual situation, however, showed that the goal was being met only about 30 percent of the time. Instead of the usual solutions, a simple feedback system was developed. A daily checklist was established on which each operator indicated every inquiry that he or she was able to complete within a ninety-minute period. The checklists were examined by the supervisors at the end of each day and *improvements* in the number of responses completed within ninety minutes were rewarded in the form of recognition and praise. Lack of improvement was not punished. Instead, the employee was told, "At least you recorded your performance accurately," and once again reminded of the goal.

Results were dramatic. In a very short time most offices in which the system was installed were responding to inquires within ninety minutes about 90 percent of the time. Furthermore, many offices began to set even higher goals for themselves. Other areas of the company showed similar results. When feedback was given to packers of containerized cargo (people who combined small packages into single shipments), container-packing efficiency jumped from 45 percent to 90 percent. In sales, a 27.8 percent gain was made in the year after installation of a feedback system.

Source: "New Tool: Reinforcement for Good Work," *Psychology Today* (April 1972), pp. 67–69, digested from Dec. 18, 1971 issue of *Business Week*.

The external control cycle works in such a way that there is a time lag between the behavior and the feedback, or measurement, of that behavior. Ordinarily, behavior is performed by one person or group and recorded and measured by some other person or group. Certain production people, for instance, might solder a number of connections onto an electronic assembly. Farther down the line these connections are inspected by quality control personnel, and then the measurement goes to the plant superintendant. The solderers typically receive feedback only when results are unsatisfactory. The steps between behavior and feedback are time consuming and indirect. However, when control is internalized, the behavior and control cycles operate simultaneously. Some psychologists suggest that employees should record their own behavior and be provided with the means to instantly feed back the results to themselves. In organizations where this method has been tried, the results have been highly satisfactory.

Feedback provided long after the behavior takes place loses its impact. Because so much else generally happens in the interim, any corrective action is geared toward behavior that is out of date or forgotten. Furthermore, rewards and punishments decrease in effectiveness when they do not immediately follow the behavior they are meant to reinforce or alter. In extreme instances, a severe lag in the control sequence can be fatal to the organization. If behavior is moving rapidly away from the standard, the corrective action may be so late that it is impossible to respond adequately. A machine that is consistently turning out defective parts cannot wait for quality control to pick up the difficulty and relay the information to top management, which then sends instructions back down the hierarchy to the operator. The employee has to know immediately whether to shut off the machine.

This feedback lag can be alleviated in part by computer and associated information system designs. Computers have the capacity to process large quantities of data and deliver it as usable information with a rapid turnaround time. The ideal of this computerized control system is an *online, real time* system. **On-line** indicates that measurements are taken at various points in a given operation as behavior occurs. **Real time** indicates that the measurements of this behavior are fed into the computer and analyzed while the action is taking place. Such a system is capable, for example, of giving a manager information as to the inventory level of all the items in warehouses all over the country within ten minutes of the closing time of the last warehouse. Central, computerized reservation systems for airplanes, hotels, and motels, which instantly report the availability of seats or rooms, are other dramatic examples of how these systems work.

Making Corrections

We have seen that corrective action can be aimed either at the standard or at the behavior. Changing the standard is often difficult because of all the prior commitments that have been made as a part of the planning process. Resources have probably been assembled, managers and employees have been sold on it, and money has been allocated or already spent on it. But if continuing with the plan after the environment has changed means incurring even further losses, then the standard must be changed accordingly.

Changing the behavior is a far more typical response when discrepancy between the standard and the behavior shows up in the control system. But this, too, is not an easy task. People become committed to what they are doing and how they are doing it. And if feedback is not internal or immediate, they may not even realize that their behavior is out of line with the standard. Furthermore, the problem may be that the people are trying to satisfy more than one goal and the standards for each are in conflict. In such cases, only partial changes in behavior may be possible. These problems and some possible solutions to them will be considered in the following section.

Integrating Control into the Organization

Control, like all other managerial activities, cannot be considered as an isolated function. In order for it to work, it must be coordinated with other organizational activities. Without such integration, control systems could not be made efficient, effective, or themselves kept in control.

Control and Organization Design

The control system needs to match the design and purpose of the organization. The major areas that need to be coordinated with control are: goals, chain of command, work flow, decentralization, and technology.

Control and Goals. We know that organizations have complex networks of goals. But trying to maintain control systems that would ensure completion of all these goals is unrealistic. Instead, control systems can be made to focus only on those goals that make a difference and that are subject to variation. At any one time certain goals become more important than others. Thus, one month control might be focused on financial expenditures; another time personnel procedures may take precedence. The trouble with this sort of rotation is that it gives a "management by crisis" air to the organization (12).

In addition to these "crisis" control systems, certain functions are associated with very important organizational goals and therefore rate elaborate control systems on a continuing basis. In an airline company, for example, the safety goal is of paramount importance and will be governed by a complex control system at all times. On the other hand, baggage handling is more likely to be a function governed by much broader tolerance limits and dealt with only periodically.

Control and the Chain of Command. Control systems need to take into consideration the authority lines of the organization. If they did not, employees might have one person telling them what to do (manager) and another person (controller) telling them whether their performance matches the standard. The possibilities for confusion and misdirection under such circumstances are great. Control groups often fail to perceive overall goals; and even when they do they may not have the authority necessary to effect change.

Control and Work Flow. Control points along the work-flow sequence are necessary to measure product consistency. This quality control activity is often assigned to a specialized staff, and for this reason may run counter to the authority hierarchy.

A major consideration in quality control is where to place the sensors in the work flow. If an error that occurs early in the sequence is not detected until the end, the product is unusable and a good argument can be made for having a number of control points all along the work-flow path. But increases in the number of control points restrict freedom, widen the overlap in jurisdiction of staff and line, and lead to higher overhead costs. Figure 19–5 suggests possible control points in a multiple-control system for a production sequence. In a single-point control system for the same sequence, the control might be placed just before the packing operation so as to include all the activities in one comprehensive inspection.

Control and Decentralization. Controlling decentralized activities presents another dilemma for management. Control is needed, but the very concept of decentralization is negated if the manager has to receive evaluation on every decision made. Still, a most important factor in the success of decentralization is maintaining knowledge about how things are going in the decentralized unit. So, how does the organization resolve this dilemma?

The guidelines discussed earlier can be applied here as well. First, control systems should focus on those activities that are especially important, and second, the control system can be built in to the decentralized unit itself. If each unit generates its own feedback, decisions can be made faster and more accurately.

FIGURE 19–5
Single- and multiple control-point systems for a production sequence.

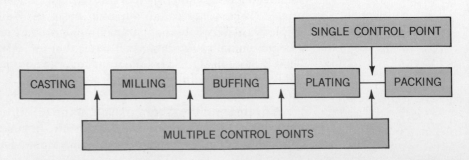

Control and Technology. A final consideration in coordinating control with the organization design concerns the technology that the organization uses. Recall that the Woodward studies showed control to be very difficult in small-batch organizations, where control instruments are generally crude and the control point is at the end of the work-flow sequence. Large-batch organizations, on the other hand, have the most specialized control units with many control points, but the whole control system is an appendage to the production system. In continuous-process organizations, control is built in to the technology. Machines rather than people do the controlling automatically. In this situation, control is an integral part of the production system (13).

Control and Communication

Because the principle of feedback is central to the control process, control, in a sense, is a form of communication. Thus, much of the material covered in Chapter 15 is relevant to an understanding of how control systems work.

Understandability. One of the first requirements of an effective control system is that it be understandable. Everyone involved in the system —whether operating it or subject to its control—must understand the standards, the type of behavior that will or will not achieve the standards, the feedback process, and the corrective activities. This suggests that all phases of the control process need to be clearly specified and made as simple as possible to understand. Further, on lower organizational levels, the system should be far less complex than it is at the upper levels.

Some disagreement may occur between line managers and staff groups over the issue of simplicity. The line manager understands the necessity for clarity and understandability while the staff group, which consists of experts in developing and maintaining control systems, is interested in obtaining a maximum of information and so argues for as sophisticated a system as possible. The staff group's control system is often incomprehensible to line management and others who are subject to its actions. The result is that people tend to find ways to get around the control system rather than to use it.

Redundancy. Analyzing feedback information provides a useful perspective not only of the behavior being measured but of how well the system is operating. It may be recalled that in the discussion of feedback in communication it was emphasized that to obtain understanding the whole communication cycle may need to repeat itself a number of times. This is also true of the control cycle. The corrective action phase is not so perfect that it automatically reveals the correct remedial action the first time around.

Running the control cycle through a number of times rather than just once puts a further premium on quick feedback. Again, simplicity is the key. It is better to operate with approximate and preliminary figures than to wait for specific and complete information that comes too late to be of any use.

Relevancy. In the preceding chapter we discussed some of the reasons why people ignore tomorrow in favor of concentrating on today. This tendency is even greater when applied to studying the past. When control systems are seen as concerned only with what has already happened, people deal with them only when they have nothing else to do. Control systems need to emphasize their relevance to present and near-future activities if they are to gain the attention of busy managers. In addition, if the feedback information is compared with very long-range organizational plans, the whole environment may have changed significantly by the time it is relevant, and its purpose will have been defeated.

Directionality of Feedback. Usually, information gathered by the sensors is relayed up the organizational hierarchy to decision makers, whereas communication about corrective action is relayed downward to the operating levels. This cross flow of information creates a **control gap** in the same manner that a planning gap is created when staff groups do the planning and line groups do the overseeing. The people performing the work are left with the feeling that corrective actions, particularly if untimely, are not in line with the reality of current operations. As mentioned earlier, an alternative is to place the entire control cycle in the hands of those performing the task. This is a major goal of those who support job enrichment. It involves entrusting a good deal more responsibility to the employees, which requires that management have a high level of trust in the work force.

Design of Information Systems. Wherever the responsibility for the decision phase of the control cycle is placed—be it upward or downward or with a staff—it is necessary to plan what information is to be received by the decision maker. When the control cycle is not well spelled out, or when the decision maker is not specified, there is a tendency to spread information out at random, hoping someone will pick it up in time to do some good. Thus, if the information is to be useful, it must be stated in usable terms and delivered to someone who knows what to do with it.

Control cycles, like plans, differ according to organizational levels. At lower levels they are immediate and specific, dealing with *how* things get done. Toward the top of the organization the control cycle focuses on *what* is to be done and covers a longer time span. The information received by the various decision makers must reflect these differences in the types and the subjects of that which is being controlled. If top management is provided with a great deal of day-to-day operational information, they must sort through it to glean the few facts they can use. On the other hand, the line supervisors need to have access to all the operational information that is gathered.

Control and the Planning and Decision-Making Functions

Since plans are the standards of the control system, they should be designed with an eye toward how they will be used in the control process. Actually, most planning techniques do have built-in control aspects.

Resource Plans. A good example of planning with built-in controls is budgeting. As a standard, a budget provides a clear and quantitative maximum or range of resource expenditures that is permissible. It is possible with accounting data to present not only actual figures of expenditures but also to make projections for control purposes. Part of this control aspect would involve simply projecting current spending patterns into the future. Also available is past history. Certain departments, for instance, may show patterns of spending money at the beginning or the end of the budgetary period, and these trends would have to be incorporated into any statement of current expenditures. With this information it could be determined whether a sudden upturn in material costs in, say, a production department with a history of stable expenditures, means that something is happening that needs looking into.

Sensors and measurement techniques are very much a part of the budgetary process. And in most organizations the accounting system probably has the best-developed feedback loop. Also, measurements and comparisons are made easy since the entire process, at least for the financial budget, is in terms of dollars. But there are certain problems associated with accounting data when they are used for control purposes. These include: timeliness, understandability, confusion of data and behavior, and the exception principle.

1. *Timeliness*. Particularly in small organizations, the control aspect of accounting takes place at relatively long intervals, perhaps semiannually or yearly. In large organizations the process is a continuous one in which monthly figures are usually available, but even here the information the manager receives may not be timely. Accountants, like other staff groups, want to present their information to the highest possible level in the organization. But the people at high levels are not necessarily the decision makers in the control system, so the information must filter down through a series of levels instead of being sent directly to the proper source, saving considerable time.

2. *Understandability*. The accounting system is designed to accomplish a number of tasks, not the least of which is to meet the demands of the Internal Revenue Service. Most information developed from the accounting system is designed primarily to satisfy this external source and only secondarily to act as an internal control system. This generates information that is very difficult to understand and that may not be useful for control purposes. As a result, a whole area of cost and managerial accounting has grown up to specifically provide internal control information and not external information.

3. *Data and Behavior*. Budgeting systems are classic examples of control systems in which the measurements and the standards are representations of behavior rather than the behavior itself. Thus, deviations need to be studied carefully to determine the proper course of remedial action. The automatic response to reduce expenditures to meet the budget is often an incorrect one. The supplementary budget idea is one that attempts to account for environmental change and thus introduces a change in the standard into the budgetary process.

4. *Exception Principle*. Budgets suffer from the problem discussed earlier of not giving feedback unless it is bad. Managers are seldom rewarded for meeting their budget or for holding expenditures below the budget. Rather they are penalized if they exceed their budget and frequently their budgets are cut for the following year if they do not spend all the money allocated for the current year. This practice encourages managers to spend more than necessary to avoid a cut in next year's funds.

Activity Plans. Activity plans, too, have control aspects built in to them. While money and personnel are the major items measured in budgets, time is the major variable in activity plans. Control, in this instance, is measured by the time it takes to complete tasks. We have seen how this control works through the implementation of critical path methods, such as PERT, which have a series of activities sketched out in the order in which they must occur and a statement as to the estimated time required to complete each activity. A focus on the important activities is maintained by the critical path.

Feedback in activity plans is usually close to the decision maker. Activity plans are drawn up and measurements taken by line management because the sequential nature of activities requires continual adaptation of the plan as well as immediate corrective action. Thus, control measurements in activity plans have the advantage over budgets of being designed directly for the job they are meant to monitor.

Control and Influence

An interesting paradox is inherent in the control process. On the one hand, control implies maintaining stability and homeostasis; but on the other hand, in order to achieve balance the manager must continually adjust either the behavior or the plan itself.

Power. Directing the behavior of others is accomplished through the various bases of power. Earlier, under organization design, it was pointed out that control needs to be consistent with authority; that is, decision makers in the control system must be able to enforce the decisions they make. The most promising bases of power for enforcing control decisions would appear to be control of rewards and punishments and established authority, rather than expertise. This fact is inconsistent with the practice of establishing staff groups, whose power base is largely expertise, as organizational control agents.

**Strategic
Leniency**
Most organizations have a great number of rules and regulations that constrain both the manager and the worker. Some of these are central to getting the work done, but others are peripheral and may constitute a source of irritation to employees. For instance, rules concerning the time and length of coffee breaks or smoking on the job are ones the manager can choose to ignore without hindering the output of the work unit. Leniency in enforcing peripheral rules is appreciated by the employees and is also strategic in that it gives the manager a power base from which to control other behavior. Thus when employees do something out of line the manager can threaten to enforce the coffee break or smoking rules. Employees are generally happy to conform with output-related regulations as long as such compliance can be traded for continued leniency in areas that make their working conditions more pleasant.

Strategic Leniency. Managers often must choose which standards to enforce and which to let slide. This type of selective enforcement, called **strategic leniency**, can be used by managers to enhance their power base. Thus, managers choose not to enforce certain rules in return for cooperation in other areas. The trick to strategic leniency is to pick areas that are of low importance to the organization and of considerable importance to the needs of the employees (14).

**Control and
People**
No discussion of control is complete without a section dealing with people's reactions to it. People both like and dislike control. They like, even need, to know what the goals are that they are working toward, and they like to receive feedback. But they do not like to be watched constantly, nor do they like to be told they are not meeting the standard.

Employees may perceive any control system, no matter how well designed and how effectively it takes them into account, as evidence of a lack of trust. Control systems seem to say that managers need to keep their eye on what employees are doing because they are not likely to do it correctly. If managers take any action when people behave wrongly, which of course happens at times, a negative feeling toward the manager is instilled in the employees. On the other hand, if no action is ever taken, employees are not likely to know that their behavior is wrong or, if they do, they may take advantage of the lenient policy. If the latter happens too often, a very strict control policy may be instituted.

Where, in fact, a definite lack of trust does exist, the organization may find itself in a constantly deteriorating situation. Tougher standards are set but only minimally met. These prompt even tighter controls, which leads to even greater laxity in meeting them. This downward spiral continues until there is a growing atmosphere of distrust between management and employees.

Since control systems are devised by one group of people (managers) to regulate the behavior of other people (employees), the two groups are more or less at odds with each other. Management has no special talent in developing control systems that are superior to employees' abilities to circumvent them. Observers have noted that employees' abilities to subvert the system, especially one designed by an industrial engineer or budget analyst, are at least as great as managers' abilities to design it. Thus a constant game goes on in organizations wherein one group designs control systems that the controlled group then figures out how to get around (15).

Not all attempts at controlling are seen as negative by the employees, however. As already mentioned, control systems provide feedback that people need and want. It is the way they perceive the control system and what it means to managers that can create negative feelings. When control systems are not clearly visible or when they are called by another name, they are far more acceptable than those loudly marked as control devices. Thus, where possible, control systems should be an integral part of the technological system—a continuous process that is not labeled "control," and that is handled by machines instead of people. People have fewer negative feelings toward machines that control their actions than they do toward control-oriented people. It has been found that when control systems are built in to the technology, the pattern of interaction reverses so that employees are initiating contacts with the manager for help rather than the manager initiating contacts with the employees for the purpose of giving orders (16).

Chapter Review

This chapter has considered the topic of managerial control. A model of a control system has been described, as have ways of achieving control and methods of integrating control into the organization. Some of the major terms and ideas presented in this chapter are listed below.

1. **Control** is a remedial activity that is instituted to see whether the behavior that occurred corresponds with what was planned for. Any deviations between behavior and plans are indicators that corrective action is required.

2. All organizations attempt to maintain a balance, or **homeostasis.** Disturbances in the existing balance will lead to actions that will regain equilibrium. The study of balance and homeostasis in systems is called **cybernetics.**

3. The elements of a control system include:

    a. **behavior,** which is measured by a **sensor,** in order to provide information feedback;

    b. a **standard** with which the measurement from the sensor is **compared;** and

    c. **corrective action** when the comparison indicates a discrepancy between the behavior and the standard.

4. A control system may be either **open** or **closed.** Closed systems operate automatically, whereas open systems rely on the judgment of the person operating the system.

5. Since it is impossible to control everything, certain guidelines are established for determining what to control.

    a. Control *what* is done, not *how* things are done.

    b. Control those variables that make a *difference*.

    c. Control variables that are subject to *variation*.

    d. Where possible, control *output,* not input.

6. Some behavior is more difficult to measure than other.

    a. **Quantitative data** are easier to measure than qualitative data; but quantitative data are not always as important.

    b. **Surrogate measures,** ones that vary consistently with the behavior one wishes to measure, often can be used as substitutes for hard-to-measure behavior.

7. **Performance standards** are plans that describe what is supposed to happen.

    a. **Tolerance limits** allow a range of behavior before deviations are recorded.

    b. Control systems operate on an **exception principle,** meaning that they are activated only when a deviation from standard is recorded.

    c. Standards need to be **realistic** if the control system is to be effective.

    d. Standards or plans may conflict with each other making any behavior violate some control system.

8. Control may be either **external** or **internal** to the individual manager or employee. Our society tends to depend on external control.

9. Standards and measurements of behavior are often hard to compare because they are stated in different terms and because behavior is often widely separated from the control point.

10. Control systems must be **consistent** with other organizational considerations. In particular:

    a. Control systems should guide behavior toward organizational *goals*.

    b. The operation of control systems should be consistent with the *chain of command*.

    c. They must take into consideration the *work flow*.

    d. Control systems are both more difficult and more necessary when decisions are *decentralized*.

    e. The type and extent of control is particularly dependent on the *technological level* of the organization.

    f. Control systems are also *communication systems* and rely on similar principles.

    g. *Budgets* are a major source of control but they must be timely, understandable, flexible, and provide some positive feedback.

11. Control relies on **power** to change behavior, but controllers are often staff personnel and not line managers, which makes the exercise of power difficult.

12. People may react negatively to attempts to control them because control measures typically focus only on negative behavior. Managers can reduce this negative response by:

    a. Using **strategic leniency,** which is the selective application of rules and regulations.

    b. Developing a high level of **trust** between employees and management.

    c. Focusing on **positive behavior.**

Discussion Questions

1. What role does control play in the adaptation cycle? How is it related to planning and change? How is it different?

2. How does control work to maintain homeostasis in an organization? How is organizational homeostasis both similar to and different from homeostasis in organisms?

3. What is cybernetics?

4. Design control systems for:
    a. driving an automobile
    b. shopping for groceries
    c. writing a class report

5. What are the differences between open and closed control systems?

6. How and why would control systems differ in the following organizations?
    a. An atomic energy plant
    b. A hospital
    c. A university

7. What variables would you isolate for control in the following situations? Which variables would you choose *not* to control in each instance?
    a. Student performance
    b. Speed of automobiles on a freeway
    c. Violations of rules in football or basketball

8. What is the exception principle? What does it have to do with reward and punishment?

9. Distinguish between internal and external control.

10. Describe a situation in which you would choose to change the standard. One in which you would change behavior. State the reasons for your choice in each case.

11. Make an argument for control points being in the chain of command. For being in the work flow.

12. Why is control considered to be a form of communication?

13. What is strategic leniency? How does it work? When would it be most useful?

14. Why do people dislike being controlled? What can be done about it?

**Involvement
Activity**

One of the more popular forms of educational experiences today is the management game. Teams of students simulate the operation of a business over a number of time periods with the aid of a computer. Each team puts its decisions into the computer for each time period. How well each team does depends on the environment as represented by the computer program and the behavior of the other teams. One management game has twelve time, or decision, periods with a set of decisions due each week of the semester and an oral report presented to the class as a final examination.

Typically, teams of students range from five to seven members, with each acting as functional specialists for either analysis or decision making. The final decisions, however, are made by group consensus.

Assume now that you are a member of such a team. During the first meeting, a strategic plan (when and how you are going to make group decisions) and an organization design are worked out (who is going to be in charge of what kinds of decisions). As the team is about to break up, you remind people that ''Just because we have a plan, there is no assurance that it will be carried out as designed.'' The others agree, and with typical democratic procedures select you to design a control system for the team.

1. What will your control system be like?
2. How are the following parts of the control process included in your system?
    a. Sensor and measurement
    b. Standard
    c. Decision maker
    d. Corrective action
3. What difficulties do you predict you will have with achieving control? Why?

20

Change

The only constant in the manager's world is change. And because managers can be sure that things will not remain the same, they must deliberately plan for and institute change in order to keep their organizations current and viable. Sensing what changes are occurring externally, accommodating them effectively, and initiating and implementing planned changes are the managerial activities that keep organizations from being subject to the caprice of both external and internal forces that, sooner or later, could make them obsolete.

In this final chapter we will take another look at several of the important models and concepts developed in earlier sections to see how they affect and are affected by change processes. The activities of changing will be examined in terms of the change sequence, the various types of organizational change, the forces acting for and against change, and the methods for achieving change.

One of the recurring themes of this book is that the manager is a "person in the middle." We have seen that the manager must respond to pressures from a variety of sources and in turn apply pressure back on these sources to maintain internal organizational equilibrium and to move the organization toward the accomplishment of its goals. This perspective has shown the manager occupying a somewhat ambiguous position with few clear-cut principles to follow. His or her time is fragmented by a constant barrage of demands, and the necessity to take action and to activate others is ever present. In addition, we have learned in this last unit how the activities of planning, control, and change make up a cycle of adaptation by which the manager must both adjust the organization to accommodate the environment and attempt to modify the environment so that it serves the needs of the organization. Figure 20–1 again illustrates this cycle.

The intention of this illustration of the adaptation cycle is to show that it is a continuous process with no end or beginning. Managers engage

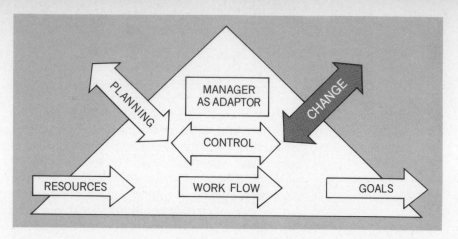

FIGURE 20–1
The managerial role
focusing on change.

The accent in this chapter is on change, an activity that is linked to planning and control and that is carried out through the activities of directing.

in planning, control, and change activities as an integral part of the functions they perform in all other areas of organizational work. For this reason, many of the concepts presented in earlier chapters will reappear here to show how they are connected to and are part of the change cycle. The purpose is to understand the nature of change, the demands and limitations of change, and the methods by which change can be facilitated.

The Change Sequence

Change starts from its opposite state—a condition of temporary stability or equilibrium. We saw in the last chapter that when a new variable is introduced into the organizational environment the balance of forces is disturbed. This occurrence triggers the homeostatic mechanism that seeks to regain balance by making a change in the opposite direction. But a true balance in organizations is never fully achieved because changes occur more rapidly than homeostatic tendencies can correct them.

A contributing factor to this inability to keep up with change is the fact that the introduction or alteration of one variable has a multiple effect on other variables. It is not a one-to-one cause-and-effect relationship. For instance, the installation of a computer will obviously affect those in the department in which it is installed. But it will also affect the people in other parts of the organization that deal with that department. Thus, it may necessitate changes in managerial functions, accounting procedures, personnel requirements, and so on. Failure to predict and account for these related effects may create more problems than the computer's primary usefulness can offset.

A Model of Change

Most change either directly or indirectly involves people. People must react to change and it is they who determine whether the change attempt will be successful or not. It makes sense then to use as a model of change one that is based on the behavior of people. The model presented here was first developed by Kurt Lewin in 1947 and later expanded upon by Edgar Schein in 1961. The change sequence suggested by these authors has three steps: **unfreezing, moving,** and **refreezing,** which are illustrated in Figure 20–2 (1).

Unfreezing. The first step in change is recognition of the need for change; that is, to see that the present situation is inadequate in some way. To recognize that change is needed, one must have a good understanding of the present situation. (Recall from Chapter 18 that recognizing and understanding the present situation was suggested as the first step in developing a plan.) People behave in certain ways because it is functional to do so. They are rewarded for it. So not only must there be a recognition of inadequacy but also a removal of the rewards that make present behavior functional. These two conditions constitute the unfreezing process. Unfreezing is usually precipitated by some crisis—a wildcat strike, a failure to meet a quota, a difficult new assignment, the passage of a new law, and so forth. Unfreezing may also stem from a steady build-up of anxieties or pressures that make the necessity for change both desirable and inevitable. Where the latter situation is true, present rewards are already insufficient to overcome the feeling that change is preferable to no change.

Moving. Because unfreezing makes old behaviors inadequate and does away with certain rewards, the second step in the change sequence is to introduce new behaviors and rewards. This step is called *moving* because it involves education and training techniques and leads the person to new modes of behavior. This is a very sensitive step since there is generally some anxiety associated with learning new behaviors. Thus, an

FIGURE 20–2
The steps of change.

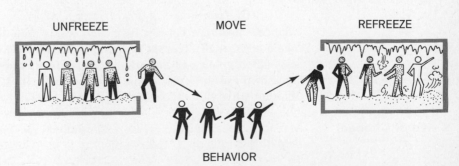

accepting and relaxed atmosphere should surround this area of the learning environment. An environment that encourages experimentation with new behaviors is not one in which there are no standards, however. High but realistic goals should be established for achieving the desired new behavior. We have seen in earlier chapters that very low standards are not challenging and lead to boredom, and standards that are too high lead to frustration. Learning occurs in neither case.

Success in this step requires the person to *identify* and *internalize* the new behavior. **Identification** means that a person sees the new behavior working successfully for others, and he or she then models, or imitates, that behavior. Identification almost always occurs in response to someone who is admired, and the imitator begins to act as though he or she were that person. **Internalization** is the incorporation of certain behaviors to the point that they are an integral part of the person's repertoire. A newly learned tennis stroke may seem clumsy at first, but once internalized — learned and used successfully over time — the player often cannot even remember having done it any other way.

Refreezing. The final step in the change sequence is refreezing. This step requires a continuous reinforcement of the newly acquired behavior. The new tennis stroke may seem easy enough when the instructor is right there encouraging its application. But when the player begins to practice on her own, she may revert back to the same old behavior patterns. The same holds true for people who are retrained away from the work site. For the change to become a permanent part of behavior patterns, either people need to be returned to new jobs or the organization needs to be changed during their absence. As we saw in Chapter 10, this tendency to return to familiar habits presents a major obstacle to effective human relations training for managers.

When refreezing is accomplished, the change sequence comes full circle and returns to a state of equilibrium. The new behavior is natural and functional, and the person is rewarded for it. The introduction of any disturbance at this point will start the whole sequence over again.

Organizational Change

Change is an alteration, a substitution of one thing for another, and it may take a number of different forms in the organization. Further, managers respond to change in various fashions. In this section we will explore some of these different forms of organizational change and some of the different ways that managers respond to change.

Kinds of Change   Managers react to and create essentially three kinds of change: *unanticipated, anticipated,* and *planned.*

Unanticipated————————Anticipated————————Planned

Even though outwardly the organization may appear to be in a stable environment, subtle alterations are constantly afoot. From a short-term perspective, these changes may be as imperceptible as the fact that employees are just a bit older today than they were yesterday, or that a resource may be slightly more costly than it was several months ago. But when neither the organization nor its environment is stable, large-scale alterations regularly beset managers and create problems that no one had foreseen. Regardless of the state of the environment, however, an **unanticipated change** is one that occurs without management having planned for it.

Managers may have little ability to prevent change, but awareness that change is coming (**anticipated change**) makes it easier to deal with. If the organization is prepared to handle an event, then many problems can be prevented or solved with little difficulty. Consider, for example, a firm that knows the cost of its needed resources is going to rise 15 percent in the next year. Several alternatives for dealing with this change are immediately available. Managers can stockpile their inventory, experiment with less expensive substitute materials, or initiate a change in the goals of the organization. Whatever course is decided on—maybe a combination of solutions—the organization is in a much better position than it would have been had the increase been unanticipated.

Planned change refers to an orderly development and implementation of changes before they are required. Planned change is an offensive response by organizations to turbulent environments. It keeps the organization even with or ahead of the changes that would have necessitated alterations anyway. By planning changes, organizations can have some influence on the environment instead of just responding to the dictates of uncontrollable forces.

Managerial Responses

Regardless of the kind of change with which managers are confronted, some response is always necessary. Managerial responses to change can be ranged along a continuum from reactive at one extreme to proactive at the other extreme.

Reactive   Proactive

In common with the managerial activities of planning and controlling, the activities concerned with change are geared toward maintaining the equilibrium of the organization. If there are no clear-cut strategies for handling change, managers can only be responsive to environmental forces. This is a **reactive** orientation, which sometimes is necessary but at other times is undesirable. For instance, the response of managers to unanticipated change is necessarily reactive because the need for change first presents itself when it is already a problem. Although being a "disturbance handler" is a most important aspect of the managerial role, the reactive orientation is not very comfortable for the manager (2). Furthermore, the occurrence of too many unanticipated changes may be symptomatic of managerial shortsightedness.

Managers with a **proactive** orientation attempt to foresee problems and develop advance strategies for coping with them. A manager with this orientation attempts to be an influencer of outcomes rather than a reactor to changes already beyond control. A proactive stance can help to maintain the organization as a vital part of its environment. Plans can be made to accommodate unexpected events by programing flexibility into the organization. Better, managers can set up sensors to detect alterations in the environment and thereby convert potentially unanticipated changes into anticipated ones. But the best course of action is to establish strategies for planning and implementing changes that will enable the organization to influence its own destiny.

Forces For and Against Change

Two somewhat different views of change exist. One view, which is perhaps best represented by Alvin Toffler's book *Future Shock,* asserts that change is the only constant in today's world (3). This conception has the world changing so rapidly that people and institutions are unable to cope or keep up with the pace. The other view of change sees people not as struggling and failing to keep abreast of the times but putting up tremendous resistance to innovation and change (4). Those who espouse this point of view maintain that people are fearful of change and therefore try to circumscribe or hold back the initiation of new ideas or technologies.

Managers of organizations seem to be caught between these two positions. While they are constantly required to change and adapt to the demands imposed from outside and inside the organization, any attempt on their part to create change is always in danger of being resented. Any one of the people or groups with whom the manager must deal is likely to see the effects of proposed change as negative (no advantage or no reward value) and put up resistance to its implementation.

A construction of a complete model of the manager's job, Figure 20–3, is useful to help pinpoint some of the areas from which the manager is likely to encounter both demand for and resistance to change. The external or adaptive view of the manager focuses on changes in the environment, resources, and goals. The overall environment is constantly changing, yet it demands a certain consistency in the organization's behavior. The more specific part of the environment, which contains the resources needed by the organization—particularly people and technology—is also an important change area. The area of goals, or outputs, is another one in which the manager must both respond to and initiate change. The internal view of the manager's job focuses on the organization's need for and resistance to change. Each of these external and internal areas of focus will be considered in this section of the chapter.

The Environment

Throughout the book we have stressed that a rapidly changing and increasingly demanding environment is more and more becoming a common fact of life for organizations. Consider but a few examples. In the political sector, new laws, new interpretations of old laws, and new government agencies to implement these laws proliferate on every side. In the economic environment, inflation, unemployment, a shortage of investment capital, and balance-of-payments problems are prevalent. Sociocultural changes abound, too, as evidenced by the gradual acceptance of alternative life styles, the demands for equality by women and minority groups, the decreasing birthrate, and the tightening of the global community. In the natural environment, a shortage of fuels and other raw materials plus the potential dangers inherent in destroying the ecosystem and the atmosphere are everyday news items.

The problems presented by all these changes—and many more—have yet to be well defined in terms of their long-term effects on organizations. Nonetheless, managers must somehow cope with those that impinge on their endeavors. The hardest part of this task is simply trying to keep up with the pace of change.

FIGURE 20–3
A complete model of managerial activities showing both internal and external processes.

Constraints on Change. The multitude of demanding environments imposes constraints on change and encourges and demands that one

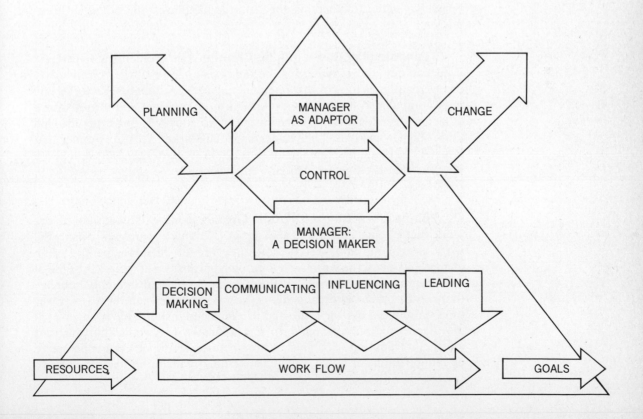

make changes. To some extent constraints are a result of the conflicting demands of the various groups, which make any course of action untenable to one faction or another. Thus, a proposed building alteration may pass all the various code regulations but be denied because of local zoning ordinances. Overlapping jurisdictions and conflicting purposes reduce the probability that an organization can achieve change even when change is demanded and managers are ready for it.

Resources

The two most significant resources in terms of demanding and prohibiting change are technology and people.

Technological Demands for Change. One of the hallmarks of American society is technological change, and we pride ourselves on being a world leader in this area. The advantages of technology make it impossible for any organization to ignore the consequences of failing to alter antiquated systems. As a result, very few industries have avoided rapid change in their methods of operation. Certainly the computer has had a revolutionary effect on most organizations, including quite small operations. A little less obvious in its consequences for change, but also of major significance, has been the development of copying equipment, which has had a tremendous effect on the handling and volume of information.

Technological Restraints on Change. The greater the investment in technology, the stronger will be the resistance to further change. But change continues to evolve at phenomenal rates. Automated factories and huge computer systems are extraordinarily expensive, and it may take a company decades to absorb the cost. But no sooner is one type installed than a bigger and better one appears on the market. It is no wonder that attempts to convince a company to trade in its two-year-old model on a new one that is twice as efficient—but twice as expensive—are met with resistance.

People as a Change Force. Organizations exist because of the work that people perform within them. Although managers create the work assigments and specify how they are to be done, people often change and adapt the work to fit their own purposes and to satisfy some of their personal needs. Probably the most apparent and influential change that people create in organizations, however, is through turnover. Over time, employees quit or retire and are replaced, usually by younger people. Each generation brings into the organization a somewhat different viewpoint from that which has existed before. As the newer people move up into positions of power, they change the organization to make it more consistent with the world as they see it (5).

People as a Force Against Change. Paradoxically, people like stability. Standard operating procedures and systematic routines for handling regularly recurring situations make people feel comfortable and provide continuity to their lives. And managers often reinforce these stabilizing routines because they make *their* lives easier too. Established ways of doing things mean that employees do not have to ask managers to make decisions about how to handle every matter that comes up. To serve a similar purpose, managers also encourage the norms of formal and informal groups because it is easier to rely on group pressure to ensure regularity of performance and orderliness of behavior than to enforce it by using managerial power. But while groups are useful to managers in many respects, they can present problems by tending to resist changes in the environment in order to keep the group situation in equilibrium.

Goals

Agents of Change. Organizational goals constantly change in response to changes in the environment, the organization, and the desires of top managers. Ordinarily these changes are relatively minor, such as a new product to fill out a product line or the acquisition of a new territory. At other times the change is dramatic, such as when an airplane manufacturer switches to missile design and production. But probably the most traumatic goal change comes about by goal succession, in which one set of goals is superseded by another (6). Goal succession, as we learned in Chapter 3, happens when current goals are fully achieved and the organization is forced to turn its attention elsewhere.

Goals are a reflection of and a validation for change. Goals change when the environment changes; and if the new goals are successfully received in the environment, the change is verified and becomes established.

Resisters of Change. Goals can also act as constraints on change by limiting or curtailing consideration of other goals. For example, if an organization defines its mission as the manufacture of automobiles, it will mobilize its forces to this end. If its mission is defined instead as providing transportation, managers might actively look for alternatives to automobile transport. If the mission is specified even more broadly, such as providing a service to people, everything from health care to travel clubs might be incorporated into the goal statement. The broader the defined mission of an organization, the fewer are its constraints and the more likely it is to welcome change.

The Organization

As we have already indicated in this section, an organization is open to its environment and is allowed to exist only as long as it satisfies the needs of that environment. The manager must be able to determine which forces from outside the organization will affect it, how the organization must affect the environment, and how and when the organization must change to better fulfill its mission.

Whatever the source of change, the web of events that connect subunits, organizations, and the environment are closely intertwined, and a change in any one sphere has consequences for all others. Sometimes a change is accommodated easily, and its force quickly expended. At other times, even a slight change can become compounded as it travels throughout the network, and dramatic effects are felt everywhere along its route. Organizations are designed in such a way that some of their functions are predominantly concerned with preserving homeostasis—these are called **maintenance functions;** and others are primarily directed toward change—these are the **adaptive functions.**

Maintenance Functions. Planning for change is no more natural to managers than is any other kind of planning. Most organizations exhibit an inertia that makes them increasingly vulnerable to the changing flow of events. Ironically, the forces that contribute to internal planning problems are inherent in the very functions that make organizations efficient. These are maintenance-oriented functions that contribute to orderliness, regularity, and predictability. Maintenance functions keep operations in balance and under control by means of standard operating procedures, policy guidelines, rewards, punishments, and other control devices. Although not always specified in writing, all organizations develop sets of standards to regularize behavior. These functions cut across work groups and activities, although they are more often found in the internal areas of the organization rather than at the boundaries. Maintenance functions are conservative in the sense that they perpetuate present methods of doing things. It is important that the behavior of all groups be understandable and predictable and that as much work as possible be prescribed to reduce the time and cost of conscious decision making. The maintenance function is valuable, too, because it contributes to efficiency. But to the extent that it perpetuates activities that are inconsistent with the changing pattern of environmental needs, it reduces organizational effectiveness (see the boxed insert on page 549). Maintenance forces are reflected throughout the organization—in goal statements, managerial activities, technology, and people.

Adaptive Functions. To prevent ineffectiveness, organizations develop adaptive techniques to search for new and better ways of operating internally and to seek new opportunities in the environment. Examples of those who perform adaptive functions are market researchers, systems and procedures groups, and planners. On occasion, organizations solicit the help of outside groups, such as management consultants, to help institute change or adapt to change. In all organizations, those units responsible for securing resources and those responsible for serving clients exhibit more adaptive than maintenance characteristics. The reason is that these groups have direct connections with the environment and therefore can often see the need for change before others do. Whether they can influence their organizations, however, depends on their power relative to the power of the maintenance-function groups.

An Unofficial Organizational Maintenance Function

In New York City before air-conditioning became commonplace, municipal agencies closed their doors an hour early on extremely hot, humid days. Over a period of time, many of them came to shorten the work day by an hour routinely during the summer months. The policy was purely a humane gesture made unilaterally by high administrative officers on their own initiative—indeed, in violation of official provisions of law and labor contracts.

Years later, when air-conditioning had become almost universal in municipal offices, an incoming administration, seeking ways to increase output without increasing expenditures, discovered this widespread, informal, unsanctioned, and possibly illegal practice. Orders were issued at the highest levels that henceforth the official hours of work would be observed all year round. The result was outrage in the ranks of the municipal workers and especially among the leaders of the more militant civil service unions. The administration was faced by threats of job action and possible strikes. Custom had hardened into a format as rigid as law. The administration had to back away.

Material from *The Limits of Organizational Change*, pp. 38–39, by Herbert Kaufman. Copyright © by The University of Alabama Press, 1971. Used by permission.

The amount of relative power adaptive-function groups should have is another question. People in adaptive groups may try constantly to institute changes and to add exciting new dimensions to the mission of their organizations. Planning and instituting changes, however, are costly endeavors. It takes time, effort, and money to collect the resources and to gear up the technology, structure, and people for a new mission. At the extreme, the adaptive system would be changing so rapidly that its costs would exhaust resources. Thus, maintenance and adaptive functions work at cross purposes; there is almost always conflict between them, and the friction must be accepted as part of the price of keeping operations both regularized and adaptable. And though the remainder of this chapter is concerned with the ways in which the organization can create change, the need for a strong maintenance function should be kept in mind.

Methods of Achieving Change

Whether the need for change comes from outside or inside the organization, putting changes into effect is a major managerial task. Implementation usually involves some change in the existing pattern of relationships among people, work assignments (structure), and technology. The way to effect change is to find out *what* can be done and *how* it can be done, requiring that information be gathered and analyzed. In this final section we will first discuss ways to gather information and then go on to explore some of the specific techniques that may be used to achieve change.

Gathering and Analyzing Information

One way of looking at the activity of gathering information is to start by reconsidering the model of the organizational environment used earlier in this book. This model, which divides the environment into four sections, appears here as Figure 20–4. In section 1, which represents the external-external environment, the forces at work are not directly connected to the organization, but their interactions do have direct organizational effects. Section 2 is the input sector, where resources flow from the environment into the organization; and section 3 is the output segment in which the organization serves its environment through its goals. Section 4 includes all of the subunits of the organization. In this segment the changes that occur must be managed, but at the same time, the changes emanating from all other sections must be implemented here.

There are so many events occurring in all these segments that without some kind of filtering device managers can easily experience a data overload. But even minor bits of data might indicate the existence of new problems or new opportunities. Thus, it is important to establish criteria and standards for the admission or rejection of data. In addition, a sensory apparatus must be established to tune in to events that could easily be missed. A screen and a sensor are both necessary. A few examples may illustrate some techniques to secure data about change.

Environmental Information (Section 1). In Chapter 18 it was seen that forecasting is a major way of dealing with environmental information.

FIGURE 20–4

The organization and its environments: four types of relationships: (1) outside: external-external links; (2) input: external-internal links; (3) output: internal-external links; (4) inside; internal-internal links among subunits.

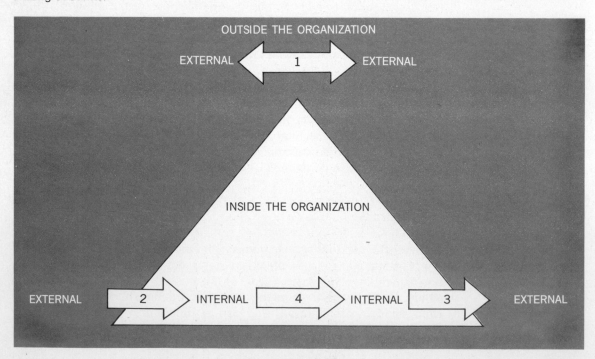

OUTSIDE THE ORGANIZATION

EXTERNAL ⟵ 1 ⟶ EXTERNAL

INSIDE THE ORGANIZATION

EXTERNAL 2 ⟶ INTERNAL 4 ⟶ INTERNAL 3 ⟶ EXTERNAL

Every organization must have accurate information about such matters as anticipated trends in the economy, the cost and availability of capital, changes in prices and wages, and local conditions. Of potentially equal value, depending on the nature of the organization, is information about changes in the political-legal, sociocultural, geophysical, and ecological systems. Larger organizations employ staffs of economists and attorneys to sort through the piles of data and assess implications of changes in these various environments. But general managers need to be cautious about allowing others to do all the sorting of information. Planning staffs and functional managers have specific biases that determine whether what they preceive is relevant. These biases may eliminate information that is of vital concern to managers for proper decisions about change. The discussion of groupthink in Chapter 13 is a good example of utilizing information that was improperly processed.

Resource Information (Section 2). Keeping abreast of changes in the supply and price of resources is of major importance. Purchasing agents, personnel specialists, and financial experts are among those usually charged with the responsibility for maintaining a steady influx of resources. These people interact with the environment at the input side and must be well prepared to accommodate any changes in resource availability. Some purchasing agents, for example, spend a good deal of time examining alternatives to materials that are in short supply or that are becoming expensive. Thus, packing companies can move from steel cans to glass, to aluminum, to plastic, and back to glass according to current prices and environmental conditions. Others are not so fortunate, such as organizations that rely on educational institutions and other organizations for trained and experienced professional employees. If human resources are in short supply, or if salary demands are excessive, few personnel recruiters have the budget and facilities necessary to switch tactics and hire inexperienced, less expensive people and then go about the process of training and educating them.

Output or Goal Information (Section 3). Output information is that which is concerned with defining the mission of an organization, identifying client populations, and determining what is wanted. Gathering this type of input is a highly specialized operation and includes such strategies as marketing research, delivery systems analysis, product research, and research and development.

Clients are continually changing in character and in importance, and the organization, to be effective, must alter its services to suit changing requirements. Continual redefinition of the mission of the organization can be taxing and uncomfortable, but effectiveness is directly related to meeting the changing needs of clients, or seeking new clients to replace those whose needs have changed. Market research and other kinds of analyses attempt to determine what clients want and whether they can af-

THAT'S NOT THE KIND OF CHANGE
I'M TALKING ABOUT SNEDLEY.

ford it. Because entire classes of clients disappear over time, many large-scale organizations have attempted to diversify their missions so that the loss of one set of customers will not be disastrous.

Organizational Information (Section 4). A great deal of information is available about changes in internal operations, especially if organization standards and control processes are explicit and well developed. If they are not, the manager must act as the sensor of changes as well as the implementer of planned change. Because managers are part of the system, they often have the same kinds of blind spots that afflict others. They may therefore fail to perceive gradual changes until such time as they lead to crises that cannot be ignored. Major problems will result from a gradual build-up of small but neglected events. Standards are of great value in preventing some kinds of problems, but as mentioned earlier, they ordinarily relate only to those activities that can be quantifiably measured. In addition, they reinforce the maintenance functions to the potential detriment of the adaptive functions.

Analyzing Information. The purpose of collecting and analyzing data about change is to determine what the organization can and should do to adjust to altered situations. It may be a difficult task to assess the implications of minor incremental changes, but often these are warning signals of great opportunities or serious problems to come. Converting the data into usable information requires interpretation. Consider, for example, a personnel specialist who regularly receives cost-of-living data from the regions where the company employs more than 100 people. To convert these raw figures (data) into meaningful information, the specialist compares them with the take-home pay of employees in these areas to determine whether some wage adjustments should be made. If the cost of living has increased 10 percent and wages have increased only 5 percent, employees' real earnings have declined. The specialist must then compare this information to budgetary figures to see whether wage adjustments *can* be made.

Assume that cost data are regularly collected from various departments inside the organization. If the data show a dramatic decline in costs in one department, the analyst cannot immediately accept this data as evidence of efficiency; rather it indicates a situation that needs investigation. If the department proves in fact to be more efficient, then its cost-saving procedures might be applicable to other areas. On the other hand, if declining costs are shown to be a reflection of overutilization of equipment, leading to soaring maintenance costs, or if the department has deliberately replaced experienced, high-priced personnel with inexperienced, low-priced employees, the situation may have to be reversed if the cost savings are not great enough to offset the maintenance costs or the lowered efficiency.

The accurate interpretation of data does not just happen; it requires the logical and analytical skills of a knowledgeable manager—someone who has the ability to recognize and define problems and opportunities that require some change in the existing order of things.

Change as Decision Making. Defining problems is one of the most difficult areas of decision making. Problem definition is rigorous, time consuming, and usually expensive. In particular, difficulties arise when one uses simplistic theories of causation, such as the tendency to look for a single person or event to blame when things are not going well. If sales are down, fire the salesperson or the sales manager. If there is dissension in the office, fire the troublemaker. The fact that problems are usually caused by whole sets of interacting variables is often ignored because it is much harder to deal with underlying causes than with external symptoms. But if only the symptoms are removed, the problem will keep recurring.

Change is effected through a sequence of managerial decisions. The process and the methods involved in decision making were discussed in Chapters 13 and 14. When the change is unanticipated and reactive, the decision processes are most likely to be programed and systematic. When change is planned and proactive, more heuristic decision processes and techniques are possible.

Implementing Change

Once a decision for change has been made, the next step is to implement that decision. Since implementation strategies differ considerably as to what is to be changed, this section will examine the areas of the environment, the resources, and the organization to show how implementation techniques can be applied to each. You will find that some techniques have been covered previously while others are introduced here for the first time.

Changing the Environment. All organizations are under some pressure from the environment to change and adapt. At the same time, the organization pressures the environment to change and adapt to *its* needs. The degree to which one force is able to influence the other depends on the power relationship between the two. Managers who are, or feel they are, highly dependent on their environment will primarily react to change; those who are not or feel they are not as dependent will be able to initiate more change.

Organizational strategies for implementing change in the environment may be ranged along a continuum from highly competitive to highly cooperative, as illustrated below.

```
      High                                              High
   Competition                                       Cooperation
      └─────────────────────────────────────────────────┘
```

The extremes, and all strategies in between, involve the organization in an attempt to be less dependent on its environment.

Competitive strategies involve some of the following techniques:

1. Managers attempt to reduce organizational dependency by having a number of alternatives; that is, by creating competition among suppliers and customers. An organization that sells 80 percent of its output to one customer, for example, is not in a competitive situation.

2. Managers attempt to build positive sentiments toward their organization within people in the outside community. In this way they obtain the support of powerful sectors of the environment. Thus both sides in a labor dispute may attempt to solicit public opinion to apply pressure on the other side (7).

3. Another way managers make use of powerful sectors within the environment is to pit one against another, a situation of countervailing power. For example, builders who are under pressure from environmentalists might appeal to the chamber of commerce and the local government by saying that a curtailment of construction will increase unemployment or cause home buyers or businesses to go elsewhere. In this way managers may persuade the city groups to go to battle with them against the environmentalists (8).

Cooperative change strategies involve making a deal with some part of the environment. Three methods of cooperation follow:

1. Negotiating contracts or agreements for future exchanges of inputs or outputs assures the organization of a stable future.

2. Coopting a particularly powerful part of the environment enables the organization to free itself of a current or potential source of dissonance. School districts, for example, maintain a host of parent and community boards that advise them in district decision making.

3. Combining with other units in the environment permits the organization to rid itself of or prevent an unwanted competitive situation.

In all three of these strategies the organization gives up a certain amount of freedom in order to gain some power in the environment.

Changing the Technological Resources. Changes in technology have to do with altering techniques, adopting new processes or machines, or improving the technical expertise of people. Putting new technologies into effect is easiest if only machines are involved because machines do not represent a threat to workers. Changing the technology of person-machine systems is made easier if real benefits accrue to all concerned. One way to get people involved is to ask for their help in designing a better technology. Just as employees can subvert the best efforts of industrial engineers, so can they be of material help in developing a better way—if they are rewarded for doing so.

The major resistance to changing technology is *sunk cost,* that is, investment already committed to current goals. Therefore a useful change strategy is to keep the level of sunk cost low (9). In simple terms, leasing machines instead of purchasing them reduces the organization's dependence on the machines. Many organizations keep their capital investment at nearly normal levels of operation, and rely on temporary resources for production above the norm. Suppose, for example, the demand and supply capacity of a local trucking company is like that illustrated in Figure 20–5. This organization normally needs three trucks, but seven are required for peak periods. If it maintains seven trucks, there is a great deal of slack or "down" time. On the other hand, if the organization rents extra

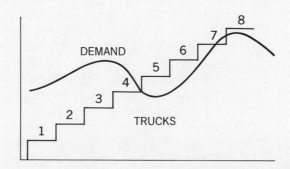

FIGURE 20–5
Demand for and supply of trucks.

trucks only when they are needed, supply can be accommodated to any demand situation without high sunk cost.

Changing People. Human behavior is difficult to change even when that behavior is no longer effective in satisfying personal needs or maintaining a balance between internal and external forces. But change *can* be effected, as discussed earlier in this book and as depicted in Figure 20–2 of this chapter.

People do not resist all changes, but they do resist those they perceive as threatening. In organizations, changes that disturb the dynamic equilibrium will upset the people who are affected. But changes that restore equilibrium, or otherwise increase the satisfaction of workers, are accepted. For example, if an organization on the verge of bankruptcy is taken over by new managers promising to restore solvency, most of its employees will go along with some fairly violent alterations. Most people would rather adapt to new programs than try to find new jobs.

There are basically three methods that managers use to change human behavior in organizations: selection, training, and rewards.

1. *Selection.* Human behavior in organizations changes naturally over time because people come and go. We have seen how the nature of an organization changes as younger generations take over the managerial hierarchy. Hiring practices, too, have a significant impact on the general behavior tone. Selection can be geared toward hiring people who are like those already employed (the most common practice), or they can be aimed at hiring people with diverse backgrounds to ensure a dynamic atmosphere.

2. *Training.* Both skills and attitudes can be changed through properly designed training programs. For instance, T-group workshops for managers and employees are regular occurrences in many large organizations as a means of increasing harmonious working relationships on all levels of the hierarchy.

3. *Rewards.* The model of change presented earlier in this chapter and the expectancy model offered in Chapter 8 are support for the contention that people behave in given ways because they are rewarded for doing so. Thus, a fairly reliable method of changing behavior is to change the established structure of rewards.

Changing the Organization. People, technology, and organization structure are inextricably interrelated in a complex network of interaction patterns. A change in one part has inevitable consequences for the other two parts. Thus, if one wants to change people, an indirect approach—say through a change in structure—may have better results than a direct attempt to change people's behavior.

Changing the organization structure essentially involves changing people's work assignments. Turned around, this statement may be read to mean that a wanted change in behavior can be effected simply by changing the situation. An employee who is a good worker but inclined to be a troublemaker can thus be transferred to a work group where the dysfunctional behavior is no longer possible. Structural changes in organizations include such alternatives as reassigning work, transferring resources, relocating units, exchanging managers, and expanding or combining departments.

New organizations and some existing ones can be structured or restructured around the work to be done rather than around the traditional hierarchical model. We have seen how project organizations arrange work and employees in accordance with the horizontal flow of work during the term of the project. These kinds of organizations (construction companies, "job shops," and so on) produce to order; employees move freely from one phase of work to another, and there are relatively few managers. Obviously, many types of work do not lend themselves to this kind of organization. Mass-production or processing industries may need specialized personnel doing the same kind of work in the same location over a long period of time. It is conceivable, however, that some of the dysfunctional effects of the authority pyramid might be overcome if even these types of organizations were redesigned around the work to be done.

Another form of structure is the **collegial organization.** Made up of persons who are professional equals, the structure is democratic and loose. Professional norms rather than authority direct behavior, although most such systems do have an elected leader. Professional associations, some research firms, departments within universities, and a variety of personal-growth-oriented centers use the collegial model. However, the applicability of this form of organization is not likely to be universal. Real differences in people's interests require a division of labor that necessitates integration and coordination by managers.

In recent decades, consultants have developed a special set of techniques aimed at changing organizations. Called **organization development,** it is a planned strategy to increase effectiveness and efficiency on all levels of an organization through the application of behavioral science techniques. Beginning with top executives and working down through the hierarchy, organization development, or OD, consultants employ a whole range of methods to examine people, technology, and structural arrangement. Consultants try to help members of an organization improve their ability to fulfill their goals. Although all aspects of an organization's functions may be examined, the primary focus is on people, and the assumptions underlying organization development are basically humanistic. These assumptions are: that people want to grow and make a contribution to the organization; that they want to be accepted and thus will work hard to facilitate a valued group experience; that feelings are facts to those who hold them, and that work is made more pleasurable if these feelings are made explicit rather than suppressed; and that collaborative solutions are far preferable to win-lose strategies. The goals of organization development include increasing the level of trust among managers and employees, getting people to face problems rather than to bury them, augmenting authority with the power of knowledge and skill, increasing communications, expanding the level of enthusiasm, finding collaborative solutions, and increasing the level of problem-solving responsibility of all organizational participants (10).

The methods used to reach these goals vary with the OD consultants and with the organization. Some common elements in many OD strategies can be identified, however. A typical scenario might proceed very much like the following.

Certain key executives in an organization become aware of some internal problems they cannot handle. They call in behavioral scientist consultants to intervene. The consultants gather data and make a tentative diagnosis, presenting their ideas to the clients. The executives agree to continue, and the consultants then outline the objectives of the OD program and the means whereby the organization can attain its goals. They gather more data, primarily about what key people in the organization are thinking and feeling. A feedback session follows, succeeded by the establishment of action teams made up of members of the organization. These teams engage in various tasks, such as generating lists of problems and assigning priorities to the problems. Task-oriented work by teams may be supplemented with voluntary sensitivity training sessions on weekends. Often, people from the same subunit attend together with their manager, or managers may be in separate groups by themselves.

From this point on, discussion, work, problem-solving suggestions, and data generation are the responsiblity of teams. The teams come up with statements of problems, objectives, and means for reaching them. Then the new behavior is introduced. If successful to this point, the OD program may be permitted to move down the hierarchy to include everyone in the organization. In some organizations, OD has become a permanent procedure for solving problems and resolving conflicts. At agreed upon times, the consultants reassess the state of the organization, provide feedback, and reinstitute the process if it has been successful or devise new procedures if the earlier methods have not worked (11).

Although still somewhat controversial, the success of OD has been notable. Whether limited to key managerial personnel, or whether it involves all persons in the organization, the OD strategy seems well devised. It starts at the top, where any official change must be approved; it involves many people; and members of the organization are encouraged to diagnose their own problems. The consultant does not try to affix standard solutions on nonstandard problems, but relies instead on those people closest to the situation to come up with whatever alternatives they think appropriate. On balance, OD appears to be a workable method of isolating areas that need change and of devising action programs that lead to shared objectives.

Organization Development in the Jailhouse

Organization development programs have been used successfully in many private and public organizations for a number of years. Some institutions employ their own internal consultants; others hire external consultants on a fee basis. Sometimes both an internal and an external consultant are used, as was the case in one recent OD program that took place in a county jail.

Most prisons are coercive institutions in which the inmates are alienated. The model of compliance in Chapter 16 indicates that attempts to generate inmate commitment in a coercive institution are generally fruitless unless coercive power is replaced with normative power. The hypothesis that OD techniques would be able to change the nature of correctional institutions from alienating to rehabilitating was tested at the Berkshire County House of Corrections in Massachusetts beginning in July 1973.

The consultants developed three process goals and four program goals to help reach the overall goal of rehabilitation. Process goals included (1) creating an environment supportive of change and personal growth; (2) using an OD program to help people socialize and learn adaptive skills; and (3) introducing self-government. Program goals were (1) to provide the inmates with access to educational and vocational training; (2) to develop new helping roles for the jailers; (3) to assemble community resources; and (4) to maintain successful new programs.

The organization development program of planned change continued for three years. The first year was devoted to diagnosis, the second to implementation, and the third to institutionalization of the changes. In other words the first year was one of unfreezing, the second of moving, and the third of refreezing.

During the first year of the Model Education Program the consultants, working with inmates, guards, and administrators, formed committees, work groups, and discussion groups to assess the current state of affairs and to tackle the problems they discovered. During that year the inmates and administrators, working together, secured funds for a workshop and shop instructors and began vocational training sessions. The inmates developed a self-help drug rehabilitation group. Adult education and degree study programs were started. The help of the local Junior Chamber of Commerce was enlisted from the community. Trust gradually began to develop between the inmates, the administrators, and the consultants.

During the second year, the program was implemented. In part, implementation required that the consultants persuade the governing board, the inmates, the police officers and guards, and the prison administrators to set aside their suspicions and assumptions about one another. Open discussion forums attended by representatives of each of the groups and by the OD staff helped to allay fears and led gradually to program credibility.

During the third year change was institutionalized. Programs were continued, run by those associated with the jail. The external change agent took an increasingly marginal role as she turned over more and more of the responsibility to insiders.

After the third year, as members of the institution worked on positive, growth-oriented programs rather than on custodial, alienting ones, the jail was more nearly rehabilitating than alienating inmates.

Source: Norma B. Gluckstern and R. W. Packard, "The Internal-External Change-Agent Team: Bringing Change to a 'Closed Institution.' A Case Study on a County Jail," *Journal of Applied Behavioral Science*, vol. 13 (Jan-Feb-March 1977), pp. 41–52.

The topic of organization development seems like a good stopping place for this text. OD promises hope in an area of management that needs hope; and it suggests that orderly change *is* possible even in a disorderly and turbulent environment. It also indicates that there are strategies by which organizations and individuals can cope with powerful forces that change continually. If we have learned anything in this book it is that there will be change. Adjusting to imposed change and initiating needed change while at the same time maintaining order and stability require a unique combination of flexibility and steadfastness. Those who are well equipped to play this dual role are the ones most likely to be successful in managing work in organizations.

Chapter Review

This closing chapter of the book is about change; what it is, what aids and constrains it, and what methods may be used to achieve it. Change is what the manager is constantly seeking to create or prevent, and, as such, has supplied the framework for most of what has been covered in this book. The specific terms and ideas developed in this chapter appear below.

1. The change sequence consists of the following three events:

a. **Unfreezing,** which requires a recognition of the need to change and a removal of rewards for current behavior

b. **Moving,** which introduces the new behavior and provides initial rewards for acting in the new way

c. **Refreezing,** which requires continued practice of the new behavior and establishes the new reward structure

2. Change can be ranged along a continuum from unanticipated to planned.

a. **Unanticipated change** requires a reactive response to a new situation.

b. **Anticipated change** allows the organization to adjust to the conditions that have been predicted.

c. **Planned change** is an active response to predicted situations in ways that help the organization best achieve its goals.

3. Managers respond to the need to change by being either reactive or proactive. A **reactive** manager adapts to a new situation; a **proactive** manager shapes the change according to the organization's needs.

4. As **people in the middle,** managers are caught between a world that is changing too fast and an organization, technology, and people that change too slowly.

5. **Environmental demands** for change have increased incrementally with the pace of change, but the multitude of environments also imposes constraints on change by making conflicting requirements.

6. **Technological demands** for change are seen as healthy and positive, but technology is expensive and involves high **sunk costs,** often making continued change impractical.

7. **People** in the organization change *over time* and thus create change in the organization. But at any *given time,* people generally like things to stay the way they are.

8. Organizational **goals** change as a response to the environment and to changing organizational values. At the same time, goals focus attention on current behavior and away from change.

9. Organizations have functional areas devoted to both change and stability.

    a. **Maintenance functions** are usually associated with the production core of the organization and seek stability and predictability.

    b. **Adaptive functions** are usually on the boundary of the organization and seek to keep the organization in alignment with the environment.

10. Change requires that information be gathered and analyzed about the environment, resources, outputs, and internal activities.

11. Organizations use both competitive and cooperative methods of implementing change.

    a. **Competitive strategies** include creating competition among others, giving support to powerful forces, and developing countervailing power.

    b. **Cooperative strategies** include contracts, cooptation, and combination.

12. Implementing technological change is easiest when only machines are involved, or when technology benefits employees.

13. Implementing change in people can be done by **selection, training,** or **altering rewards.**

14. **Organization development** is a process of planned change of organizational relationships through an in-depth examination of organizational problems. OD utilizes the behavioral science techniques designed to develop open relationships within a trusting environment.

Discussion Questions

1. What role does change play in the manager's job?
2. How can managers effect change in people?
3. What kinds of change situations do managers face? What are some of the ways they can react to these situations?
4. For each of the following areas indicate three forces working for and three forces working against change:
    a. Environment
    b. Technology
    c. People
    d. Goals
    e. Organization
5. What part does information play in instituting change?

6. Where would you seek information about change in:
    a. The environment?
    b. Resources?
    c. Goals or outputs?
    d. The internal organization?

7. Under what circumstances would competitive strategies for change be effective? When would cooperative strategies be more effective?

8. How might managers avoid a dependence on technology? Why should they?

9. Suppose you were a plant manager who must install a new production process to accommodate a new product line. What strategies of changing people might you employ? Why might these strategies be successful or unsuccessful?

10. When would changing the organizational structure be a useful way to introduce change?

11. What is organization development? What are its goals? How does it seek to accomplish them?

12. In what situation would organization development most likely be successful? Unsuccessful?

Involvement Activities

1. Peter Drucker suggests that rapid change, which will cause confusion and discontinuity for the manager, will occur in the following four areas:

a. Introduction of new technologies which will create new industries and render existing industries obsolete.
b. Emergence of a world economy that involves a world market or global shopping center.
c. Development of a changing political and social matrix involving much disenchantment with our major institutions.
d. Creation of a "knowledge economy" in which about one-half of our American dollars are spent on procuring ideas and information and in which knowledge has become the central "factor of production" (12).

For each of these predicted areas of change indicate the impact they will have on:
    a. Organization, structure and operation
    b. Managers and the managerial job
    c. You

2. Consider your class as an organization. Set up an organization development program whereby course objectives can be attained effectively with the full involvement of all students and faculty.

References

CHAPTER 1

1. Henry Mintzberg, *The Nature of Managerial Work* (New York: Harper & Row, 1973).
2. R. L. Katz, "The Skills of the Effective Administrator," *Harvard Business Review,* vol. 52, no. 5 (Sept.–Oct. 1974), pp. 90-102.
3. Henri Fayol, *General and Industrial Management* (New York: Pittman, 1949).
4. Henry Mintzberg, *op. cit.*
5. Elliott Jaques, *Equitable Payment* (Carbondale, Ill.: Southern Illinois University Press, 1961), p. 52.

CHAPTER 2

1. William J. Bossenbook, Development of Contemporary Civilization (Lexington, Mass.: D. C. Heath & Co., 1940), pp. 179-180.
2. Adam Smith, *An Inquiry Into the Nature and Causes of the Wealth of Nations* (New York: P. F. Collier, 1901).
3. Frederick W. Taylor, *The Principles of Scientific Management* (New York: Harper & Row, 1911).
4. W. R. Spreigel and C. E. Meyers, eds., *The Writings of the Gilbreths* (Homewood, Ill.: R. D. Irwin, 1953).
5. Henri Fayol, *General and Industrial Management* (New York: Pitman, 1949); Luther Gulik and L. Urwick, eds., *Papers on the Science of Administration* (New York: 1937; reprinted by Augustus M. Kelley, 1969); Max Weber, "Bureaucracy," in H. H. Gerth and C. Wright Mill, eds., *From Max Weber: Essays in Sociology* (New York: Oxford University Press, 1958), pp. 196-224.
6. Elton Mayo, *The Human Problems of an Industrial Civilization* (New York: Macmillan, 1933).
7. *Ibid.*
8. T. North Whitehead, *The Industrial Worker* (Cambridge, Mass.: Harvard University Press, 1938).
9. F. Roethlisberger and W. J. Dickson, *Management and the Worker* (New York: Wiley, 1939).
10. Charles Perrow, "Framework for the Comparative Analysis of Organizations," *American Sociological Review* (April 1967) pp. 194-208.
11. F. Emery and E. L. Trist, "The Casual Texture of Organizational Environments," *Human Relations,* vol. 18 (Feb. 1965), pp. 21-32.
12. Shirley Terreberry, "Evolution of Organizational Environments," *Administrative Science Quarterly,* vol. 12 (March 1968), pp. 590-613.
13. T. Burns and G. Stalker, *The Management of Innovation* (London: Tavistock Publications, 1961).
14. P. R. Lawrence and Jay W. Lorsch, *Organization and Environment: Managing Differentiation and Integration* (Homewood, Ill.: R. D. Irwin, 1969).
15. Henri Fayol, *op cit.,* pp. 3-5.
16. Henri Fayol, *op cit.,* p. 6.
17. Luther Gulick and L. Urwick, eds., "Notes on the Theory of Organization," *Papers on the Science of Administration* (New York: Institute of Public Administration, 1937).
18. Chester Barnard, *The Functions of the Executive* (Cambridge, Mass.: Harvard University Press, 1938).
19. Herbert Simon, *Administrative Behavior,* 3rd edition (New York: The Free Press, 1976).
20. *Ibid.*

21. Herbert Simon, *The Shape of Automation for Men and Management* (New York: Harper & Row, 1965).

22. R. Cyert and J. March, *A Behavioral Theory of the Firm* (Englewood Cliffs, N.J.: Prentice-Hall, 1963).

23. Fred Fiedler, *A Theory of Leadership Effectiveness* (New York: McGraw-Hill, 1967).

24. Joe Kelly, "The Study of Executive Behavior by Activity Sampling," *Human Relations,* vol. 17 (Aug. 1964), pp. 277-288.

25. Leonard R. Sayles, *Managerial Behavior: Administration in Complex Organizations* (New York: McGraw-Hill, 1964).

26. Henry Mintzberg, *The Nature of Managerial Work* (New York: Harper & Row, 1973).

27. *Ibid.*

CHAPTER 3

1. Ephriam Yuchtman and Stanley E. Seashore, "A Systems Resource Approach to Organizational Effectiveness," *American Sociological Review,* vol. 32 (Dec. 1967), pp. 891-903.

2. David L. Sills, "Preserving Organizational Goals," reprinted from *The Volunteers* (New York: Macmillan, 1957), in Oscar Grusky and George A. Miller, eds., *The Sociology of Organizations* (New York: The Free Press, 1970), pp. 227-331.

3. Frederick Taylor, *Scientific Management* (New York: Harper & Row, 1947); F. J. Roethlisberger and W. J. Dickson, *Management and the Worker* (New York: Wiley, 1939).

4. V. Thompson, *Modern Organizations,* 2nd edition (University, Alabama: University of Alabama Press, 1977).

5. Robert Michels, *Political Parties* (New York: The Free Press, 1958).

6. David L. Sills, *op. cit.*; Amitai Etzioni, *Modern Organization* (Englewood Cliffs, N.J.: Prentice-Hall, 1964), p. 13.

7. N. J. Demerath III and Victor Thiessen, "On Spitting Against the Wind: Organizational Precariousness and American Irreligion," in Oscar Grusky and George Miller, *The Sociology of Organizations* (New York: The Free Press, 1970).

8. Richard Steers, *Organizational Effectiveness: A Behavioral View* (Santa Monica, Calif.: Goodyear Publishing, 1977).

9. Douglas McGregor. *The Professional Manager* (New York: McGraw-Hill, 1967.

10. Seymour Tilles, "The Manager's Job—A Systems Approach," *Harvard Business Review,* vol. 41, no. 1 (Jan.–Feb. 1963), pp. 73-81.

CHAPTER 4

1. Elliott Jaques, *Equitable Payment* (Carbondale, Ill.: Southern Illinois University Press, 1970).

2. Elliott Jaques, *Earnings Progressions Handbook* (Carbondale, Ill.: Southern Illinois University Press, 1968).

3. Jaques, *op. cit.* (1970).

4. H. J. Leavitt, *Managerial Psychology,* 3rd edition (Chicago: University of Chicago Press, 1972).

5. Wilfred Brown, *Explorations in Management* (New York: Wiley, 1962).

6. G. D. Latham and G. A. Yukl, "A Review of Research on the Application of Goal Setting in Organizations," *Academy of Management Journal,* vol. 18 no. 4 (Dec. 1975) pp. 824-45.

7. B. M. Gross, *The Managing of Organizations* (New York: The Free Press, 1964).

8. W. E. Scott, "Activation Theory and Task Design," in W. E. Scott and L. L. Cummings, *Readings in Organization Behavior and Human Performance* (Homewood, Ill.: R. D. Irwin, 1973).

9. K. Lewin, "The Psychology of Success and Failure," in Harold Leavitt and Louis Pondy, *Reading in Managerial Psychology* (Chicago: University of Chicago Press, 1964).

10. P. R. Kelly, "A Reappraisal of Appraisals," *Harvard Business Review,* vol. 36, no. 3 (May–June 1958), pp. 59-68.

11. V. Thompson, *Modern Organization.* 2nd edition (University, Ala: University of Alabama Press, 1977).

12. R. E. Miles, "Human Relations or Human Resources," *Harvard Business Review,* vol. 43, no. 4 (July–Aug. 1965) pp. 115-130.

13. Henry Mintzberg, *The Nature of Managerial Work* (New York: Harper & Row, 1973).

14. D. McGregor, *The Human Side of Enterprise* (New York: McGraw-Hill, 1960).

15. Peter Drucker, *The Practice of Management* (New York: Harper & Row, 1954); Douglas McGregor, *The Professional Manager* (New York: McGraw-Hill, 1967); H. H. Meyer, E. Kay, and J. R. P. French, Jr., "Split Roles in Performance," *Harvard Business Review,* vol. 43, no. 1 (Jan–Feb. 1965), pp. 123-129; S. I. Carroll and H. L. Tosi, *Management by Objectives: Applications and Research* (New York: Macmillan, 1973).

16. McGregor, *op. cit.*

17. H. Levinson, "Appraisal of *What* Performance?" *Harvard Business Review,* vol. 54, no. 4 (July–Aug. 1976), pp. 30-48.

CHAPTER 5

1. H. Simon, *The Shape of Automation for Men and Management* (New York: Harper & Row, 1965).

2. W. A. Rushing, "The Effects of Industry Size and Division of Labor on Administration," *Administrative Science Quarterly* vol. 12, no. 2 (Sept. 1967) pp. 273-295.

3. C. Argyris, *Integrating the Individual and the Organization* (New York: Wiley, 1964).

4. L. Davis and A. Cherns, *The Quality of Working Life, Vol. 1* (New York: The Free Press, 1975).

5. R. Blauner, *Alienation and Freedom* (Chicago: University of Chicago Press, 1964).

6. James Biggane and Paul Stewart, "Job Enlargement: A Case Study," in L. Davis and J. Taylor, *Job Design* (Baltimore: Penguin Books, 1972).

7. L. Davis, "The Design of Jobs," in L. Davis and J. Taylor, *Job Design* (Baltimore: Penguin Books, 1972).

8. M. Fein, "Job Enrichment: A Reevaluation," *Sloan Management Review,* vol. 15 (1974) pp. 69-88.

9. E. J. McCormick, *The Development, Analysis, and Experimental Application of Worker Oriented Job Variables,* Report #8, Contract #Nonr-1100 (19), Prepared for the Office of Naval Research (Lafayette, Ind.: Occupational Research Center, Purdue University, July 1964).

10. C. H. Stone and Dale Yoder, *Job Analysis, 1970* (Long Beach, Calif.: California State College Press, June 1970).

11. W. K. Kirchner and M. D. Dunnette, "Identifying the Critical Factors in Successful Salesmanship," *Personnel* (Sept.–Oct. 1957), pp. 54-59.

12. P. H. Engelstad, "Socio-Technical Approach to Problems of Process Control," in L. Davis and J. Taylor, *Job Design* (Baltimore: Penguin Books, 1972).

13. F. Herzberg, "One More Time: How Do You Motivate Employees?" *Harvard Business Review,* vol. 46-1 (Jan.–Feb. 1968), pp. 53-62.

14. "Stonewalling Plant Democracy," *Business Week* (March 28, 1977), p. 78.

15. Pehr G. Gyllenhammar, "How Volvo Adapts Work to People," *Harvard Business Review,* vol. 55 (July–Aug. 1977), pp. 102-113.

16. Peter Schoderbek, A. Kefalas, and Charles Schoderbek, *Management Systems* (Dallas: Business Publications, Inc., 1975).

CHAPTER 6

1. D. Marquis, "Ways of Organizing Projects," *Innovation #5* (1969), pp. 26-33.
2. A. H. Walker and J. Lorsch, "Organizational Choice: Product Versus Functions," *Harvard Business Review* (Nov.–Dec. 1968), pp. 129-138.
3. Marquis, *op. cit.*
4. J. Litterer, *The Analysis of Organizations*, 2nd edition (New York: Wiley, 1973), pp. 645-648.
5. Ivar Avots, "Why Does Project Management Fail?" in Patrick Connor, *Dimensions in Modern Management* (Boston: Houghton-Mifflin Co., 1974), pp. 176-85.
6. J. Kelly, "The Study of Executive Behavior of Activity Sampling," *Human Relations*, vol. 17, no. 3, pp. 277-288.
7. Leonard Sayles, *Managerial Behavior* (New York: McGraw-Hill, 1964).
8. R. L. Katz, "The Skills of the Effective Executive," *Harvard Business Review*, vol. 52, no. 5 (Sept.–Oct. 1974).
9. Henry Mintzberg, *The Nature of Managerial Work* (New York: Harper & Row, 1973).
10. N. H. Martin, "The Levels of Management and Their Mental Demands," in W. L. Warner and N. H. Martin, *Industrial Man* (New York: Harper & Bros., 1959).
11. J. M. Pfiffner and F. Sherwood, *Administrative Organization* (Englewood Cliffs, N.J.: Prentice-Hall, 1960).
12. L. F. Peter and R. Hull, *The Peter Principle* (New York: William Morrow & Co., 1969).

CHAPTER 7

1. Chester Barnard, *The Functions of the Executive* (Cambridge, Mass.: Harvard University Press, 1938); Herbert Simon, *Administrative Behavior*, 3rd edition (New York: The Free Press, 1976).
2. D. McGregor, *The Professional Manager* (New York: McGraw-Hill, 1967).
3. D. Sirota and J. M. Greenwood, "Understand Your Overseas Work Force," and Peter Drucker, "Managing the Educated," in R. Sutermeister. *People and Productivity*. 3rd edition (New York: McGraw-Hill, 1976).
4. A. W. Gouldner, "The Norm of Reciprocity: A Preliminary Statement," *American Sociological Review*, vol. 25 (April 1960), p. 163.
5. Barnard, *op. cit.*
6. V. Thompson, *Modern Organization*, 2nd edition (University, Ala.: University of Alabama Press, 1977).
7. P. Blau and M. W. Meyer, *Bureaucracy in Modern Society*, 2nd edition (New York: Random House, 1971).
8. T. W. Adorno, Else Frenkel-Brunswik, D. J. Levinson, and R. N. Sanford, *The Authoritarian Personality* (New York: Harper, 1950).
9. L. Urwick, *The Elements of Administration* (New York: Harper, 1943).
10. B. A. Gross, *The Managing of Organizations* (New York: The Free Press, 1968).
11. H. Metcalf and L. Urwick, eds., *Dynamic Administration: The Collected Papers of Mary Follett* (New York: Harper, 1942).
12. F. W. Taylor, *Scientific Management* (New York: Harper & Row, 1947).
13. Simon, *op. cit.*
14. L. Sayles, *Managerial Behavior* (New York: McGraw-Hill, 1964).
15. R. L. Kahn, R. P. Wolfe, J. D. Quinn, J. D. Snoek, and R. A. Rosenthal, *Organizational Stress: Studies in Role Conflicts and Ambiguity* (New York: Wiley, 1964).
16. R. C. Davis, *Fundamentals of Top Management* (New York: Harper & Row, 1951).
17. L. Urwick, "The Manager's Span of Control," *Harvard Business Review* (May–June 1956).

18. J. Woodward, *Industrial Organization: Theory and Practice* (London: Oxford University Press, 1965).
19. J. Worthy, "Organization Structure and Employee Morale," *American Sociological Review,* vol. 15 (1950).
20. J. Woodward, *op. cit.*
21. P. R. Lawrence and J. W. Lorsch, *Organization and Environment* (Homewood, Ill.: R. D. Irwin, 1969).
22. E. W. Bakke, "The Human Resources Function," in E. W. Bakke, C. Kerr, and C. W. Anrod, *Unions Management and the Public,* 3rd edition (New York: Harcourt, Brace & World, 1967).
23. C. A. Myers and J. G. Turnbull, "Line and Staff in Industrial Relations," *Harvard Business Review,* vol. 34 no. 4 (July–Aug. 1956).
24. Wendell French and Dale Henning, "The Authority-Influence Role of the Functional Specialist in Management," *Academy of Management Journal,* vol. 9, no. 3 (Sept. 1966), pp. 187-204.
25. M. Dalton, *Men Who Manage* (New York: Wiley, 1959).
26. A. Chandler, *Strategy and Structure* (Cambridge, Mass.: The MIT Press, 1962).
27. J. B. Miner and M. G. Miner, *Personnel and Industrial Relations,* 3rd edition (New York: Macmillan, 1977).
28. Miner, *op. cit.*
29. R. E. Miles, "Human Relations or Human Resources," *Harvard Business Review,* vol. 43, no. 4 (July–Aug. 1965), pp. 115-130.

CHAPTER 8

1. W. French, *The Personnel Management Process,* 3rd edition (Boston: Houghton-Mifflin, 1974).
2. F. J. Roethlisberger and W. J. Dickson, *Management and the Worker* (New York: Wiley, 1939).
3. H. P. Knowles and H. O. Saxberg, *Personality and Leadership Behavior* (Reading, Mass.: Addison-Wesley, 1971).
4. J. March and H. Simon, *Organizations* (New York: Wiley, 1958).
5. V. Vroom, *Work and Motivation* (New York: Wiley, 1964).
6. L. W. Porter, and E. Lawler, *Managerial Attitudes and Performance* (Homewood, Ill.: R. D. Irwin, 1968).
7. R. Dubin, V. E. Champoux, and L. W. Porter, "Central Life Interests and Organizational Commitment of Blue Collar and Clerical Workers." *Administrative Science Quarterly,* vol. 20 (1975), pp. 411-421.
8. L. A. Broedling, "The Uses of the Intrinsic-Extrinsic Distinction in Explaining Motivation and Organizational Behavior," *The Academy of Management Review,* vol. 2 (April 1977), pp. 267-276.
9. A. Maslow, *Motivation and Personality* (New York: Harper & Row, 1954).
10. D. C. McClelland, *The Achieving Society* (Princeton, N.J.: D. Van Nostrand, 1961).
11. Michael Korda, *Power: How to Get It, How to Use It* (New York: Ballantine Books, 1976).
12. D. C. McCelland, "That Urge to Achieve," *Think,* vol. 32 (published by IBM, Nov.–Dec. 1966), pp. 19-23.
13. W. R. Nord, "Beyond the Teaching Machine: The Neglected Area of Operant Conditioning in the Theory and Practice of Management," *Organizational Behavior and Human Performance,* vol. 4 (November 1969), pp. 375-401.
14. Frederick Herzberg, *Work and the Nature of Man* (Cleveland: The World Publishing Co., 1966), p. 71.
15. W. G. Scott and T. R. Mitchell, *Organizational Theory: A Structural and Behavioral Analysis,* 3rd edition (Homewood, Ill.: R. D. Irwin, 1976).
16. E. Lawler, *Motivation in Work Organizations* (Belmont, Calif.: Wadsworth, 1973).

17. J. B. Rotter, "Generalized Expectancies for Internal versus External Control of Reinforcement," *Psychological Monographs,* vol, 80 (1966), pp. 1-28.

18. J. S. Adams, "Inequity in Social Exchange," in L. Berkowitz, ed., *Advances in Experimental Social Psychology,* vol. 2 (New York: Academic Press, 1965), pp. 267-99; P. Blau, *Exchange and Power in Social Life* (New York: Wiley, 1967); and G. A. Homans, *Social Behavior: Its Elementary Forms* (New York: Harcourt Brace, and World, 1961).

19. M. E. Katzell, "Expectations and Dropouts in Schools of Nursing," *Journal of Applied Psychology,* vol. 52 (1968), pp. 154-157.

20. D. W. Belcher and T. J. Atchison, "Compensation for Work," in Robert Dubin, *Handbook of Work, Organization and Society* (Chicago: Rand McNally, 1976).

21. H. Leavitt, *Managerial Psychology,* 3rd edition (Chicago: University of Chicago Press, 1972).

22. K. E. Scheibe, *Beliefs and Values* (New York: Holt, Rinehart and Winston, 1970).

23. K. Lewin, "The Psychology of Success and Failure," in Harold Leavitt and Louis Pondy, *Readings in Managerial Psychology* (Chicago: University of Chicago Press, 1964).

24. Chris Argyris, *Personality and Organization: The Conflict Between System and the Individual* (New York: Harper and Row, 1957) and Robert Presthus, *The Organizational Society* (New York: Alfred A. Knopf, 1962).

25. F. Herzberg, *op. cit.*

CHAPTER 9

1. B. M. Springbett, "Factors Affecting the Final Decision in the Employment Interview," *Canadian Journal of Psychology,* vol. 12 (1958), pp. 13-22.

2. D. J. Peterson, "The Impact of Duke Power on Testing," *Personnel,* vol. 51 (1974), pp. 30-37.

3. A. H. Chayes, "Make Your Equal Opportunity Program Court Proof," *Harvard Business Review,* vol. 32 (June–July, 1974), pp. 81-89.

4. L. F. Peter and R. Hull, *The Peter Principle* (New York: William Morrow & Co., 1969).

5. F. F. Foltman, *Manpower Information for Effective Management, Parts I and II* (Ithaca, N.Y.: New York School of Industrial and Labor Relations, Cornell University, 1973).

6. J. B. Miner and M. G. Miner, *Personnel and Industrial Relations,* 3rd edition (New York: Macmillan, 1977).

7. M. Dunnette, *Personnel Selection and Placement* (Belmont; Calif.: Wadsworth, 1966).

8. *Ibid.*

9. J. B. Miner and M. G. Miner *op. cit.*

10. H. H. Gerth and C. W. Mill, *From Max Weber: Essays in Sociology* (London: Oxford University Press, 1946).

11. E. Schein, "Management Development as a Process of Influence," *Industrial Management Review,* vol. 2 (May 1961).

12. S. J. Carroll, F. T. Paine, and J. M. Ivancevich, "The Relative Effectiveness of Training Methods in Expert Opinion and Research," *Personnel Psychology,* vol. 25 (1972), pp. 495-509.

13. D. W. Belcher, *Compensation Administration* (Englewood Cliffs, N.J.: Prentice-Hall, 1974).

CHAPTER 10

1. Dorwin Cartwright and Alvin Zander, *Group Dynamics: Research and Theory,* 3rd edition, (New York: Harper & Row, 1968), p. 48.

2. Leonard Sayles, *Research in Industrial Human Relations* (New York: Harper & Bros., 1957).

3. Leonard Sayles, *Behavior of Industrial Work Groups* (New York: Wiley, 1958).

4. George C. Homans, *The Human Group* (New York: Harcourt, Brace & Co., 1950).

5. Robert Coffey, Anthony Athos, and Peter Raynolds, *Behavior in Organizations: A Multidimensional View,* 2nd edition (Englewood Cliffs, N.J.: Prentice-Hall, 1975).

6. Homans, *op. cit.,* p. 429.

7. Homans *op. cit.,* pp. 224-225.

8. Harold Leavitt, *Managerial Psychology,* 3rd edition (Chicago: University of Chicago Press, 1972).

9. J. A. Litterer, *Analysis of Organizations,* 2nd edition (New York: Wiley, 1973).

10. R. A. Van Zelst, "Sociometrically Selected Work Teams Increase Production," *Personnel Psychology,* vol. 59 (May 1954), pp. 530-535.

11. H. H. Kelley, "Communications in Experimentally Created Hierarchies," *Human Relations,* vol. 4 (1951), pp. 39-56.

12. R. Coffey et al. *op. cit.,* p. 117.

13. R. Coffey et al. *op. cit.,* p. 118-119.

14. Rensis Likert, *New Patterns of Management* (New York: McGraw-Hill, 1961), p. 26.

15. L. P. Bradford, J. R. Gibb, and K. D. Benne. *T-Group Theory and Laboratory Method* (New York: Wiley, 1964), and C. Argyris, *Interpersonal Competence and Organizational Effectiveness* (Homewood, Ill.: Dorsey Press, 1962), p. 156.

16. Robert J. House, "Leadership Training: Some Dysfunctional Consequences," *Administrative Science Quarterly,* vol. 12, no. 4 (March 1968), pp. 556-571.

17. G. Odiorne, "The Trouble with Sensitivity Training," *Training Directors Journal,* vol. 14, no. 10 (October 1963), pp. 12-19.

CHAPTER 11

1. Jacques Ellul, *The Technological Society* (New York: Vintage Books, 1967).

2. E. L. Trist and K. W. Bamforth, "Some Social and Psychological Consequences of the Longwall Method of Coal-Getting," *Human Relations,* vol. 4 (1951), pp. 3-38.

3. Charles Perrow, "A Framework for the Comparative Analysis of Organizations," *American Sociological Review,* vol. 32 (April 1967).

4. James D. Thompson, *Organizations in Action* (New York: McGraw-Hill, 1967), p. 146; and Mariann Jelinek, "Technology, Organization and Contingency," *Academy of Management Review,* vol. 2 (January 1977).

5. Raymond G. Hunt, "Technology and Organization," *Academy of Management Journal,* vol. 13 (September 1970), p. 235.

6. James D. Thompson, "Organizations and Output Transactions," *The American Journal of Sociology,* vol. 68 (November 1962).

7. James D. Thompson, *Organizations in Action,* p. 54.

8. Beverly P. Lynch, "An Empirical Assessment of Perrow's Technology Construct," *Administrative Science Quarterly,* vol. 19 (September 1974); Lawrence G. Hrebiniak, "Job Technology, Supervision and Work-Group Structure," *Administrative Science Quarterly,* vol. 19 (Sept. 1974); and Lawrence B. Mohr, "Organizational Technology and Organizational Structure," *Administrative Science Quarterly,* vol. 16 (December 1971).

9. William A. Faunce, "Automation and the Division of Labor," *Social Problems,* vol. 13 (Fall 1965).

10. Charles Walker, *Technology, Industry and Man: The Age of Acceleration* (New York: McGraw-Hill, 1968).

11. Charles Walker and R. Guest, *The Man on the Assembly Line* (Cambridge, Mass.: Harvard University Press, 1952).

12. Herbert A. Simon, *The Shape of Automation for Men and Management* (New York: Harper & Row, 1965).

13. Peter M. Blau, Cecilia McHugh Falbe, William McKinley, and Phelps K. Tracy, "Technology and Organization in Manufacturing," *Administrative Science Quarterly,* vol. 21 (March 1976), p. 21.

14. H. Simon, *op. cit.*
15. T. Whisler, "The Impact of Information Technology on Organizational Control," in C. A. Myers, ed., *The Impact of Computers on Management* (Cambridge, Mass.: MIT Press, 1967).
16. H. J. Leavitt and T. Whisler, "Management in the 1980's," *Harvard Business Review,* vol. 36 (Nov.–Dec. 1958), pp. 41-48.
17. H. Leavitt and T. Whisler, *op. cit.*
18. M. Anshen, "Automation and the Manager," in J. T. Dunlop, ed., *Automation and Technological Change* (Englewood Cliffs, N.J.: Prentice-Hall, 1962).
19. Joan Woodward, *Industrial Organization: Theory and Practice* (London: Oxford University Press, 1965).
20. D. S. Pugh, D. J. Hickson, and C. R. Hinings, "An Empirical Taxonomy of Structures of Work Organizations," *Administrative Science Quarterly,* vol. 14 (March 1969).
21. David J. Hickson, D. S. Pugh, and Diana C. Pheysey, "Operations Technology and Organization Structure; an Empirical Reappraisal," *Administrative Science Quarterly,* vol. 14 (September 1969).
22. Charles Perrow, *op. cit.*
23. Beverly P. Lynch, "An Empirical Assessment of Perrow's Technology Construct," *Administrative Science Quarterly,* vol. 19 (September 1974).
24. L. G. Hrebiniak, *op. cit.*
25. Gerald Hage and Michael Aiken, "Routine Technology, Social Structure, and Organizational Goals," *Administrative Science Quarterly,* vol. 14, no. 3 (Sept. 1969), pp. 366-376.

CHAPTER 12

1. Paul R. Lawrence and Jay W. Lorsch, *Organization and Environment: Managing Differentiation and Integration* (Homewood, Ill.: Richard D. Irwin, 1969).
2. Richard D. Hays, "The Executive Abroad: Minimizing Behavioral Problems," *Business Horizons* (June 1972).
3. J. K. Galbraith, *American Capitalism* (Boston: Houghton Mifflin, 1956).
4. Philip Selznick, *TVA and the Grass Roots* (Berkeley, Calif.: University of California Press, 1949).
5. J. K Galbraith, *The New Industrial State* (Boston: Houghton Mifflin, 1967).
6. Committee for Economic Development, "Excerpts from Social Responsibilities of Business Corporations," *Social Responsibilities of Business Corporations* (New York: Committee for Economic Development, 1971), chapters 1-4.
7. M. Friedman, "The Social Responsibility of Business Is to Increase Its Profits," *The New York Times Magazine* (September 13, 1970), pp. 33, 122-126.
8. Committee for Economic Development, *op. cit.,* p. 20.
9. Committee for Economic Development, *op. cit.,* pp. 19-21.
10. Earl F. Cheit, "Why Managers Cultivate Social Responsibility," *California Management Review,* vol. VII (1964), pp. 3-22.
11. A. D. Chandler, *Strategy and Structure* (Cambridge, Mass.: MIT Press, 1962).
12. Arthur L. Stinchcombe, "Social Structure and Organizations," in James G. March, ed., *Handbook of Organizations* (Chicago: Rand McNally, 1965), pp. 142-193.
13. Lawrence and Lorsch, *op. cit.*
14. T. Burns and G. Stalker, *The Management of Innovation* (London: Tavistock Publications, 1961).

CHAPTER 13

1. Herbert Simon, *The Shape of Automation for Men and Management* (New York: Harper & Row, 1965).
2. S. Kassouf, *Normative Decision Making* (Englewood Cliffs, N.J.: Prentice-Hall, 1970).
3. James March and Herbert Simon, *Organizations* (New York: Wiley, 1958).
4. Simon, *op. cit.*

5. T. Sorenson, *Decision Making in the White House* (New York: Columbia University Press, 1963).

6. C. E. Lindblom, "The Science of Muddling Through," *Public Administration Review,* vol. 19 (1959), pp. 78-88.

7. K. Boulding, *The Image* (Ann Arbor, Mich.: University of Michigan Press, 1961).

8. C. H. Kepner and B. B. Tregoe, *The Rational Manager* (New York: McGraw-Hill, 1965).

9. Simon, *op. cit.*

10. Simon, *op. cit.*

11. B. Entoven, "Analysis Judgment and Corporations," West Bank Computer Center Dedication, University of Minnesota, 1969, p. 37.

12. Simon, *op. cit.:* and Henry Mintzberg, *The Nature of Managerial Work* (New York: Harper & Row, 1973).

13. E. Scannell, *Communication for Leadership* (New York: McGraw-Hill, 1970).

14. J. Hall, "Decisions, Decisions, Decisions," *Psychology Today,* vol. 5 (November 1971), pp. 51-58.

15. N. R. F. Maier, "Assets and Liabilities in Group Problem Solving: The Need for an Integrative Leader," *Psychological Review,* vol. 74 (1967).

16. David R. Hampton, *Contemporary Management* (New York: McGraw-Hill, 1977).

17. W. F. Whyte, *Organizational Behavior: Theory and Application* (Homewood, Ill.: R. D. Irwin, 1969).

18. V. Thompson, *Modern Organization,* 2nd edition (University, Ala.: University of Alabama Press, 1977).

19. W. Bennis, *Beyond Bureaucracy* (New York: McGraw-Hill, 1966).

20. T. J. Atchison, "The Fragmentation of Decision," *Personnel,* vol. 47 (July–Aug. 1970), pp. 8-14.

CHAPTER 14

1. J. L. McKenney and P. G. W. Keen, "How Managers' Minds Work," *Harvard Business Review,* vol. 52 (May–June, 1974), pp. 102-112.

2. G. W. England, "Personal Value Systems of Managers—So What," unpublished manuscript, *Industrial Relations Center* (Minneapolis: Univeristy of Minnesota, January 1973).

3. Lyman Porter, *Organizational Patterns of Managerial Job Attitudes* (New York: American Foundation for Management Research, 1964).

4. C. E. Summer, J. J. O'Connor, and N. S. Peery, *The Managerial Mind,* 4th edition (Homewood, Ill.: R. D. Irwin, 1977).

5. D. A. Kolb, I. M. Rubin, and J. M. McIntyre, *Organizational Psychology: An Experimental Approach* (Englewood Cliffs, N.J.: Prentice-Hall, 1974).

6. H. M. Schroder, M. J. Driver, and S. Streufert, *Human Information Processing* (New York: Holt Rinehart & Winston, 1967).

7. McKenney and Keen, *op. cit.*

8. J. L. Adams, *Conceptual Blockbusting* (Stanford, Calif.: Stanford Alumni Association, 1974).

9. McKenney and Keen, *op. cit.*

10. K. Lewin, *Resolving Social Conflicts* (New York: Harper & Row, 1948).

11. E. DeBono, *Lateral Thinking* (New York: Harper & Row, 1970).

12. Adams, *op. cit.*

13. DeBono, *op. cit.*

14. C. H. Kepner and B. B. Tregoe, *The Rational Manager* (New York: McGraw-Hill, 1965).

15. DeBono, *op. cit.*

16. E. DeBono, *The Mechanisms of Mind* (New York: Simon & Schuster, 1969).

17. R. P. Crawford, *The Techniques of Creative Thinking* (Englewood Cliffs, N.J.: Prentice-Hall, 1954).

18. E. K. BonFange, *The Creative Process in Engineering* (New York: General Electric, 1954).
19. DeBono, *op. cit.* (1970).
20. *Ibid.*
21. W. J. Gordon, *Synectics* (New York: Harper & Row, 1961).
22. C. W. Emory and P. Niland, *Making Management Decisions* (New York: Houghton-Mifflin, 1968).
23. F. M. Tonge, "The Use of Heuristic Programing in Management Science," *Management Science* (April 1961), pp. 231-237.
24. Emory and Niland, *op. cit.*

CHAPTER 15

1. L. Thayer, *Communication and Communication Systems* (Homewood, Ill.: R. D. Irwin, 1968).
2. D. K. Berlo, *The Process of Communication* (New York: Holt, Rinehart & Winston, 1960).
3. J. R. Gibb, "Defensive Communication," *Journal of Communication,* vol. 11, no. 3 (Sept. 1961), pp. 141-148.
4. *Ibid.*
5. R. G. Nichols, "Listening is Good Business," *Management of Personnel Quarterly,* vol. 2 (Winter 1962), pp. 2-9.
6. Harold Leavitt, *Managerial Psychology,* 3rd edition (Chicago: University of Chicago Press, 1972), pp. 115-121.
7. W. H. Read, "Upward Communication in Industrial Hierarchy," *Human Relations,* vol. 15 (Feb. 1962), pp. 3-15.
8. Henri Fayol, *General and Industrial Management* (New York: Pitman Co., 1949).
9. Leavitt, *op. cit.,* pp. 189-198; and Alex Bandlas, "Communication Patterns in Task Oriented Groups," and Harold Guetzkow, "Differentiation of Roles in Task Oriented Groups," in D. Cartwright and A. Zander, *Group Dynamics: Research and Theory,* 3rd edition (New York: Harper & Row, 1968), pp. 503-526.
10. K. Davis, "Communication within Management," *Personnel,* vol. 31, no. 3 (Nov. 1954), pp. 212-217.
11. G. W. Dickson, "Management Information-Decision System," *Business Horizons* (Dec. 1968), pp. 17-26.

CHAPTER 16

1. J. R. D. French and B. H. Raven, "The Basis of Social Power," in D. Cartwright, ed., *Studies in Social Power* (Ann Arbor: University of Michigan Press, 1959).
2. E. E. Lawler, "The Mythology of Management Compensation," *California Management Review,* vol. 8 (Fall 1966), pp. 11-22.
3. V. A. Thompson, *Modern Organization,* 2nd edition (University, Ala.: University of Alabama Press, 1977), pp. 114-115.
4. David McCelland, *Power: The Inner Experience* (New York: Irvington Publishers, 1975), pp. 13-23, 253-61.
5. *Ibid.*
6. This model is adapted from that of Amitai Etzioni, "Compliance Theory," in Oscar Grusky and George A. Miller, eds., *The Sociology of Organizations* (New York: The Free Press, 1970), p. 108.
7. Herbert A. Simon, *Administrative Behavior,* 3rd edition (New York: The Free Press, 1976), p. 12.
8. Michael Korda, *Power How to Get It; How to Use It* (New York: Ballantine Books, 1977).
9. Michael Murphy, "Workers on the Board: Borrowing a European Idea," *Labor Law Journal,* vol. 27 (Dec. 1976), p. 751.

10. M. Dalton, *Men Who Manage* (New York: Wiley, 1959).

11. Leonard Sayles, *Managerial Behavior: Administration in Complex Organizations* (New York: McGraw-Hill, 1964), pp. 56-57.

12. The "linking pin" concept is from Rensis Likert, *New Patterns of Management* (New York: McGraw-Hill, 1961).

13. L. Sayles, *op. cit.*, pp. 58-111.

14. *Ibid.*

15. Kenneth E. Boulding, "A Pure Theory of Conflict Applied to Organizations," in R. L. Kahn and Elise Boulding, eds., *Power and Conflict in Organizations* (London: Tavistock, 1964), pp. 136-145.

16. Martin Shubik, "The Uses of Game Theory in Management Science," *Management Science* (October 1955), p. 40.

17. Douglas McGregor, *The Professional Manager* (New York: McGraw-Hill, 1967), p. 184.

CHAPTER 17

1. Jeffrey Pfeffer, "The Ambiguity of Leadership," *The Academy of Management Review*, vol. 2 (January 1977), p. 105.

2. Abraham Zaleznik, "Managers and Leaders: Are They Different," *Harvard Business Review*, vol. 55 (May–June 1977), pp. 67-78.

3. Jeffery C. Barrow, "The Variables of Leadership: A Review and Conceptual Framework," *The Academy of Management Review*, vol. 2 (April 1977), pp. 231-251.

4. Leo Tolstoy, *War and Peace* (New York: The Heritage Press, 1938), p. 461.

5. Barrow, *op. cit.*, p. 232.

6. Eugene Jennings, *An Anatomy of Leadership* (New York: McGraw-Hill, 1960).

7. For a review of the trait approach and its critics, see Barrow, *loc. cit.* Also see R. M. Stogdil, "Personal Factors Associated with Leadership: A Survey of the Literature," *Journal of Psychology*, vol. 25 (1948), pp. 35-71. For another version of the trait approach, see Edwin E. Ghiselli, *Explorations in Managerial Talent* (Pacific Palisades, Calif.: Goodyear, 1971).

8. See S. Kerr, C. Schriesheim, C. Murphy, and R. Stogdill, "Toward a Contingency Theory of Leadership Based Upon the Consideration and Initiating Structure in Literature," *Organizational Behavior and Human Performance*, vol. 12 (1974), pp. 62-82.

9. Ralph White and Ronald Lippitt, "Leader Behavior and Member Reaction in Three Social Climates," Dorwin Cartwright and Alvin Zander, eds., *Group Dynamics: Research and Theory*, (Evanston, Ill.: Row, Peterson & Co., 1953), pp. 585-611.

10. Robert Tannenbaum and W. W. Schmidt, "How to Choose a Leadership Pattern," *Harvard Business Review*, vol. 36 (1958), pp. 95-101.

11. *Ibid*, p. 101.

12. Robert R. Blake and Jane S. Mouton, *The Managerial Grid* (Houston: Gulf Publishing, 1964), p. 10.

13. Barrow, *op. cit.*, p. 234.

14. See Fred E. Fiedler, *A Theory of Leadership Effectiveness* (New York: McGraw-Hill, 1967).

15. Douglas McGregor, *The Human Side of Enterprise* (New York: McGraw-Hill, 1960), pp. 33-57.

16. *Ibid.*

17. Chris Argyris, *Personality and Organization* (New York: Harper, 1957) and Chris Argyris, "Personality and Organization Theory Revisited," *Administrative Science Quarterly*, vol. 18 (June 1973), pp. 14l ff.

18. Frederick Herzberg, *Work and the Nature of Man* (Cleveland, Ohio: The World Publishing Co., 1966).

19. Rensis Likert, *The Human Organization: Its Management and Value* (New York: McGraw-Hill, 1967).
20. Herzberg, *op. cit.*; Argyris, *op. cit.*; McGregor, *op. cit.*
21. See Leonard R. Sayles, *Managerial Behavior: Administration in Complex Organizations*, (New York: McGraw-Hill, 1964), p. 143.
22. *Ibid.*
23. *Ibid*, pp. 154-155.
24. Pfeffer, *op. cit.*, p. 111.
25. *Ibid.*, pp. 107-108.
26. *Ibid.*
27. *Ibid.*, p. 100.
28. From an article by Jerry Caroll, "The Jogger Who Rescued Memorex," *San Francisco Cronicle* (August 6, 1977), p. 4.

CHAPTER 18

1. S. Thume and R. House, "Where Long Range Planning Pays Off," in B. Taylor and K. Hawkins, *A Handbook of Strategic Planning* (London: Longman, 1972).
2. R. L. Katz, *Managing the Total Enterprise,* (Englewood Cliffs, N.J.: Prentice-Hall, 1970).
3. F. F. Foltman, *Manpower Information for Effective Management, Parts I and II* (Ithaca, N.Y.: New York School of Industrial and Labor Relations, 1973).
4. F. J. Augilar, *Scanning the Business Environment* (New York: Macmillan, 1967).
5. A. R. Fusfeld and R. N. Foster, "The Delphi Technique: Survey and Comment," *Business Horizons,* vol. 14, (June 1971), pp. 63-74.
6. L. S. Silk and M. L. Curley, *A Primer on Business Forecasting* (New York: Random House, 1970).
7. R. S. Sobek, "A Manager's Primer on Forecasting," *Harvard Business Review,* vol. 51 (May–June 1973), pp. 6-14.
8. Katz, *op. cit.*
9. Henry Mintzberg, *The Nature of Managerial Work* (New York: Harper & Row, 1973).
10. E. P. Ward, *The Dynamics of Planning* (New York: Pergammon Press, 1970).
11. A. R. McKenzie, *The Time Trap* (New York: Amacom Books, 1972).
12. C. Argyris, *Organization and Innovation* (Homewood, Ill.: Richard D. Irwin, 1965).
13. R. W. Ackerman, "Role of the Corporate Planning Executive," in P. Larange and R. F. Vancil, *Strategic Planning Systems* (Englewood Cliffs, N.J.: Prentice-Hall, 1977).
14. S. C. Wheelwright and D. G. Clarke, "Corporate Forecasting: Promise and Reality," *Harvard Business Review,* vol. 54 (Nov.–Dec. 1976), pp. 40-69.

CHAPTER 19

1. W. G. Scott and T. R. Mitchell, *Organization Theory: A Structural and Behavioral Analysis* (Homewood, Ill.: Richard D. Irwin, 1976).
2. N. Weiner, *The Human Use of Human Beings* (Garden City, N.Y.: Doubleday & Co., 1954).
3. P. P. Schoderbek, A. G. Kefalas, and C. G. Schoderbek, *Management Systems* (Dallas: Business Publications, Inc., 1975).
4. J. L. Livingstone, "Integrating the Hierarchies of Control," in J. McGuire, *Contemporary Management: Issues and Viewpoints* Englewood Cliffs, N.J.: Prentice-Hall, 1974).
5. N. M. Bedford, "Managerial Control," in J. McGuire, *Contemporary Management: Issues and Viewpoints* (Englewood Cliffs, N.J.: Prentice-Hall, 1974).
6. R. Albanese, *Management: Toward Accountability for Performance,* 2nd edition (Homewood, Ill.: Richard D. Irwin, 1978).
7. Peter Drucker, *Managing for Results* (New York: Harper & Row, 1964).

8. V. F. Ridgway, "Dysfunctional Consequences of Performance Measurements," *Administrative Science Quarterly* (September 1956), pp. 240-247.

9. T. Caplow, *Principles of Organization* (New York: Harcourt, Brace & World, 1964).

10. P. Blau and W. R. Scott, *Formal Organizations* (San Francisco: Chandler Publishing, 1967).

11. E. E. Jennings, *An Anatomy of Leadership* (New York: McGraw-Hill, 1960).

12. Caplow, *op. cit.*

13. J. Woodward, *Industrial Organization: Theory and Practice* (London: Oxford University Press, 1965).

14. P. Blau and M. W. Meyer, *Bureaucracy in Modern Society,* 2nd edition (New York: Random House, 1971).

15. Blau and Scott, *op. cit.*

16. *Ibid.*

CHAPTER 20

1. K. Lewin, "Group Decision and Social Change," in T. M. Newcomb and E. L. Hartley, eds., *Readings in Social Psychology* (New York: Holt, Rinehart & Winston, 1947), pp. 340-44. Also, Edgar Schein, "Management Development as a Process of Influence,"*Industrial Management Review,* vol. 2 (May 1961).

2. H. Mintzberg, *The Nature of Managerial Work* (New York: Harper & Row, 1973).

3. Alvin Toffler, *Future Shock* (New York: Random House, 1970).

4. H. Kaufmann, *The Limits of Organizational Change* (University, Ala.: University of Alabama Press, 1971).

5. H. Leavitt, "The Company President as a Berkeley Student," *Harvard Business Review,* vol. 45, (Nov.–Dec. 1967), pp. 152-157.

6. Amitai Etzioni, *Modern Organizations* (Englewood Cliffs, N.J.: Prentice-Hall, 1964).

7. V. Thompson, *Bureaucracy and Innovation* (University, Ala: University of Alabama Press, 1969).

8. J. K. Galbraith, *The New Industrial State* (Boston: Houghton-Mifflin, 1967).

9. Kaufmann, *op. cit.*

10. W. L. French, *The Professional Management Process,* 4th edition (Boston: Houghton-Mifflin Co., 1978).

11. W. L. French and C. H. Bell, Jr., *Organization Development: Behavioral Science Interventions for Organization Improvement* (Englewood Cliffs, N.J.: Prentice-Hall, 1973).

12. Peter F. Drucker, *The Age of Discontinuity: Guidelines to Our Changing Society* (New York: Harper & Row, 1969).

Index